LONDON PLOTTED
Plans of London Buildings c.1450-1720

The title page of William Leybourn's plan book for the Fishmongers' Company, 1686. This was drawn not by Leybourn but by a professional arms painter, Thomas Penson.

LONDON PLOTTED
Plans of London Buildings c.1450-1720

by
Dorian Gerhold

Edited by
Sheila O'Connell

LONDON TOPOGRAPHICAL SOCIETY
Publication No. 178
2016

©
LONDON TOPOGRAPHICAL SOCIETY
103 Harestone Valley Road
Caterham CR3 6HR
2016

ISBN
978 0 902087 65 1

PRODUCED BY
OUTSET SERVICES LIMITED

CONTENTS

	page
INTRODUCTION	1
The development of estate plans in London	2
Customers for plans	5
Surveyors	9
Surveying	17
Plans and London's houses	20
Plans and the changing character of London	28
Editorial and other matters	30
Glossary	36
EARLY PLANS, c.1450-1630	37
PLANS OF AREAS	85
The City	85
Outside the City	124
PLANS OF BUILDING TYPES	135
London Bridge	135
London Wall	137
Wharves	142
Industries	152
Markets	165
Inns, alehouses and stables	172
Livery company halls	183
Official buildings	192
Churches	203
Other buildings	206
PLANS OF HOUSES	213
Mansions	213
Other large houses	224
Two-room plan houses	234
City Lands houses of two-room plan	242

	page
PLANS OF HOUSES *continued*	
One-room plan houses	252
Almshouses	264
New residential developments	268
APPENDICES	279
1. Document references, scales and dimensions	279
2. Payments for London plans, 1587-1721	284
3. Fines and rents	286
4. Sources of pre-1720 plans	291
LIST OF ABBREVIATIONS	294
NOTES	295
Notes to the Introduction, pages 1-36	295
Notes to 'Early Plans, *c*.1450-1630', pages 37-84	299
Notes to 'Plans of Areas', pages 85-134	301
Notes to 'Plans of Building Types', pages 135-212	303
Notes to 'Plans of Houses', pages 213-278	307
IMAGE ACKNOWLEDGEMENTS	310
AUTHOR'S ACKNOWLEDGMENTS	311
INDEX	312

INTRODUCTION

Detailed plans of London buildings survive in quantity from the seventeenth century onwards. They range from individual buildings to whole alleys or city blocks, and cover a wide variety of structures—houses from large to small, warehouses, wharves, inns, company halls and so on. They are often extremely evocative, taking one down a level from the larger-scale maps of London to individual homes and places of work. Also, although they generally show buildings at a particular moment, they often tell a story about how London was changing. And yet, other than the earliest ones such as Ralph Treswell's from 1607-12,[1] most have never been published. The purpose of this book is to make this large resource better known, and to show what the plans can contribute to our knowledge of London's history.

'Plan' is used here to mean a drawn survey covering a small area, and 'detailed plan' to mean one providing extensive information about buildings, usually showing individual rooms. Many plans were much less informative, depicting only the outlines of buildings or the plots they stood in (the latter are referred to here as plot outlines). The contemporary term for all of these was most often plot, plat or ground plot, but many other words were used and often two or three together, including draught, scheme, schedule, survey, platform, description, map, table, model, and plan. The words were evidently interchangeable, whereas the only four occurrences of 'design' found were all for building projects.[2] Plans were usually drawn for one of three reasons: to be attached to a deed or lease to show what was being transferred; to form a record of existing buildings for other purposes, as in the case of livery companies' plan books; or to show proposed buildings (these ones being referred to here as building plans).

The main criterion for selecting plans for this book has been how informative each is about London's buildings and the uses made of them, but the aim has also been to cover as many different types of building as possible and as many different surveyors as possible. The selection has been influenced by the availability of views of the buildings shown, as this not only helps to bring the plans to life but also contributes to understanding how the facades of buildings related to the activities going on behind them. Plans of palaces and the Tower of London are excluded because they have usually been researched and published already. Building plans showing proposed buildings are generally included only when there is reasonable confidence that they show what was actually built. No printed plans are included.[3]

The area covered is the City and what by 1720 were contiguous built-up areas, including Westminster, Southwark, Bermondsey, Ratcliff, Wapping, and Finsbury. The only exceptions are almshouses at Mile End and bargehouses at Lambeth and Vauxhall, where the buildings were erected by London organisations for purposes directly connected with the city (Plans 121-22, 186). In the 1690s, about 20% of London's population lived within the City's walls, 16% in the City outside the walls, 26% in Westminster and the West End, 16% in the southern suburbs, 14% in the eastern suburbs and 8% in the northern suburbs.[4] Over time the City's proportion declined as the suburbs grew. By the late seventeenth century there were essentially three Londons: the mercantile city within the walls, the aristocratic West End, and a horseshoe of suburbs dominated by manufacturing and maritime activities, from Southwark through Bermondsey, Ratcliff, Wapping and Whitechapel to Finsbury.[5]

How many plans of buildings there are for each part of London is largely determined by the presence or absence of institutional landowners. These were the landowners who were most likely to commission plans, and also whose plans were most likely to survive. Institutions owned at least 46% of properties in the City in the 1660s, but only about 1% of those in St Margaret's parish in Westminster in the 1690s.[6] The City is consequently well covered, thanks mainly to the City Corporation, Christ's Hospital and the livery companies. Those organisations, the Bridge House (which maintained London Bridge) and St Thomas's Hospital ensure that Southwark has a reasonable number of plans, and the City Corporation does the same for Finsbury. The Bermondsey plans are mostly of the Earls of Salisbury's property there. Some of the Westminster plans were commissioned by institutions, and some of the plans relating to the eastern suburbs, the area least well covered, are of the City's holding in Ratcliff and Bridewell Hospital's in Wapping. In this book there are twenty plans relating to Westminster and the West End, sixteen to Southwark and Bermondsey, eight to the northern suburbs and six to the eastern suburbs, compared with 144 for the City. If all the extant plans were assembled, the City would be even more dominant.

The cut-off date of 1720 is to some extent arbitrary, but there is sufficient material before 1720 to provide a varied and reasonably representative picture of London's buildings. Also, the date coincides roughly with the end of the practice of copying plans from City Lands leases into volumes, which gave rise to the two magnificent plan books at London Metropolitan Archives, and the last of the livery company plan books before a long gap. In the last half-century or so covered here London dominated England more than ever before or since, having in about 1700 one-ninth of its population, three-quarters of its foreign trade, nearly half its merchant fleet, a dominant position in its internal trade, its largest concentration of industry, its banking centre, its seat of government and its centre of upper-class social life for half the year. It was then about twenty times the size of the next largest English city (Norwich), and was the fourth largest city in the world. Daniel Defoe described London as the heart which circulated England's blood: it drew in foodstuffs, raw materials and manufactured goods from the rest of Britain and the world at large, which were either consumed within London or pumped out again, either in the same form or after processing.[7]

THE DEVELOPMENT OF ESTATE PLANS IN LONDON

The drawing of plans of urban estates and buildings can be seen as a distinct subject, but it also relates to other aspects of cartography, especially designs for buildings and fortifications and maps of rural estates. The story has two aspects: the development of the scaled ground plan, which happened relatively quickly, and the much longer-term increase in the number of plans drawn.

Until the 1570s the idea of an estate map for general reference, whether of urban or rural property, was unknown; that need was served by the written estate survey instead. Deeds and leases virtually never included plans, relying instead on written description. Maps had become common by the first half of the sixteenth century, but they were drawn to meet particular needs, such as a legal dispute over boundaries. Until the 1540s they were almost all pictorial ones and they were not drawn to a consistent scale, the value of which was not appreciated.[8]

The earliest plan of a London building was drawn in order to show the pipes supplying the Charterhouse with water in about 1450 (Plan 1). The fact that the pipes could not be seen on the ground obviously made a plan useful. The plan shows some buildings pictorially, but for the cells of the Great Cloister it is a ground plan. A new version was drawn in about 1511 (Plan 2). For most of the century after 1450 all there is covering small areas is simple outlines of plots. Four of these survive from the 1470s in a register of the Bridge House estates, though only one within the area dealt with here, for Carter Lane in the City. The text on three of the four provides lengths, compass points, abuttals, and total area. On one there is an elevation, of two recently-built tenements at Deptford Strand in 1475. One was explicitly drawn to settle boundaries. Three describe themselves as a 'patron' (i.e. pattern), and one as a 'platte'.[9] No more surviving plot outlines have been identified until 1534, when two were drawn of property purchased by Thomas Cromwell.[10] None of these early outlines were drawn to scale. The shape would resemble that on the ground, but the resemblance evidently did not need to be exact; the measurements written on the outline were what mattered. Plot outlines continued to be included occasionally on deeds and leases until at least the eighteenth century, though they were rare until after the Great Fire, when numerous plot outlines (not to scale) were drawn of foundations staked out in the burnt area.[11] Later they were more likely to be to scale, and outlines for groups of properties were sometimes used as a basis for organising information about tenants and leases.[12]

There was a sudden increase in the use of maps and plans for warfare and administration in the late 1530s and 1540s, prompted initially by fear of invasion. Surveys of the coasts ordered in 1539 (the largest government-sponsored cartographic survey before the nineteenth century) were followed in the 1540s by maps and plans of individual fortifications, of demarcation lines and contested lands in France and on the Scottish border and (in 1541) of liberties and places of sanctuary. The more sophisticated of these were to scale.[13] The government's increasing interest in maps and plans and the call for plans such as those of coasts and places of sanctuary began to influence others, and may have contributed to the creation of a few detailed plans of London buildings. The first such plan after the one of the Charterhouse shows a house in Cheapside belonging to the Savoy Hospital (Plan 3). It was probably a building plan, of 1531 or earlier, but was attached to a lease of the completed house in 1542. The next Savoy plan, showing houses in Fleet Lane in 1542, is more remarkable, as it is the first surviving plan drawn of existing buildings in order to be attached to a lease (Plan 4). Whereas the Cheapside property would have been easily recognisable on the ground, the Fleet Lane one seems to have included one house which straddled a property boundary. Neither of these plans was drawn to scale. Other Savoy leases did not have plans, and, like plot outlines, detailed plans remained rare on deeds and leases until after the Great Fire.[14]

Drawing to scale

The importance of scale seems to have been appreciated first as regards elevations of buildings rather than their plans.[15] Plans for proposed buildings might be detailed, but at first they were not to scale. The earliest surviving scale plan for a proposed building in England was for an exchange between Lombard Street and Cornhill in about 1537, probably drawn by an artist from Antwerp.[16] Scale plans of English military fortifications in the Calais area probably in early 1541 and at Hull later in the same year were drawn by Richard Lee and John Rogers, master masons employed by Henry VIII as military engineers; in 1542-43 Rogers drew scale building plans of the king's manor house at Hull; and in 1546 Rogers and Lee drew scale plans of areas around Boulogne showing fortification projects in their wider context. Military engineers had to consider the range of cannon and lines of fire, which made scale increasingly important to them. The first scale map of a town was drawn of Portsmouth in 1545, and one of London was drawn in about 1555.[17] The first scale plan of an existing London building shows Cecil House in the Strand in the mid-1560s (Plan 6). William Cecil has long been recognised as a pioneer in the use of maps, and the plan of his London house pre-dated by about a decade the first maps of rural estates drawn to scale, which are from the mid-1570s.

Apart from building plans for Nonsuch House in about 1577 and Cursitors' Hall in about 1578 (Plans 7, 8), the only other extant London plans drawn to scale in the sixteenth century are those of Hermitage Dock, Wapping, in about 1590 and a mansion called the Erber in 1596 (Plans 10, 12), though the sixteenth-century plan of the Steelyard may also be to scale (Plan 5). The Hermitage Dock plan was pictorial whereas the Erber and Steelyard ones were ground plans. The last two plans included here which were not to scale were those of Holy Trinity Aldgate in about 1585 and part of the precinct of St Bartholomew's Hospital in about 1610 apart from one of c.1660 (Plans 9, 16, 19). After about 1610, all plans drawn with any care, whether ground plans or pictorial, were to scale, though there were some where the stated measurements were not consistent with the scale indicated or with each other (e.g. Plan 29).

Ground plans instead of pictorial ones

The map of Portsmouth in 1545 is remarkable not only for being drawn to scale but also for being entirely a ground plan without any pictorial features at all. Maps of other English towns were always pictorial for the next century or so, although in some cases the pictures were added to a ground plan so that the scale could be uniform, as in the case of London's Copperplate Map of about 1555, rather than being a bird's-eye view from a single point.[18] Maps of London remained pictorial until Ogilby and Morgan's ground plan of the City in 1676, though many later maps had some pictorial features. Maps of rural estates, though usually drawn to scale from the 1570s, continued to show buildings and some other features pictorially. The first using block plans of buildings were from around 1700.[19]

In contrast, ground plans quickly became the norm for London buildings. The first such ground plan to scale, of Cecil House in the mid-1560s, has all the features one would expect on later plans, including room divisions, doors, hearths and windows (Plan 6). In the second, of the Erber in 1596, even the convention of red for brick, yellow or brown for timber and grey for stone seems to be present (Plan 12).[20] In the second ground plan to scale, and perhaps even the first, the art of drawing ground plans had already reached its fullest development; there was nothing more to add, just as the rural estate map emerged fully fledged in the 1570s.[21] All that was missing was demand. When plans were made subsequently, not all urban landowners and surveyors considered such extensive detail necessary, and many later plans would omit features seen on these two, such as windows and even staircases.

Pictorial plans continued to be drawn occasionally, but the last substantial body of pictorial work was Llewellyn's plans of the St Bartholomew's precinct and nearby areas in 1613-17 (Plans 19, 20). Later pictorial plans were sometimes the result of a surveyor more used to rural mapping receiving a London commission, such as John Coffyn in 1670 and John Friend in 1711 (Plans 28, 60, 61). The reasons for most plans being ground plans were probably that ground plans were familiar from an early period in the form of building plans, and that they were simply a better way of showing urban properties. The latter point is well illustrated by Coffyn's plan of Nevill's Alley in 1670 (Plan 28). Nothing was more important in an urban estate plan than the outline of the plot, and it was therefore essential that any views of buildings did not obscure that line. This made it hard to show the buildings accurately, especially if they were towards the back of the plot. Coffyn did manage to show the outline of the Nevill's Alley property, but only by abandoning accuracy in portraying some of the buildings. Moreover, his plan conveyed less information about the layout than a ground plan would have done. In two early plans reproduced here, the less important buildings are shown pictorially and the areas that really mattered by means of ground plans (Plans 11, 15).

Was London distinctive in adopting the ground plan so thoroughly? Not enough examples are available from other places to be certain. Plans of urban buildings elsewhere were sometimes pictorial, even at a late date,[22] but so they were occasionally in London. On the other hand, they were sometimes ground plans, even at early dates, such as those of Corpus Christi College, Cambridge, in 1574-77.[23] The small numbers are surely the point: urban estate plans of any sort were rare outside London, which was so much larger than any other English city. For example, no detailed plans of buildings in Bristol from before 1700 are known to exist, and only one outline plan.[24] The distinctiveness of London was that its size and the many organisations with large London estates generated a substantial number of plans earlier than elsewhere, and wherever there was a need for plans of urban estates it must quickly have become apparent that a ground plan served the purpose best.

Numbers

Many pre-Fire plans, perhaps the majority, have been lost, but there is no doubt that they were produced only occasionally and usually for specific reasons until Treswell's two great commissions of 1610 and 1612. Why Christ's Hospital and the Clothworkers' Company decided to have their entire London estates plotted then is unclear. Perhaps they were influenced by the growing interest in maps among rural landowners. Christ's Hospital had already had some of its rural properties mapped by Treswell, and it was experimenting with the use of plans on its London leases.[25] Whatever the reasons, their example seems not to have been followed until after the Fire. Even Llewellyn's plans for St Bartholomew's were confined to the immediate vicinity of the Hospital rather than covering its extensive estate elsewhere in London. A mapped survey cost more than a written one—Norden estimated twice as much in about 1616.[26] Many landowners, including many of the largest ones, had surveys made but were content with written ones, such as the Mercers' Company from the early seventeenth century.[27] The parliamentary surveys of confiscated property in 1649-54 were also written ones.

The Great Fire generated increased interest in plans, as individual plots were no longer clearly marked on the ground. The Rebuilding Act of 1667 required that foundations be staked out and plans be made by the City surveyors, and many of these plot outlines were subsequently used in leases. The Merchant Taylors noted in 1669 that 'the Companie may much suffer in theire tofts of grounds if there be not plots exactly taken thereof' and agreed that John Oliver should be their surveyor and make such plots, probably giving rise to the surviving plan book.[28] The Cordwainers' Company had conducted a survey of its burnt properties by 18 October 1666 in the hope of claiming compensation, and its plans from the following year possibly had the same purpose.[29] Obviously at first there were no buildings to draw, and even when there were, many owners saw no need for further plans or continued to be satisfied with plot outlines or little more, as in the Merchant Taylors' plan books of c.1670 and c.1694, the Skinners' of c.1695 and the Drapers' of 1698.[30]

On the other hand, the post-Fire plot outlines must have increased awareness of the potential value of plans.

The number of detailed plans made increased only gradually, like the number of rural estate maps in this period.[31] Plan books of London properties giving more than plot outlines were drawn for livery companies as follows: the Stationers in 1674, the Tallow Chandlers in 1678, the Armourers in 1679, the Fishmongers in 1686, the Goldsmiths in 1692, the Salters in 1709 and the Dyers in 1721. Magdalen College, Oxford, had plans drawn in 1678. The committee administering the City's lands required plans for all leases from December 1675,[32] and St Thomas's Hospital began to use detailed plans on some leases from 1686. The City's Court of Aldermen ordered in 1698 that all leases by the Bridge House and the Hospitals have plans attached, though the order was at best only fitfully observed.[33] The key period seems to have been from about 1674 to 1698, suggesting that the aftermath of the Great Fire and the growing interest in estate maps nationwide both had an impact. Nevertheless, most deeds and leases continued to lack plans of any sort.

CUSTOMERS FOR PLANS

Estate surveys and lease plans

As indicated above, only three institutions commissioned significant numbers of plans in the early seventeenth century, but many more did so from 1674 onwards. In some cases this resulted in a plan book; in other cases in many leases having plans annexed. As regards lease plans, the City was alone in requiring a plan on all its leases. From 1675 every lease was to have a plan 'with a description of the exact dimensions of the ground thereof'.[34] At first, up to 1677, these were just plot outlines, but thereafter they were detailed ground plans, drawn successively by William Leybourn, John Olley and Isaac Olley. From 1700 to 1723 the lease plans were copied into books. The Bridge House, Bridewell Hospital, Christ's Hospital and St Thomas's Hospital were all more selective in using plans on leases, and St Bartholomew's Hospital only occasionally included a plan. Livery companies (other than the Clothworkers) and private owners rarely included detailed plans on leases, and only occasionally even plot outlines.

As for plan books, these were a speciality of livery companies, but only of a minority of them. Taking the number of parishes in which the companies held property as a crude measure of the size of their holdings,[35] five of the ten companies with property in twenty or more parishes had plan books made up to 1721 (including plan books consisting of plot outlines); to these five we can add the Clothworkers, who already had such a plan book (though they considered making a new one in 1690)[36] and often included plans in leases. Of the seven companies with property in eight to fifteen parishes, three had plan books made; a fourth, the Ironmongers' Company, had a new plan drawn of its Old Street estate to replace an old one.[37] Of the numerous companies with property in fewer than eight parishes, only two seem to have commissioned plan books—the Stationers and the Dyers. Some companies evidently considered plan books useful, but they were not essential for estate management. Few parishes had plans drawn of all their properties,[38] and no private owners are known to have done so.

The lease plans have clearer purposes than the plan books. The most obvious was to provide unambiguous and agreed information about the outlines of plots being leased. Another purpose was perhaps to avoid complicated and potentially ambiguous written descriptions, though practice varied as to whether attaching a plan to the lease or deed resulted in less description. Among the early examples, one of the deeds with a plan relating to Thomas Cromwell's house fully describes the bounds and dimensions, whereas the other records only the parish and ward, stating that the dimensions were as in the plan.[39] Of the two Savoy leases with plans, the Cheapside one gives the approximate position and abuttals, but for dimensions refers to the plan, whereas the Fleet Lane one includes the dimensions but for the location gives only the parish. There is similar variation later: organisations such as Christ's Hospital left out information which was conveyed instead by the plan, whereas City Lands leases continued to give dimensions in great detail rather than relying on the plans, resulting on one occasion in inconsistent information.[40] City Lands leases became more informative in the mid-seventeenth century, often specifying the rooms a property contained, whereas once plans became routine the leases, while continuing to record dimensions and abuttals, became less informative about rooms.

These advantages of plans on leases could be obtained by attaching a mere plot outline, and some organisations which considered plans worthwhile regarded those as sufficient, such as the Drapers' Company. Sometimes there was clearly a specific reason for a more detailed plan, such as a new building straddling a boundary so that the exact property boundary was no longer visible on the ground (e.g. Plans 28, 132), redevelopment which had made an earlier grant of land obscure (Plan 20) or a complication such as intermixed upper storeys or shared access (e.g. Plans 131, 150). More generally, some organisations apparently decided that plans providing details of the building's footprint within the site and its ground-floor layout gave a better idea of the property and what belonged to it and were therefore, for some or all leases, worth what was presumably a higher cost. At the same time as it required plans on all its leases, the City Lands Committee ordered that a plan of a particular house 'expresse therein all the rooms and severall particulars thereof, that so this Committee may have a distinct view thereof', and a general survey of all the City Lands (which never happened) indicating not just the ground but the buildings.[41] There is little sign of such plans being used to assess a property's value in advance of a lease.[42] For the Committee at least, the motivation was instead fear of undetected encroachment. In 1681 it stated that the City Lands were 'exposed to hazard uncertainties and losses for want of an exact survey ... and a discripcon not only of the ground thereof but of the severall parts of building thereupon'.[43] With

Fig. 1. The title page of Leybourn's plan book for the Tallow Chandlers' Company, together with the Company's coat of arms, 1678.

standing buildings it was presumably easier to identify any encroachment if the relationship of rooms to the plot boundary was known.

If a detailed plan was useful, the question arises of why it was almost always confined to the ground floor, and the likely reason is that the even higher cost of covering all floors was not worthwhile because a ground plan combined with written information about upper storeys or personal observation was sufficient to ascertain the extent and value of a property. The same calculation can be observed in nineteenth-century sale catalogues. Of the seven plans found showing all floors of a property, four involved intermixed upper floors (Plans 22, 131, 138, 146) and three were plans for new buildings or improvements (Plans 8, 13, 130).[44]

Different reasons are needed to account for plan books, and they may have varied from company to company, as the plan books differed greatly in form. None followed Treswell's work for the Clothworkers in combining detailed ground plans with written information about upper storeys and about tenants and sub-tenants. Generally they either concentrate on the buildings or give plot outlines and tenants. Of the eleven plan books, four — Drapers, Merchant Taylors (two), and Skinners — give little more than plot outlines, to which in the latter three cases (and probably originally in the case of the Drapers too) information on tenants and leases is added. Seven provide detailed ground plans, of which four give information about upper storeys, in greater or lesser detail, but not about tenants, and three provide information about tenants but not about upper storeys.

One possible reason for plan books can be dismissed at the outset. A plan book might have been a useful source of plans to be appended to leases, but in practice they were not used in this way. The Fishmongers ordered in 1668 'that plotts be taken and made of all the ground and houses belonging to this Company in London and the just & true measure thereof bee sett downe upon the same plotts and kept in the fashion of a booke for the Companies lease[s] and plotts affixed to the severall leases',[45] but in fact they did not do so, even when they eventually obtained a plan book in 1686. Similarly, no such use of the plans in the Armourers', Stationers' and Goldsmiths' plan books has been found. The nearest examples identified are two Christ's Hospital leases of 1660 and 1683 which refer back to the Hospital's plan book but without attaching copies of the plan (Plan

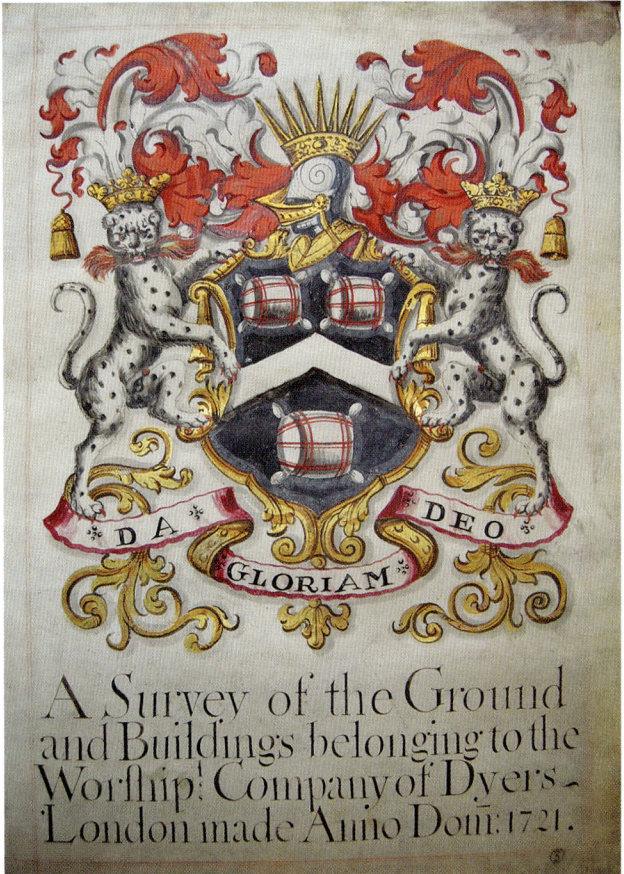

Fig. 2. The title page of James Gould's plan book for the Dyers' Company, 1721. Gould was drawing plans for the Dyers by 1716, and the Company ordered a plan book from him in 1718. In 1720 they warned that 'if he does not bring it the next court day the Company will employ some other person'.

146). In fact the causation seems to be the other way: organisations which began to attach plans to leases, and presumably found this useful, sometimes decided they wanted them gathered into a plan book and made comprehensive. The several Christ's Hospital plans pre-dating Treswell's main work suggest this, and the same applies to the Fishmongers in 1675-86 and the Dyers in 1716-21. The City Lands Committee never obtained the comprehensive survey it wanted, but it did eventually start copying its lease plans into a book, and when this was first proposed in 1692 the stated reason was 'so that they may be better preserv'd'.[46]

An important purpose of plan books was probably to make a definitive record of what was owned so as to prevent losses, and to do so more clearly than a written survey could. As indicated above, preventing losses was the reason for the proposed survey of the City's lands in 1681. Plan books may also have been seen as providing a clearer view of an organisation's estate in order to assist in managing it, for example by stating when leases would expire (though only a few plan books did this) or by showing the configuration of buildings and generating ideas on how this could be improved and rents increased. The City Lands Committee's decision in 1700 not only to enter its lease plans into a book but also to have the book produced at every meeting of the Committee suggests a similar purpose,[47] though if so the intention was often thwarted by the Olleys not keeping the book up to date (see below).

Probably the most important motive is suggested by the character of most of the plan books. They were prestige items, with the Company's arms finely drawn at the front (sometimes if not always by a professional arms painter)[48] and showing in attractive coloured plans the properties owned (frontispiece and Figs 1, 2). To an extent a plan book was nice to have rather than necessary for managing the estate. Even today, the Tallow Chandlers keep their plan book, which they ordered to be bound 'very handsomely' with clasps,[49] in the court room where William Leybourn presented it to them in 1678, together with their later plan books. The Fishmongers have retained their plan book of 1686 despite depositing almost all their other records in Guildhall Library.

Building plans

A distinct category of plans is the building plan, showing an intended building rather than one which already existed. Sometimes they are explicitly building plans, attached to building agreements or leases or labelled or otherwise recorded as such (Plans 8, 93, 94, 115, 173, 188, 189, 192-95, 197); in other cases there are stylistic or other reasons for identifying them as building plans (Plans 3, 7, 13, 169, 190, 191). In particular, building plans tend to have lines drawn using a ruler, and not to say what the rooms were used for. The fullest discussion of building plans in this period is by Elizabeth McKellar, but almost all the plans she considered were layouts of building plots or were plans required to obtain royal approval for building, in neither case providing the ground plans of individual buildings.[50]

Building plans were not unusual, but nor were they common. They were usually confined to ground plans, and said nothing about style or manner of construction, which was described in writing if at all, so they gave only limited information about what was to be built. There is little evidence of builders compiling plans (other than layouts of plots) for their own benefit, though that may have been the reason for the one of Nonsuch House, which was possibly needed because the wooden frame was being fabricated elsewhere and the dimensions of the base and the frame needed to match (Plan 7). Otherwise plans were for the benefit of landowners: they were either commissioned by landowners to help them decide whether or how to go ahead with building projects of their own, or they were required from the builder by a landowner who wished to understand what was proposed or to keep some control over the process. For example, as regards the first of those categories, in 1641 the Fishmongers' Company instructed the viewers of its house called the Leaden Porch to draw 'a plott of such buildinge as they shall conceive most fitt to make and erect there' and calculate the cost. In the same year, elevations and plans of each floor of a residence for the Clothworkers' Beadle adjoining Clothworkers' Hall gate were drawn explicitly to assist in a decision about whether to build it. The same may apply to Nathaniel Hanwell's plans of 1681 of four houses and the gateway of St Thomas's Hospital in the High Street, Southwark, 'as how they are and as they may be conveniently built'.[51] For both their new streets off the Strand the Cecils had plans drawn showing buildings as well as building plots, and in one case they compared two different plans (Plans 189-91). Of the plans in this book, those of the Cecils' new streets and Rose Street (Plan 56) are closest in purpose to those discussed by McKellar.

Examples of the second category—plans required from the builder by a landowner—are those of the Star Inn and the Peacock brewery drawn for the Fishmongers, and new houses in Tothill Street and Barnham Street drawn for Christ's Hospital (Plans 79, 94, 147, 174-75, though only in the Star Inn case is the building plan the one reproduced here). In none of these cases was the building plan attached to the subsequent lease (and only in two of them does it survive), though building plans were sometimes used in that way.[52] One pair of West End developers, William Pym and Johnshall Crosse in the 1680s, obtained plans from prospective builders, of widely varying character, and attached them to the building leases (Plans 192-95), whereas in other cases involving a plan the landowner may have had more influence on the proposal shown (Plan 197).

The landowner was likely to be more interested in potential income than style (apart from, occasionally, a degree of regularity in facades), so a ground plan was usually sufficient, but that might not be so when an attractive or impressive building was a matter of prestige or the landowner was paying. Four 'uprights' or elevations, or references to them, have been found: the house for the Clothworkers' Beadle, where the Company was paying and the appearance of the Company's Hall was probably affected; the Meal Market mentioned below; Emanuel Hospital, where the City was paying (Plan 188); and houses in Frith Street, where the landowner was funding the development (Plan 197).

Building plans were sometimes insubstantial, drawn on paper rather than vellum and in pencil rather than ink, but there seems little reason to doubt that agreed ones were intended to be binding, even if this was apparently never tested in court and enforcement was likely to be difficult.[53] Where they can be compared with what was actually built there are usually differences, but these were generally minor and could even have been approved (e.g. Plan 173). Often the landowner retained some control by not agreeing leases until some or all of the proposed buildings were up.

The City evidently regarded building plans as binding: the ground plan and elevation of the planned new Meal Market in 1700 were to be copied into the Committee's journal, signed by the Comptroller and delivered back to the proposer, who was then to proceed (Plan 93). The ground plan as built corresponded closely with the proposal, but not exactly. In 1701 John Olley certified to the City that his plan for Emanuel Hospital had been followed, and therefore that the agreed sums should be paid for the work (Plan 188).

Building plans were sometimes attached to written agreements which specified matters such as the materials to be used, the height of storeys and the date of completion,[54] but written agreements without plans were probably at least as common. And many landowners seem to have been satisfied with no more than a commitment in a building lease to spend a certain amount on building and to build well and substantially. Some building leases required new houses to conform to one of the types of house specified in the Rebuilding Act of 1667, or to conform to neighbouring buildings already erected, or made other stipulations (Plans 60, 189-95).

SURVEYORS

The surveyors who produced the earliest plans of London buildings were a varied group. They included Humphrey Coke, carpenter, who drew what was a probably a building plan for a house in Cheapside in about 1531 (Plan 3); John Symonds, mason, joiner, architect and military surveyor, represented here by plans of c.1578 and c.1585 (Plans 8, 9); Arthur Gregory, counterfeiter and surveyor in the service of Francis Walsingham, who drew a plan of London Bridge (now lost) in 1587;[55] William Haiward, a surveyor usually of rural estates in Norfolk, who (with Joel Gascoyne) drew a plan of the Tower of London in 1597;[56] Baptista Boazio, the Italian compiler of maps of one of Drake's voyages and of Ireland, who was commissioned by the City to draw a plan of London Wall and its ditches in 1602;[57] Ralph Treswell, usually a surveyor of rural estates, who drew London plans for Christ's Hospital and the Clothworkers' Company in 1607-12 (see below); Martin Llewellyn, former marine cartographer and steward of St Bartholomew's Hospital, who drew plans of some of the Hospital's London properties in 1613-17 (see below); Edward Mansell, a surveyor of rural estates in England and Ireland, whose plan of the former Greyfriars precinct in 1616 was redrawn as Plan 20;[58] Samuel Parsons, estate surveyor and 'practitioner in the mathematicks', who drew a plan of Dame Elizabeth Craven's property off the Strand in 1621;[59] Adam Bowen, estate surveyor, who drew plans of property at Queenhithe, St Katherine's and Old Street for the Fishmongers' and Ironmongers' Companies in 1630-33 (only that of Old Street survives), as well as plans of rural estates, usually near London and for London owners such as the Bridge House, St Thomas's Hospital and the Mercers' Company;[60] and Joseph Darvoll, the Bridge House's carpenter of the land works, who drew several London plans for his employer in 1633 and 1653 (Plans 62, 78).

Two conclusions can be drawn. First, fewer plans are known to have been drawn by men from the building trades than was to be the case later —none between John Symonds and Joseph Darvoll—though this could partly reflect accidents of survival. Secondly, it was often the same men who produced plans of London buildings, rural estate maps and other types of map, probably a consequence both of limited demand for maps and plans and a limited number of capable surveyors. Even when, in the early seventeenth century, there is for the first time a surveyor producing numerous plans of London buildings, he had previously mapped rural estates.

Ralph Treswell

That surveyor was Ralph Treswell (1544/5-1616/17). Treswell's life has been reconstructed and his London work published in full by John Schofield, and only a few additions have been made to that story.[61] Treswell was by trade a painter-stainer, which included among other things heraldic painting and house painting, and he is first recorded working in 1567/8. By 1571 he was in the service of the courtier Sir Christopher Hatton, though whether at first as painter-stainer or surveyor (or both) is unknown. In 1571 no-one had yet drawn a scale map of a rural estate, and Treswell could have been Hatton's surveyor without drawing maps. Whatever the case, it was in Hatton's service that he learnt the skills needed to do so, and he produced a series of maps of Hatton's rural estates from 1580 to 1587. From 1585 he was also drawing maps and plans for other clients, including London ones: Christ's Hospital from 1585/86 to 1611, St Bartholomew's Hospital in 1587-95, the Bridge House from 1592 to 1612, Bridewell Hospital before 1601, the Clothworkers' Company in 1612 and the City at an unknown date.

Some of these commissions were for London plans. The earliest of these, from 1585, were pictorial. Treswell continued to draw maps of rural estates with the buildings shown pictorially, but for his two great London surveys of 1607-12, carried out at the age of about 65 to 70, he drew ground plans. The first survey was for Christ's Hospital, of which he was a governor, carried out mainly in 1610-11 but including lease plans from 1607 onwards. It resulted in eighteen plans, covering twenty-one blocks of property. The second was for the Clothworkers' Company, in one campaign in 1612, giving rise to thirty plans (Plans 17, 18). The plans show doorways, staircases and chimneys, but only in a few cases windows. They were accompanied by detailed descriptions of upper storeys and named the tenants and occupiers. Drawing ground plans in such number was unprecedented, and was not repeated until the 1670s. Whether Treswell influenced other surveyors is unknown.

Two of Treswell's sons were also surveyors. Ralph Treswell junior, born in about 1574, drew many maps of rural estates but none of London ones. The elder son, Robert Treswell, born in about 1568, drew fewer maps and plans, but they included a London one of 1610 (Plan 15). He was a herald (Bluemantle Pursuivant 1591-97, Somerset Herald 1597-1624) and Surveyor-General of Woods South of the Trent from 1610 until at least 1626. He died not later than 1633.[62]

Martin Llewellyn

The only other surveyor who drew a substantial number of London plans before the Fire was Martin Llewellyn. Of the ten pictorial plans drawn for St Bartholomew's Hospital (one dated 1617), one covers only the church of St Bartholomew the Less (Plan 21), seven relate to the area around Smithfield (Plan 19), one shows property bounded by Newgate and St Martin's le Grand, and one shows the former Greyfriars (Plan 20).[63] Other parts of the Hospital's extensive London estate were not mapped. At least two of the plans relate to lawsuits. All ten plans are in the same style, and it has been argued convincingly that they were drawn by Llewellyn, who was steward of St Bartholomew's Hospital from 1599 to 1634. The argument is based on similarities of style with Llewellyn's atlas of the Far East, the first known sea atlas by an Englishman, probably dating from 1598. The similarities include the borders, where round beads alternate with long ones, the palette of unusual colours and the handwriting.[64] Also, in May 1618 the Hospital's court examined 'a booke of certaine plotts made by Marten Llewellen of divers lands of this Hospitall',[65] which is presumably the surviving plan book containing London and rural plans. However, some of these were copies by Llewellyn of maps drawn by others, including Treswell's maps of the Hospital's rural estates.

The Hospital's accounts clarify to some extent what Llewellyn did. In 1610, he was paid £3 'for makeinge twoe modells of the tenements in Newgate Markett London the one sheweinge the proportion of the brewehouse before the buildinge of the houses nowe standinge uppon the soyle thereof, and the other the proportion of the same tenements as now they stand builded'. This was in connection with the same lawsuit that seems to have prompted the plan of Greyfriars. 'Model' could refer to a ground plan, but this one was a model in the modern sense, as in 1615 money was spent on 'past boards to mend the modells of the brewhouse the backhouse and the millhouse'.⁶⁶ In 1613 Llewellyn was paid 'for making a ground plotte of the church yards and garden neere Sr Thomas Bodlies house and Pilkynton place the xxii^th of May 1613', apparently in connection with a lawsuit over Pilkington Place, which was just south of Bodley's house.⁶⁷ It was not a copy of the Hospital's slightly earlier plan of that area (Plan 16). This makes it likely that all the Smithfield plans were wholly Llewellyn's work. In one case, however, the accounts record a payment to another surveyor, Edward Mansell, for a plan of Greyfriars which seems to have been copied by Llewellyn (Plan 20). The £5 paid to Llewellyn in 1621 'for his extraordinary imployments in draughts' was small, but this was perhaps because some of the plans were only copies and at least one of those which was not had been paid for previously.⁶⁸

William Leybourn

After the Great Fire, William Leybourn (1626-1716) (Fig. 3) dominated the drawing of plans of London buildings for a quarter of a century, in a way that no-one would achieve again. Before the Fire he was a printer, in partnership with Robert Leybourn, possibly his brother. Apart from books, they printed the *Moderate Intelligencer* newspaper for several years. William wrote books as well as printing them: the first book in English on astronomy in 1649 (with Vincent Wing), a book on surveying in 1650, an enlarged version of the latter entitled *The compleat surveyor* in 1653, *Arithmetic* in 1657 (five editions by 1700) and subsequently other mathematical works.⁶⁹ *The compleat surveyor* was highly influential: according to A.W. Richeson, although Leybourn added little new to surveying, he probably exerted a greater influence on the practising surveyor than any other seventeenth-century writer (with one possible exception).⁷⁰ However, there is no evidence of Leybourn actually doing any surveying before 1666.

Leybourn acquired a small dwelling in Northcott in the parish of Southall early in 1666, and it has been suggested that this could be connected with his departure from printing. It seems more likely, however, that it was the Fire which ended his career as a printer. In a list of printers of 1668, 'Leybourne' is one of those listed under the heading 'disabled by ye fire'.⁷¹ If so, the Fire, having closed off one career, quickly opened up another as an actual surveyor. Leybourn was one of the

Fig. 3. William Leybourn in 1674, the year he completed his first plan book for a livery company (print by Robert White).

six men who carried out the survey of the City in December 1666. His first London plan was of land in Whitefriars bought by Thomas Hatton in December 1668, and his first plan for the Clothworkers' Company dates from August 1669. He continued to draw plans for the Clothworkers until at least 1689. One was drawn for the Ironmongers' Company in 1671-73. In 1672 John Ogilby put him in charge of his planned map of the City of London, working with other surveyors, and the map was eventually published by Ogilby and Morgan in January 1677.⁷² In 1674 Leybourn compiled a plan book for the Stationers' Company (Plans 30-33). By 1675 he was 'one of the sworne measurers of this City', which involved costing building work carried out for the City, and he was soon being described as 'City Measurer'.⁷³ By 1676 he was drawing plans for the Fishmongers' Company, though none seem to have survived until the plan book of 1686.⁷⁴

Even more important was that in 1676 Leybourn began to draw plans for the City, starting with a plan of London Wall and encroachments on it in 1676 (apparently based on surveying by others—see Plan 63) and plans of markets and of laystalls in 1677 (Plans 90, 123). From 1678 he drew the plans attached to each lease of City Lands.[75] Apart from the Clothworkers, the Fishmongers and the City, his other longer-term customer was St Thomas's Hospital from 1686 to at least 1688.[76] One-off commissions not already mentioned were for Christ's Hospital in 1675 (a plan of houses at Shoreditch) and 1680 (several plans),[77] the Dean of St Paul's in 1677 (a plan book), the Tallow Chandlers' Company in 1678 (a plan book), the Merchant Taylor's Company in 1680-82 (intended to result in a plan book, though no such book now exists),[78] the Bridge House in 1680-81 (plans of Battle Mills), 1683-84 (measuring of houses on London Bridge) and 1687 (plans of mills between Bow and Stratford),[79] Magdalen College, Oxford, in 1684 (five plans) and Rochester Bridge Trust in 1687 (a plan of a house).[80] There are few examples of him surveying rural estates.[81] He continued to write books, including in 1693 the first ready-reckoner in English, which still bore his name in the 1817 edition.[82]

Leybourn disengaged from surveying in the early 1690s. The City transferred its work to John Olley in 1694 (see below). Other surveyors began to obtain significant commissions, such as John Ward for the Clothworkers and the Goldsmiths in 1691 and Mr Biggs for the Skinners in about 1694. Leybourn retired to Northcott, informing his readers in 1694 that he provided mathematical instruction and took boarders there.[83] He died in 1716, aged about ninety.

Like other surveyors with a mathematical background, Leybourn sometimes added ornamental elements to his plans and nearly always made them colourful. They vary in the detail included, perhaps reflecting the clients' wishes. His plans of larger areas sometimes provide only outlines of buildings without any interior detail, but usually the arrangement of rooms, doors, stairs and fireplaces is shown, and occasionally windows. He sometimes described his plans as a 'planography' or 'ichnography', or even as 'planographicall draughts'.[84]

John and Isaac Olley

Plans drawn by John Olley and his son Isaac for the City form the largest component of this book. John Olley (c.1657-1719)[85] was a carpenter from Shoreditch, and continued to be based at Shoreditch, with the possible exception of 1706-11. His early carpentry work included rebuilding the steeple and mending the gallery and pews at Kentish Town Chapel in 1680, rebuilding work and repairs at Botolph Wharf and Hamond's Key in 1687 and work at several wharves in the 1690s for the cartel which ran most of London's Legal Quays. In 1719 the Mercers' Company owed him money for carpenter's work and surveying.[86] He also viewed houses frequently, often jointly with a bricklayer, Richard Smith, assessing the value of works required or the value and quality of works executed, and sometimes carried out the repairs he recommended.[87] From at least 1707 to 1713 Olley was one of the City of London's official viewers, who investigated disputes over boundaries and nuisances.[88] He was a member of two livery companies, the Basketmakers and the Carpenters.[89]

Olley's skill in viewing and measuring buildings made him well qualified to be the City's Clerk of the Works, and he purchased that office in 1693; subsequently he often described himself in depositions as surveyor of the City. The Clerk of the Works had no staff, but gave directions to the City Artificers, who carried out all the City's own building work. In 1698 he added the role of tracking repairs and improvements needed to houses on City land.[90] More important for our purposes is that in 1694 he succeeded Leybourn in a task which was carried out for the City but not necessarily by the Clerk of the Works: drawing the plans for City Lands leases. Years later, when seeking to prevent plans being drawn for the Bridge House by its own carpenter, Olley told the City Lands Committee what had happened: he was

> brought in upon his discovery of severall errors in a plott of Mr Leyburn's drawing [(]the Committee being then upon a view of the same premisses described by the said plott) who for his detecting the same and carefully drawing a plott thereof to the satisfaction of the abovesaid Committee, they was pleased upon the same to make a grant or order for him to do all such business for this honourable City for the future.[91]

The plan in question covered houses in Poor Jewry Lane, and Leybourn seems to have included more ground than was intended to be leased.[92] It should be noted that on one occasion Olley's own plans were returned to be corrected, though this was when he had been ordered to produce ten overdue plans within a week. In 1706 Olley was holding up the granting of leases by not providing plans.[93]

In 1700 the City Lands Committee ordered that Olley enter all plans drawn for City Lands leases into a book to be laid before it at each meeting, though it subsequently sometimes found both Olley and his son dilatory in doing so.[94] The two resulting books, covering 1700-12 and 1712-23, are an extraordinary monument to the surveying work of the Olleys.[95] All of John Olley's surviving plans were drawn for the City, though the viewing of houses sometimes resulted in him drawing plans for other clients.[96] The work was reasonably well rewarded. As well as fees from the City, the one detailed example of the expenses in acquiring a lease from the City (for the Wormwood Street almshouses) includes a payment of £1.10s.0d to John Olley for the plan.[97] In 1706 Olley secured a lease from the City of a dwelling in Basinghall Postern, backing onto the City's yard known as the Green Yard, partly because he had promised to live there 'for the more commodious service of the City in this station' (Plan 155).

Olley also had other activities. He designed at least four buildings: Emanuel Hospital in Westminster in or about 1698 (Plan 188), Waterstock House in Oxfordshire in about 1700 (with Richard Smith),[98] the tower of Woodford church in Essex in 1708 and an extension to the Angel Inn, Little Brickhill, Buckinghamshire, in 1708-09 (for the then Lord Mayor). In the case of Woodford he set out during a lawsuit exactly the role he had played: he drew 'a modell or draft' of the new tower, which was given to the bricklayer, though he believed its purpose was to be shown to the parishioners for their approval; he was 'the surveyor of the rebuilding thereof to see that the work was well done', making many journeys there for that purpose; and he viewed, measured and valued the work done and inspected the workmen's bills. In effect he acted as architect, with design and production being separated.[99] In the case of Little Brickhill, he drew 'a draught' for the Lord Mayor's approval and then visited Little Brickhill several times 'to see the said building & repairs carryed on & perfected'.[100]

Olley was also a speculative builder. In 1701 he took a lease of City land at Windmill Hill (probably the one near Moorfields) where he was to build two new houses. Four tenements in Shoreditch Street had been erected by him before 1714, and ten in Hanover Court, Grub Street, by 1719. He had probably also built the seven tenements in Shoreditch mentioned in his inventory of 1719.[101] Olley took a greater risk in leasing the Fleet Channel and its wharves from the City in 1705 for £100 a year, with a requirement to spend £1,500 on repairs. His widow Mary later claimed (when being sued by the City over it in 1729) that he had been a great loser by it, and his inventory stated that the channel was very much out of repair and the lease was worth nothing. Nevertheless, Olley had assigned the lease to Robert Sandford in 1713 for £160 a year, and Sandford's rent was only one quarter in arrears at Olley's death.[102] Olley was living in reasonable comfort in 1719. His house had three and a half storeys, with a kitchen and two parlours on the ground floor. It contained fashionable items such as an oval table, a Dutch tea table, a weather glass, a coffee pot and a silver watch. However, the value of his property was exceeded by mortgages totalling £1,500.[103]

Olley left one son, Isaac (c.1690-1724), and two daughters. Like his father, Isaac described himself as being of Shoreditch and a citizen and carpenter. The City's Clerk of the Works could, for a fee, nominate his successor, and Isaac succeeded as Clerk of the Works at the end of 1711. John and Isaac both signed some of the City Lands plans of 1712 and 1713, but thereafter all were signed by Isaac; Isaac may in fact have been involved earlier in the lettering on the plans. Isaac's bills record his work drawing plans, viewing properties, attending committees and auditing workmen's bills for the City. Payments were sometimes withheld because of delays in entering plans in the book, and in December 1715 he was given ten guineas as 'encouragement' to do so. There is one record of him measuring ground and drawing a ground plot for another client (at Richmond) in 1713. His term as Clerk of the Works was cut short by his early death.[104]

Mathematicians

Those drawing plans can be classified in two ways. The first distinction is between those who frequently drew plans of London buildings, such as Leybourn and the Olleys, and those who drew only one or a few such plans over a short period. In some cases the latter chanced to be on the spot when a landowner wanted a plan drawn, as in the cases of John Coffyn in Fetter Lane and John Friend in East Lane (Plans 28, 60, 61). The second distinction is between, on the one hand, mathematicians such as Leybourn and, on the other hand, those in the building trades such as the Olleys, together with a few who were more architects than builders.

In the seventeenth century mathematics was about the practical application of scientific knowledge, and it encompassed subjects such as navigation, gunnery, fortification and surveying. Besides Leybourn, two of the mathematician-surveyors are especially notable. John Ward (*c*.1648-*c*.1727) (Fig. 4) was a mathematics teacher and a bestselling author of mathematical works. The Clothworkers' Company considered commissioning him to compile a plan book in 1690, and, although this never materialised, he drew plans (generally plot outlines) for the Company from at least 1691 to 1707.[105] He is represented here by the magnificent plans he produced for the Goldsmiths' Company in 1692, which were his only work for that Company (Plans 44-46, 99, 108). He also drew a few maps of rural estates.[106] Only the barest outline of his life is recorded. His date of birth is given by the date and age on his portrait, and the approximate date of death by the fact that he was alive in 1723 and *Ward's posthumous works* appeared in 1730. When his first book was published in 1695 he described himself as formerly General Gauger of Excise (gauging was the calculation of the volume contained within particular containers, such as the number of gallons in a cask). The portrait of 1706 describes him as 'John Ward of Chester', but he was still then teaching mathematics in London, so it may indicate that he was brought up in Chester. In that year he referred to 'my house near the Kings-gate in Red-Lyon Fields'.[107] In 1707 he published *The young mathematician's guide; being a plain and easie introduction to the mathe-maticks*, which became one of the most popular mathematics textbooks of the Georgian period. Other works dealt with algebra, navigation and plane and spherical geometry. By 1713 he was teaching mathematics in Chester.[108] Ward's work for the Goldsmiths is notable for its elaborate cartouches, coats of arms, compass roses and scale bars (Fig. 5), not necessarily drawn by Ward himself, and the attention paid to floral borders in gardens. Also notable is the sum of £130 the Goldsmiths agreed to pay for his eighteen large plans (or ten if those covering the same areas are discounted).[109] Whereas some of the plans provide little more than the outlines of buildings and their doors, others include staircases and windows; in some cases the level of detail varies within a single plan (Plan 45).

Heber Lands (1672-*c*.1736) was less successful as an author but had a longer career as a surveyor of London buildings. His *A short treatise of practical gauging* was appended to John Darling's *The carpenter's rule made easie* from at least 1694 to 1738. In 1694 he advertised himself as teaching the

Fig. 4. John Ward, surveyor and teacher of mathematics, in 1706 (print by Michael van der Gucht).

mathematical arts and sciences in Holford Court, which was off Fenchurch Street almost opposite Rood Lane. In 1709 he was teaching at Salisbury Court, Fleet Street. There is no such advertisement in the 1727 or 1738 editions.[110] His earliest plans, starting in 1712, were of rural estates.[111] He drew London plans for Christ's Hospital from at least 1716 to 1723 (Plans 54, 80, 81), for the Earl of Northampton in 1720, for St Bartholomew's Hospital from at least 1725 to 1735, for the City Lands Committee and for Rochester Bridge Trust in 1730, for the Skinners' Company in 1736 and for Magdalen College, Oxford, at an unknown date.[112] Like Ward's, his plans are notable for their ornamentation.

Several other mathematician-surveyors are represented in this book. John Smith of Marine Square (later Wellclose Square) drew plans for the Clothworkers at least from 1710 to 1720 and described himself as 'teacher of ye mathematicks in Marine Square' (Plan 148).[113] Thomas Badeslade, who plotted Rochester Bridge Trust's houses in Leadenhall Street in 1719 (Plan 55),

Fig. 5. Cartouche from Ward's plan of Jewin Street, 1692.

described himself as a professor of mathematics in 1724, and at his death in 1744 was described as a surveyor and mathematician of St Clement Danes and Finnant, Montgomeryshire. He drew rural estate maps in several counties, and was also an engineer.[114] Walter Henshaw (born c.1634), a parishioner of St Botolph Aldgate who drew a plan of that church in 1706 (Plan 117), was described as a mathematical instrument maker in 1694 and a citizen and clockmaker in 1696 and 1699.[115] Others not represented here are Samuel Parsons, mentioned above; Henry Bond senior, 'practicioner in the mathematicks and survaighor', who drew a plan of the Pardon Churchyard, St Paul's, in 1666 and one of Hare Street in 1671;[116] Ralph Greatorex (d.1675), mathematical instrument maker and inventor, who worked on Leake's map of the City after the Great Fire and drew plans of the Royal Arsenal at Woolwich, Whitehall Palace and Windsor Castle;[117] Hugh Handy, 'Philomathematicus', who compiled a book of plot outlines for the Drapers' Company in 1698; and John Rowley (alive 1698-1728), mathematical instrument maker in Fleet Street, who drew at least one plan for Christ's Hospital and was described by John Ward as 'one of the best workmen of his trade in Europe'.[118]

Builders

One of the surveyors from the building trades who appears most in this volume is Joseph Titcombe or Tidcombe (c.1638-95)[119] (Plans 35, 36, 106). He was the son of Thomas Titcombe, a carpenter of Hammersmith, and was apprenticed in 1651 to another Hammersmith carpenter, Thomas Whitehead, whose daughter Elizabeth he later married. Whitehead, though a carpenter by trade, was a member of the Armourers' Company, which explains Titcombe's own connection with that Company. Titcombe lived in the parish of St Stephen Coleman Street (where Armourers' Hall lay) at least from 1658 to 1679, and left £10 for twenty poor householders of that parish in his will, but had moved to St Giles Cripplegate by 1687.[120] His recorded carpentry work included building two farmhouses and two barns at Hartford near Huntingdon in 1665, a house in Cheapside in 1668, for which the contract with a plan survives, and turnstiles and turnpikes for the City's laystall at Bunhill Fields in 1672.[121] In 1672 he and others were asked to consider the agreement made for building the City's houses in Aldermanbury and to advise on payments, and he was also, like John Olley, one of the City's viewers, from at least 1674 to 1691.[122] He sometimes acted in a similar capacity for the Armourers, viewing building work and advising on repairs, and did the same for individuals.[123] He was a Common Councilman from 1672 to 1675. He became one of the Armourers' Assistants in 1678, Renter Warden in 1683 and Master in 1686. After he became an Assistant and started attending Court meetings in 1678 the Armourers quickly recognised his usefulness, and the plan book he compiled for the Company is probably related to his becoming an Assistant, though the minutes contain only a decision to pay him £12 for having plotted the Company's lands on sheets of vellum and that the sheets should be bound up and 'perticulerly discribed for this Companyes use'.[124] Titcombe made little use of colour, but his plans were more detailed than Leybourn's as he showed windows as well as doors, stairs and fireplaces. No other plans of his survive, with the probable exception of the building plan of the house in Cheapside.

Another example is Nathaniel Hanwell, also a carpenter, born in about 1640. He was living at the Mint, Southwark, in 1665, Chick Lane, Smithfield, in 1668, the parish of St Martin Vintry in 1677 and College Hill (partly in the same parish) in 1680. Like John Olley and Titcombe he sometimes undertook views of building work — like Olley in the company of a bricklayer.[125] In 1681 he drew plans of four houses and the gateway of St Thomas's Hospital in the High Street, Southwark, 'as how they are and as they may be conveniently built', and he was evidently one of the carpenters who worked on the subsequent rebuilding, judging by the £60 bill paid in 1682. That plan has not survived, but his beautifully-drawn plan of the Hospital's property in Grange Road, Bermondsey, has (Plan 144).[126] He seems to have done no other work for the Hospital, and no other plans by him are known.

Several of those employed by Christ's Hospital to draw London plans also fall into the builder category, though not all. The somewhat fragmentary records, chiefly the Hospital's accounts[127] and names and dates on the plans themselves, identify the following: Richard Daynes 1656-59 and 1664, a surveyor mainly of rural estates; William Conyers 1663-68, bricklayer of St Sepulchre (born c.1635);[128] Joseph Hutchinson 1667-71, carpenter (born c.1611);[129] John Daynes 1668-71, who also drew ground plots for the Earl of Southampton and New College, Oxford (Plan 126);[130] John Leake c.1671, surveyor; Thomas Pluckenett 1674; William Leybourn 1675 and 1680; John Saxton 1675-82, carpenter (born c.1648);[131] Isaac Rowe 1682-83, surveyor and architect (see below); Roger Lawrence 1692; and John Hobbs 1698-1702 (Plans 147, 174, 175). Joseph Lem, citizen and tyler and bricklayer, started a plan book for the Skinners' Company in the early 1680s.[132] Many unattributed plans were probably also by builders. The leases for Arlington Street in 1682 indicate that it was normal for bricklayers and carpenters, at least those building substantial properties, to be able to draw a building plan or at least to procure one (Plans 192-95). The skill of measuring and valuing building work and that of surveying, both being based on mathematics, probably went together, as in the case of Thomas Arnald, who described himself as 'carpenter & measurer' on a plan of 1687.[133]

Architects

As well as John Olley, three surveyors represented here can be considered as architects. Isaac Rowe, who drew a London plan in 1671 and several for Christ's Hospital in 1682-83 (Plan 146), is recorded between 1663 and 1686, usually drawing architectural plans or ground plans for proposed buildings, especially alterations to Northamptonshire houses. In 1686 he produced a ground plan for what later became Smith Square, Westminster, and was described as a surveyor. He was probably the painter stainer of London born in about 1637.[134]

James Gould, surveyor and architect, produced a plan book for the Salters' Company in 1709, did surveying work for the Fishmongers' Company from 1710 to 1717, was surveyor to the Dyers' Company from 1716 to 1723 (Plan 72), producing a plan book in 1721, mapped one of St Thomas's Hospital's rural estates in 1723 and other rural estates in several counties, and was surveyor to the South Sea Company from 1723 until his death in 1734. As an architect, he designed South Sea House (1724-25) and St Botolph Bishopsgate (1725-28). His daughter married George Dance senior.[135]

William Dickinson (c.1671-1725), though he regarded himself as an architect, spent more of his working life as a surveyor or clerk of works than as a designer of new buildings. He was Clerk of the Works at Greenwich Hospital in 1696-1701/2, a measurer at St Paul's Cathedral from 1696, assistant to Wren in connection with the rebuilding of the City churches, Deputy Surveyor of the Fabric and Surveyor to the Dean and Chapter of Westminster in 1711-25, one of the Surveyors to the Commissioners for Building Fifty New Churches in London in 1711-13 and Clerk of the Works at Whitehall, St James's and Westminster in 1713-15.[136] Most of his plans for the Dean and Chapter provide little detail, apart from his survey of the Deanery reproduced here (Plan 130).

One surveyor represented here falls into none of the categories above. John Friend lived at East Lane, Bermondsey, which explains his plans covering East Lane and nearby areas (Plans 60, 61). He described himself as a 'hydrographer', and was one of a sequence of seven generations of masters and apprentices who were members of the Drapers' Company and drew sea charts. Friend was born in about 1665, the son of a cordwainer, and was apprenticed to the chartmaker and surveyor, Joel Gascoyne, in 1681-89. Friend's dated charts are from 1703 to 1709. Like Gascoyne, faced by increasing competition from printed charts, he also drew estate maps, in his case both of urban and rural estates.[137]

Drawing a plan required certain technical skills, but these were evidently not hard to acquire. This, together with the limited number of plans landowners wanted, helps to explain why many surveyors apparently drew just one plan or group of plans very competently while never regarding that as their main occupation. Of all the post-Fire surveyors of London buildings in the period covered here, the only ones apart from Leybourn and the Olleys who produced more than an occasional plan or group of plans and were active for more than a few years were James Gould and Heber Lands.

SURVEYING

Methods

The surveyors who worked on Ogilby and Morgan's map of 1676, the first detailed non-pictorial map of London, found three tools essential: the fifty-foot wire chain for measuring distances, the semicircle (a brass semi-circle with two sights) for measuring angles, and the five-foot or ten-foot offset rod for measuring the distances of buildings and side streets from the chain. The method was described by one of them, John Holwell, as follows: having decided what measurements were needed, the surveyor would place a man at a point along the street visible from his own position, and would then measure the distance to him using the chain; he would measure the distances between the chain and the buildings and side streets along the way using the offset rod; and he would measure the angle between the line of the chain and the line to the previous sighting point using the semicircle. He would then move to the point where he had first placed his assistant and begin the process again to a new sighting point. All the time, having previously made an 'eye-draught' or rough sketch, he would be noting down his measurements. Having dealt with the main streets, he could move on to lesser streets, and finally measure the size of alleys and (if necessary) the width and depth of houses. Alleys and houses were measured with the rod or bevel, a flat rule with a movable tongue for determining angles. The measurements could then be transferred to vellum or paper, using ruler and protractor.[138]

Gregory King's preparatory sketch for a map of St Katherine's (Fig. 6) shows how it was done, including the measuring of distances between sighting points and angles between sighting lines and the more straightforward measuring of short distances such as the widths of buildings. In this case a separate set of sketches distinguished individual houses and recorded their dimensions.[139] For the plans of larger areas included in this book the methods described by Holwell were probably used, but for individual buildings there was no need for sighting lines; instead, the surveyor had only to measure lengths and angles. Nothing was more important than correctly showing the outer boundary of the plot, and with buildings which were not freestanding this must have created difficulties, especially where landlords such as the City were concerned with inches or even halves of an inch. The surveyor could see the external walls from inside, but it must often have been unclear how thick they were and whether they were party walls or belonged wholly to the property being surveyed, and therefore exactly where the boundary was.[140] How this difficulty was overcome is unknown.

The surveyor drawing plans for a particular landowner, unlike one drawing a map of a whole town or city, needed to know exactly what belonged to that landowner, which might not be straightforward. Presumably for this reason, when Mr Biggs surveyed the Skinners' Company's properties in about 1695 he was assisted by the Company's Clerk, who was paid £65 for his 'extraordinary services', whereas Biggs was paid only £40. The Merchant Taylors likewise ordered their Beadle to accompany Leybourn around the Company's properties in 1680.[141] The Goldsmiths' Company seems not to have provided similar help for John Ward when he surveyed its lands in 1692. The Company's minutes for 1738 state that 'the plans drawn at a large expence in 1692 are very imperfect and in particular do not show six houses standing in a court in Great New Street demised in 1668 to Ferdinando Gorges besides the Clerk (as he says upon inquiry) was told those houses were not the Company's but were freehold whereas the contrary (as he alledged) now appears'.[142] The imperfection was not in the accuracy of Ward's drawing but in the identification of the Company's houses. The errors which caused Leybourn to stop drawing lease plans for the City seem to have been similar (see above).

Much of what a plan of a building showed could be checked, and the plans often were checked, which is the main reason for regarding

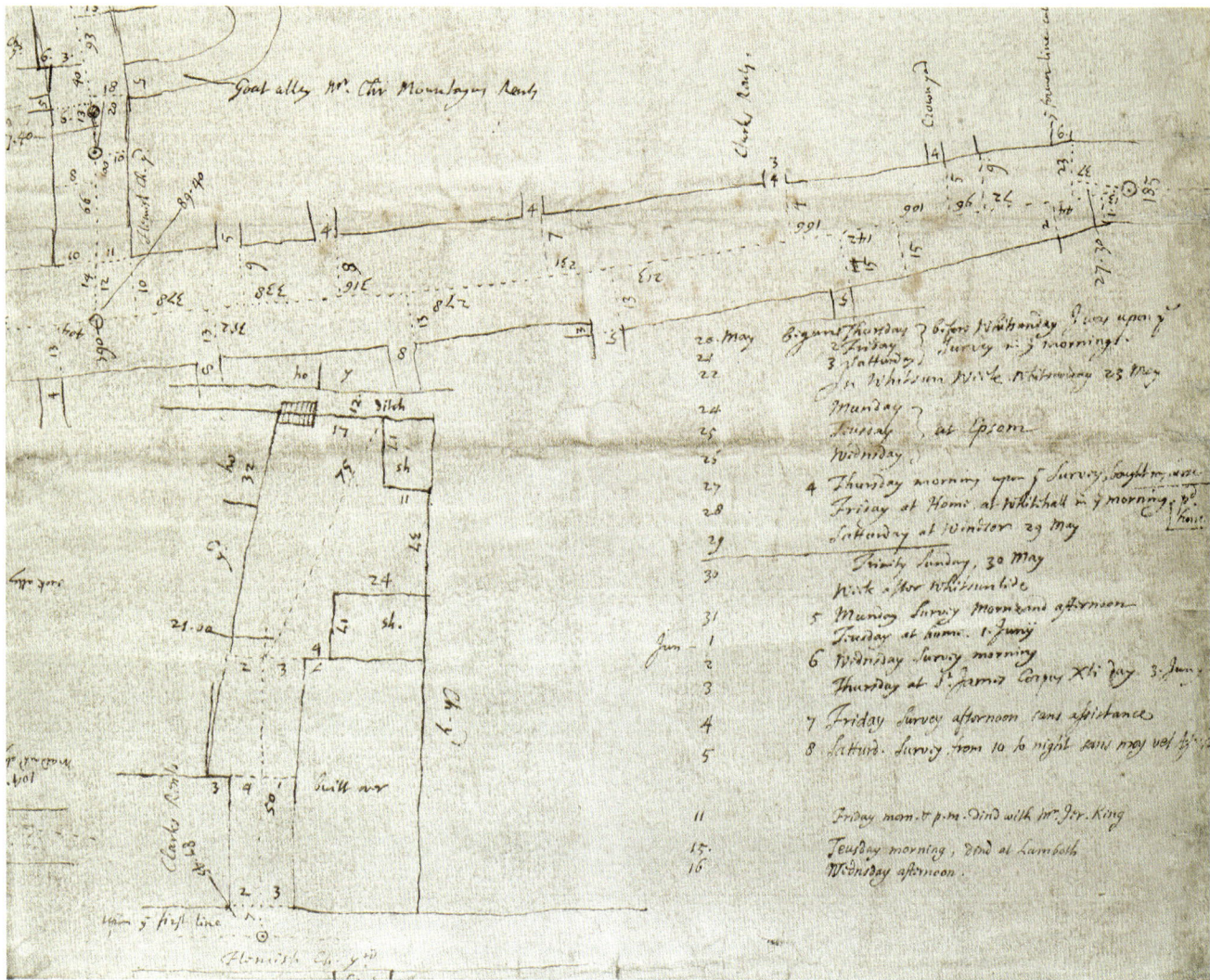

Fig. 6. Part of one of Gregory King's preliminary sketches for a plan of the precinct of St Katherine, east of the Tower, 1686. At the top is St Katherine's Lane, with the chain laid along the street from one measuring point marked by a circle to the next. Figures indicate distances from the starting point, distance at right angles from the chain to the street frontages, the width of side streets or alleys, and the angles between the line of the chain and other lines measured. At the bottom left is a court, Clark's Rents, with similar chain lines and figures but more measurements made along walls. The sketch itself is of course not to scale.

them as generally accurate. When the Tallow Chandlers received Leybourn's plan book and had a preliminary inspection, they decided that 'the same should be examined more perticulerlie upon the premises'. The Ironmongers similarly, having received his plan of Old Street, 'went into Ould Streete, & compared severall ould mapps with one new drawne by [William Leybourn], which they fynde to be done exactly'.[143] Titcombe's plans were stated on the title page of the plan book to be 'approved off to be well done by the three other veiwers of the said Citty'. Written measurements might also be checked, such as Leybourn's of the houses on the middle part of London Bridge in 1683-84: John Oliver, the City's surveyor, went from house to house with workmen to see 'if the said Mr Leyburne had taken the same exactly'.[144] As indicated above, some of Leybourn's plans for the City were corrected by John Olley, and some of Olley's plans were returned to him for amending. If a lease relied on the plan rather than also giving measurements in writing, it was obviously essential that the plan be accurate, but it was almost as important, if measurements *were* given in the lease, that plan and lease agreed: when they differed in 1700 for some houses in Houndsditch, Olley's plan was found to be correct.[145]

However, when plans were drawn for a specific purpose, such as Leybourn's showing market stalls, anything not relevant to that purpose is less likely to be accurate, such as the exact dimensions of the market buildings in that case (Plan 89). This applied especially to maps drawn in connection with lawsuits. Also, longer distances and exact plot shapes, which were hard to check on the ground, rarely correspond exactly to more accurately surveyed modern maps (e.g. Plans 24, 89).

Styles

As already discussed, plans varied in the level of detail included. In general, the larger the area plotted, the less detail was provided. Almost all surveyors showed doorways, chimneys and stairs, though neither John Daynes nor Saxton included stairs, whereas it was not always considered necessary to show windows and the exact thickness of walls. The extent to which customers specified what they wanted probably varied. In 1680 Leybourn promised to plot the Merchant Taylors' properties according to a specimen provided,[146] and, while he usually ignored windows and drew walls simply as lines, he produced more detailed plans for the Stationers and the Dean of St Paul's (Plans 31-33, 127). The variation in the level of detail in John Ward's plans for the Goldsmiths, even within the same plan, suggests that he received no clear instructions (Plan 45). Scale varied from one plan to another, the most common being ten feet to the inch. The Olleys usually drew at six, eight or ten feet to the inch.

The convention that brick walls should be red, timber ones yellow and stone ones grey was usually followed, though not by Leybourn. Where there were different materials at different levels, the surveyor presumably used the colour of either the predominant material (Plan 64) or the material at ground level, which might be a wooden shopfront (the Rebuilding Act allowed timber in the ground floor 'for conveniency of shopps').[147] There was obviously variation in styles as regards borders (if any), use of colours, lettering and the design of scale bars, compass roses and cartouches, and the same surveyor might vary his style and even his lettering.[148] The decorative elements may sometimes have been applied by someone with more artistic skill than the surveyor,[149] and in two cases there is documentary evidence that the person who drew the final version of the plan was not the one who did the surveying (Plans 62, 63). Surveyors often gave no indication that the upper storeys of buildings extended over alleys and yards, but Leybourn devised his own way of doing so (Plan 90) and some surveyors used dotted lines (e.g. Plan 55). They rarely provided any context by mapping parts of adjacent properties, other than by sometimes stating abuttals and street names, and what is shown is sometimes clarified when located on a map covering a larger area (e.g. Plan 135).

Costs

Payments for plans varied according to the size and complexity of the area covered, and probably also the level of detail required and the number of copies provided. Sometimes they were agreed in advance and sometimes (apparently) after the work was completed. The basis of calculation is rarely explained, but in 1676 the Fishmongers agreed with Leybourn that he should have 4s. per house each time he plotted the Company's properties, for which he was to provide a plan on vellum with a description in writing.[150] The Merchant Taylors agreed in 1680 to pay him 5s. per house for a plan book, to be abated in the case of plots already made, and in the same year he claimed to have made surveys at that rate for the Stationers, Ironmongers and Fishmongers.[151] In other cases we have to rely on what was actually paid (Appendix 2). Up to the 1660s, the few plans for which the cost is known tend to be of relatively large areas, requiring relatively large payments. The main exception is most of Treswell's plans, for which the Clothworkers paid just over 23s. each.

Later there is more evidence, especially for Christ's Hospital from 1663 to 1680. The Hospital seems to have paid a standard 10s. per plan, unless the buildings to be plotted were extensive, such as a mansion at Greyfriars, what was probably a mansion in Fenchurch Street, houses at Shoreditch and a large area of the Town Ditch, each of these costing from £2 to £3. For plan books, Leybourn received just over 18s. per plan from the Tallow Chandlers in 1678 and about 21s. per plan from the Fishmongers in 1686, not far from Treswell's 23s., while Titcombe received £2 per plan from the Armourers in 1679. Leybourn was paid more for his plans of markets in 1677 (just over £5 each), and Hanwell was well paid for three copies of his plan of three houses in Bermondsey in 1682 (£1.10s.0d) (Plan 144). A payment by the Clothworkers in 1691 suggests 2s.6d per house, and one to Olley in 1697 5s. per house. From about 1692 payments seem to have increased, starting with about £13 per plan for John Ward in that year, though most of his plans covered numerous buildings and were provided in two or more versions. In 1717 Heber Lands received the largest sum recorded for a single plan (£25), covering fifty-one houses and an inn (Plan 54).

Landowners obviously paid for plans commissioned for their own purposes, but only in the case of Christ's Hospital in 1663-80 is it clear that the landowner rather than the lessee normally paid for lease plans.[152] In 1669 the Fishmongers' Company ordered that tenants pay the surveyor for plans in parchment to be attached to their leases (at 3s.4d per house), but this was for the plot outlines often attached to leases in the immediate post-Fire period.[153] The one record of the costs of obtaining a City Lands lease (for the Wormwood Street almshouses) indicates that the lessee paid £1.10s.0d for the plan (Plan 187),[154] but whether this was normal for such leases is unknown.

PLANS AND LONDON'S HOUSES

The plans of houses reproduced here span two centuries, and many show houses built long before they were drawn. The plans begin when almost all houses were of timber, except a few stone ones of medieval origin, and end when almost all were being built of brick, at least in central areas. Many surveyors, though not Leybourn, consistently indicated whether walls were of timber or brick, and the width of walls occasionally indicates the presence of stone (Plan 12). Up to the time of Treswell's surveys, brick was generally used for garden walls, wells, chimneys and ovens, and occasionally for the sides of buildings, and a few brick buildings had appeared in the preceding century or so, at royal palaces, the inns of court and livery company halls, and as almshouses.[155] From 1619 royal proclamations and statutes required all new buildings in London and the surrounding area to have brick outer walls, but at first this had limited effect, and it obviously applied only to new buildings.[156] The parliamentary surveys of 1650-51 indicate that less than 10% of houses in Shadwell, the Tower Liberty and the Strand were of brick, but over 60% of those in Piccadilly, Long Acre and High Holborn (areas developed in the early seventeenth century).[157]

The plans in this book indicate brick being used for almshouses in Wormwood Street in about 1610, a house in Houndsditch in about 1624, tenements off Long Acre in 1638, tenements in Dolphin Court and Great Swordbearers Alley (both on City land) in the 1640s, a City inn in the 1640s and tenements in Goldsmiths' Alley and Primrose Alley by 1651 (Plans 43-45, 50, 56, 94, 177, 178, 187). Sometimes this reflected the landowner's policy; for example, the City stipulated that the new buildings at Dolphin Court must conform to the proclamations, which meant brick.[158] The Bridge House, on the other hand, did not insist on brick, and the impressive timber houses in Bishopsgate of 1657 were built on its land (Plan 47).[159] The brick tenements of the 1650s between Coleman and Goat Alleys in Finsbury warn against assuming that brick houses were necessarily of better quality (Plan 84). Indeed a house encased in a shell of bricks was likely to be a more impermanent structure than a wholly timber one, and even in brick-faced houses the entire interior (except fireplaces) was generally of timber, as many plans in this book show; hence the many major fires after 1666.[160] The Rebuilding Act of 1667, which was relatively well enforced, largely put a stop to the building of all-timber houses in the City, but there was a house of the 1690s in Mitre Court with only brick side walls and a timber front and back (Plan 134), and a timber building with a jettied first floor was put up at the corner of Fenchurch Street and Billiter Lane as late as 1700 (Plan 41). In the southern suburbs timber building remained the norm well into the eighteenth century.[161]

Treswell's plans and others of the same period depict institutions' properties or groups of properties and the tenancies and sub-tenancies into which they were divided, rather than necessarily recognisable houses. Many houses had been subdivided or amalgamated with others, and this sometimes resulted in tenancies being intermixed on different levels of the same building (e.g. Plans 22, 24). Even if the tenancies were straightforward, the sub-tenancies and the actual occupation might not be; indeed this might be the reason for having a plan drawn (Plan 146). After the Great Fire there was not only some tidying of boundaries[162] but also untangling of intermixed tenancies, sometimes, as on the Fishmongers' property in Thames Street, resisted by a tenant who wished to recreate exactly what he had had before.[163] However, there are also a few examples of intermixed tenancies being recreated after the Fire (Plan 131) or developing gradually in post-Fire buildings.

Fig. 7. Part of the north side of Cheapside in 1638, looking east from Friday Street, during the processional entry to the city of Marie de Medici (detail from a print published in 1639).

Fig. 8. Pre-Fire houses on the south side of Aldgate, seen from the end of Leadenhall Street in the late nineteenth century. The last of these houses was demolished in about 1906.

Fig. 9. 37 Cheapside, on the corner of Friday Street: an example of a post-Fire house of one-room plan, photographed in about 1883. It still retained its original windows in the upper storeys. It was demolished in 1928.

Fig. 10. An example of a large post-Fire house, in Sherborne Lane, on the west side facing the east-west part of the street. It was said to have been built in 1667 and was drawn by John Wykeham Archer in 1862, by which time its original windows had been replaced by sash windows.

A plan of a house in Paternoster Row in 1709 needed a green line to indicate the outline of the first floor, as it scarcely coincided at all with the ground floor, mainly because of the subdivision of the ground-floor shop.[164] The Fire had tidied up the previous complexity without completely stopping the process that created it. That probably depended on greater use of brick and greater emphasis on party walls as barriers against fire.

As for subdivision within houses, Edward Hatton reckoned in 1708 that about ten per cent of London's houses were subdivided, and other evidence is consistent with this, though the proportion varied by district and by period and was sometimes higher.[165] Small houses sometimes had stairs at the front, which would have made subdivision easy and was perhaps intended to (e.g. Plans 169, 176, 178). The plans do not necessarily reveal subdivision, and even the number of dwellings stated in associated documents may not acknowledge it, but sources which say who was in occupation, such as the Goldsmiths' survey of 1651 and the journals of the City Lands Committee (from 1699) indicate very little subdivision except in small houses (Plans 45, 51, 84, 176). Occasionally the hearth tax lists of the 1660s and 1670s reveal subdivision otherwise unrecorded (Plan 35).

The number of storeys is often not stated. In the City it should have been determined by the Rebuilding Act of 1667, which provided for 'houses of the greatest bigness' to have up to four storeys, houses on 'high and principal streets' to have four storeys, houses on 'streets and lanes of note' three storeys and houses in 'by-streets and lanes' two storeys, in each case with cellars and garrets as well (the latter was usually counted as a half-storey). In practice there were no 'by-streets and lanes', as a decision of the City's Common Council in March 1667 allocated all streets and alleys to the other two categories, so there should not have been any two and a half storey houses.[166] Where the number of storeys is known it generally conformed to the rules, but with a few exceptions. There were two and a half storey houses in Church Entry and off Harp Lane, where there should have been three and a half storeys (Plans 29, 116). Houses in Pudding Lane (on City land) and Harp Lane had four and a half storeys (Plans 29, 154), and some of the Stationers' houses had four and a half storeys or even (at the 'Dark House' at Billingsgate) five storeys,[167] in all which cases there should have been three and a half.

Types of house

The plans used here are not of course a random sample of the different sizes and qualities of housing. Higher-quality housing is over-represented, partly because of geographical bias, with too few plans of suburban houses, and partly because plans tended to be commissioned by institutions rather than private individuals and they were less likely to acquire the lower-quality housing. Nevertheless, most large holdings did include some small houses, and many of them appear on plans (e.g. Plans 17, 34, 35, 45, 169, 173-85). With its extensive extra-mural and suburban holdings the City probably had the most representative estate in social terms, though even this probably did not include the worst sorts of accommodation, such as sheds and converted stables.

John Schofield's classification of houses into four plan types is largely followed here,[168] though counting rooms is not straightforward, and many houses could arguably have been placed in a different category. In particular, they might have a single large shop on the ground floor but two rooms on the upper floors, rooms might be partitioned on one floor, there might be additional small rooms such as closets or butteries, and there might be an additional back kitchen and other offices separated from the main house by a yard. Also, houses with a similar type of plan varied greatly in size.

Type 1 had only one room on each floor. These were generally the smallest houses, but the one room could be large (Plans 182, 183) and, at least until the Rebuilding Act, there could be as many as five and a half storeys.[169] They were likely to be better lit than houses of two-room plan. The smallest included here were on Holborn Hill (nine feet square) and in Fore Street (eight by twelve and a half feet) (Plans 142, 181). Some were back-to-backs. These were never a common house-type in London, but might appear where sites were cramped (Plans 26, 30, 32, 34) or even where alternative layouts would have been possible (Plan 174-75).[170] Lessees sub-letting the smallest houses obtained only a precarious income, as some of them pointed out (Plans 177, 178).

Type 2 had two rooms in plan, and was the most common type. In Treswell's time, the ground floor of this sort of house was usually occupied by a shop with a warehouse behind, and the first floor usually by a hall at the front and a kitchen at the back.[171] In the period 1666-1720, if there was no shop the ground-floor rooms were almost invariably parlour and kitchen. A shop at the front meant that the parlour was on the first floor instead (at the front); if the shop occupied the whole ground floor, as many did, the kitchen also retreated upstairs to the first floor (at the back), so that the layout was the same as in Treswell's time apart from the change of name from hall to parlour. Other rooms were usually described as chambers. While there was not much variation in rooms, there was great variation in plan. Common plans included central stairs (between the front and back rooms), central stairs with central chimney stack (instead of chimneys in the side walls or corners), and stairs at the side at the back. In the City the majority of houses were of irregular plan, and stairs tended to be winding stairs, which could be anywhere. Different plans might be used in the same development, and even by the same builder (Plans 147, 192-95), sometimes because in narrower plots it was hard to squeeze in a rear staircase without making the back room too small. The earliest example here of the rear staircase plan is from 1638, which seems to be the earliest known (Plan 56). It became standard by 1720 for houses for the middling sort of about twenty-feet width, as well as for some narrower houses, although the central stairs layout also continued to be used throughout the eighteenth century. The central chimney plan became unusual north of the river after about 1720, but remained popular south of the river.[172] Another variation was that, while most London houses presented their short sides to the street in order to make the best use of the valuable street frontage, some on shallow plots presented their long sides to the street or alley (Plans 28, 47, 168).[173] Some of these, as at Nevill's Alley, were lobby-entry houses, where entry was to a small hall communicating with both rooms, and stairs and chimney stacks were behind the hall (Plan 28).

Type 3 had three to six rooms in plan. The examples here include pre-Fire timber houses in the City (Plans 18, 22, 38, 141), a pre-Fire brick house (Plan 139), post-Fire houses in the City (Plans 28, 41, 111, 131, 132, 134-38) and late seventeenth-century brick houses in Bermondsey (Plan 60). In the few cases where the hearth tax assessment is known it was from nine to thirteen hearths.

Type 4, the largest houses, are a miscellaneous group in this book: a medieval mansion (Plan 130), converted monastic buildings (Plan 125), four mansions wholly or largely of the sixteenth century (Plans 6, 12, 16, 24), two early seventeenth-century mansions in the Strand (Plans 13, 14), four post-Fire houses in the City which were two rooms deep (Plans 46, 127-29) and one post-Fire courtyard house (Plan 126). They ranged in size from sixteen hearths up to twenty-eight at the Deanery at Westminster and sixty-three at Northumberland House. Similar to this group, and all arranged around courtyards, were the seven company halls included here (Plans 23, 24, 105-09). The Strand mansions were intended to be visible and impressive, but most of the others were tucked away in courtyards so that valuable street frontage could be used more profitably, albeit sometimes with a gatehouse (Plan 46). Several of the houses display careful planning on constricted sites, especially as regards light and street access for stables.

Rooms

Most plans cover only ground floors. For upper floors in the early seventeenth century this section relies on Treswell's written descriptions as calendared by Schofield and on descriptions of houses in Cheapside and around Drapers' Hall (Plans 22, 24). For the later seventeenth century it relies mainly on descriptions in plan books of the Stationers' property in 1674 and the Armourers' property in 1679, abstracts of Goldsmiths' Company leases from about 1650 to 1675, the few City Lands leases with schedules of fittings and the few plans covering all floors. It has only occasionally been possible to link probate inventories to the houses shown on the plans.

Houses were not of course only for living in. On streets of any importance there was usually a shop occupying some or all of the ground floor. There were unusually large shops at Nonsuch House, the White Bear in Cheapside and behind Leadenhall Street (Plans 7, 22, 55). At the other extreme were lock-up shops in Bread Street, in the churchyard of St Botolph Aldgate (only between four and five feet deep) and in the forecourt of St Paul's Deanery (about five feet deep) (Plans 22, 118, 127). Shop fronts were unglazed until the late seventeenth century (Figs 11-13).[174] They often projected forward from the building (Figs 11-12), and this is presumably reflected on some of the plans. The ones most clearly depicted on a plan were at Wapping in 1676 (Plan 57). In Treswell's time shops often had warehouses behind them, and these were probably equivalent to the back shops sometimes found later in the century. Larger houses usually had warehouses. These were almost always on the ground floor, the only exception found being on the second floor of Thomas Papillon's house (by 1745) (Plan 128). Cellars and vaults seem to have been used almost invariably for storage, though Treswell provides one example of a cellar being lived in and one of a cellar being used as a kitchen, and there are several later examples of cellars with windows, which perhaps had other purposes. One of the latter had an oven, though in this case and most others the kitchen was certainly on the ground floor (Plans 31-33, 153). A large house of about 1680 off Leadenhall Street had a kitchen and service rooms in the basement (Plan 38), and two written references have been found to basement kitchens in post-Fire houses (in Goldsmith Street in 1671 and Ave Maria Lane in 1699).[175] Nevertheless, use of basements for kitchens and servants' rooms seems to have been largely an innovation of the early eighteenth century.[176] Some garrets may have been used for storage rather than sleeping. Many houses had one or more counting houses, and there was probably not much difference in practice between a counting house and a study or closet. A house in Fenchurch Street had three closets in a row behind a counting house in 1710 (Plan 160). There were sometimes workshops or bakeries in back yards, especially outside the City walls (Plans 53, 85-88, 147), and larger enterprises also sometimes mingled with domestic accommodation (e.g. Plans 37, 133).

Fig. 11. Houses on the north side of Cornhill in 1643, on the site of the triangular space now in front of the Royal Exchange (detail from a print by Wenceslaus Hollar). This is a rare view of pre-Fire houses drawn before the Fire showing them down to ground level.

In Treswell's time, kitchens in smaller properties were usually on the ground floor behind a shop or parlour, or at the back of the first floor or in a separate building in a yard. All these arrangements can be found later, though only a few kitchens are recorded in detached buildings (Plans 107, 154, 161). Nonsuch House is as usual exceptional, with kitchens on the second and third floors. Kitchens were not just for preparing food but were for cleaning dishes and clothes and were where servants, apprentices and younger children ate their meals.[177] Ovens seem to have become rarer after Treswell's time, suggesting an increasing reliance on professional bakers. Other service rooms included washhouses and butteries and, less often, larders, sculleries and pantries; two houses had brushing rooms (for brushing clothes) (Plans 24, 29). The plan of Drapers' Hall c.1620 provides an exceptional view of a large pastry with three ovens (Plan 24). Some washhouses perhaps had the industrial purpose of processing yarn and cloth.[178]

In Treswell's surveys, houses of types 3 and 4 had a hall either at the inner end or the side of a

Fig. 12. Shops in Cheapside east of St Mary le Bow, 1680 (detail from a print by Nicholas Yeats and J. Collins after R. Thacker).

Fig. 13. Shops by the Stocks Market in about 1720, showing wooden shutters, and in one case a fishmonger's counter (detail from a print by Sutton Nicholls).

courtyard or, for long but wide properties, along the side behind the street range. Smaller houses often lacked a hall, but if they had one it was on the first floor at the front. In the latter cases the hall was probably the main living room, whereas in the larger houses it was more likely to be an open hall with the main purpose of displaying the occupant's status.[179] Sometimes, probably where the house was old, the hall lacked a chimney (Plans 17, 18). Already some large houses had no hall. For example, Baptist Hicks in c.1617 had great and little parlours (over the front shop) but no hall, and the same applied in c.1620 to William Cockin in Austin Friars, whose parlours were on the ground floor (Plans 22, 24). In the second half of the century halls became rarer. The larger houses often had one but in many cases it was an entrance hall used to display a grand staircase rather than a traditional hall (Plans 38, 55, 129, 135, 139).[180] Thomas Papillon had both a hall and a great hall on the ground floor, and Peter Du Cane had a ground-floor hall, though it was smaller than his parlour (Plans 126, 128). At least one of the Fishmongers' Leadenhall Street houses had a first-floor hall, with wainscot benches, which sounds like an old-fashioned hall, and a house in Bermondsey had a ground-floor hall (Plans 38, 144). The two Nonsuch House tenancies had three first-floor halls between them (Plan 7). Of the two-room plan houses in this book, three are known to have had halls: a post-Fire house on Fish Street Hill had a first-floor room at the front referred to as a hall or chamber, and a pre-Fire house in Mark Lane and a post-Fire one in Grocers' Alley had ground-floor halls (Plans 95, 152, 153). That in Grocers' Alley had a writing desk and an enclosed office with a desk, so it was not a traditional hall. Livery companies of course continued to have halls.

The rooms which were supplanting the hall were the parlour and the dining room, though in some cases the change was one of name rather than function. The parlour had a long history as a living room less formal and more private than the hall. In Treswell's time only a few of the smaller houses had parlours, whereas larger houses often did so, usually on the ground floor by the garden (if there was a garden). Later in the century, it was more common for smaller houses to have parlours, which were apparently the main living space—in effect the former hall renamed. Larger houses continued to have parlours, and sometimes two or three of them, but increasingly they had dining rooms or dining chambers too. The term was being used in London by 1631, Norwich by 1630 and Exeter from 1590 (though mainly from the 1620s); in Exeter it was synonymous with hall or parlour. In effect a dining room was a specialised kind of parlour, though not necessarily confined to a single use.[181] At George

Jeffreys' house in Aldermanbury the plans consistently record a dining room, whereas schedules of fittings consistently refer to the same room as the great parlour (Plan 129). In a house at Whitefriars, the dining room on the plan was a parlour in the lease; there was no hall (Plan 27). The Westminster Deanery had both great and high dining rooms (Plan 130). Several type 3 houses are recorded as having dining rooms (Plans 33, 38, 138, 139), and perhaps most of them did so. So did at least eight type 2 houses (Plans 28/Mundy, 44/house 109, 55/houses D and K, 108/house 15, 150, 154, 167), though in one of these cases it was referred to as a hall or dining room.[182] The Goldsmiths' leases of 1653-62 mention six first-floor halls and one ground-floor hall, but no dining rooms, whereas its leases of 1669-72 refer to eleven halls (all but one on the first floor) and thirteen dining rooms (all on the first floor); only their type 4 houses had both a hall and a dining room.[183] Withdrawing rooms were rarer, but Jeffreys' house in Aldermanbury had one, and so did the largest of the Stationers' houses in Ave Maria Lane (Plans 33, 129). Long galleries were of course confined to type 4 houses, including a post-Fire one (Plan 46).

Most other rooms are referred to simply as chambers, and were probably what would now be called bedrooms (a room was so called in one of the Stationers' houses in 1709), though the best bedroom might be used for entertaining as well as sleeping.[184] There were also closets, first recorded in London in 1509. A closet was a small room, commonly off a bedroom, to which its user could retire for privacy or rest, and above all where valuable possessions could be stored securely. Treswell records twenty-six closets in about 225 tenancies, as well as twenty-three studies, two rooms described as 'closet or study' and seven counting houses. According to Pratt the least a closet could be was nine by three and a half feet, though even in Treswell's time there were some smaller than this.[185] Later in the century some closets were much smaller, and seem to have been closets in the modern sense (e.g. Plan 168), sometimes with shelves for storage; the 'darke clossetts' in Harp Lane were probably of this sort (Plan 29). There were still some larger closets however, sometimes in a separate back extension (Plans 141, 147, 196), which would eventually develop into the standard back extension of the Victorian terraced house.

Almost all houses had garrets. Some were heated and others were not, which might indicate that some were chiefly for storage rather than sleeping, or simply that it had not always been thought worthwhile to provide a hearth in every garret. Sometimes there was access to the leads, with rails to make this safe, and the keeper's house at Wood Street Compter had a 'summer roome on ye leads' (Plans 37, 136-38). As for stairs, type 4 houses usually had several sets of these, whereas few smaller houses did so. The exceptions are the two Mincing Lane houses and the largest houses in the Billiter Square, Arlington Street and Frith Street developments (Plans 41, 136, 137, 195, 197); even in these cases the second staircase probably extended no further than the first floor. Central stairs were often lit by what was called a 'skylight' (e.g. Plan 153).

Services

On Treswell's plans, even the smallest houses had at least a chimney and several heated rooms. The type 1 to 3 houses had about half their rooms heated. Old-fashioned halls often lacked chimneys, as in West Smithfield and Fenchurch Street (Plans 17, 18). Later in the century usually all rooms were heated, except for shops, warehouses, some garrets and small rooms such as closets, counting houses, studies and butteries; hence the good fit sometimes with the hearth tax (e.g. Plans 35, 38, 135). In the few cases where shops had fireplaces this may have been because a heated room had been converted into a shop or a back shop (Plans 161, 162, 165, 166, 171). As for garrets, in the twenty-six houses—all post-Fire—described in the Stationers' plan book, only five of the thirty-four garrets were unheated, and in the Armourers' forty-eight post-Fire houses only twelve of the forty-nine garrets were unheated, while in their nineteen pre-Fire houses eleven of the twenty-five garrets were unheated. Otherwise, apart from the types of room normally unheated, there were almost no rooms lacking fireplaces among the Stationers' and Armourers' properties.[186]

Water supply is rarely referred to except in the larger houses. Most inhabitants in the City probably relied on public cisterns and water carriers or on the piped New River water, though a few had private wells. In Chandlers' Rents there was a 'water cock' which seems to have been communal (Plan 34). Some type 3 or 4 houses had a cistern in the yard. Those with first-floor kitchens needed to raise water to them, and at the keeper's house in Wood Street a pump and a pipe to the kitchen are mentioned (Plan 138). At Thomas

Papillon's house rainwater was collected and conveyed downwards, as well as water being pumped upwards to a cistern under the roof (though this was in 1745) (Plan 128).

As for privies, referred to as houses of office, houses of easement or boghouses, there was a long-established system of public privies, one of which is recorded on a plan (Plan 124). They had for centuries been supplemented by private ones. Stone cesspits were widely adopted in the fourteenth century, adding to or replacing timber ones. They were emptied periodically, at great cost. From about 1470 privies were no longer allowed to empty into the Fleet, the Walbrook or the town ditches, though this seems to have been ineffective as regards the Fleet. From 1570-71 the Aldermen, prompted by the Privy Council, insisted that all dwellings have their own facilities, and that alleys have at least two privies.[187] Treswell's surveys indicate that by about 1610 most houses did indeed have a privy, though few had more than one. Where possible it was in the garden or yard, usually at the furthest end; otherwise it was most likely to be placed in a garret. If it was on an upper floor (a long-established practice in London) there would be a funnel to the cesspit.[188] The same preferences can be observed later, though it became more common to have more than one privy. Information about upper floors is of course patchy after Treswell's time, but what seems to have been a typical arrangement in the larger type 2 houses and type 3 houses was a privy in the cellar or under the stairs (perhaps for the servants) and one in a garret, from which a lead pipe or funnel connected with the cellar (Plans 32, 33, 138, 153). Often the privies of neighbouring properties adjoined each other, suggesting that they shared a cesspit (e.g. Plan 45/Acorn Alley); there were also privies shared by more than one house, sometimes with complicated access arrangements (Plan 150). Several alleys had three or four common privies between them, whereas in Glasshouse Alley each of five small houses had its own (Plan 145).

Few houses except type 4 ones had their own stables, either in Treswell's time or later. The smallest on the plans to do so were a house of two-room plan in West Smithfield in 1612, one of three-room plan by St Mary Abchurch in 1678 and the baker's house in Perpoole Lane in 1719 (Plans 17, 88, 132). Only one of the Billiter Square houses of 1690 had its own stables, and only one of the company halls included here did so (Plans 41, 107). Most stables were commercial, at inns, at industrial sites such as breweries or operating independently (e.g. Plans 36, 103, 104).

Gardens

In Treswell's time and before, many type 4 houses had gardens, and so did some smaller ones, especially in suburban areas, as well as some company halls, the Inns of Court and (until the Dissolution) monasteries. More widespread evidence from later in the seventeenth century includes not just substantial gardens belonging to a few of the largest houses, but gardens behind some smaller houses with deep plots. There were even some type 1 houses in suburban areas with gardens (e.g. Plan 178), though most small houses had at best a paved yard. But the plans and associated documents also show gardens disappearing or being reduced in size, especially in central areas, such as Leadenhall Street in or about 1590 and Billiter Lane in 1689-96 (Plans 12, 27, 37, 38, 41, 43, 44, 128).

Only a few plans are informative about garden layouts. The best are the earliest one of a central London garden, showing Cecil House and its grounds in the 1560s, and that of the Erber in 1596, depicting an elaborate formal garden (Plans 6, 12). More often they simply show a garden divided into squares and walks, the former no doubt containing plants arranged with varying degrees of formality, sometimes with a gallery or balustraded walk alongside (Plans 16, 37, 46, 133) and often overlooked by the parlour. A slightly more complicated layout is shown on a plan of three livery company bargehouses and their gardens at Vauxhall in 1654 (Plan 121). The surveyor most interested in gardens was John Ward, who drew floral borders or trees in pots or in the ground in many of them (Plans 44, 45). These were not necessarily accurate representations of the gardens in question, but probably show typical urban layouts. Plants in pots were certainly common.[189]

Leases

Some Londoners occupied property they owned as freeholders, but it was much more common to lease a dwelling, and even the grandest, such as Sir Thomas Bludworth and Thomas Papillon, might do so (Plans 46, 128). Perhaps three-quarters of London householders were tenants in the 1690s.[190] Given that the plans were largely commissioned by institutional landowners, they almost invariably show leased properties. The lessee usually paid an entry fine on taking up the lease and subsequently an annual rent (see Appendix 3). These were related: the fine might be large if the rent was low, or vice versa; occasionally one was traded off against the other (Plan 41). The fine was also affected by the length of the lease. The City decided in 1624 that it preferred a large fine to a large rent,[191] and this was common among institutional owners. Once the fine was paid and the lease granted, the lease was therefore a valuable possession, and the property could be let out for more than the annual rent payable to the freeholder, as shown in Appendix 3, unless the lease forbade sub-letting. The lease could also be sold on to a new lessee, though some landowners made this subject to permission. City Lands leases, other than building leases, were almost invariably for twenty-one years, while other owners tended to grant somewhat longer ones — usually twenty-six to thirty-one years in the case of the Fishmongers' Company and thirty-three or forty years in the case of Magdalen College.[192] About a third of the leases considered by the Fire Court were for twenty-one years, while half were for longer.[193] The lessee was required to keep the property in repair. In lower-quality housing, occupants were often 'tenants at will' without a lease.

Building leases included an obligation to spend a certain amount of money on new buildings by a certain time. They lasted longer, so that the lessee could recoup the cost of building. Fifty-one or sixty-one years was common (the City's were usually sixty-one years). The longest terms found in this study were for rebuilding the Star Inn and adjoining houses (ninety-one years) and for building a house in Arlington Street (ninety-nine years) (Plans 95, 195).[194] Often the lease was granted when a certain stage of building had been reached, such as enough houses erected to ensure the ground rent.

PLANS AND THE CHANGING CHARACTER OF LONDON

Plans and the Great Fire

Given the extensive coverage of the City, the plans are particularly informative about the rebuilding following the Great Fire, which destroyed about four-fifths of the City within the walls and an area outside the walls to the west, though only about a quarter of London as a whole. Examples can be found of slight adjustments of property boundaries and disentangling of intermixed dwellings,[195] but often what was built seems to have been similar to what existed before (e.g. Plans 34, 99). There are examples both of several plots being combined for large houses and of plots being split up to increase the number of houses. The former include Peter Du Cane's mansion in Pancras Lane combining two house-plots, the City's house in Weighhouse Yard combining four, and Henry Whistler's house in Abchurch Lane combining three (Plans 126, 132, 135). The latter include a mansion, the Erber, with a large garden split up following the Fire or shortly before, a development of seven houses replacing three in Harp Lane, five houses replacing one in Whitefriars and a new street, Bull and Mouth Street, with numerous small houses along it (Plans 12, 29, 54, 145). The testimony of the plans makes it implausible that the number of houses in the burnt area could have been significantly lower after the rebuilding

Fig. 14. Painting of the Master, Wardens and Court of Assistants of the Joiners' Company, in their livery gowns, receiving plans for their new Hall in about 1670, following the Great Fire.

than it was before the Fire, as is sometimes suggested.[196]

Several plans show properties affected by the creation of a forty-foot quay along the Thames, the widening of streets (see Fig. 15) or the turning of the Fleet River into a canal, most notably in the case of the Dean and Chapter of Rochester's property on Ludgate Hill (Plan 40). New urban several sidelights on the Fire itself, such as the fact that one of the early victims, the Star Inn, New Fish Street Hill, had been wholly or partly rebuilt in brick several decades before, together with nearby houses in Pudding Lane (Plan 94). As indicated above, the amount of timber that even a brick house contained meant that brick construction provided only limited protection. Another aspect is the erection of sheds after the Fire to enable business to be continued, for example at Queenhithe and Botolph Wharf (Plans 70, 124). Also interesting is that, in addition to the shells of major buildings known to have been re-used after the Fire—the Guildhall, Blackwell Hall, Goldsmiths' Hall, Grocers' Hall, Merchant Taylors' Hall and some churches—there were also a few smaller buildings within the burnt area which survived, including a recently-built brick house in Whitefriars and Arthur Higgins' cottage by the City wall near Christ's Hospital (Plans 27, 54).[197] These were reached towards the end of the Fire, when the wind was less strong. The line between burnt and unburnt was sometimes less tidy than it appears on Ogilby and Morgan's map, as in Nevill's Alley (Plan 28).

Plans and the changing city

The plans reproduced here of course provide only small and scattered glimpses of a vast metropolis. They largely ignore some aspects of London's development, such as the growth of financial services, the professions and the entertainment industries. They nevertheless shed light on the development of the city as a whole. One of their main contributions is that, although each shows a piece of land at a particular moment, they enable us to see how London was changing on the ground. The city's population was increasing —from perhaps 70,000 in 1550 to 200,000 in 1600, 400,000 in 1650, 575,000 in 1700, and 675,000 in 1750.[198] One result was building in new areas, and the plans record both new developments and ones completed earlier, for example in Finsbury, Westminster, Southwark and Ratcliff (Plans 84, 147, 174-75, 177). Another result was denser building in areas already developed, and here the plans are especially useful, as this sort of change is less well recorded. We find, for example, new buildings replacing mansions and their gardens (Plans 12, 41), new buildings added within existing plots, often replacing gardens (e.g. Plan 38), new alleys and courts (Plans 35, 47, 56) and tiny shops squeezed into narrow roadside sites (Plans 118, 127).

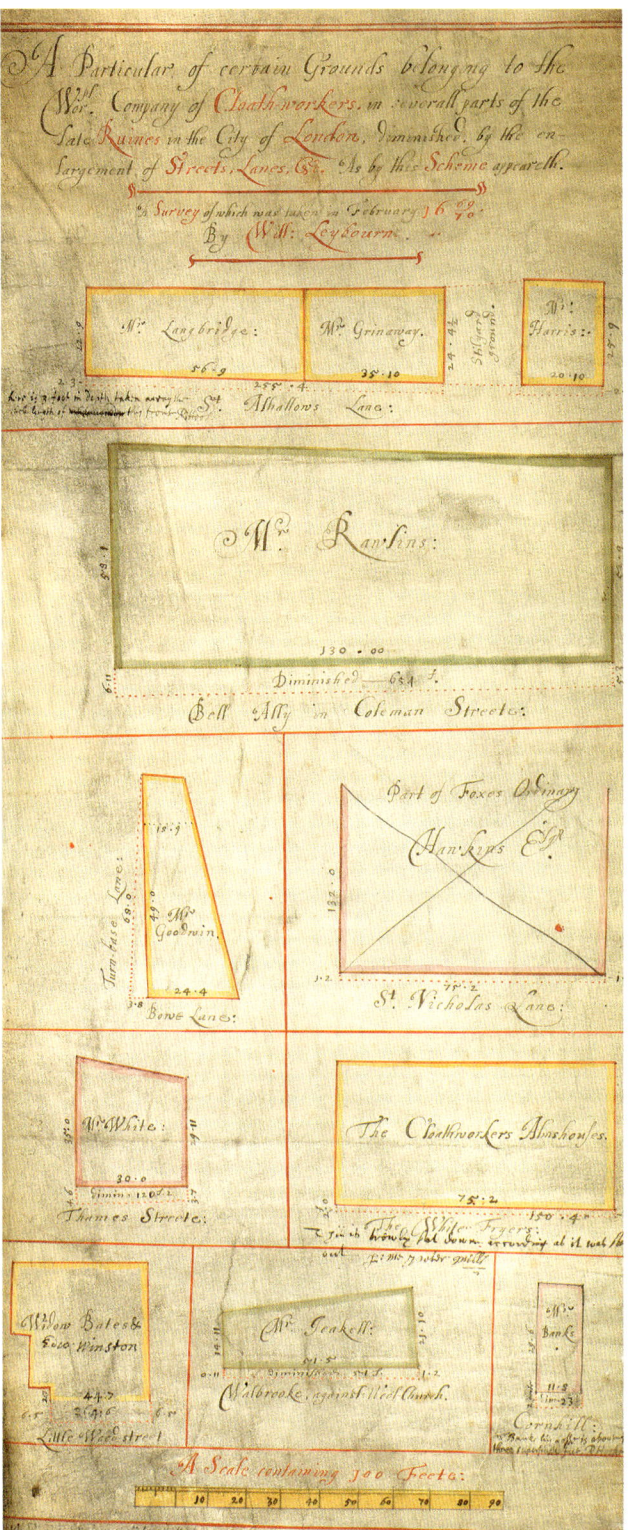

Fig. 15. Leybourn's plan of 1669 showing Clothworkers' Company properties affected by street widening after the Fire.

amenities are recorded, such as off-street markets and public laystalls (Plans 89, 123). The site on which the Fire started is also shown (Plan 154). The plans and associated documents provide

Changing use within buildings can occasionally be identified, such as the gradual taking over of large houses in the City by warehousing (e.g. Plans 126, 135), though this generally depends on having a series of plans extending beyond 1720. Where new streets were built, we can observe the varying strategies of landowners as regards their arrangements with builders and as regards design and quality of construction (Plans 60, 189-95, 197).

The plans also enable us to examine London's many different urban landscapes. For example, at the time of Ogilby and Morgan's map of 1676, even within the walls the City varied from the relatively scattered buildings and extensive gardens in the east and north-east to tightly packed buildings elsewhere, and the latter varied according to whether there was a dense street layout along which most buildings stood, as in most southern parts of the City, or whether roads were few and a network of alleys had developed, as was often the case further north. Elsewhere, there were densely developed areas immediately outside the walls and in parts of Southwark and along the riverside, areas with more scattered development around the city's edges, and fairly regular terraces of houses in the West End and occasionally elsewhere. Distinctive parts of the city included the former monastic sites, the land between Thames Street and the river with its elongated property holdings, and the Strand with its aristocratic mansions. The plans reproduced here cover all these sorts of area, and a great part of their value is that they enable us to enter such places in our imagination and to understand better what it would have been like to live and work there.

EDITORIAL AND OTHER MATTERS

Sources. The source and document reference for each plan is given in Appendix 1.

Scale. No attempt has been made to print the plans at standard scales. Scales drawn on the plans themselves are almost invariably in feet. The original scale is indicated in Appendix 1, which also provides dimensions. The scale of plans as printed here, where this is not indicated by a scale bar or measurements, is as follows: Plan 6, 1:860; Plan 7, 1:145; Plan 10 (Fig. 39), 1:890, (Fig. 40) 1:640; Plan 15, 1:505; Plan 18, 1:194; Plan 24 (Fig. 77), 1:745, (Fig. 82) 1:279; Plan 25, 1:1300; Plan 44, 1:550; Plan 46, 1:400; Plan 62, 1:900; Plan 64, 1:140; Plan 74, 1:640; Plan 93, 1:360; Plan 99, 1:215; Plan 111 (Figs 229-30), 1:472; Plan 112, 1:1900; Plan 113, 1:370; Plan 114, 1:980; Plan 127, 1:410; Plan 191, 1:720; Plan 197, 1:275.

Orientation. This varies, and the original orientation (in so far as it is clear) is used here. The captions indicate which direction is north if it is not otherwise obvious. In practice, the direction from which one approached the building was usually at the bottom. For all the details taken from printed maps such as Ogilby and Morgan's or the Ordnance Survey, north is at the top unless the contrary is stated.

Vellum and paper. Almost all the plans included are on vellum. Exceptions are the paper ones in the St Bartholomew's Hospital and Skinners' Company plan books, as well as Plans 4, 22, 93, 144, 173, 190, 192, 197. In 1694 the Skinners wanted their plans 'to be preserved & done in a fair book in vellum & also another in the nature of a survey book to be used upon the view day';[199] if the book in vellum was made it has not survived. Plans on vellum attached to leases have often been folded, making them hard to photograph without distortion.

Keys and descriptions (all set out here under the heading 'Key'). Only a small minority of plans have either a key or a description. Where there is one, it is calendared here, unless a lengthy description has already been published (Plans 17, 18, 22). It is from the same source (as given in Appendix 1) and of the same date as the plan unless the contrary is indicated. Note that descriptions usually ignore the ground floor, regarding the plan itself as sufficient for that.

Storeys. Modern British terminology is used for storeys, i.e. ground, first, second etc. Contemporary usage was usually to call our ground floor the first floor, though this was not entirely consistent; Leybourn, in particular, sometimes referred to storeys in the modern sense, using terms such as 'the first story above stair'.[200] Where keys or descriptions have been included here, references to storeys have where necessary been amended to modern usage, for example to change 'first' to 'ground', and either italicised (at the start of the description of a storey) or placed in square brackets. The garrets at the top were usually regarded as a half storey, and that usage is followed here, though Leybourn counted garrets as a full storey.

Quotations. Capitalisation is modernised.

Street names and numbers. The street names at the time of the plan are used, with the modern name given in the text if necessary; in two cases the contemporary street name is unclear and a later one has been used (Mitre Court and Grange Road). Where street numbers are given they have been identified from the maps of the City's wards ('the Secondary's plans') in 1855-58[201] unless another source is indicated.

Dates. Lease plans are assumed to be of the same year as the lease, unless there is reason for doubt or a different year is stated (e.g. Plans 3, 64, 123).

Sometimes an earlier plan was attached to a lease, and a few were drawn slightly later (as leases were sometimes sealed after the ostensible date.)[202]

Occupations. Where a person is described here in terms such as 'citizen and fishmonger', this indicates his livery company but not necessarily his trade. Actual trades are given where different and known.

Hearth tax. This was a tax levied on hearths or chimneys from 1662 to 1689. The lists it generated indicate the number of rooms, at least of those which were heated, and therefore provide a rough indication of size of house and status of occupant. In 1666, dwellings in central City parishes averaged 5.5 hearths, compared with 2.7 or 2.8 in eastern and southern suburbs and in City parishes outside the walls. Merchants averaged 8.0 hearths.[203]

Fig. 16. Part of Morgan's map of London in 1682, with sites covered by plans in this book marked. The boundary of the City is indicated by a red line and the area destroyed in the Great Fire by a blue line (the latter taken from Ogilby and Morgan's map of 1676).

Numbers appear more than once for Plans 45 and 63. Locations shown for
Plans 4, 86, 88, 149, 157, 162, 163, 167, 181 and 185 are approximate.

Fig. 17. Map of London from John Strype's *Survey* of 1720. Sites covered by plans in this book outside the area shown in Fig. 16 are marked. The red rectangle shows approximately the area covered by Fig. 16.

INTRODUCTION

Numbers appear more than once for Plan 2.

GLOSSARY

airy: an area within a house open to the elements; a light well.

back-to-backs: houses one room deep sharing a back wall with houses facing in the opposite direction.

box: a compartment partitioned off in the public area of a tavern or coffee-house.

bridge: a landing stage *or* a structure carrying a road over a river.

Bridge House: the organisation which maintained (and continues to maintain) London Bridge.

buttery: a store-room for alcoholic drinks and sometimes other provisions.

capital messuage: a large house.

chamber: usually an upper room used mainly or wholly for sleeping.

citizen: a freeman of the City (usually bracketed with the individual's livery company, e.g. 'citizen and grocer').

City: the area under the jurisdiction of the Corporation of the City of London, partly within London Wall and partly outside it.

city: when referring to London, the whole of the city, including areas outside the jurisdiction of the City of London.

City Lands: properties belonging to the City of London.

closet: a small room, commonly off a bedroom, providing greater privacy and security for valuables; by the late seventeenth century some were mere cupboards or 'dark closets'.

cockloft: a small room under the ridge of the roof, usually reached by a ladder.

double house: a house with two rooms on each floor.

fine: a lump sum paid by the tenant at the start of a lease.

Fire Court: the Court established in 1667 to resolve property disputes arising from the Great Fire.

garret: a room within the roof of a house.

house of office or house of easement: a toilet.

jetty, jettied: the carrying forward of the upper storey of a timber building beyond the storey below it.

laystall: a place where refuse and dung are deposited.

leads: an area on the roof of a house (usually referred to when it is available for use by the occupants, and is therefore presumably flat).

lights: the right to light, hence sometimes windows.

lobby-entry house: modern term for a house with central chimneys and a central front door opening into a small lobby between the door and the chimneys from which rooms to left and right are accessed.

Lutheran lights: dormer windows.

messuage: term used for a house in deeds and leases (often 'a messuage or tenement').

parlour: a living room less formal and more private than the hall; the main living space in smaller houses by the late seventeenth century.

pastry: a place where pastry is made.

piazza: an area of ground under a part of a building whose upper storeys have been carried forward on pillars.

privy: a toilet.

Rebuilding Act: The Act of Parliament of 1667 providing for the rebuilding of the area burnt in the Great Fire.

scullery: a small room used for washing plates, dishes and kitchen utensils.

tenants at will: tenants without a formal lease specifying a term (usually in small houses).

tenement: term used for a house in deeds and leases (often 'a messuage or tenement'); particularly but not exclusively applied to smaller houses.

toft: a house plot not containing a house (e.g. after a fire).

upright: a drawing showing the facade or elevation of a building; also used in descriptions of buildings to indicate rooms one over another, e.g. 'three rooms upright'.

victualler: a provider of food and drink for payment, such as an alehouse-keeper.

view: an inspection of a property by or on behalf of its owners.

viewers: those appointed to inspect a property on behalf of its owners; also City officials appointed to report on disputes over party walls, light and similar property matters.

EARLY PLANS, c.1450-1630

Plans 1 and 2

The Charterhouse, c.1450 and c.1511

FIGS 18, 21, 22

Plan 1, the earliest of any London building, shows the Charterhouse, a Carthusian monastery founded in 1370-71 but not completed until about 1420.[1] In 1430 the Charterhouse secured a plentiful water supply from high ground in Barnsbury known as Overmede, and pipes were laid to convey it to the monastery. What is reproduced here is part of a larger plan, ten feet long, showing the entire course of the pipes from source to taps. Other monasteries compiled written surveys of their water supplies, but the Charterhouse was apparently the first in England since Canterbury Cathedral in the mid-twelfth century and Waltham Abbey in the early thirteenth century to commission a plan.[2] The plan dates from after 1442, when the northernmost of the conduits serving St John's priory was built, and before 1457, when the original spring had begun to fail and others nearby were brought into use. The northern part of the plan was redrawn in or after 1457 to show the new arrangements, and the text on the plan continued to be altered or added to until at least 1512.[3] Despite the early date, the plan is largely a ground plan, though also partly pictorial.

The monastery was dominated by the great cloister, measuring 340 by 300 feet, and by the

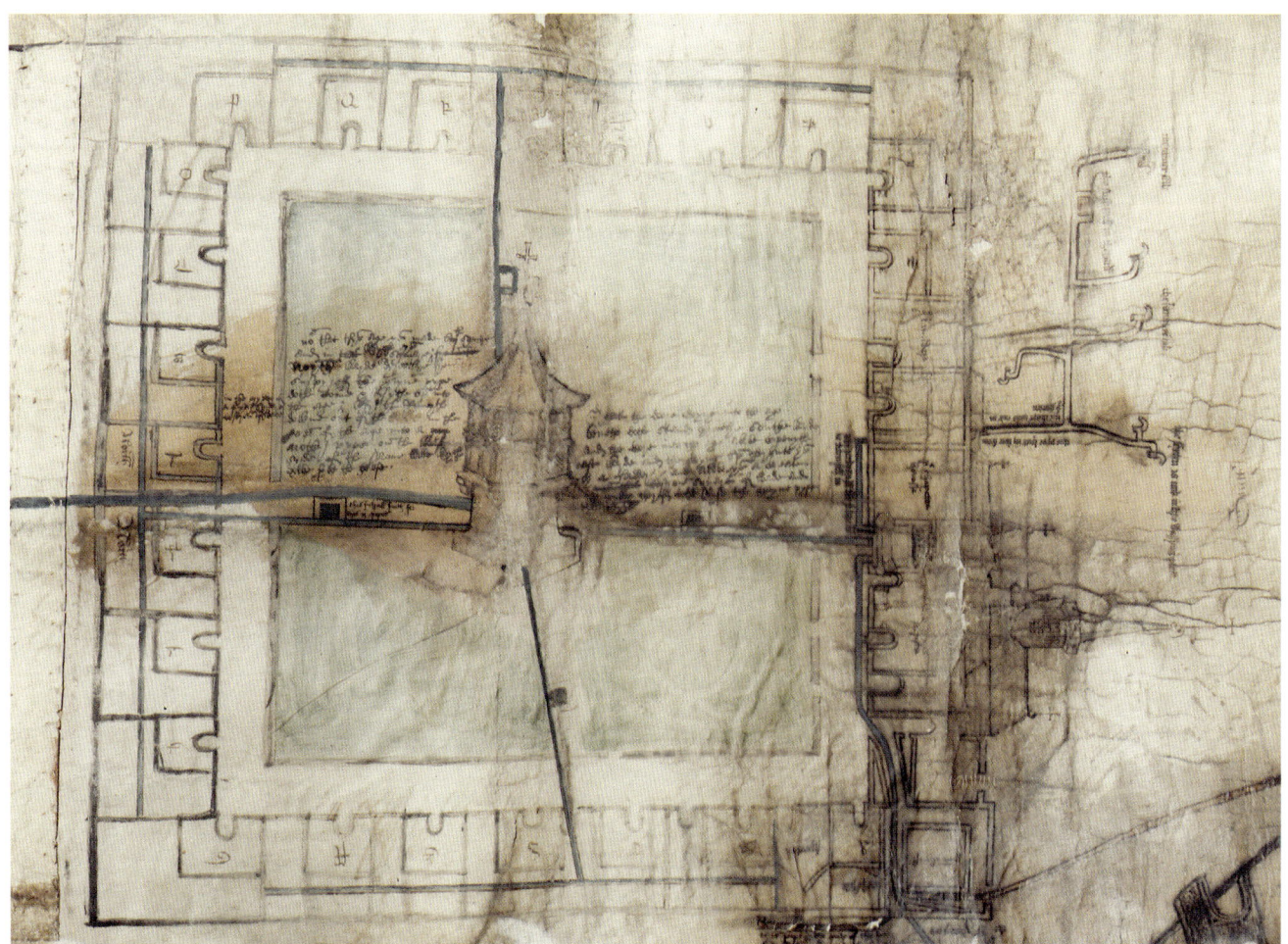

Fig.18. Part of the plan of the Charterhouse's water supply, c.1450, showing the Charterhouse itself. North is to the left.

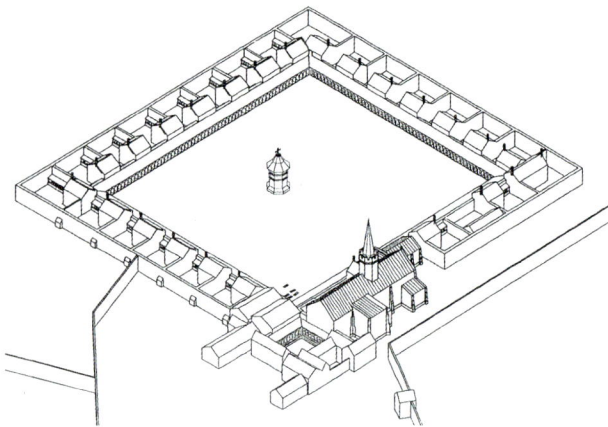

Fig. 19. Reconstruction of the Charterhouse in about 1450, seen from the south-west (drawn for Museum of London Archaeology).

twenty-four 'cells' around it (Figs 18-19). Carthusian monks were known as hermits, and lived in individual cells, as can best be seen today at Mount Grace in Yorkshire. Each cell, known by a letter of the alphabet, was in its own walled enclosure, and had two storeys containing three or four rooms, which provided separate spaces for working, praying, eating and sleeping. Meals were placed in a serving-hatch with a flap beside the front door (see Fig. 20), and a few of these are shown on the plan. The church and other buildings were south of the cloister, with service buildings such as the kitchen off the south-west corner (at the bottom right in Fig. 18).

The main pipe entered the great cloister from the north (on the left in Fig. 18), terminating in a conduit house with a lead cistern on top near the centre of the cloister. From there pipes radiated to all four sides of the cloister, and then passed through the cells' gardens, undoubtedly with a tap in each garden. On the south side there was a second cistern, in the sacrist's tower adjoining the chapter house (now the chapel tower and chapel respectively). In the south-west corner branches led to 'Egypt the fleyshe kychyn', belonging to the priory but outside the precinct, and to several public houses. Some of the pipes south of the cloister are shown outside it for clarity. They served cell Y, cell Z, the laundry, an unlettered cell and 'the washing place'. The square forms on some of the pipes were 'suspirals', intended to prevent pressure build-ups or air locks and to trap sediment.

A second plan, now lacking the section showing the monastery, was drawn in the early sixteenth century, possibly in connection with repairs made in 1511 (Figs 21-22),[4] and two more were made in the early seventeenth century. The monastery was suppressed in 1538. The church and cloister were soon demolished, and a mansion was subsequently created in the south-west corner, occupied successively by Lord North, the Duke of Norfolk and the Earl of Suffolk. Thomas Sutton, an immensely rich businessman, bought it in 1611 and arranged for it to be converted into

Fig. 20. The surviving entrance to cell B, with its serving hatch. This cell was donated in 1371 by Sir William Walworth, the Lord Mayor of London who killed Wat Tyler during the Peasants' Revolt in 1381.

Fig. 21. Detail from the plan of the Charterhouse's water supply, c.1511, showing the Pardon Chapel. The chapel was built in 1348 within a burial ground for plague victims. It was converted into a house by 1565 and the last traces disappeared around 1770. In modern terms it stood to the rear of 36-48 Clerkenwell Road and 19-24 Great Sutton Street, a little west from Berry Street.

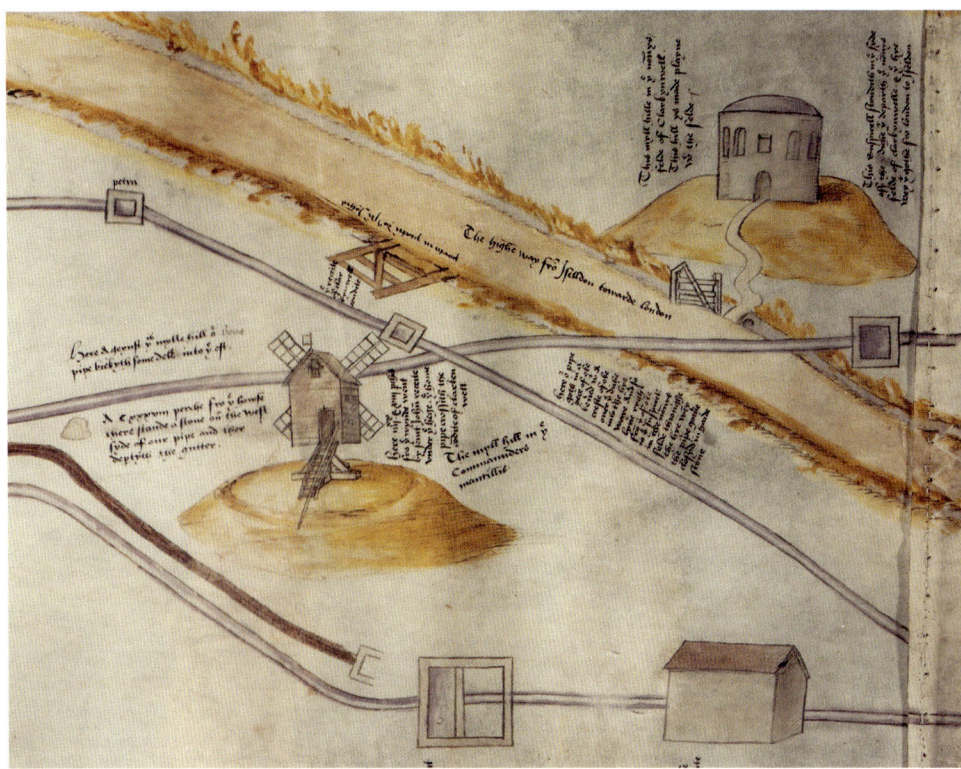

Fig. 22. Another detail from the plan of *c*.1511. The wooden post mill stood about where St John Street now meets Myddelton Street, and had gone by 1624. The other structure seems to be a partly-dismantled brick windmill, between St John Street and Northampton Square.

a hospital for eighty poor people, together with a school for poor boys, though these provisions were quickly altered after his death to make it mainly a home for poor gentlemen. The monastic spring and pipes continued to supply water to the Charterhouse until 1767.[5] The school moved to Godalming in 1872, but the gentlemen remain at the Charterhouse today. The surviving parts of the monastery include the chapter house (now the chapel of Sutton's Hospital), some of the service buildings and half of the cell-front wall on the west side of the cloister. The central courtyard of St Bartholomew's medical school approximately corresponds to the former great cloister, though the cloister extended further east than the courtyard does.

Plan 3
Cheapside, *c*.1531
Humphrey Coke
FIG. 23

This plan is attached to a lease made by the Savoy Hospital to Christopher Holgill, citizen and merchant taylor of London, in 1542. The house was described as a tenement, shop, solars and warehouse newly built by the Hospital and occupied by Holgill—presumably a relative of William Holgill, the first Master of the Hospital from 1517 to 1548.[6] The plan shows a house of two-room plan, with the upper storeys reached by a winding stair entered from a side passage. In the back yard are two privies. The plan pays particular attention to the walls, noting, for example, that half of the wall to the east belonged to the next property. The house was described as being on the north side of the highway from Cheapside to Newgate and in the parish of St Michael le Querne, and it abutted west on a Bridge House property and east on another Savoy property, newly built at the same time and also granted to Christopher Holgill.[7] This pattern of ownership makes it easily identifiable from nineteenth-century rate lists as 156 Cheapside, a little west from Foster Lane.[8]

The lease specifies abuttals, but for measurements refers to 'a platt therof made by the hands of Humfry Cooke carpenter'. Humphrey Coke, recorded from 1496 to 1531, was, among other things, Warden of the Carpenters' Company of London (1506-10 and 1519), master carpenter of Corpus Christi College and Cardinal College (now Christ Church), Oxford, and the King's Master Carpenter (1519-31). The hall roofs of the two colleges are among his surviving works. On several occasions he is referred to as drawing plans, sometimes for others to work from. He was closely connected with the Savoy, as he became chief carpenter there in 1517 and was buried in the Savoy Chapel in 1531.[9]

The lease to which the plan is attached was made eleven years after Coke's death, and the house concerned was described as newly built. Coke had a younger son called Humphrey, who could conceivably have carried on his father's trade. On the other hand there is no evidence of Humphrey junior being a carpenter and the lease was not a building lease; the unusually long term of seventy years was evidently a favour to a relative. The reference to the house being newly built in 1542 probably meant only that it had been built fairly recently. The plan may therefore be Coke's building plan of 1531 or earlier, or more likely, as the two adjoining houses had been rebuilt together, a copy made by Coke of part of the building plan, perhaps originally attached to a

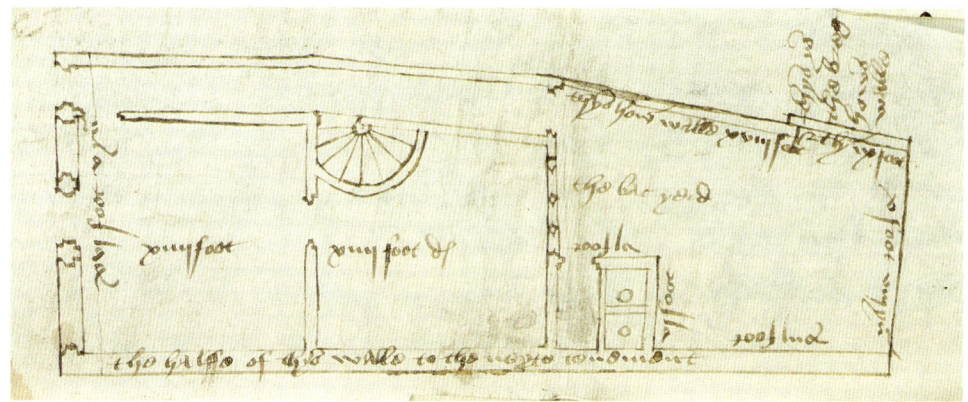

Fig. 23. A house in Cheapside, *c*.1531. North is to the right.

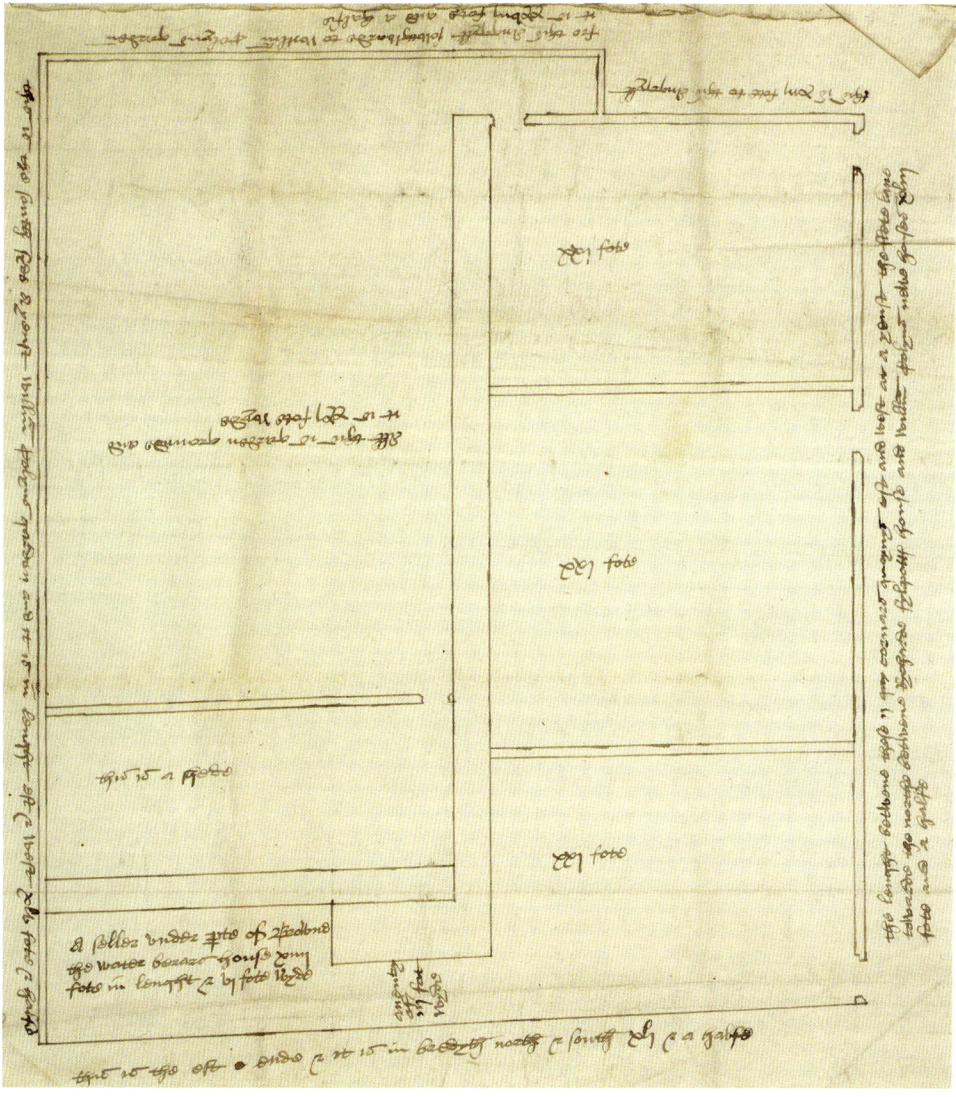

Fig. 24. Houses in Fleet Lane, 1542. North is to the right.

slightly earlier lease. There are later examples of building plans being attached to leases, even sometimes before the erection of the buildings, presumably because they were readily available and cost no extra.[10] In this case, attaching the plan resulted in measurements being omitted from the lease. Like many early plans, this one was not drawn to scale. The information that was being relied on was the stated measurements rather than the actual lengths of the lines drawn.

The Savoy Hospital was seized by the Crown in 1553. Although it was re-founded under Queen Mary, its lands other than the Hospital site and Savoy Rents were transferred to St Thomas's Hospital, and the plan survives among St Thomas's records.

Plan 4
Fleet Lane, 1542
FIG. 24

This plan, drawn on paper, is from another Savoy Hospital lease, made to Peter Green of St Sepulchre parish in 1542. It is apparently the first surviving plan specially drawn for a lease and containing more than just a plot outline. It shows all or part of three houses on the south side of Fleet Lane, towards the lane's east end (now St George's Court).[11] Unlike the lease containing the Cheapside plan, this one gives dimensions, but it is vague about where the property was, other than that it was in St Sepulchre parish between the Hospital's properties held by Roger Philpott and William Collyn; only the plan indicates that it was in Fleet Lane. The plan states the dimensions, but is not drawn to scale. The houses (on the right here) were of one-room plan and twenty-one feet deep, ending at a thick wall, probably of stone. One of the three may have extended onto the next property, as it ends at a single line rather than a double one and it included a cellar under the next house. This complication was perhaps why a plan was thought necessary. The garden and shed apparently belonged to one of the three houses.

Plan 5
The Steelyard, sixteenth century
FIG. 25

The Steelyard was a community of German merchants with valuable trading privileges.[12] It originated in or before the 1170s, when the citizens and merchants of Cologne were confirmed in the possession of their house or guildhall in London. The property, much enlarged, later passed to the Hanseatic League. The site is now covered by Cannon Street Station. This plan of the Steelyard, found among the Tudor state papers, may have resulted from one of the two major political crises affecting the Steelyard in the sixteenth century, in 1552-53 and 1598 (though it seems too crude for 1598), but could equally have been drawn for some other reason. The annotation on it refers to packs, barrels, pipes and chests. No scale or measurements are given. The outline of the property closely matches the walled area shown on later plans (sites 1 to 3 on Fig. 27), but this would mean that there was no access between the easternmost strip of land (site 3) and the rest of the Steelyard, and that the whole site was radically replanned after the Great Fire, whereas the man who rebuilt it then stated that it was rebuilt as before.[13] It is more likely that the plan shows the land added in 1475 (sites 2 and 3) together with that between the walled enclosure and Allhallows Lane (site 4), omitting the original holding (site 1).[14] The eastern wall, the two north-south lanes, the northernmost cross lane and some other features then match those shown on the post-Fire plans, and even the lack of access between the 1475 property and the earlier holding (sites 2-3 and 1 respectively) is partly continued on the later plans. Indeed the match is close enough to suggest that Plan 5 is to scale. In either case the layout differs significantly from the printed plan purportedly based on one by Wenceslaus Hollar of 1667, to which too much credence has been given.[15]

The Germans first occupied the north-west part of the later Steelyard (site 1), where excavations in 1988 revealed the foundations of a large twelfth-century hall, about 100 by thirty-five feet, facing Thames Street. That property was gradually extended southwards as land was reclaimed from the river. In 1475 Edward IV granted the Hanse traders properties either side of Windgoose Lane (site 2) and a separate property to the east already known as the Steelyard (site 3). The latter name came to be applied to the whole complex. Given that the area was associated with cloth-finishing, the name may have been derived from the German verb *stalen*, signifying the application of a seal to cloth to indicate that it had been dyed or subjected to some other process. From 1475 or thereabouts there was a walled enclosure known as the Steelyard (sites 1 to 3), though there was also some Steelyard property outside the wall.[16]

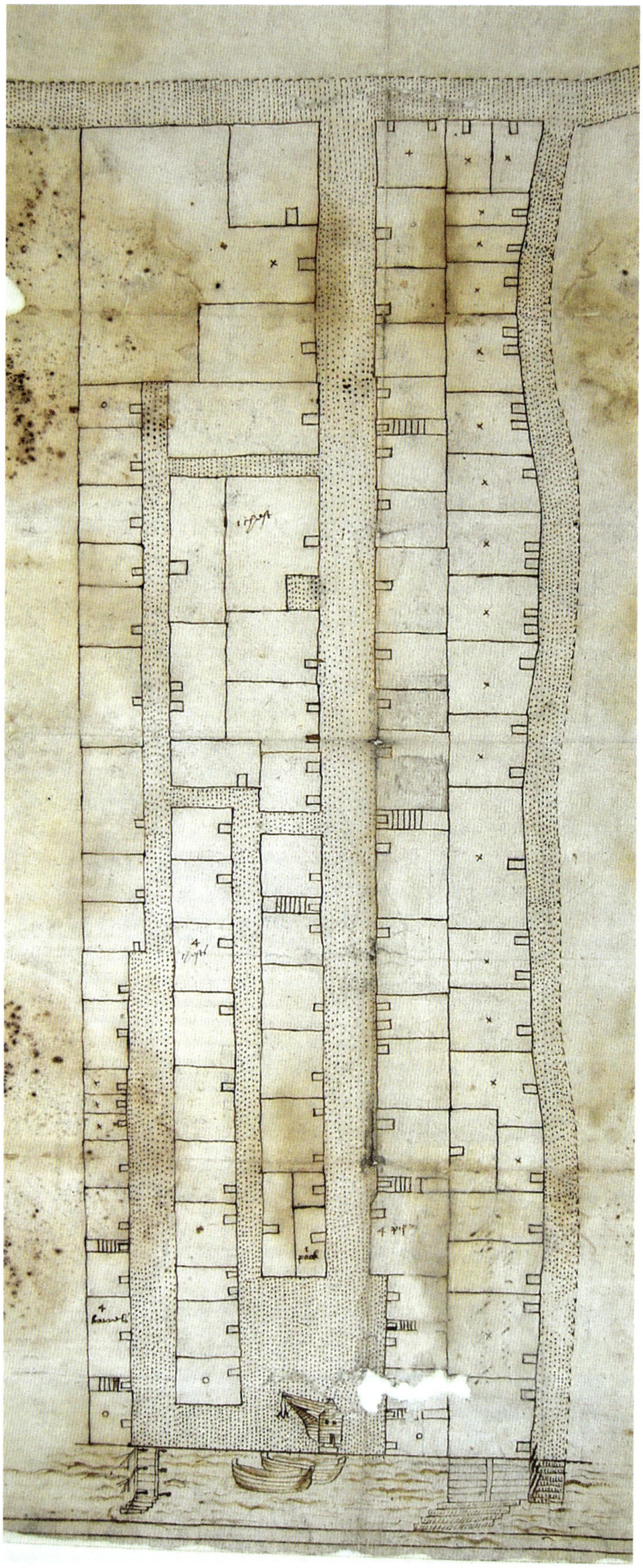

Fig. 26. Detail from Claes Janz. Visscher's panorama of 1616, showing the Steelyard.

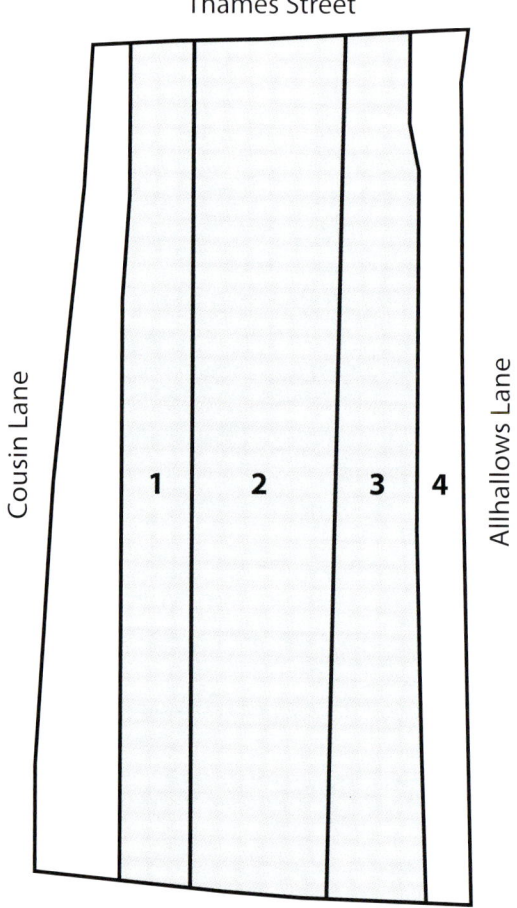

Fig. 25. The Steelyard in the sixteenth century. North is at the top.

Fig. 27. Outline of the different properties in and around the Steelyard. 1 is the original holding, as extended to the Thames; 2 is properties either side of Windgoose Lane; 3 is the property known as the Steelyard before the Germans obtained it; 4 is properties between the Steelyard and Allhallows Lane (formerly Haywharf).

The Steelyard formed a self-governing quasi-monastic community. Young Germans from good mercantile families came there to learn their trade, and ceased to be part of the Steelyard community if they married. According to L. Grenade in 1578, the German merchants 'live and take meals together and consist of roughly between eighteen and twenty masters, and as many others who are below them ... This second rank eat at a separate table but still in the same room ... They have a governor or superintendent who presides over them and whom they call Alderman ... he is also their sole magistrate ... The common name of this house is the Steelyard, and it is most magnificent, noble and rich.'[17]

The merchants generally had a warehouse with a chamber above, and the plan shows four rows of these within the Steelyard. The stairs depicted probably led down to vaults and cellars. This pattern of lanes close together with the land between them heavily subdivided was typical of the central section of the City's riverside in the late medieval period.[18] Almost all the properties in Allhallows Lane are marked with a cross, as are most of those in Thames Street and three on the western part of site 2. This perhaps indicated properties let to Englishmen, which in most cases would make sense in terms of access.

Edward VI removed the Steelyard merchants' privileges in 1552, though they were shortly afterwards restored by Mary. Elizabeth expelled the merchants in 1598, and James I allowed them back in 1606. The Steelyard was no longer so important in English trade in the seventeenth century, but it remained a corporate body of German merchants. The property was destroyed in the Great Fire and rebuilt (see Plans 73–74).

Plan 6
Cecil House, the Strand, c.1565
FIG. 28

In 1559 or 1560 Sir William Cecil, Queen Elizabeth's Principal Secretary and a privy counsellor (Fig. 30), began building a mansion on the north side of the Strand.[19] It seems to have been largely complete by 1562. At first Cecil House, it became Burghley House when Cecil was created Lord Burghley in 1571, and was later Exeter House under his son. It is shown on a detailed plan rediscovered at Burghley House, Northamptonshire, in 1999.

The plan can be approximately dated from the fact that it shows the northern part of the site (including the mound and the orchard), which Cecil purchased from the Earl of Bedford in 1562, as part of the garden, together with a bay projecting from the north side of the garden wall (also authorised in 1562 and built by the end of 1565), whereas it does not show small projecting areas to the east, west and north, wanted by Cecil as sites for garden buildings which were built by 1567. The plan was therefore drawn between 1562 and 1567. The fact that a scale is shown is therefore especially important, as it precedes by about a decade the first rural estate maps drawn to scale in England. Given Cecil's known interest in maps this is not surprising. The plan is also the earliest showing a central London garden.

The most likely reason for the plan is that it was created to be displayed. The most likely surveyor is Lawrence Bradshaw, Surveyor of the King's Works (later the Queen's Works) from 1547 to 1560, as the conventions for stairs, doorways and privies on plans known to have been by him are the same, and at least some of his plans were to scale.[20] Another possibility is Henry Hawthorne, Purveyor to the Queen's Works from 1562, who used similar conventions, though he did not always draw to scale.[21] Both drew other plans for Cecil. On the plan, walls are red, indicating brick, the stairs alternate in yellow and green, windows are green for the panes and yellow for the sills, chimneys and ovens are black, divisions within the garden are red (brick), dark green (hedges) or buff (gravel walks), and in the tennis court each paving slab is marked in red or white.

The house itself was of brick, with three storeys around two courtyards and towers at the four corners. The main facade was towards the garden, with an open loggia. In the centre was the hall (possibly a single-storey hall), and to its east the great parlour, where the family would have dined, with what may have been a guard room between them. The location of the main staircase is unknown. The main rooms would have been on the first floor, the rooms where the family lived on the ground floor towards the garden (with the kitchen in the north-west corner), and service rooms and offices around the Strand courtyard. East of the house were a tennis court (possibly open air, so the play could be viewed from the house) and a bowling alley (the plan shows the bowls). Gardens were extremely important to Cecil—his gardens at Theobalds were among the most famous in England—and house and garden were evidently planned as a unity. As well as the main garden aligned with the house

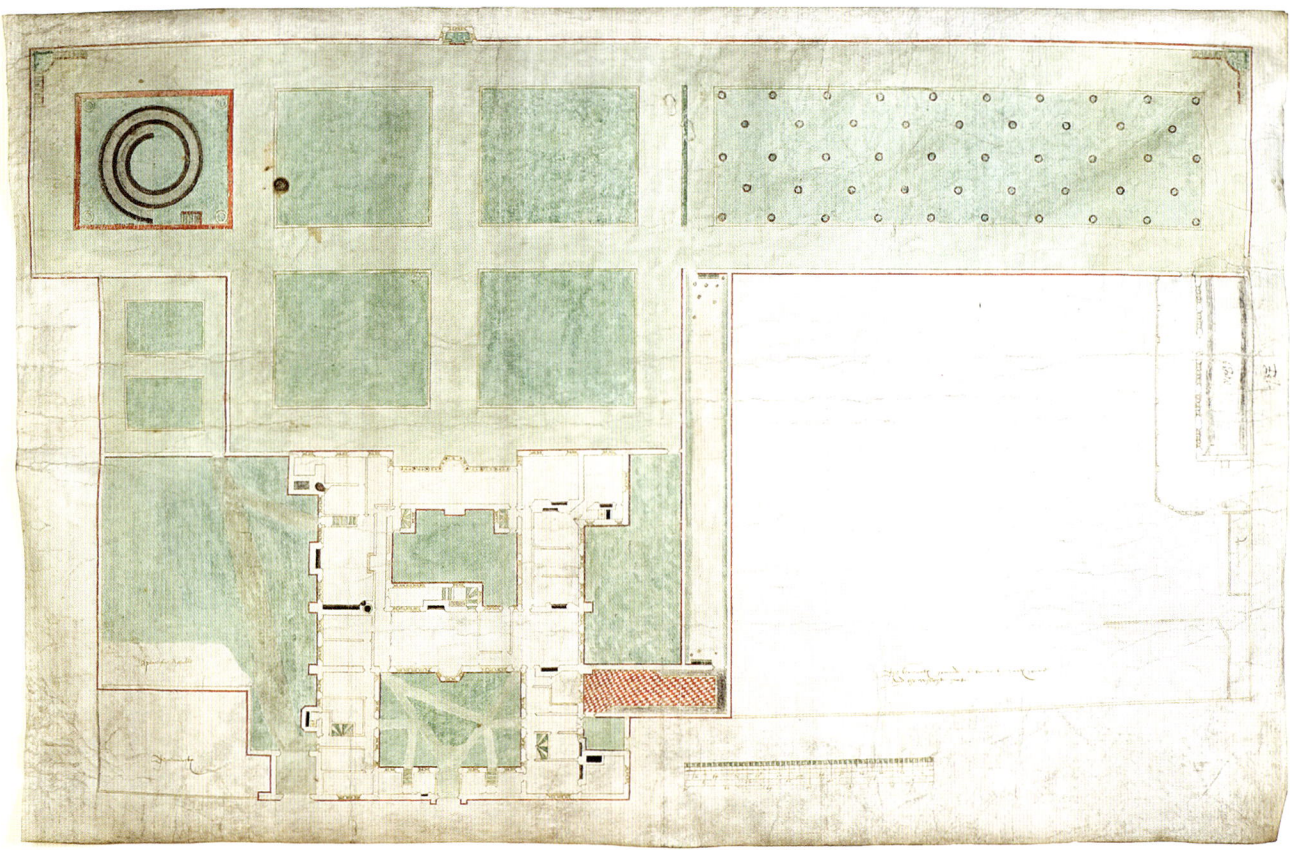

Fig. 28. Cecil House, the Strand, *c.*1565. North is at the top.

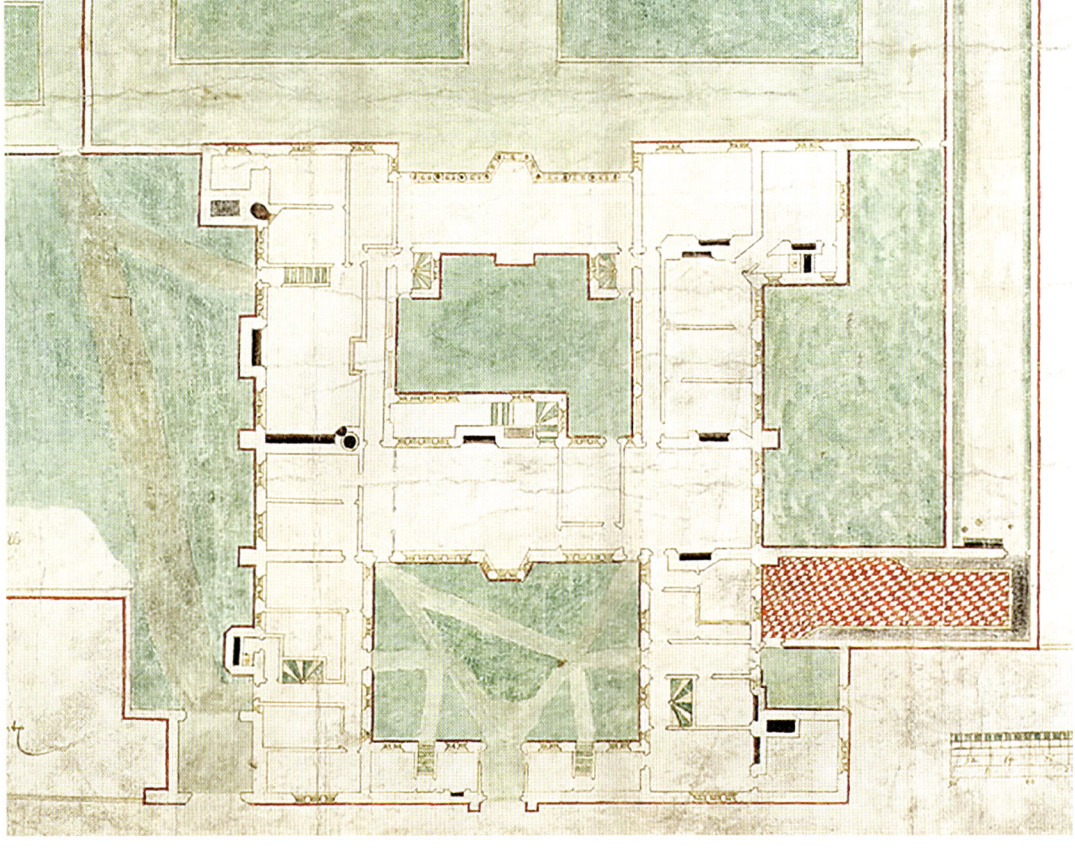

Fig. 29. Part of the plan of Cecil House, showing the house itself.

Fig. 30. William Cecil, Lord Burghley (1520-98), painted probably by Hans Eworth.

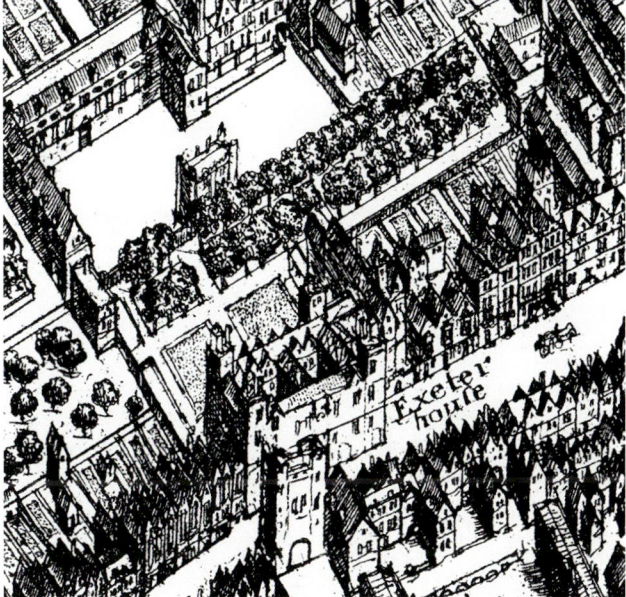

Fig. 31. Detail from Hollar's map of the area west of the City in about 1658, showing Cecil House, labelled as Exeter House. Hollar clearly shows the house abutting directly onto the Strand, and its garden and garden buildings, but does not correctly show the house arranged around two courtyards.

and later including a banqueting house on an axis with the Strand gateway, there was a kitchen garden to the west, the mount garden with a spiral walk to the top, the orchard, and what may have been Cecil's privy garden east of the house. There were viewing platforms seventeen steps up in the north-west and north-east corners. On the east side were the stables.

The Strand houses began to disappear in the 1670s, and Cecil's descendants demolished Cecil House in 1676. The site, including the garden and adjoining tenements, is between the Strand, Exeter Street and Wellington Street, and Strand Palace Hotel stands on the site of the mansion.

Plan 7
Nonsuch House, London Bridge, c.1577
Fig. 32

Nonsuch House was built from 1577 to 1579, replacing London Bridge's New Stone Gate.[22] The name meant 'no other such house', and probably referred to its elaborate and colourful decoration. There seems to be no good evidence for the traditions that the house was prefabricated in Holland and built without nails.[23] The plan is most likely connected with the house's construction and the relationship of timbers prepared elsewhere with the stones of the bridge supporting them, so 1577 is the probable date. No scale is given, but in the absence of any stated dimensions a plan not to scale would have been of little use. Nonsuch House always consisted of two houses let to tenants, the first of whom, in 1579, were William Clayton, grocer, in the western house and Thomas James, vintner, in the eastern house. Each paid a £200 fine and £10 a year and was forbidden to make any alterations without permission.[24] The Bridge House continued to take responsibility for external embellishments.[25]

The plan indicates a shop and a passage to the stairs in the turret in each house. Subsequent leases (see the description below) give the size of the shops as thirty-one feet (or just over) by twenty-five feet, and these dimensions work on the plan if the passages had been taken into the shops, which would have made sense. The roadway is then about twelve feet nine inches wide, which is consistent with other evidence (see Plan 62 below). The western house is described in a lease of 1653 to Jane Weedon, widow—presumably the widow of John Weedon, citizen and mercer, who had leased it in 1627.[26] On the first floor were two halls over the shop, a second staircase, and two chambers over the street, together the same north-south length as the shop 'besides the galary over the draw bridge' (see Fig. 33). On the second floor were four chambers and a kitchen. On the third floor were three garret chambers, a kitchen and two other chambers, and above it was one garret with leads and turrets. Hollar's view (Fig. 33) provides a good match with the plan and the description, apart from the number of ground-floor windows. The third-floor chambers were apparently at the front with garrets behind, and the topmost garret was above the roadway.

The description of the eastern house, from a lease of 1713 but clearly copied from an earlier

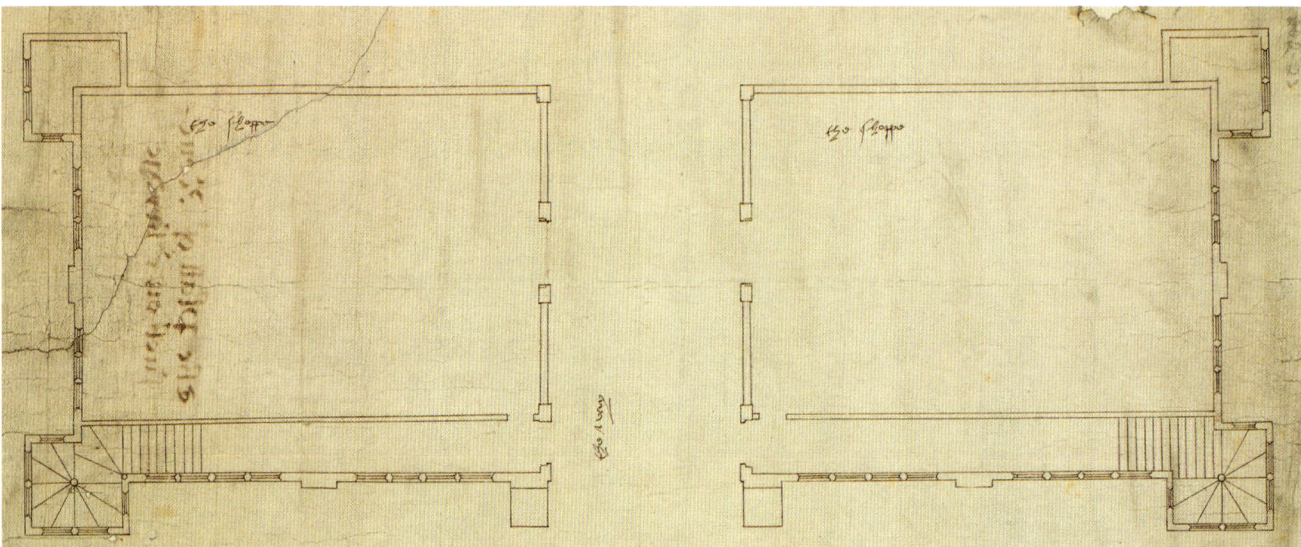

Fig. 32. Nonsuch House, London Bridge, c.1577. North is at the top; the facade shown in Fig. 33 is at the bottom.

KEY (1653)[27]

Western house: cellar, east-west within the walls 25 feet, north-south 17½ feet; shop over cellar, east-west 31 feet 9 inches, 25 feet on street side; two halls on a floor wainscoted over shop, of same length besides staircase and jetties and of same breadth, with one other staircase and chimneys; two chambers on same floor over street, together north-south besides gallery over drawbridge 25 feet; two chambers wainscoted, kitchen and two other chambers all on a floor over halls and street chambers of same length and breadth; three garret chambers, a kitchen and two other chambers all on a floor over them of same length and breadth; one garret with leads and turrets.

Eastern house: cellar, 23 by 18 feet; shop 31 by 25 feet; little counting house adjoining shop, 5½ feet; washhouse over street, 12 by 7 feet; chamber on same floor over street of same length and breadth; hall over shop, 19 by 13 feet besides chimney and staircase; parlour on same floor, length 22 feet, breadth besides two studies adjoining 16½ feet; two chambers over washhouse and chamber over street of same length and breadth; chamber over hall of same length and breadth; kitchen and chamber over parlour, besides the waterhouse and closet, together of same length and breadth as parlour; two chambers over the two chambers over street of same length and breadth; three garrets, buttery and two closets over said chamber[s]; leads over said garrets 31 by 12 feet besides two turrets; garret over street, 14 by 7 feet.

Fig. 33. Nonsuch House in 1647—detail from Hollar's long view of London.

one, indicates only a few differences from the western house. The ground floor included a little counting house, probably in one of the corner towers. On the first floor, instead of two halls there was a hall and a parlour, together with two studies, and one of the rooms over the street was a warehouse. The second floor included a 'waterhouse' and a closet. The third floor had a buttery instead of a kitchen. The rooms in both houses must have had spectacular views.

It is testimony to the continuing admiration for Nonsuch House that it was retained when the decision was taken to widen the bridge's roadway and rebuild the other houses in 1683-84. But to widen the roadway to twenty feet and make it one storey higher, Nonsuch House's shop fronts had to be set back and its first-floor rooms over the roadway removed. In November 1685 John Foltrop, a carpenter, was paid £182.10s. for 'setting back the front and taking downe the lowest story of Nonsuch house and beautifying the outside thereof', and a further £31.18s. for brickwork on the north side of the house.[28] Perhaps the work included updating the windows. The last occupants were Andrew Bray, stationer, in the eastern house and William West, drysalter, in the western one. Nonsuch House was demolished early in 1757, and the other houses on the bridge had all gone by 1760.[29]

Plan 8
Cursitors' Hall, Cursitors Alley, c.1578
John Symonds
FIGS 34-36

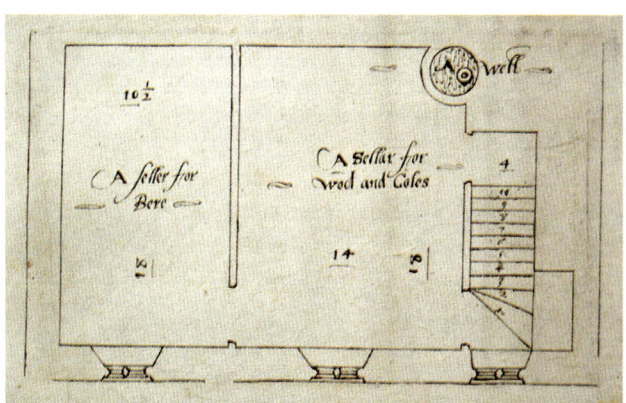

Figs 34-36. The basement (right), ground floor (below) and first floor (overleaf) of the Cursitors' proposed kitchen and hall, c.1578. The basement and first-floor plans were originally flaps to be placed over the ground-floor plan. North is at the bottom.

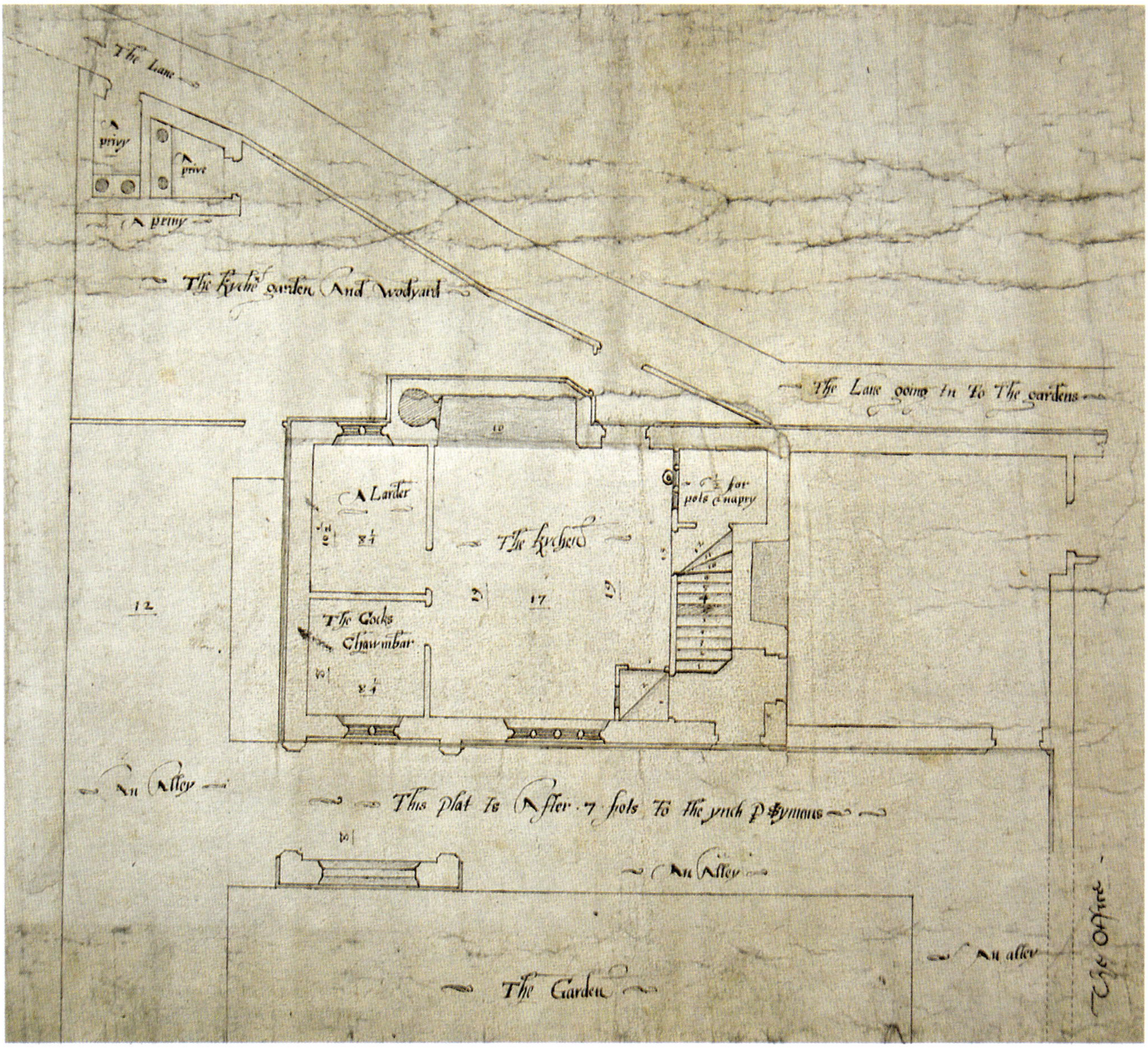

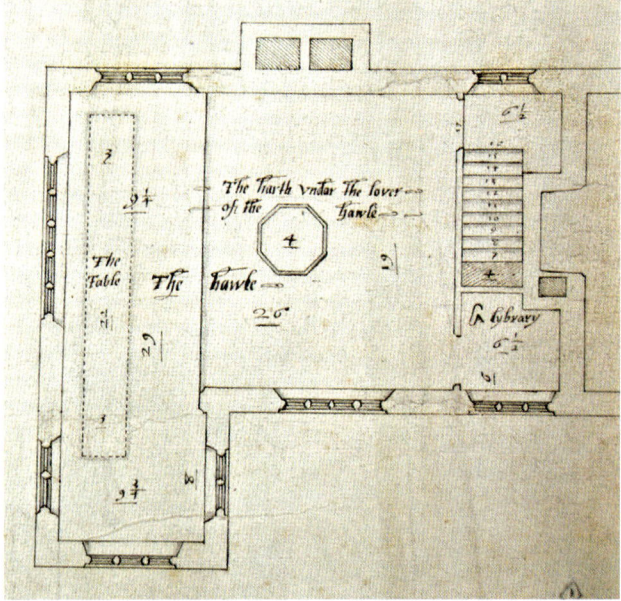

The role of the twenty-four Cursitors was to prepare and issue writs on behalf of the Court of Chancery. In 1573 Sir Nicholas Bacon, Lord Keeper under Queen Elizabeth, secured a charter of incorporation for the Cursitors. He also provided an office, which the Cursitors occupied from 1575, so that they should 'keape together in the terme tyme bothe for the encrease of knowledge and for the easie and readie dispache of all our clientes'. The office was eighty-four by twenty feet, with a withdrawing chamber twenty by nineteen feet adjoining, and above these were chambers and garrets let out by separately by Bacon. They stood on the east side of Chancery Lane, north of what is now Cursitor Street, directly opposite the gateway of Lincoln's Inn. The garden behind was also let to the Cursitors. Stow described the property as 'builded with divers fayre lodgings for gentlemen, all of bricke and timber, by Sir Nicholas Bacon'. When Bacon and the Cursitors agreed a lease in December 1577 it committed the Cursitors to building within three years 'one newe house for a kytchyn' in the garden; also, jointly with the tenants of the rooms over the office, they were to build a set of privies, to be shared between them and Bacon's other tenants, the latter having separate access from the back lane, exactly as shown on the plan; hence the assigning of the plan to c.1578.[30] The plans are labelled 'a plott for building'. Above the cellars of the new building was to be a ground floor consisting mainly of a kitchen, and above that was to be the hall, twenty-six by nineteen feet, with an open hearth, a louvre above and a bay projecting northwards over one of the garden walks. By 1618 the withdrawing chamber seems to have been in use as the 'hall or dineing roome', so perhaps that part of the planned new building was left out, but the Cursitors still had the kitchen, larder, cellar and privies described as lately built by them.[31] Whichever building was used, the Cursitors' hall was not merely for dining: from 1596 there were readings of writs and formularies three nights a week after supper.[32]

The architect was John Symonds, who was skilled in several trades, being a mason by training and a joiner by company, as well as the Queen's Master Plasterer from 1590. He was employed in the Queen's Works for many years from 1571/2, acted as architect to Lord Burghley from 1577 and drew several architectural and military plans. He died in 1597. He was probably the John Symons said to have designed an extension to the hall of Lincoln's Inn in 1583. One of his cousins was a cursitor.[33]

When the Cursitors' lease expired in 1639 the then owner, Nicholas Bacon, wanted to rebuild the property as tenements to increase the rent, but the Cursitors brought pressure to bear on him through his brother Francis Bacon, and he agreed to lease part of the site to the Cursitors with their premises rebuilt. A 'modell or plott forme' was provided to show the Cursitors what was intended, but that cannot be the plan reproduced here, as the man who signed it was long dead. This was presumably when the kitchen block of c.1578 disappeared. After the rebuilding a new lease was drawn up in 1643, though the Cursitors were disgruntled about paying the same rent for smaller premises and legal action was required before they sealed the lease.[34] The site was not affected by the Great Fire. Ogilby and Morgan's map of 1676 shows houses where the kitchen block of c.1578 had been. The Cursitors left the office in 1813 and were abolished in 1835.[35]

Plan 9
Former precinct of Holy Trinity Aldgate, c.1585
John Symonds
Fig. 37

This plan shows the site of the monastery of Holy Trinity Aldgate about fifty years after it was dissolved.[36] The monastery, founded in 1107/8, was the richest in London and the first post-Conquest foundation within the walls. Its church dated from the twelfth and thirteenth centuries. The plan, together with a similar one of the first

Fig. 37. The former precinct of Holy Trinity Aldgate, c.1585. North is at the bottom left.

storey, is at Hatfield House, and may have been made for Lord Burghley when the City of London was considering purchasing the site in the 1580s. The City's interest in the property continued from 1579 until it finally made the purchase in 1592, but the names given on the plan date it somewhat more closely to 1582-90. Unlike Symonds' building plan for the Cursitors, this one was not drawn to a consistent scale, and seems instead to have been derived from sketch plans drawn in the field, perhaps themselves based on pacing. Within the precinct it also conforms to a rectangular grid, which introduces further inaccuracies. Symonds seems to have been as interested in the former

Fig. 38. Reconstruction of the former precinct of Holy Trinity in about 1585, by Richard Lea. Leadenhall Street and Aldgate are to the left, with the church of St Katherine Cree to the top left. Numerous houses had been built within the remaining walls of the priory church. North is to the right.

monastery as in the current situation (perhaps for the same reason as the surveyor of Greyfriars —see Plan 20 below); he identifies the various parts of the monastic complex, and sometimes adds vanished features in dotted lines or makes remarks such as 'The north end wher the great tower fell downe'. The layout of the monastery is clearly visible on the plan, including the church, gatehouse, cloister and outer court.

After the monastery was dissolved in 1532, most of the site was acquired by Sir Thomas Audley, who created an aristocratic mansion in the west part of the cloister. The mansion was occupied by the Duke of Norfolk from 1558 to 1564, giving rise to the name, Duke's Place. The church had been unroofed, the nave becoming a garden, but the mansion included a gallery along the north side of the nave leading to the Ivy Chamber (possibly a banqueting house) sited in the crossing at first-floor level. Other substantial houses were also created among the ruins, as well as smaller ones (see Fig. 38 and Plan 100). The various tenancies are indicated on the plan by different colours. The holder of the west range of the cloister, which had apparently been Norfolk's mansion, was William Kerwin, Master of the Masons' Company in 1579 and the City Mason who rebuilt Ludgate in 1585-86;

he was buried in St Helen's Bishopsgate, where his tomb survives, in 1594. As on other monastic sites in London, holdings gradually became more fragmented. The cloister eventually became the Little Court, Duke's Place and is now Mitre Square, while the monastery's outer court became Broad Court and is now Creechurch Place. An arch from one of the transept chapels survives within a modern building.

Plans 10 and 11
The Hermitage and the Crash Mills, Wapping, c.1590 and c.1605
FIGS 39, 40, 42

These two plans cover overlapping areas, and show a stretch of water later known as Hermitage Dock but which originated as a millpond rather than a dock. The mills were the Crash Mills, first recorded in 1233. The name of the dock came from a medieval hermitage, known as the Swan's Nest by 1375. The land belonged to the abbey of St Mary Graces from 1375 until the Dissolution.[37]

The earlier plan (Figs 39, 40) was drawn in connection with lawsuits in 1589-92, and survives among the records of the Court of Exchequer.[38] It shows land stretching from East Smithfield in the north to the Thames in the south, though only part is reproduced here. The north-south road was then Nightingale Lane and is now Thomas More Street, between the former London Docks and St Katherine's Docks. Like most plans drawn for legal purposes, it shows only the lands and buildings relevant to the dispute and ignores others, notably the breweries all along the riverbank.[39] But the buildings it does show were drawn with exceptional clarity and detail, suggesting that they are accurate representations. By the Thames, for example, are the Hartshorn brewery and the Abbey's brewery east of the dock, together with warehouses, wharves, cranes, steps and ships.[40] Nearby are the Crash Mills, just south of the bridge over the inlet, with the millpond behind and several water channels. Further north is the Hermitage alias the Swan's Nest. The later plan helps to interpret what is shown there: the western part closest to the bridge over the millpond was a large house, twenty-two feet wide, occupied by John Stepken, whose grandfather Thomas had acquired a lease of the Swan's Nest or Hermitage directly from the last Abbot in 1538,[41] while the eastern part was the Hermitage brewhouse. The house was probably what was described in 1548 as new

EARLY PLANS, c.1450-1630

Fig. 39. Detail from the plan of the Hermitage, c.1590, showing the Crash Mills and the wharf east of Hermitage Dock. North is at the top. The plan is heavily stained.

lodgings adjoining the hall of the brewhouse westwards, built by Thomas Stepken together with two chambers over the brewhouse hall.[42] In modern terms the Swan's Nest was between the Hermitage Basin and Vaughan Way (Fig. 41). The area as a whole bordered on Wapping Marsh to the east.

The later plan (Fig. 42) looks like a pictorial one, but this is deceptive. The unusual amount of text makes clear that the plots or buildings of direct concern are shown in ground plan with dimensions. Only the buildings which did not matter are shown pictorially. There seem to be more buildings than on the earlier plan, but that may simply indicate that the earlier plan had a more limited purpose. Buildings are evidently shown in standardised form, with the possible exceptions of Stepken's house and what seems to be a brewhouse west of the dock. The main clue to the date is that the Crash Mills are still there, indicated by two water wheels. The mills still existed in 1609, but had gone by 1613.[43] Once the mills had gone, the whole stretch of water could be used as a dock, instead of just the water below the mills.

The block of land which seems to have generated the plan was north of the bridge at the upper end of the millpond. There had been an alum house there, presumably for storing alum, a salt combined with alumina used mainly as a mordant in the dyeing of cloth, but some or all of it had become a brewhouse. The brewhouse, with watercourses on three sides, consisted of dwellings for two families, brewhouse, millhouse, malt lofts, storehouses, stable and yard for loading drays. West of the main millstream was a storehouse 110 feet long, with at its north end the alum house's former 'plumerye' (presumably for lead working) and its forge, now a cooper's shop. Elsewhere around the dock were lime shops, a coal yard and a deal yard. A deed of 1644 refers to three great warehouses with two small houses at the north end of the dock known as the 'allom house and since ... the sope house one of which warehouses is now used for a pott house', occupied by Edward Ball. It also mentions a former glasshouse.[44] When the London Docks were built, their western entrance coincided with that of the Hermitage Dock, and it has outlasted London Docks, though the Hermitage Basin further inland only slightly overlaps the site of the former millpond (Fig. 41). The plan evidently passed with the property to the Port of London Authority.

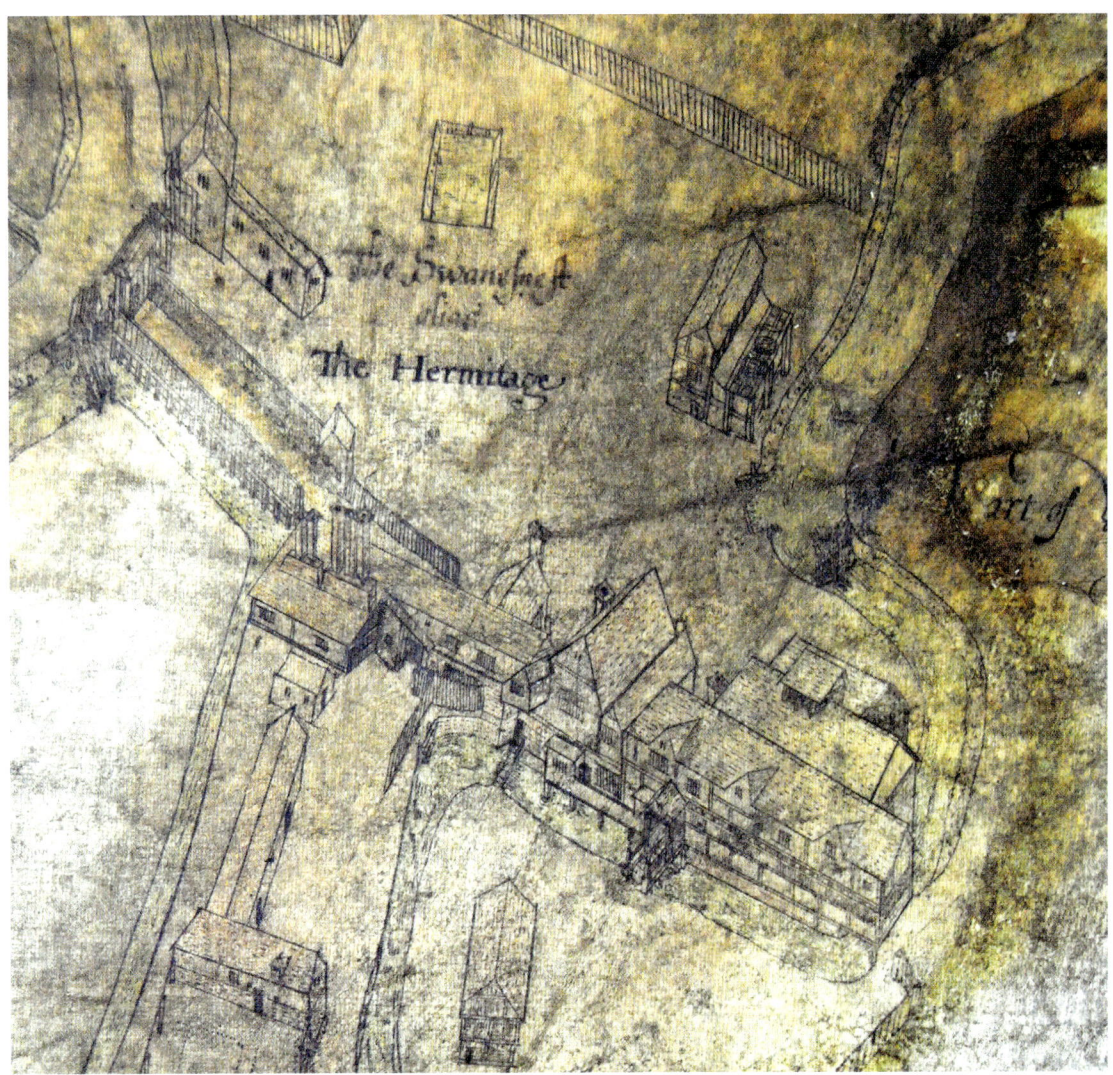

Fig. 40. Another detail from the plan of the Hermitage, *c.*1590, showing the Swan's Nest.

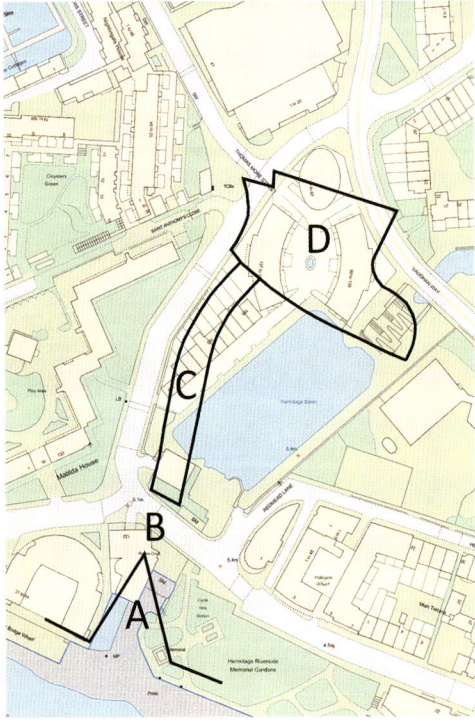

Fig. 41. The approximate location of features of the *c.*1590 plan shown on the Ordnance Survey map of 2015. A is Hermitage Dock; B is the Crash Mills; C is the millpond; D is the Swan's Nest and its enclosure. On the 2015 map, St Katharine's Way and Wapping High Street are near the bottom; the north-south road is Thomas More Street.

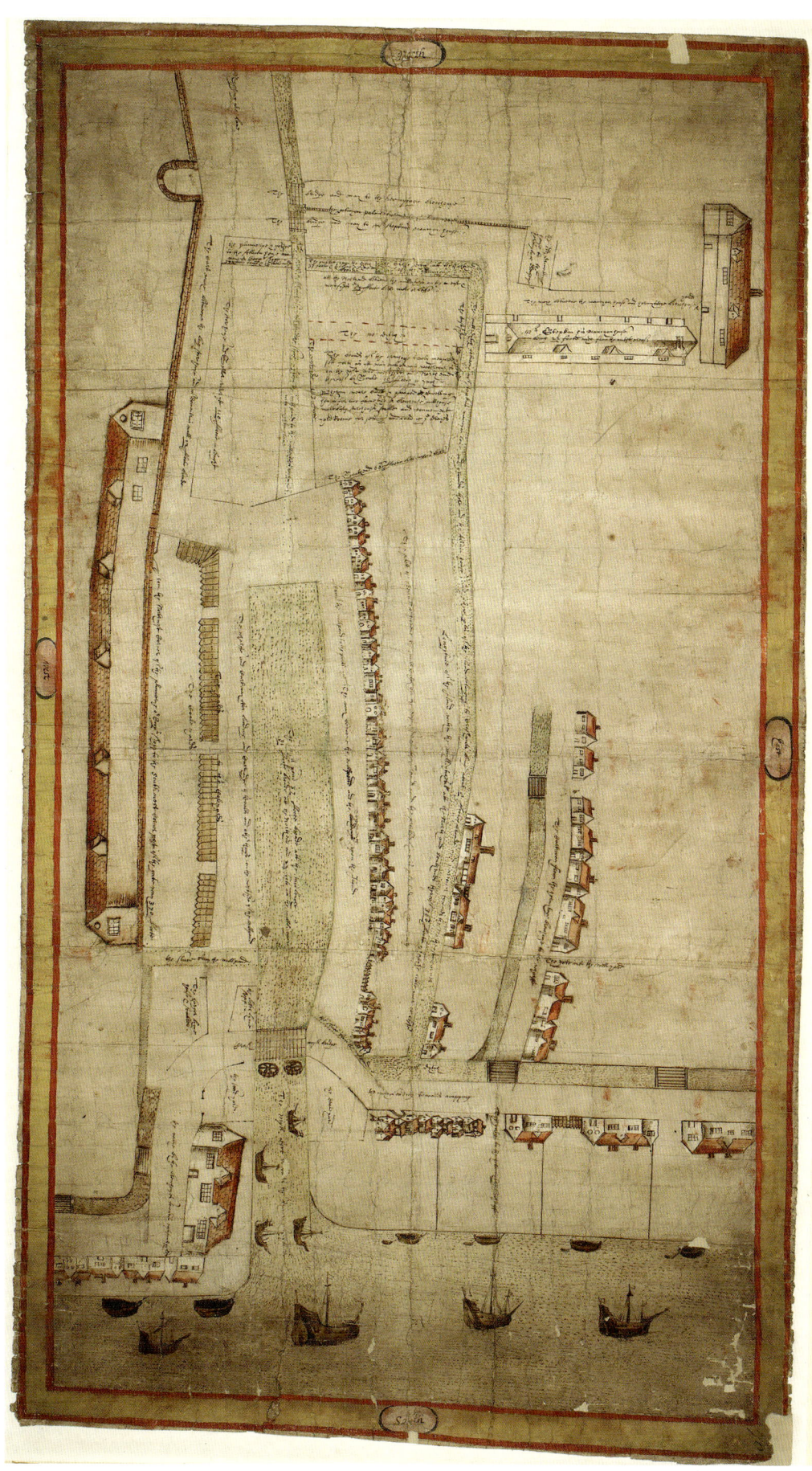

Fig. 42. The Hermitage and the Crash Mills, c.1605. North is at the top.

Plan 12
The Erber, Dowgate Hill, 1596   FIG. 43

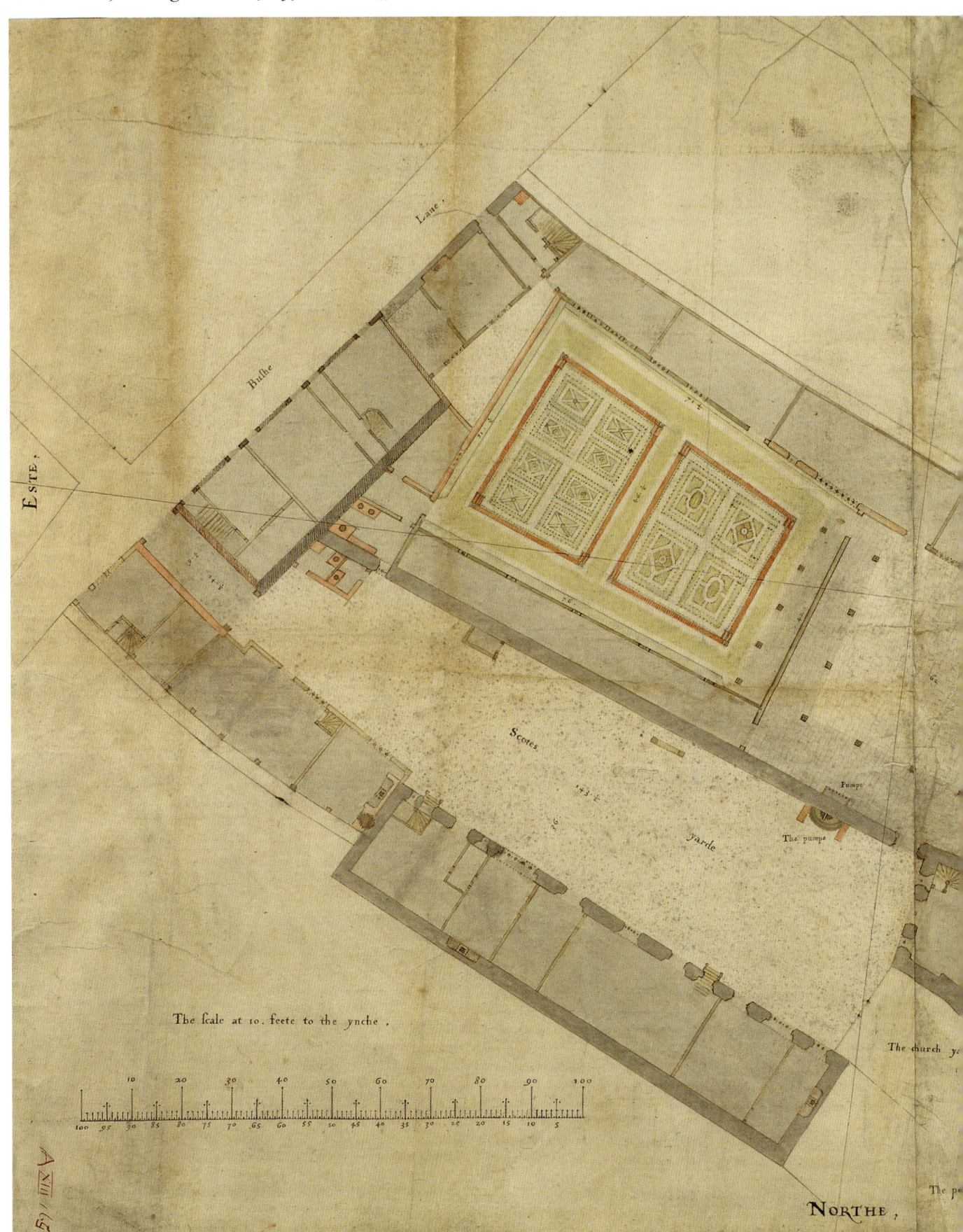

Fig. 43. The Erber, Dowgate Hill, 1596.

The Erber was an important medieval mansion in the City. It was between Dowgate Hill and Bush Lane, and the site is now under the front part of Cannon Street Station (Fig. 44). It is first mentioned in 1340, and was owned by the Earl of Wiltshire in 1399, the Earl of Salisbury in 1429, the Earl of Warwick ('the Kingmaker') in 1460 and the Duke of Clarence in 1472-78. Its last noble occupant was Margaret Pole, Countess of Salisbury, executed by Henry VIII in 1541. Henry VIII sold it to the Drapers' Company in 1542.[45] Stow, writing in 1603, described it as a 'great olde house ... lately new builded by Sir Thomas Pullison Maior'. Pullison acquired an eighty-year lease of the house in 1580, which required him to spend 1000 marks (£667) 'in new building and altering thereof'.[46] The plan shows many thick walls—usually at least three feet wide—and colours most of them grey, contrasting with the few walls coloured yellow or orange, which were presumably of timber and brick respectively. This indicates that the Erber was largely a stone building, especially at the front, which suggests that the rebuilding was not a complete one but included some 'altering'. The lease was transferred in 1589 to Sir Francis Drake, who occupied the house until 1593.[47]

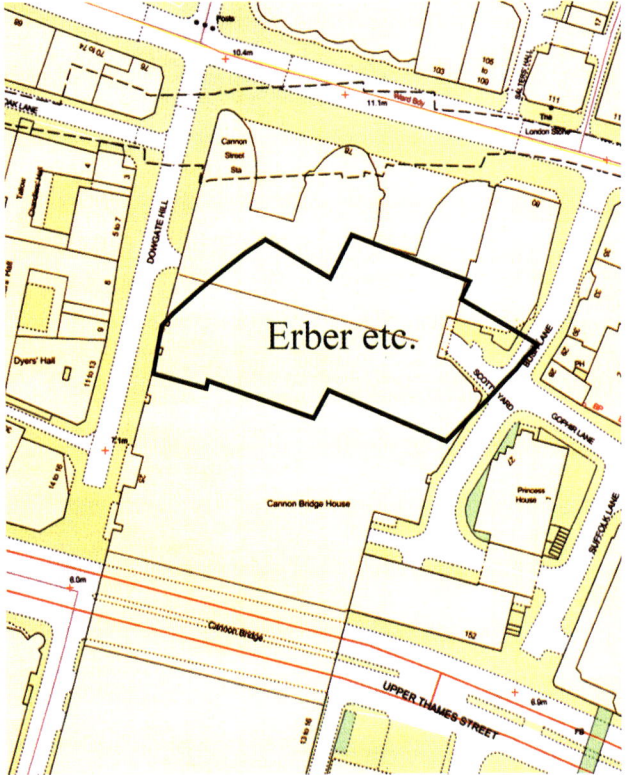

Fig. 44. The approximate location of the buildings in Fig. 43, including the Erber, shown on the Ordnance Survey map of 2015. Cannon Street is at the top and Upper Thames Street (passing under Cannon Street Station) at the bottom.

The Drapers' ownership was challenged in the 1590s on the basis of whether Henry VIII's title was good, which depended on whether Henry IV had granted it to Lord de Raby in tail or not in tail nearly two centuries earlier. The matter was considered by the Court of Exchequer in 1597, and the legal proceedings evidently gave rise to the plan in the previous year, though its exact purpose remains unknown. Queen Elizabeth settled the matter by ruling in the Company's favour in 1598.[48] Already in 1596 every feature of the most detailed ground plans is present, including staircases, fireplaces, ovens and windows. Even the convention of grey for stone, orange or red for brick and yellow for timber seems to be followed. The Drapers' minutes and accounts record that the plan cost them £3.6s.8d, but not who drew it.[49] The plan may in fact be a re-drawing of the late seventeenth century, as the style of the text (especially the long 's' used) suggests,[50] but it is evidently a carefully-drawn copy and therefore likely to be a faithful one. The plan remained important to the Drapers even after the site was redeveloped in the 1660s because it showed clearly what land Henry VIII had granted to the Company.

In 1550 the Erber holding included a house adjoining the main part of the Erber (shown here to its north-east), one north of the Erber's back gate together with four adjoining it (evidently the north-east side of Scotes Yard), two others (probably in Bush Lane), a garden in Carter Lane alias Checker Alley, and an inn called the Checker (on the opposite side of Checker Alley and not shown on the plan).[51] The Erber itself was approached through a gatehouse on Dowgate Hill, which brought one into an enclosed and partly colonnaded courtyard, from which steps ascended to what was probably a medieval hall over an undercroft. Further accommodation lay around a paved and colonnaded courtyard behind, as well as south-west of the garden. There was an elaborately designed garden, with what may have been a gallery on the north-east side. Service areas lay west of the main block, including a kitchen and a store yard, together with two new stables. Rear access was though the Bush Lane gatehouse and Scotes Yard, and possibly from a passage in the south corner.

Seventeenth-century occupants of the Erber included Sir Edward Bromfield, Lord Mayor in 1636, before 1645, Alderman Richard Chambers in 1645 and Sir Richard Chiverton, Lord Mayor, in 1658.[52] In 1657, despite Chiverton's wish to renew his lease, the Drapers decided the property should be let for a forty-one year term, to encourage the lessee to build and improve it, suggesting that its career as a mansion may have ended then. It was eventually let in 1658 to John Burton and John Chevall, both drapers, for a fine of £2,400; the lease was extended to fifty-one years in 1660.[53] No mansion appears in the hearth tax list of 1666. Whatever stood on the site was burnt in that year.

A rebuilding lease was secured in 1668 by Burton and Chevall who, unknown to the Drapers, were part of a consortium including Sir Thomas Bludworth. There were fifteen dwellings there in 1707.[54] Most of the site was acquired from the Drapers in 1867 for Cannon Street Station,[55] but a fragment of Scotes or Scott's Yard remains between Cannon Street Station and Bush Lane.

Plan 13
Great Salisbury House, the Strand, c.1601
Simon Basil   FIG. 45

This plan was a design for a proposed building, but a convincing case has been made that it shows at least approximately what was built.[56] The house was Great Salisbury House, constructed for Robert Cecil, first Earl of Salisbury (Fig. 46), largely in 1600-02. Cecil was temporarily without a London home, as Burghley House (Plan 6) had passed to his half-brother, the Earl of Essex, following the death of Lord Burghley in 1598. The plans were by Simon Basil, then Comptroller of the King's Works, who was the leading figure in the house's creation, though many others

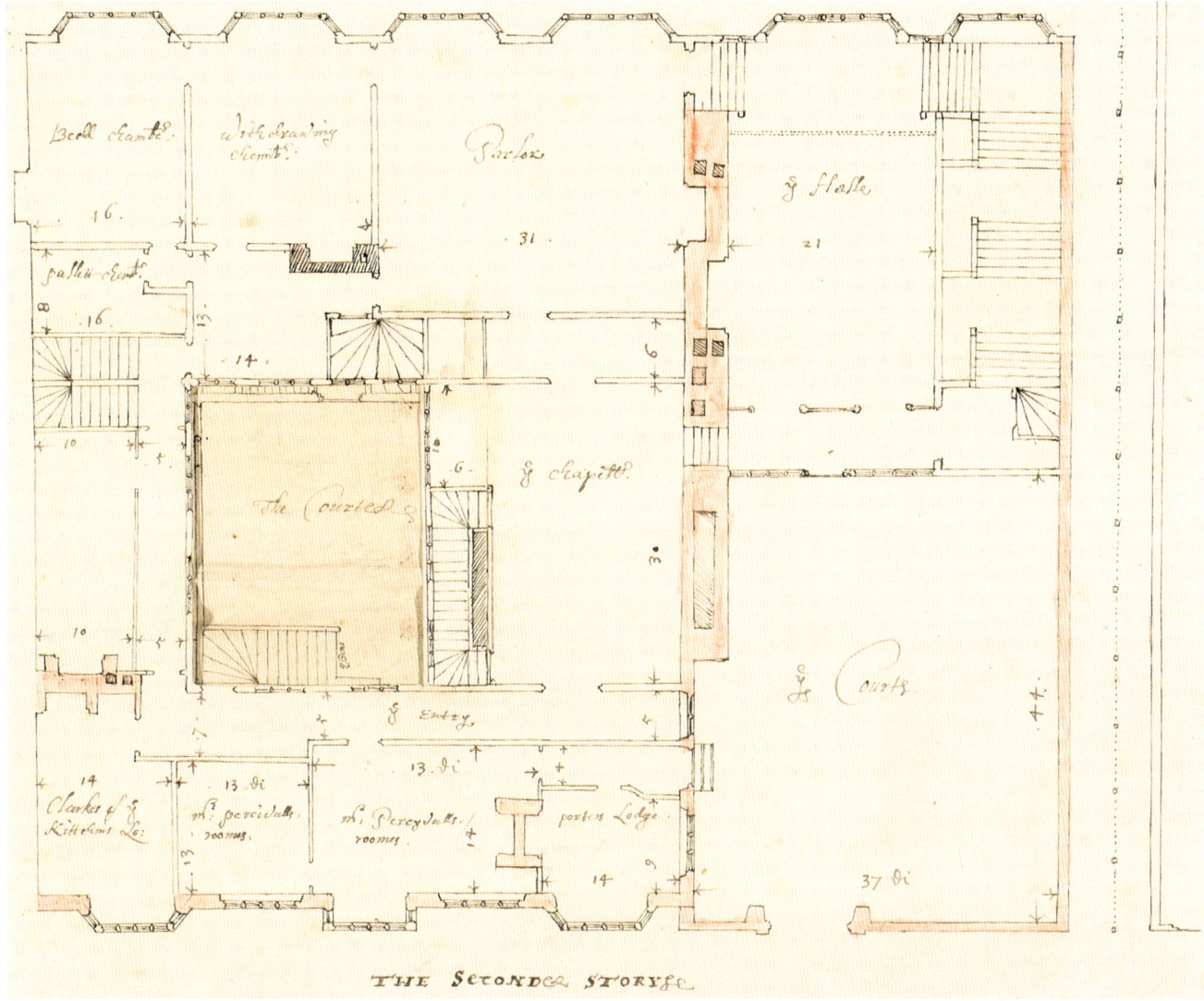

Fig. 45. Plan of the ground floor of Great Salisbury House, the Strand, as proposed *c.*1601. The ground floor is labelled 'The second story' because the slope of the ground resulted in the basement level at the front extending into a terrace at the back, and this was therefore regarded as the ground floor or, in contemporary parlance, the first floor; the floor above was therefore referred to as the second. North is at the bottom.

were also involved, including Cecil himself. The site was at first a narrow one, comprising approximately the main block of the house around the internal courtyard, but further acquisitions and the diversion of Ivy Lane (seen in its new course on the right of the plan) made it possible to add the block including the hall.

The ground-floor plan shows that the house was entered from the Strand by a courtyard on the west side, flanked by the porter's lodge. Behind was a single-storey hall, evidently acting as an entrance lobby, beside which was the main staircase. Also on this floor were the parlour, withdrawing chamber, bed chamber and chapel. The first storey consisted of the great chamber over the hall, the gallery, eighty-four feet long, occupying the whole west range adjoining, and lodgings. The second storey contained lodgings and wardrobes, and there was a garret storey over the main part of the house. The kitchen was under the hall, with other service rooms nearby, and on the same level was a terrace adjoining the garden (Fig. 47). When Queen Elizabeth dined at the house in December 1602 this was described as the 'warming of Master Secretaries new house'.

A north-south range was added on the east side of the house in 1605, possibly containing a library and another long gallery. Around 1607, turrets were added at the corners of the house of 1602, together with a great lantern at the top of the house and a garret storey over the wing containing the hall. In 1611-13 Little Salisbury House was added on the west side, Ivy Lane being moved again. Decline set in early: the Middle Exchange was built in 1637-39 between Great and Little Salisbury Houses. In 1670 the ground floor of Great Salisbury House was converted into shops

Fig. 46. Robert Cecil, first Earl of Salisbury (1563?-1612), painted by John de Critz the elder in about 1602.

Fig. 47. Reconstruction by Manolo Guerci of the river front of Great Salisbury House as proposed c.1601.

and tenements, in 1673 Little Salisbury House was replaced by a new street, and in 1694 the same fate befell Great Salisbury House and the Middle Exchange (see Plans 189-91).

Plan 14
Northampton House, the Strand, 1609
John Smythson
FIG. 48

Northampton House, later called Suffolk House and afterwards Northumberland House, was built by Henry Howard, Earl of Northampton (Fig. 49), one of James I's most important ministers.[57] The site of the house was assembled from 1605 to 1608, with further purchases in 1609 to 1611 to enlarge the garden. The structure of the house seems to have been complete by 1609. The plan was not a design but instead shows what had been built, largely corresponding to what is known from other sources. It was drawn during a visit to London by John Smythson, son of the architect Robert Smythson and the designer of several buildings himself.[58]

The plan shows the ground floor of the mansion arranged around a large courtyard, with several projecting windows and four corner turrets (Figs 50, 51). It had three storeys, topped by lead roofs, together with a basement storey under part of the house. The internal arrangements have been reconstructed by Manolo Guerci, mainly from the surveys by Smythson and John Thorpe and an inventory of 1614. The basement storey consisted largely of cellars but with

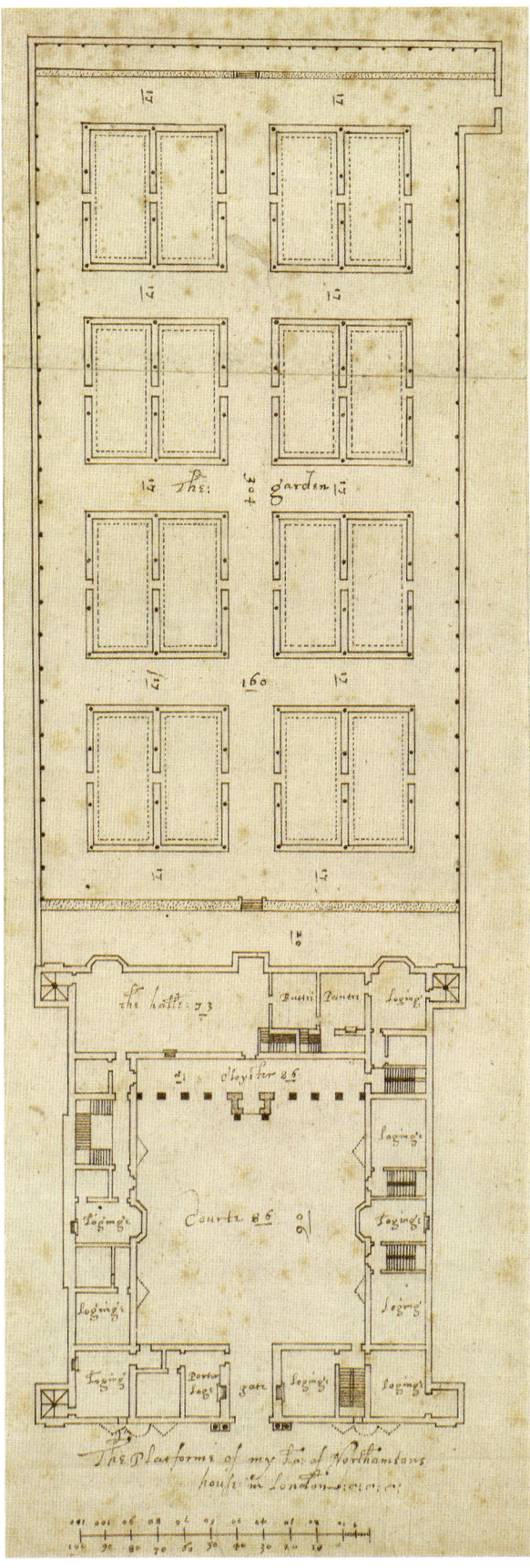

Fig. 48. Northampton House (later Northumberland House), the Strand, 1609. North is at the bottom.

kitchens under the garden wing, and had an arcaded loggia overlooking the garden. The ground floor, as Smythson shows, was mainly lodging chambers, together with the porter's lodge and the Strand gateway, the hall (possibly sharing part of the space indicated with a library or parlour), a buttery and a pantry. Smythson shows the main staircase, five others in the ranges and three in the turrets. On the south side of the court was a cloister. The middle floor was relatively private, but included the great chamber and dining chamber in the south-west corner. The top floor, accessed only by the main staircase and the turret stairs, was used almost entirely for the main rooms of state. Anti-clockwise from the south-east corner, they were the higher library, the main staircase, the long wardrobe, a parlour, the bigger great chamber, the great withdrawing chamber and a long gallery of 160 feet occupying the whole west range; the south range was a storey lower than the others, and at this level had a lead terrace from which the garden could be viewed. The house was richly furnished in 1614, with numerous tapestries and paintings. It had sixty-three hearths in 1664.[59] The large formal garden recorded by Smythson did not reach as far as the Thames, but a purchase by the Earl in 1611 made its extension to the riverside possible (the site is now separated from the Thames by the nineteenth-century embankment).

The house was acquired in 1642 by Algernon Percy, tenth Earl of Northumberland, who effectively rebuilt the south range. From the 1730s there were almost continuous alterations. In 1874 the Duke of Northumberland reluctantly agreed to sell the house to the Metropolitan Board of Works, which drove Northumberland Avenue through the site.[60] The approximate location of the house is shown in Fig. 237.

Fig. 49. Henry Howard (1540-1614), later Earl of Northampton, the builder of Northampton House, painted in 1594 by a follower of Hieronimo Custodis.

Fig. 50. Drawing by Hollar of Northumberland House seen from the river, 1647.

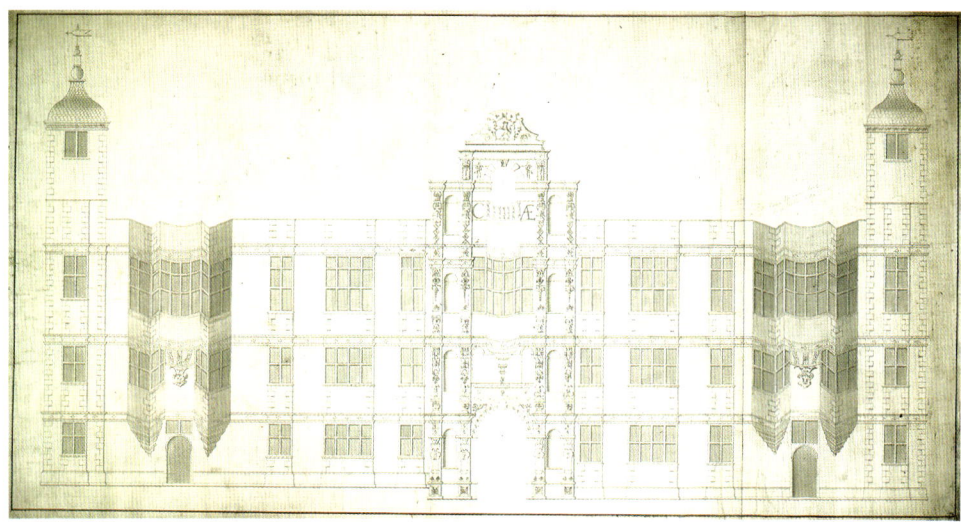

Fig. 51. Elevation of the Strand front of Northumberland House before the mid-eighteenth-century alterations.

Plan 15
Whitehall, 1610
Robert Treswell
Fig. 52

These houses were on the east side of Whitehall near the north end. 'The Armitage', or hermitage, was first recorded in 1253 and originally extended westward to the street; it formed part of the holding called 'Scotland' until 1519. The plot labelled here 'The Armitage' was later the site of Craig's Court, which still exists, with the passage to it occupying the southern part of what was in 1610 Gardyner's house. The two houses shown here in ground plan rather than elevation were therefore on the site of that passage and immediately north of it (later 19-20 Whitehall). 'Scotland', to the south, probably named after a medieval owner called Scot, was later absorbed into Whitehall Palace. 'Rownceval', to the north and east, was the Hospital of St Mary Rounceval, founded by William Marshall in 1231 and surrendered to the Crown in 1542. The houses between the hermitage and Rounceval had belonged to the Abbot of Westminster until acquired in 1531-32 by Henry VIII, who rebuilt them as houses for court servants.[61]

The plan was drawn in connection with a lawsuit, and according to Treswell was signed both by himself and by Gardyner's surveyor.[62] It combines a pictorial view with a ground plan of the two houses concerned, held by Sir John Parker (left) and Richard Gardyner (right). In 1609 Parker was granted a lease of a messuage and 'diverse shopps' in Whitehall belonging to the Crown, together with any property which could be proved to form part of the premises, and he claimed that Gardyner's property did so. Gardyner replied that his grandfather of the same name, who had been Sergeant of the Queen's wine cellar, had held his property as a freehold capital messuage and shops and had granted a lease of it in 1565; it had passed to

Fig. 52. Houses on the east side of Whitehall near the north end, 1610.

his father and then to himself. Gardyner's house had been let in 1565 to a single tenant, Thomas Putterell, but in 1610 it had two: Edmund Newsham in the front part, with just one room per floor, and David Hughes in the back or 'inward' part, some or all of which had been added by Putterell. Gardyner seems in fact to have had no freehold interest, and Parker evidently won the lawsuit and was in control of Gardyner's house by 1612.[63]

Hughes's widow, Katherine, gave a detailed explanation of a former door between the two properties, which was presumably the 'dore place now walled up' south of Parker's staircase. She said it had been made in about 1580 when Parker's house, then occupied by Mr Ruff of Queen Elizabeth's pantry, was visited by 'the sycknes'. Ruff's house, which lacked water, was likely to be shut up, so it was agreed to make a door allowing water to be fetched from the well behind Gardyner's house. It was closed again after two months.[64]

As with Plan 11 above, the combination of ground plan and pictorial plan was determined by the matters in dispute. The case centred on Parker's and Gardyner's houses, covering issues such as whether they had once been a single house, and Treswell therefore provided a ground plan of them. Parker argued that all the houses between Scotland and Rounceval had been obtained by Henry VIII from the Abbot of Westminster and were therefore Crown property, so these are all shown too, but there was no need to go inside each property and make a ground plan, and no great accuracy was needed in this area. In particular, the wall of Scotland had several kinks not shown here, and the eastern boundary of the Hermitage was not parallel to the street.[65] The number of houses may have been accurate and, less certainly, their varying number of storeys. The way Treswell shows their back parts at an angle to the front parts was clearly done for artistic effect, as it is not consistent with the shapes of Parker's and Gardyner's plots.

George Parker sold what had been Gardyner's house to James Craig in 1664, and Craig's Court existed by 1694.[66]

Plan 16
Petty France or Little Britain, c.1610
FIG. 53

This plan, drawn for St Bartholomew's Hospital, dates from between April 1604, when Thomas Bodley was knighted, and January 1613, when he died. Neither the surveyor nor the reason for the plan being drawn are known. It was not drawn to scale, and everything is rectangular, which was not so in reality, as Llewellyn's plan of a few years later (Plan 19) and the detail reproduced here as Fig. 54 show. Nor should the details of the buildings be taken too seriously, as they are too regular, though the numbers of storeys may sometimes be correct. The whole area was within the present hospital site, and the street shown as Petty France, usually regarded as part of Little Britain or Britten Street, no longer exists. Features shown here are Little St Bartholomew's churchyard, with the mortuary chapel of St Nicholas, the Hospital's 'Britten gate', Sir Thomas Bodley's mansion and garden and other houses in Petty France. 'H' seems to indicate Hospital land.

Bodley's mansion probably dated from about 1564, when a lease of at least ninety-one years was granted to Lord Mordaunt. Through an outer gateway a courtyard was approached, with stables to the right and a small garden behind them (part of a churchyard leased by Bodley). The main range facing the courtyard is depicted as having three storeys, with a two-storey gatehouse. Beyond, on the right-hand side of the walled main garden, was a gallery, apparently looking both into the garden and in the opposite direction into Little St Bartholomew's churchyard. A lease of 1655 records a gallery on the west side of the courtyard; the main block, fifty-three by thirty-three feet, including a hall (described as divided) with benches, a parlour behind it, a kitchen, and

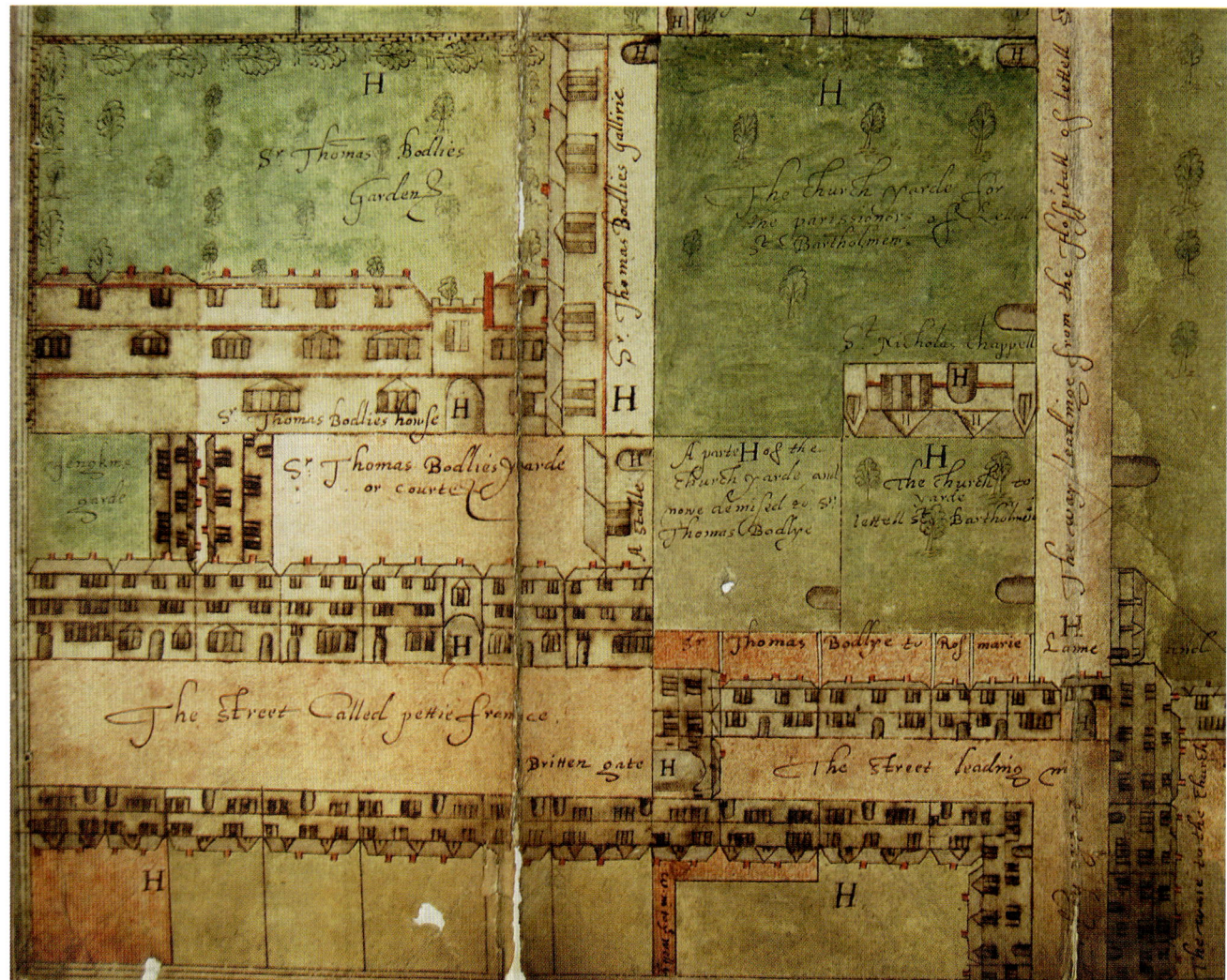

Fig. 53. Part of the plan of St Bartholomew's precinct, c.1610, showing Sir Thomas Bodley's house in Petty France. North is at the bottom.

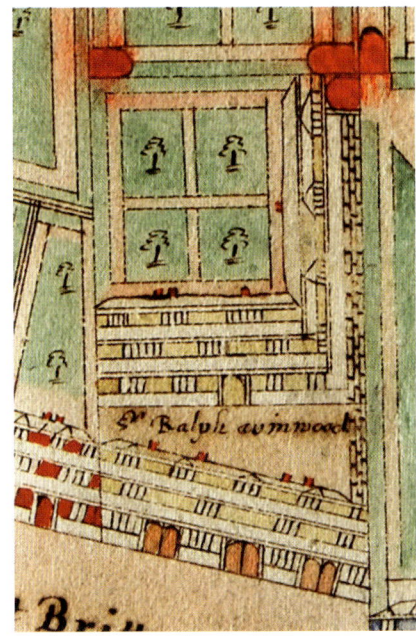

Fig. 54. Detail from one of the plans by Martin Llewellyn of c.1613, showing the mansion formerly Sir Thomas Bodley's.

Fig. 55. Sir Thomas Bodley (1545-1613)—miniature of 1598 by Nicholas Hilliard.

over the hall a dining room; a gallery fifty-two feet long at the east end of the house with buildings over (evidently not there in c.1610); a gallery fifty-three by fourteen feet on the west side of the garden with buildings over and a staircase at its south end; and a 'tarrys room' (terrace room) adjoining that staircase. The house had seventeen hearths in 1666.[67]

Thomas Bodley, diplomat and scholar and founder of the Bodleian Library (Fig. 55), lived there from 1599 until his death. He was succeeded there by his step-daughter's husband, Sir Ralph Winwood, Secretary of State to James I, by Sir Ralph's widow, Elizabeth, until 1655, and by John Lewys, merchant (and later baronet) from 1655.[68] In 1666 the mansion was divided into two parts, and the western section was partly rebuilt in 1676-77 (see Plan 133). Anything which remained would have been removed by Gibbs in 1730-59 to create the present hospital courtyard. The site of Bodley's house is now under the courtyard's south-east block.

Plan 17
West Smithfield and Cow Lane, 1612
Ralph Treswell
FIG. 56

This plan shows property in Smithfield west of the sheep pens—in modern terms largely under the market building a little west from the remaining open space at Smithfield (see Fig. 197). It was acquired by the Clothworkers' Company under a will of 1580.[69] The plan provides a good example of Ralph Treswell's style and the conventions he followed, as well as his ability to provide an insight into the lives of Jacobean Londoners. Treswell used grey rather than yellow for timber walls. Around Pheasant Court (the yellow and brown properties in Fig. 57) there were twelve households, all in dwellings of one-room plan. Charles Hill, for example, had a ground-floor room fourteen by twelve and a half feet, a chamber above one foot longer (evidently the building was jettied) and a garret above one foot longer again; each of his three rooms had a fireplace. The other dwellings were similar, though of varying sizes and with four of the garrets lacking a chimney. There was some subdivision: under Hill's and Samson Pott's dwellings was a cellar with a chimney 'wherein dwelleth Edward Lee', and Widows Howell and Lee occupied the chambers above William Procter's and William Ashpoole's rooms. William Haslom's ground-floor room was a shop. Everyone shared the three privies. Pheasant Court had been the Maidenhead, perhaps a hostelry, in the sixteenth century.

There were five substantial houses of two-room plan facing Smithfield (red or pink in Fig. 57). Edward Drewry had a first-floor hall, but chimneys only in the kitchen and the chamber over the kitchen. Upper rooms in the other houses were all described as chambers, and all were

Fig. 56. Houses in West Smithfield and Cow Lane, 1612. North is at the top.

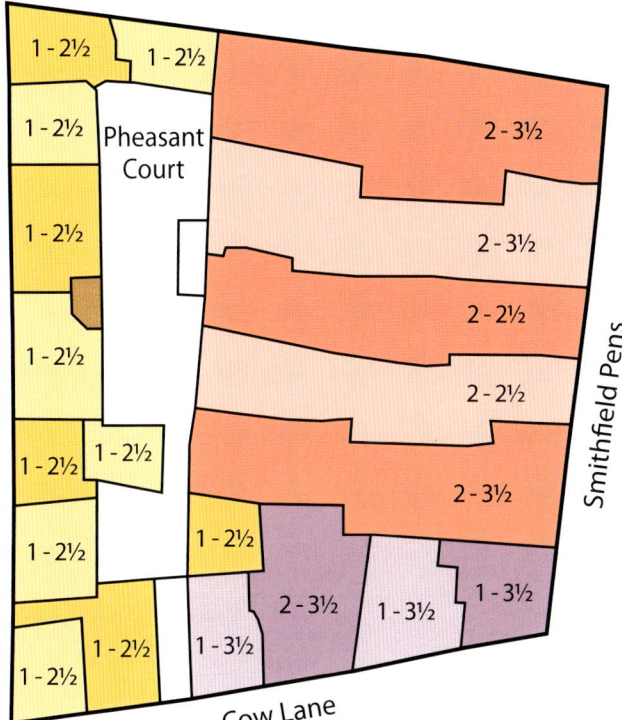

Fig. 57. Dwellings belonging to the Clothworkers' Company in West Smithfield in 1612, based on Treswell's plan. The figures in each case are the number of rooms in plan and the number of storeys.

heated, except in Peter Clarke's case where chambers had been divided. No garrets were heated except one of Clarke's. Only Christopher Askwith and Clarke seem to have had privies in their yards. The four smaller houses facing Cow Lane (purple in Fig. 57) had been rebuilt in or about 1603. Robert Seger and Thomas Brettnor had first-floor halls, both with chimneys, though in Brettnor's house only one room on each floor was heated. Otherwise all rooms were heated except all but one of the garrets. John Showell had a privy in the cellar, Seger one under the stairs and Brettnor one in a garret. In 1612 four leaseholders held the entire site from the Company: Drewry held one house, Askwith, a saddler, three houses, Clarke one house and Mrs Banckes all the rest. The Company sold part of the premises before 1841 and the remainder in 1875.[70]

Plan 18
Fenchurch Street, 1612
Ralph Treswell
Fig. 58

These six properties in Fenchurch Street, backing onto Clothworkers' Hall, were bequeathed in 1520 to the Shearmen's Company, later merged into the Clothworkers' Company, and the site remains in the Company's ownership today (now 46-48 Fenchurch Street).[71] The reconstructions were drawn on the basis of Treswell's plan by Peter Jackson (Figs 59, 60). At the bottom of the plan, William Jennings had shop and kitchen on the ground floor, hall and chamber above, two chambers above those, and garrets at the top, together with a cellar. The next two houses were similar, except that Anne Robinson had one storey fewer. The front rooms, the garrets and in John Yeoman's case all rooms above the first floor lacked chimneys. The top part of the plan shows a larger house, with two smaller tenancies occupying most of the street frontage. James Sutton's house was a small one of three and a half storeys and two-room plan without any backland, while James Dyer's shop and kitchen on the corner occupied only the ground floor. Jacques de Bees, in the large house, had hall, kitchen and washhouse on the ground floor, five chambers on the first floor (only two of them with chimneys) and a long garret above (unheated), together with garden and cellar. By 1619 de Bees' house had been rebuilt by Robert Hungate (the front part in brick, the rest in timber), and in the same year he agreed to rebuild Sutton's house. The rebuilt houses survived the Fire, but the others shown here were destroyed.[72]

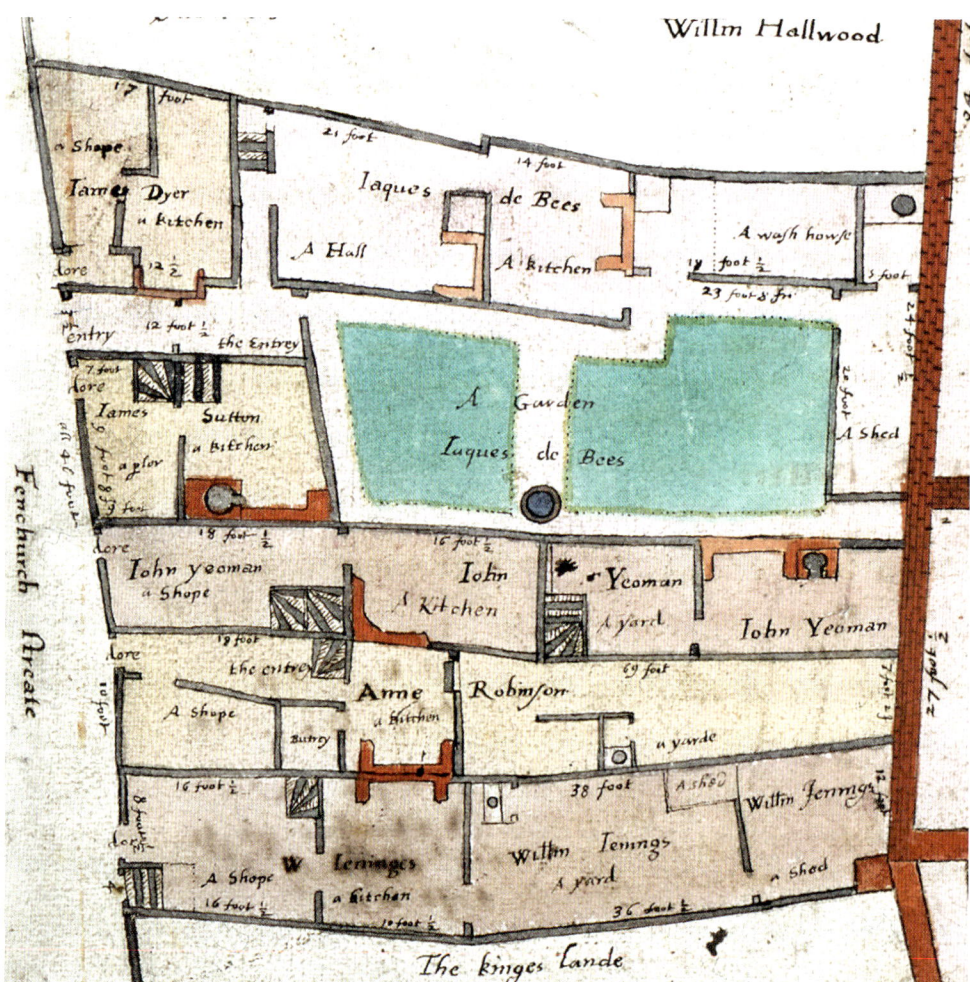

Fig. 58. Part of a plan by Treswell, showing houses in Fenchurch Street, 1612. North is to the left.

Fig. 59. Reconstruction by Peter Jackson of houses in Fenchurch Street shown on Treswell's plan of 1612.

Fig. 60. Reconstruction by Peter Jackson of the ground floor interiors of houses in Fenchurch Street shown on Treswell's plan of 1612.

Plan 19
St Bartholomew's precinct, c.1613
Martin Llewellyn
Fig. 61

This plan and others covering parts of the same area account for four of the ten pictorial plans drawn for St Bartholomew's Hospital. For these four there is direct evidence that Martin Llewellyn carried out the original survey. He was paid 'for making a ground plotte of the church yards and garden neere Sr Thomas Bodlies house and Pilkynton place the xxii[th] of May 1613', apparently in connection with a lawsuit over Pilkington Place, which was just south of Bodley's house.[73] The description fits one of the plans showing just part of the area shown here,[74] making it likely that Plan 19 is also wholly the work of Llewellyn.

Like the earlier plan of the Petty France area (Plan 16), Llewellyn's shows buildings in standardised form. Unlike that plan, his is to scale. Nevertheless, like other plans of this period covering relatively large areas, Llewellyn's is hard to relate exactly to a modern map, and London Wall did not change direction as he indicates (see Fig. 62). Important features shown are London Wall; the Town Ditch; Little Britain and Petty France; the house formerly of Sir Thomas Bodley but now of Sir Ralph Winwood; Little St Bartholomew's churchyard and the Hospital's burying ground; a large

Fig. 61. St Bartholomew's precinct, c.1613. North is at the bottom.

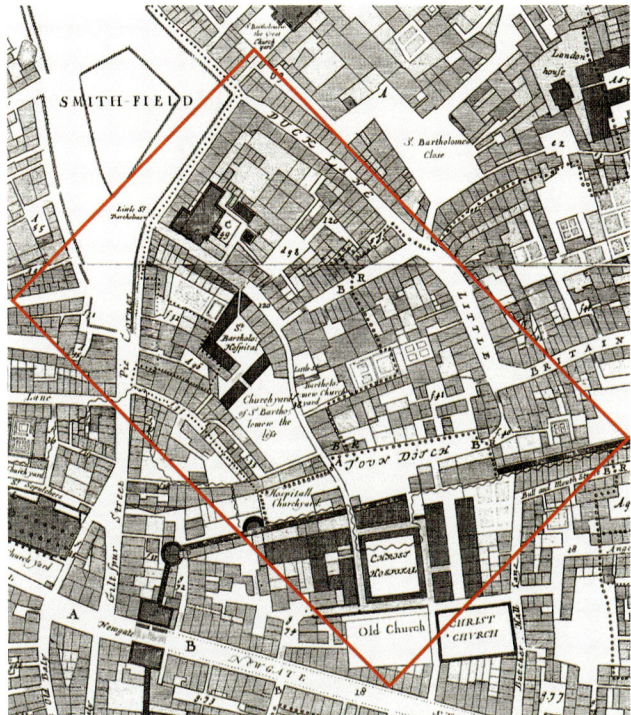

Fig. 62. Detail from Ogilby and Morgan's map of 1676, with a red line indicating the approximate area covered by Llewellyn's plan of St Bartholomew's precinct (Fig. 61).

arcaded courtyard containing a garden; the Hospital's 'great cloyster' just south of St Bartholomew the Less, with what seems to be its great hall adjoining; St Bartholomew the Less (compare Plan 21 below); the Hospital's gate to Smithfield; and Smithfield. The Hospital's buildings had fifty-eight hearths in 1674, but little is known about them.[75]

Plan 20
The former Greyfriars precinct, 1616
Edward Mansell and Martin Llewellyn
Fig. 63

In 1616 St Bartholomew's Hospital paid £6.13s.4d to 'Edward Mansell surveyor for makinge a large plott of the scyte of Christs Hospitall to sett out the backhouse and millhouse in question wch Adams holdeth buylded into tenements the viii[th] day of July 1616'.[76] The description matches the plan reproduced here, though this plan is entirely in the style of Martin Llewellyn and is almost certainly a copy of Mansell's plan.

The plan has sometimes been regarded as anomalous because it covers a different hospital, shows only part of the Greyfriars precinct (excluding its eastern part) and seems as interested in buildings and tenants of the 1540s as in contemporary ones.[77] For example, the gatehouse had been granted in 1540-41 to Thomas Eyre and Anne Leago, and the latter's name appears on the plan. All this is probably explained by the fact that St Bartholomew's owned former Greyfriars property in Newgate, that the ownership of that property was contested and that at least one of the lawsuits turned on exactly what the recipients of former monastic lands had been granted by Henry VIII in 1540-47. St Bartholomew's Hospital claimed the Greyfriars brewhouse and gatehouse, and stated that its tenant had sub-let two chambers over the house called the gatehouse to John Hunter, who had pulled them down and replaced them by 'a heap or cluster of chimnes'. Hunter's son and heir, Richard Hunter, claimed that Henry VIII's grants of the brewhouse and gatehouse had passed to him. Hunter recited evidence on changes to the premises; for example, a shoemaker's shop had been part of an oven place in Leago's house, and a poulterer's shop had been its coal-house. The Hospital obtained a decree in its favour in 1608, but Llewellyn's making of a model of the brewhouse in 1610 and the wording of 1616 as regards the bakehouse and millhouse suggest that the Hospital's possession continued to be challenged, probably because what was granted in the 1540s was no longer clear on the ground.[78]

After the dissolution of Greyfriars in 1538, many of its buildings survived little changed in the occupation of Christ's Hospital, and so appear on this plan, as well as on Plans 26 and 119.[79] The friary's main features were the church rebuilt in the early fourteenth century, the second largest in London after St Paul's Cathedral (its choir later became Christ Church); the great cloister, with the refectory to its west, library to its north and chapter house and dormitory to its east; the little cloister, with the infirmary to its west (see Plan 125); the gatehouse in Newgate Street leading into the service court; and gardens to the north-east. Christ's Hospital, an orphanage and poor-school, was established in and around the great cloister in 1552 and eventually owned most of the former precinct.

The Great Fire destroyed most of the buildings, but the north side of the great cloister survived together with some other pre-Fire fabric until about 1830 (Fig. 64).[80] Other features on the plan are Newgate; London Wall and the Greyfriars gate; the meal and flesh markets of Newgate, which were moved to off-street locations after the

Fig. 63. The former Greyfriars precinct, 1616.

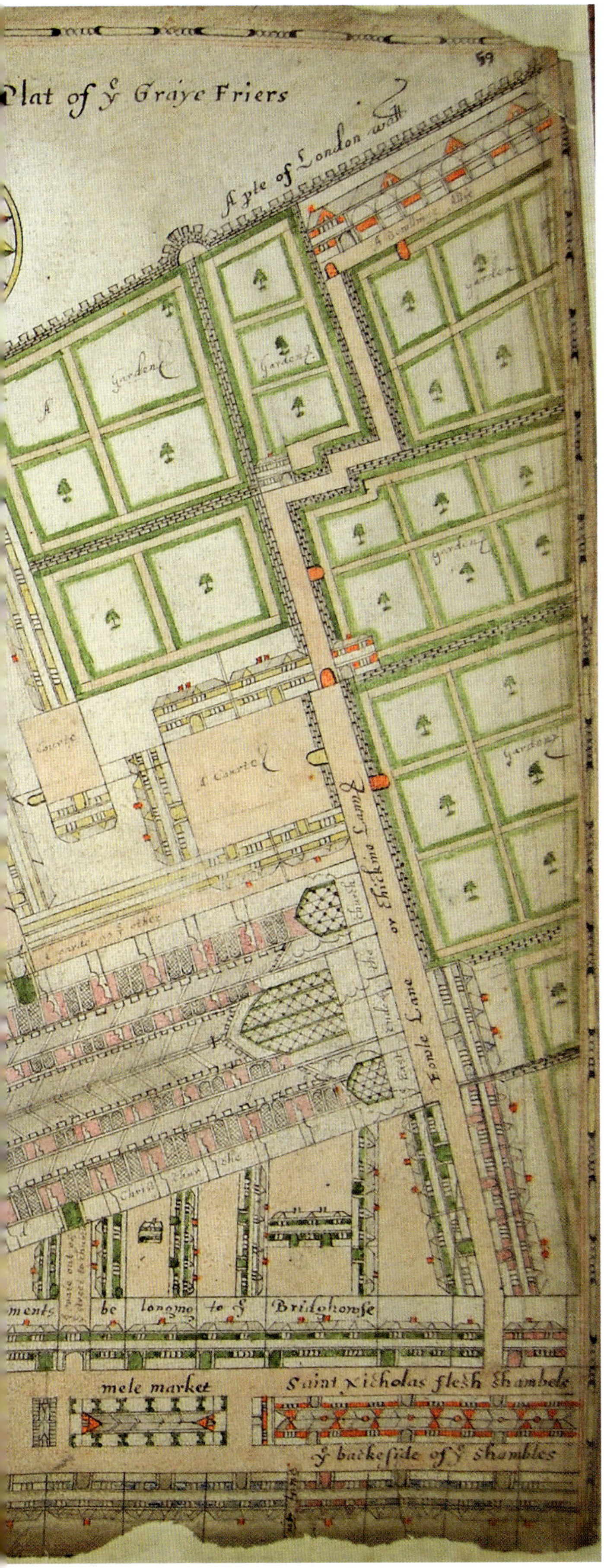

Great Fire; and a bowling alley in the top-right corner. The houses are standardised, and even Newgate bears no resemblance to the view drawn of it in 1650.[81]

Fig. 64. The cloister of Christ's Hospital, looking north (print by Henry Shaw of 1833-34). The range on the north side had survived the Great Fire.

Plan 21
St Bartholomew the Less, 1617
Martin Llewellyn
Fig. 65

St Bartholomew the Less began as one of the Hospital's chapels, apparently first built in the fifteenth century, and became a parish church after the Dissolution.[82] The plan of the church differs from Llewellyn's other plans not just in scale but also in character. It is essentially a ground plan, but of a peculiar type. The walls, at least the lower parts, are also shown, as if folded flat onto the ground. Previously Llewellyn had made a model for the Hospital,[83] and this plan is set out exactly as a model-maker might do it. Actual ground seems to be faintly marked by pink shading.

Though a ground plan, there are many pictorial elements, including windows, doors, the altar rail, the font and pew ends (shown yellow). The communion table is in the middle of the chancel, in the early seventeenth century manner, rather than set against the back wall like an altar, and is protected by rails and surrounded by what may be kneeling benches. The pulpit seems to be shown in blue south-west of the chancel. In 'ye poors chappell' there are benches rather than pews. The print from the 1730s shows three windows rather than two on the south side, which is accounted for by the subsequent disappearance of the vestry (Fig. 66). The print shows doors at the west end of the tower and

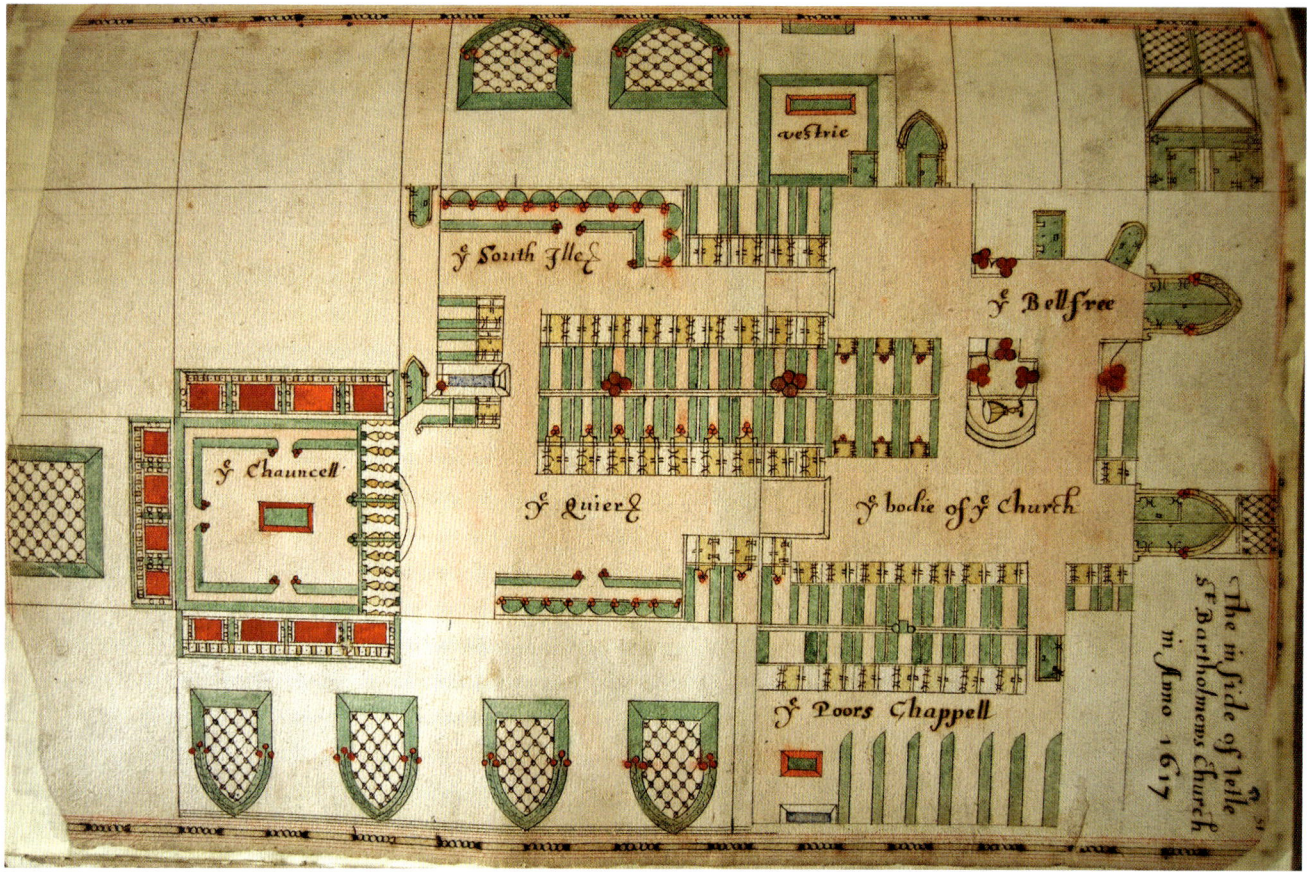

Fig. 65. St Bartholomew the Less, 1617. North is at the bottom.

Fig. 66. St Bartholomew the Less, seen from the south—print by William Henry Toms after a drawing by Robert West of 1737. The present gateway of the Hospital, dating from 1702, is not shown, which could indicate that the view was drawn much earlier.

the main body of the church as shown by Llewellyn; indeed these can still be seen today. On the other hand, the windows shown on the print indicate that at least some of the plan's pictorial detail was a representation rather than conveying the real appearance. The church was rebuilt in 1789-91 and again in 1823, but the fifteenth-century tower and the west wall plotted by Llewellyn remain.[84]

Plan 22
Cheapside and Bread Street, c.1617
FIGS 67-72

This is the earliest example of a plan covering all floors of an existing London building.[85] It also records an exceptional shop and the childhood home of John Milton. It shows Eton College's property at the south-east corner of Bread Street and Cheapside, known as the White Bear, though the site on the corner itself was in separate ownership. The White Bear had come to Eton among the possessions of the Hospital of St James, Westminster, in 1449. A written survey was made in October 1617, when the tenant, Sir Baptist Hicks, was seeking to renew the lease granted in 1568. Making a written survey was common enough before granting a new lease, but in this case plans were made too—not at exactly the same time, as one of the sub-tenants had changed, but presum-

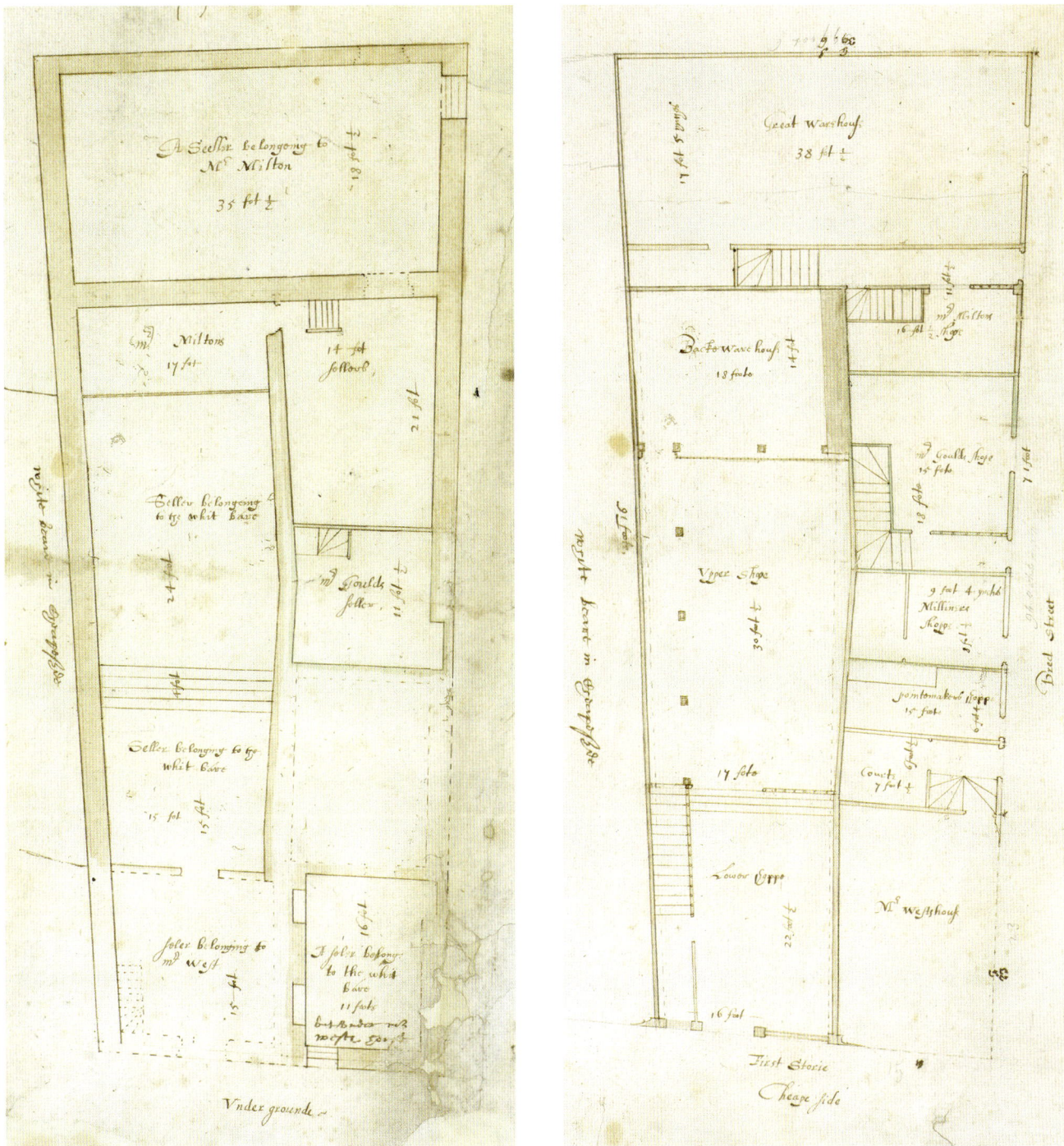

Figs 67-68. Houses in Cheapside and Bread Street, c.1617, showing the cellars and ground floor.

ably before the new lease was granted in March 1618.

One possible reason for the plans was uncertainty over the exact boundary between the corner house and Eton's property, and even the ownership of the corner house. Mr West, tenant of the latter, also had a staircase and a first-floor kitchen on College property, and a cellar under the adjoining White Bear, while the White Bear had a cellar under the corner house: 'But for convenience they change one with an other. Which sheweth yt the corner house is the College inheritance because it is builded over the College seller which belongeth to the White Beare.'[86] Another reason for the plans may have been concern about Hicks's additions at the top of the structure. No plans of this period exist for any of Eton's other London properties.

Baptist Hicks (Fig. 73) was a rich merchant and moneylender, and later (in 1628) became Viscount

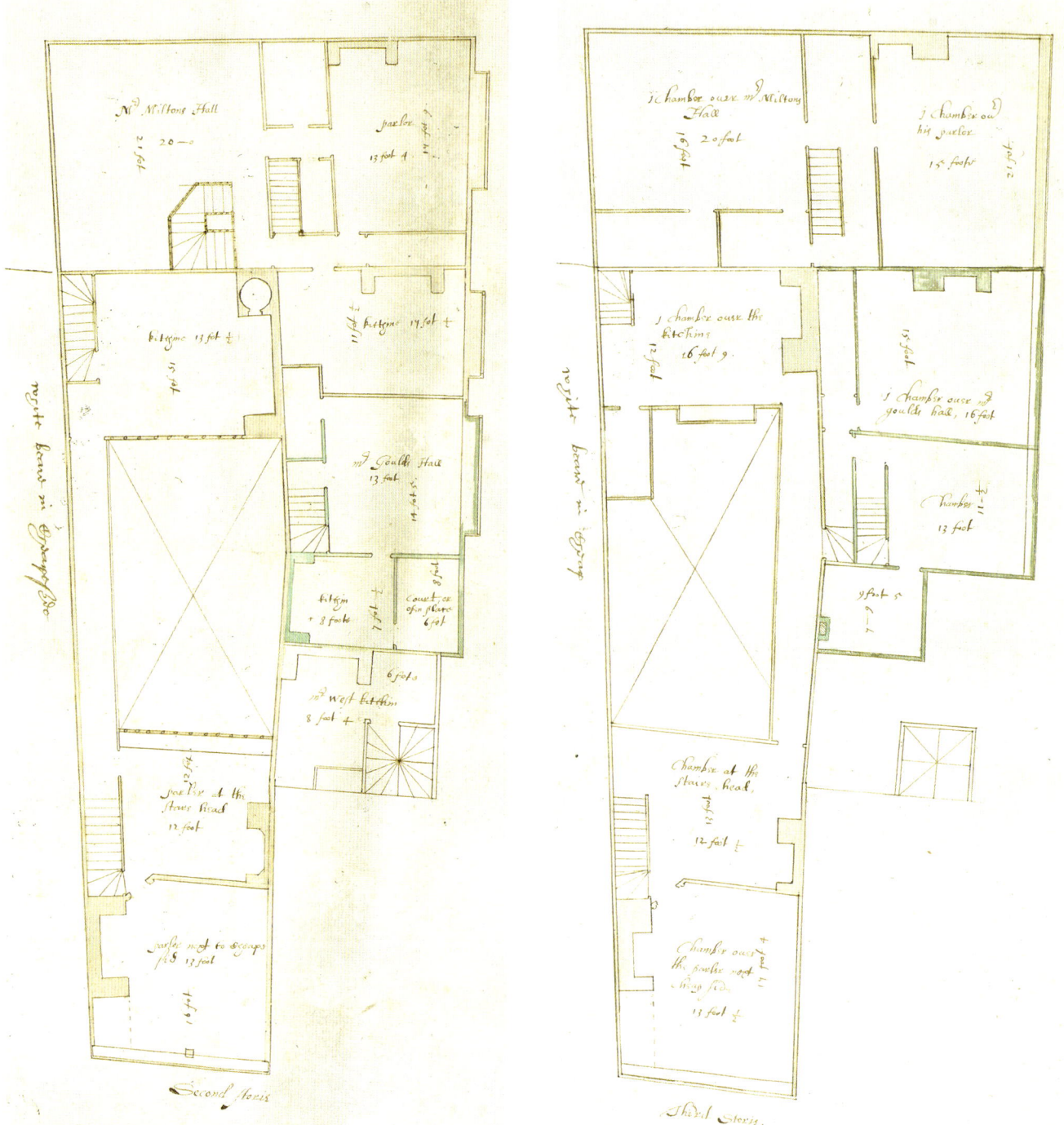

Figs 69-70. Houses in Cheapside and Bread Street, *c.*1617, showing the first and second floors.

Campden. He was the third son of a Cheapside silk mercer, and succeeded to his father's business in 1592, accumulating one of the greatest fortunes of the time. He was Master of the Mercers' Company three times, was mercer to Queen Elizabeth from 1596 and to James I from 1603, and was knighted in 1603. His shop in Cheapside was correspondingly fashionable, with Lord Chancellor Bacon among the visitors. In 1611 he wrote 'from my house in Cheapside', but when criticised by some of the aldermen for continuing the business after being knighted he claimed that the shop was kept by his servants rather than himself, that he was seeking to dispose of the business, and that shopkeeping was more acceptable than the moneylending of the aldermen (though he was himself involved in this too). He built Campden House, Kensington, and a mansion at Chipping Campden, as well as the Middlesex Sessions House known as Hicks' Hall.[87]

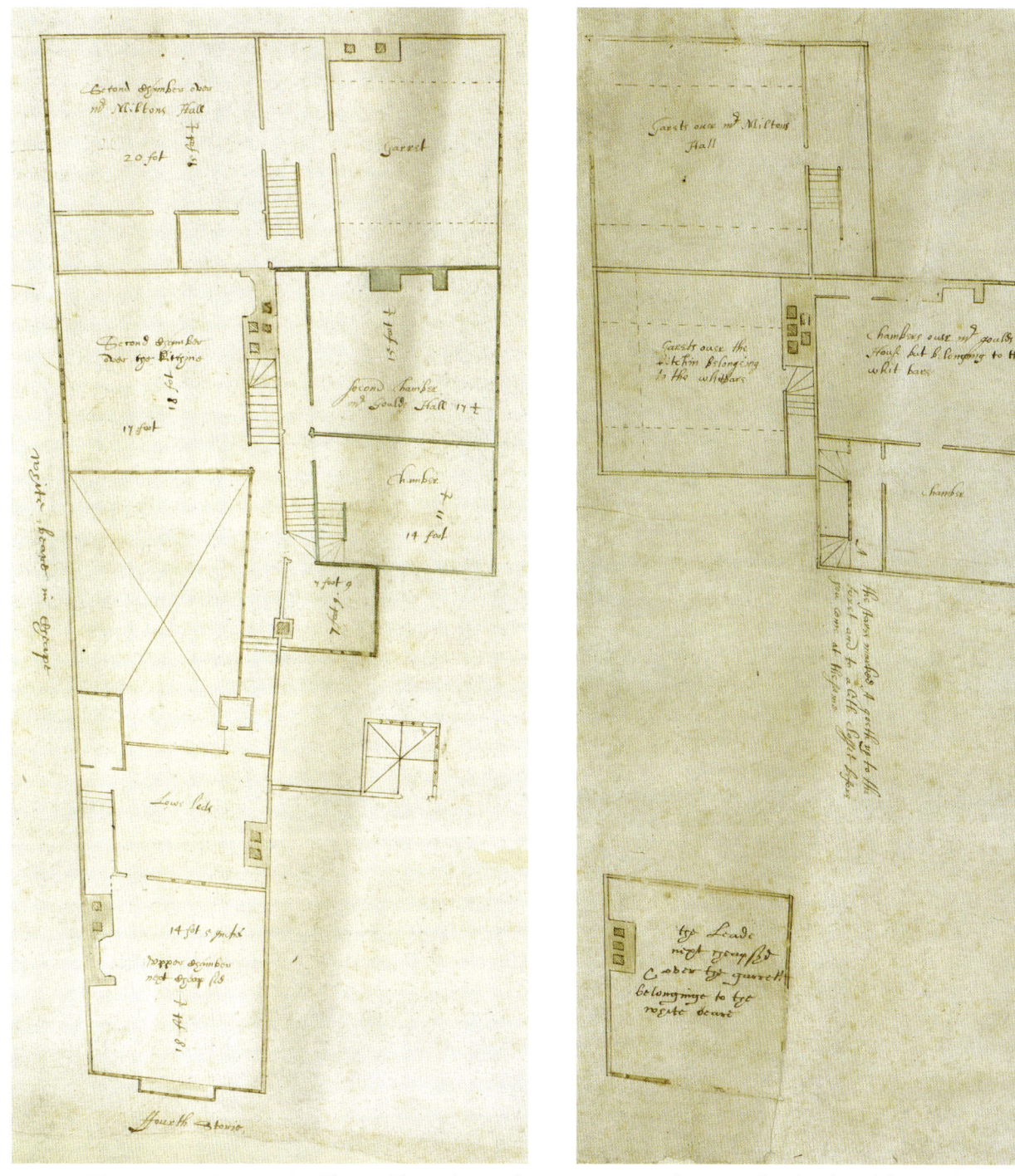

Figs 71-72. Houses in Cheapside and Bread Street, c.1617, showing the third and fourth floors.

Externally, the buildings probably resembled those shown in the view of Cheapside in 1638 (Fig. 7). They were of several dates. A lease of 1528 of four houses had provided for the building of one new house (according to a 'platt' provided by William Collyns, carpenter), while a lease of 1545 had required the building of a frame at the front of one of the four houses, 'which frame shalbe of three storeyes of heighte above the nether flore or shoppe of the same messuage'. This was probably the front of the property later occupied by Hicks. More recently, Hicks had added rooms at the top. The premises consisted in 1617 of three substantial properties and three smaller ones, and provide a good example of the intricate arrangements within many City properties. The main holding was the White Bear in Cheapside, occupied by Hicks, consisting of: on the ground floor, lower shop, upper shop and back warehouse—sixteen feet wide at the front and together seventy-two

Fig. 73. Sir Baptist Hicks (1551-1629), later Viscount Camden, c.1618 — painting attributed to Paul van Somer.

Fig. 75. John Milton (1608-74) in about 1629, by an unknown artist.

feet long; over the lower shop, jettied out, great and little parlours, two chambers above them and one chamber or garret above at the front; over the back warehouse, kitchen, two chambers and garret, one over the other; communicating with the last-mentioned garret, two chambers over the house in Bread Street, topped by a turret and a small room adjoining (the written survey indicates another garret chamber there as well); and cellars below (Fig. 74). One of the first-floor parlours had 'a window looking into the shopp'.

Mr Gould's house in Bread Street (in the written survey belonging to Thomas Hambleton, girdler) had a small shop and entry on the ground floor, and above that, hall and kitchen, three chambers on the second floor, and at the top two chambers, above which were some of Hicks's new rooms. Each storey had a different shape. The top two chambers were both described as 'a fine roome'. The house of Mr Milton, scrivener, had on the ground floor just a small shop; on the first floor, a kitchen over the shop, and hall, parlour and buttery over Sydway's 'great warehouse'; on the second floor, two chambers, 'lodging chamber' and buttery; on the third floor, two chambers and a house of office; on the fourth floor, a garret; and extensive cellars. The rooms were spacious, including the hall twenty-one by twenty feet and the parlour eighteen by thirteen feet. This was the house where the poet John Milton (Fig. 75) was born and grew up. Aubrey noted that Milton 'when he was very young studied very hard and sate up very late, commonly till 12 or one a clock at night, and his father ordered the mayde to sitt up for him'; his father had a 'plentiful estate', which the size of the house bears out.[88] The other tenants were Mr Sydway, grocer, in the 'great warehouse' or 'great shopp' at the back, and two small shops in Bread Street occupied by Richard Westcomb, milliner or leather seller, and Richard Scales, pointmaker.

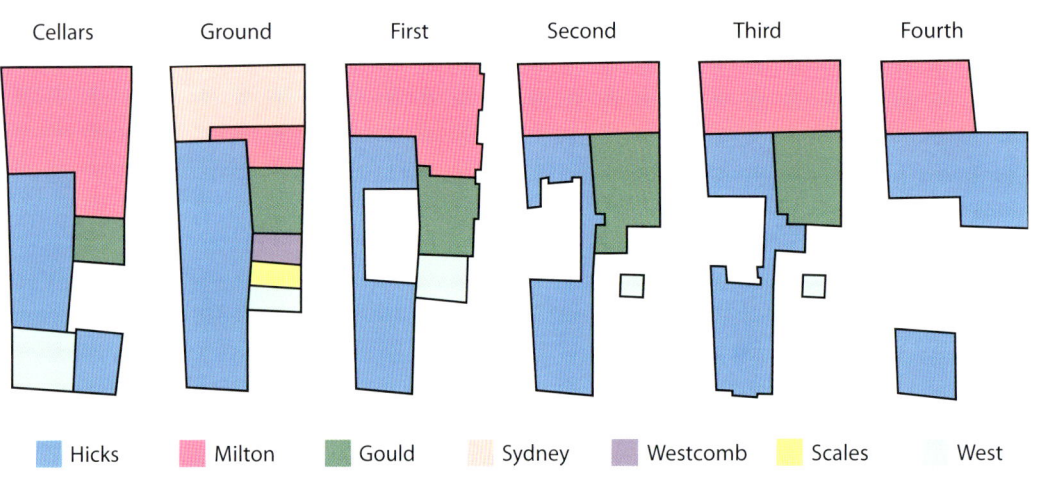

Fig. 74. Tenants of the various floors of the houses in Cheapside and Bread Street, based on the plan of c.1617.

All the third- and fourth-floor rooms in the back half of the premises, together with the turret and small room adjoining, had been added by Hicks, and had apparently overburdened the structure. The written survey notes that the turret was 'intended to be taken downe least yt hurt the house', together with the small room. The plans are somewhat more detailed for the third and fourth floors, consistently indicating windows and showing the individual chimney flues. Little colour is used, except that Gould's walls are coloured green, for reasons unknown.

Hicks died in 1629. Milton's father retired from business in 1632 and moved to Horton, Buckinghamshire, taking his son with him. The premises were destroyed in the Great Fire.

Plan 23
Glaziers' Hall, Old Fish Street Hill, 1618
FIG. 76

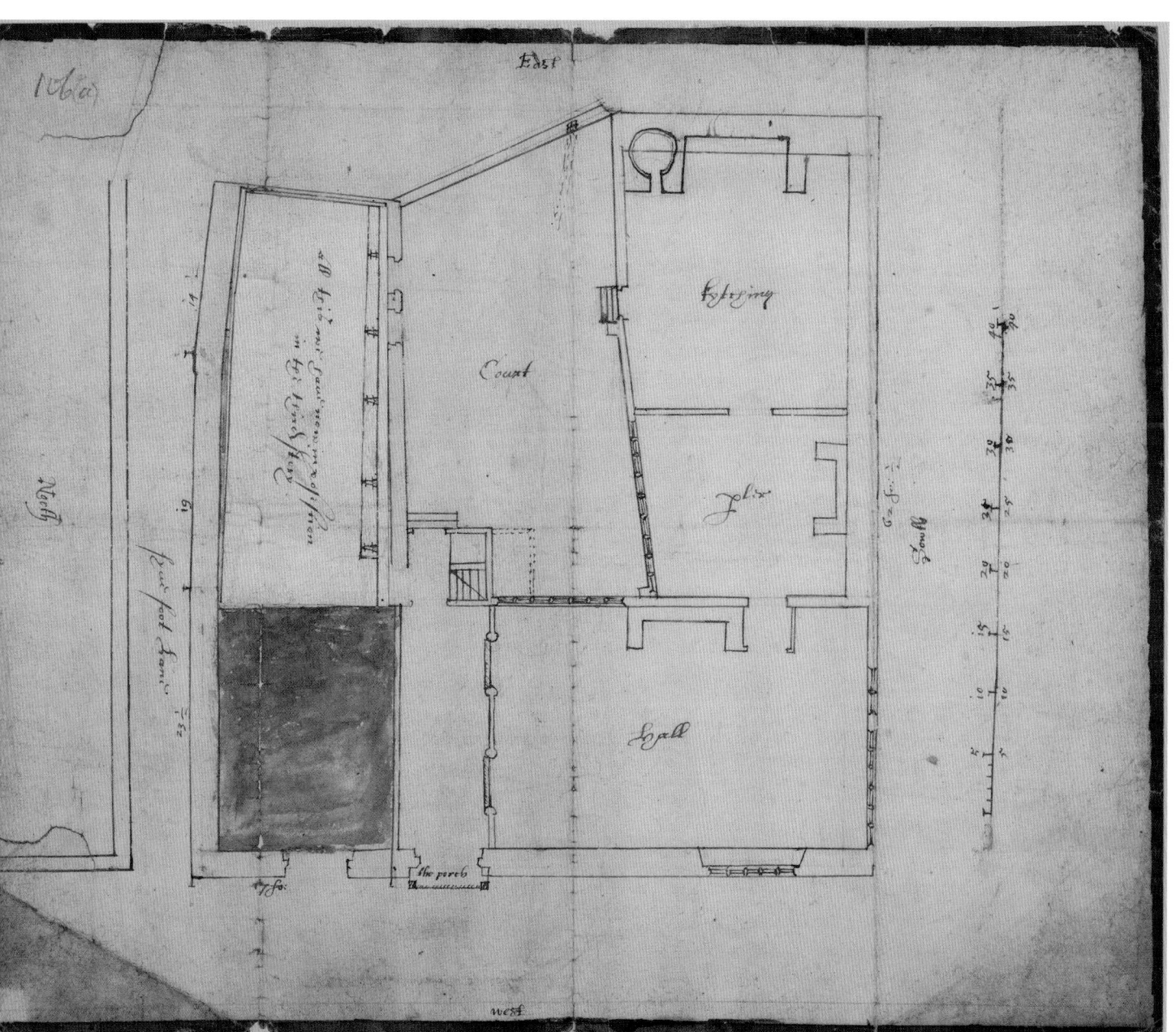

Fig. 76. Glaziers' Hall, Old Fish Street Hill, 1618.

This plan, labelled 'The Glasiers plott', shows a medieval house which served at least twice as a livery hall. It stood on the south-east corner of Old Fish Street Hill and Five Foot Lane; the site is now under the south carriageway of Queen Victoria Street between St Nicholas Cole Abbey and the tower of St Mary Somerset. Stow described it as a 'greate house, now letten out for rent', which had been one of the Fishmongers' Company's halls during the reign of Richard II.[89] By 1601, when William Blewe, citizen and fishmonger, leased most of it from the Fishmongers' Company, part was already let out as separate tenements. From 1612 to 1653 the main part was let to the Glaziers' Company as their hall. In 1618 the Glaziers successfully requested a new lease including extra rooms, and presented a plan showing 'that which they have alreadye and of that which they requyre to be added to it', which is almost certainly this plan.[90] On the north range, on a flap, the plan says 'All this we have now in possession in the third story'; under the flap is the ground floor with a passage to Five Foot Lane. The space to be added was presumably that coloured brown. The outer walls between two and three feet thick suggest a largely stone building. The hall was about forty by twenty feet, with a screens passage and several windows of five to seven lights. The kitchen occupied an odd position, separated from the hall by the parlour instead of being across the screens passage from the hall. The Glaziers left in 1653 after the Fishmongers demanded too much for a new lease, and the property was leased instead to George Foxcroft, citizen and fishmonger. After the Great Fire four tenements were built on the site.[91]

Plan 24
Throgmorton Street and Austin Friars, *c.*1620
Christopher Flemming FIGS 77, 82

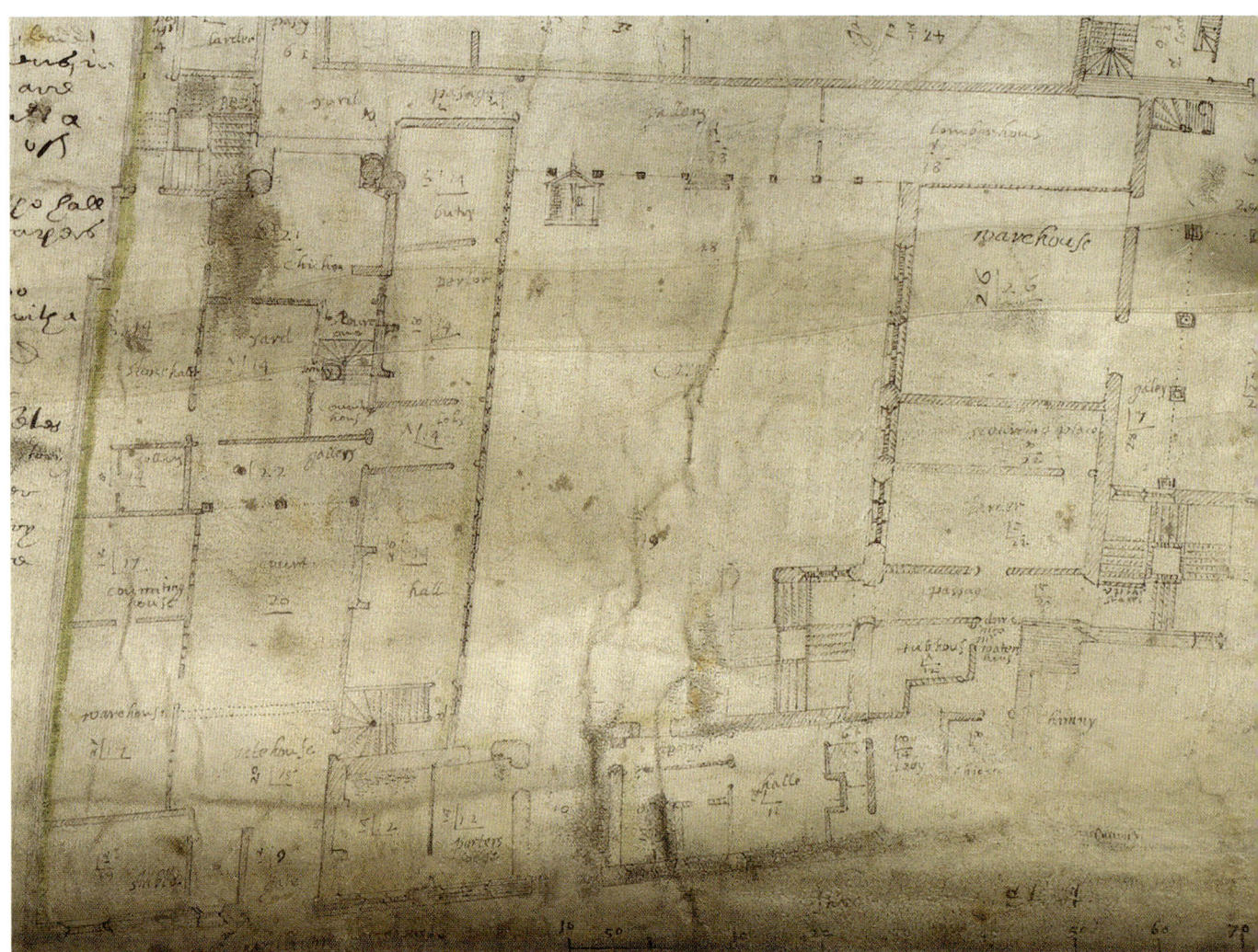

This unprepossessing but very detailed plan shows land purchased by the Drapers' Company from the Crown in 1542 following the fall of Thomas Cromwell. Much of it had formerly belonged to the monastery of Austin Friars. The main evidence of the plan's date is the fact that Sir William Garway is named as a tenant: he was knighted in 1615 and died in 1625. It also seems to be after the rebuilding of part of Henry Garway's house in 1617-20 (see below). The reason for commissioning it is unknown, though in 1618 the Company ordered that a general view be made of its property and that, to avoid losses, this be recorded in a book, and that its leases state measures, rooms and abuttals; in 1621 the Warden was ordered to make a survey of all the Company's lands, taking a skilful surveyor with him.[92] Neither of these orders implies plans as opposed to a written survey, and no expenditure on plans appears in the Company's accounts from 1613/14 to 1625/6. Nothing is recorded about Christopher Flemming, who drew the plan.

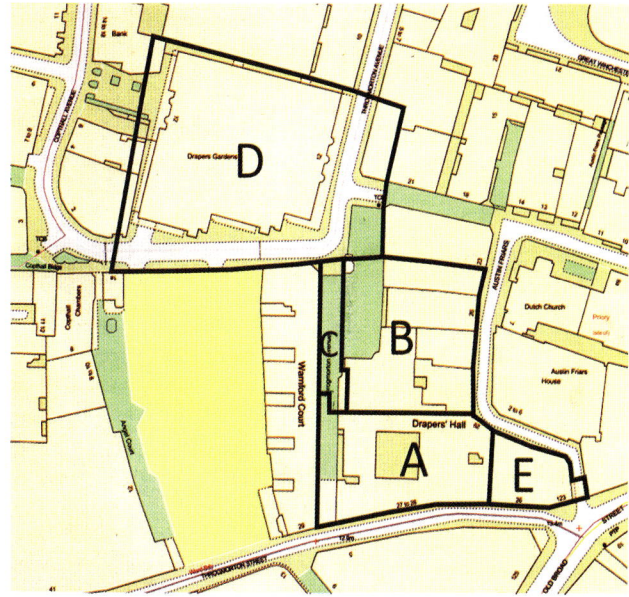

Fig. 78. The plan of the Drapers' Company's Throgmorton Street estate interpreted in relation to the 2015 Ordnance Survey map with the help of later property boundaries. A is what had been Cromwell's house; B is the houses in Austin Friars; C is the passage to the Drapers' garden; D is the Drapers' garden; E is Mr Williams's and Mr Garway's houses. The passage to the garden survives as part of Throgmorton Avenue.

Fig. 77. Part of the plan of Throgmorton Street and Austin Friars, c.1620, showing the mansion built by Thomas Cromwell in Throgmorton Street. North is at the top.

Fig. 79. Reconstruction of the ground plan of Thomas Cromwell's house, by Nick Holder.

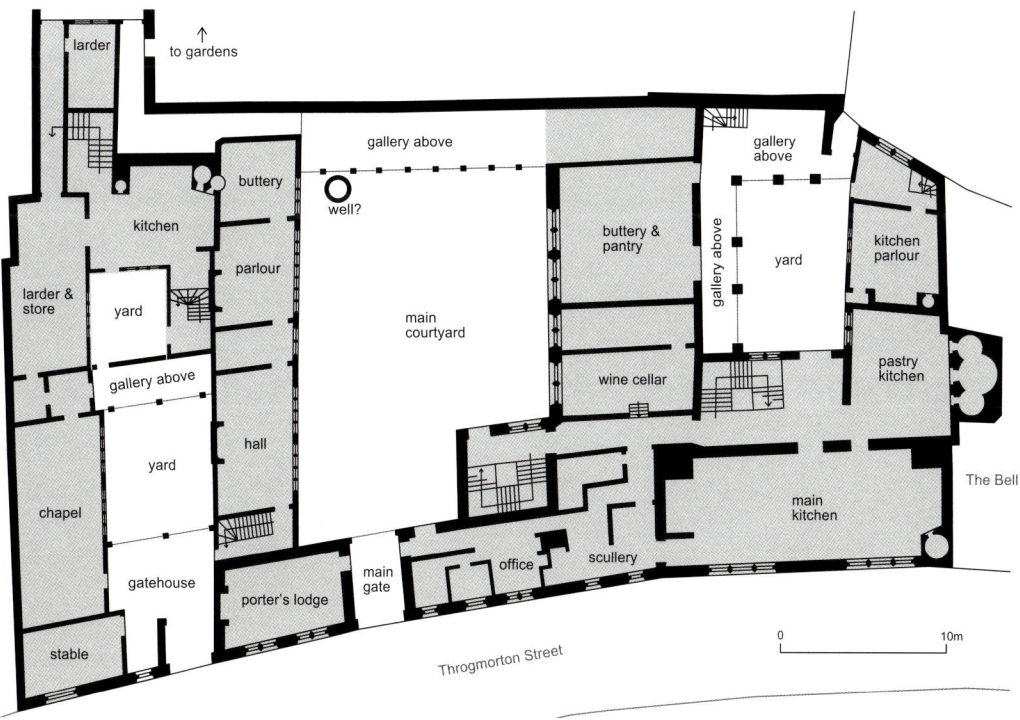

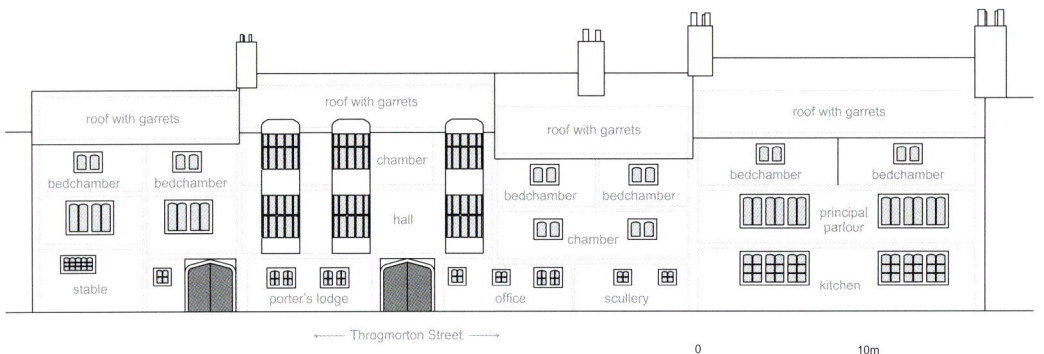

Fig. 80. Reconstruction of the Throgmorton Street facade of Thomas Cromwell's house, by Nick Holder.

Thomas Cromwell's connection with the site has recently been traced by Nick Holder. First, by 1522, Cromwell occupied a house in Austin Friars (see below). Then, as he rose in the service of Henry VIII, he began acquiring land, including a large garden, and in 1535-39 he built a mansion in Throgmorton Street with more than fifty rooms and about a dozen garrets. It stood largely on land formerly owned by the friary but outside the precinct. Cromwell's mansion, though sub-divided and with some alterations by the Drapers, is shown on the plan (Fig. 77), and the original layout can be reconstructed (Fig. 79). It stood around three courtyards, and most of it had two storeys, though the street front had three storeys and garrets. Much of it was brick. The main entrance led to the central courtyard, which included a large stair tower. On the first floor were the great hall, great chamber, parlours and galleries. There was also a chapel. The most spectacular room must have been the great chamber above the entrance, with three oriel windows facing the street (Fig. 80) and probably others facing the courtyard. The family apartments were probably on the first floor to the north-west, with views towards the gardens. The chambers on the second floor of the street frontage are likely to have been for Cromwell's staff and senior household servants. The main service buildings were around the eastern courtyard, including a large kitchen and a pastry with three ovens (Fig. 81). In the garden were stables and a bowling alley.[93]

After 1542 the Drapers used part of the mansion as their Hall and let out the remainder. They occupied the eastern side of the main courtyard and most of the street range from the main gate eastwards. This included kitchen, pastry and other service rooms on the ground floor, the staircases from the courtyard and the kitchen to the hall and, on the first floor, the great hall, the great parlour over the kitchen and the ladies' chamber west of the parlour. The western part of Cromwell's house became a separate mansion, including the whole of the western courtyard, rooms over the south and north sides of the main courtyard and, by 1620, rooms over William Wollistone's and William Cockin's warehouses to the north. It included Cromwell's great chamber and the long gallery along the west side of the main courtyard, and a lease of 1619 mentions a second great chamber with two bay windows looking towards Wollistone's yard.[94] It was occupied from 1570 by Sir Martin Calthorp, who was Lord Mayor in 1588. The next occupant was William Garway (1542-1625). Garway was Master of the Drapers' Company in 1594 and 1599, a farmer of the customs and a member of the East India and Levant Companies.[95] The lease of 1619 provided for the Drapers to use the great chamber over the great gate annually 'on the day that they shall keepe theire great dinner in theire hall' and for four days before and after.[96] The next lease, to William Wale, citizen and vintner, in 1658, extended the Company's use to the funerals of important members and election days. By then the mansion had been subdivided to form three houses, including shops. General Monck lodged in Wale's house in the period leading up to the Restoration. In 1666 Drapers' Hall and Wale's part of the mansion each had sixteen hearths.[97]

In 1620 Isaac Jones, citizen and merchant taylor, had the eastern part of Cromwell's house, mainly on upper storeys. East of Jones, in buildings which had not formed part of Cromwell's mansion, were two more houses. One was occupied by John Williams, citizen and draper, and

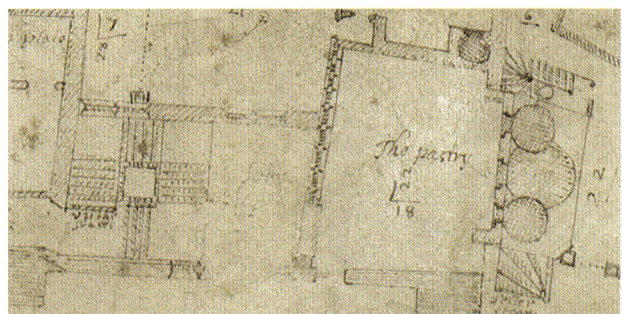

Fig. 81. Detail from Fig. 77 showing the pastry and one of the staircases of Cromwell's mansion.

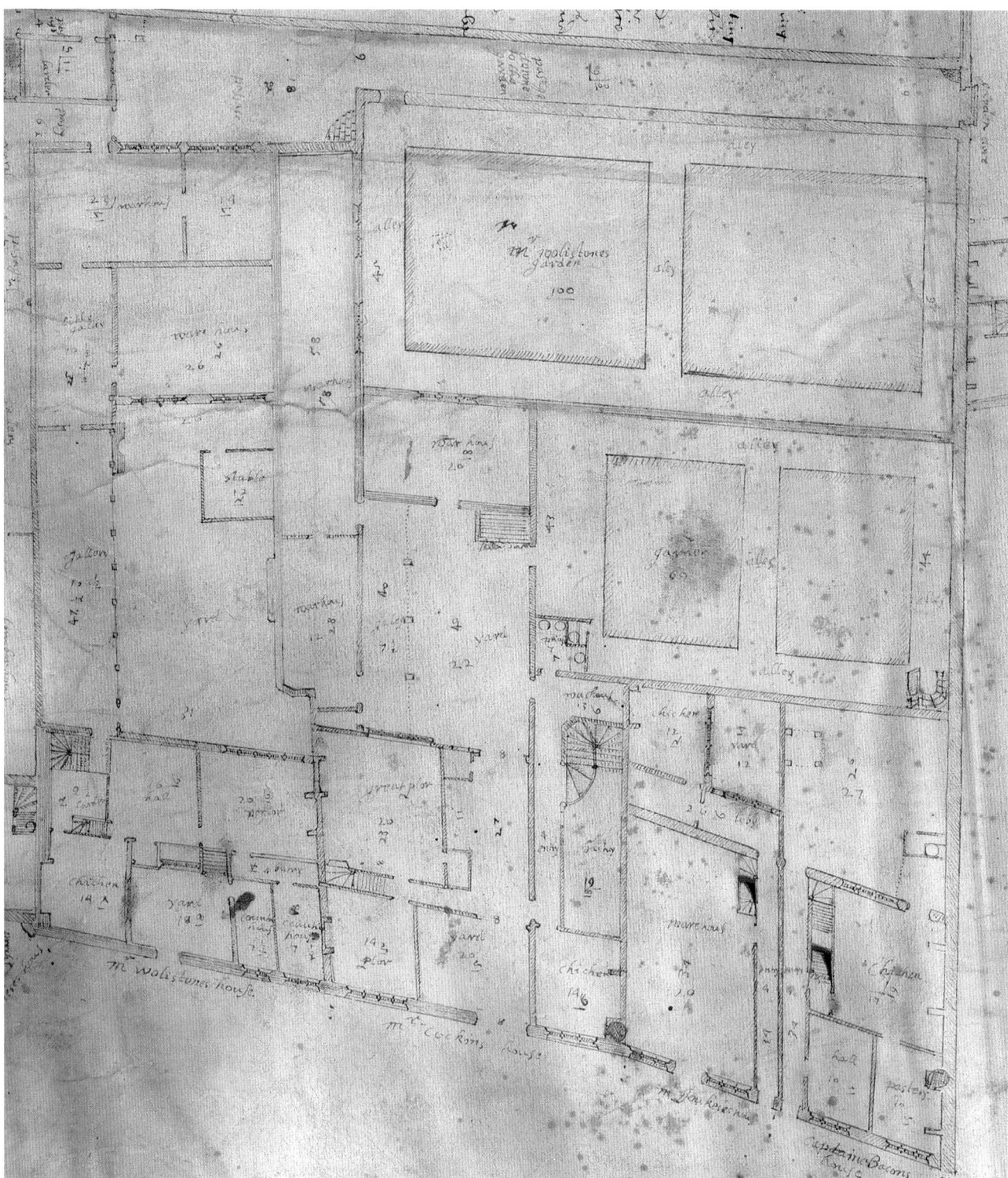

Fig. 82. Part of the plan of Throgmorton Street and Austin Friars, c.1620, showing houses in Austin Friars. North is to the right.

KEY[101]

Captain Baker's: over hall, two chambers and a half storey one above the other; over pastry, the like one above the other; over kitchen, two chambers and two garrets; half storeys in the [ground] and [first] storeys; two counting houses standing out into the yard; cellars under all.

Mr Foulkes's: over warehouse and entry, two fair chambers, hall and parlour; in hall, a counting house; over parlour, in [second] storey a fair chamber, counting house and house of office; over hall, two fair chambers; over them, two garrets with a house of office; cellars under all.

(continued overleaf)

(continuation of the key to Plan 24)

Mr Cockin's: two chambers over little parlour and great parlour; closet over entry between the two inner gates; two chambers over kitchen and buttery; entry in [second] storey; chamber over great parlour; house of office over little parlour; chamber over gateway; chamber, closet and entry over buttery; chamber over kitchen; garrets over all; cellars under two parlours, buttery and warehouse at end of yard.

Mr Wollistone's: fair chamber over counting houses and buttery; over parlour, a chamber; over Cockin's warehouse, a chamber 24 by 14 feet; over hall, a chamber; over kitchen, a chamber; in [second] storey, chamber over counting houses and buttery; chamber over parlour; over hall, a brushing room, a lodging and a little counting house; chamber over kitchen; over larder, a small chamber; garrets over all; benefit of cellar under counting houses, long buttery, parlour, hall and larder.

Mr Jones's: hall over gate [and?] over little hall and part over kitchen with a little counting house; parlour over the other part of kitchen and over part of the Drapers' pastry, with a buttery over the pastry; in [second] storey, over hall, two chambers; over parlour and buttery, two chambers; garrets over all; cellars under warehouse and little hall; over great gallery, two chambers in [first] storey; lead over them.

Sir William Garway's: *First storey*, matted gallery over hall, parlour and buttery; fair chamber over porter's lodge of Drapers' Hall; three chambers over warehouse, office and 'tubhouse'; two chambers over stone hall; chamber over kitchen; two counting houses over one end of gallery, leaded overhead; chamber over gatehouse; fair chamber over larder and part of entry and part of Wollistone's warehouse; fair matted chamber over the other part of Wollistone's warehouse and two closets; three chambers over part of Cockin's long warehouse; *Second storey*, three chambers over warehouse and office over great chamber; over Flood's house [*Flood was the Company's porter and apparently had only ground-floor rooms*],[102] three chambers and closet; over great stairs [*illeg.*]; *Third storey*, chamber and closet, leaded over that; cellars under all parts of Flood's house, staircase, hall, lobby, parlour and buttery.

---

included rooms over the gateway into Austin Friars; the other by Henry Garway, the eldest of Sir William's seventeen children and later, in 1639, Lord Mayor. Henry Garway's house included a passage over the Company's ovens, as well as rooms which 'lye uppon the frame of the hall buildings'. The front part was rebuilt in brick and stone in 1617-20 at a cost of £1,000, resulting in some of Jones's rooms being darkened and 'annoyed by ye smell of an howse of office'. In 1666 it had sixteen hearths.[98]

The row of substantial houses in Austin Friars (Fig. 82) was developed by the friary from the 1510s for leasing out. All had three and a half storeys and cellars, and three or more rooms per floor. In 1666 they had from nine to twelve hearths. The two at the north (formerly one) were the least complicated. The next, of William Cockin or Cokayne, citizen and skinner, had been Cromwell's house from 1522 until his mansion in Throgmorton Street was completed. It was approached through its own front yard, and had its main rooms (great and little parlours) on the ground floor to the left, with kitchen and service rooms to the right. Behind were warehouses, which at least in Cromwell's time had a long gallery over them. There was a garden behind the two houses to the north. The next house, held in c.1620 by William Wollistone, citizen and girdler, but belonging to an Italian merchant, John Cavalcanti, in Cromwell's time, was also entered through a front yard. It had hall, parlour and kitchen on the ground floor, and chambers above, including one over part of Cockin's warehouse, together with warehouses and galleries behind. It had a garden. But parts of the upper floors at the back belonged to Sir William Garway's house.[99]

The entire site was destroyed in the Great Fire, with the possible exception of the northernmost house in Austin Friars. The Drapers rebuilt their hall around the central courtyard, taking in hand ground which had belonged to Sir William Garway's and Jones's houses (see Plan 131, p. 224).[100]

Plan 25
St Paul's Cathedral, before 1633   Fig. 83

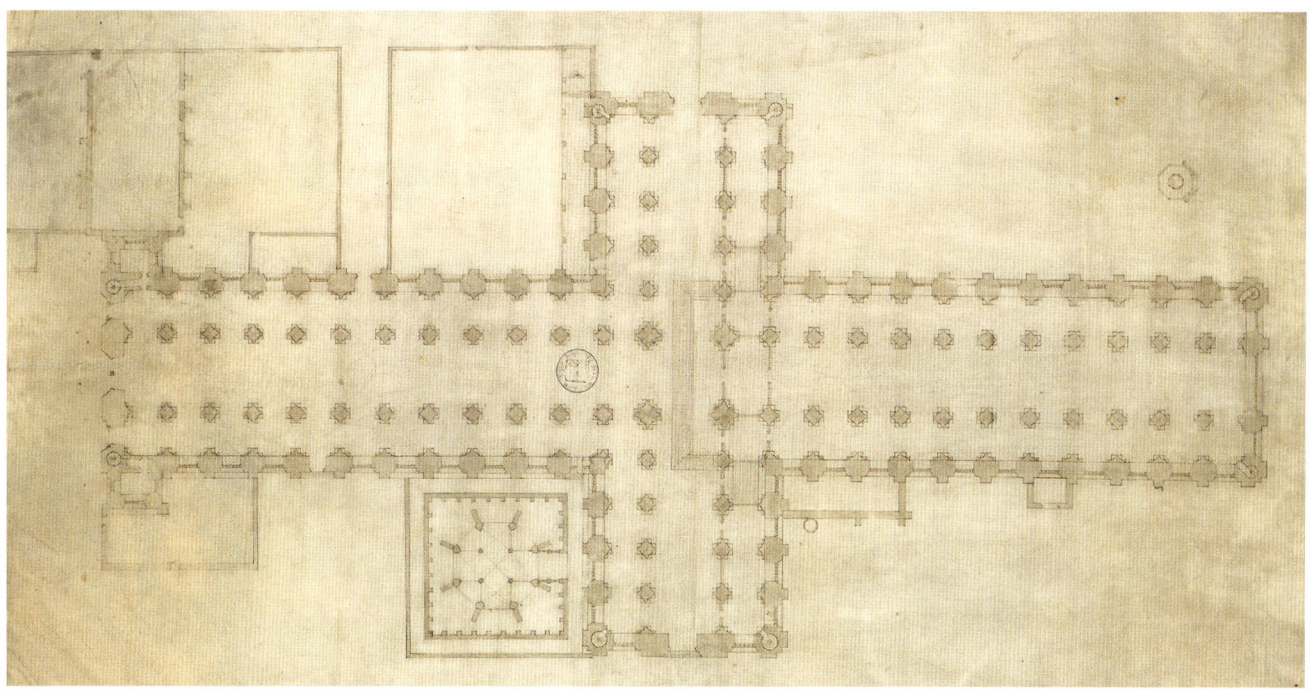

Fig. 83.   St Paul's Cathedral, drawn before 1633. North is at the top.

Fig. 84.   The south side of St Paul's Cathedral, 1658—print by Hollar.

St Paul's Cathedral was by far the largest church in England: 596 feet long—sixty-six feet more than Winchester Cathedral—with a tower of 260 feet topped by a lead spire of 208 feet—fifty feet taller than the spire of Salisbury Cathedral.[103] The nave of the cathedral destroyed by the Great Fire was begun in 1087 and was still under construction in 1136, though much of it must have dated from after the fire of that year. The tower was completed by 1221. The choir was rebuilt in two phases in 1240 and 1255. The spire was struck by lightning and destroyed in 1561.

The plan is undated, but seems to be from before 1633, when Inigo Jones began to add a portico to the west front. It survives among the drawings from Sir Christopher Wren's office at All Souls College, Oxford. It differs in some respects from Hollar's printed plan of 1657, and in particular omits the buttresses of the choir and parts of the transept. It also makes the choir too long and the bays too regular. As well as the Cathedral it shows some of the surrounding buildings. On the south side these included the cloister and the octagonal chapter house of the 1330s, which largely survived the Fire. They were being used by Wren as a site office in 1672-73, and parts remained until 1714-15; part of their layout can be seen today marked out on the ground by modern stone. The church of St Gregory nestled against the west end of the nave. North of the nave, shown in outline, were the hall of the Bishop's palace (probably shortened here), the bishop's garden with the bishop's chapel adjoining the nave, the site of the Pardon Cloister (demolished in 1549), and the library adjoining the north transept. Towards the top right is Paul's Cross, a medieval outdoor preaching cross, rebuilt as shown here in 1448 (Fig. 85). The cathedral was much more hemmed in by surrounding buildings than it appears here.

Fig. 85. Preaching at Paul's Cross—print of 1621.

PLANS OF AREAS

THE CITY

Plan 26
Christ's Hospital and Butchers' Hall Lane, 1656
Fig. 86

Fig. 86. Christ's Hospital's property north of Newgate Street, 1656. North is to the left.

This plan extends from London Wall in the north to Christ Church and from the west side of Christ's Hospital's great cloister to and beyond Church Alley (now King Edward Street; Fowle Lane in 1616). Nothing is known of why it was commissioned, who drew it or why two plots are edged in pink, and the key to the letters has not survived. Much of the same area also appears in plans of 1616 and the 1660s (Plans 20, 119), and there are two plans of the 1650s showing a small area east of the cloister.[1]

On the south side of the plan are Christ Church, formerly the choir of the Greyfriars' church, and 'Old Church', formerly the nave of that church and by this time probably just a walled churchyard. North of that is the cloister, which had been the centre of Christ's Hospital since it opened in 1552. The Grammar School was on the east side of the cloister, and nearby were the schoolmaster's yard and the house of Jonathan Picks, writing-master from 1633 to at least 1668,[2] part of the property marked A. Just east of that and north of the plot edged pink, the large space also marked A is described on one of the contemporary plans as 'the printing roome'; on the other it is a 'great roome' on the ground floor divided into several rooms or warehouses, over which and the passage were several rooms, warehouses and a printing house. On the east side of Church Alley is an alley containing houses mostly of one-room plan, some of them back-to-backs. In Pincock Lane, which no longer exists, were Mary Gwillim's slaughterhouse, reflecting the proximity of Newgate Market, 'Mr Pies 5 tenements' shown as backing on to Northumberland Place (see Plan 54), and at the end of the lane a large house facing a garden. It was double-fronted, with two bay windows looking onto the garden, had parlour, hall and kitchen on the ground floor and was let to an alderman (Fig. 87). Everything shown was destroyed in the Great Fire except the buildings on the north side of the cloister. Christ's Hospital subsequently expanded to occupy more of the former Greyfriars precinct.

Plan 27
Whitefriars, c.1658
FIG. 88

This plan shows two properties obtained by the Clothworkers' Company at different dates. The southern part consisted of a row of almshouses for poor clothworkers' widows, established within the precinct of Whitefriars shortly before the Dissolution. In modern terms they were on the north side of Tudor Street just east of Bouverie Street. The founder was Margaret, Countess of Kent, one of whose previous husbands had been a member of the Company and who lived just east of the almshouse site. The land, leased from the friary and later bought by the Company, had been part of a garden south of the infirmary. The almshouses had been built by October 1536, and consisted of ten rooms on two floors, the upper ones reached by stairs and a gallery. Each was about thirteen feet square and had its own chimney and privy. In 1612 they were occupied by nine women aged from fifty to ninety-seven and a porter aged eighty-six.[3]

In 1654 the Company bought the former infirmary site to the north for £330. The deed describes the land as a great messuage formerly four messuages and other houses and buildings belonging to it, though it seems already to have been re-divided into two separate properties. The main house was the one to the north-west, containing in the 1650s cellar; parlour, kitchen and entry; two chambers over the parlour and kitchen; two garrets over them; a back chamber at the head of the first pair of back stairs; a back kitchen or washhouse and an entry leading to it; and a pump yard with pump and coal house. The plan shows the large garden in front of it (almost black here, but evidently green originally), and also a pear tree in the yard; given the slope of the land there was probably an uninterrupted view of the Thames. The house was leased in 1660 to Walter Fowkes, gentleman, who made it his dwelling, and had seven hearths in 1666. The lease

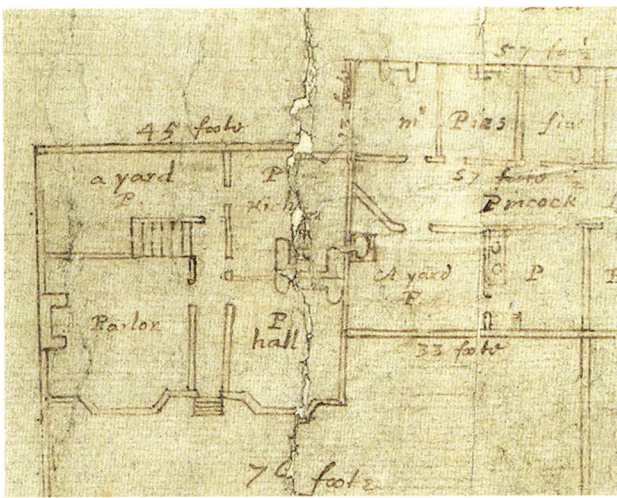

Fig. 87. Detail from Fig. 86, showing a large house facing a garden at the north end of Pincock Lane and adjoining houses.

Fig. 88. The Clothworkers' Company's property in Whitefriars, c.1658. North is at the top.

required him to build a new roof and upper floor. The house had been described in almost identical terms in 1577, except that excluded from Fowkes's lease was 'the stone hall' adjoining the pump yard and the room above it (already separately occupied in 1577). The stone hall, with thick grey walls on the plan, was undoubtedly part of the Whitefriars infirmary, as probably was the rest of the house. Most of the eastern part of the Company's new land, including the stone hall, was leased in 1657 to William Mayes, citizen and cordwainer, who was required to build one or two new houses on the garden plot on the south side. The brick house to the south-east is presumably what Mayes built, and is the reason for attributing the plan to about 1658. In 1663 Fowkes was granted two extra rooms (probably in the north-east corner) on condition that he turn them into a separate house of two and a half storeys.[4]

Whitefriars was within the area destroyed by the Great Fire, but a lease granted in 1668 for the eastern part of the site (except the almshouses) states that a brick tenement at the south end there survived the Fire. That must have been the tenement added by Mayes in or about 1658 and shown on the plan. It was presumably protected by being of brick, not directly adjoining other dwellings and being threatened only when the wind had died down. The new lessee, Robert Phelps, citizen and apothecary, was to build three more houses there to replace those destroyed.[5] A row of five houses was built on the western part (see Plan 145). The almshouses were rebuilt, and stood until 1770, when they were replaced by new ones at Islington. The eastern part of the site was occupied by a glassworks in the nineteenth century. The whole site was sold by the Company in 1922.[6]

Plan 28
Nevill's Alley and Fetter Lane, 1670
John Coffyn
FIG. 89

Nevill's Alley (later Court) is shown here shortly after most of it had been rebuilt following the Great Fire.[7] The Fetter Lane frontage was first built on in the 1570s, whereas the first houses on the eastern part (from Henry Trevers' and Peter Burrows' houses eastwards) dated from about 1605-10. There were originally five houses there, probably all set back with gardens in front to maintain an air of spaciousness. The alley was sometimes known in the seventeenth century as Nevill's Gardens. Edward Potkin's and Stephen Mundy's houses in the north-east corner, both one room deep, were described in 1668 as 'paper buildings', and as lacking drainage, but nevertheless stood for three centuries (Fig. 90). In 1676 Mundy, an official of the Court of Common Pleas, had kitchen and parlour on the ground floor, dining room and chamber on the first floor, two chambers on the second floor (one hung with tapestries) and two garrets above, together with service rooms in the right-hand corner; there were six hearths. By 1666 there were also buildings in the alley at the back of the Fetter Lane plots.

Ogilby and Morgan's map shows the whole of Nevill's Alley within the area burnt in 1666 (see Fig. 16), but Fire Court proceedings and the parish rate book make clear that Potkin's and Mundy's houses and the two held by Richard Henthorne on the north side of the alley survived the Fire. The line between burnt and unburnt was an untidy one here. The finest of the post-Fire houses was that later known as the Great House, built for Burrows in 1668-69, with ten hearths (Fig. 91). The rebuilding in the south-east corner apparently gave rise to the plan. Stephen Mellichipp built there two new 'duble houses' (houses of two-room plan) on the site of one of the burnt ones, but sub-let an irregularly-shaped plot left over to the holder of adjoining property in East Harding Street, so the property was no longer defined on the ground. Mellichipp and the sub-lessee were required to sign the plan to acknowledge that it showed the bounds correctly.

The landlord was Sir Nicholas Bacon of Shrublands, at Barham in Suffolk, and the arms shown were his. Unusually for urban properties Bacon seems to have had a sentimental attachment to them; on leaving them to his son in 1688 he added: 'hopeing as they have been in the family a great while he will keep them in the family'. In fact they belonged to the Bacons from 1574 to 1696. Bacon used one of his own tenants in Fetter Lane to draw the plan. This was John Coffyn, aged about thirty-seven, who was at this time a surveyor based in London and working in various counties. He lived in the Fetter Lane house until 1678/79, and later at Great Burstead in Essex, where he concentrated on surveying in south-east Essex. Coffyn's distinctive style included the calligraphic cartouche, the design of the compass rose, and the use of a roman font for text and Gothic script for his own name. He was also distinctive in making the plan a pictorial one,

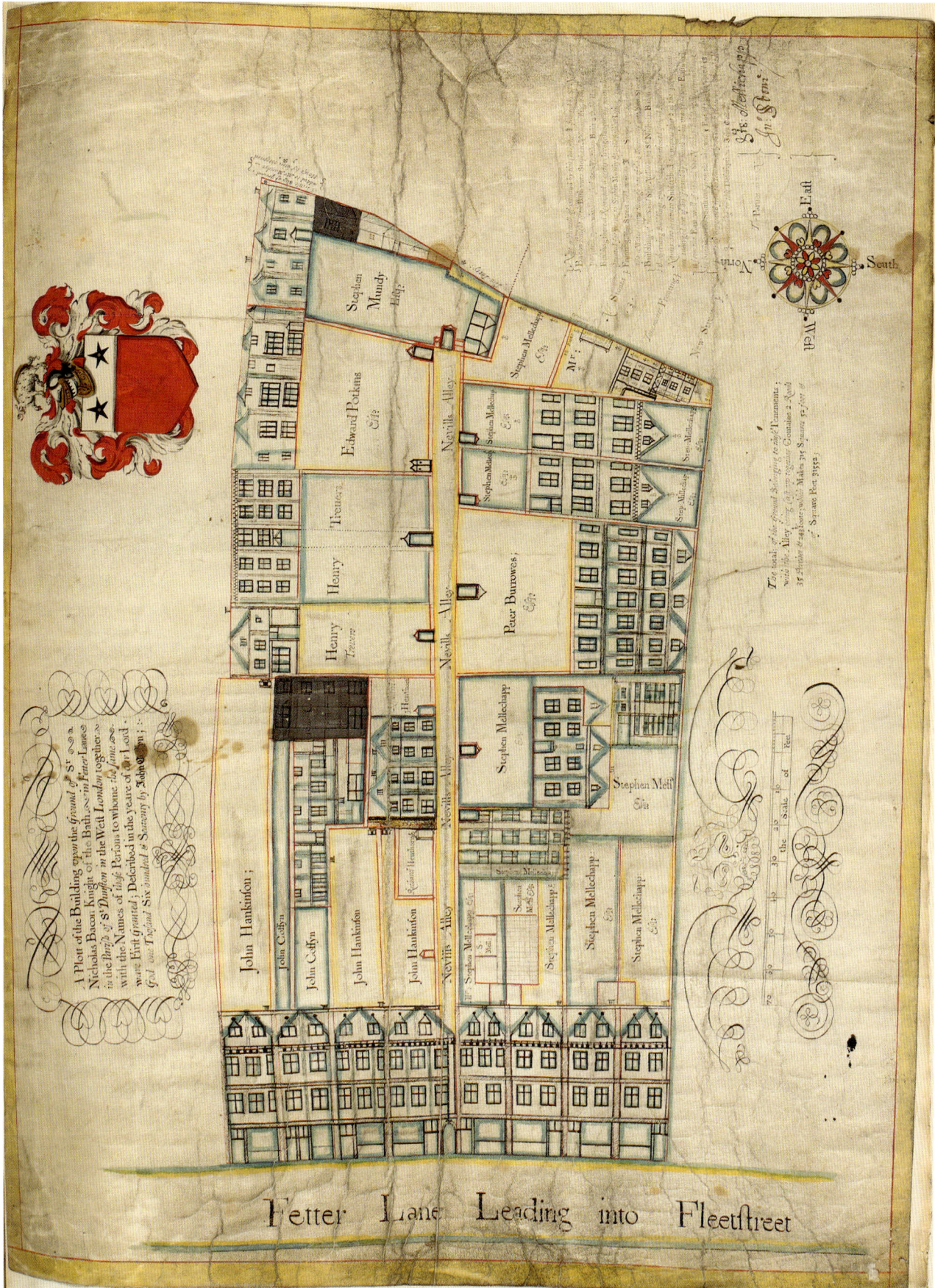

Fig. 89. Nevill's Alley and houses in Fetter Lane, 1670.

Fig. 90. Houses in the north-east corner of Nevill's Alley which had been Edward Potkins' and Stephen Mundy's in 1670, photographed in 1910.

Fig. 91. The house in Nevill's Alley which had been Peter Burrows' in 1670.

probably because, though living in London, he usually surveyed rural estates. Later photographs show that he drew the buildings accurately rather than in standardised form; even the houses in Fetter Lane have small differences, which correspond to the photographic evidence. However, like most surveyors, he placed the view of each building on the line of its facade, with different buildings being seen from different directions. This worked well for the Great House, accurately depicted with its narrower windows either side, but in the north-east corner, where the houses were tall and set well back, he had to leave out a storey to avoid obscuring the boundary of Bacon's property, and some other buildings have become an odd collection of windows and walls.

Most of Nevill's Alley was little changed at the start of the twentieth century. Potkins' and Mundy's houses were demolished in 1911, and the Fetter Lane houses in 1910 and about 1928, but the Great House and Mellichipp's two houses next to it survived until destroyed by bombing in 1941. Subsequently New Fetter Lane was driven through the site, meeting Fetter Lane about where Nevill's Alley used to be.

Plan 29
Tower Street and Harp Lane, 1671
Fig. 92

This is a rare example of a detailed plan drawn while the rebuilding of houses immediately after the Great Fire was still in progress. The rebuilding here, on land belonging to St Bartholomew's Hospital, was financed by Robert Russell, citizen and skinner, whose father had leased the property in 1661. Three houses, one described as a capital messuage, had been replaced since the Fire by seven brick ones, though the house in the yard was not yet finished. Their rooms are listed in the lease, showing that they were of one-room or two-room plan and mostly had three and a half storeys, but that one had a storey more and one a storey less (Fig. 93). The planning was determined by the desire to fit as many houses as possible onto the site while providing light to their backs. The passage and yard were sub-let to the leaseholders of the properties to the south. The measurements stated are not consistent either with each other or with the scale bar. Tower Street is now Great Tower Street; the part of Harp Lane shown here no longer exists.

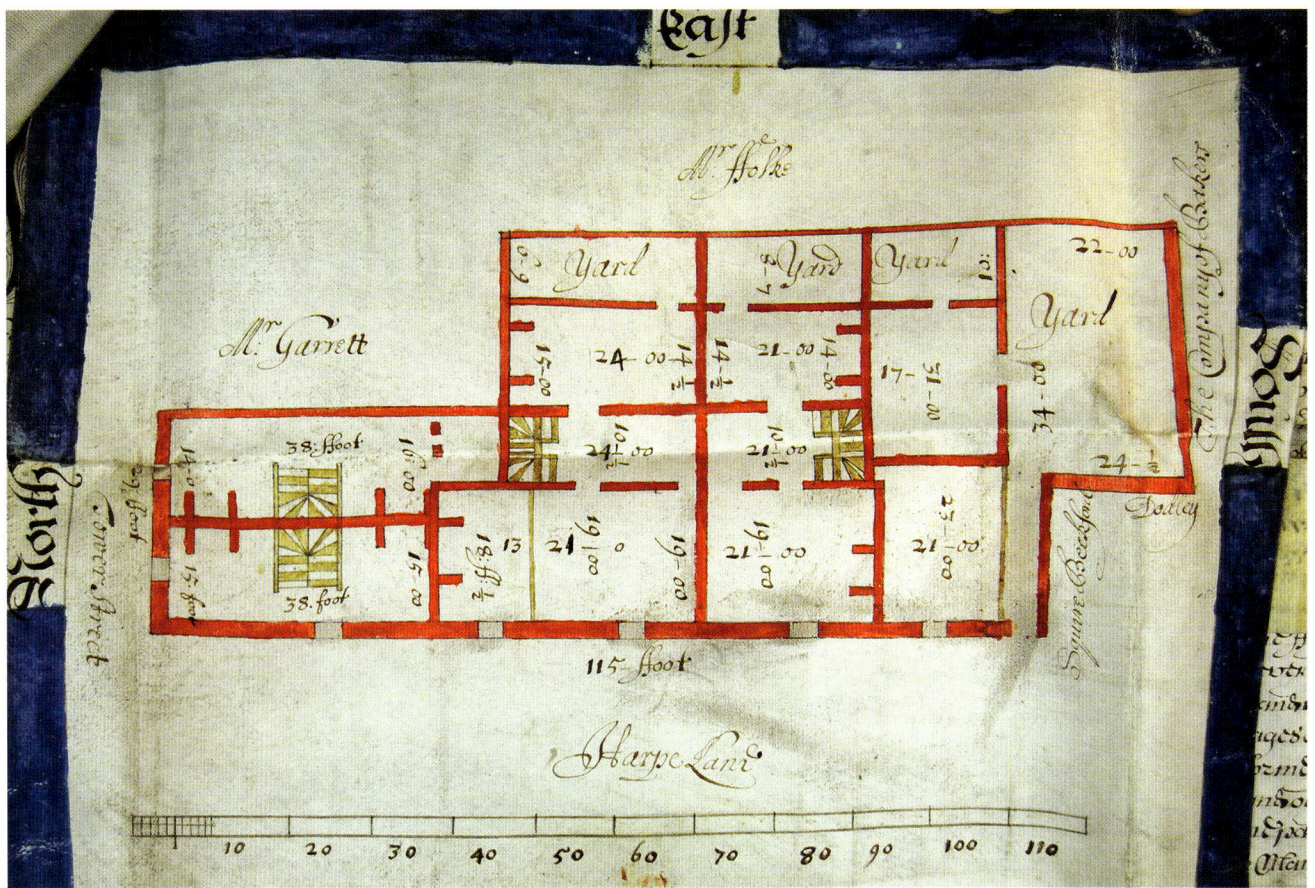

Fig. 92. Houses in Tower Street and Harp Lane, 1671.

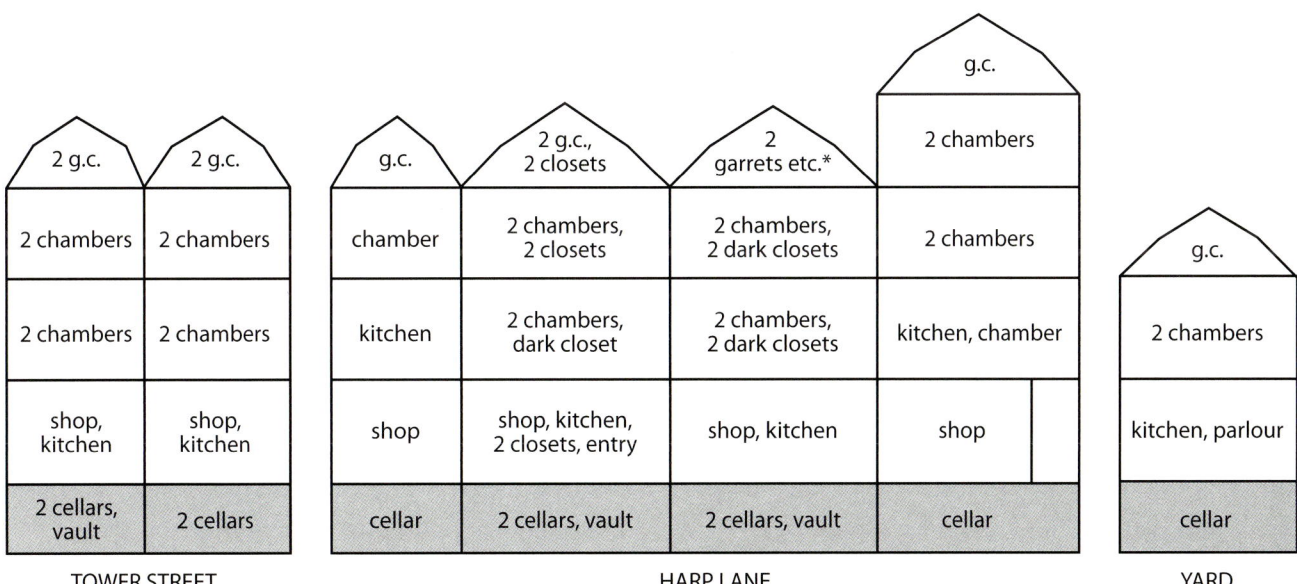

g.c. is garret chamber; second house in Harp Lane has house of easement in yard; * little dark closet and 'brushing room' at stairs head

Fig. 93. Rooms in the houses in Tower Street and Harp Lane, as recorded in the lease.

Plans 30-33
Stationers' Hall and Ave Maria Lane, 1674
William Leybourn

FIGS 94-97

In his first plan book for a livery company, Leybourn drew very basic plans of each holding together with detailed ones (more detailed than most of his later work) of each house, accompanied by descriptions comparable to the lists of fixtures often appended to leases. The Stationers' main holding (Fig. 94) had been an aristocratic mansion, belonging to the Earls of Richmond in the fourteenth century, the Earls of Pembroke in the fifteenth and the Barons of Burgavenny in the sixteenth. The property stretched from London Wall in the west to Ave Maria Lane in the east, where tenements had been built. The Stationers occupied it from 1606 and bought it in 1611 for £3,500. They added warehouses on the eastern part of the garden, between what were later the Inner and Outer Courts.[8]

The entire property was destroyed in the Great Fire. The six Ave Maria Lane houses from O to V were rebuilt by the Company in 1669-70, costing £3,000, the Hall in 1670-75, and other houses by Robert Wapshott from 1671.[9] The Ave Maria Lane houses were of three and a half storeys, and also had cellars with windows. Apart from house V they were of two-room plan, except on the ground floor, which was a shop in every case (Fig. 96). Where the kitchens were is unclear; one leased in 1699 had kitchens both in the cellar and on the first floor. Each house, including house V, had a 'seat of easement' under the stairs and another in one of the garrets, connected to the cellar by a lead pipe or funnel. House V, twenty-two feet wide, had three rooms on most floors. It consisted of front and back shop on the ground floor; kitchen, dining room and withdrawing room on the first floor; three rooms, one of them a with-

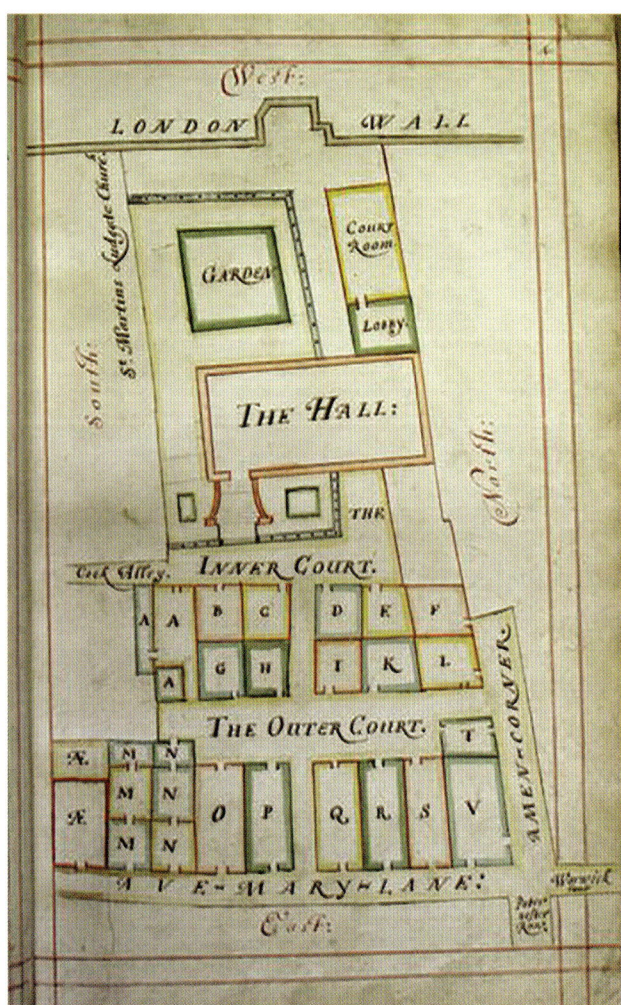

Fig. 94. Stationers' Hall and the Company's property adjoining, 1674.

KEY [10]

K. *Cellar*: two lights into Outer Court; vault and seat of easement under stairs; *First storey*, partition to divide it into two rooms; four four-light windows; *Second storey*, same as below but no partition; *Third storey*, garret; chimney on north side; two Lutheran windows.

R. *Cellar*: seat of easement under stairs; two lights at each end; *First storey*, two rooms over shop; in each a chimney and closet with door on south side; two four-light and one two-light windows in each; entry or passage at stair's head, between the rooms, and room behind the passage divided by a partition equally between the two rooms; *Second storey*, as below; *Third storey*, garrets; chimney on south side of each; two Lutheran windows in each; seat of easement in one with funnel of lead down to vault in cellar; double skylight over stairs between the two garrets.

V. *Cellar*, two lights to Ave Maria Lane and two to Amen Corner; seat of easement and vault under stairs; partition for beer and coals; *First storey*, over back shop, kitchen with chimney on south side; one three-light window and one single; lead pipe to bring water up from street; over fore shop, dining room with two lights towards Ave Maria Lane and two to Amen Corner; chimney on south side; withdrawing room at stair's head, with three-light window at north end; *Second storey*, three rooms as in storey below; chimney on south side in two rooms over kitchen and dining room; withdrawing room or nursery as in storey below; *Third storey*, garrets; chimney on south side in each; four Lutheran windows in corner garret and one in back garret; a seat, and lead funnel from garret down to vault in cellar; double skylight over newel of stairs.

PLANS OF AREAS 93

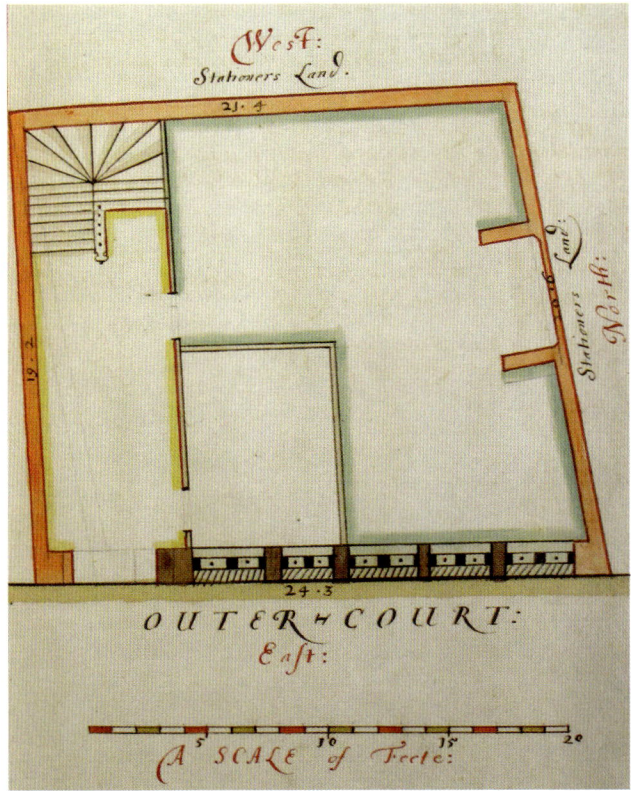

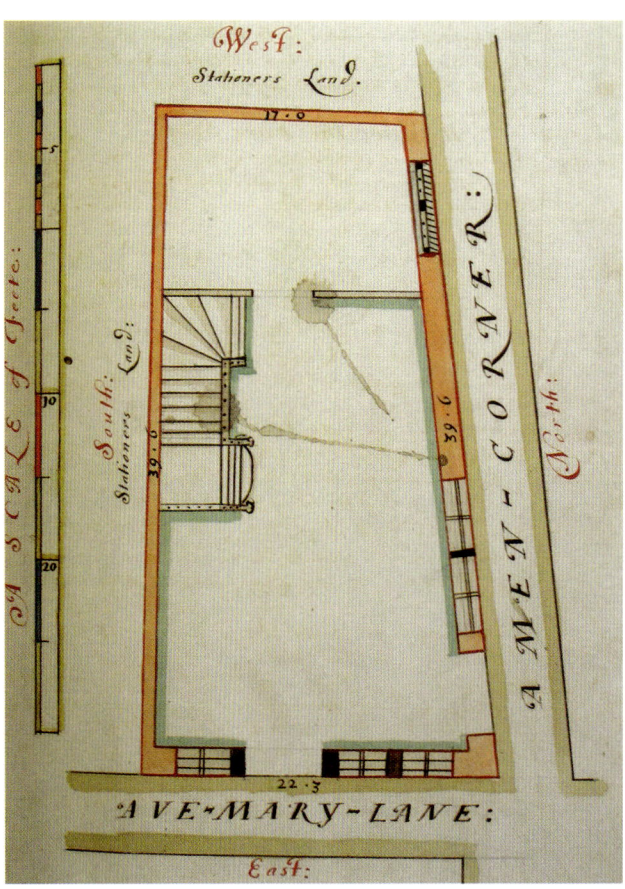

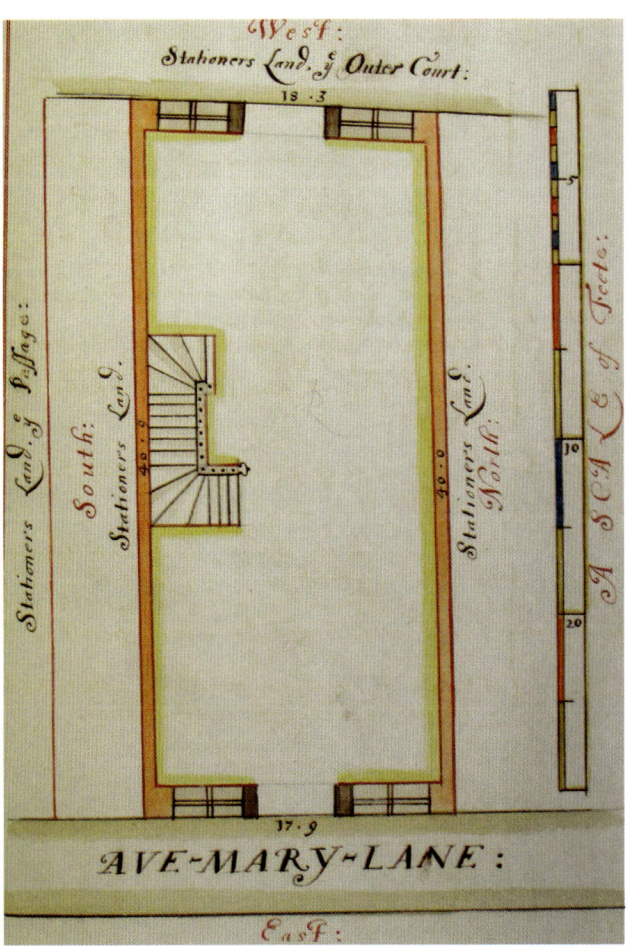

Figs 95–97. The detailed plan of houses K (top left), R (above), and V (top right) in Fig. 94.

drawing chamber or nursery, on the second floor; and garrets (three in 1699) (Fig. 97).[11]

Houses were built between the Inner and Outer Courts instead of warehouses. They were back-to-backs, with one-room plans but generous room sizes (Fig. 95). Houses B, C, G and H were of four and a half storeys, but with garrets only over the east part in the case of B and C and the west part in the case of G and H. The others had three and a half storeys. All had cellars with windows, and all had a 'seat of easement' only under the stairs. House L, for example, had just one room on each floor, including a shop on the ground floor, but it was twenty-two by twenty feet, and by 1709 all the upper floors including the garret had been partitioned so as to contain a separate bedroom.[12] Houses D and I, like T and Q, extended over the adjoining passages or gateways.

Strype described the Outer Court in 1720 as 'an open square court, with good houses, called Stationers Rents'. The post-Fire houses seem to have remained until about 1860, when the arrangement of Inner and Outer Courts was simplified.[13] Stationers' Hall itself remains largely as Leybourn showed it.

Plan 34
Chandlers' Rents, near Addle Hill, 1678
William Leybourn
Fig. 98

Fig. 98. Chandlers' Rents, 1678.

KEY

A. Cellar under the two ground rooms; two floors above the ground floor, with two lodging chambers on each with chimneys; garrets.

B-S. Each has cellar; two chambers [over the ground floor], one over the other, with chimneys; garret. B, D, F and H have lights only to the east; C, E, G, K, N, O and P only to the west; A, L, Q, R and S only to the north; and M to the north and west.

This plan shows a densely-built area of the City, including back-to-back houses, immediately east of St Andrew by the Wardrobe. The property was acquired by the Tallow Chandlers' Company in 1596, when it was described as five houses and six cottages. Seven leases granted between 1657 and 1664 indicate eighteen houses before the Great Fire. In 1669-71 Thomas Gamon, citizen and carpenter, rebuilt the houses and was granted sixty-year leases.[14] There were seventeen houses in 1678, suggesting that the pre-Fire arrangement had largely been replicated. All were of three and a half storeys, and all were of one-room plan, except houses A and S. Few had even so much as a small yard. The inhabitants seem to have shared three privies, and also a water cock nearby. House S was a lobby-entry house. Leybourn's plan and description pose a few problems: some houses have no stairs shown to their upper floors, the few small yards were not assigned to anyone (perhaps they were common) and house S is described as if it was of one-room plan. When a new plan was drawn in 1790 Gamon's houses were still there but most had separate access from outside to the ground floor and to the stairs, indicating subdivision. The Metropolitan Board of Works bought the property from the Tallow Chandlers in 1864 in order to create Queen Victoria Street, which crosses approximately the southern third of the site.[15] The alley called Chandlers' Rents has vanished, but part of the 'passage about St Andrew's Wardrobe church yard' remains as Wardrobe Terrace.

Plan 35
Bottle Alley and Bishopsgate Street, 1679
Joseph Titcombe

FIG. 99

This land had been given to the Armourers' Company in 1588 by Roger Tyndall, one of Queen Elizabeth's gentlemen-at-arms and three times Master of the Company. It seems then to have consisted only of tenements facing Bishopsgate Street and gardens behind. Even in 1619 the Company still had only five houses there, though Stow observed in 1603 that many houses in the north part of Bishopsgate 'have beene builded with alleys backeward of late time too much pesterd with people'.[16] By 1679 there were seventeen houses, all of timber except for the brick range comprising K, L and M. The Bishopsgate Street houses, from ten to thirteen feet wide, were each of two-room plan and three and a half storeys, with each storey jettied outwards. All the others had either three and a half or two and a half storeys, and two of those in the second court were jettied. There was a large bakehouse in the first court. Almost every room except for the shops and a few of the garrets had a chimney. All the houses relied on the two common houses of easement, with two places each, except the Bishopsgate Street ones. The hearth tax list for 1674 matches the descriptions exactly for the Bishopsgate houses (six, seven, seven and seven hearths for B, C, E and F respectively), and almost so for part of the first courtyard: probably Widow Mitford, three hearths in house H; Nicholas Page, seven in house I; Nicholas King, one hearth unlocated; Henry Soames, four in house K; Widow Linger, four in house M; Edward Jones, three in house N; Widow Breame four in house O. However, whereas the plan shows seven other houses in Bottle Alley, only one with as few as two hearths, the tax list then records twelve more householders, three with two hearths and nine with one hearth, indicating that most of the smaller houses of Bottle Alley were subdivided.[17] The houses were mostly let individually by the Company, but some in groups of two or three.[18]

Strype wrote in 1720 that Bottle Alley 'hath a narrow entrance, but openeth into a free stone court, with well built houses, which said alley leadeth into another down steps bearing the same name'. Subsequently, as the Company's lands within the City walls became more valuable, its almshouses were moved here, in 1736 and 1809. In the nineteenth century the Alley was known as Britannia Place, after a public house of that name. In 1886 the site was sold, and became part of Liverpool Street Station.[19]

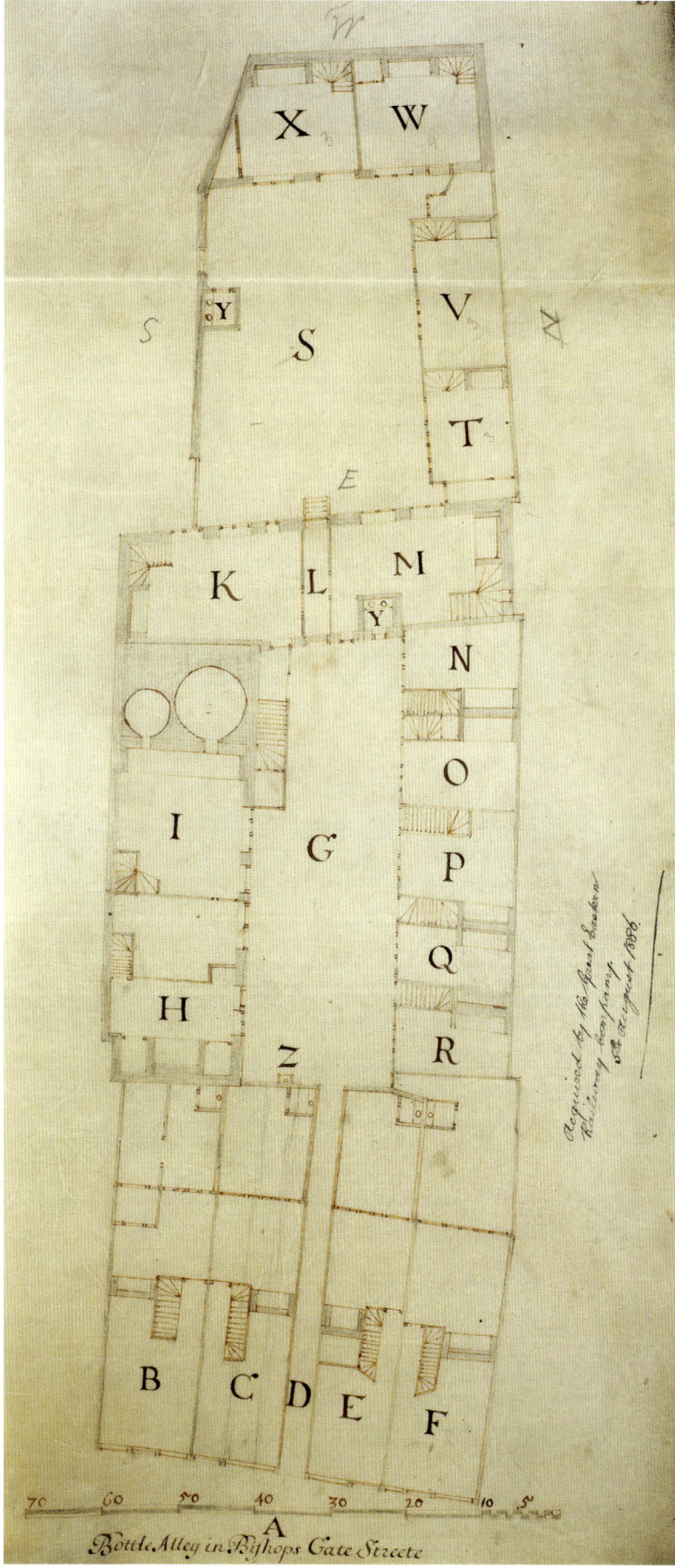

KEY

A. Front of four houses in Bishopsgate Street.

B, C, E, F. Each is house of three storeys besides cellar and garrets; *Ground floor*, shop; kitchen paved with purbeck stone with chimney; yard paved with purbeck stone, with house of easement; *First storey*, jetties in front one foot; two rooms each with chimney, front one with jetty window; *Second storey*, two rooms each with chimney, front one jetties 18 inches and has jetty window; *Third storey*, garret divided in two, each with chimney, front one jetties 18 inches and has jetty window. (B has a buttery in the yard with two small rooms over, and no chimney in the back garret; upper storeys of C and E go half way over Bottle Alley.)

D. Bottle Alley.

G. First courtyard.

H. House of two storeys and garrets; *Ground floor*, room paved with purbeck stone with chimney; cellar under next house westward; *First storey*, room with chimney; room on same floor over part of the house westward; *Second storey*, two garrets, one with chimney; porch at outward door.

I. Bakehouse of two storeys besides arched vault and garrets; *Ground floor*, two rooms, one with large chimney and two large ovens; *First storey*, two rooms, each with chimney; *Second storey*, garret divided in two, one with chimney; staircase breaks out into courtyard.

K, M. Each is brick house, three storeys besides garret and cellar; each storey and garret has chimney; upper storeys go half way over passage.

L. Passage between two courts.

N, O, P, Q, R. Each is house of three storeys and garret; one room with chimney in each storey.

S. Second courtyard.

T, V. Each is house of two storeys and garret; one room in each storey with chimney (T also has a chimney in the garret).

W, X. Each is house of two storeys and cellar and garret; first storey jetties one foot, with jetty window; one room in each storey, and chimney in each room and garret; W also has small room outside the door with chimney and small cellar under.

Y. Common house of easement in each court.

Z. Lead pump in first courtyard.

Fig. 99. Bottle Alley and houses in Bishopsgate Street, 1679. North is to the right.

Plan 36
Old Jewry, 1679
Joseph Titcombe FIG. 100

KEY

A. Front of four houses.

B. Passage into back yard.

C, D, E, F. Each is house of three storeys besides cellar and garret;[20] two rooms on each floor; chimney in each room and the garret; yard paved with ragstone. (Cellars and all floors except ground floor of D and E go halfway across the passage; ground floors of C and E are each shop and kitchen with one chimney; D has no chimney on ground floor; ground floor of F is all one shop without chimneys.)

G. House of three storeys besides cellar and garret; one room on each floor; chimney in each room except garret.

H, K. Each is large stable with hayloft over.

I. Stable yard.

L. Windmill Alley.

M, N, O, P. Almshouse three storeys high besides cellar and garret; chimney in each room and garret.

Fig. 100. Houses and stables in Old Jewry, 1679. North is to the left.

This land had been left to the Armourers' Company in 1551 by Dame Elizabeth Morris, widow of Sir Christopher Morris, Master of the Ordnance and Chief Gunner at the Tower of London. The Company was required to allow thirteen poor and honest persons to dwell rent-free, but paying for repairs, in the houses in Love Alley alias Love Lane —presumably the later Windmill Alley (named after a nearby tavern). In 1619 the property was described as five houses in St Olave Jewry and thirteen habitations occupied by widows. There were probably never thirteen houses; in 1663 the thirteen poor persons had seventeen rooms between them, ten of them having just one room.[21]

After the Great Fire, four houses, each about thirteen feet wide, were built at the front and one in the yard behind, perhaps replicating the earlier arrangement. Augustine Newbold, whose father had leased house D or E in 1636, fought off a demand by the Armourers for a large increase in rent in order to pay for the rebuilding of the almshouses; the Fire Court decreed an increase from £3.8s.0d to £5 instead of the £10 requested. He then sold his interest, and the four front houses were rebuilt by Ralph Hartley on a seventy-nine year lease. The Company complained in 1679 about the 'irregular building' of Hartley's houses in Old Jewry.[22] In the back yard were two large stables, perhaps serving people with business nearby. The almshouses were rebuilt as a three and a half storey block with sixteen rooms and two staircases entered directly from the alley. Evidently the upper rooms were occupied separately, and this arrangement too seems to have replicated the pre-Fire one. Each room was a mere eleven by nine feet at its maximum extent. When the almshouse vault or cesspit was to be emptied in 1680 the Company ordered a search 'to prevent any mischeife by filling the same from the stables neere thereunto'.[23]

In 1746 a meeting house was built on the back part of the site, and the almshouses were rebuilt on the south-west corner (F on the plan). By 1791 everything shown on the plan had been rebuilt since 1679, with the possible exception of house E. In 1809 the almsfolk were removed to Bottle Court, Bishopsgate, the requirement being interpreted as thirteen rooms, and the whole site was sold to the Bank of England.'.[24] Windmill Alley is the passage later called Bank Buildings and now enclosed by a gate.

Plan 37
Billiter Lane, 1686
William Leybourn
FIG. 101

This plan shows pre-Fire buildings on the west side of Billiter Lane (now Billiter Street) on land acquired by the Fishmongers' Company under a will of 1468 (Fig. 102).[25] The three houses by the street, each of two and a half storeys, were of one-room plan, lacking any backland. The two larger properties, described by Leybourn as 'back tenements' but in the Fishmongers' minutes as a 'great messuage' in each case, both consisted of warehouses at the front and dwellings and gardens set back from the street, and one of them included a 'sugar house', presumably for refining sugar. Leybourn described them as 'promiscuously disposed'.

The most important property, marked K, was described in the Fishmongers' accounts as 'the greate place'. It was leased in about 1590 to Roger Owfeild (or Oldfield), a wealthy fishmonger and merchant, who lived there. The lease included a tenement at the gate (presumably house H), which Owfield rebuilt a storey and a half higher, and a garden facing Leadenhall Street (see Plan 38). A survey of 1650 indicates that the main house was partly two and a half and partly three and a half storeys, and that, unrecorded by Leybourn, it extended twenty-seven feet along the street front over the front warehouse of house I. The lease was later renewed by John Oldfield, but in 1662 he assigned it to Thomas Turges esquire and Richard Turvile, citizen and fishmonger. They claimed in that year to have spent more than they were required to on rebuilding, and their changes may well have included the sugar house. There were fourteen hearths in about 1670, and Turvile was living there in 1678 with his wife, an apprentice, four male servants and two female servants. After Turvile's death in 1692 his son surrendered the lease to avoid having to pay for repairs.[26]

Property I, known as the Dolphin, was leased by 1608 to John Dike, citizen and fishmonger, together with houses F and G. His changes included raising the front part of the house from one and a half to two and a half storeys in or about 1610. In 1650 the property (apparently including the two small houses) consisted of cellars, eight rooms and a gallery on the ground floor, the same on the first floor, eight garrets on the second floor and half the leads over the Owfields' house. The first-floor gallery was probably the one built before 1610 by Roger Owfield on the north side of Dike's garden over part of Dike's house, at first with shared use but divided between the two houses after a dispute in 1610-12. By 1650 the

---

KEY

F, G, H. Tenements fronting the street, with cellars under and two floors over the ground floors; H is built over the passage or gateway.

I, K. Back tenements with yards, gardens and other appurtenances, principally consisting of workhouses, sheds, warehouses and storehouses over them, promiscuously disposed; divers vaults and cellars under several parts, and two floors over [the ground floors].

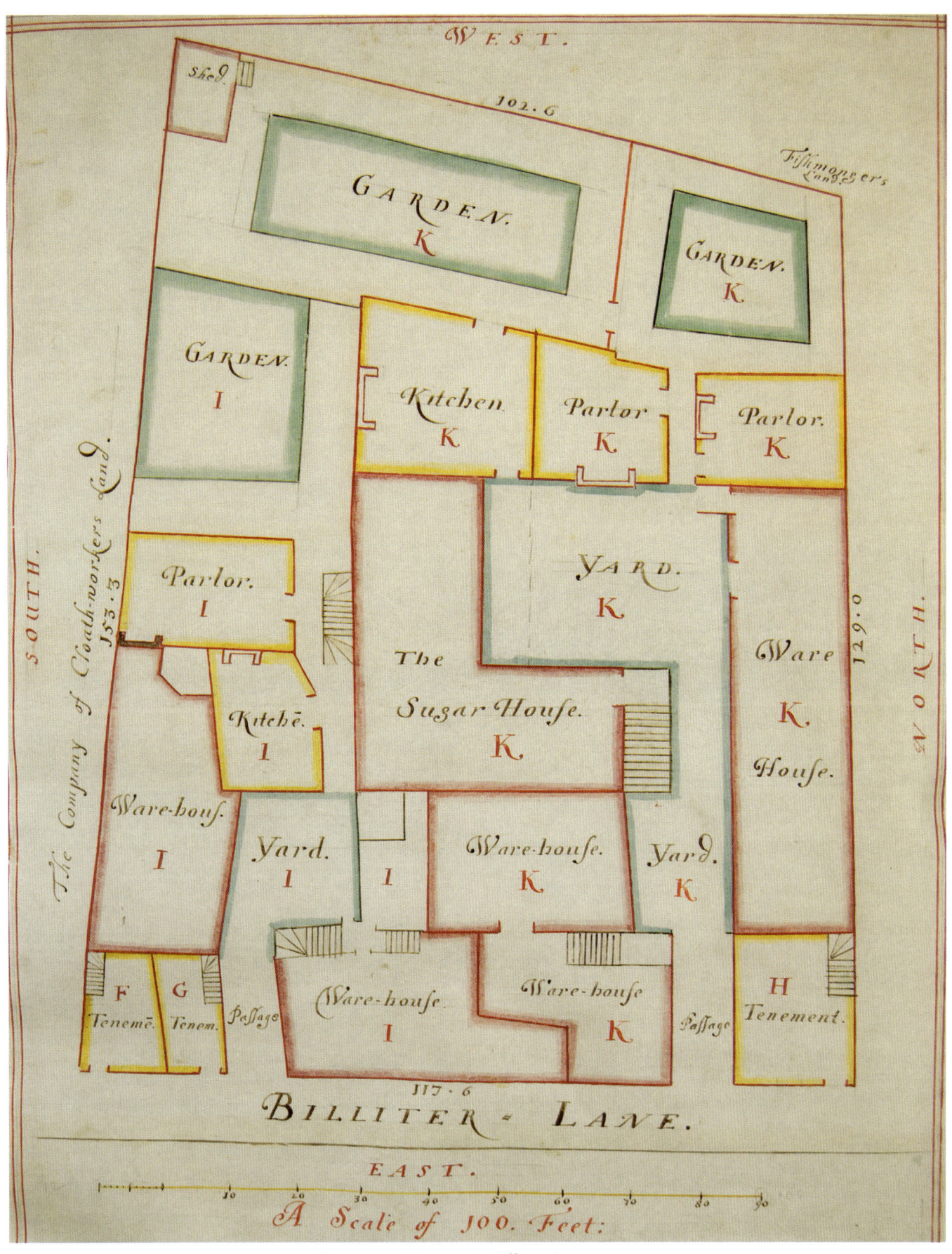

Fig. 101. Houses in Billiter Lane, 1686.

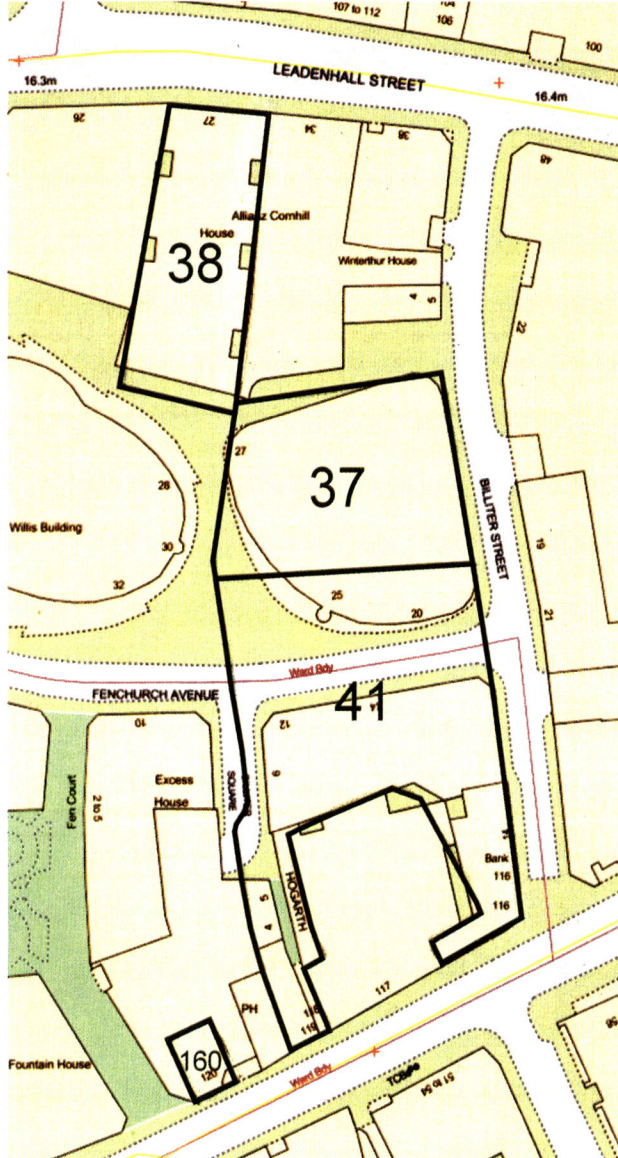

Fig. 102. Areas covered by plans in and around Billiter Lane, marked on the 2015 Ordnance Survey map. The numbers indicate plans in this book.

Dolphin was occupied by Peter Middleton, merchant, apparently from the Middleton family of Chirk Castle. He was succeeded by his brother, John Middleton, citizen and grocer, on whose death in 1686-87 the lease passed to three daughters.[27]

In 1696 Edward Belitha, citizen and haberdasher, agreed to lease the entire property for sixty-six years (subject to the Middleton lease of part of it running until 1704), to pay fines totalling £1,000 and to spend at least £1,500 on rebuilding it within ten years. He rebuilt it on a much more regular plan. Thereafter there were four ranges around a central yard, with tenements facing the street and warehouses on the other three sides.[28]

Plan 38
Leadenhall Street, 1686
William Leybourn
Fig. 103

This plan, from the Fishmongers' plan book, makes it possible to relate a ground plan to a view of the street frontage (Fig. 104), and to observe the increasingly intense use of backland in the City's deeper plots. The houses, later 27-33 Leadenhall Street (Fig. 102), were pre-Fire ones, and survived until 1859. Stow mentioned in Leadenhall Street, between Billiter Lane and Lime Street, 'a frame of three fayre houses, set up in the yeare 1590, in [a] place where before was a large garden plot inclosed from the high streete with a bricke wall',[29] and there is good evidence, in addition to the location and number of houses, that these were the 'three fayre houses' referred to. The building lease was from before 1592, when the Fishmongers' minute books begin, but not long before, and at the time of the lease the site was a garden, held by Roger Owfeild with adjoining property in Billiter Lane (Plan 37). The Fishmongers later agreed that Owfeild had been persuaded by 'divers ancients' of the Company to build 'strongly and substancially', which included enlarging the houses backwards, 'to his wonderfull great charge', and that this justified extending the lease so that it would expire in 1653 instead of 1636.[30]

When the three houses were viewed in 1650, their occupants were, from left to right, John Cressey, merchant, Henry Boone, barber chirurgeon, and Thomas Murthwaite, merchant. Each house had, apart from entries, closets and butteries, three rooms on each of the two lower floors and two rooms on each of the upper floors (Fig. 105). The upper storeys were jettied. Murthwaite's house in 1669 still had a hall with wainscot benches on the first floor at the front. Most of the rooms in Cressey's house had chimneypieces of carved stone.[31] Each house had from ten to twelve hearths in 1674, the difference probably indicating that some garrets were heated and others were not, and four years later each had from four to eight occupants.[32] Subsequent lessees of Cressey's house were Abraham Dolings, merchant, in 1667, Edward East, citizen and grocer, in 1681, and Edward Greene, citizen and haberdasher, in 1697; Murthwaite's passed to Robert Steevens, barber chirurgeon, in 1685.[33] Each house had a garden, but instead of three narrow gardens, Boone had the land furthest from the houses, with a path

PLANS OF AREAS

KEY

A. Great house and garden: cellars and other offices; three floors over ground floor.

B. Shop and tenement, being a tavern: cellars; four floors over part next the street; two floors over boxes in yard; one room over back kitchen.

C, D. Tenements consisting of two shops, kitchens, yards and a shed; cellars under shops and kitchens; four floors over shops and kitchens; entry to back house.

E. Tenement: cellar; four floors over shop.

F. Tenement behind: cellar under parlour and kitchen; two floors over parlour; four floors over kitchen.

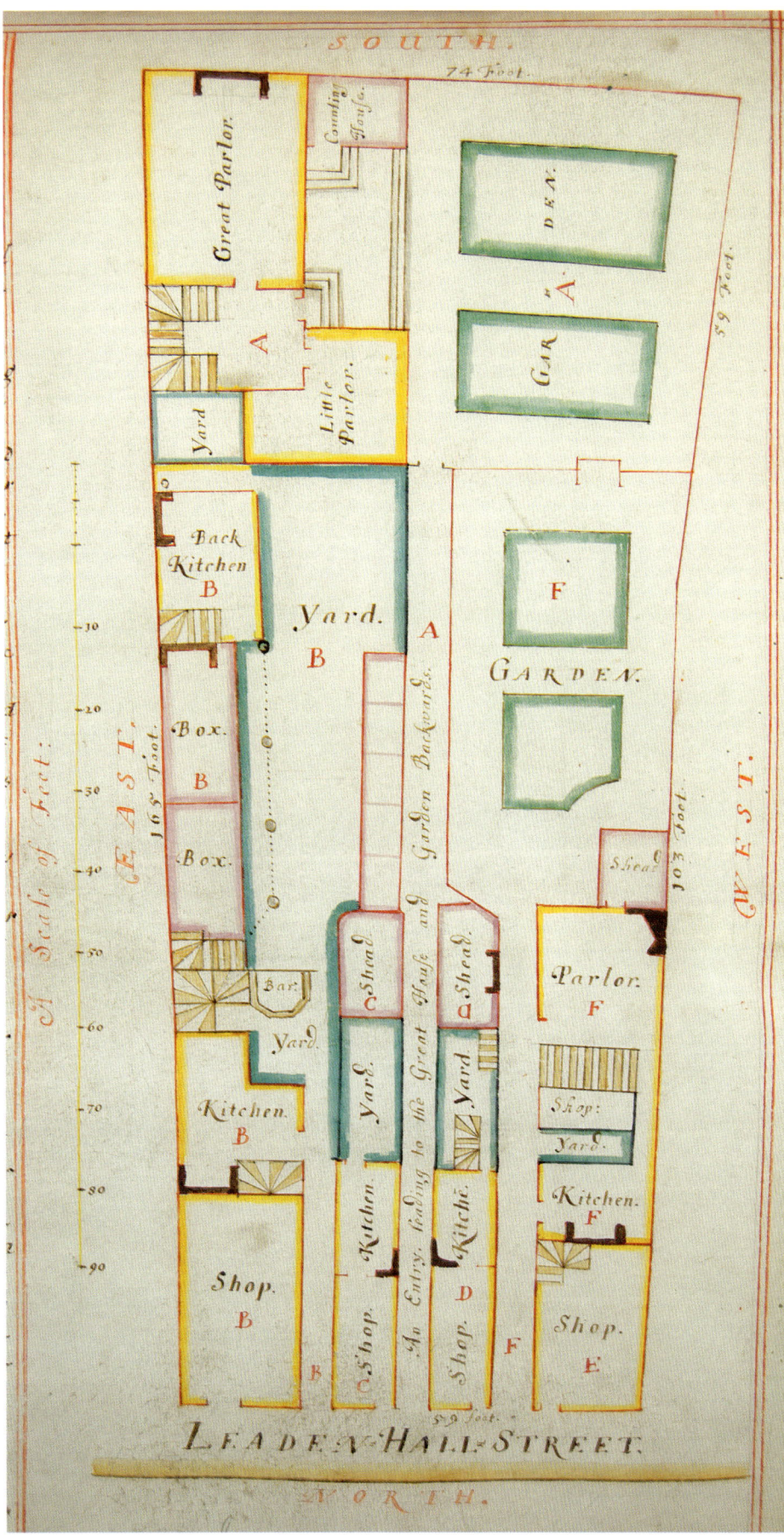

Fig. 103. Houses in Leadenhall Street, 1686.

Fig. 104. The houses in Leadenhall Street shown in Fig. 103, drawn by T.H. Shepherd in 1859 when about to be demolished.

2 garrets	2 garrets	2 garrets
2 rooms	2 rooms	2 rooms
2 rooms (with house of office)	2 rooms	2 rooms
3 rooms (kitchen & 2 chambers)	3 rooms	3 rooms (inc. hall)
3 rooms (inc. shop & parlour), buttery	3 rooms, buttery	3 rooms (inc. parlour & kitchen), buttery
2 cellars	2 cellars	2 cellars

Hearths 1674
Abraham Dolings 12   Robert Scott 11   John Murthwaite 10

Inhabitants 1678
Abraham Dolings, wife, 2 children, apprentice, 3 female servants   Robert Scott, wife, 2 children, apprentice, 2 female servants   Mary Murthwaite, daughter, male servant, female servant

Fig. 105. Rooms, hearths and inhabitants at the houses in Leadenhall Street.

providing access, and his two neighbours had the land nearer the houses. The projection from Murthwaite's garden was a privy.

By 1686 there had been major changes, especially a new house on Boone's garden. Boone's proposal for building a back house was rejected by the Company in 1658, and there was still no back house in 1670, and probably in 1678, but it existed by 1686. In 1694 it was occupied by Mr Rett, a merchant.[34] A list of rooms in 1699 indicates that it had three and a half storeys and a basement. The kitchen and other offices were in the basement; the ground floor included parlour and dining room, both with marble chimney-pieces, together with hall and stairs; and there were two or more rooms on each floor above. By 1734 the garden contained 'several elms and figg trees ... with grass platts and a handsome seat'.[35] Presumably at the same time as the back house was built, Boone's front house had been divided at ground floor level into two narrow shops, each about eight feet wide, and a central passage, as shown on the plan; how the upper floors were arranged is not known. Cressey's house was a tavern by 1686, with drinking boxes and a back kitchen and rooms above them on the former garden; by 1697 it was two separate dwellings.[36] Murthwaite's house was the least altered, but it was divided between 1681 and 1686 into a back house and a front one, the latter consisting of the shop and the rooms directly above it. In its garret the front house had the only surviving original windows in the street facade in 1859, consisting of ten lights.

Plan 39
Thames Street and Black Raven Alley, 1686
William Leybourn
Fig. 106

This plan provides an example of the narrow plots which stretched from Thames Street to the Thames, reflecting the centuries-long process of reclaiming additional land from the river. The property was acquired by the Fishmongers' Company under a will of 1518. It was a little west from Fishmongers' Hall, between the Hall and Swan Lane. The width of the main plot (later 106 Upper Thames Street) varied from seventeen feet in Thames Street to eleven feet at its south end. In the mid-seventeenth century it was still called Our Lady, a name presumably reflecting medieval piety, but it was beginning to be known as 'The Lady'. The northern part was leased in 1646 to William Whitney, citizen and fishmonger, who lived there, whereas the southern part towards the river was let separately as three or more small tenements. By 1666 Whitney's lease was held by John Parrett (1622-84), citizen and fishmonger, and in 1667, after the Fire, Parrett obtained a new lease which included the sites of the small tenements, though the property was somewhat truncated at both ends to provide for the widening of Thames Street and the creation of the forty-foot wharf. Parrett's lease required him to build one or more substantial dwellings within two years. He not only rebuilt the Lady but added a dyehouse in place of the small tenements, contributing to the increasingly industrial character of the waterfront. The Lady and the dyehouse were separated by the small yard approached from Black Raven Alley. William Parrett, presumably a descendant of John, secured a new lease in 1713.[37]

The land to the west bordered Black Raven Alley, which made it easier to split it up into smaller properties, and the Fishmongers owned only the middle section. Until the Fire there were several separate tenants here, leasing tenements or 'rooms'. In January 1671 William Darvoll, citizen and plaisterer, undertook to build four or more tenements on the site, and by the end of May he had built the six houses shown, each about thirteen feet wide and with three and a half storeys. During archaeological excavations in 1974-75 parts of these houses were found, corresponding exactly to Leybourn's plan.[38]

KEY
T. Shop, warehouse and two yards: cellar under shop; three floors of rooms over shop; room over warehouse.
V. Yard and dyehouse: cellar; three floors of rooms over ground floor.
W-Z and A-B. Six tenements: each has cellars; three floors of rooms over ground floor.
C. Passage into dyehouse yard.

Plan 40
Ludgate Hill and Fleet Ditch, 1689
John Tasker
FIG. 107

The Dean and Chapter of Rochester had this plan drawn to show the land taken from them following the Great Fire in order to widen Ludgate Hill and turn the Fleet River into a canal, and it demonstrates the scale of the changes made after

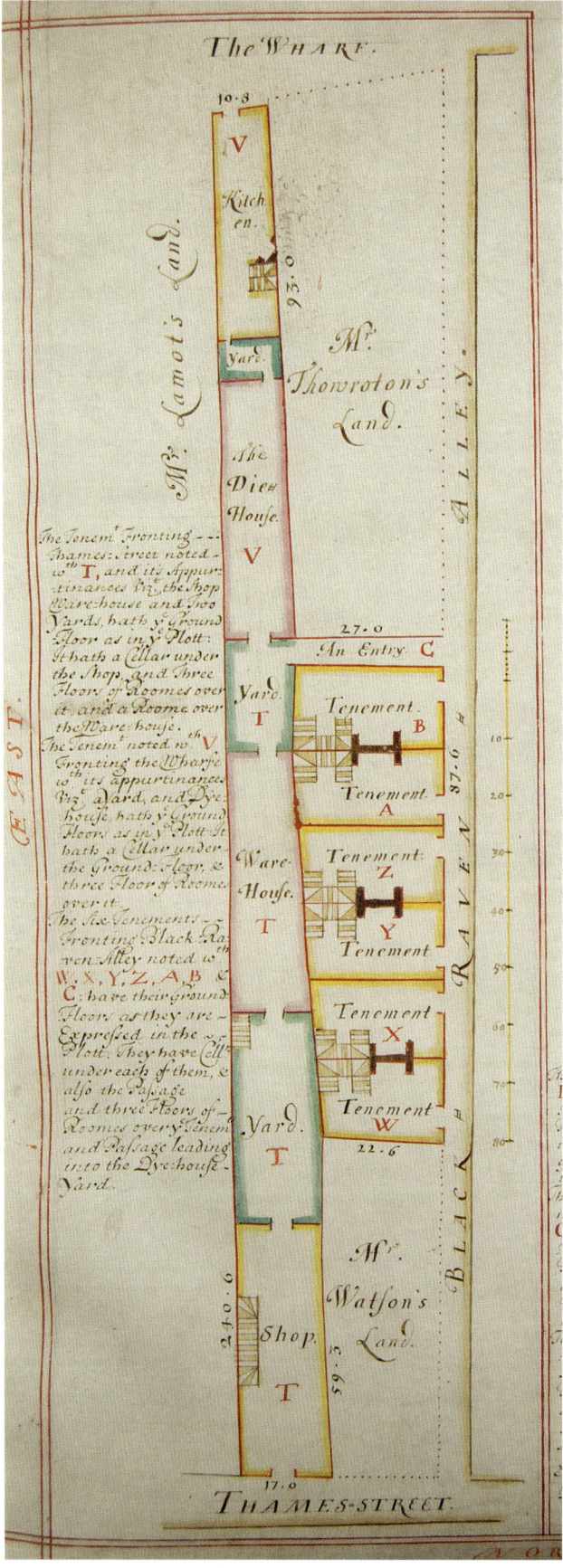

Fig. 106. The Lady tenement in Thames Street and houses in Black Raven Alley, 1686. North is at the bottom.

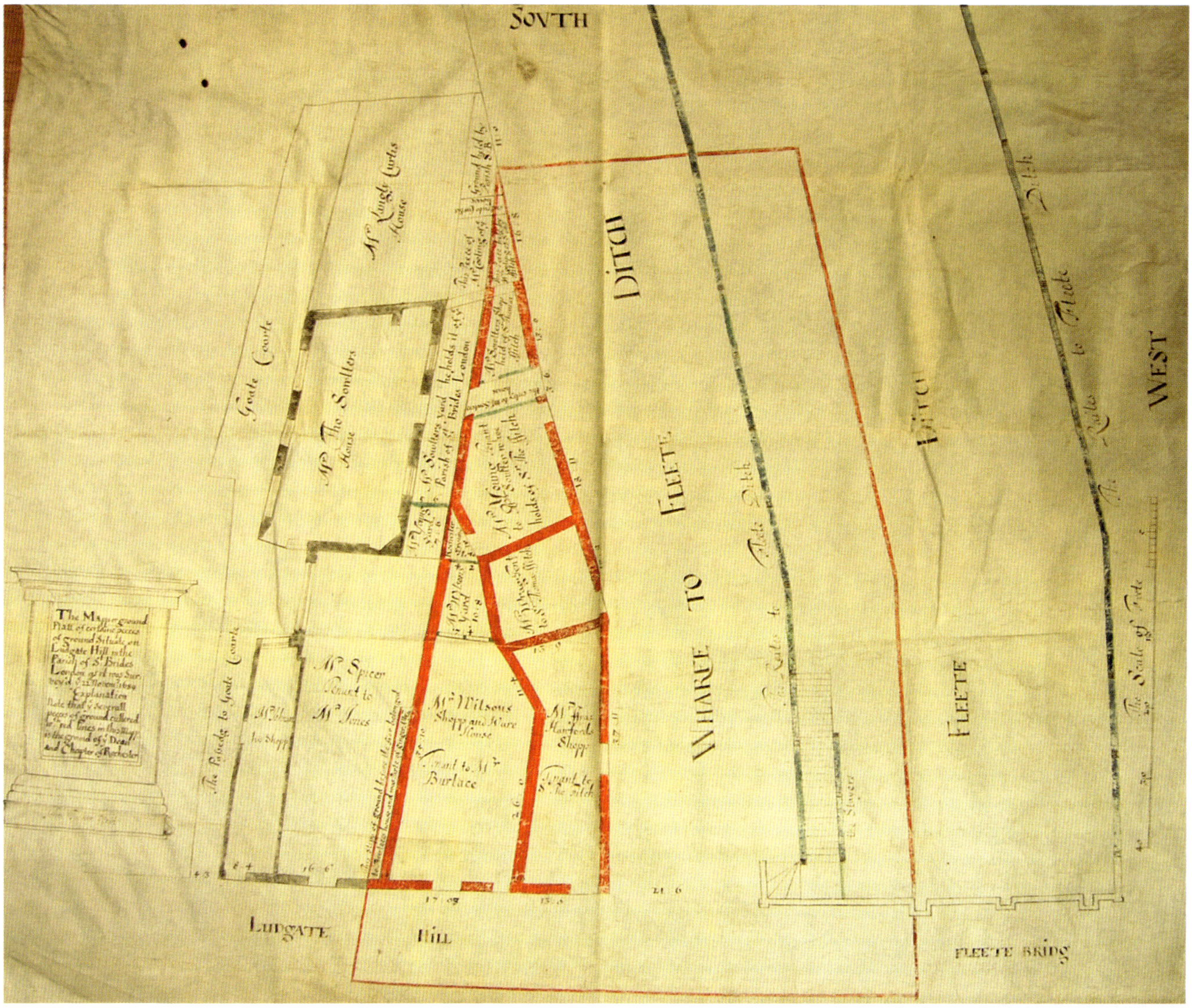

Fig. 107. Property on Ludgate Hill and by the Fleet Ditch, 1689.

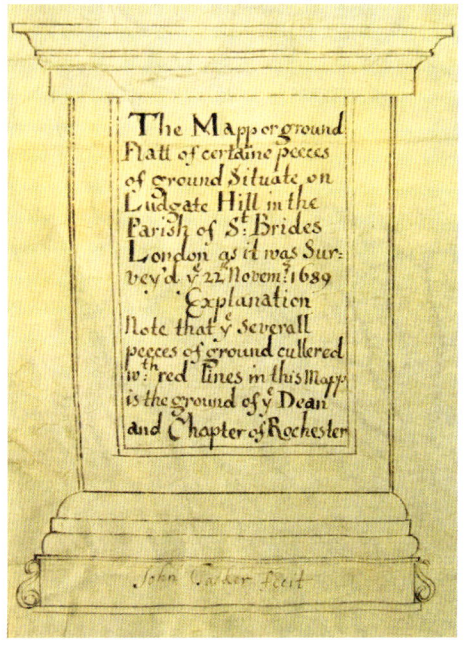

Fig. 108. Title from Fig. 107.

the Fire. It also provides a cautionary tale about absentee landownership.

The property was the former Rose brewhouse, which by 1649 had been divided into at least ten tenements. It abutted south on an alley leading to 'the Fleet Privihouses'. Abraham Church renewed his lease of it in 1662. Following the Fire he assigned his interest in the site of the Red Bull, in the north-east corner, to John Burlace in 1669, and his interest in the rest of the property to Henry Edwards in 1672. In the same year Edwards sold his part to the City as if it was freehold, for £600, 'by which act Mr Edward hath done ye Church wrong', as a note in the Dean and Chapter's archive laments. Their large plot, outlined on the plan by a red line, was reduced to little more than a sliver. The City transferred the land it did not need to Thomas Fitch, lessee of the Fleet Ditch and its wharves, for £200. Fitch and Burlace continued to pay ground rent, which is perhaps why the Dean and Chapter seem not to have noticed what had happened until 1681. Efforts to persuade the City to pay the Dean and Chapter for the land were unsuccessful in 1681-82 and 1700. The Dean and Chapter were still seeking payment in 1774, when the City took the view that their interest 'was extinct by their giving up the same to the public after the Great Fire of London'.[39] John Tasker is referred to as a surveyor in a lawsuit of 1695, but nothing more is known about him and no other maps or plans by him are recorded.[40]

Plan 41
Clothworkers' Court, 1690
FIG. 109

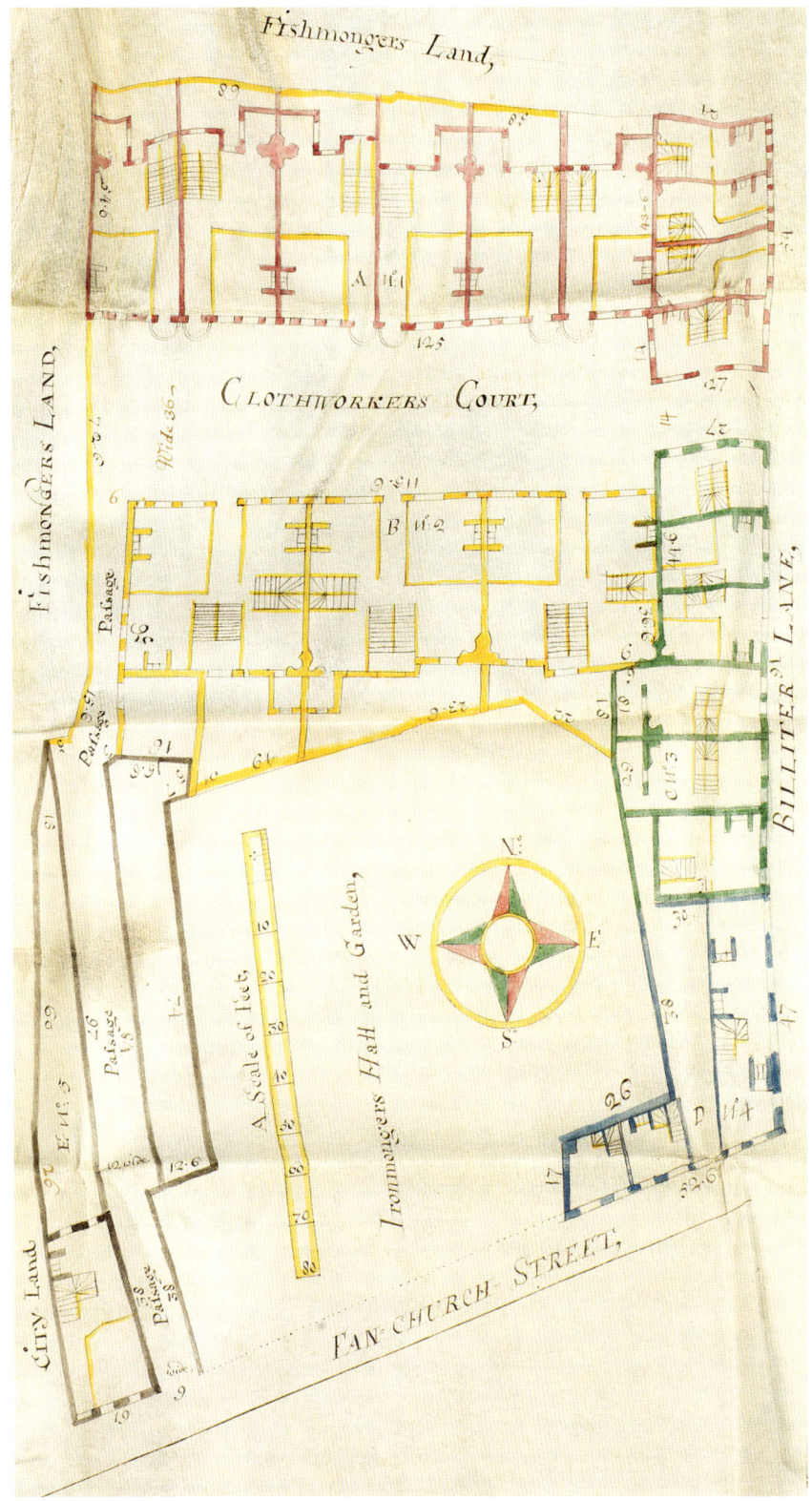

Fig. 109. Clothworkers' Court (later Billiter Square), 1690.

This plan provides an example of a major new development several decades after the Great Fire which gave rise to part of the City's present street layout. When Ralph Treswell surveyed the site for the Clothworkers' Company in 1612 it was largely occupied by a mansion leased to Sir Edward Darcy, together with small houses facing Billiter Lane (Fig. 110).[41] The site was not affected by the Great Fire.

By 1689 John Smith, a scrivener, was lessee of the mansion, and he agreed with the Company that he would pay a £2,000 fine and rent of £120 a year, and would pull down the old houses and build as many new brick ones as he thought fit in return for his lease being extended to sixty-one years. He would also buy out the leaseholders of five of the houses at his own cost. By August 1690 enough progress had been made that the Company was willing to agree new leases covering the five separate parts of the property, and the plan marks this stage in the process, indicating each of the five parts by a different colour. Also, 'out of their great respect to Mr John Smith', it granted him the freedom of the Company. At his suggestion, it repaid him £1,620 in return for the annual rent being increased to £200.[42]

The main part of Smith's venture was to build two rows of brick houses facing each other on the site of the mansion and its garden, either side of a courtyard thirty-six feet wide, with a new access way from Billiter Lane and a back passage from Fenchurch Street. By August 1690 this had largely been achieved. Three 'great houses' had been built south of the courtyard, marked yellow, and six 'double houses' (i.e. of two-room plan) north of the courtyard, marked red. Also new were six houses in Billiter Lane, marked green, the plots of which had been extended backwards into the site of the mansion, blocking its former access. The new courtyard was to be known as Clothworkers' Court, but by the 1740s was called Billiter Square. Three areas remained to be rebuilt, all of which, with the possible exception of the Swan at the south-east corner and the adjoining gatehouse, had already been rebuilt since 1612. They were: three houses (though the plan seems to show four) in Billiter Lane, marked red, to be replaced by four new ones; three houses and the former gateway in Fenchurch Street, marked blue; and one house in Fenchurch Street, described in 1631 as lately rebuilt,[43] together with vacant land formerly occupied by two other houses, marked black. In 1700 the Clothworkers were asking Smith why the house on the corner of Fenchurch Street and Billiter Lane had still not been rebuilt, and a timber house with a jettied front was put up there in that year. The passage to Fenchurch Street was known as Smith's Rents but later as Fishmongers' Alley (it is now partly Billiter Square and partly Hogarth Court).[44]

Smith's 'great houses' south of the Court, each about forty feet wide, had six bays, including two half-width bays. On their ground floors they had four rooms and two staircases. The westernmost one had a coachhouse and stables. The houses north of the Court, each just over twenty feet wide, had three or three and a half bays. They had stairs by the side at the back and back extensions rather than just two rooms per floor. According to Strype in 1720, Billiter Lane was full of timber houses which ought to be demolished, 'but the chief ornament of this place is Billiter Square on the west side, which is a very handsome, open, and airy place, graced with good new brick build-

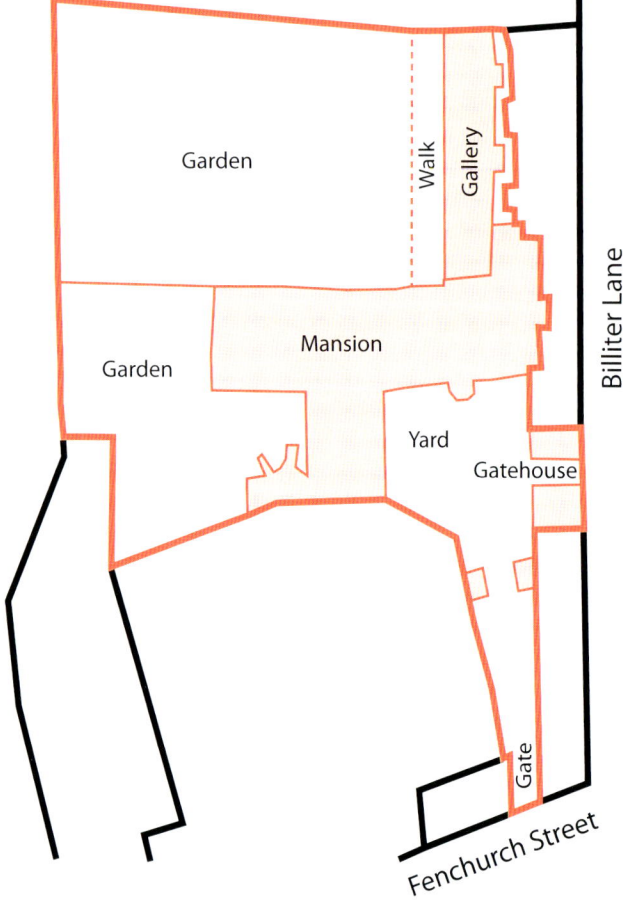

Fig. 110. Sir Edward Darcy's mansion off Billiter Lane in 1612, redrawn from Treswell's plan. North is at the top.

ings, very well inhabited'.[45] Billiter Square continued to have prosperous inhabitants into the nineteenth century.[46]

In or about 1877 a new road was created between Billiter Lane and Lime Street.[47] That road is now Fenchurch Avenue, and the former Clothworkers' Court or Billiter Square is its eastern end. All of Smith's Billiter Square houses were demolished between 1867 and 1890.[48]

Plan 42
Cousin Lane, 1692
William Leybourn
FIG. 111

This plan, from one of the City's leases, records another narrow plot between Thames Street and the Thames, twenty to twenty-one feet wide, though only the southern part of it. The City itself had only a lease of this land, bought in 1673 for £800, rather than the freehold.[49] Cousin Lane still exists, though slightly realigned, immediately west of Cannon Street Station. Dowgate Dock was the lowest part of the Walbrook. On Ogilby and Morgan's map of 1676 the brewhouse in Cousin Lane is apparently built but not the house south of it. Under an agreement of 1681 Anthony Shercliffe, citizen and brewer, built the house and repaired the wharf, and he was eventually granted a forty-one year lease in 1692. Land was to be left open for the forty-foot wharf.

In 1692 the brewery equipment included four square tuns, one copper containing thirty barrels, a mash tun, a liquor back and a horse mill. There were two floors of rooms over part of it. The house was described as having four storeys (probably meaning three and a half), and included a best room and a best parlour. There were also a malt loft, a stable, a kitchen, a counting house and a store house. By 1718, when the tenant was Thomas Underwood, citizen and brewer, an additional house had been built south of the stable, reducing the depth of the wharf by half, and showing how the continuous forty-foot wharf insisted on by Charles II was gradually encroached on.[50]

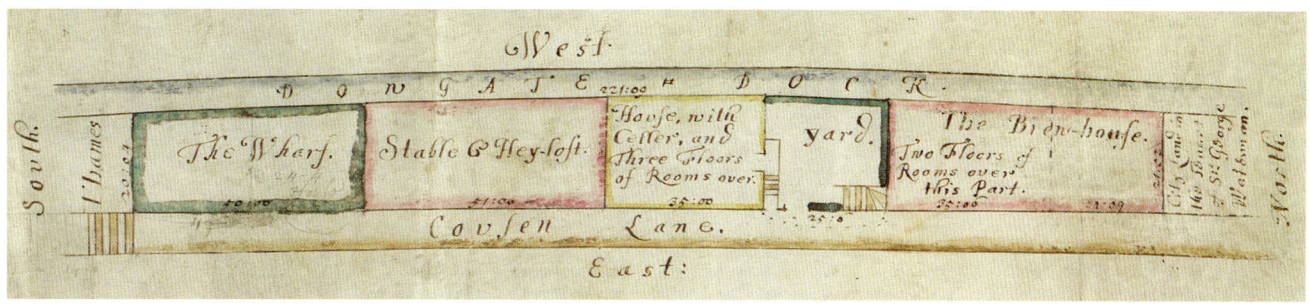

Fig. 111. Property in Cousin Lane, 1692.

Plans 43-44
Goldsmiths' Alley and Jewin Street, 1687 and 1692
Anonymous and John Ward
FIGS 112-13

These plans provide an example of spacious gardens in a lightly-developed area on the edge of the City. It was known as the Jews' Garden or Jewin Garden—before 1177 the only place in England where the Jews were allowed to bury their dead—and is now in the western part of the Barbican. It was acquired by the Goldsmiths' Company under a will of 1422, and Stow referred to it in 1603 as being 'now turned into faire garden plots and summer houses for pleasure'.[51] The Goldsmiths used part of the site as their own garden until 1641 (the block of land from Nos. 66-69 to 109-11 on Fig. 113) and had a bowling alley there until 1655 (the land comprising Nos. 24-27 and 65 and part of the area marked Bullhead Court on Fig. 113). John Ward's plan shows the area after considerable development, including the creation of Jewin Street in 1652. He provides much detail on the gardens and very little on the dwellings, but that is partly remedied for the Company's former garden by a lease plan of 1687 (Fig. 112). This was possibly by George Prestwood, a carpenter and the Company's surveyor, who accompanied the viewers to the site two years earlier and made at least one other plan for the Company.[52]

When Robert Arden, citizen and weaver, leased the area shown in Fig. 112 in 1641, it

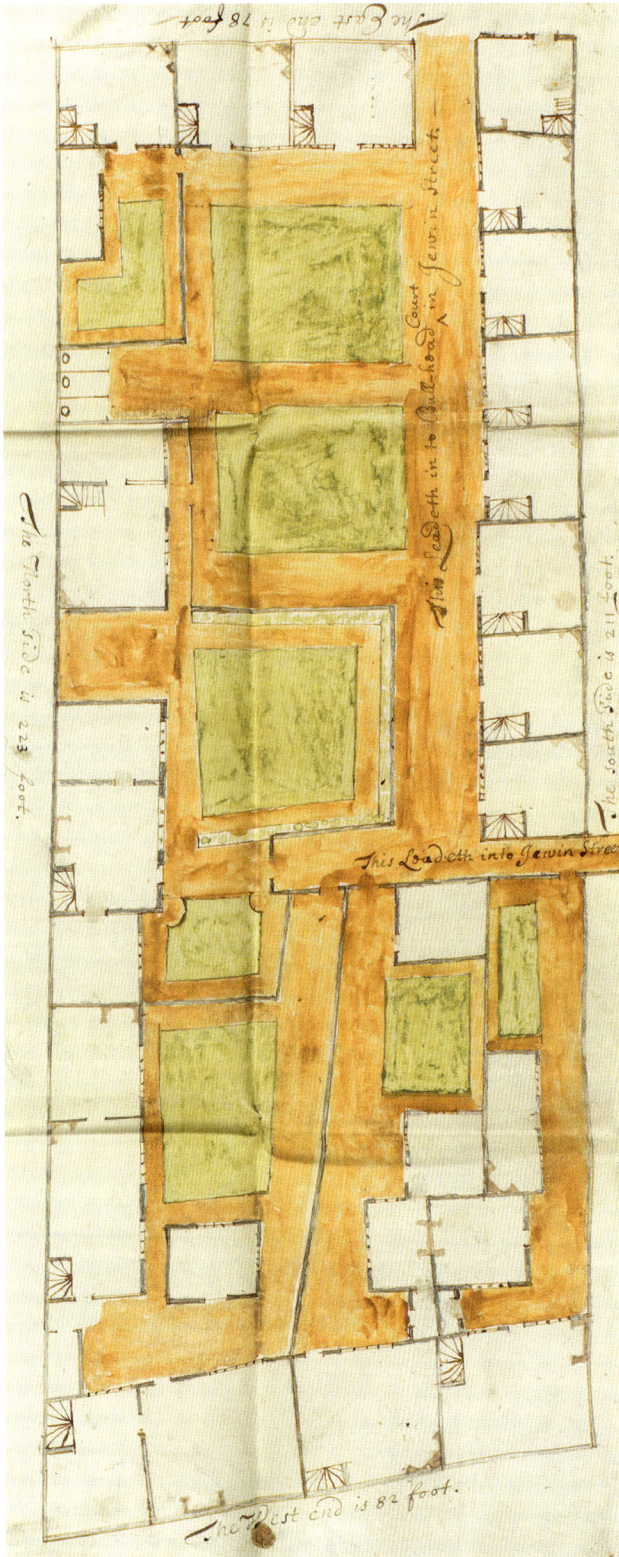

Fig. 112. Goldsmiths' Alley, Jewin Street, 1687.
North is to the left.

consisted of a single house and garden called 'the Companyes garden house', whereas by 1651 there were fourteen houses, the same number as in 1687. Arden himself lived in the large house on the north side, probably the former garden house, where he had 'a workshop with weaveing loomes and fframes'.[53] The house had three and a half storeys, with hall and kitchen on the ground floor. All the houses were timber, except the row on the south side referred to in a note on the plan as seven brick houses (though the plan shows eight). The brick houses were all of one-room plan, with four storeys and cocklofts and lacking gardens. In 1651 their occupants included three weavers, two wiredrawers and a carpenter. Access to Arden's houses was at first somewhat awkwardly from the south via Horn Alley and the passage shown in Fig. 113 between Nos. 101 and 114. Arden described the premises in his will of 1654 as 'Goldsmiths Alley commonly called Jewen Gardens'.[54] In 1687 the new lessee was Henry Shalcross, citizen and merchant taylor, the husband of Arden's granddaughter.

In 1652 the Goldsmiths laid out Jewin Street, between Red Cross Street near St Giles Cripplegate and Aldersgate Street, threading it between existing developments. Many of the buildings shown in Fig. 113 were constructed within the next few years, including the row north of Jewin Street from No. 114 to 131 and that to the south from No. 115 to 129 (the latter all of one-room plan with three and a half storeys plus cellars). John Lawrence, jeweller, built the first two on the north side in 1652-53 (Nos. 130 and 131) and later successfully requested extra years on his lease, having exceeded his expected costs 'because hee would bee an example unto others (that soe the street might bee gracefully built)'.[55] In 1655 the Goldsmiths let out their bowling alley for building, causing one member to complain that 'those which voted the demolishing of the Company's bowling alley were a company of knaves'. Robert Lawrence, brewer, built Nos. 24 to 27 there and Sarah Arden built No. 65, and new access was provided to Goldsmiths' Alley via Bullhead Court. Gardens gradually gave way to more houses: south of Goldsmiths' Alley, Nos. 70-75 and 141 had comprised just two dwellings and Nos. 80-85 and 101-04 just one dwelling in 1667.[56] Strype described Bullhead Court in 1720 as 'a handsome place, with good buildings, and well inhabited', and Jewin Street as 'well built and inhabited, and of some trade for button mould makers'. Goldsmiths' Alley (later Nixon's Square) was replaced by Jewin Crescent around 1800.[57] Jewin Street and Jewin Crescent disappeared after Second World War bombing.

KEY, Fig. 113 (1651)[58]

[69, 76-79, 105-07] William Marshall, Thomas Shedd, carpenter, Mark Cham, weaver, William Cordray, wiredrawer, Mark Colledge, wiredrawer, Oliver Arden, weaver, John King, weaver: each has brick tenement containing cellar, kitchen, three rooms upright over it, cockloft; Cham has garden plot; together £54 p.a.

[68, 67, 66] East end: Francis Hill, wiredrawer: cellar, kitchen, three rooms upright; Edward Ironmonger: the like; John Marshall, glover: shed, garden plot, large kitchen divided, two rooms over it upright, closet; together £24 p.a.

[111] South-west end: [blank] Smith: passage yard with washhouse and shed, kitchen, four rooms, garret, whereof part is over next house to north; £10 p.a.

[110] West end: Richard Pretty, gent: little garden before house, passage yard paved, washhouse, kitchen, hall, buttery, little cellar under kitchen, chamber over hall, three garret chambers over that (and closet), whereof two run northward over next house to north; £14 p.a.

[109] North-west end: William Drax: garden plot before the house, three cellars, kitchen, parlour, large dining room over kitchen and parlour on north side adjoining a chamber, over that another chamber, over that a garret, and over Arden's workshop a chamber and garret; £18 p.a.

[108] Mr Arden's own dwelling: garden plot and paved passage, two cellars under, workshop with weaving looms and frames, kitchen, hall, chamber over kitchen, two closets at stairs head, chamber over hall and little chamber within it, chamber over kitchen chamber, chamber over hall chamber, ceiled garret, little closet in yard by grass plot, two counting houses, washhouse and a buttery within it, cockloft over it, little yard for poultry; £30 p.a.

Drying yard and pump in common for all the tenants.

Fig. 113. Goldsmiths' Alley and part of Jewin Street, 1692. North is to the left.

Plan 45
Primrose and Acorn Alleys and Walnut Tree Yard, Bishopsgate Street, 1692
John Ward
Fig. 114

Fig. 114. Primrose Alley, Acorn Alley and Walnut Tree Yard, Bishopsgate Street, 1692.

John Ward provided more detail here than in the other plans he drew for the Goldsmiths, including windows in Acorn Alley and much of Primrose Alley. The site of Primrose Alley is marked by the present Primrose Street; Acorn Alley was south of the present Pindar Street (despite its placing here); and Walnut Tree Yard, east of Bishopsgate Street, was between Devonshire Row and New Street. Nearly all the houses were of one-room plan. Walnut Tree Yard is the area best recorded. It was leased in 1652 to Thomas Andrews, draper and financier, a devout puritan and republican, who was Lord Mayor in 1649 and 1650 and sat in the court which tried Charles I. The property was then said to be a capital messuage called the Harp, also known as the Walnut Tree, with three small tenements adjoining, but evidently an old description was used, as all the properties shown on the plan of 1692 were listed in the Company's survey of 1651. At the east end in 1651 was

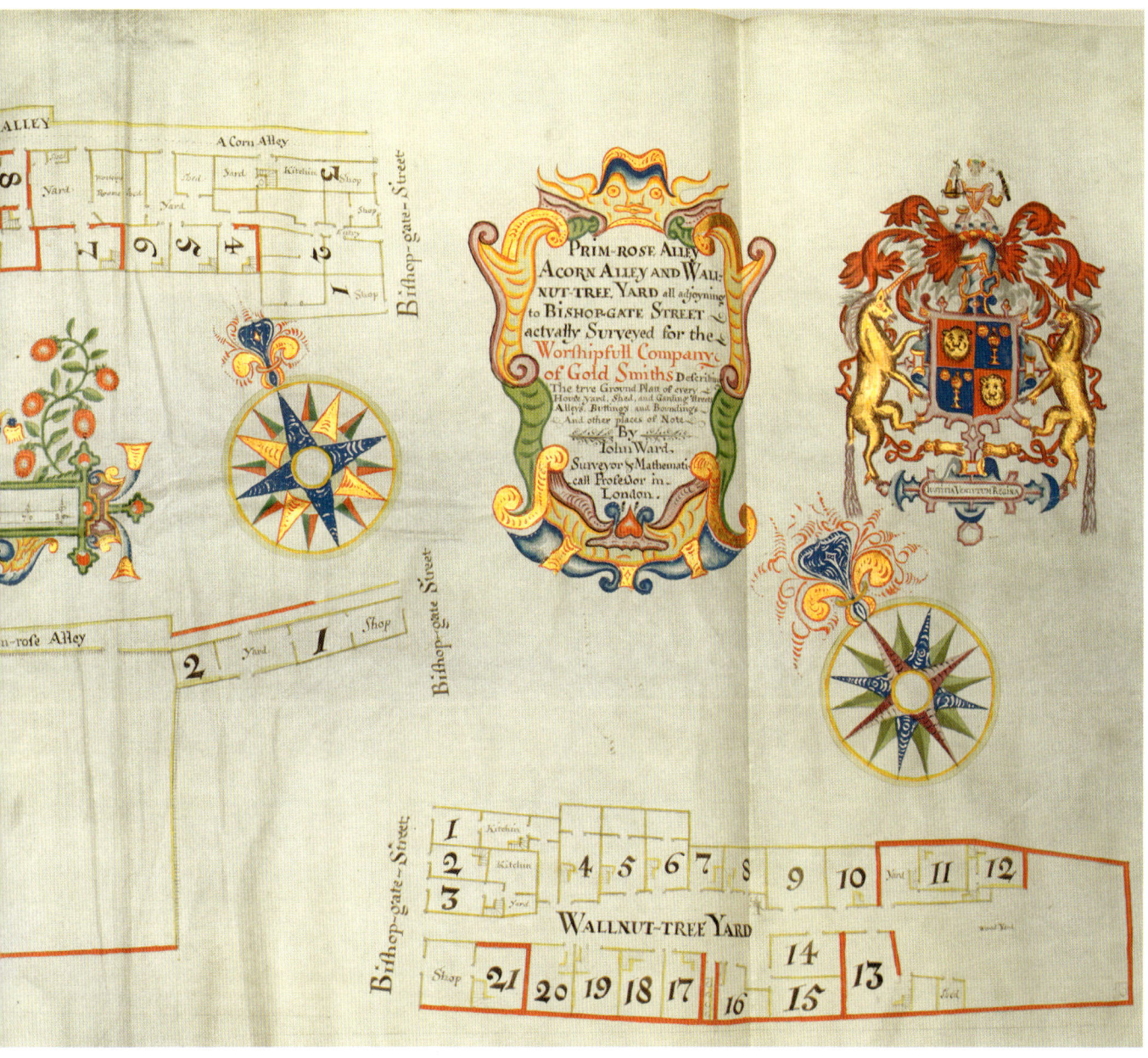

Edward Buckle's carpenter's yard, with a sawpit and a six-room brick house (No. 13 in 1692); Buckle had eight hearths there in about 1670. At the west end were the Walnut Tree (No. 21 in 1692), which was the only other partly brick house, and three houses with shops. In between were small timber houses, several of them subdivided: No. 10, with three storeys, had six occupants, only Widow Elizabeth Grainger on the ground floor having two rooms; there were three occupants at what seems to be No. 14, with three rooms and a cellar between them; and five houses had two occupants. Several dwellings had rooms over or under another. Many inhabitants had a single hearth in about 1670, though some had three or more. In 1692 there were four privies. Ward carefully draws the pump. The Andrews family still held all the houses in 1692. None was worth more than £5 a year except the four facing Bishopsgate Street (£16 to £29 each) and No. 13 (£20).[59]

Acorn Alley had nine houses in 1663, including four facing Bishopsgate Street, and twelve in 1692. Nos. 4 to 7 were probably the older houses, being largely of timber. None was worth more than £8 a year except Nos. 3 and 10 (£14 and £10 respectively).[60] The character of Primrose Alley reflected the piecemeal development of a series of gardens. At least sixteen of its houses were brick-built by 1651 and most of them were by 1692. Again the yearly values were small: probably only No. 1, at £15, exceeded £8 a year.[61] There was a 'Weaving Place' at the west end, apparently attached to No. 35, and a large wash-house at the back of No. 37. Three of the Company's boundary stones are marked. The word 'Shore' applied to the watercourse on the west and north sides, signifies a common sewer. In 1720 Strype described Primrose Alley as 'very long, narrow and ordinary', Walnut Tree Court as 'small and mean' and Acorn Court as 'very narrow and ordinary'.[62] Primrose Alley had developed into Primrose Street by 1745, and still exists as a road. By 1814 Walnut Tree Court and most of Acorn Alley had gone.

Plan 46
Sir Thomas Bludworth's mansion, Maiden Lane, 1692
John Ward   FIG. 115

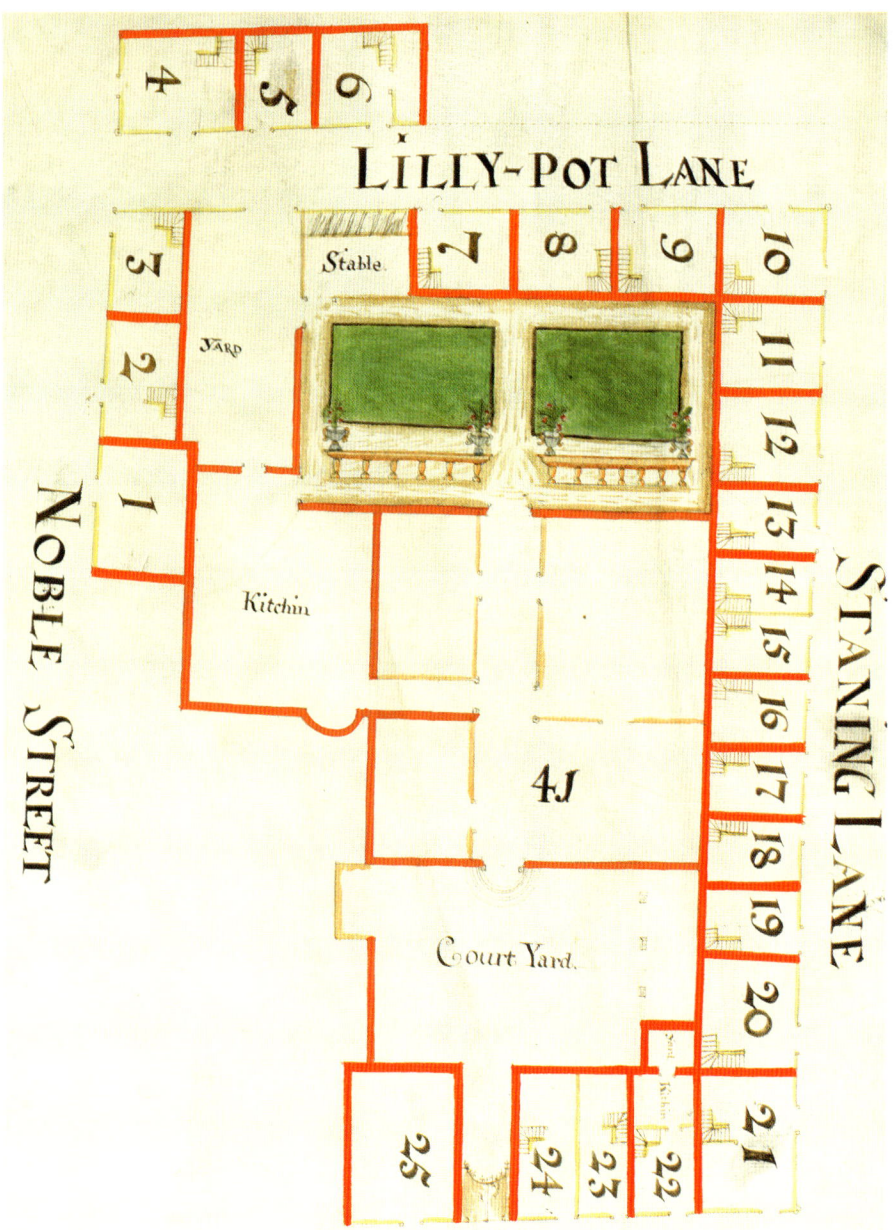

Fig. 115. Part of a plan of property in Maiden Lane, showing Sir Thomas Bludworth's mansion and adjoining houses, 1692. North is at the top.

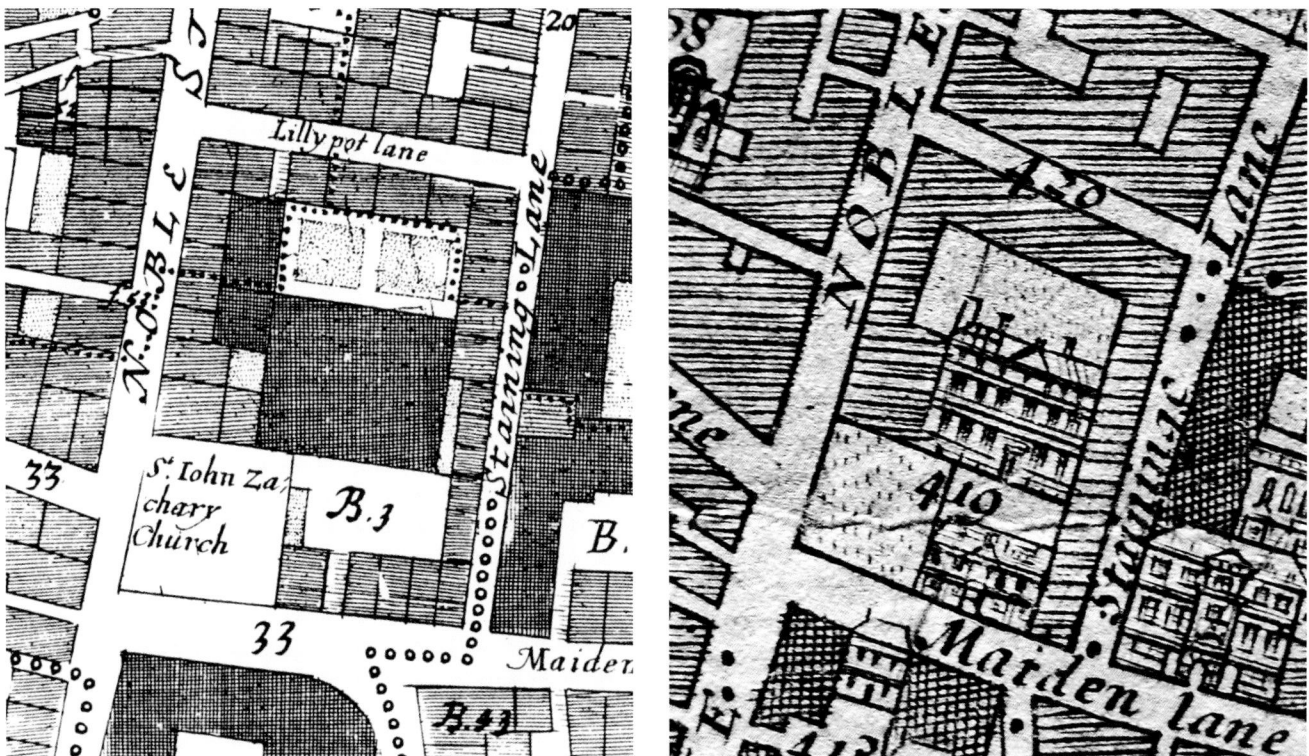

Figs 116-17. Details from Ogilby and Morgan's map of 1676 and Morgan's map of 1682 showing Bludworth's mansion.

This plan, another of John Ward's for the Goldsmiths' Company, provides an example of a City grandee's mansion almost entirely surrounded by small houses, reflecting the high value of street frontage in the City. John Olley's rule of thumb was that back ground was worth only half as much as front ground.[63] The property was between what are now Gresham Street, Noble Street, Oat Lane and Staining Lane. There had been a mansion here before the Fire, with twenty-two hearths, consisting in 1651 of hall, two parlours, withdrawing room, kitchen and other service rooms on the ground floor; great dining room, eight chambers and closets on the first floor; long gallery, two chambers and six garrets or garret chambers on the second floor; and two chambers leading to the turret. It was occupied before the Fire by Sir Thomas Bludworth (1624-82), the Lord Mayor who proved ineffective in the Fire's early stages. He had an estate worth £3,000 a year in 1660.[64]

After the Fire Bludworth rebuilt the mansion, with seventeen hearths, and he also financed the rebuilding of Nos. 1, 7-9, 11, 14, 15 and 17-25.[65] Morgan's map suggests that Nos. 22-25 were intended to give the impression of a gatehouse (Fig. 117). The plan shows the mansion's gateway, courtyard, garden, kitchen and stable, including the plants on the garden terrace, but not in any detail its internal arrangements. Sir Richard Levet, Lord Mayor in 1700, later lived in the mansion and kept his mayoralty there. His inventory of 1711 records twenty-four rooms, including great and little parlours, dining room, long gallery, servants' hall and brewhouse. He had an equally large house at Kew, where the inventory compilers found his two coaches, chariot and three horses.[66] The corner omitted on the plan was occupied by the churchyard of St John Zachary, not rebuilt after the Fire, and several houses in Noble Street (Fig. 116). Almost all the surrounding houses were of one-room plan, with three and a half storeys and cellar,[67] including timber-fronted shops on the ground floor. St John Zachary's churchyard still exists, and the land to its east is also open, while the rest of the block is occupied by a single office building.

Plan 47
Angel Court and Bishopsgate Street, 1697
John Olley
FIG. 118

The Angel, immediately north of St Ethelburga's, was a medieval inn, first recorded in the fourteenth century. By 1466 it was in the hands of the Bridge House, though like many corporate owners the Bridge House later had to re-purchase its

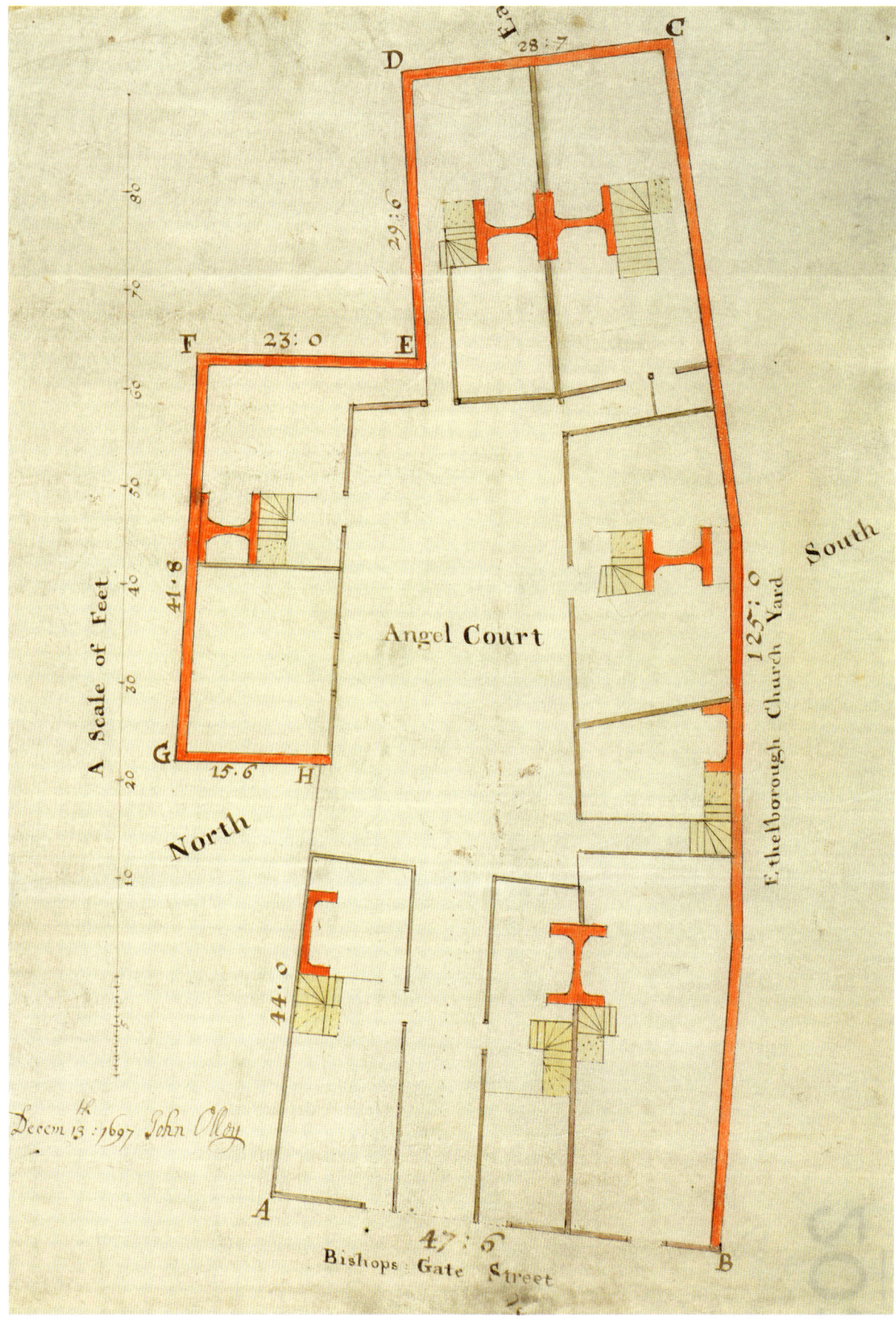

Fig. 118. Angel Court and part of Bishopsgate Street, 1697.

Fig. 119. Houses in Bishopsgate Street in front of Angel Court, with St Ethelburga's on the right —detail from a print of 1736 by William Henry Toms after Robert West.

property from the Crown because it was subject to payments for a 'superstitious use' (prayers for the soul of a deceased owner), which enabled the Crown to seize it.[68] When the site shown on the plan was leased in 1649 it consisted of the Angel Inn at the front, a yard and two stables in the middle and another stable at the back. Richard Hardmett, citizen and skinner, agreed in that year to demolish the inn within five years and spend £800 on a new house 'of oken tymber and other materialls'. In fact he built more houses, described in 1698 as eight houses and a warehouse, and these are what the plan shows.[69] On the Bishopsgate Street frontage he created three elaborately-decorated timber houses of two-room plan and three and a half storeys (Fig. 119). These were evidently not completed within the five years allowed, as the pilasters bore the date 1657. In Angel Court the plan shows four houses of two-room plan and one smaller one, though by 1697 a ground-floor room of the house north of the yard had been turned into a warehouse let separately to a grocer.[70] The larger houses in the yard had central staircases and chimneys, and two were lobby-entry houses. Apart from the outer wall of the site as a whole, all the walls were of timber. The new lessee in 1698 was Thomas Haughton of Writtle, Doctor of Divinity. Hardmett's buildings were eventually rebuilt under a lease of 1772.[71]

Plans 48-53
Houndsditch, 1712-18
John and Isaac Olley
FIGS 120-25

These adjoining properties were on the south side of Houndsditch near its eastern end.[72] The whole of the south side of Houndsditch had been built on the former ditch outside London Wall and therefore belonged to the City. On the Copperplate Map of c.1555 the site of the ditch contains tenters (wooden frames on which cloth was stretched so as to dry evenly) but virtually no buildings. This changed in or about the 1580s,[73] and probably many of the timber buildings recorded in Houndsditch just over a century later were of that period, albeit with much alteration. Houndsditch was described by Strype in 1720 as 'a place of a good trade, and of note for salesmen and brokers, whose dealings are in apparel, linen and upholsterers goods, and chiefly second hand goods'.[74]

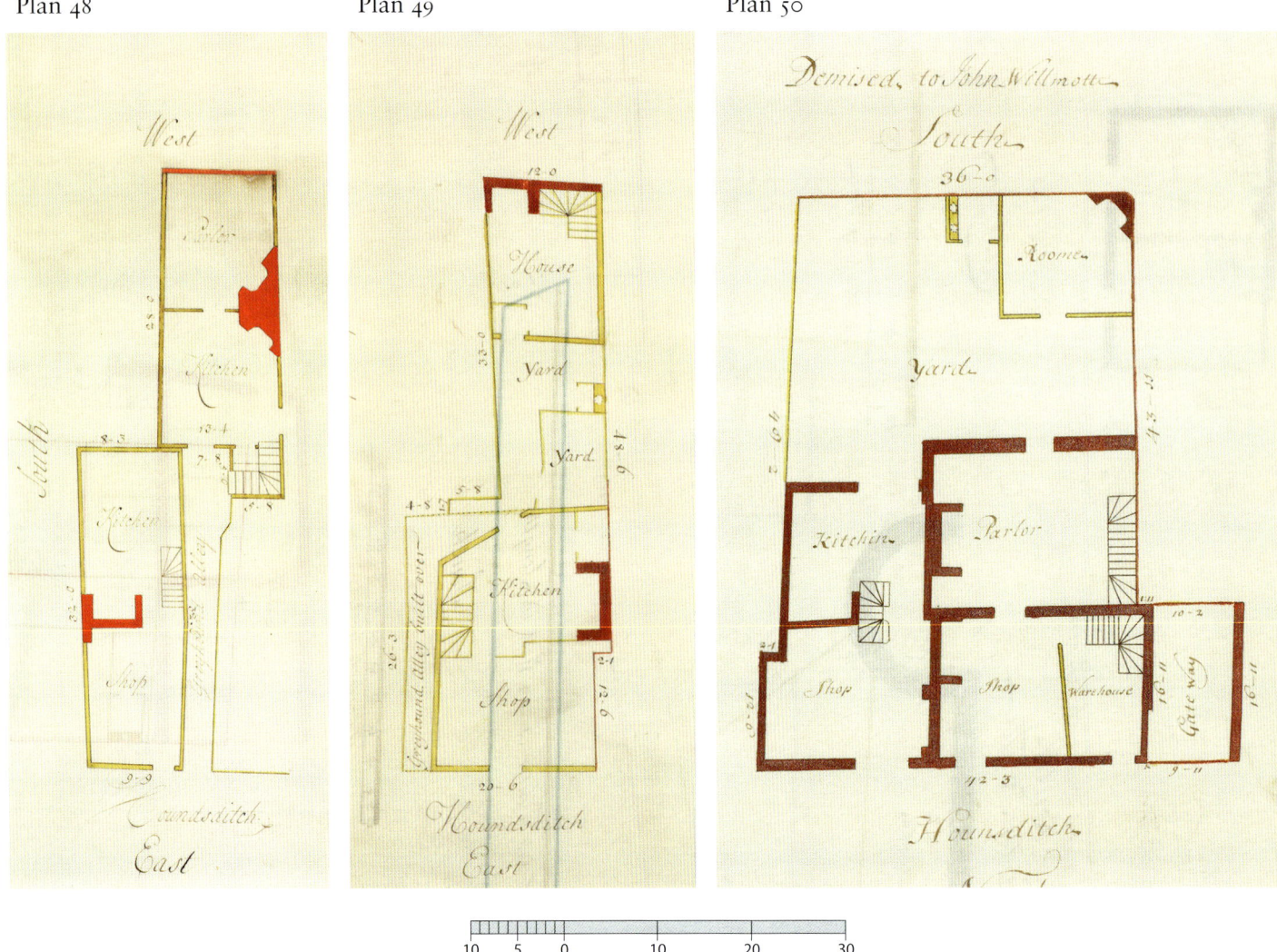

Plan 48. Two houses, let in 1715 to Thomas Ambrose, brewer. Re-let to him in 1719 on a building lease.

Plan 49. Two houses, let in 1661 to Nicholas Harding, citizen and merchant taylor, who had rebuilt them, in timber, by 1672. In 1717 the front house was sub-let for £20 a year and the back one for £3 a year. Mary Rozer, widow, who occupied the front house, acquired the lease in that year.[75]

Plan 50. Two houses, on separate leases until 1712. The left-hand one was let in 1624 to William Marshe, citizen and merchant taylor, on condition that he rebuild it completely. Evidently he did so in brick. In 1652, when leased and occupied by Robert Marshe, it contained shop and kitchen, four chambers, two garrets and two cellars, and presumably had three and a half storeys. The right-hand house, also of brick, had probably been rebuilt too, and was known as the Shears. The gateway led to Thomas Ambrose's brewery, which occupied all the ground behind this part of Houndsditch. Both houses were let in 1712 to John Willmott, citizen and joiner of London, who was already in possession of the Shears and two rooms of Marshe's house.[76]

Plan 51. Buckley's Court. This property was let to John Buckley, citizen and carpenter, on a building lease in 1623. In 1652 it contained two houses of three and a half storeys, probably at the front, and a carpenter's yard. In that year it was re-let to Buckley for sixty-one years, and the timber tenements of Buckley's Court were presumably created shortly afterwards. Buckley died in about

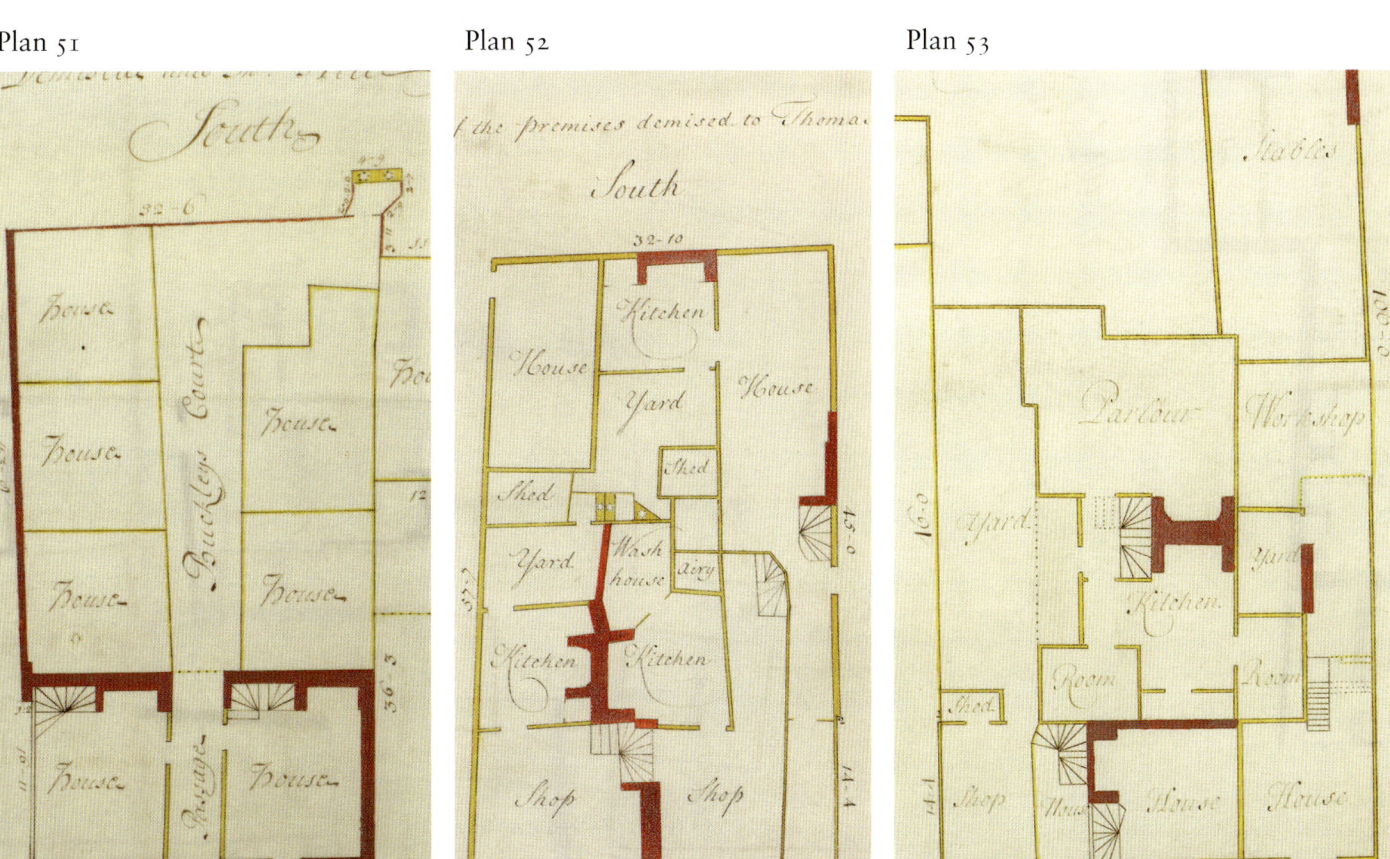

Figs 120-25. Adjoining houses on the south side of Houndsditch, 1712-18. North is to the bottom right. Plan 51 wrongly included a house accessed from Buckley's Court but belonging to the property in Plan 52 and correctly shown there, so it is omitted here from Plan 51. On some of these plans, as with others from the City Lands plan books, the other side of the page shows through.

1673. In 1712 the two front tenements, known as the Cock and the Three Ladles, were sub-let at £14 a year each. Three of the back tenements were sub-let at £6 each, two at £5 each and one was let to 'several inmates'. The City Lands Committee referred to 'the precariousness of tenants in such small houses'.[77] John Hill of Enfield, brewer, became the lessee in 1712. A house on the next plot, accessed from Buckley's Court, was wrongly included in the lease at first and so is incorrectly marked on the plan.[78]

Plan 52. Four houses, somewhat eccentrically arranged. They were let to John Barnes, citizen and cooper, in 1652, and Thomas Hatley, citizen and mercer, in 1718, when they were described as the Three Horseshoes and two houses adjoining. The house in the top left corner was entered from Buckley's Court on the next plot. The lease of 1718 was a building lease.[79]

Plan 53. Three houses, as described in the lease, though the plan seems to show four. At the back, adjoining London Wall, were extensive stables in Flying Horse Yard (omitted here). The central house was a lobby-entry house. The property was let to Richard Dewin, cordwainer, in 1615, Alice Dewin, widow, in 1652, and Thomas Love, citizen and leatherseller, in 1712.

Plan 54
Bull and Mouth Street, 1717
Heber Lands
FIG. 126

Fig. 126. Bull and Mouth Street, 1717.

Annual Rents

No.	L	S	D		L	S	D		L	S	D		L	S	D		L	S	D
1	22	0	0	15	10	–	–	29	10	–	–	43	9	–	–
2	24	–	–	16	14	–	–	30	14	–	–	44	9	–	–
3	24	–	–	17	120	–	–	31	14	–	–	45	9	–	–
4	20	–	–	18	10	–	–	32	14	–	–	46	9	–	–
5	20	–	–	19	10	–	–	33	12	–	–	47	10	–	–
6	35	–	–	20	7	–	–	34	13	–	–	48	12	–	–
7	32	–	–	21	8	–	–	35	14	–	–	49	10	–	–
8	10	–	–	22	7	–	–	36	10	–	–	50	10	–	–
9	13	–	–	23	7	–	–	37	10	–	–	51	8	–	–
10	20	–	–	24	10	–	–	38	10	–	–	52	9	–	–
11	24	–	–	25	9	–	–	39	10	–	–	53	9	–	–
12	40	–	–	26	9	–	–	40	10	–	–	54	9	1	–
13	12	–	–	27	9	–	–	41	10	–	–
14	10	–	–	28	9	–	–	42	9	–	–

Survey'd By Heber Lands 1717.

Bull and Mouth Street was one of several new streets created by private owners after the Great Fire.[80] Nevertheless, the layout was strongly affected by the medieval past. Until the Dissolution of the Monasteries, the precinct wall of Greyfriars ran north-south through the middle of the area shown here, separating the two plots edged in red in Fig. 127.[81] East of the wall was a medieval mansion known as Northumberland Place. The later deeds identify its exact site by making clear that Northumberland Place was converted into the Bull and Mouth Inn.[82] The mansion is first recorded in 1252; was owned by members of the Percy family, Earls of Northumberland, from 1343 to 1403; briefly belonged to Henry IV's queen, Joanna of Navarre; was recovered by the Earl of Northumberland in the late fifteenth century; and was sold to the king between 1534 and 1544. It was the headquarters of the King's Printing House from about 1600 to 1625, and became the Bull and Mouth Inn in or shortly before 1629, when it was leased to Thomas Greene, whose son Henry was later innkeeper there.[83] Its entrance was from St Martin's le Grand, on approximately the site of the passage shown on the 1717 plan. The property probably always included houses facing St Martin's le Grand —on the green plot to the east in Fig. 127.[84]

Converting a mansion into a livery hall was easy, because the needs were similar (see Plans 23-24, 105-09), but that did not apply so clearly to

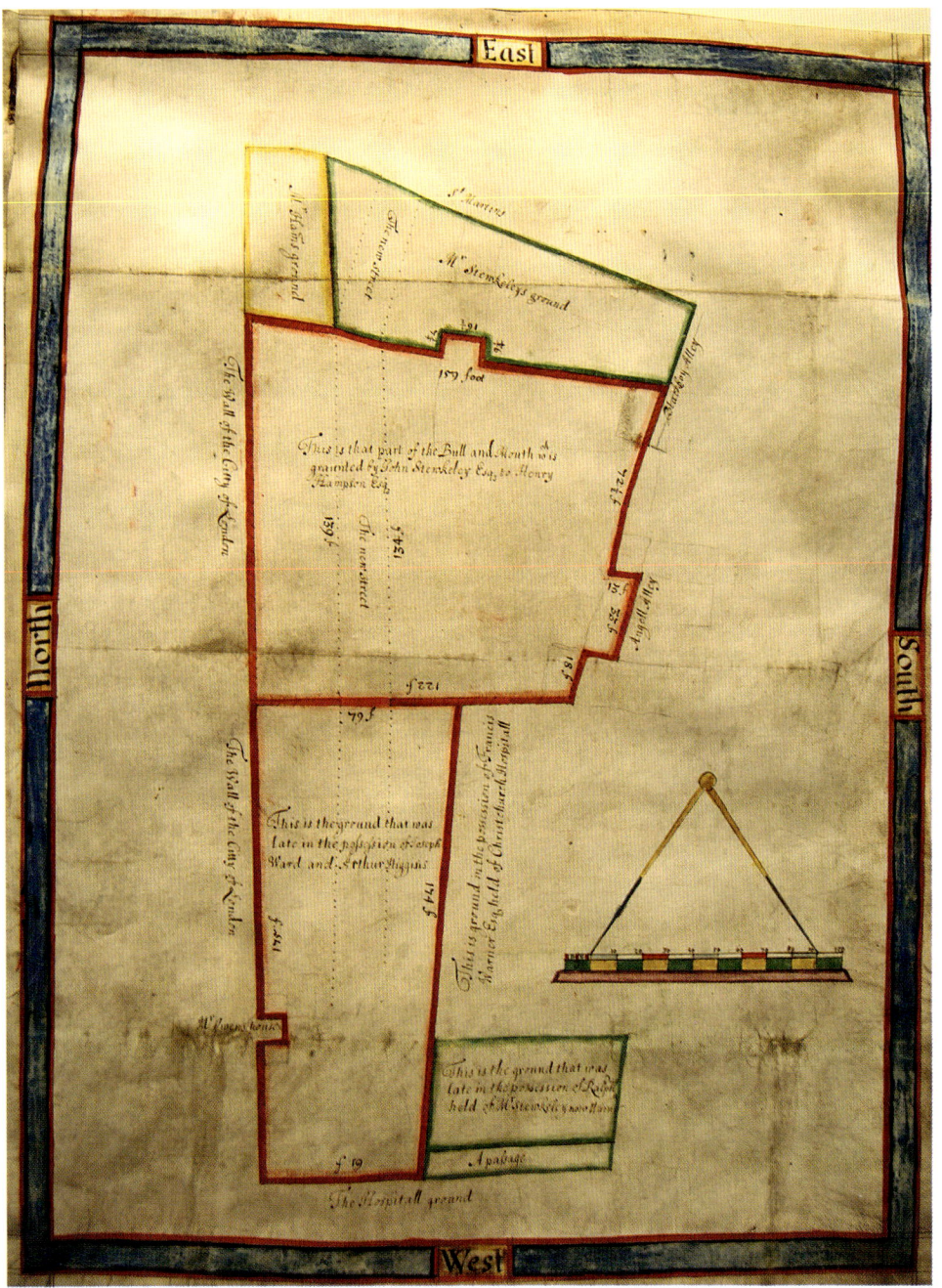

Fig. 127. Plan drawn in 1668 distinguishing the various parts of the Stewkley property in and around the planned Bull and Mouth Street and showing (faintly) the line of the new street. North is to the left. The properties to the west edged in green and red are the former Greyfriars land bought by Thomas Stewkley in 1650; the other land edged red is the former Northumberland Place; that edged green is houses in St Martin le Grand; and that edged yellow is a former garden belonging to the City and not part of the Stewkley estate.

an inn. In particular, an inn did not really need a great hall, and this resulted in the other major building on the 1717 plan. In 1655 the Society of Friends, or Quakers, secured the hall as their first London meeting place. As one of them put it later, 'Some part of an ancient great house or building within Aldersgate was taken for a meeting place the other part of it with a yard being before made a publick inn for carriers and travellers ... having for a sign the Bull and Mouth'. This 'great meeting place' was said to hold a thousand people.[85] Thus both major buildings on the plan had their origins in the decline of a medieval mansion.

The land west of the precinct wall, formerly gardens belonging to Greyfriars, long remained unbuilt on and secluded. The 1616 plan (Plan 20) shows a bowling alley on part of it, and Butchers' Hall Lane (then Fowle Lane and now King Edward Street) obstructed by a gate. Even in 1650 there were just three dwellings there: that of Joseph Ward, a twister of silk, next to Northumberland Place, that of Arthur Higgens, clothworker, at the west end, and in the plot facing Butchers' Hall Lane (edged green in Fig. 127) that of Ralph Day, carpenter, who had a timber yard there. The latter plot contained five dwellings by 1666.[86]

Sir Thomas Stewkley owned Northumberland Place by 1629, and in 1650 Thomas Stewkley, esquire, acquired the former Greyfriars land west of it for £360.[87] All the buildings on the Stewkley land were burnt in 1666 except Arthur Higgens' dwelling, which was protected by gardens on three sides and London Wall on the fourth.[88] The Stewkleys decided to increase the value of their property by creating a new street eighteen feet wide, intended to be called Stewkley Street, from St Martin's le Grand to Butchers' Hall Lane, as set out in Fig. 127. Building leases were agreed in 1668.

The deeds make clear that the inn and the meeting house were rebuilt on their old sites. Most of the property was let to Henry Hampson of Mitcham, who constructed the new street, but the former timber yard was let to Francis Warner, who also held adjoining land, and the St Martin's le Grand plots to three separate tenants, one of them, John Nesbett, rebuilding his house in almost the same place as before the Fire.[89] Fifty-one new houses were built, mostly of one-room plan, as well as a new Bull and Mouth Inn and a new Quaker meeting house.

In 1692 the property was purchased by Christ's Hospital for £5,700.[90] The plan was commissioned by the Hospital in 1717, when the leases granted in 1668 were about to expire. Heber Lands was paid £25 for drawing it.[91] His plan is the best of a major carrying inn. In 1690 the Bull and Mouth Inn (Figs 128, 129) had six packhorse, waggon or caravan services each week and one fortnightly service.[92] The plan shows the extensive stables, the taphouse, the kitchens, the parlour and the two lace chambers. The latter highlight the role of London inns as centres of marketing. In 1720 Strype described the Bull and Mouth as 'large, and well built, and of a good resort by those that bring bone lace, where the shopkeepers and others come to buy it'.[93] The Bull and Mouth was later one of London's main coaching inns, and was rebuilt by Edward Sherman in 1830. As for the meeting house, this was for decades a scene of determined persecution, with frequent visits from soldiers, numerous imprisonments and much violence. Apart from 1697-1700 the Quakers continued to use the meeting house until 1740, after which other denominations took it over. In 1890-95 Bull and Mouth Street disappeared when a new General Post Office headquarters (now Nomura House) was built there.[94]

Fig. 128. The courtyard of the Bull and Mouth Inn in 1830, looking north-west—print by W. Watkins after T.H. Shepherd.

Fig. 129. The entrance to the Bull and Mouth Inn, Bull and Mouth Street, 1806—watercolour by Frederick Nash.

Plan 55
Leadenhall Street, 1719
Thomas Badeslade   FIG. 130

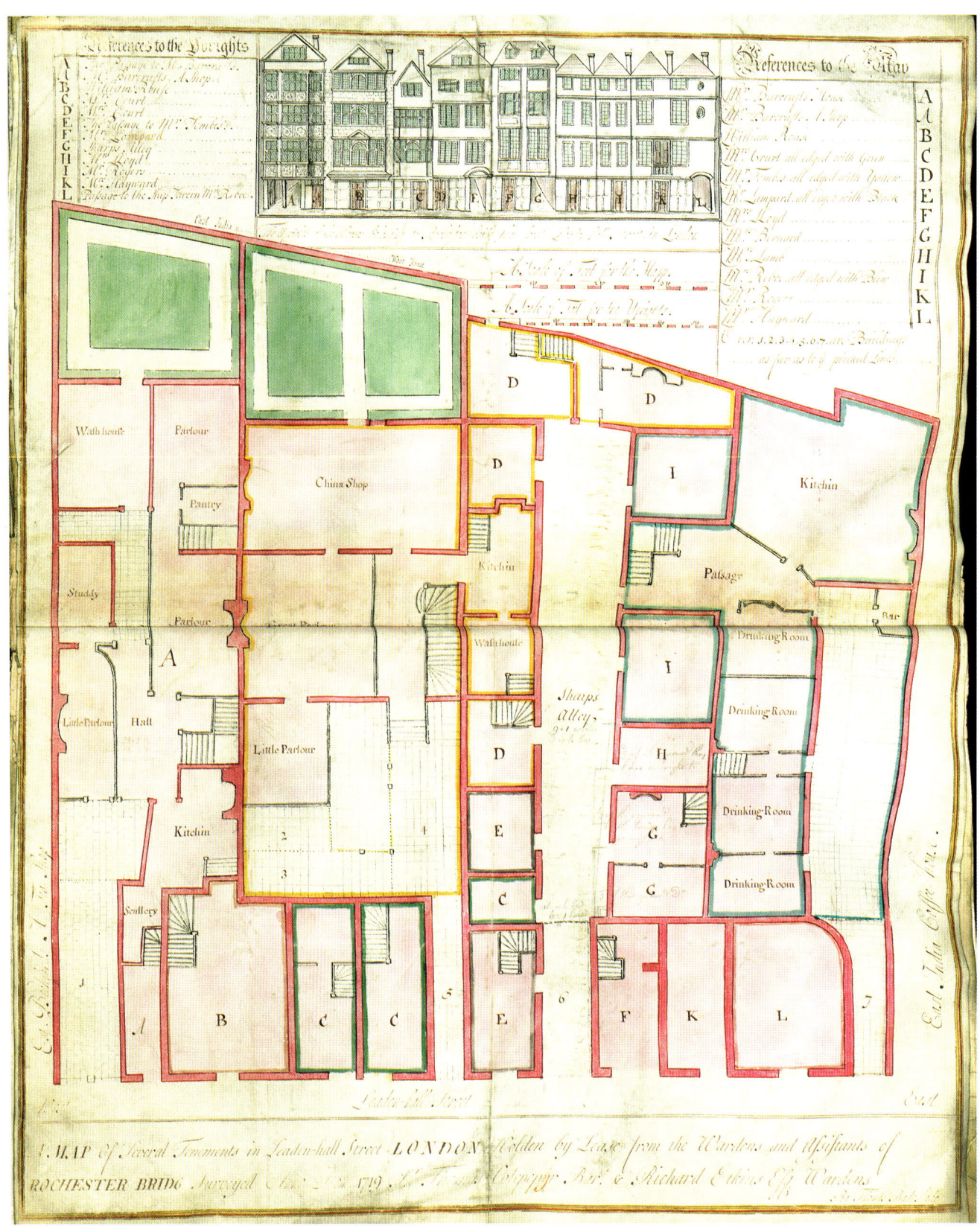

Fig. 130.   Houses in Leadenhall Street, 1719. North is at the top.

Fig. 131. Elevation of the Leadenhall Street houses from Fig. 130.

This plan shows property on the north side of Leadenhall Street acquired by Rochester Bridge Trust in about 1400.[95] The Trust's plan of the property of about 1712 was a pictorial one with what were clearly imaginary facades for the buildings.[96] Here instead, seven years later, is a ground plan with an elevation (or 'uprights') of a fine row of wholly or largely pre-Fire houses. It was drawn by Thomas Badeslade, who was described as a surveyor and mathematician (he was also an engineer). His main work was estate maps in a range of counties, but he lived in London; in 1719 his address was the Inner Temple. His first known map was drawn in 1712 and he died in 1744.[97] Badeslade seems occasionally to omit stairs and fireplaces.

The street houses were all of three and a half or four and a half storeys, and almost all were one room deep at ground level, though at least some of these had two rooms on each floor above. One, marked D on the elevation, can be dated to 1590, as a new fifty year lease was granted then as recompense for rebuilding it.[98] For two there are probate inventories. Robert Davies, citizen and haberdasher, leased and occupied house C on the elevation. He had five hearths in 1666 but four in 1674. Davies' inventory of 1681, which does not indicate storeys, can probably be related to this house as follows: cellar; on the ground floor, kitchen and dining room (with two tables, eleven turkey-work chairs and tapestries); on the first floor, parlour and chamber over the dining room; on the second floor, chamber over the parlour and 'the greene chamber & little roome adjoyneinge'; and a garret. The most valuable furnishings, including tapestries, were in the chamber over the dining room, almost certainly at the front.[99] Henry Smith, a merchant taylor by company but a grocer by trade, both leased and occupied house K in the elevation and L on the plan (shown on a plan of 1687 as square rather than with a rounded corner). The plan of 1719 shows a single room on the ground floor, but upper floors extended over the passage, and at about twenty-three by twenty-two feet two or more rooms per floor were possible; perhaps extra rooms over the Ship and Turtle were leased, as they were in 1741. There were five hearths in 1674. Smith's inventory of 1676 records shop, kitchen (presumably at the back of the ground floor), dining room (with an oval table and twelve leather chairs), room at the front of the first floor, 'the long chamber' (perhaps over the Ship and Turtle), two rooms at the front and back of the second floor, and a garret. All upper rooms except the dining room had beds in them, the best room with by far the most valuable furnishings being the front room on the second floor.[100] William Hayward, likewise a merchant taylor by company but a grocer by trade, was lessee of the same house in 1716, and dwelt in Leadenhall Street in St Andrew Undershaft parish in a house of about the correct rent, so probably occupied the house too. The rooms in his inventory of that year were similar, except that the dining room was now called the parlour (it was similarly furnished with tables and chairs), there is no sign of the long chamber, and the garret had been divided into two. Hayward's grocery wares were worth the spectacular sum of £4,981.[101]

The plan shows how, where plots were deep, the backland might be entirely separate from the street houses. The backland divided broadly into four plots, their north-south boundaries sometimes not corresponding to those of the street houses, and each of the four had developed in a different way. From west to east, the first plot accommodated a large house with at least three parlours and a garden. The second contained a high-class shop set back from the street, run by Henry Tombs, china man, who evidently relied on reputation rather than passing trade. His premises had been rebuilt in or about 1675 (Fig. 132), though not as a shop; in 1678 the future china shop was a parlour.[102] The third plot contained Sharps Alley, usually known as Shafts Alley, a reference to the storing there until the 1550s of the maypole belonging to St Andrew Undershaft. Fig. 133, showing the west side of Shafts Alley, provides a rare view of one of the City's alleys, almost certainly with pre-Fire buildings. The alley's dwellings had from one to three hearths in 1666.[103] By 1719, two houses in the alley had been taken over by the house to the west, one (marked C) by one of the street houses, and several by the inn to the east. The fourth plot was occupied by an inn called the Ship and Turtle, with a large kitchen and four drinking rooms.

Subsequent plans show piecemeal changes, including some re-facing of the street houses, the apparent rebuilding of those marked A, B, F and K on the elevation, and the conversion of the gardens to warehouses and a yard, but some of the pre-Fire buildings survived until the entire site was redeveloped in 1881.[104] The Ship and Turtle continued to operate until 2008, though latterly under a different name.[105] The whole site is now occupied by the Leadenhall Building (the 'Cheesegrater').

Fig. 132. Elevation of the front of what had been Tombs' china shop, as rebuilt in about 1675, from a plan of 1796.

Fig. 133. Elevation of houses on the west side of Shafts Alley in 1797, from a plan by Daniel Alexander.

OUTSIDE THE CITY

Plan 56
Rose Street, Covent Garden, 1638
Fig. 134

This is a remarkably early plan of speculative building and shows one of the developments of small houses in the 1630s which Charles I was seeking to prevent. The Earl of Bedford's regularly laid-out development of the 1630s in Covent Garden stopped to the north at an earlier brick wall along the north side of what is now Floral Street; the wall turned south-west along the east side of what became Rose Street (Fig. 135). Beyond the wall much less control was exercised over development. Long Acre was laid out in 1615, and by 1635 only one plot between Long Acre and the wall remained undeveloped, towards the west; it was 'handsomely plainted with trees and flowers'. This was the land shown on the plan. Nicholas Stone, the King's Master Mason, who lived on the east side of it in Long Acre, described it as 'beinge in proporcon like a carpenters square'. The Earl sold it in 1635 to Gabriel Essingwood, one of the king's coachmen, and he sold it in May 1638, apparently little altered, to John Ward, citizen and girdler, and John Parker. Their intention was to build sixteen

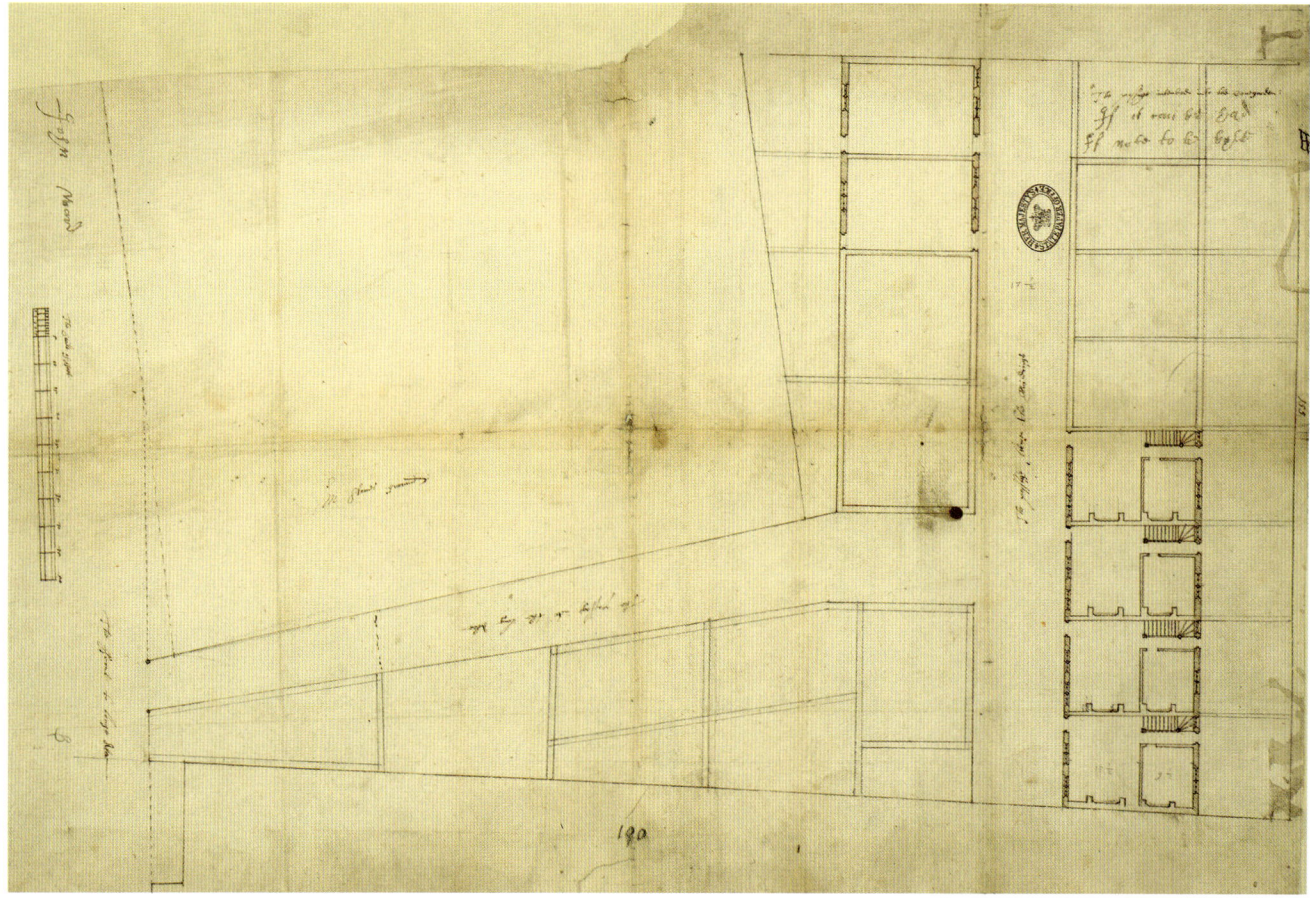

Fig. 134.   A housing development in White Rose Street and Red Rose Street, Covent Garden, 1638.
North is to the left, as is Long Acre.

houses: one in Long Acre, three in an alley leading southwards, to be called White Rose Street, and twelve in an east-west alley, at the end of the first, to be called Red Rose Street. Ward built other houses on the Bedford estate, including a house in the piazza.[106] The plan was probably drawn to assist Ward and Parker in laying out an awkwardly-shaped site. It was signed by Ward but apparently not drawn by him, as his signature and his note about the passage to Covent Garden differ from the other writing on it.

By October 1638, when the Privy Council sent Inigo Jones to investigate, four houses in the east-west alley had been completed and two started (one of them, on the site of the present Lamb and Flag public house, already sold to Thomas Constable); these are evidently the ones shown in more detail. Jones used the plan to examine what was proposed, and possibly it was then updated (perhaps by Jones himself) to show the buildings completed or under construction. Clearly it was never returned, as it remains among the State Papers. Although Jones referred to the 'pestering of such places with allyes of meane houses', the houses completed were seventeen and a half feet wide, with two rooms per floor, thirteen and a half and nine and a half feet deep, together with small yards. They provide an early example of the two-room plan with a rear staircase to one side. They must have been of brick, as otherwise Jones would have mentioned it. Jones criticised the fact that the development was creating a blind alley. Ward marked the house-site in the south-east corner as a passage to Covent Garden if that could be obtained (if not it was to be built on), but Jones argued that Lady Stanhope was unlikely to give up part of her garden for this purpose. The Privy Council summoned Ward and criticised his 'houses fitt for mechanicks only & persons of meane quallitie', with 'but one narrow entry or passage to them all', and ordered that they be reformed in a manner to be approved by Jones. Parker at some stage bound himself not to build houses in Long Acre without a licence.[107]

These problems were overcome by selling the site in February 1639 to Richard Harris, who was already involved in some of Ward's ventures (the occupant of a house built by Ward and Harris in

Catherine Street complained in 1635 that 'yt raynes into every roome of ye said house'). By November he had sold three brick houses of three and a half storeys next to Constable's on the north side of Red Rose Street to Nicholas Stone, together with the ground adjoining Long Acre on which Stone was to build two houses, one of them partly over a stone arch. In 1640 Harris succeeded in obtaining the Earl of Bedford's permission for the link Jones had thought unlikely, between the east end of Red Rose Street and New Street, and completed the development. He later claimed to have lost £2,000 on it, to his 'utter ruyne & undoeing', though the Rose Street properties are marked 'Harris' on John Lacy's plan of Covent Garden in 1673.[108]

By the nineteenth century Rose Street had become a slum. Part of it was removed in the 1860s by the creation of Garrick Street and the westward extension of Floral Street, but much of the layout of the 1630s remains today (Fig. 135).[109]

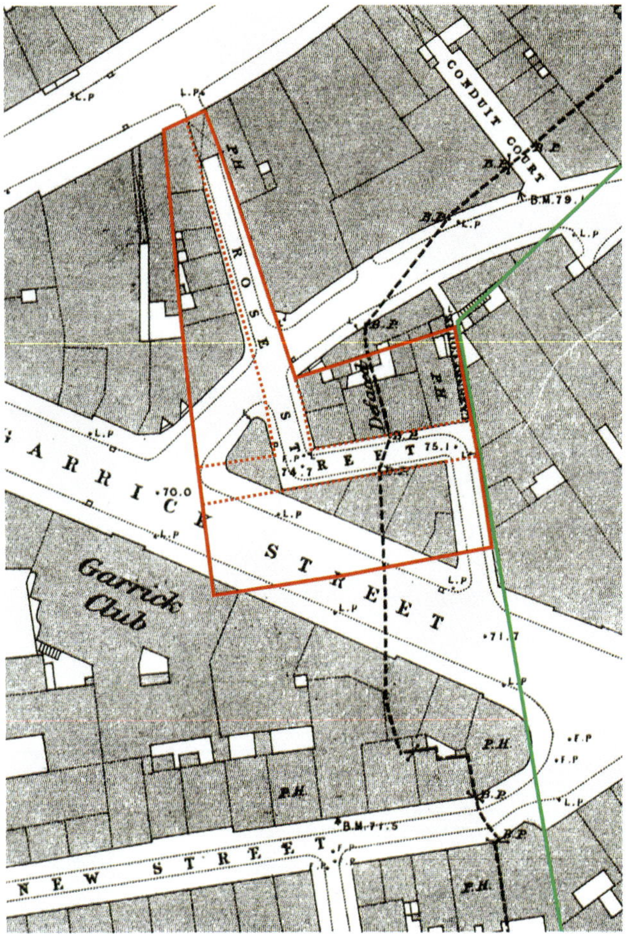

Fig. 135. The approximate site of John Ward's development of 1638 marked in red on the Ordnance Survey map of 1871, with Long Acre at the top; Ward's streets are marked by dotted red lines. The green line is the wall of *c.*1610. The orientation of Long Acre was incorrectly shown in 1638 and has been adjusted here. White Rose Street, most of Red Rose Street and part of the passage obtained by Harris to link Red Rose Street and New Street remained in 1871, as they do today, but Garrick Street and Floral Street (shown here curving across Rose Street) had obliterated much of the development.

Plan 57
Wapping Street and Gravel Lane, Wapping, 1676
FIG. 136

Bridewell Hospital owned a large, compact estate in Wapping, stretching about 400 yards along the river front. In July 1673 a fire destroyed nearly 200 of Bridewell's houses in Wapping together with many others.[110] This plan records part of the rebuilding. The property concerned was a long strip between the Thames, about where Wapping Station is now, and Cinnamon Street, extending west at two places to Gravel Lane (by the 1740s known as Wapping Dock Street). Before the fire it contained a house on the north side of Wapping Street and two on the east side of Gravel Lane, together with a wharf by the Thames and a yard behind the houses. It was let to John Buckinham, a mariner of Rotherhithe. He sub-let it by 1668 to John Wilson, who was living in one of the Gravel Lane houses by 1672.

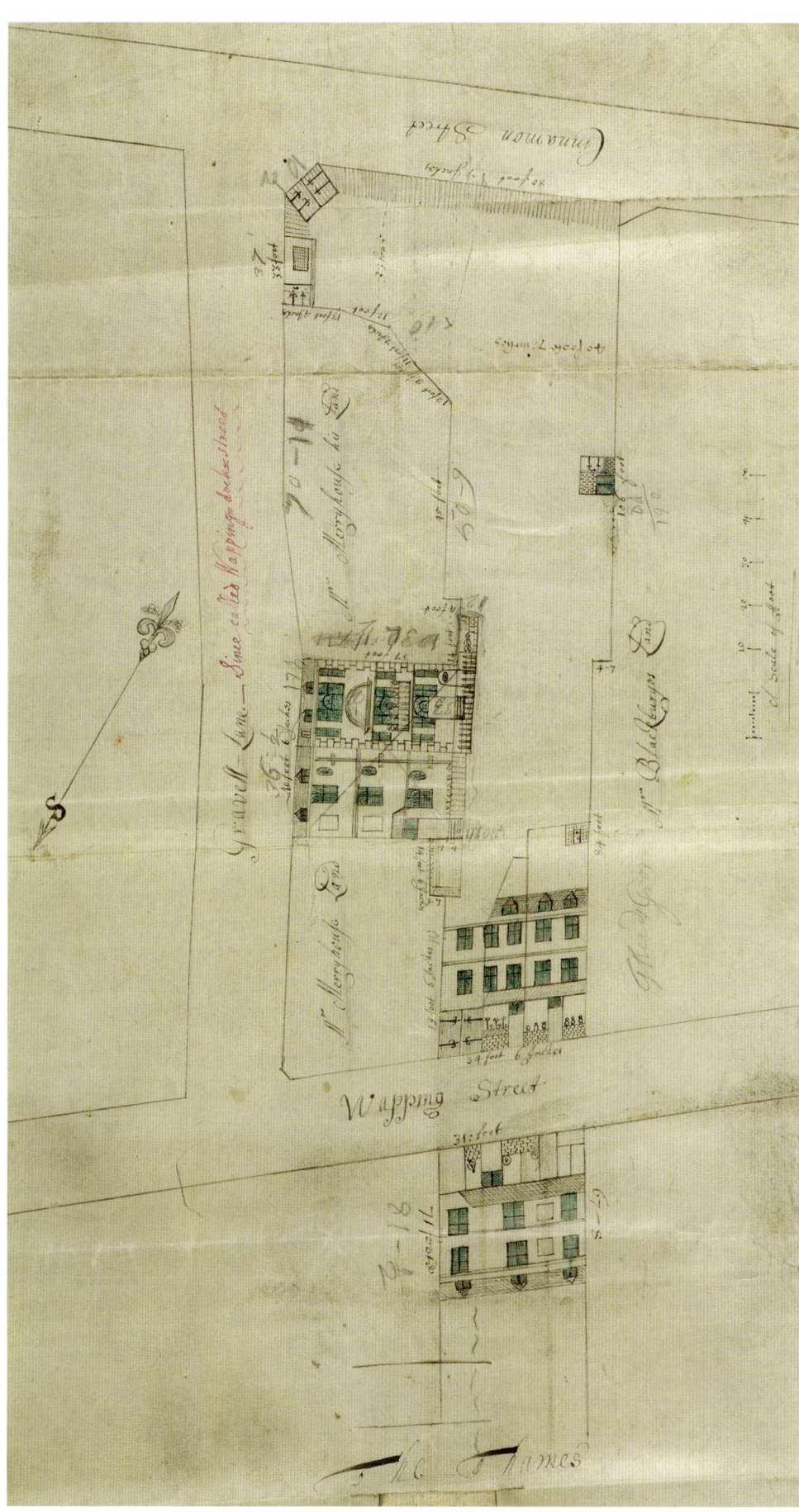

Fig. 136. Property in Wapping Street and Gravel Lane, Wapping, 1676.

Wilson is described in a later lease as a citizen and haberdasher, but he traded as a timber or deal merchant, and a plan of 1668 records the yard as Mr Wilson's deal yard. Wilson described the fire as resulting almost in his 'utter ruine and undoeing'. After the fire, he acquired the lease himself, borrowed heavily and built the six or seven new houses shown on the plan. The King and Lord Mayor had required that the new houses in the burnt area be of brick and 'upright' without jetties or bay windows, and the lease included this requirement. They also required that the streets be widened to twenty feet, and a strip of nine feet had been taken from the property to widen Wapping Street.[111]

Bridewell's other post-fire leases generally contain street plans with the relevant plots outlined. Why this plan alone was different and who drew it are unknown. It provides a lovingly detailed view, extending even to the metalwork of the yard gates. The impressive house in Gravel Lane, with a balcony, elaborate windows and quoins (Fig. 137), was presumably Wilson's own; whether this was really the side facing the yard rather than the street is uncertain. The shops appear to have jars and other items displayed on the counters. Some of the houses in Wapping Street have been distorted to fit within the property boundaries. Houses on adjoining holdings are of course ignored. Mrs Blackborrow's property to the east was also a timber yard.[112]

Plan 58
Blackman Street, Southwark, c.1678
Fig. 138

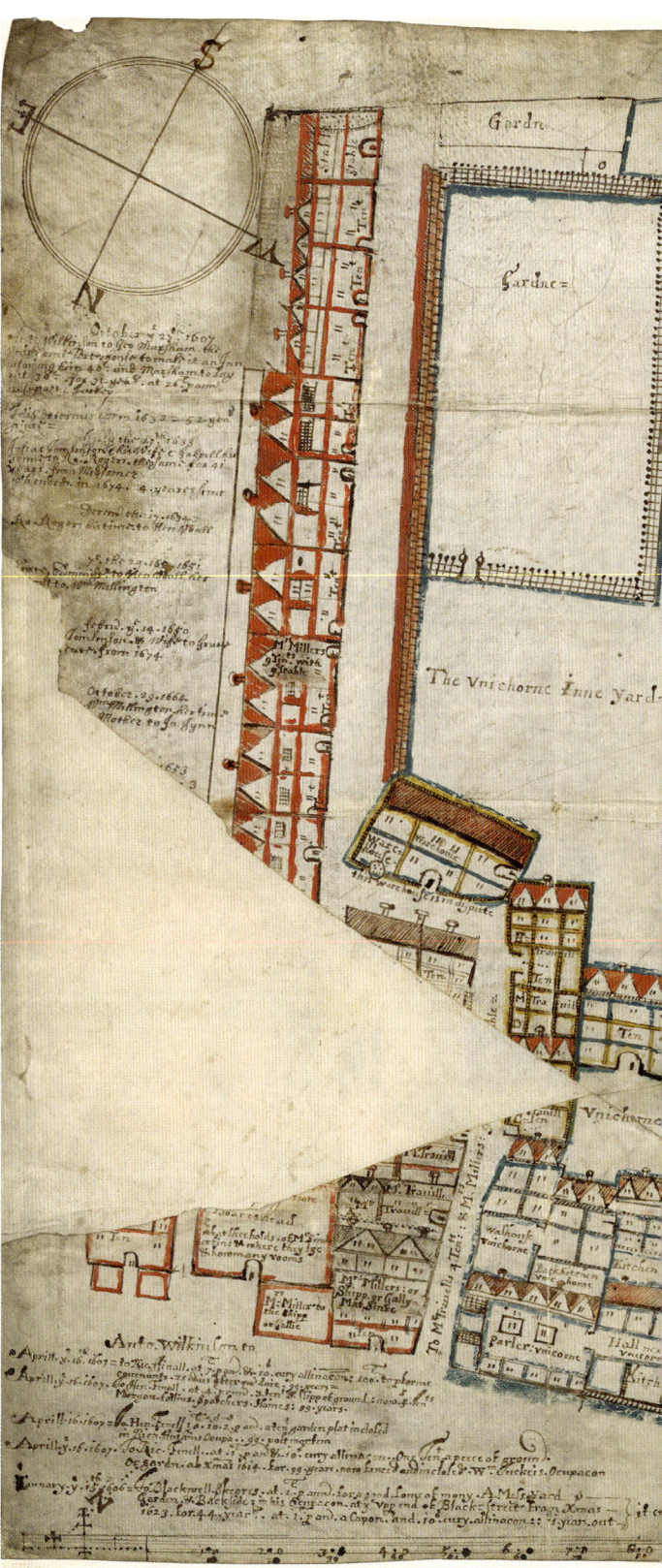

Fig. 137. Detail from Fig. 136 showing houses in Gravel Lane, including what was probably John Wilson's house.

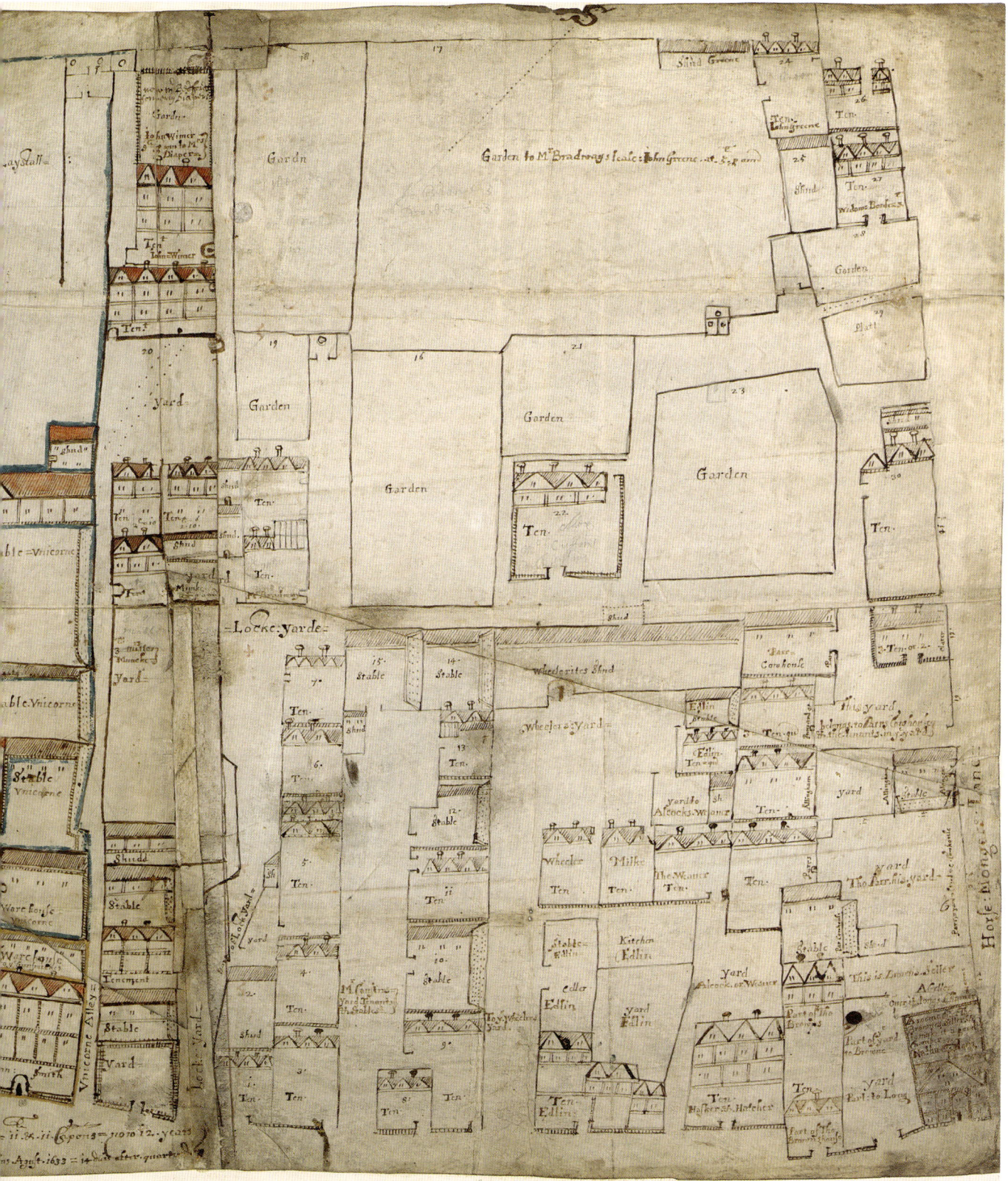

Fig. 138. The Unicorn Inn and adjoining property, Blackman Street, 1678. North is to the left.

The area shown was on the east side of Blackman Street (now part of Borough High Street) just north of Horsemonger Lane (now Harper Road). On Rocque's map of the 1740s, which names both Unicorn Yard and Locks Yard, it is at the very edge of the built-up area, apart from ribbon development. The text on the plan refers to one lease ending in 1674, '4 yeares since', and one ending in 1638, '52 yeares scince', which could place it either in 1678 or 1690. Comparison of the names on the plan with those in the St Mary Newington poor rate indicates that the earlier date is the correct one.[113] The back of the plan says 'A mapp of my estate in Blackman Streete in Southwark'. That it is an estate plan is confirmed by the information on it about leases and comments such as 'what shee holds of Mr Sinderfin: & where they lye & how many rooms', 'A roome over Tho Brownes seller [*illeg.*] to make it a good chamber', and 'this warehouse is in dispute'. A possible reason for it being drawn was the search for 'concealed' Crown lands in Southwark and Bermondsey, which resulted in a lawsuit in 1686. The Crown's claim to the Unicorn was clearly based on confusion with a different Unicorn Inn in Southwark, and is contradicted by the information on the plan.[114] This indicates that the plan covers land split up and leased out by Anthony Wilkinson in 1607, including the Unicorn Inn, then a brewhouse, and five other holdings, then containing six or seven dwellings and mostly let for ninety-nine years. One of the owners in 1686 was Charles Bowles, who had inherited his interest from Sir William Bowles (d.1681),[115] named on the plan as recipient of some of the rent from the Red Cross Alley houses; the other was Daniel Stephens, who first appears in the rate lists in 1680, evidently as innkeeper at the Unicorn. As the Bowles interest was confined to the northern part of the premises, the plan was most likely drawn by or for either Stephens or the person he purchased his interest from, who was probably Thomas Siderfin of the Middle Temple, named on the plan. There are at least two different hands on the plan.

The plan is both pictorial and to scale. Sometimes buildings are clearly depicted, such as the two and a half storey gunsmith's house south of the Unicorn Inn and Mrs Miller's tenements on the left-hand side. In other cases only the gables have been drawn and the rest left unfinished. The names are presumably lessees, but in some cases there seem to be references to the occupier's trade. Behind 'Wheeler' is a wheeler's yard and a wheelwright's shed, and behind 'Gunn: Smith' is 'Warehouse to ye gunsmith'.

The buildings were what one would expect at the very edge of a major city: an inn, alehouses, stables, wheelwrights' and blacksmiths' premises and small farms. On the north side was an alehouse, the Boar's Head. In 1628 this had been the Red Cross, with two rooms on each of three storeys, and a long narrow plot behind containing yard, bowling alley and garden, twelve feet wide. By 1637 it was the Boar's Head, with ten tenements on the former garden. On the plan these are Mrs Miller's nine tenements and a stable, named Red Cross Alley on Morgan's map of 1682. The wording on the plan seems to indicate that the Boar's Head had been added in front of the old Red Cross, which had been divided into two tenements. Next was another alehouse, the Ship or Galley, followed by the Unicorn Inn.[116] James Miller's inventory of 1678 lists kitchen, parlour, rooms over the kitchen, parlour and bar, and front and back garrets, and probably relates to either the Boar's Head or the Ship.[117] The Unicorn Inn had been converted from a brewhouse under a lease of 1607 in which George Marsham undertook to spend £30 on the premises. The main part of the inn was in the block facing the street, including hall, parlour, two kitchens, back kitchen and washhouse. On the south side of the inn and inn yard were stables and warehouses, and at the back was an enclosed garden. Strype described the Unicorn as 'very neat and fine, being adorned with carved figures, and sundry sorts of birds stuft, and set about, as if they were alive, with a small ship, such as are hung up in great halls'.[118]

Further south was a fascinating mixture of dwellings, stables, workshops, yards and gardens, including the houses and stables of Locke Yard, those of Mr Costin, a blacksmith, the wheelwright's yard, John Edlin's dwelling, another yard behind Hasker and Hatcher's house, and a yard partly let to Nathaniel Long, blacksmith.[119] Edward Costin's dwelling in 1684 consisted of shop, kitchen, bedchamber and garret, and in the shop were an anvil, hammers, bellows, other working tools, bars of iron and horseshoes.[120] Other dwellings faced Horsemonger Lane, and there were gardens away from the streets. Thomas Parr, who lived in this area from 1673 to 1685, described himself as a yeoman, and may have been a small farmer.[121]

Plan 59
Millbank, 1696
George Fisher   FIG. 139

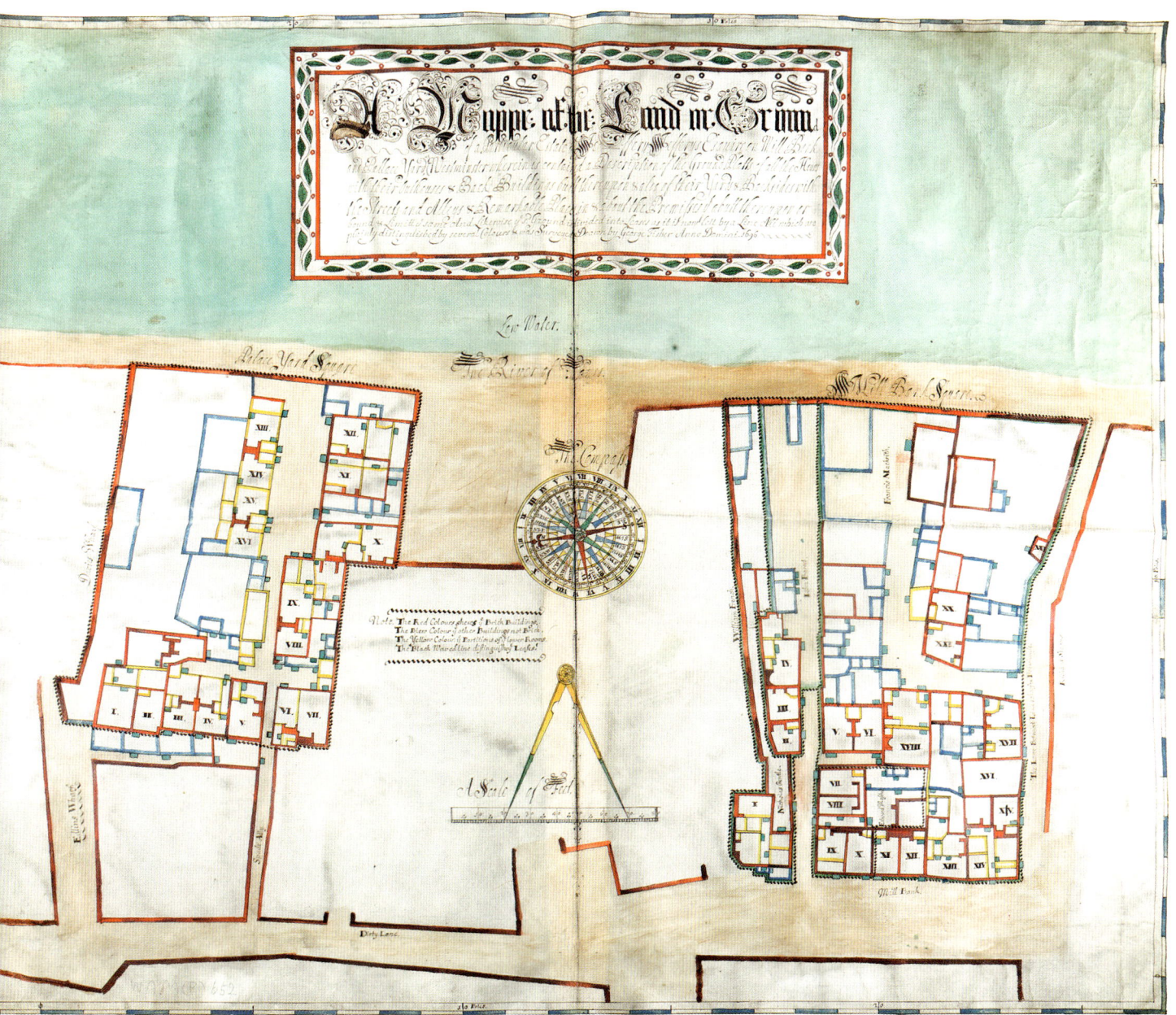

Fig. 139.   Property between Millbank and the Thames, 1696.

This plan shows two areas between Dirty Lane (now Millbank and Abingdon Street) and the Thames just south of the present Palace of Westminster. In modern terms the properties are on the western part of the Victoria Tower Gardens, with the northernmost houses just overlapping the Victoria Tower; the two streets heading west are now Great College Street and Great Peter Street. The property belonged to Jeffrey Jeffreys, a City merchant. He had traded in tobacco in partnership with his uncle John Jeffreys until the latter's death in 1688, when the nephew was his uncle's sole heir. Subsequently he was knighted and became an Alderman and an MP, said to be worth £300,000.[122] The plan survives in the archives of Westminster Abbey, but its presence there is unexplained, as the property shown has no connection with the Abbey. Nothing is known about George Fisher, and no other maps or plans by him are recorded. The book of reference to the plan has not survived.

The property was divided into 'Palace Yard Square' and 'Mill Bank Square', and the plan indicates by 'the black waved line' the area covered by each existing lease. Fisher states that red shows brick buildings, blue other buildings not of brick and yellow the partitions of lower rooms, though he is not wholly consistent: a row of buildings on the west side of Spade Alley is shown almost entirely in yellow, presumably indicating timber buildings. At first sight Fisher appears not to show doors, making it hard to distinguish one house from another, but in fact, uniquely, he marks each door by a small blue square, and the individual houses can therefore be identified. Most were of one-room or two-room plan, but No. I in the Palace Yard square and Nos. I and XIII in the Mill Bank square were larger, and No. I in the latter had a long plot stretching to the river. On Morgan's map of 1682 the alley towards the north side of the Mill Bank square is marked Maskell's Alley, and Edward Maskell is marked on the plan as a lessee there, and was living there in 1690.[123] The riverside part of the Mill Bank square evidently consisted largely of commercial buildings, in both brick and timber, rather than dwellings. On Rocque's map of the 1740s, Edlins Wharf is marked as a timber wharf, Spade Alley as a stone wharf and the two alleys further south as a timber wharf and a stone wharf.

Plans 60-61
East Lane, Salisbury Lane and Bermondsey Wall, 1711
John Friend
FIGS 140, 142

These two plans were drawn in connection with the Earl of Salisbury's sale of land in Bermondsey in 1711 in order to pay off debts.[124] The two areas covered were sold for £1,752 to Sir William Steavens (*c*.1659-1713), a timber merchant. Steavens also had shipping interests, and was High Sheriff of Surrey in 1708.[125] He already held most of the land concerned on long leases. The plans were drawn by a local man, John Friend, who lived in East Lane and who was more used to drawing coastal charts and rural estate maps.[126] Friend evidently coloured brick buildings red, timber buildings blue and fences and sheds brown. He followed the normal practice in pictorial plans of placing the view of each building on the baseline of its facade, so that buildings face in different directions on the plan. Examination of the long row of dwellings on the smaller plan (Fig. 142) indicates that the buildings are shown accurately rather than in standardised form, as Fig. 141 confirms.

The larger area covered was just inland from the Thames, a little south of Bermondsey Wall and east of Jacob's Island. What remains of East Lane is still so called today, but the remaining fragment of Salisbury Lane is now Flockton Street. The deed states that the area had been part of the Wilds. The two streets were developed in the second half of the seventeenth century: Salisbury Lane is first mentioned in 1654 and East Lane in 1676, when it already contained a few buildings. In that year Thomas Miller, a bricklayer of London, leased the whole of the east side of East Lane, where there were only four houses, toward the north end. The lease required him to build on two-thirds of the unbuilt frontage and to pave that half of the street. He also leased two plots west of the street containing six houses in 1676-78. Miller sub-let some of the ground east of the street, requiring the sub-tenants to build in a 'uniform manner' with the houses already there, but he was probably himself the builder of most of the row of large brick houses shown on the plan.[127] These were each about thirty-three feet wide, and in 1821 they had four rooms per floor and were described as suitable for merchants. They may, however, have been intended for prosperous sea captains, who were numerous in the area; twelve of the eighteen residents on the east side of East Lane were captains in 1712, more than in the whole of the rest of the Waterside division of Bermondsey.[128] One house, the southernmost in the row, survived long enough to be photographed in 1948 (Fig. 141).[129]

On the other side of the street, the plan depicts the home and business of a wealthy timber merchant. In his will of 1713 Steavens refers to his dwelling in East Lane, and the parish poor rate places him on the west side of the street, with the most valuable property in Bermondsey's Waterside division,[130] so he clearly occupied the large house shown there on the plan, with extensive gardens, fish and horse ponds and what may have been workshops in Salisbury Lane. The

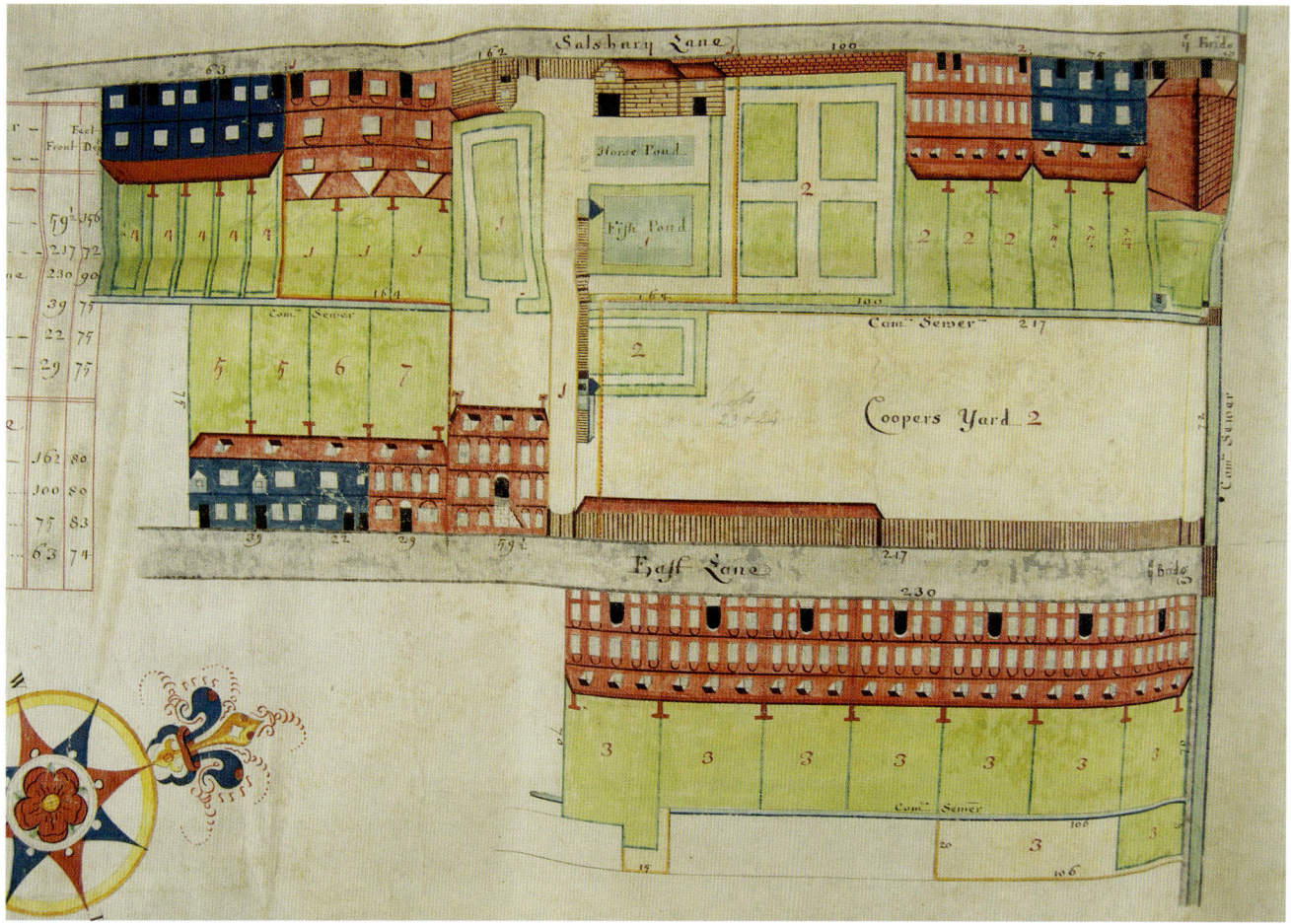

Fig. 140. Property in East Lane and Salisbury Lane, Bermondsey, 1711.

KEY: former leases, with front and depth in feet

East Lane
1. Mr William Stephens [Steavens], 59½ × 156.
2. Coopers Yard ditto, 217 × 72.
3. Ditto on east side of East Lane, 230 × 90.
5. [Blank], 39 × 75.
6. Mr George Stephens, 22 × 75.

7. Mr John Gruchey, 29 × 75.

Salisbury Lane
1. Mr William Stephens, 162 × 80.
2. Ditto, 100 × 80.
4x. Mr Thomas Stephens, 75 × 83.
4. Ditto, 63 × 74.

site, previously undeveloped, was leased to Steavens in 1701 and the house was described in 1711 as lately erected by him. In 1819 it had kitchen and cellars in the basement, three parlours and counting house on the ground floor, drawing room and three bedrooms on the first floor, and four attics.[131] The area known as 'Coopers Yard' was a timber yard in 1711, and was probably the centre of Steavens' business. The deed refers to three brick houses in Salisbury Lane south of Steavens' garden (No. 1 on the plan) as lately erected by him, and to the five timber ones there (No. 4) also as recently erected. Two timber houses in East Lane (No. 5) were described as recently repaired by Steavens. The latter were one-room plan houses; in 1819 each had kitchen, bedroom and attic, with a small washhouse and garden.[132]

The smaller area was further east, with Salisbury Street, now Wilson Grove, on the east side. When first recorded in 1636 there was a house and a timber yard here, and in the plan of *c*.1670 (Plan 75) the site included the yard and wharf of Richard Dober, a shipwright.[133] Steavens obtained a lease of the area in 1703, including Dober's former yard, which is shown on the plan with the 'knees' (pieces of timber with a bend in them) needed for shipbuilding. One of the houses

south of the street was set back and had what looks like a garden pavilion behind.

Steavens also purchased other Bermondsey land in 1711. When he died in 1713 he had property in Southwark, Deptford, Essex and Kent too, and his lands were said to be worth £1,500 a year. The estate passed to his son-in-law Thomas Steavens, and eventually by marriage to the West family, who remained major landholders in Bermondsey until 1960.[134]

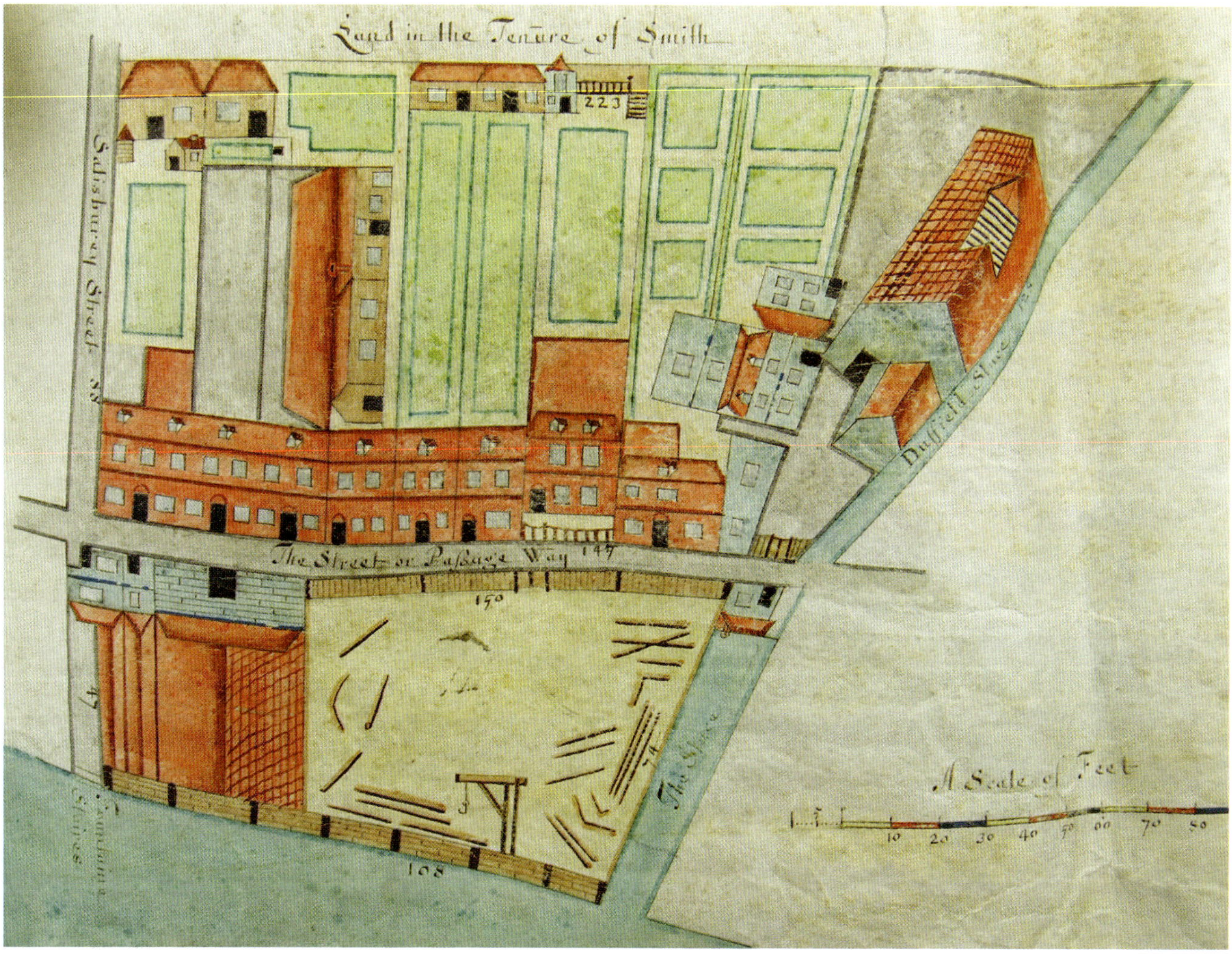

Fig. 141.   89 East Lane, probably built in the 1670s, photographed in 1948.

Fig. 142.   Property in and around Bermondsey Wall, Bermondsey, 1711.

PLANS OF BUILDING TYPES

LONDON BRIDGE

Plan 62
The northern end of London Bridge, 1633
Joseph Darvoll and Thomas Sterne
Fig. 143

On 11 February 1633, the maidservant of John Briggs, needlemaker, at the northern end of London Bridge, put a tub of hot ashes under the stairs before going to bed, and the resulting fire destroyed more than a third of the houses on the bridge. By 21 March two Privy Counsellors had ordered the bridgemasters 'to make an exact plott of the bridge as it is nowe burned'. A plan showing the burnt area was ready by 26 March, and was almost certainly the one reproduced here.[1] Two payments were made for it, both specified as for the plan required by the Privy Counsellors. In May Joseph Darvoll, the Bridge House's master carpenter of the land works from 1627 to 1665, was paid 40s. for this and another plan, but the writing differs from that on the one plan he is known to have drawn (Plan 78). On 23 March Thomas Sterne was paid 8s. for 'the newe draweinge of a plott of the bridge'.[2] A reasonable explanation is that Darvoll compiled the plan, but Sterne was employed to draw a more attractive version for the Privy Council.

The plan shows the first seven of the nineteen piers and starlings (the line of the present river wall passes through the middle of the fourth starling). The piers were those built by Peter of Colechurch between about 1176 and 1209, and around them were the starlings, consisting of rubble enclosed by piles, which had grown larger over time. The order of 1633 required that the plan show 'the solid peares of the bridge it selfe and the out letts which have been added to [it] for strength and commodity and which have been arched and which not and without all a line expressinge the terminateinge of the pyleinge with the severall measures of all by scale'.[3] The arched 'out letts' may be what are shown between the piers on the west or upstream side.

The plan shows pictorially the waterworks at the north end of the bridge (Fig. 144). These were created in 1578-82 by Peter Morris, a Dutchman, and provided the City's first supply of piped water from the Thames. The City leased him the first two arches of the bridge. The water wheels rotated a shaft, which gave rotary motion to a disc connected to the piston rods of the pumps, which forced the water into the pipes. The pipes led up to a barrel on top of a tower, from which wooden pipes carried the water down to street level and then to cisterns at St Margaret Fish Street Hill and the Greenyard at Leadenhall.[4]

South of the burnt area, the plan does not show the piers and starlings at all, but instead, beyond the small open space which had checked the fire, it gives the outline of the surviving houses and of

Fig. 143. The northern end of London Bridge, 1633. North is to the right.

Fig. 144. Detail from Fig. 143 showing the water works.

the narrow roadway. It shows that at bridge level the houses were basically square ones of one-room plan.[5] The larger one, labelled 'The chaple house', was the chapel dedicated to Thomas Becket (Fig. 145). It was built with the bridge, rebuilt in 1384-96, secularised in 1549-53 and demolished with the bridge's other houses in about 1757.[6] The plan shows that the roadway in this area was about twelve and a half to fourteen feet wide, roughly corresponding to Strype's statement about its width and to measurements made at the southern end of the bridge in 1831-32 (both twelve to fourteen feet).[7]

Charles I was determined that the burnt houses should not be rebuilt, and wanted the bridge entirely cleared of houses, 'in regard of the conveniance for passage and the uniformitie and beautie that wolde be caused thereby'. The Bridge House evidently resisted this considerable reduction in its income, and the plan reflected its defiance, as it covered only the burnt area rather than the whole bridge as required. Compromise was reached in 1635: the remaining houses could stay, but the burnt area would not be rebuilt. There were to be parapet walls thirty-two feet apart, containing footways six feet wide on each side and a twenty-foot roadway. Arches were to be added between the piers on the downstream side, and 'void places' (presumably the former house cellars) were to be filled in. The 'modall thereof accordinglie drawne by the masters of the Bridge-house' was to remain with the Privy Council's records.[8] This seems to have been the 1633 plan amended, as the Bridge House accounts contain no further payments for plans between 1633 and 1635. The parapets and the edges of the roadway

Fig. 145. The houses on the east side of the Bridge shown in Fig. 143, including St Thomas's Chapel, as they were in 1597 (detail from a print of c.1803 after John Norden).

Fig. 146. Detail from Wenceslaus Hollar's long view of London in 1647 showing the northern end of the Bridge, with the roadway as widened and enclosed in 1633.

are apparently marked on the plan by a line indicating brickwork and a grey line respectively, giving footways and roadways of the specified widths. The planned arches between the piers downstream are not shown.

The intended changes were never made, and Hollar's print of 1647 shows only what was done in February 1633: a roadway widened to eighteen feet and enclosed by boards ten and a half feet high, with three refuges for foot passengers on each side (Fig. 146).[9] Only in 1645, when Charles I was on the brink of military defeat, were new houses built in the burnt area, and even then only on the northernmost part. This became unexpectedly important in 1666, as it prevented the Great Fire spreading to the whole bridge and to Southwark.

LONDON WALL

London Wall had long since lost its military value by the end of the seventeenth century, but it remained largely intact. The outer ditch had begun to be enclosed in the sixteenth century, and to be built on by the end of that century, and the non-military uses of the bastions were increasingly permanent from the late sixteenth century. By 1676, when Leybourn drew his plan of the Wall, large parts of it had been reduced in width to gain space ('Wall diged away' is applied to a stretch by the College of Physicians' garden), but only in a few places had it gone completely (around Aldersgate, at Christ Church, near Ludgate and along the Fleet River).[10] In 1683 the City's viewers could still regard it as dishonourable to the City for any part of the Wall to be demolished (Plan 65). However, when John Olley took down part of it near Houndsditch in 1688 the City's concern was only to maintain the Wall as a barrier to normal traffic and a property boundary and to prevent passages being made through it. Olley was ordered to replace what he had destroyed with a wall three bricks thick.[11] Other breaches were soon being made (Plans 65, 67), but the Wall was largely maintained as a barrier until at least 1731, when it was considered worthwhile to rebuild Bishopsgate.

Plan 63
Bishopsgate and Ludgate, 1676
William Leybourn
FIGS 147, 149

The plan made for the City in 1676 of the Wall and encroachments on it was drawn by Leybourn but seems to have been based on surveying by John Oliver and Robert Hooke.[12] It included the City gates. Aldgate had been rebuilt in 1617 and four gates—Ludgate, Newgate, Aldersgate and Moorgate—were rebuilt or repaired after the Great

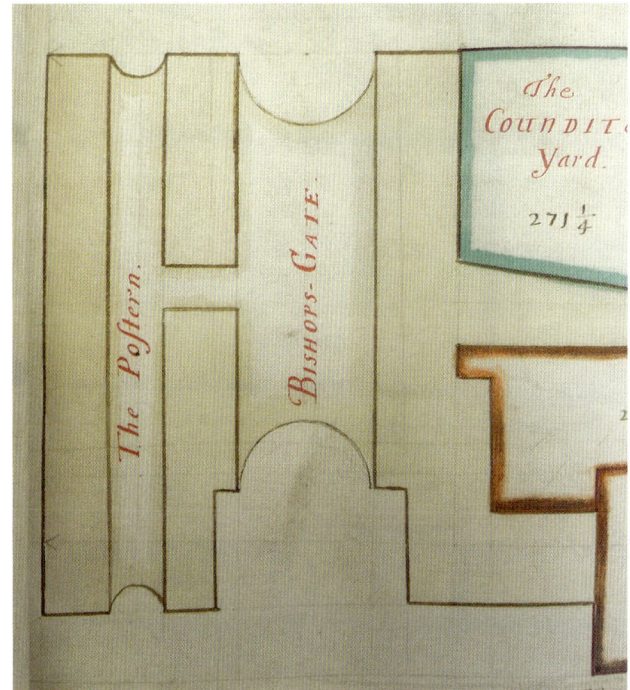

Fig. 147. Detail from Leybourn's plan of London Wall, showing Bishopsgate, 1676. North is at the bottom.

Fig. 148. The outer side of Bishopsgate, from a print of 1731 by Sutton Nicholls.

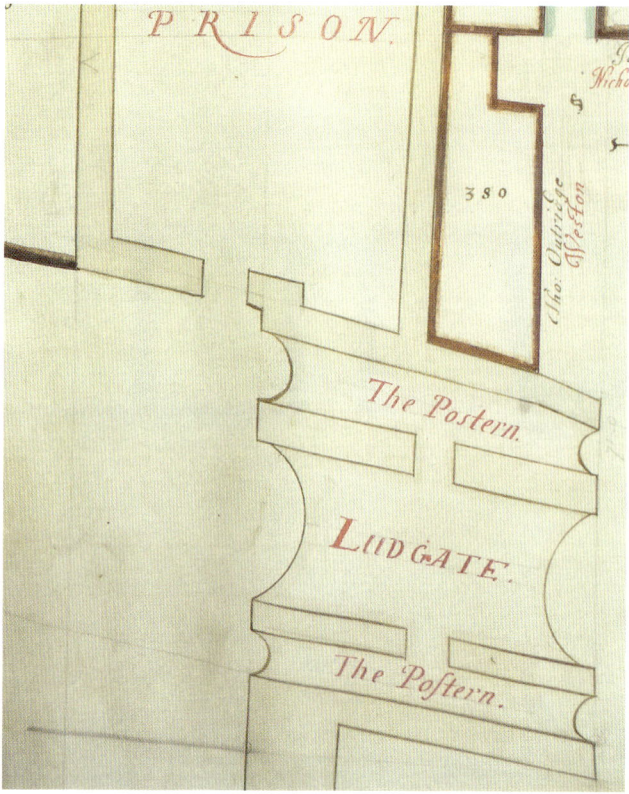

Fig. 149. Detail from Leybourn's plan of London Wall, showing Ludgate, 1676. North is at the bottom.

Fig. 150. Ludgate, from a print of 1731 by Sutton Nicholls.

Fire. The two older ones were Cripplegate, rebuilt in 1491 and 'beautified' in 1663, and Bishopsgate.

Bishopsgate (Figs 147, 148) had been rebuilt in 1479 by the Hanse merchants of the Steelyard. It had a roadway and, like most of the gates, just one postern for pedestrians (though Fig. 148 apparently shows two). The north or outer face bore a statue of a bishop and two of kings. The rooms over the gate were occupied in 1720 by one of the Lord Mayor's carvers, Edward Gostling, who was also one of the Serjeants of the Chamber.[13] The gate was demolished in 1731 and the lower structure which replaced it was removed in 1760.

Ludgate (Figs 149, 150), which stood almost adjacent to St Martin Ludgate, was rebuilt in 1586 and much restored in 1670-73 after the Fire. It had two posterns. Ludgate had been a prison since 1378, and a rectangular building was added on the south side in 1463, with lodgings on the upper floor and a lead roof to walk on above; the prison continued until 1760.[14] Ludgate and its prison were demolished in 1760 with all the other gates except Newgate, which survived until the new prison there was nearing completion in 1777. The statue of Queen Elizabeth which formerly adorned Ludgate is now outside St Dunstan in the West.

Plan 64
Bastion off Poor Jewry Lane, 1694
John Olley
FIG. 151

This bastion, on the east side of Poor Jewry Lane (now Jewry Street), is interesting mainly because the red colour on the plan indicates that the stone wall had been replaced by a brick wall roughly following its outline but occupying less space. In fact much of the bastion had fallen down in 1651, and a stone had been attached stating 'Glory be to God on high, who was graciously pleased in a wonderful manner to preserve the lifes of all the people in this house, twelve in number, when the ould wall of this bulwork fell down three stories high, and so broad, as two cartes might enter a-breast, and yet without any harm to their persones'. More of the old bastion survived than Olley's plan suggests, as in 1756 the old work was eight feet high, topped by a new building of three storeys.[15] The house was one of a row of six leased together, and was occupied by a victualler in 1676. In 1697 the lease was granted to Thomas Langham, citizen and apothecary. The plan was John Olley's first for a City Lands lease and corrected an error by Leybourn, which resulted in Olley taking over the drawing of such plans from him.[16]

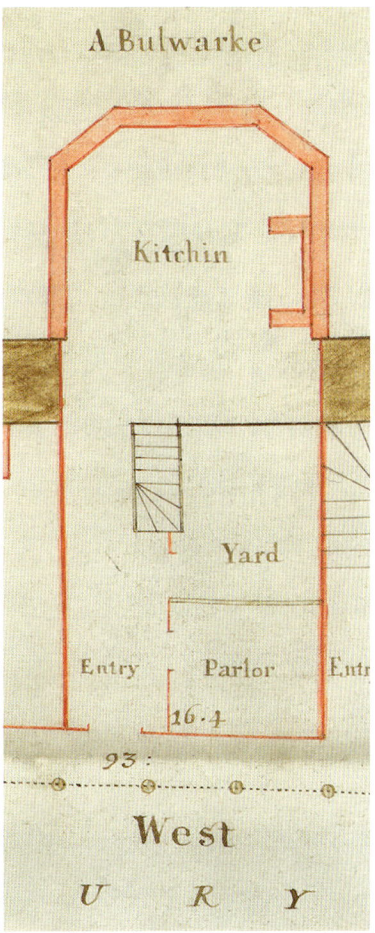

Fig. 151. Detail from a plan of houses in Poor Jewry Lane, showing the bastion, 1694.

Plan 65
Bastion in Shoemakers' Row, 1699
John Olley
FIG. 152

This was the southernmost of the two bastions between Bevis Marks and Aldgate, beside a part of Duke's Place also known as Shoemakers' Row.[17] The bastion contained a cellar, three rooms one above another and a cockloft; in 1683 the description had been vault and four rooms one above another. In that year the lessee, Francis Beech, citizen and cordwainer, demolished the upper part of the bastion and was planning to pull down ten feet of the Wall. The City's viewers considered that this would be 'a very great weakning to the Citty wall and likewise a dishonour to the Citty if they suffer any particular person to pull downe any part thereof'.[18] A new sixty-one year lease was taken in 1699 by Robert Smith, citizen and cordwainer, and included thirty-two feet of the Wall (or the site of the Wall). Smith was expected to be at great charge in building a brick extension in front of his house in the bastion, equal to it in height, and also building two-storey brick shops on the site of the part of the Wall leased to him, to be equal in height to the houses already built on the adjoining stretch of Wall. The plan seems to show these structures already in place, perhaps indicating that they were built by Smith before the lease was granted. In 1756 the bastion was described as twenty-one feet high and 'perfectly sound'.[19]

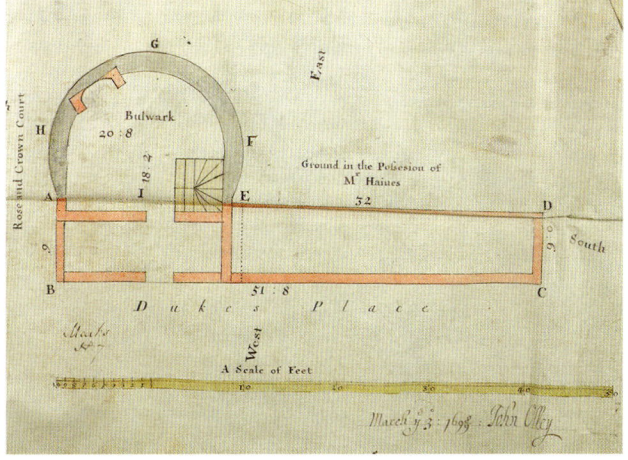

Fig. 152. Bastion in Shoemakers' Row, 1699.

Plan 66
Bastion in Windsor Court, Monkwell Street, 1712
Isaac Olley   Fig. 153

This bastion can still be seen just east of the Museum of London, though no obvious seventeenth- or eighteenth-century fabric is visible (Fig. 154). It was leased in 1712 to Christopher Morrison, citizen and founder, who was living there.[20] The stated width of the bastion is not consistent with the scale. The bastion was still occupied by a house in the mid-nineteenth century, though arranged differently: on the ground floor were a five-bay facade, a central passage to the back, a room either side and, at the back, stairs (probably those visible today) and small rooms.[21]

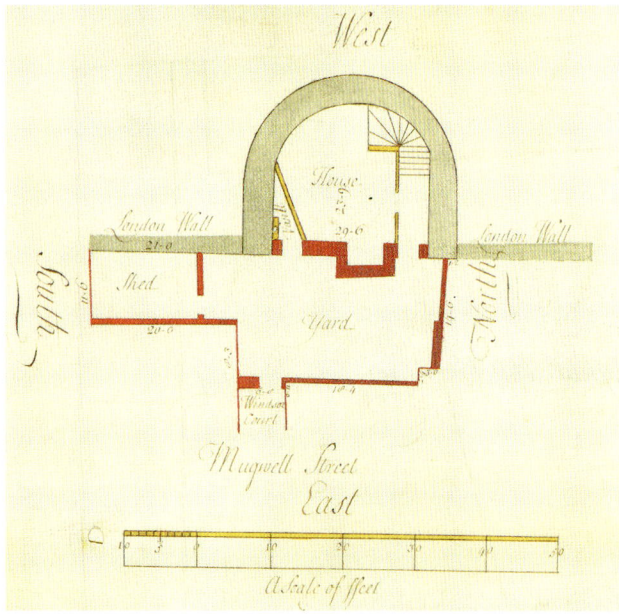

Fig. 153. Bastion in Windsor Court, Monkwell Street, 1712.

Fig. 154. Remains of the bastion off Monkwell Street, 2013.

Plan 67
Bastion in Shoemakers' Row, 1716
Isaac Olley
Fig. 155

This was the northernmost bastion between Bevis Marks and Aldgate. It was leased in 1716 to Robert Stuart, citizen and barber surgeon (but also described as a chemist), together with a stretch of the former Wall, though the plan shows that the Wall had disappeared on both sides of the bastion; indeed Plan 9 shows the Wall reduced in thickness here as early as the 1580s. The premises consisted in 1716 of Hudson's Coffee House (apparently in the bastion), a barber's shop adjoining it and a poulterer's shop. In 1756 the bastion, then occupied by a baker, was described as three storeys high and badly decayed.[22]

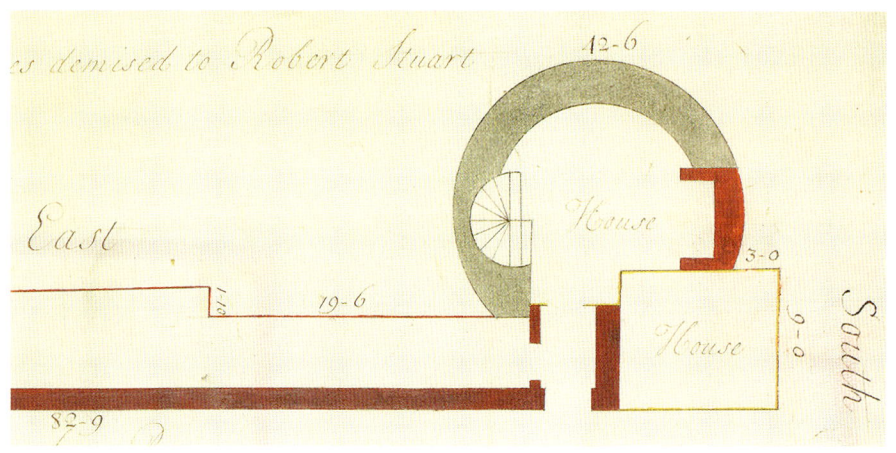

Fig. 155. Bastion in Shoemakers' Row, 1716. About sixty-four feet of the Wall north of the bastion was included in the lease and is shown on the plan.

Plan 68
Bastion off Bull and Mouth Street, c.1720
Isaac Olley   FIG. 156

This property consisted of the bastion itself, a staircase which had replaced a small part of the Wall and two chambers and a garret, one over the other, above a kitchen belonging to a house in Bull and Mouth Street. The yard is the passage shown on Plan 54 between plots 45 and 46. The lease has not been identified.

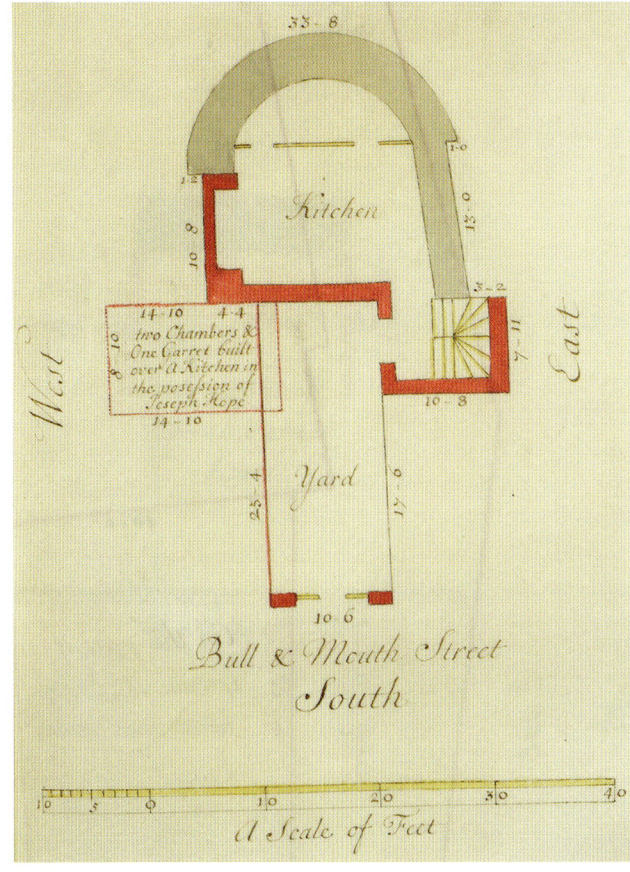

Fig. 156. Bastion off Bull and Mouth Street, c.1720.

Plan 69
London Wall opposite Coleman Street, 1719
Isaac Olley
FIG. 157

In 1719 Coleman Street ward petitioned the City for part of the Wall and adjoining ground opposite Coleman Street to build a watchhouse, a cage (for locking up offenders) and stocks, taking down part of the Wall to do so. In return they would remove their existing watchhouse, cage and stocks, which stood nearer to Moorgate, and add the site to the roadway. A sixty-one year lease was agreed. The six-foot width of the Wall had become valuable property, and, as the plan shows, the cage and stocks and part of the watchhouse were within the former width of the Wall. After 1723 the ward failed to pay the 4s. per year rent, and the City decided eventually, in 1738, to recover its property at law.[23]

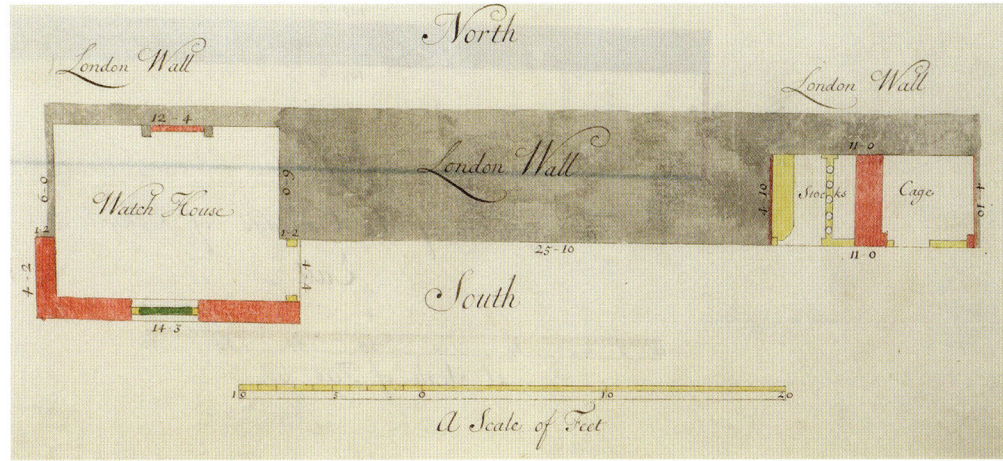

Fig. 157. London Wall opposite Coleman Street, 1719.

WHARVES

Plan 70
Botolph Wharf, 1680
William Leybourn   FIG. 158

London's most important wharves were the Legal Quays, on the north bank of the Thames between London Bridge and the Tower. From about 1559 until the 1790s all dutiable goods had to be landed there, with limited exceptions permitted at the Sufferance Quays (mainly in Southwark). The Legal Quays consequently became extremely valuable. One of them was Botolph Wharf, midway between London Bridge and Billingsgate. It was leased from the City in 1622 by Thomas Soane, citizen and grocer, and in 1645 Soane obtained a new lease for thirty-one years for a £2,000 fine and rent of £50 a year. Soane's widow, Elizabeth, added an extra thirty-eight years to the term, for £900, and then sold both leases to Josiah Child, her son-in-law. Child (Fig. 159) was the son of a London merchant and had made his fortune as a supplier of beer and victuals to the Navy. He was a great financial manipulator, especially as Governor or Deputy Governor of the East India Company from 1681 to 1690, and became immensely wealthy, with a fortune estimated at £200,000. In 1678 he was made a baronet.[24]

After the Great Fire, Child first spent £1,000 on cranes and sheds at Botolph Wharf, but then had to rebuild again to comply with the Rebuilding Act, and claimed to have spent a further £6,000 by 1672. He sought a longer term or a reduced rent from the City, observing that the post-Fire requirement to leave open a forty-foot wharf had reduced the value of the property. The City argued that Child had in fact gained from the Fire by letting out sheds at high rates. It also complained of his 'irregular building and intermingling the interest of the [City] with his owne next adjoying buildings, whereby they will not be able at the expiracon of the terme to know their owne ground'; the inclusion of part of a crane on the plan bears this out. The Fire Court ordered that Child's lease be extended from the remaining forty-two years to sixty years and that the rent be reduced to £30, and the lease of 1680 gave effect to this. Child also leased Hammond's and Lyon's Quays.[25]

The plan of 1680 shows that the property consisted of the wharf with its cranes and a lane from Thames Street to the wharf flanked by warehouses and tenements. Two of the tenements overlooked the wharf and two were in Thames Street. A later plan, of 1720, records fifty-two warehouses, of which twelve were west of the lane, twenty-five east of it and fifteen over it. The forty-foot wharf remained open in 1720, but with an extra crane.[26]

Fig. 159. Sir Josiah Child (1630-99) – portrait attributed to John Riley.

Fig. 158. Botolph Wharf, 1680.

Plan 71
Porter's Key, 1686
William Leybourn FIG. 160

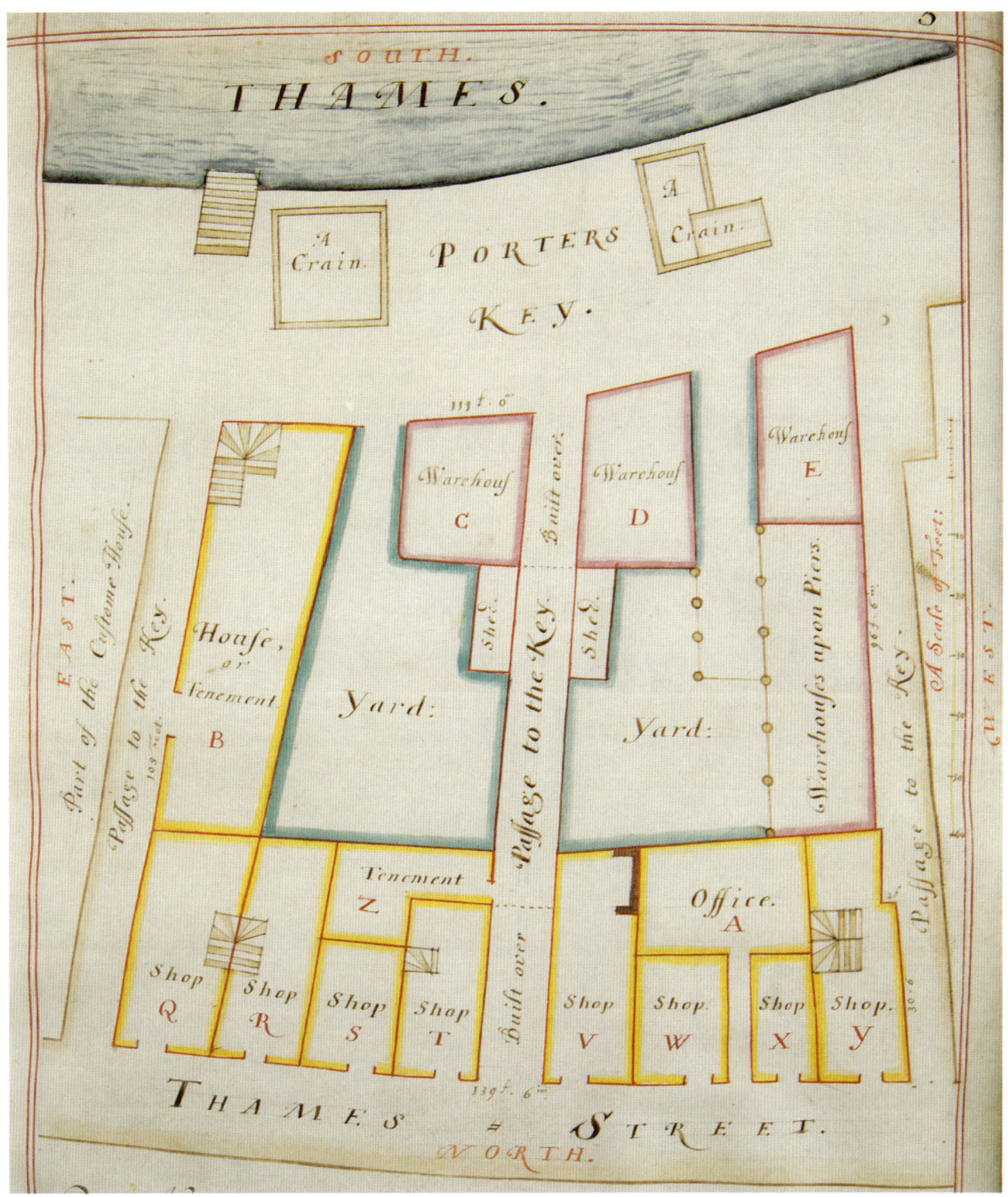

Fig. 160. Porter's Key, 1686.

KEY
Q–Z and A. Cellars under; three floors of rooms over ground floor.

B. Warehouse: vaults or warehouses under; dwelling house over.
C–E. Warehouses: vaults under; warehouses with cranes over.

Fig. 161. Detail from Morgan's panorama of 1682, showing Porter's Key in the centre with five gables to the left of the Custom House.

Porter's Key was another of the Legal Quays, and belonged to the Fishmongers' Company. It was on the eastern part of the present Custom House site but in 1686 was immediately west of the then Custom House. The plan provides a fine view of an important quay, with cranes on the forty-foot wharf, warehouses, an office and what was probably the manager's house overlooking the wharf. There were houses of three and a half storeys facing Thames Street. Morgan's panorama of 1682 (not always accurate) shows five gables rather than the four the plan seems to suggest, but the warehouses probably formed a continuous row above the ground storey, with the gables not necessarily corresponding to the divisions at ground level (Fig. 161).

Porter's Key had formerly been Crown and Greenbury Keys, and the new name recorded a recent lessee, John Porter. John Saintloe, citizen and fishmonger, secured a twenty-one year lease in 1629, paying a fine of £2,000. The Company extended his lease two years later because the £300 he had spent on new buildings was 'very well bestowed' and he was likely to prove a good tenant.[27] In 1668 Mary Saintloe, his widow, told the Fire Court that 'she and her late husband have bin tenants of the premisses about forty yeares now last past and that she was burnt out of the place and that her livelyhood and the imployment of her sonn depended on her continuance there'. She had paid £1,700 for a renewal of the lease in 1655 and now sought a forty-year extension at the old rent of £47 a year in return for rebuilding at an estimated cost of £5,000 (the City surveyors' estimate was only about £2,900, including £500 for the double crane and single crane already built). The Fishmongers' Company, on the other hand, wanted to do the rebuilding itself and to make the wharf 'one of the noblest publique places in the City'. It eventually offered to buy out the Saintloes' remaining term for £600 a year, but the Saintloes would not accept less than £800 a year. The Fire Court ordered in December 1668 that the Saintloes have an additional forty-year term, at a slightly increased rent of £60 for the extra years.[28] The Fishmongers did not give in easily. In April 1669 they ordered that Mary Saintloe erect no buildings on the wharf without their consent, and when she sought the lease provided for in the decree they asked if she had taken notice of their instruction about building. They began to prepare a petition to the House of Commons 'for avoyding the great injury done to this Company by the said decree'. Agreement was eventually reached in February 1670, apparently because Mary Saintloe wanted to include the tenements in Thames Street in the new lease and so was willing to pay more than the Fire Court had decreed. She paid a £600 fine and rent of £100 a year for the forty-six year term.[29]

By 1674 Mary Saintloe seems to have been in financial difficulty, and by 1684 the wharf was held by Francis Millington of London esquire. Millington was sub-letting it to John Moore, citizen and fishmonger, who was occupying what was described as a capital messuage there and paying Millington £950 a year. In 1715 Porter's Key was destroyed by a fire which also consumed the Custom House, and the Fishmongers rebuilt the property themselves. In 1813 the site was used for the new Custom House.[30]

Plan 72
Dyers' Hall Wharf, 1716
James Gould

Fig. 162

Away from the Legal Quays, riverside property in central London tended to be used for industrial purposes, and Dyers' Hall Wharf, half-way between the present Fishmongers' Hall and Cannon Street Station, provides an example. The Dyers acquired most of the site as the gift of Sir Robert Tyrwhitt in 1545, when it consisted of a 'great messuage' called the Three Stars together with wharves and a small tenement. Tyrwhitt provided for the Company to build almshouses there for four poor men and three poor women and maintain them for ever. In 1586 the Dyers added to the property by purchasing the White Cock adjoining the almshouse, probably the dyehouse of that name recorded in the early seventeenth century; it included a wharf. The Company used the central part of the site itself, letting out the 'lower part' of the property towards the river and

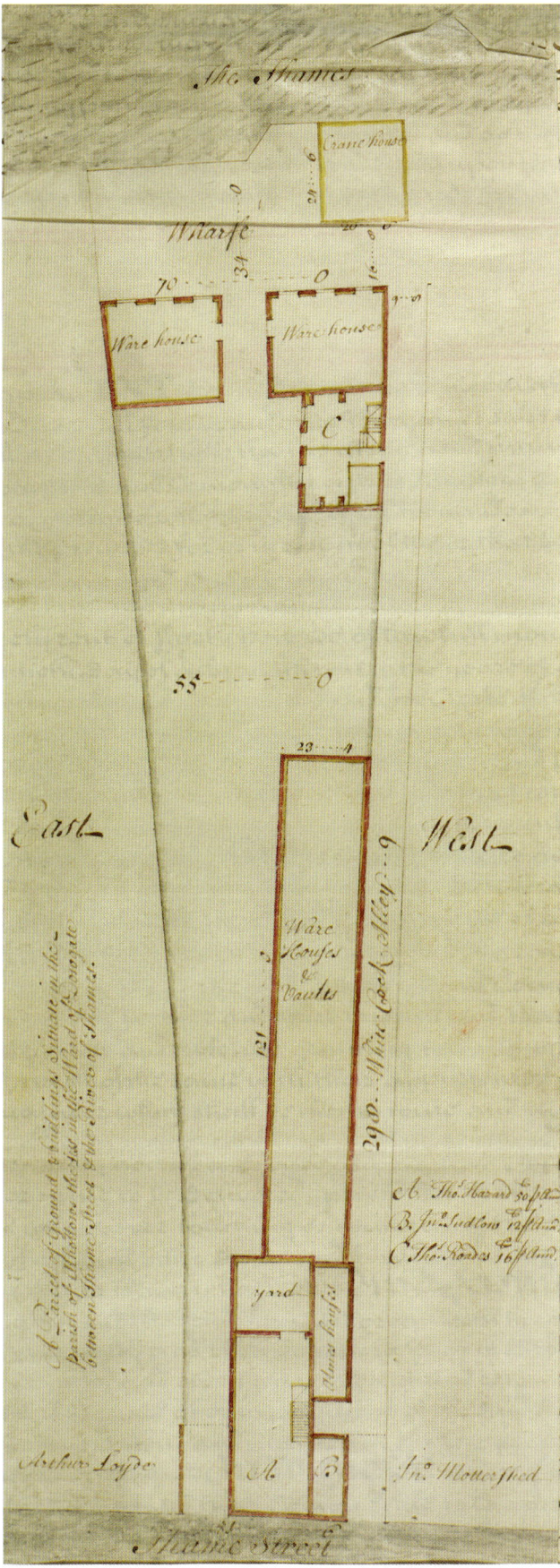

Fig. 162. Dyers' Hall Wharf, 1716.

the two houses in Thames Street. The almshouses seem to have been raised up, as there were two warehouses belonging to the dyehouse under part of them in 1633, and there was a little house under them in 1652 (the lease of it excluded the vault and privy with a funnel from rooms used by the almspeople).[31]

After the Fire the Dyers regained control of almost all the property from the lessees. They built a new Hall on the old site, with a 'great warehouse' under it (Fig. 163).[32] The almshouses were also rebuilt, on or near their original site. As the new site was only ten feet by thirty-one feet, the seven almspeople must have been on several floors, as a request of 1723 for one of the garrets in Whitecock Alley confirms.[33] The southern part of the property still contained no buildings in 1676; in that year it was leased to Job Clark, citizen and joiner, who was required to build a brick house there (presumably the one marked C), and who used the site as a timber yard. The small house marked B was rebuilt, apparently disentangled from the almshouses. It had three and a half storeys and was just under ten feet wide at ground level but with upper storeys extending over Whitecock Alley. It consisted in 1684 of a shop on the ground floor, a kitchen and a small room or chamber on the first floor, two chambers

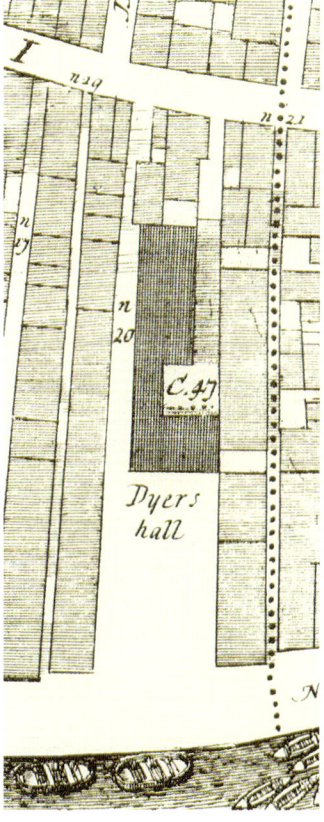

Fig. 163. Detail from Ogilby and Morgan's map of 1676 showing Dyers' Hall Wharf and Dyers' Hall as rebuilt after the Great Fire.

over them, a garret and a cellar. In 1676 it was occupied by Edward Hawkins, a barber. Only the house marked A, known as the White Dove, where the Company had planned to rebuild its almshouses, eluded the Company for a time: the pre-Fire tenants, James Clements, scrivener, and his wife Elizabeth went ahead and rebuilt it, and persuaded the Fire Court in 1672 that their existing lease should be extended by forty years.[34]

Dyers' Hall was probably the shortest-lived company hall ever, as it burnt down in April 1681. The Dyers were in severe financial difficulties and were unable to rebuild: the Dyers' Hall property was mortgaged from 1679 to at least 1716, and it took the Dyers until 1731 to provide even a court-room for themselves (on their present site on Dowgate Hill).[35] The former Hall site, together with house A, was let to a group of merchants in 1684, and by 1716 had been combined with the southern part of the property, with a large warehouse erected. By about 1720 it was occupied by William Edwards & Co, ironmongers, and there were several iron warehouses and a large iron wharf (Fig. 164). While the Dyers had departed for ever, the almspeople remained in place until 1777, when they were removed to a new building in City Road.[36] The Dyers retained ownership of Dyers' Hall Wharf until at least the 1950s.

Fig. 164. Detail from the Bucks' panorama of 1749, with, in the centre, Job Clark's building of about 1676 on the Dyers' land, later used as iron warehouses. Iron bars can be seen stacked on the wharf.

Plans 73-74
The Steelyard, 1680/81 and c.1714
FIGS 165, 166

The Steelyard was burnt in the Great Fire, though some buildings may have been temporarily patched up and part of what seems to have been the west wall survived until the nineteenth century.[37] Jacob Jacobsen, from Hamburg, 'housemaster' since 1647, sought instructions from the Hanse towns on rebuilding, pointing out the risk of the property being forfeited if it was not rebuilt, but the towns could not reach agreement. Eventually, in March 1670, Lubeck, Bremen and Hamburg told Jacobsen to grant leases of up to forty years at rents specified, though longer leases subsequently proved necessary to attract builders. In 1670 John Ball, a joiner, agreed to build the Thames Street frontage on a fifty-one year lease, and two sites in Allhallows Lane were let to others in 1670 and 1671, for fifty-one and sixty-one years.[38] Jacobsen found that no-one was willing to build on the remaining part of the Steelyard with less than a ninety-nine year lease except his brother Theodore. The Jacobsens turned to the Fire Court, which ordered in 1673 that Theodore have a forty-year lease of it. Jacob Jacobsen and two German merchants then granted him a further thirty-one years, though it is not clear on what authority.

Ogilby and Morgan's map of 1676 shows the eastern warehouses built, as well as the Rhenish winehouse and what may have been a patched-up pre-Fire range on the west side of the site. By November 1680 Theodore Jacobsen could tell the three cities that 'God be thanked the whole yard is now rebuilt as it was formerly with gates to shut up house & warehouses within, so that no English have any habitation therein. I have also

---

KEY, Fig. 165
1. Mr Jacobsen's dwelling.
2. Warehouse.
3. Stable and coach-house.
4. Rhenish winehouse and garden.
5. Warehouses.
6. Crane.
7. Covered place for watermen.
8. Small writing-office.
9. Bridge.
10. 'Secret'.

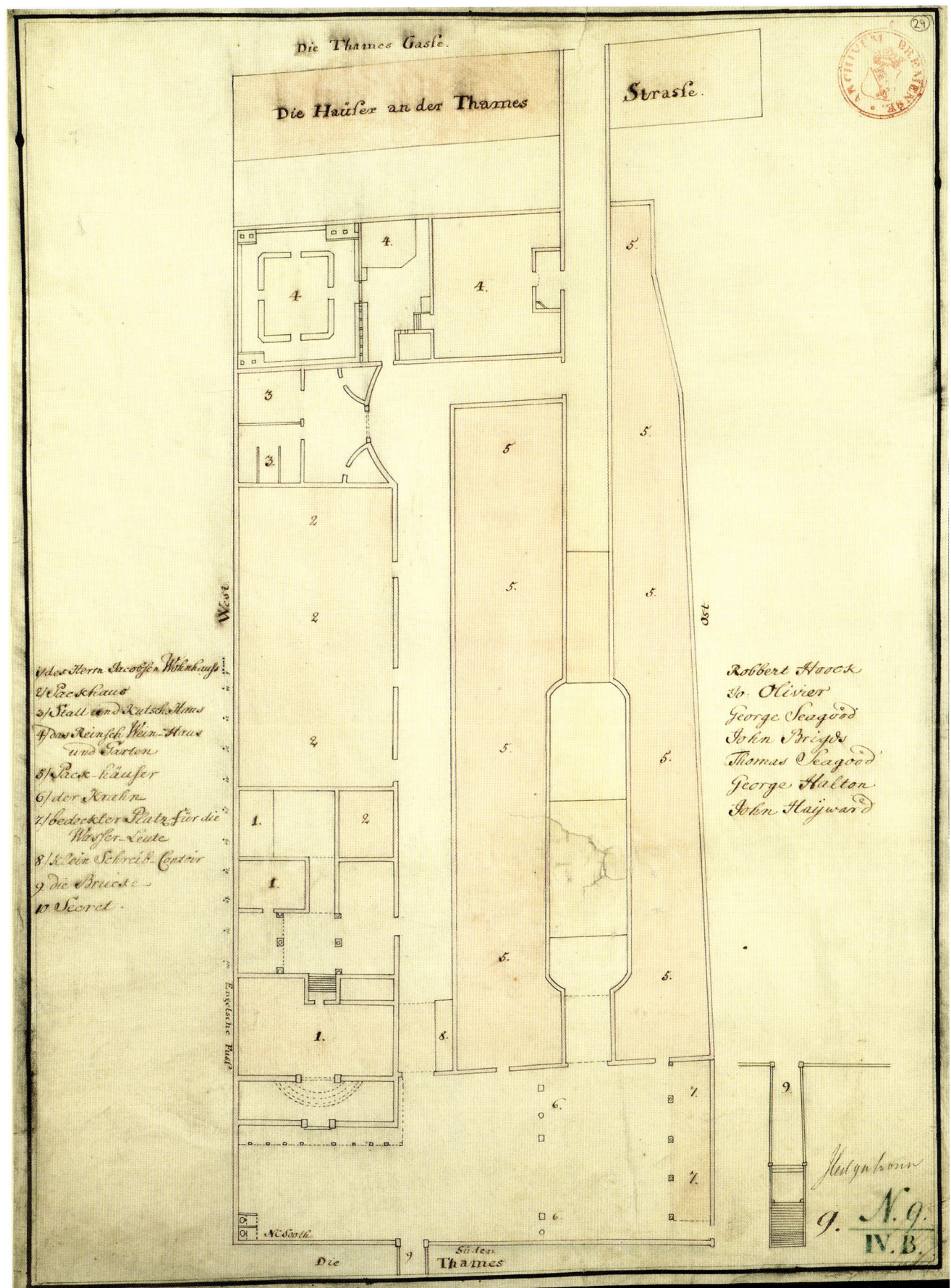

Fig. 165. The Steelyard, 1680/81.

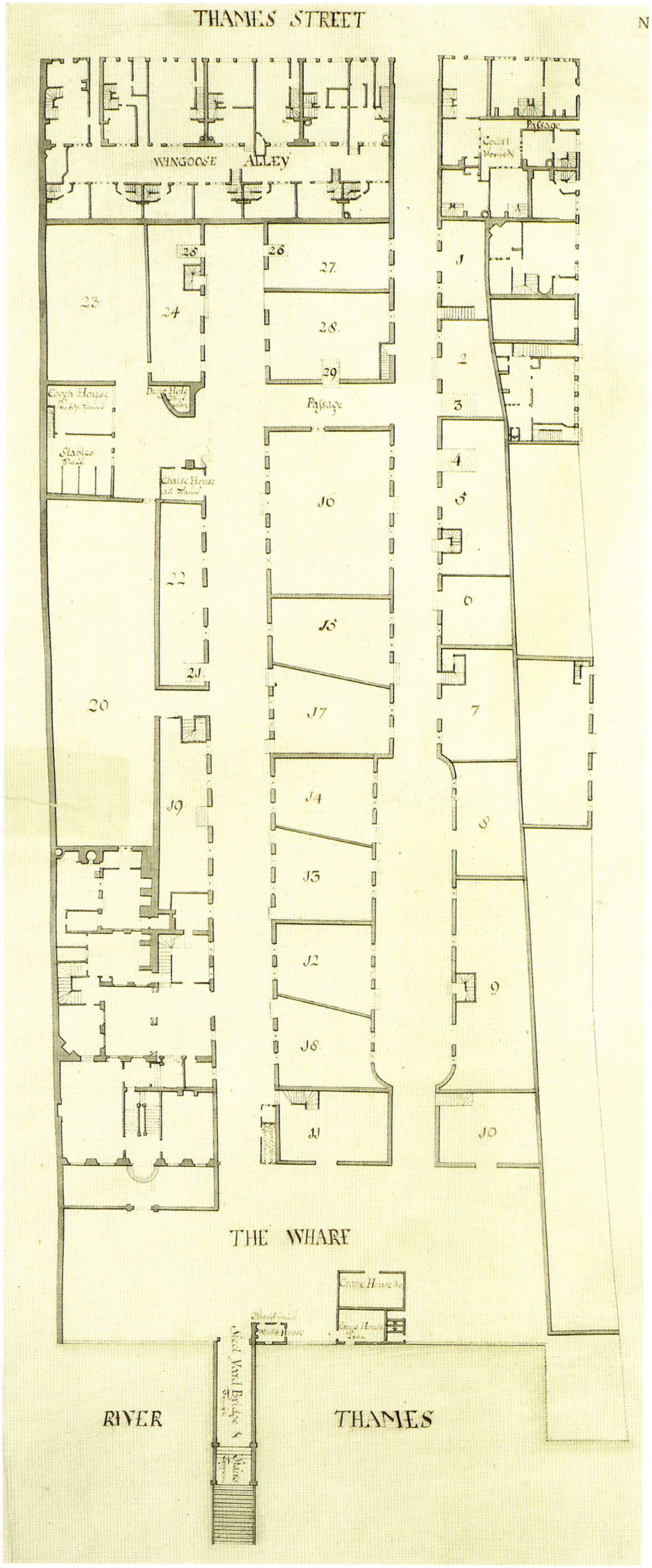

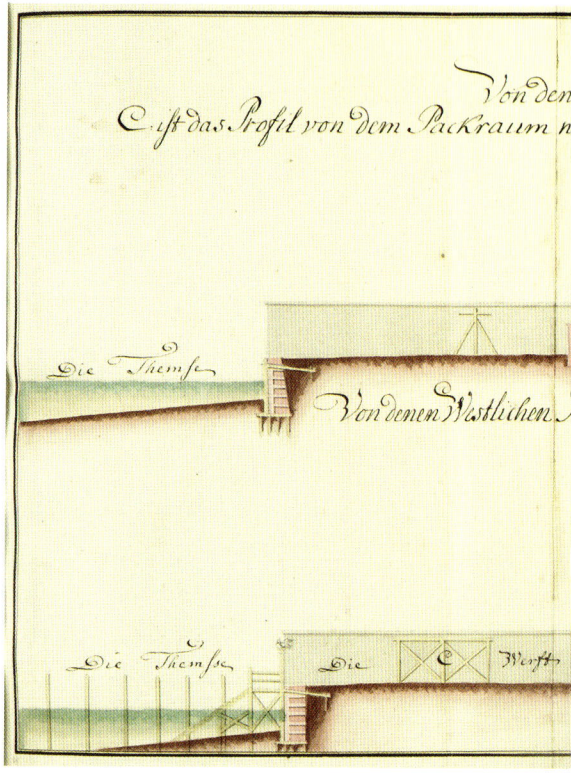

Fig. 166. Part of the plan of the Steelyard, c.1714, showing the ground floor. On the same sheet is the plan of the first floor of the warehouses, the elevation of the buildings facing the river and the arms of the Hanseatic League (see Fig. 171).

KEY, Fig. 166

Ground floor: 1–29 are warehouses, except 3, 4, 21, 25, 26 and 29, which are stairs to vaults under 1, 2, 5, 6, 22, 24, 27 and 28.

First floor: warehouses over 1–22 and 24–29.

Second floor: warehouses over 19–22; above 22 is the long garret.

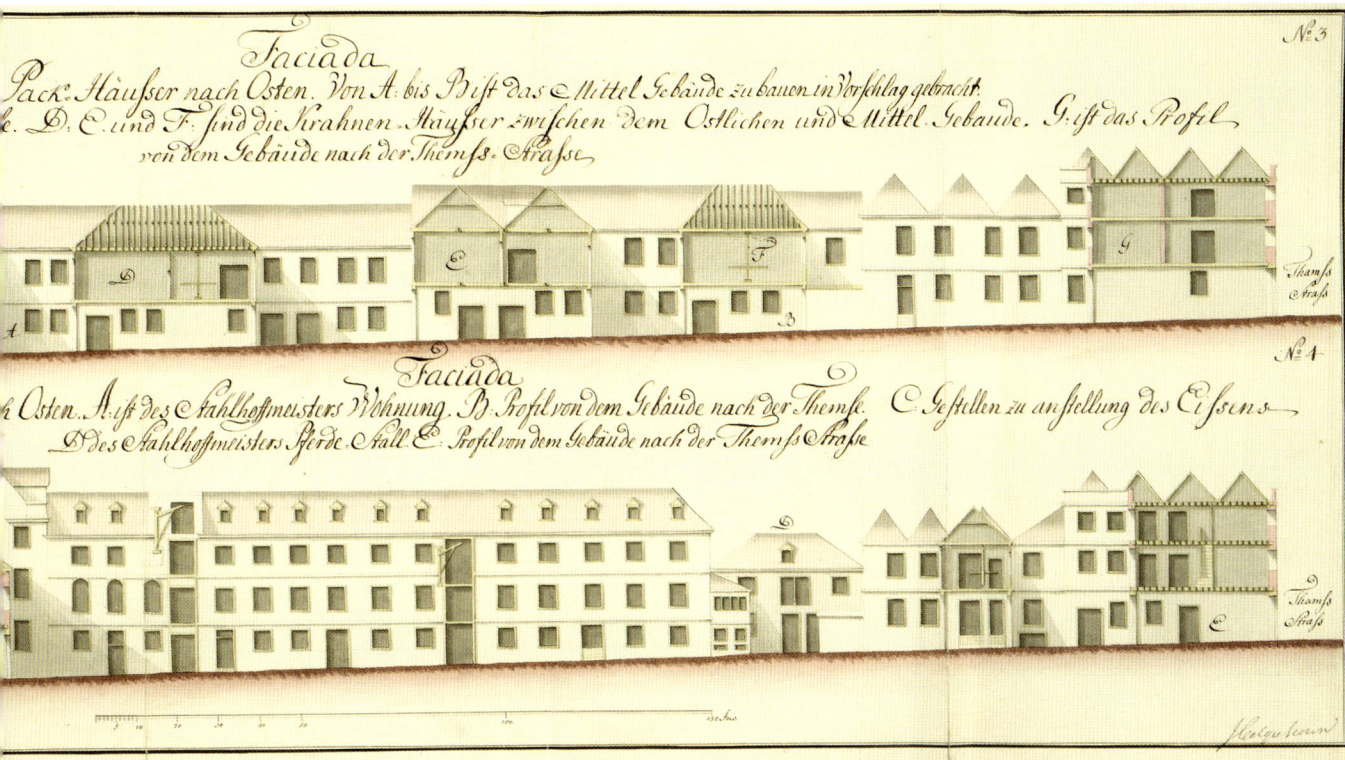

Fig. 167. Elevations of the Steelyard's middle and western ranges (top and bottom respectively), both from the east, 1778. The buildings were the post-Fire ones except the range in Thames Street, rebuilt in 1754, and the warehouses immediately behind it, which replaced the Rhenish winehouse before 1714.

Key to top: A to B – middle building proposed to be rebuilt; C – cross-section of warehouse by Thames; D, E, F – crane houses between eastern and middle buildings; G – cross-section of building next to Thames Street.

Key to bottom: A – Steelyard Master's dwelling; B – cross-section of building next to Thames; C – frames for iron; D – Steelyard Master's stable; E – cross-section of building next to Thames Street.

built a fine bridge [landing stage], and as well there as to the street for ornament have caused the arms of the Hanse towns to be set up'. In February 1681 he responded to their request for accounts and 'a draught of the buildings thereof and its substantialness', which is undoubtedly Plan 73.[39] It bears the names of two of the City's surveyors, Robert Hooke and John Oliver, the City Carpenter, George Seagood, two of the City's viewers, Thomas Seagood and George Hatton, and two others, who presumably vouched in some way for the 'substantialness' of the buildings.[40] The new buildings are shown in more detail on Plan 74 of about 1714.[41] The rebuilding largely followed the earlier layout (see Plan 5), slightly simplified, with three north-south ranges of warehouses, but the warehouses were larger and fewer than before and apparently without associated lodgings (for example just four large rooms on the first floor of the range numbered 16 to 18 in Fig. 166). The warehouses mostly had two storeys, except in the west range, and there were vaults under those further from the river and several cranes over the lanes to convey goods to the upper storeys (Fig. 167). There was a wider wharf than before, exceeding the forty feet required, though it was walled off from the neighbouring wharves. Facing the river was a fine new house-master's residence, occupied by Jacob or Theodore or both of them. It had three and a half storeys and cellars, and was approached through a small yard and a central front door facing the Thames (Figs 168-69). There were seven houses in Thames Street west of the entrance, of two-room plan, and seven behind them in Wildgoose Alley of one-room plan. East of the entrance was a block of six houses of two-room or one-room plan around a small courtyard (Fig. 170). The main change by c.1714 was the replacement of the Rhenish winehouse by additional warehouses (Nos. 23-29 on Fig. 166). The plan of c.1714 also shows some property in Allhallows Lane, outside the Steelyard's enclosing wall.

Fig. 168. The Steelyard seen from the river in 1778, with iron bars stacked on the wharf.

Key: A – Steelyard Master's dwelling; B – building next to the Thames proposed to be rebuilt; C – frames for iron; D – crane house.

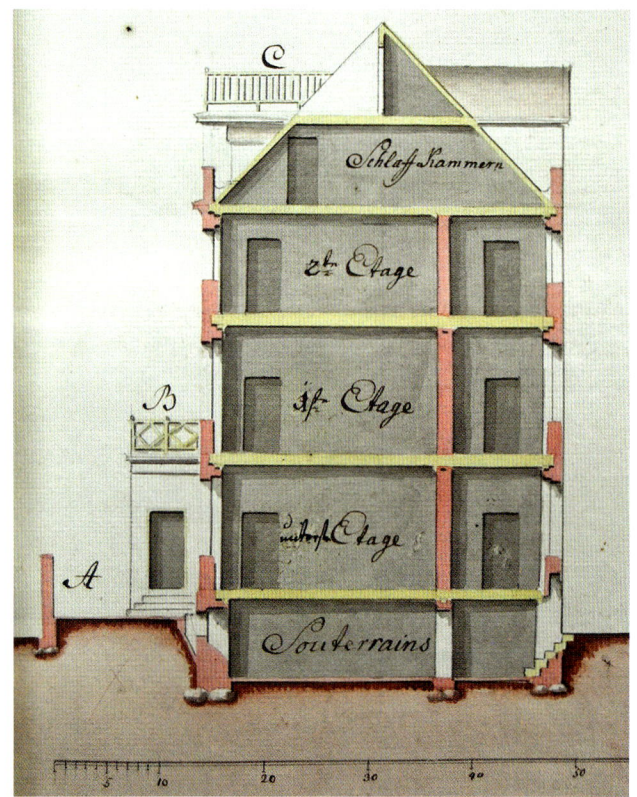

Fig. 169. Cross-section of the Steelyard Master's dwelling, 1778.

Fig. 170. The two houses built by John Ball in Thames Street east of the Steelyard's gateway, drawn in 1778.

Fig. 171. Cartouche with the arms of the Hanseatic League, from one of the copies of the plan of *c.*1714.

After Jacob's death in 1680, Theodore acted as house-master until his own death in 1706, when his interest passed to two nephews, Jacob and Theodore Jacobsen. The three cities questioned the Jacobsen lease, especially the additional thirty-one years, and began legal proceedings in 1720, which were protracted. The plan of *c.*1714 may have been part of the cities' preparation for recovering their property. It has labels in English, to which German translations have been added. The lease ended in 1745, and the lawsuit in 1748, when the three cities were ordered to pay £3,000 to the Jacobsens in settlement of all claims. On recovering their property the three cities first built a new warehouse in Thames Street west of the entrance, replacing fourteen houses, in 1754,[42] and then in or about 1778 rebuilt the middle and east warehouses and the south range. The three cities sold the Steelyard in 1853 and the buildings were demolished in 1863, the site being used for Cannon Street Station. The plans were evidently transferred from Bremen State Archives when the property was sold, eventually finding their way into the railway collections at the National Archives. The stone placed on the Thames Street houses bearing the arms of the Hanseatic League, for which Gabriel Cibber, stonecutter, was paid £5 in 1670,[43] is now in the Museum of London.

Plan 75
Wharves in Bermondsey, *c.*1670
FIG. 172

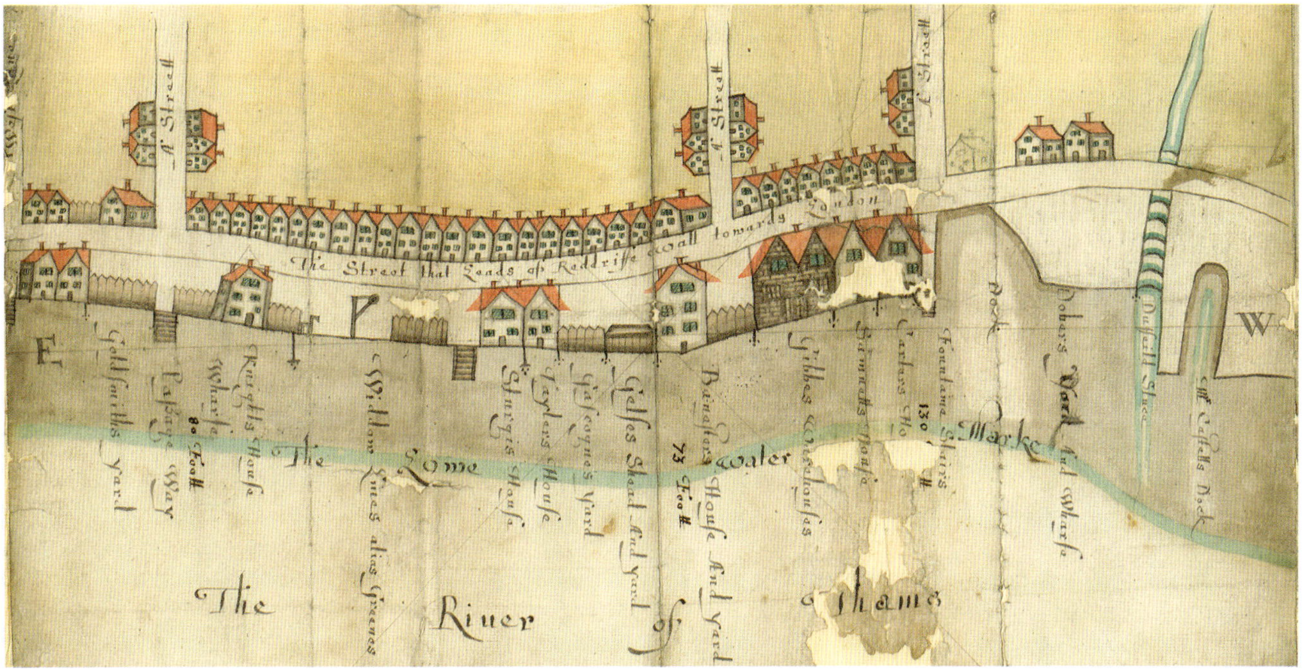

Fig. 172. Wharves in Bermondsey, *c.*1670. North is at the bottom.

This plan shows some of the Earl of Salisbury's property on Bermondsey's riverside, from just east of Duffield Sluice to Mill Stairs or West Lane Stairs—in modern terms from Bevington Street to West Lane. Its date is known only approximately, based on what is recorded about the occupants.[44] All the land east of Duffield Sluice had formed part of Lady Croft, which by the seventeenth century was the Cherry Garden. In the 1570s Lady Croft had been leased by Symond Mawe, a shipwright, who used its wharf to mend ships, as well as to lay fish on and to load hay. Subsequently the riverside parts of the Cherry Garden became separate holdings, with a passage eight feet wide (later Bermondsey Wall) maintained for access.[45]

The plan names occupants rather than lessees, and provides an illustration of riverside trades in east London. The buildings are evidently standardised, but on the riverside the plan may indicate the number and type of buildings. From west to east, Castell may have been William Castell, shipwright, and Richard Dober was certainly a shipwright.[46] John Gibbs, gentleman, was a lessee by 1652, with a holding 193½ feet from east to west. It contained two houses, a wharf and a workhouse, occupied in 1636 by two shipwrights, and two smiths' forges adjoining.[47] The next property, held by George Greene, waterman, from 1653, included a dwelling called the Fleur de Luce, two other small dwellings and wharves. One of the small dwellings was occupied by John Turgis, who was probably the 'Sturgis' of the plan. By 1689 the site was Watton's anchor forge.[48] Next were a house and wharf leased in 1658 by Philip and Joan Lynes, the latter probably being 'Widdow Lines alias Greenes' on the plan.[49] The last holding before Cherry Garden Stairs was leased by John Baldwyn, pulley-maker, in 1658, but subsequently by John Knight.[50] The last property on the plan consisted of three houses, a wharf and a workhouse, leased in 1636 to William Case, variously described as gentleman and mariner.[51]

INDUSTRIES

In the period covered by this book and for long afterwards London was the country's greatest industrial centre, and around 1700 perhaps 40% of its workforce was engaged in manufacturing.[52] Wages, rents and the cost of coal were all high in London, but London was the largest market, had the best distribution system, had plenty of skilled labour and was the largest port; the Thames-side and the southern suburbs also had water. Much of London's production took place in small workshops (e.g. Plan 87), and many industries are represented on plans only by a square building labelled as, for example, 'die house', 'sugar house' or 'printing house' (Plans 37, 39, 133). This section concentrates instead on those industries which made a distinctive mark on the townscape.[53]

Plan 76
Battle Mills, Southwark, c.1680
William Leybourn
FIG. 173

Battle Mills were at the north end of what was Mill Lane in the seventeenth and eighteenth centuries but is now Battle Bridge Lane, just east of Hay's Wharf (with Hay's Wharf jutting into the lane where the mills once did). Battle Bridge was the landing stage on the east side of the mills. The name derived from Battle Abbey, whose Abbot had had a house on part of the present Hay's Wharf site, together with two mills by 1230. The Bridge House secured ownership of the former monastic property in 1576. The mills were tide mills: water flowed inland through them at high tide and spread into various channels and into the Maze Ponds (east of the present Guy's Hospital), where it was penned until low tide and then released, flowing back through the mills. Tide mills had once been common in Southwark, with up to seventeen on six sites in the medieval period, but by the mid-seventeenth century Battle Mills and Pickleherring Mill (Plan 77) seem to have been the only survivors.[54] Leybourn drew a plan dated 1680 of the mills, millstream and ponds, as part of a commission from the Bridge House for 'making the surveys and drafts of Battle Mills and mill streame Eglinsgate and the Maze Ponds', receiving payments amounting to £20 from October 1680 to July 1681, and this undated plan, showing the mill in more detail, was undoubtedly part of the same commission.[55]

In 1655, when the mills were leased to Damaris Boggest, they consisted of a capital messuage of three and a half storeys with a stone wharf (perhaps the house edged in red west of the mills), a

Fig. 173. Part of the plan of Battle Mills, Southwark, c.1680, showing the mills.

crane, a warehouse, a stable, a millhouse of two storeys besides the roof, two water mills, and ponds and watercourses; there were also a large workhouse and warehouse north of the millhouse, a tenement of two and a half storeys east of the lane and abutting north on the Thames, a coalhouse at the north end of the wharf and four tenements on the east side of the wharf (perhaps replaced by the house edged in red). Dotted lines on the plan indicate that the millstream was built over almost all the way from the millhouse to the Thames. A lease of 1669 included 'three paire of dyers washing staires as they are now fastened to ye wharfe of Battle Bridge mill pond',[56] and the plan dated 1680 shows numerous encroachments on the millstream between the mill and Tooley Street. From 1668/9 the miller was Timothy Franklin, who was succeeded by Richard Franklin by 1682.[57]

Battle Mills continued to be listed in the Bridge House's rentals until 1767, but Ralph Hilditch, who leased the site from 1731 to 1767, was a wharfinger, and when the site was advertised for letting in 1766 it was referred to as Beale's or Hilditch Wharf without any mention of mills, so it seems likely that the mills disappeared around 1731.[58] Tide mills were expensive to maintain, as the channels had to be scoured regularly (unlike a normal millstream), the machinery suffered from fluctuating water levels, and they could operate for only limited hours per day, but the main reason for the mills' disappearance may have been London's increasing need for wharf space.

Plan 77
Morgan's Lane, Southwark, 1684
William Leybourn
FIG. 174

This plan was one of several drawn of the London estates of Magdalen College, Oxford, in 1684. It relates to five or more industries, and to a watercourse on which most of them depended, though it refers directly only to one of them. The property shown, a little eastward from Battle Mills, was bought in about 1200 by Malling Abbey, which built a town house and two water mills there. Henry Yevele, the mason, acquired it in 1387 and had the mills rebuilt as a double mill on the model of Battle Mills. The brewery existed by 1425. The property came to Magdalen College in the 1480s as part of the estate of Sir John Fastolf. In 1638 the College leased it to Edmund Morgan of Lambeth, esquire, who evidently gave his name to Morgan's Lane. It then included the High Brewhouse on the west side and two water mills, together with wharves and watercourses.[59] The mills were known as Pickleherring Mill (probably taking the name from the Thames stairs a little to the east), though in the petition referred to below the name was changed from Pickleherring Mill to St Mary Magdalen Mill.[60]

In 1667 the College leased the property to Alderman Edmund Lewin and gave him permission to pull down the water mills and replace them by a wharf. However, Lewin had already sub-let the mills to Thomas Franklin, a miller, for four and a half years. Lewin and Franklin were soon in the lawcourts over repairs. Franklin stated that 'hee stayed there untill it was like to fall downe and was necessitated to take another mill to keepe on his trade and custome'. In late 1668 or early 1669 he moved to Battle Mills, boarding up Pickleherring Mill as he left.[61]

By 1669 Lewin's changes were having an impact on other industries. He first made a dam across the millpond, narrowing the water channel to four feet, and was forced to remove the dam by the Commissioners for Sewers. Then he began to drive posts and piles into the water channel and to build a house over the pond. This prompted a petition from the College's other tenants nearby, who pointed out that they had previously had the benefit of the water which ran in through the mills at each tide, 'dilateing itselfe to divers sewers ditches and draynes', and that they were mostly feltmakers, fellmongers, whitsters or in similar trades who depended on that water for their

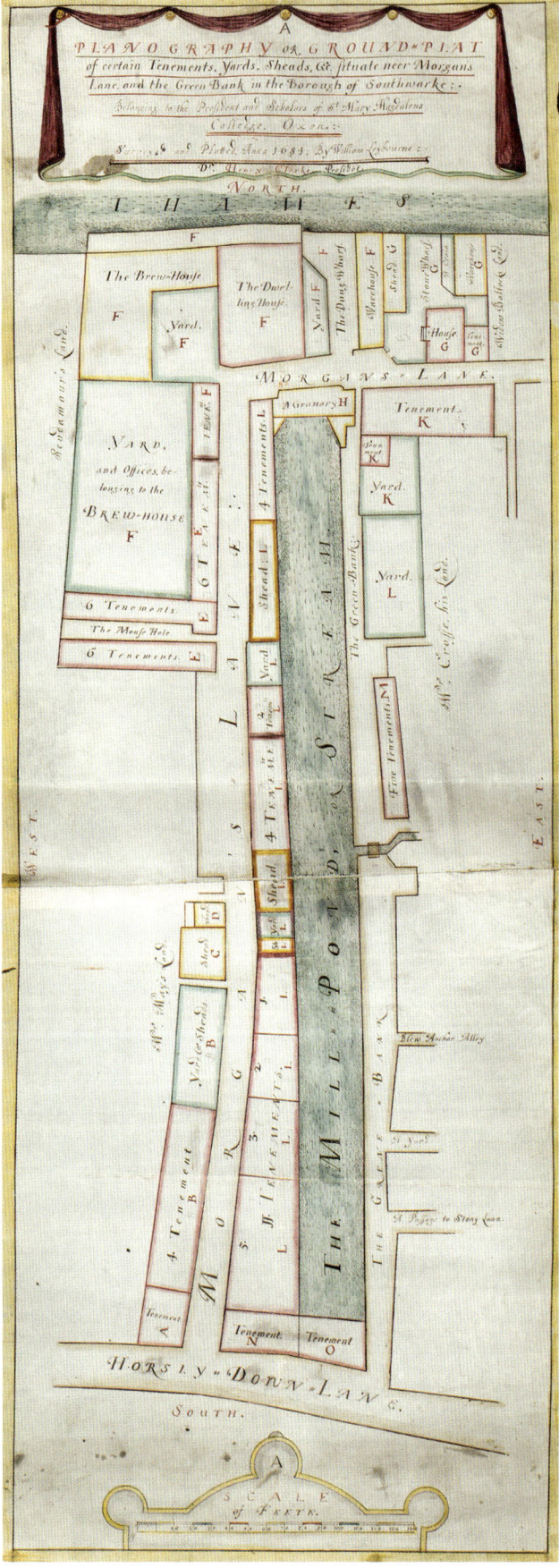

Fig. 174. Morgan's Lane, Southwark, 1684.

livelihoods. Feltmakers (who made hats) were certainly prominent among the College's Southwark tenants. (Fellmongers dealt in hides and skins, and whitsters bleached cloth—see Plan 82.) According to a letter of 1679, many of the College's tenants had 'shedds or little howses, and other conveniencies, supported by posts, sett in the soyle of the watercourses'.[62] The plan shows one watercourse heading eastwards, and Morgan's map of 1682 shows a network of watercourses to the south and east, though it is not clear how they connected. The petition refers to families relying on the water living on the east side of Barnesby Street (now Bermondsey Street), the Isle of Ducks (south of Tooley Street east of the millstream), Horsley Down (now part of Tooley Street), Weavers Lane (north of Tooley Street), Stony Lane (the next street east from Green Bank, now gone), Green Bank and Horsley Down Lane (further east). Undoubtedly Lewin did demolish the mills, as his renewed lease of 1679 indicates that they no longer existed. However, the College told Lewin in August 1669 that it had not intended to damage its other tenants by letting him remove the mills, and the problem was probably resolved; the 1679 lease provided for the College's other tenants to have undiminished use of the water and watercourses.[63]

The millstream still appears on Rocque's map of the 1740s, but had gone by the time of Horwood's in 1814. Morgan's Lane and what remained of Green Bank, renamed Braidwood Street, disappeared during recent redevelopment, but the street signs can still be seen either side of 115 Tooley Street, which stands on the site of the millstream.

Plan 78
The Bridge House Brewhouse, Southwark, 1653
Joseph Darvoll   Fig. 175

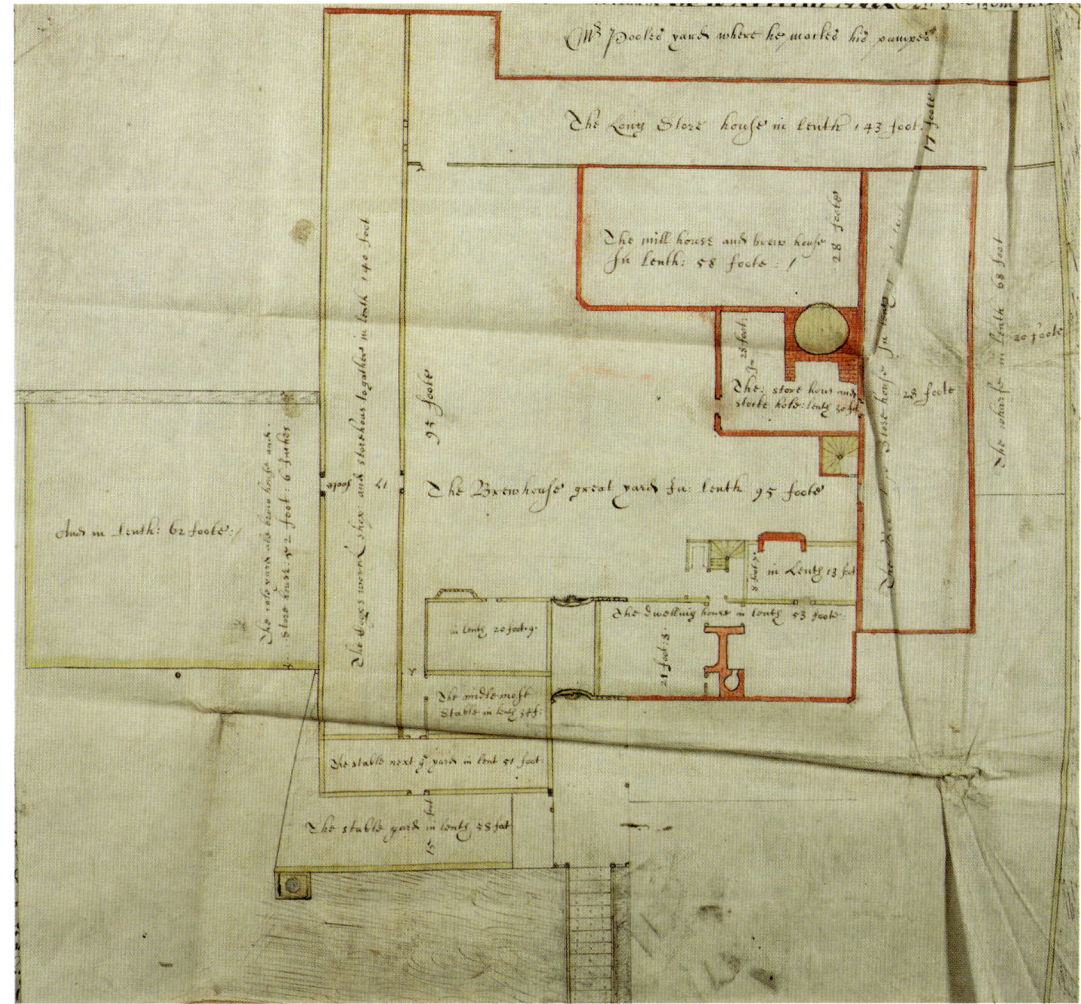

Fig. 175. The Bridge House Brewhouse, Southwark, 1653. North is to the right.

This plan, by the Bridge House's carpenter of the land works, shows a large brewery belonging to the Bridge House. It was between the Bridge House and Battle Mills, and was approached from the east by a bridge across the millstream of Battle Mills, at the bottom of the plan (see Plan 76). Around a courtyard were a large brewhouse, storehouses, coopers' workshops, a separate ale brewhouse, three stables (totalling 143 feet in length) and the brewer's house. Some of the buildings were timber and others brick. The wharf was known as Pipeborers Wharf.[64] The site had contained only two houses and a garden in 1591, but the brewery was there by 1629. Robert Houghton was the brewer by 1633 and renewed the lease in 1653 for sixty-one years, but died within a year.[65] The brewery was still operating in 1803. The site is now occupied by Hay's Wharf.[66] The plan records one other industry: to the west was 'Mr Pooles yard where he mackes his pumpes'.

Plan 79
The Peacock Brewhouse, Whitecross Street, 1686
William Leybourn FIG. 176

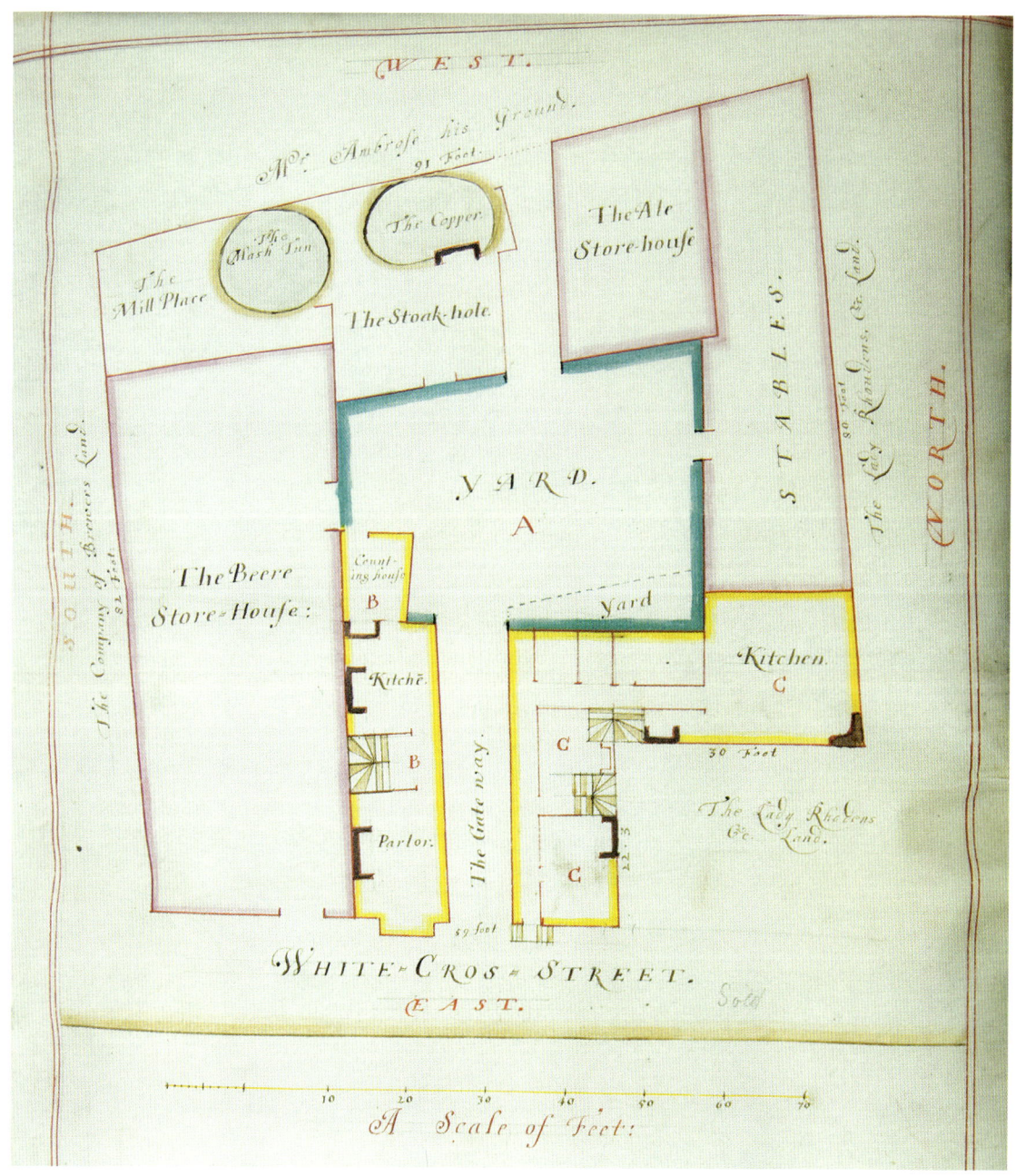

Fig. 176. The Peacock Brewhouse, Whitecross Street, 1686.

petitioned the Company a year later about his 'extraordinary charges of new building' there. It is presumably Walker's buildings which are shown on the plan. Shortly after that, William Ambrose, brewer, became the occupant. His son-in-law, Thomas Calvert or Calverd, stated in his will of 1668 that he held the freehold of part of the brewery, evidently the land to the west marked on the plan as Ambrose's, which Ambrose claimed he had added to the brewery to make it more convenient. Ogilby and Morgan's map suggests that it contained part of the main brewhouse and a second small yard (Fig. 177). Ambrose renewed the lease in 1681, paying a £520 fine, and obtained permission to sub-let the house north of the gateway. In 1685 the Fishmongers allowed him to sell a one-third share to Felix Calvert (probably Thomas's son) and another one-third share to Anne Cleeve, and these three were partners in the brewery until at least 1697.[67] Felix Calvert took a new lease of the brewery in 1715, and the Peacock was later one of the Calvert family's two breweries, the other being in Thames Street. By about 1750 it had been rebuilt by Felix Calvert, and ten years later it had the largest production of any London brewery. In 1810 the Calverts abandoned the Peacock to concentrate their activities in Thames Street. The Peacock site was used for a debtors' prison from 1815 to 1870, then for a railway goods depot until the Second World War, and is now part of the Barbican.[68]

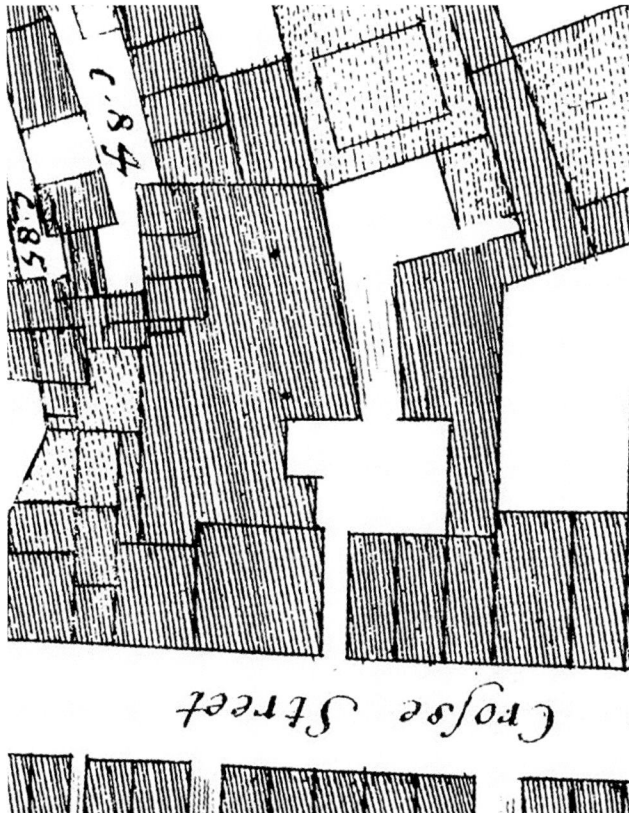

Fig. 177. Detail from Ogilby and Morgan's map of 1676 showing the Peacock Brewhouse, including the part not on Fishmongers' Company land. It has been given the same orientation here as Fig. 176. Ogilby and Morgan show the courtyard correctly but not the houses either side of the gateway.

This plan shows the Fishmongers' Company's Peacock Brewhouse, with its copper, mash tun, storehouses and stables. Malt was crushed and ground in the 'mill place' and then combined with warm water in the mash tun to make wort, and the wort was boiled with hops in the copper. There were a malt loft over the beer storehouse, 'coolers' over the ale storehouse (probably for cooling the wort) and hay lofts over the stables. Houses of three and a half storeys stood either side of the gateway; house B had rooms over the gateway and seems to have been entered through the counting house.

The brewery was already an 'ancient' one by the 1650s. In 1653 the Fishmongers' tenant, Francis Webb, stated that the greater part of it needed to be rebuilt, and was asked to bring 'his proposalls & plott of new building'; a new lease was agreed the following year. It is not clear whether anything was done until in 1657 Webb assigned his interest to James Walker, brewer, who

Plans 80-81
Pye Corner brewhouse, 1718
Heber Lands
FIGS 178-79

These two plans, from separate leases, provide an example of Heber Lands' ornate style. The brewery was described as being at Pye Corner, and was just north of London Wall near Christ's Hospital, to which it belonged (Fig. 180). In 1671 the western property, previously a garden, was leased to Anthony Dolle, citizen and saddler, who was required to build a substantial brick dwelling there (presumably the one shown).[69] By 1680 this was held by Daniel Cary, brewer, who also took a lease in that year of the eastern property, previously a garden used by the steward and matron of Christ's Hospital to dry clothes in. In the same year he built on the eastern property the two-storey brick and timber storehouse for keeping malt and coal,[70] and it was probably then that he built the brewhouse on the western

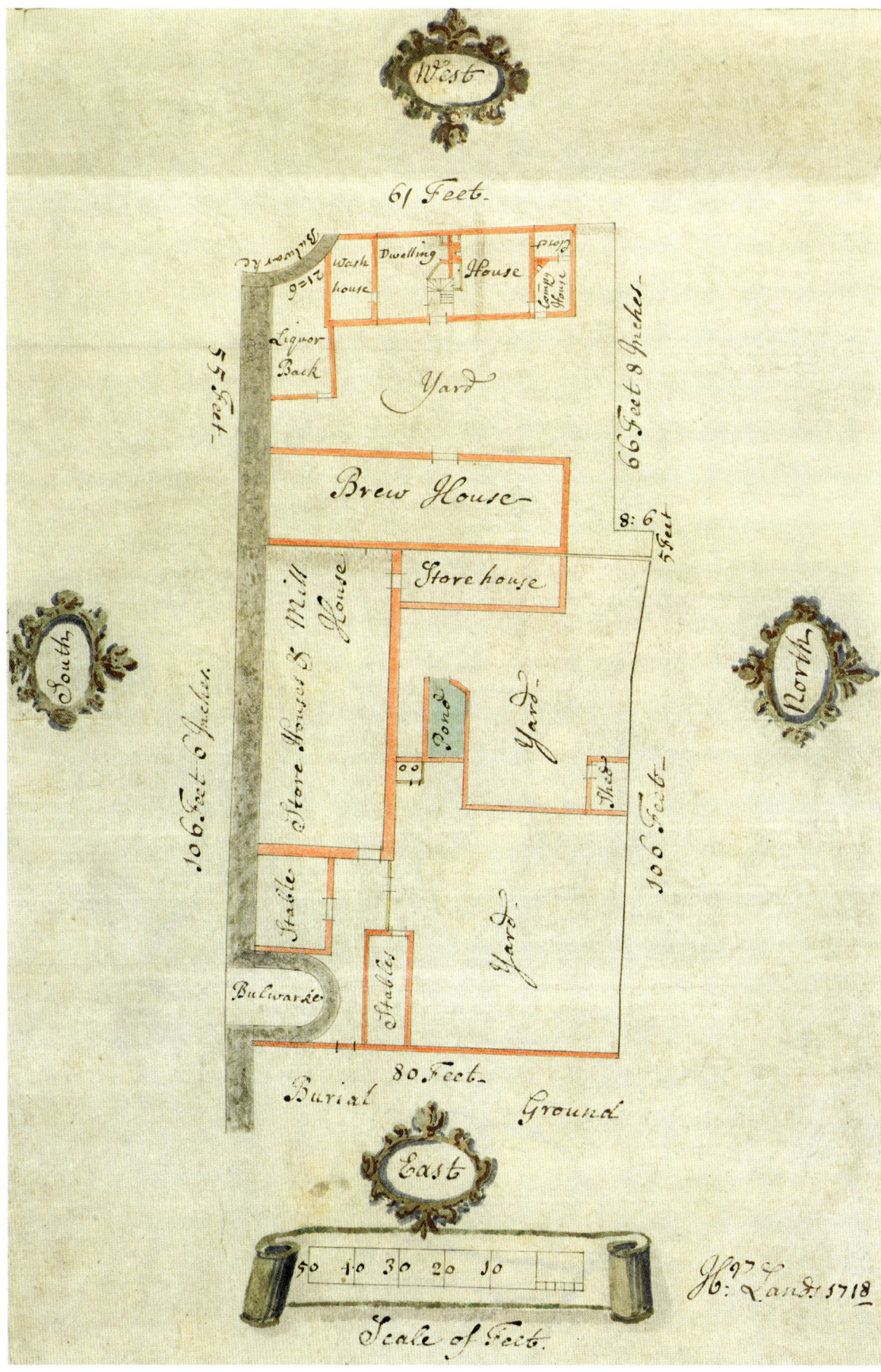

Fig. 178-79. A brewhouse near Pye Corner, 1718 (assembled digitally from two separate lease plans).

property, as it shared a wall with the storehouse. The brewhouse was about sixty-five feet long. In 1718, John Wightman junior, citizen and brewer, obtained leases of both properties, and was required to replace the existing brick house with a new one.

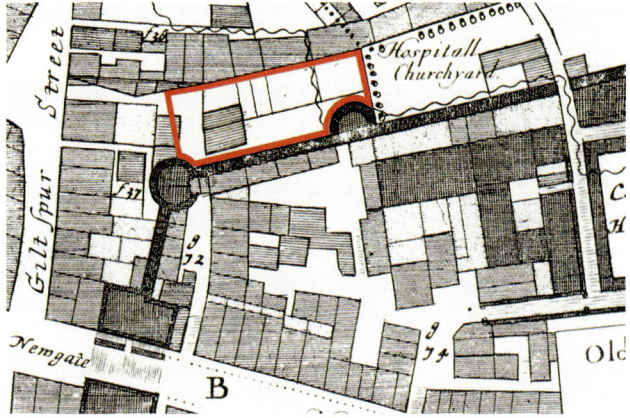

Fig. 180. Detail from Ogilby and Morgan's map of 1676, with the approximate site of the brewery near Pye Corner (not then built) edged in red. The churchyard belonged to Christ's Hospital.

Plan 82
Whiting ground and rope walk in Bermondsey, 1701
Fig. 181

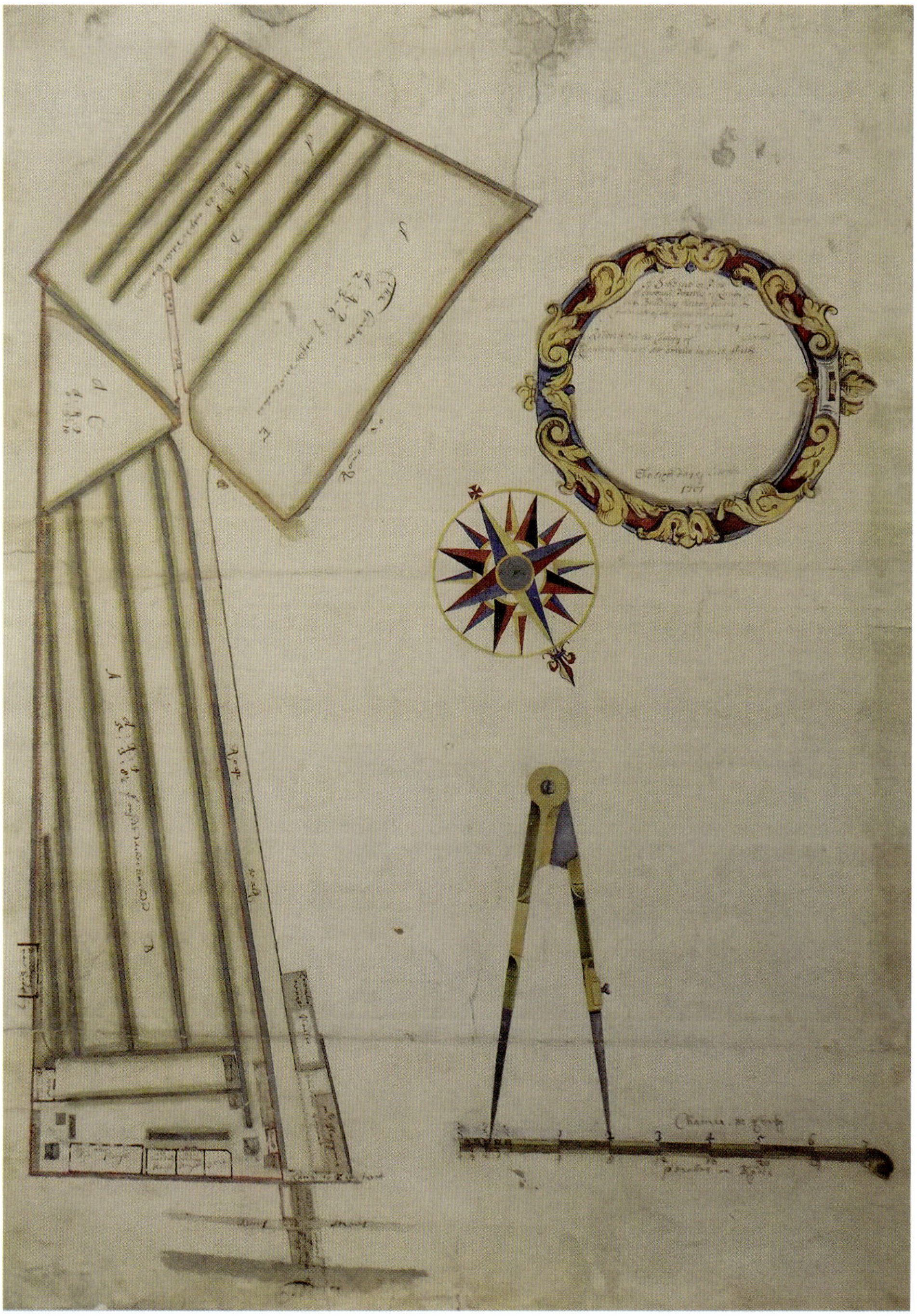

Fig. 181. A whiting ground and a rope walk in Bermondsey, 1701.

The whiting ground and rope walk shown here were on the Earl of Salisbury's land in Bermondsey. In modern terms they were just south of Bermondsey Wall between East Lane and Bevington Street. Until later in the eighteenth century bleaching or 'whiting' cloth so that it could be dyed or patterned was a lengthy process taking about eight months, and was done using sunlight rather than chemicals. There was a cycle of 'bucking' (covering the cloth in a vat with hot water mixed with lye) and crofting or grassing (laying the cloth on the grass for wetting and drying), which was carried out ten to sixteen times. This was followed by souring with buttermilk and working with bare feet, and finally soaping. The long water channels shown on the plan were used for scooping up water to drench the cloths laid out on the banks.[71] When leased to Robert Langstraffe, whitster, in 1677, the six acres converted into a whiting ground included two houses, each with five rooms and a washhouse, and also a drying house, a beating house (partly converted into a stable), an ash house, a bucking house and a long shed divided into five washing rooms. If his water supply was obstructed, Langstraffe was entitled to lay pipes from the Neckinger Wall Ditch across William Terrell's ropeway, but he would then have to pay additional rent. He was required to build a substantial double house of brick on the south side of Bermondsey Wall within seven years.[72]

By 1701 the premises were being used for dyeing as well as bleaching, as there was a new dyehouse on the north side (at the bottom here), of five bays by three. To the west was a new dwelling, perhaps built by Langstraffe, adjoining an old one. There was an old storehouse further west, another dwelling nearby, a shed in the north-east corner, a new building almost adjoining, and a building under construction nearby.[73]

The rope walk belonged in 1677 to William Terrell, ropemaker, who was occupying one of Thomas Miller's houses on adjoining land in East Lane in 1676 (Plan 60).[74] As explained in 1747, 'Rope-yarn is spun in a long walk: The spinner fastens one end of two threads to two spindles of a wheel; the hemp is turned round his middle, and he retires backward from the wheel, spinning out both his threads as he goes, till he reaches the farther end of the walk: The wheel is turned by another hand. When the threads are all spun, they are twisted together, and smeared over with tar.'[75] Maps show that the rope walk remained in use into the nineteenth century.

Plan 83
Tannery in Grange Road, Bermondsey, 1683
FIG. 182

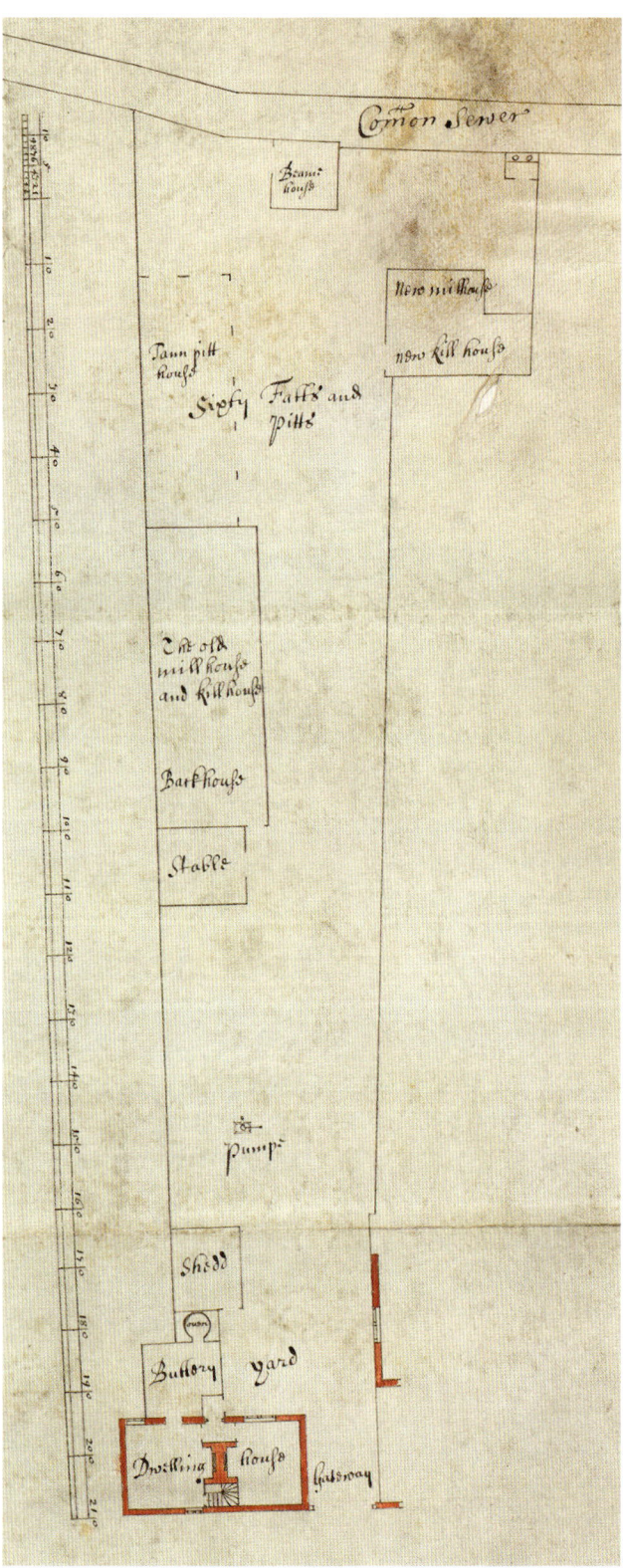

Fig. 182. A tannery in Grange Road, Bermondsey, 1683. North is at the bottom.

In seventeenth-century England the leather industry was second only to the woollen cloth industry, and its most important centre was London. Within London it was concentrated in Bermondsey, which not only had access to the hides which were a by-product of London's meat consumption but also had plenty of water, relatively cheap land and access to oak bark from Surrey. In the late seventeenth century there were about eighty tanneries in Bermondsey and Southwark,[76] one of which is shown here. It was west of the junction of what are now Tower Bridge Road and Decima Street, facing the latter, on land belonging to St Thomas's Hospital, and was run by Elizabeth Smith. The plan was evidently based on Nathaniel Hanwell's—see Plan 144—but is in a different hand.

The initial processes included soaking in lime to remove hair and wool and washing using animal dung. These were called beam-house operations because for some tasks the hides were placed over a wooden beam and worked on using two-handled curved knives. Smith's beam-house was sited as far as possible from her house. There followed the actual tanning process—prolonged soaking in a solution containing tannin, which was usually from oak bark. The bark was ground in a mill, which in Smith's case must have been animal-powered. The soaking was done in pits, and took from six months to two years. Smith had sixty vats ('fatts') and pits, some of them in the open-sided building marked as 'tann pitt house'. The hides then had to be dried in a dark shed.[77] The shed next to Smith's house had the advantages of an oven next door and proximity to the house for security against theft. The function of the killhouse is unclear.[78]

Elizabeth Smith was succeeded by her son Nathaniel and grandson, also Nathaniel, whose possessions were inventoried on his death in 1733. Given the length of the tanning process, much of his capital was tied up in hides and skins. He had 829 hides at six different stages—in 'the limes and grainers', 'the small wooze', 'the strong wooze', the 'settaway', the first layer and the second layer, rising in value with each stage from 10s. to 14s. each and valued at £575. There were also 1,596 skins at five different stages, worth £385, and there were ten bushels (or eighty gallons) of pigeon dung. The stock in the tanning yard totalled £1,007. Smith was evidently prosperous, with £696 of ready money, £104 of plate, rings and watches, and items of clothing such as waistcoats, buckles and wigs.[79]

Plan 84
Silver-spinners' sheds between Coleman and Goat Alleys, Finsbury, 1713
Isaac Olley
Fig. 183

This plan is in the somewhat spare style used by Isaac Olley for large properties with many buildings, giving little information about internal arrangements. As well as showing the mingling of residential and industrial buildings, the plan depicts the complex layout which often resulted even where there was a single landholder. The property was a little south of Old Street, between Whitecross Street and Bunhill Row (Fig. 184). It was leased by the City in 1652 to Daniel Stepping on what was probably a building lease, lasting sixty-one years. It then contained two tenements and gardens, whereas by 1713 there were thirty-three tenements. The houses were mostly brick, but the sheds timber. According to those who viewed them for the City in 1713, 'Wee find the same to be but indifferently tenanted being all lett to tenants at will and severall of them are inmates inhabiting each a seperate room, and that many of the houses are much out of repair and the water comes into the cellars'. They were leased in 1713 to Nathaniel Withers, described as a gentleman of St Giles Cripplegate, who promised to spend £1,000 on new buildings.[80]

The silver-spinning sheds formed part of one of London's luxury trades. The materials required were gold or silver wire and silk. The wire was produced by drawing a silver bar, or for gold wire a gold-coated silver bar, repeatedly through a die set with ever-smaller holes. This manufacture was well established in London by the 1570s, though until long into the seventeenth century Venetian gold and silver wire was thought better than English.[81] The wire was next flatted by being passed between two rollers, and it was then ready for the silver-spinners in their long sheds. The material was supplied by the gold and silver lace-men, who paid the spinners for their work by the ounce. At the end of the spinning shed was a steel wheel, attached to the spindles to which a thread of silk was fastened: 'one person turns the wheel, while another holding the thread of silk in one hand, and the flatted silver in the other, allows the silver to wind gently about the silk as it is turned round by the wheel: in this manner the whole thread of silk is covered'. The 'gold and silver sleysy' was then ready to be applied to high-class clothing, furniture and other items.[82] The metal-

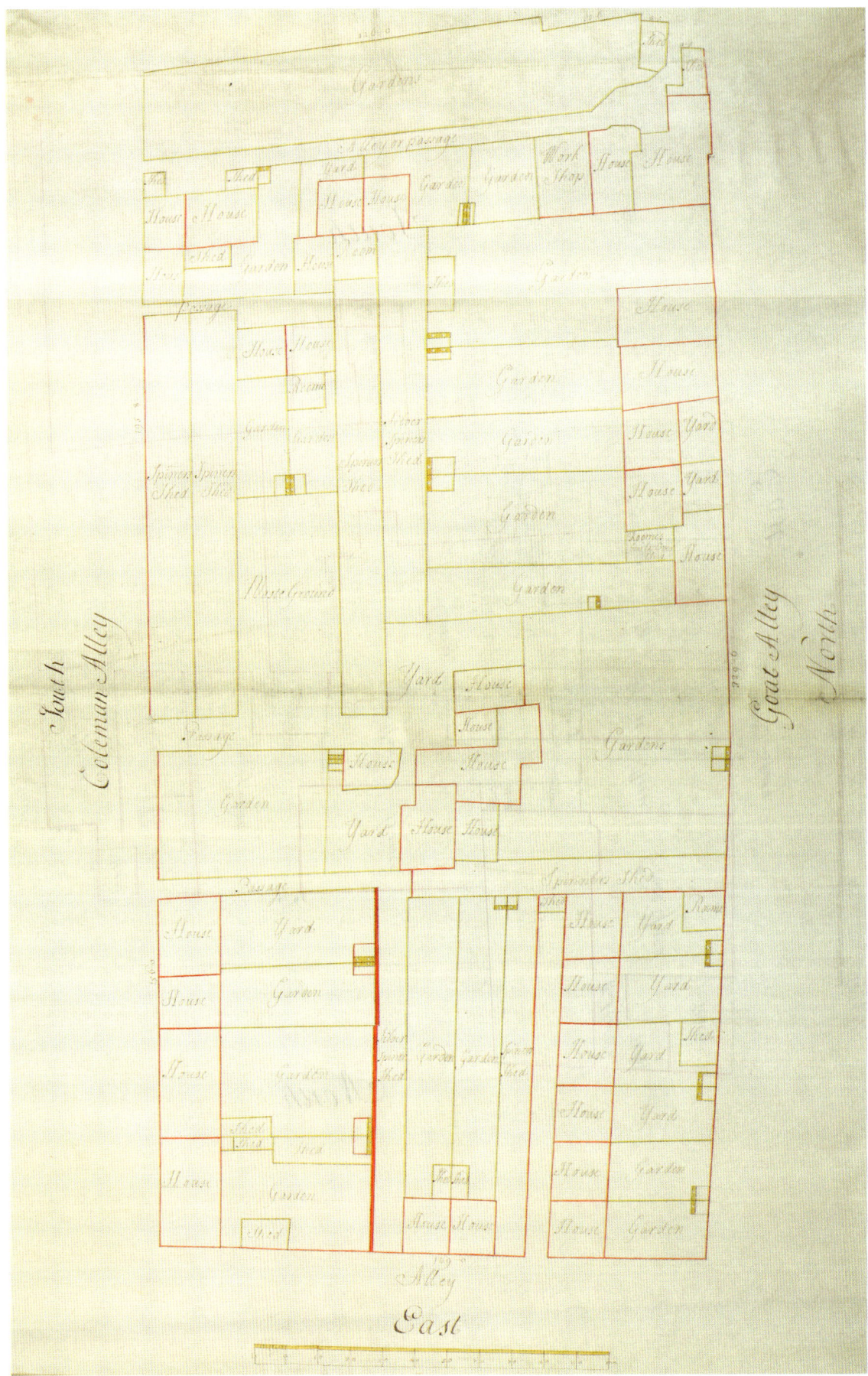

Fig. 183. Houses and silver-spinners' sheds between Coleman Alley and Goat Alley, 1713.

PLANS OF BUILDING TYPES   163

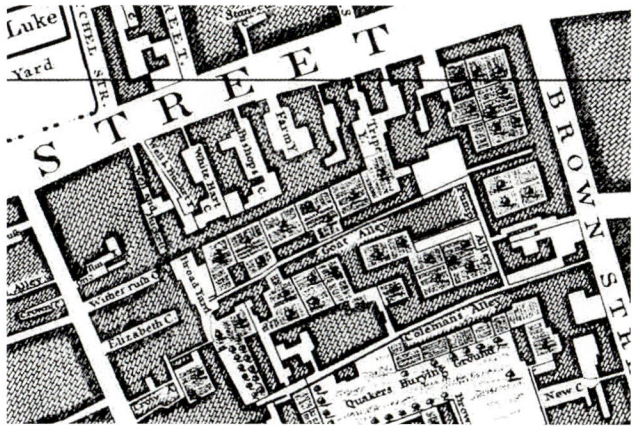

Fig. 184. Detail from Rocque's map of *c.*1745 showing Coleman and Goat Alleys. The streets to west, north and east are, respectively, Whitecross Street, Old Street and Brown Street (now Bunhill Row).

working trades were important in the northern parts of London; in 1692 they accounted for 16.5% of those stating occupations in nearby Aldersgate and Cripplegate Within Wards, and almost two-thirds of these were silversmiths or wiredrawers.[83]

Plan 85
Silver-spinner's shed in Grub Street, 1715
Isaac Olley
Fig. 185

This plot, containing two houses and a silver-spinner's shed, was just under twelve feet wide and 201 feet long, and the spinning shed was about 120 feet long. It was on the west side of Grub Street (now Milton Street), near the north end just south of Cross Dagger Court.[84] In 1715 the front tenement was let to John Knowles and the back tenement with the shed was untenanted.[85] The City leased them in 1715 to Thomas Brookes, citizen and carpenter.

Plan 86
Foundries in Old Bethlehem, 1720
Isaac Olley   Fig. 186

Fig. 185. Houses and a silver-spinner's shed in Grub Street, 1715.

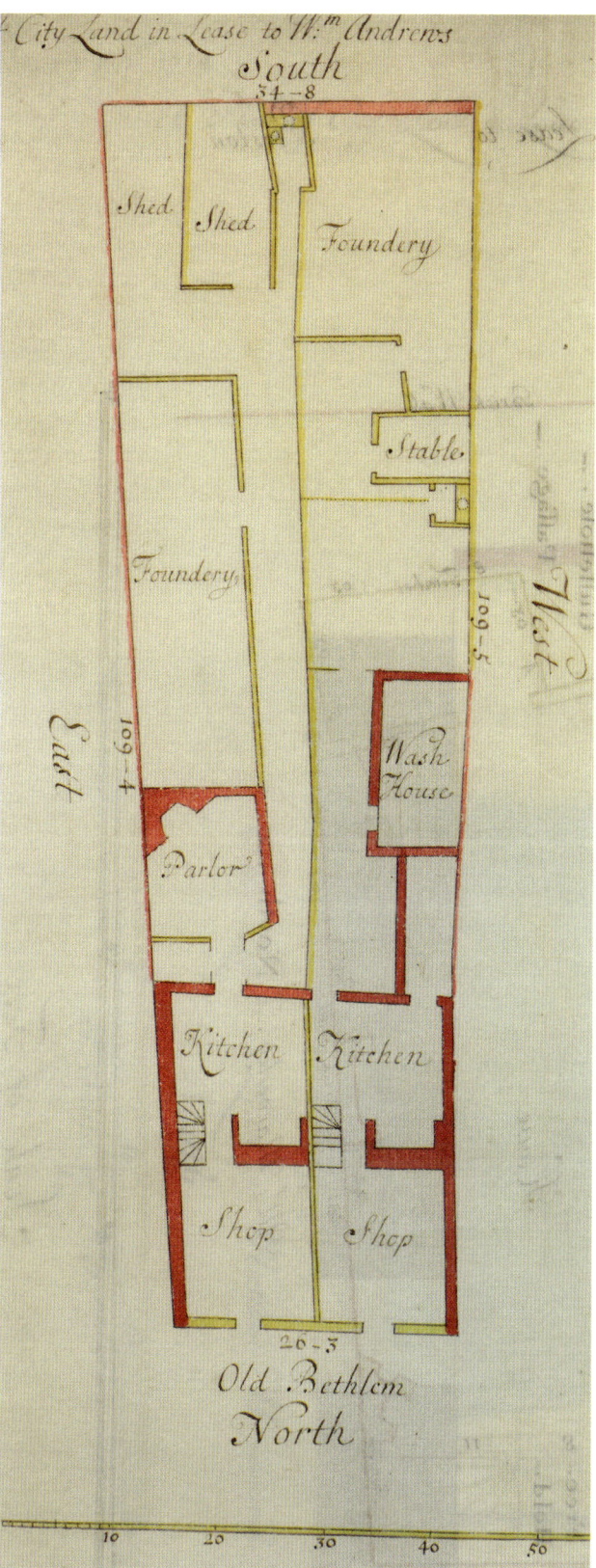

Fig. 186. Houses and foundries in Old Bethlehem, 1720.

Old Bethlehem was approximately on the site of today's Liverpool Street, and these foundries were on the south side of it and, judging by Ogilby and Morgan's map, in the part of it west of the present Old Broad Street. There was a foundry behind each of the two houses. While the houses were largely of brick, the foundries were built of timber. The City leased the property in 1720 to Williams Andrews, a founder. He was the son of a founder of the same name, was apprenticed to Eleanor Andrews, apparently his mother, in 1706, and took an apprentice of his own in 1713.[86]

Plan 87
Workshops in Houndsditch, 1712
John or Isaac Olley
FIG. 187

This plan provides another example of the mixing of the residential and the industrial, with a founder's shop, a currier's workshop (where leather was dressed and coloured after tanning) and a bakehouse behind three houses in Houndsditch. It probably also provides an example of what had once been a more common arrangement: small masters selling the produce of their workshop in a shop at the front of the property. The houses, east of Castle Court, may have been constructed under building leases of 1616 and 1619, though perhaps under the sixty-one year lease granted in 1652. They were largely of timber but with brick facades. Each had two and a half storeys and cellar; two had shop and kitchen, two chambers above and one garret, while the other had four chambers above and two garrets. The two left-hand tenements were known as the Three Bells and Horse Shoe and the Porter and Dwarf respectively. The City's lessee was in 1652 John James, citizen and armourer (hence perhaps the founder's shop), and in 1712 John Barker of London, gentleman, the son of a Lichfield mercer.[87]

Plan 88
Bakery in Perpoole Lane, 1719
Thomas Henley
FIG. 188

The bakery shown here occupied a plot about thirty-four feet square on the south side of Perpoole Lane (now Portpool Lane), off Leather Lane. The 'sincke into ye white hart sewer' marked on the plan suggests that it was at the east end of Perpoole Lane, near the White Hart Inn shown in Leather Lane on Ogilby and Morgan's map of 1676. On the right-hand side was a bakehouse, with a round oven about ten feet in diameter, and a chimney or hearth, and there was a 'shop for bread' at the front. The house on the left-hand side had parlour, kitchen and buttery on the ground floor, together with a yard and a stable. John Willey, baker, who was already occupying the property, bought it in 1719 for £200. Thomas Henley, who drew the plan, was probably the carpenter who in 1717 was living in Liquorpond Street, the next street to the north.[88]

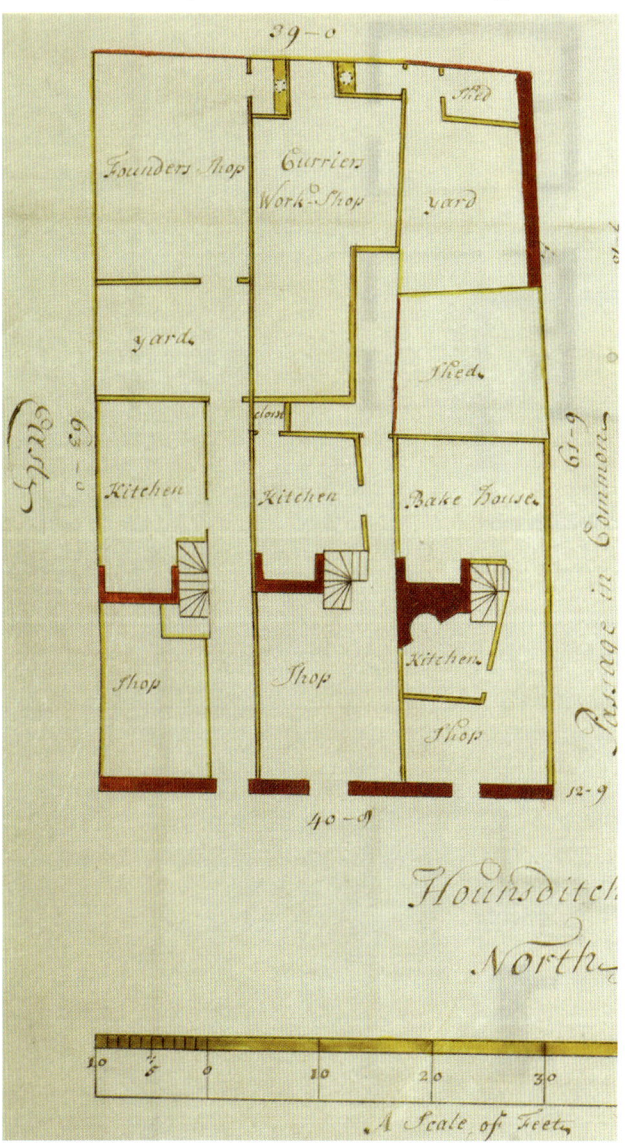

Fig. 187. Houses and workshops in Houndsditch, 1712. A fourth house shown on this plan has been omitted.

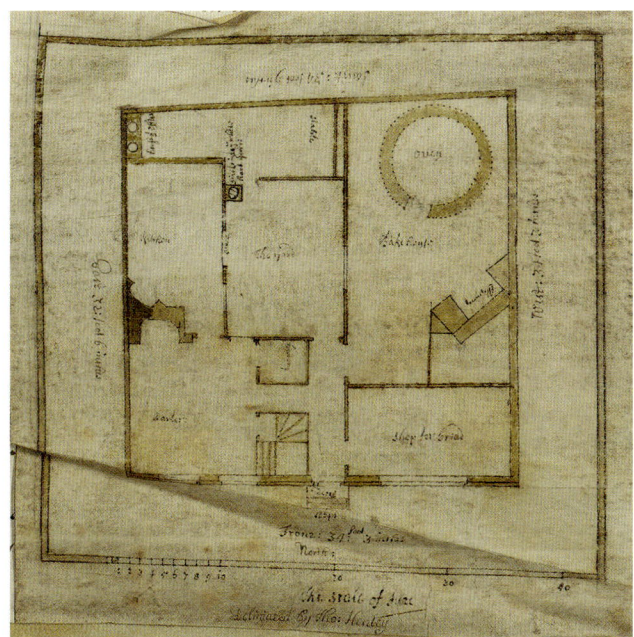

Fig. 188. A bakery in Perpoole Lane, 1719.

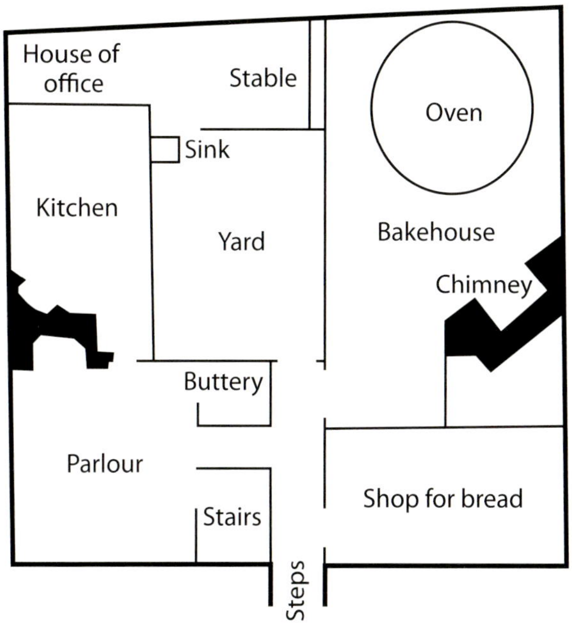

Fig. 189. The plan of the Perpoole Lane bakery redrawn.

MARKETS

The main purpose of the City's markets was to enable country people to sell their produce directly to London's inhabitants, within prescribed days and hours in prescribed places. Retailers were allowed to buy for resale only for a short period before the markets closed. Londoners were not supposed to take stalls and country people were not supposed to sell anything other than country produce, including some non-food items such as leather and nails.[89] Before the Great Fire almost all the markets were in the streets (e.g. Plan 20); after the Fire they were moved out of the streets to new locations. Inns also had a role in marketing (Plans 54, 93), and there were some markets in London outside the City.

Plans 89-91
Leadenhall Market, 1677, 1698 and 1700
William Leybourn and John Olley
FIGS 190, 191, 193

Of these three plans, one shows all three parts of Leadenhall Market (Fig. 190), one shows its oldest part (Fig. 191) and one shows just a small area (Fig. 193).[90] The City acquired the mansion called Leadenhall in 1411 and rebuilt it in 1440-55 as four ranges around a large courtyard, with its own chapel (Figs 192 and 194). The market took place within the courtyard, though there was also a street market until 1666. The ranges, originally intended as granaries, were used for other commercial activities. The Greenyard to the southeast, which had probably been the garden of the mansion, was also in use as a market by the seventeenth century. The stout walls of the Leadenhall and the open space of the Greenyard halted the Great Fire in this area, though according to Strype all but the stonework of the Leadenhall was destroyed.[91] After the Fire, as part of the plan to move the City markets out of the streets, the Herb Market was added on former garden ground to the south.

In 1676 the City leased out jointly all its markets other than Smithfield, Queenhithe and Billingsgate, setting out in the lease the rates to be paid by stallholders and other vendors (such as those who sold from movable trestles, carts or baskets), but by the following year the lessees were asking for abatements of rent. As the profits of the markets were partly determined by rents from the stalls, which varied according to size, the City urgently needed an accurate survey and it ordered Leybourn to make one. Fig. 191 is one of Leybourn's six plans, showing the Beef Market in the medieval courtyard. Leybourn's measurements were later examined and sometimes corrected by Robert Hooke and John Oliver, whose names appear on the plan, showing that on this plan, which is concerned with stalls, Leybourn's measurements cannot be relied on for the buildings.

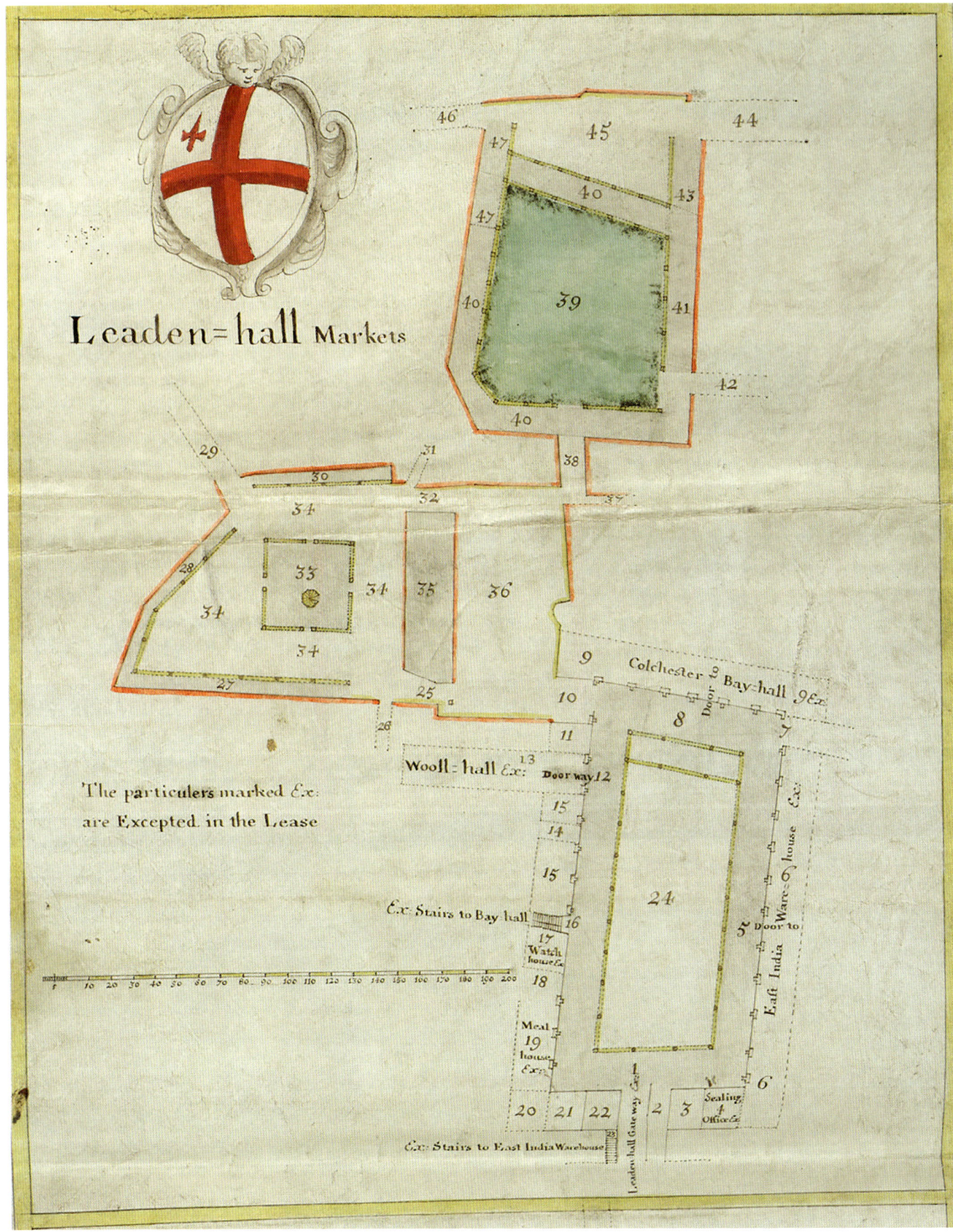

Fig. 190. Leadenhall Market, 1698. North is at the bottom.

KEY, Fig. 190
1. Gate way out to Leadenhall Street.
2. Postern.
3. Warehouse to the market.
4. Sealing Office.
5. Door to East India warehouse.
6. East India warehouse.
7. Passage to Gracechurch Street.
8. Door into Bay Hall.
9. Colchester Bay Hall.
10. Passage into Fish Market.
11. Market warehouses.
12. Door to Wool Hall.
13. Wool Hall.
14. Price's paved alley.
15. Red Lion house.
16. Stairs to Bay Hall.
17. East India watchhouse.
18. Tokenhouse Yard.
19. Meal house.
20-21. Collerman behind the leather seller.[92]
22. Brandy shop.
23. Stair to East India warehouse.
24. Body of the market.
25. Passage into mutton market.
26. New passage to Price's Buildings.
27-28. Country butchers.
29. Passage to Lime Street.
30. Country butchers.
31. House of office.
32. Passage to Fish Market.
33. Market house.
34. Market place.
35. Nail Gallery.
36. Fish Market.
37. Passage to Spread Eagle Inn.
38. Passage to Herb Market.
39. Herb Market.
40. Dorcery.
41. Bacon Market.
42. Passage to Bull Head.
43. Against Vandeputt's buildings.
44. Passage by the Ship Tavern.
45. Place for higlers.
46. Passage to Lime Street.
47. Against Buckworth's Rents.

The plan of 1698 (Fig. 190) also resulted from leasing out the markets. Leybourn drew a plan to be attached to the lease in 1686, and this was copied by John Olley for the 1698 lease.

The courtyard used for the Beef Market also served one day a week for tanned leather and one day for raw hides. Changes made after the Fire included a 'piazza' consisting of wooden columns and a roof around the four sides (Fig. 194); the columns can be seen among the stalls on the 1677 plan. Changes were still being made in 1677, and Leybourn shows only ninety-four of the 106 stalls eventually provided. The egg-cup shapes in Figure 191 are Leybourn's way of indicating covered passages. The ranges around the courtyard, shown better on the 1698 plan, had three storeys, with eight great store-rooms on the upper floors, the longer ones 180 by nineteen feet, and there were staircases in the corners. The north side was largely occupied by the Colchester Bay Hall, used to store woollen cloths from Colchester and Suffolk. The Wool Hall to the east was the former chapel.

The Greenyard, with 143 stalls in 1677, contained the Fish Market, the Nail Gallery, two and a half storeys high, where iron and steel and cutlery wares were sold, and the White Market for mutton, lamb, veal, pork and poultry. A market house was added after the Fire, consisting of twelve wooden columns supporting two upper storeys and a cupola containing a clock. In 1664 houses had been built on empty ground on the north and east sides of the White Market, with the upper storeys extended forward on pillars, 'reserving conveniency for the market people to sit under the piazza' (Fig. 193). This arrangement was extended to the south side after the destruction of the south side and part of the east side in the Great Fire. The eastern houses were said in 1699 to be ill-situated and often untenanted. The property in Fig. 193, described as two houses, had three cellars, three lower rooms, thirteen chambers and three garrets, and seems to have survived the Great Fire, as there was no new lease after the Fire.[93] The Herb Market had replaced a market formerly held in Gracechurch Street, and was for fruit, vegetables and dairy produce, though the western piazza was used by bacon sellers. There was a piazza or arcade around four sides, and there were twenty-eight stalls in 1677, mostly with cellars. Several parts of the piazza were described

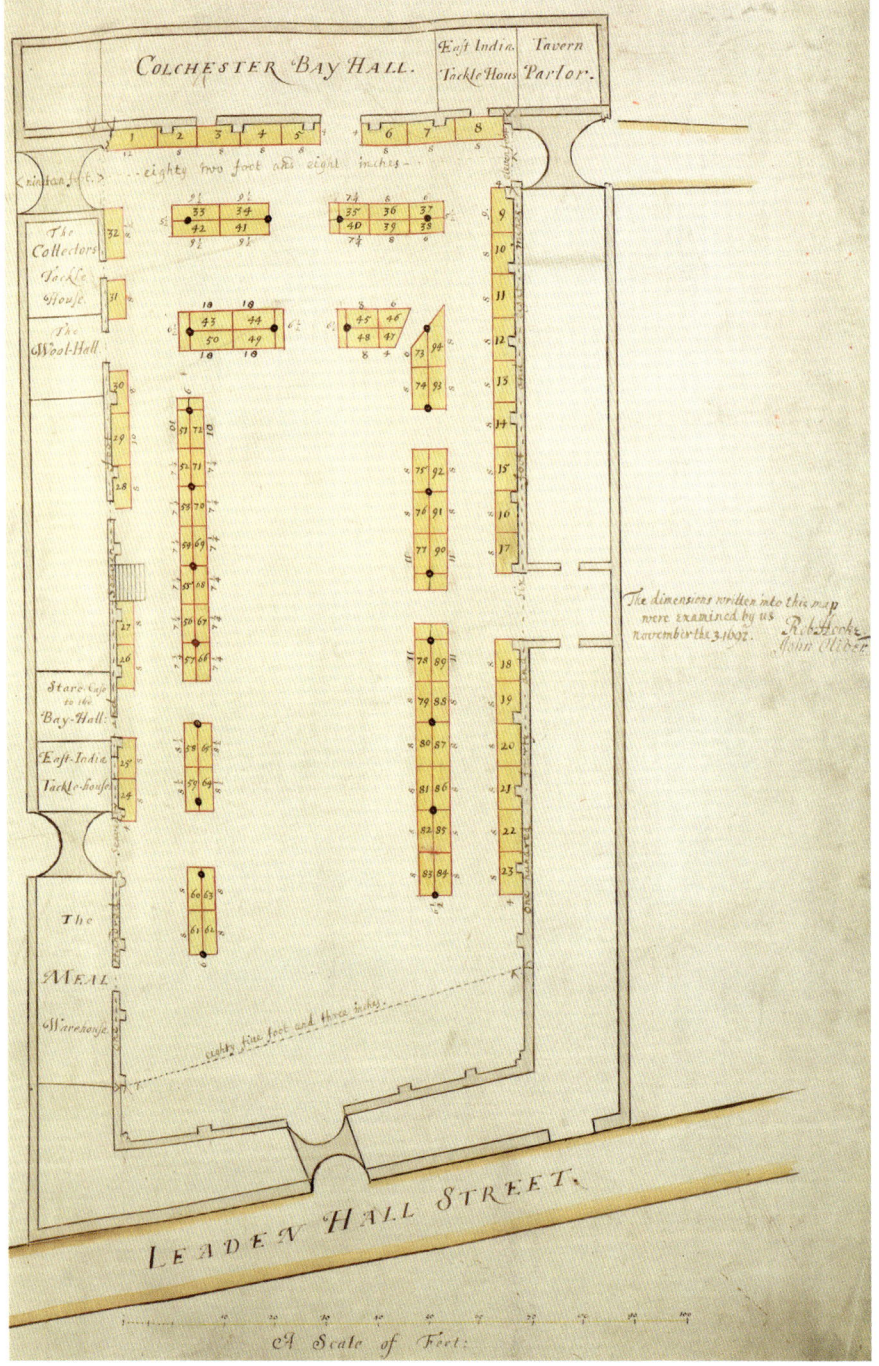

as the 'Dorcery', dorsers being large baskets carried on the back in which produce was brought to market and sometimes displayed. A laystall, five feet deep, could be moved about on wheels. South of the Herb Market was a space for 'higlers' or pedlars.

The northern part of the medieval quadrangle was demolished in 1794, and the rest of it, together with the former chapel, in 1812-14, though parts of the outer wall lasted longer, and on the south side a stretch of that wall still exists behind 16-19 Leadenhall Market. A new Green Market was added east of the old quadrangle. The whole complex was demolished in 1879-80, to be replaced by the present market building (Fig. 195).

Fig. 191. The main quadrangle of Leadenhall, 1677. North is at the bottom.

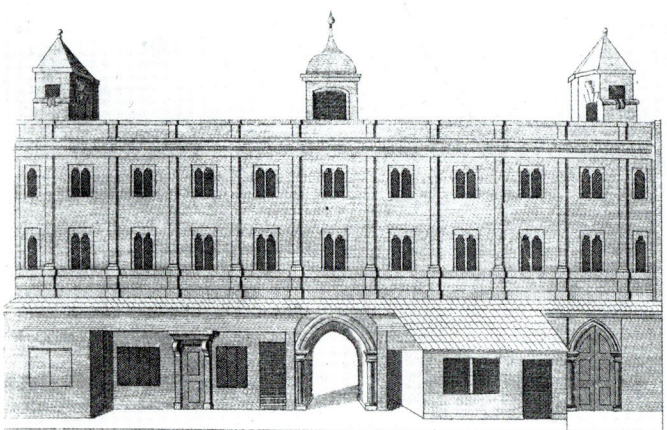

Fig. 192. The Leadenhall Street front of the market building of 1440-55, engraved in about 1750.

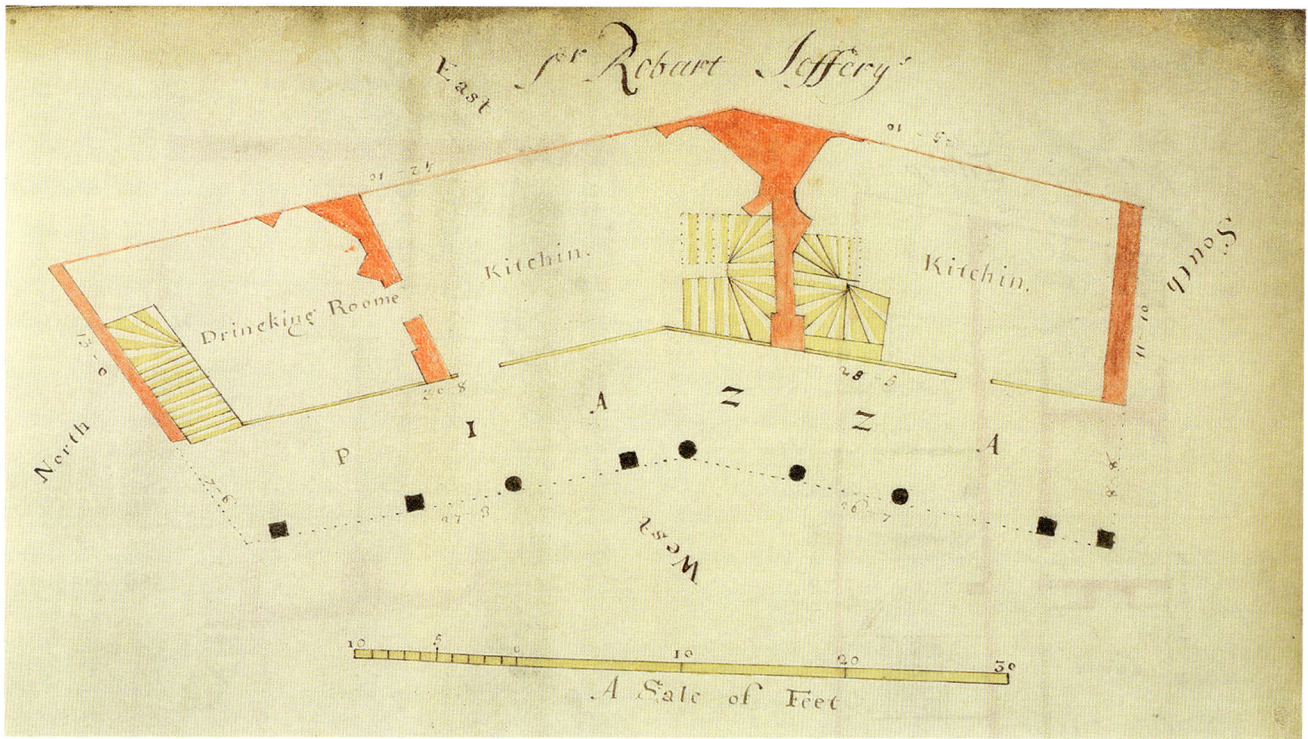

Fig. 193. Properties on the east side of the Greenyard, Leadenhall Market, 1700, with the 'piazza' introduced in 1664.

Fig. 194. The Beef Market with its stalls in the main quadrangle of Leadenhall, drawn before 1814 (print published in 1825 by Thomas Dale after George Samuel). The Beef Market was used on certain days of the week for raw hides or tanned leather, as shown here.

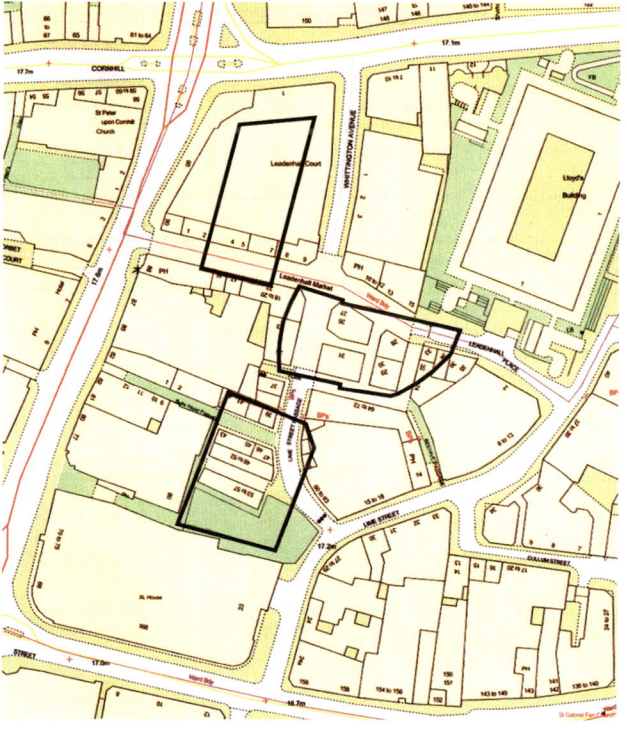

Fig. 195. The three courtyards of Leadenhall Market in 1698 marked on the 2015 Ordnance Survey map. The locations shown are very approximate, as neither the 1698 plan nor the same area on Ogilby and Morgan's map can be related directly to the modern map. Leadenhall Street is at the top and Fenchurch Street at the bottom.

Plan 92
Smithfield sheep pens, 1682
William Leybourn Fig. 196

This plan accompanied a lease of the Smithfield sheep pens by the City to the parish of St Sepulchre, Holborn. The pens were west of the main part of Smithfield (Fig. 197). The City decided in 1616 that St Sepulchre should have the lease when an existing one ended in 1621,[94] and there were several renewals subsequently. The decision may have been connected with the improvement of Smithfield by paving it in 1615, though the sheep pens area had already been paved in 1567.[95] For St Sepulchre, a poor suburban parish, the benefit was that it could make more from the lease than it cost and thereby keep down the poor rate. In the 1650s the parish was paying rent of £100 a year and another £50 or £60 for keeping the area clean, while letting out the pens for £160 and the associated properties for another £50 or £60, leaving about £60 in hand.[96]

The 1682 lease refers to sheep pens, 'as well those that have sheds and workeshopps over them as those that are covered over and made close penns as those that are left open or onely railed or paled about'. In addition to 'standing penns', which were the ones shown on the plan, there were 'hurdle penns that shall be ty'd about such standing penns', and on market days hurdles were set up to within eight feet of the surrounding houses.[97] There were also six tenements and stables, some of them with pens under them,[98] and a fish stall occupied by Robert Curd, together with 'the pond ground and buildings thereupon with the railes'. 'Pond ground' probably refers to the former Horsepond on the east side of the pens, filled in after the Great Fire.[99] Excepted from the lease was the use of the area for booths selling leather at the time of Bartholomew Fair. The plan shows what appear to be the stocks and cage, and towards Smithfield Bars (on the route towards St John Street) the fish shops or sheds. A bellhouse is mentioned in the churchwardens' accounts.[100]

In 1683 St Sepulchre vestry decided that the pens should be managed by a committee instead of being let out as previously. The committee kept the pens in repair, appointed collectors of fees, resolved disputes over who should have which pens, challenged new markets elsewhere, dealt with the lessees of the houses and proceeded against market offenders, such as forestallers who bought before the market opened, people who tied their horses to posts other than the two provided for that purpose and 'the lamb men that lye in the street and not

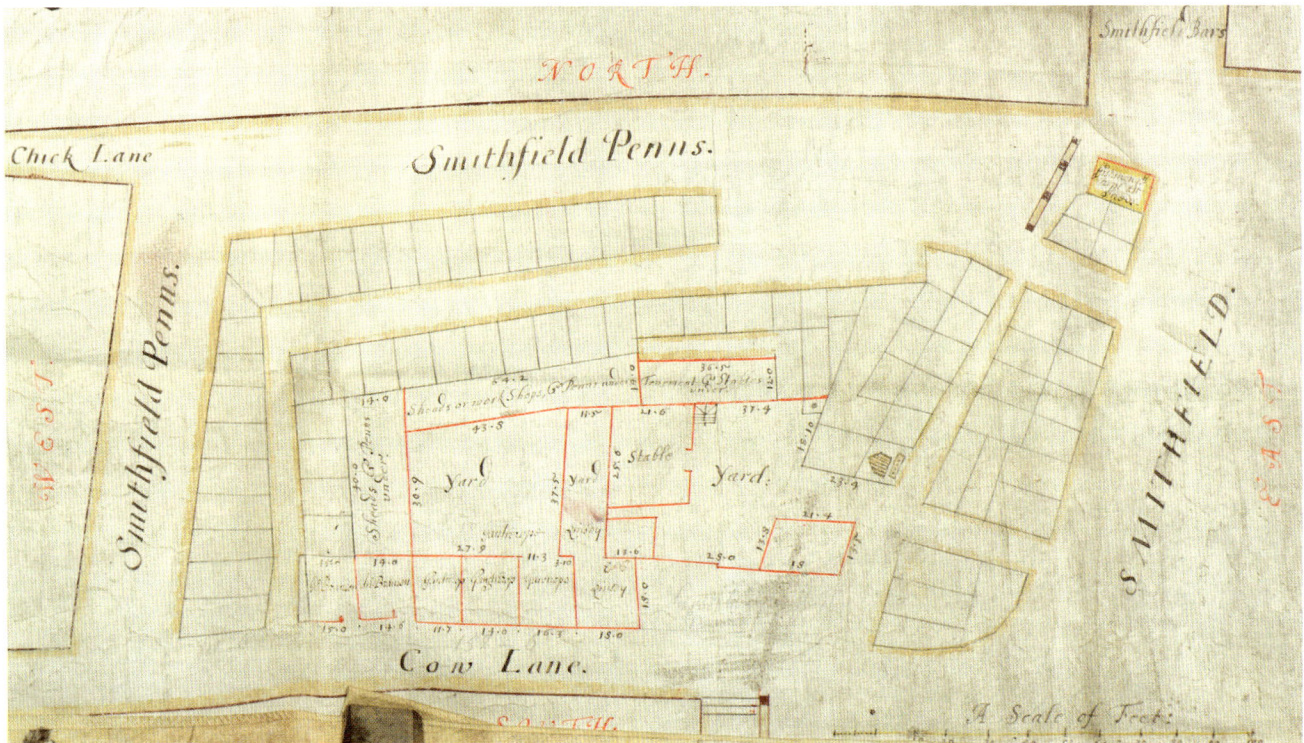

Fig. 196. Smithfield sheep pens, 1682.

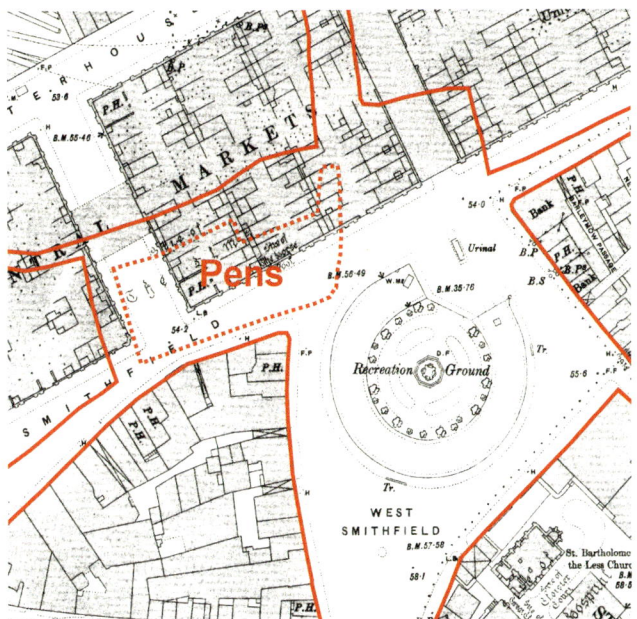

Fig. 197. The approximate location of the streets and sheep pens of 1682 marked on the 1896 Ordnance Survey map.

penn'. In 1695 it decided to transfer the stocks and whipping post to Holborn Conduit and the cage to one of the pens. The placing of market people could be contentious. In 1718 Widow Spiggs pointed out that the Oxfordshire men who brought sheep and lodged at her house, as their fathers had done forty years before, had always used the row of pens between Cow Lane and Chick Lane. In 1719 the committee decided that if any chapmen or other sellers of goods wanted pens they would be placed 'upon Hogg Hill or in the Rounds'. The accounts for 1693 indicate a clear profit of £487, and in 1711 the committee reckoned the average over the previous sixteen years had been £400.[101]

The next lease plan, of 1712, shows a more complicated arrangement of stalls, but occupying almost the same area. For this renewal the parish had to pay a £3,000 fine, and the annual rent increased from £103 to £460. The houses within the pens area were eventually replaced by more pens, apparently in 1736. In 1754 the parish offered a £4,800 fine and £530 rent for the next renewal, but there was a higher bidder offering £5,500 and £560. Two years later, after 135 years, St Sepulchre relinquished the sheep pens.[102] The sale of live animals moved to Islington in 1855 and new market buildings were constructed at Smithfield in 1851-66, opened as a meat market in 1868 and later extended (Fig. 197).[103]

Plan 93
The Meal Market, Fleet Ditch, 1700
John Olley Fig. 198

After the Great Fire, with the ending of the street market at Newgate, the City had no market for meal or flour except at Queenhithe.[104] Meal and flour were sold instead at inns around Holborn Bridge and Aldersgate. In 1698 the City ordered that, to prevent excessive prices and market offences such as forestalling, meal and flour should be sold at markets rather than inns, but there was not enough room in the markets. The lessees of the markets therefore agreed with the City to implement a long-discussed proposal for

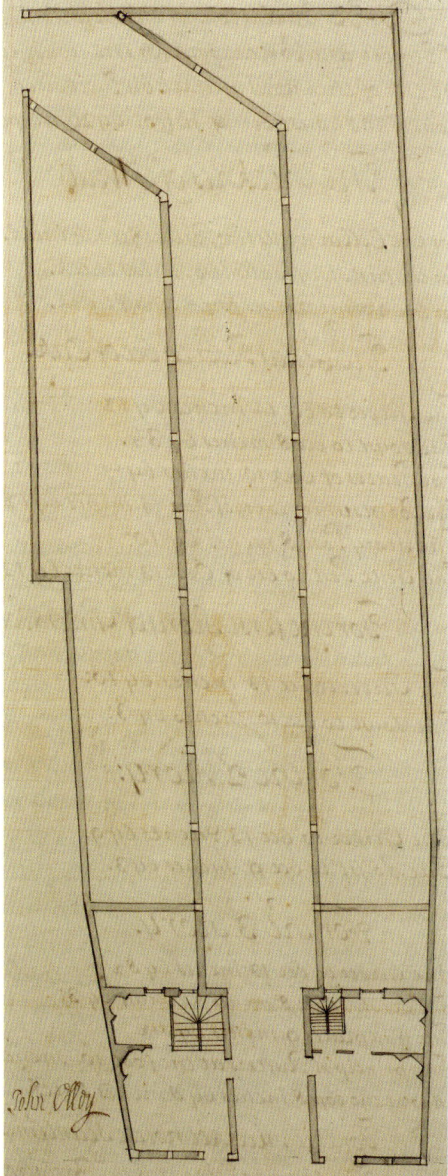

Fig. 198. The planned Meal Market, Fleet Ditch, 1700. North is to the left.

Fig. 199. Elevation of the planned Meal Market, 1700.

a meal market on vacant land east of the Fleet Canal—now on the east side of Farringdon Road between Old Fleet Lane and Bear Alley. Probably they were expecting much of the meal to be brought in via the Canal.

In February 1700 the lessees submitted a 'model' of the proposed market, consisting of ground plan and elevation and providing for two colonnades and an imposing four-storey facade towards the Fleet (Fig. 199). The City Lands Committee ordered that the plan and elevation be copied into their journal and that they be signed by the Comptroller and delivered back to the lessees for them to proceed. In June 1700 the Committee declared that the lessees had fully performed the agreement 'in respect both as well of the moneys therein expended, and as of the architecture'. In fact the ground plan on the lease shows minor variations in the building facing the Fleet, such as the absence of a front entrance or staircase in the part south of the gateway and the absence of partitions dividing the two front rooms into two.[105]

The new market was a failure. The lessees surrendered their lease of it in 1705, and it was briefly run by Mr Smith, carman to the market. Smith halved the duty from 1d to ½d per sack in order to attract trade. When the new lessee, John Nicholls, gentleman, doubled the duty again, Smith 'drew of[f] allmost all the mealmen to inns and other markets, there not remaining above six persons in the Meale Market and they very likely to go away'; Nicholls added that Smith lived at the George, Snow Hill, and 'carrys out and sells the goods of severall persons that pitch meal there and at other inns'. Nicholls reduced the duty again, but became insolvent and absconded. In 1707 the new lessee, a brewer, was not required to maintain the premises as a market, and no more is heard of the Meal Market. It was Meal Yard on Rocque's map of the 1740s and later Wheatsheaf Yard. The market building was apparently still standing in 1838, though without the cornice and topmost part.[106]

INNS, ALEHOUSES AND STABLES

There was a hierarchy of inns, taverns and alehouses.[107] The largest and most valuable were the inns, similar to modern hotels, providing food and drink but also accommodation and stabling. The most important inns were the 150 or so which accommodated commercial road services (Plans 54, 94-97), but there were some smaller ones also dominated at ground-floor level by stabling (Plans 58, 98). Next in importance were taverns, the name indicating a licence to sell wine. They concentrated on food and drink rather than stabling, and were a combination of coffee-house, club and restaurant. They would have a bar near the entrance, where the landlord sat ready to receive guests, and behind it a series of small private rooms or boxes, where customers could amuse themselves with friends or transact business (Plans 38, 55, 99-101, 113). Larger taverns might have a 'great room' suitable for meetings or feasts (Plan 99). The line between taverns and alehouses is hard to draw. Alehouses could have a few drinking rooms (Plan 102) or just a single drinking room which might or might not be noted as such on a plan (e.g. Plans 166, 179).

Plans 94-95
The Star Inn, New Fish Street Hill, c.1639 and 1686
Anonymous and William Leybourn
FIGS 200, 201

These two plans, one undated and one from 1686, show a coach and waggon inn, though not one of the more important ones. The inn's outline and the location of its back entrance from Pudding Lane are different on the two plans. Such changes

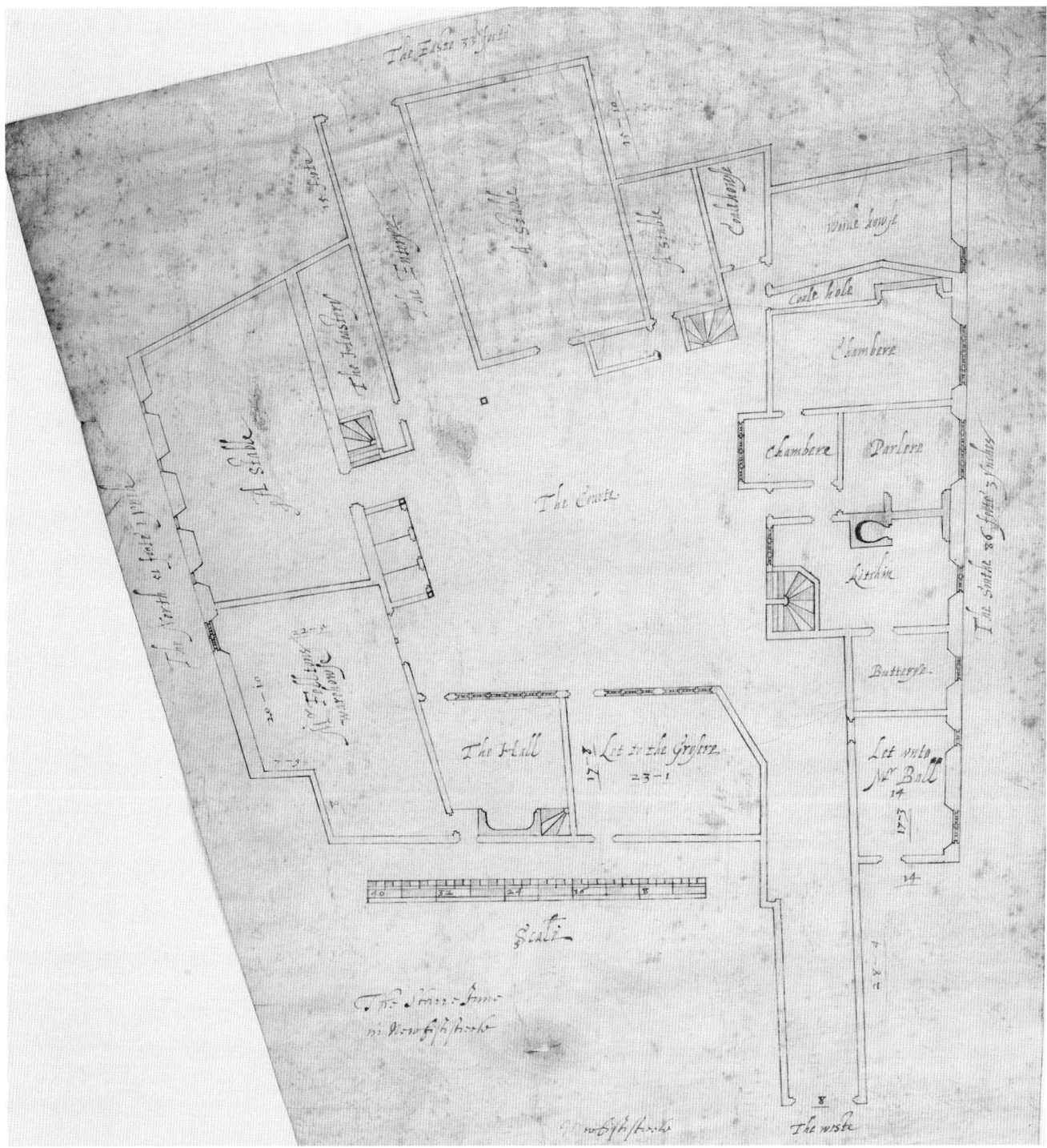

Fig. 200. The Star Inn, New Fish Street Hill, c.1639. North is to the left.

are most likely to have been made when the inn and adjoining property were rebuilt after the Great Fire, which suggests that the undated plan is a pre-Fire one. The most useful clue on the plan itself is the room in the south-west corner let to Mr Ball, as John Ball, ironmonger, leased the property south of the inn gateway in 1617, hired that adjoining room not later than 1639 and had gone not later than 1645.[108]

The minutes of the Fishmongers' Company, to which the inn belonged, provide the likely context. In 1639 the Company's lessee, William Molins, told it that the east side of the inn needed to be rebuilt and that he would rebuild it if his lease was extended. The Company appointed people to examine the premises and 'to consider of the draughte of new buildings to bee presented unto them by the said Mr Mollins'. The plan is

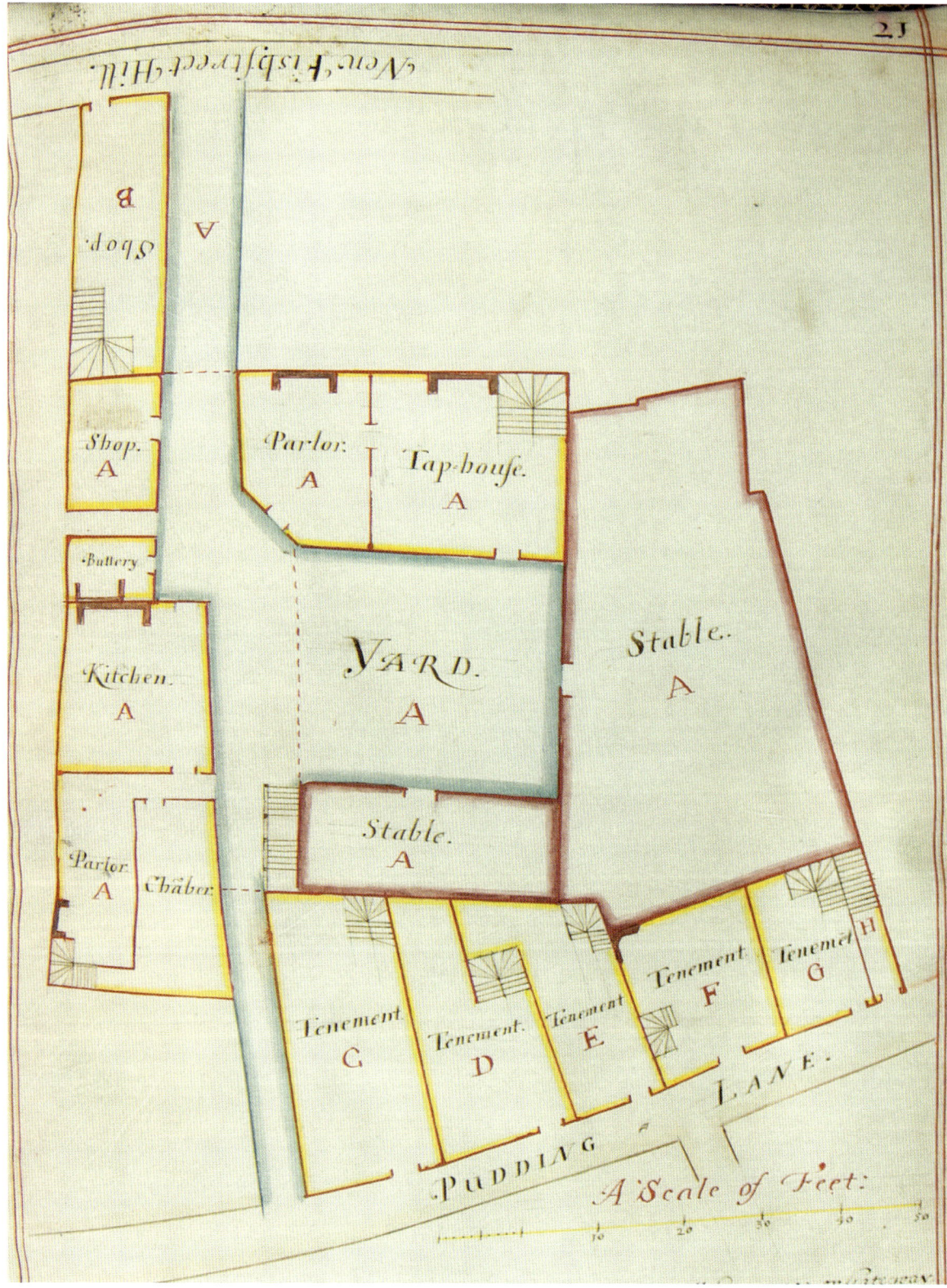

Fig. 201. The Star Inn, New Fish Street Hill, 1686. North is to the right.

probably that 'draughte'. Molins' reason for rebuilding indicates the changing expectations of those who stayed in London inns: 'he desireth to build his owne parte presently to accomodate his guests with small chambers whereof he hath much need and for wante thereof looseth many guests'. In 1640 it was agreed that Molins would spend £400 rebuilding the east part of the inn in brick and pay the Company £550 in return for twenty-one years being added to his lease. As

KEY, Fig. 201

A. Star Inn: principal entrance or gateway fronting New Fish Street Hill and other entrance fronting Pudding Lane; two floors over taphouse, parlour and stables, also over shop, entry, buttery, kitchen, parlour and chamber, which rooms on the south side project over the passage from east to west (into the yard) about 12 feet.

B. Tenement: cellar under shop; four floors over shop and inn gateway.

C-G. Tenements: cellars; three floors over [ground floor].

H. Entry, leading up into tenement over stables.

Molins spent £730 more than he was required to do, the Company agreed in 1644 to extend his lease by thirty-one years instead of twenty-one. Molins also rebuilt four houses in Pudding Lane in brick for the Company. In 1666 the inn had twenty-nine hearths.[109]

All this was destroyed in 1666; indeed, though largely brick-built, the inn, with hay and other combustible items in its yard, was one of the Fire's earliest victims and contributed to its spread. In 1669 Sir John Shaw, merchant, financier and lessee of the customs, agreed to rebuild the inn and three or more houses in return for a lease of ninety-one years. The lease included not just the site of the inn but also sites B (Ball's former tenement) and C to E on the 1686 plan (a separate lease to Shaw added F and G).[110] This made changes possible at the Pudding Lane end, where in 1686, instead of a stable and a wide passage, there was a row of tenements and only a narrow passage on a new alignment. Leybourn states that there were two floors of rooms over the west, south and east ranges, projecting over part of the yard (as the dotted lines indicate), though in fact Fig. 202 shows three and a half storeys. There was a tenement over the large northern stable.

An inventory of 1700 provides a detailed picture of the inn. The chamber on the south-east side had tapestry hangings, the parlour a large map and a playing table, the taphouse five tables, two forms and a bar, and the yard a 'globe lantern'. There was a 'horse pond'. In the upper storeys were 'the Kings Armes or dyneing roome' and thirty-three chambers, all with names such as the Anchor, the Greyhound and the Unicorn and containing forty-five beds. Five of these chambers were used by the chamberlain, the tapster, the ostler, the coachman and Mr Adcock (a carrier). There was a clock, with a bell and a dial in the top storey and weights in a room below. Occupants of the chamber called 'the Dover' had the benefit of '11 Roman Empier heads'.[111]

A print of 1677 shows the south side of the inn (one of the smoking chimneys probably marks its kitchen), together with the house by the inn gateway (Fig. 202). Before the Fire the house had three and a half storeys and a cellar; it consisted of a

Fig. 202. The entrance to the Star Inn from New Fish Street Hill and the south side of the inn in 1677, with part of the Monument on the right—detail from a print by William Lodge.

narrow shop on the ground floor, hall or chamber next to the street and kitchen and staircase behind it on the first floor, two chambers above, and two garrets. After the Fire it had an additional storey, as required by the Rebuilding Act. In 1657 two great posts had to be provided to protect it from 'shakeing and shattering with the turning of carts downeward passing out of the said inn'.[112]

In 1690 the Star was used by Mr Varnham, Canterbury and Maidstone coachmaster, and John Adcock, packhorse carrier of Ashford in Kent. There were still stage coaches there in 1755 but not in 1765. The building lease expired in 1760, and by 1772 the site had been redeveloped as warehousing around a courtyard, approached only from Pudding Lane.[113]

Plan 96
The Cross Keys Inn, Whitecross Street, 1667
John Jennings   FIG. 203

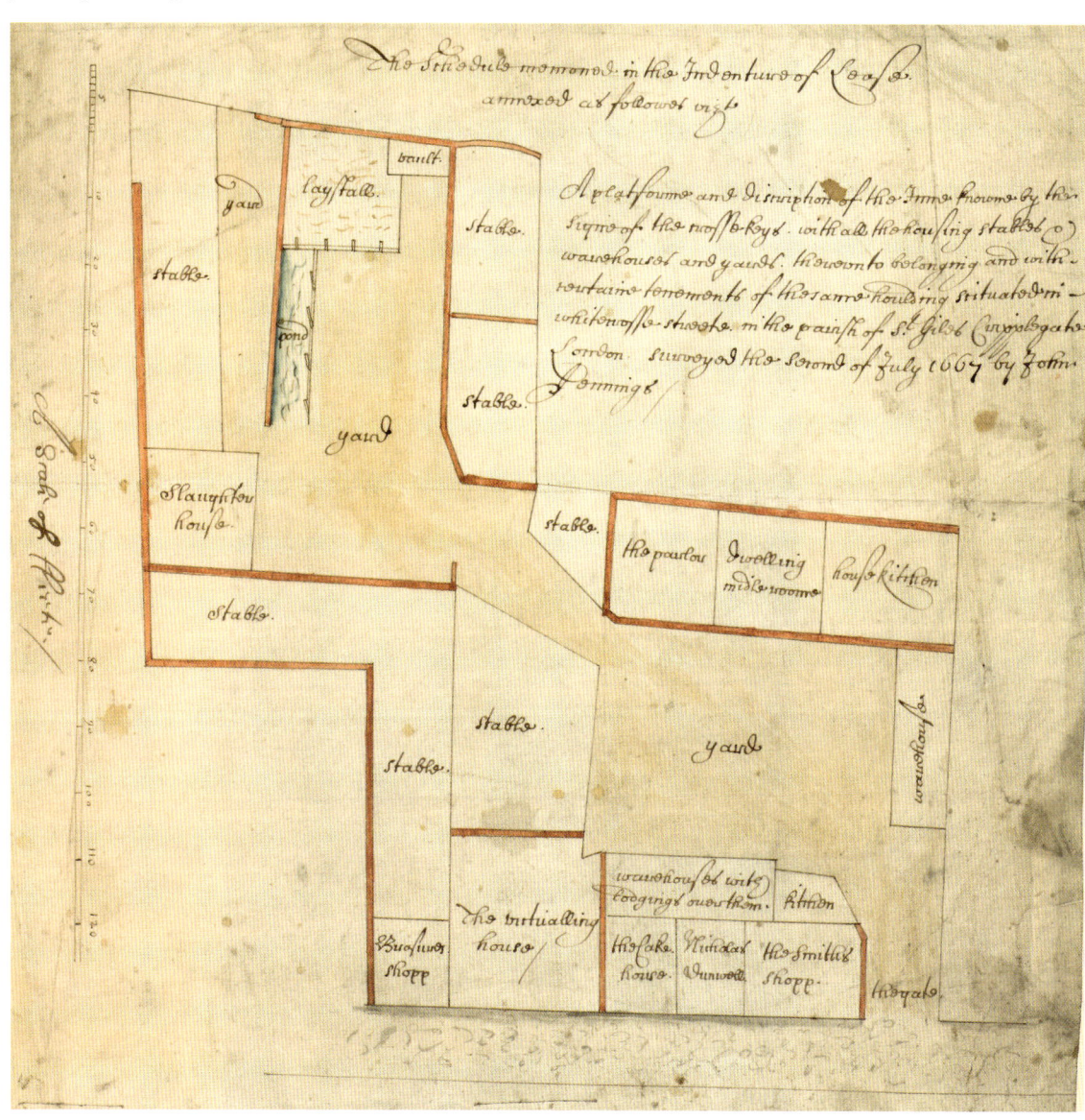

Fig. 203. The Cross Keys Inn, Whitecross Street, 1667. North is to the left.

The Cross Keys was an important carrying inn in 1681, but was probably so for only a brief period after the Great Fire destroyed most of its competitors. It then had eight services a week by waggon, packhorse or coach-waggon, all from different counties.[114] The plan accompanied a lease, now lost, and shows the usual expanse of stables at ground level. There were presumably lodgings on more of the upper floors than the plan indicates. The slaughterhouse is an unexpected feature. John Jennings, recorded from 1654 to 1667, was one of the surveyors who assisted

Leake in preparing the map of the City immediately after the Great Fire, and he also drew estate maps in several counties.[115]

The inn seems to have declined in the 1680s, losing most or all of its carrying services. In 1720 Strype described it as 'pretty large, and of an indifferent trade, with some private houses in it'.[116] Rocque recorded it merely as Cross Keys Yard in the 1740s. The site is now part of the Barbican, a little north from St Giles Cripplegate.

Plan 97
The Catherine Wheel Inn, Borough High Street, Southwark, 1686
William Leybourn
FIG. 205

The Catherine Wheel, on the west side of Borough High Street (a little north from the present Little Dorrit Court), belonged to St Thomas's Hospital by 1564. It was a minor inn for coaches and carriers, with just a packhorse carrier from Shere in Surrey and short-stage coaches from Croydon and Dulwich using it in 1681.[117] Like many inns, it was entirely screened from the street by separately-occupied houses, which were leased with the inn. Behind were a front yard including kitchen and parlours, a back yard dominated by stables and a barn, and a garden. In 1670 the lease was held by Robert Beard, coachman, who was recorded running a stage-coach to Tonbridge in 1663.[118] The occupier in 1686 was Ellen Baker, widow. The inn was far enough south to escape the great Southwark fire of 1676, but in the fire of 1689 the three houses south of the gateway were destroyed and the inn was 'considerably

Fig. 204. One of the courtyards of the Catherine Wheel Inn in 1853 (watercolour by T.H. Shepherd).

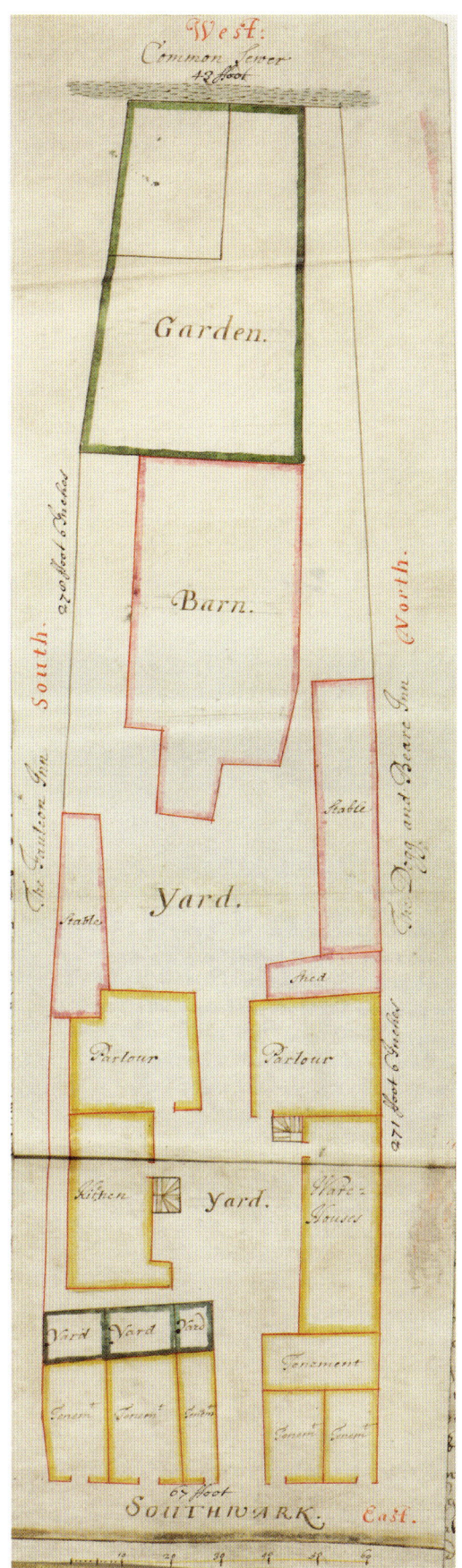

Fig. 205. The Catherine Wheel Inn, Borough High Street, Southwark, 1686.

damaged'. Michael Terry, gentleman, then the lessee, agreed a new lease requiring him to rebuild all the houses in brick.[119] How much of the inn of 1686 survived long enough to appear in the view of 1853 is unknown, but the overall plan of the inn was probably little changed (Fig. 204). The inn was demolished in 1869.[120]

Plan 98
The Boar's Head Inn, Borough High Street, Southwark, 1684
William Leybourn
FIG. 206

Fig. 207. Wash drawing of the former Boar's Head Inn, c.1800.

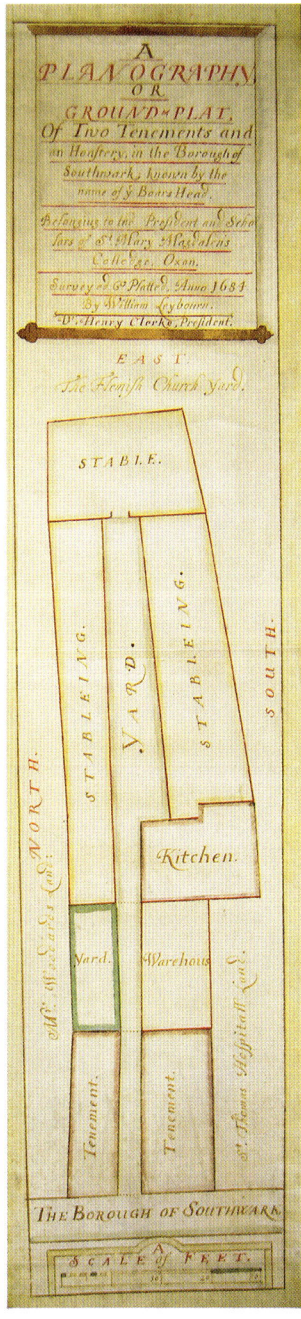

Fig. 206. The Boar's Head Inn, Borough High Street, Southwark, 1684.

The Boar's Head was on the east side of Borough High Street opposite what is now Southwark Cathedral. It is first recorded in 1393, and was purchased by Sir John Fastolf in 1450,[121] passing after his death with Morgan's Lane (Plan 77) and other property to Magdalen College, Oxford. Leases of 1674 and 1694 describe it as a tenement called the Boar's Head with two tenements belonging commonly called shops, indicating that the two houses with shops at the front (Fig. 207) were separately occupied and that the Boar's Head was entirely behind the street frontage. The inn consisted of a long, narrow yard largely surrounded by stabling. At the east end part of the stable had formerly been the taphouse; above it were a warehouse, with two rooms, and a hayloft over that. Presumably the kitchen marked on the plan was serving the role of taphouse in 1684. There were haylofts over the stable on the north side. The warehouse at the west end was later described as a place where 'market ffolkes used before to lay baskets and other things in'. The lessees were Daniel White of Bexley, gentleman, in 1674 and Thomas Saunders of London, dyer, in 1694. Some time after 1684 the sub-tenant, Daniel Williamson of Southwark, citizen and haberdasher, made alterations. He converted the warehouse and hayloft at the east end into four lodging rooms, with new chimneys and staircase; converted the warehouse at the west end into a new taphouse, with a new chimney; added backhouses to the two houses; and gave the two shops new fronts and higher ceilings. By 1721 the inn had been divided into tenements.[122] The buildings were cleared in 1830 for the London Bridge approach, and the site is now occupied by the approach to London Bridge Station.

Plan 99
The Horn Tavern, Fleet Street, 1692
John Ward FIG. 208

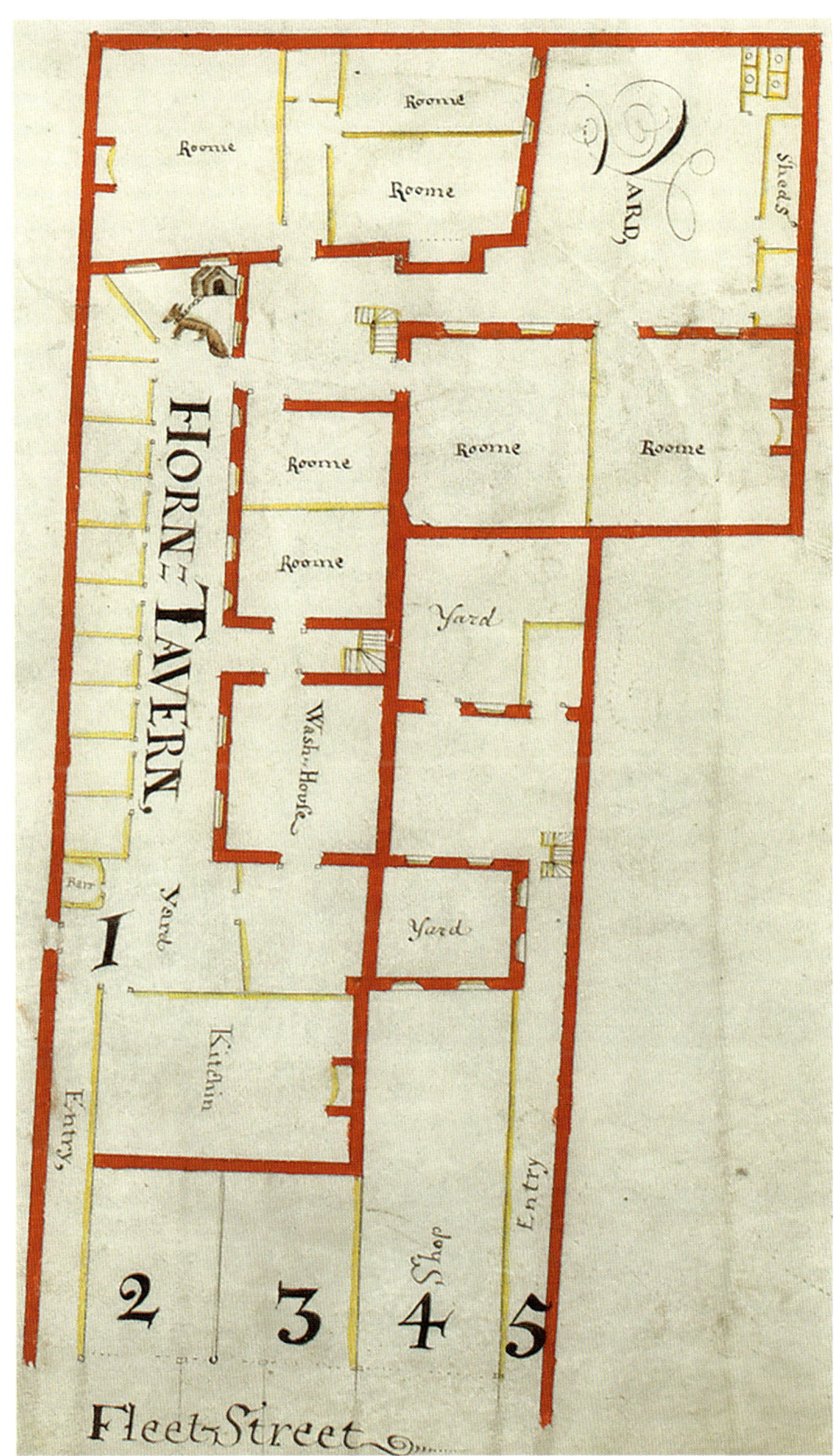

Fig. 208. The Horn Tavern, Fleet Street, 1692. North is at the top.

This plan shows a large tavern on the north side of Fleet Street, devoted to eating and drinking rather than to transport and stabling.[123] The site was later 164 Fleet Street, two doors east of Johnson's Court. The inn was acquired by the Goldsmiths' Company under a will of 1405, when it was the Horn in the Hoop, and the adjoining properties were acquired under a will of 1430.[124] In 1692 the front of the Goldsmiths' property was occupied by three houses, of which at least Nos. 2 and 4 had four and a half storeys and cellars; there was also a back tenement, No. 5. After the Fire, the Horn was rebuilt by the widow of Philemon Powell, a former lessee, and her new husband, and a fifty-five year lease was granted to her son, also Philemon Powell, a draper, in 1672.[125] The tavern then had three main parts. On the east side of the yard was a building of three and a half storeys, with three rooms on each floor. West of the yard was a single-storey building described as five drinking rooms and a bar, though the plan (of twenty years later) shows more rooms. Here also (in 1692) was the dog kennel, containing the only dog to be drawn on any plan of this period. At the north end of the yard was a building of three and a half storeys and cellar, with a 'great room' on the first floor. In the north-east corner were a yard, a grass plot, a house of easement and coal and wood sheds. There was also a 'low room' intended for a kitchen, though by 1689 this had been taken into house No. 2. The arrangement was similar to the pre-Fire one, which consisted of bar and drinking rooms west of the yard, old buildings east of the yard, a new building of three and a half storeys north of the yard and a back yard with sheds; the changes were that there was no longer a kitchen west of the yard or chambers over the drinking rooms, the building east of the yard had an extra storey and there was no longer a parlour under part of one of the Fleet Street houses. By 1722 two 'great rooms', both wainscoted, not there in 1672, had been added in the north-east yard, and these seem to be the rooms shown on the south side of the yard on the plan.

The tavern was run from 1684 to 1708 by John Carpenter, vintner, and then by his widow Elizabeth until about 1718. It was capable of providing dinner for about 200 members of the Goldsmiths' Company in 1721. The tavern was superseded in the 1790s by Anderton's Coffee House, later Anderton's Hotel, which continued until 1939.[126]

Plan 100
The Mitre Tavern, Mitre Court, Duke's Place, 1721
Isaac Olley
Fig. 209

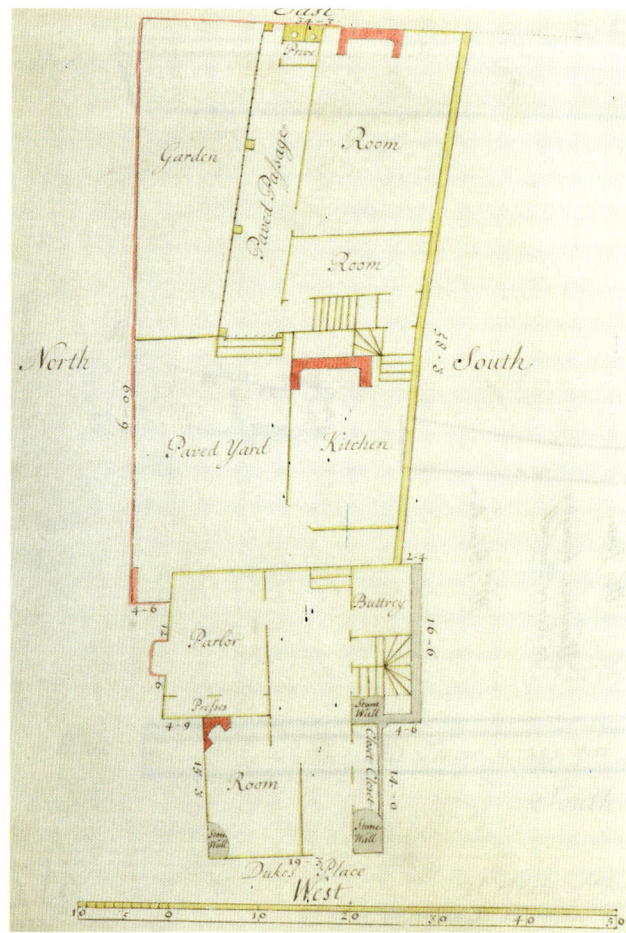

Fig. 209. The Mitre Tavern, Mitre Court, Duke's Place, 1721.

Fig. 210. The Mitre Tavern after a fire destroyed adjoining properties in 1800, with remains of Holy Trinity Aldgate on the right (print by S. Rawle).

What makes this plan interesting is that it shows surviving fabric of Holy Trinity Priory, Aldgate, built into a later house, and that a view of that house is available (Fig. 210).[127] Two blocks of stone which had evidently once been round pillars and several walls are coloured grey on the plan and labelled 'Stone Wall'. The pillars have been identified by John Schofield as a bay in the north aisle of the presbytery or choir of the priory church. There was a Mitre Tavern here from the 1650s, occupied in 1720 by James Manwaring. Like many taverns and alehouses it had several ground-floor rooms labelled just as 'Room', probably indicating drinking rooms. The lessee from 1721 was John Boover, citizen and poulterer, who leased many of the City's properties. The Mitre was demolished in or about 1803, when several drawings were made of the exposed remains of the priory.

Plan 101
The Blue Anchor, Duke's Place, 1697
John Olley Fig. 211

This property was described as two tenements: one was the Blue Anchor alehouse, which occupied almost the entire ground floor;[128] the other had a staircase from the street and rooms only on the upper storeys. According to the lease, there were two kitchens and four drinking rooms on the ground floor, two cellars below and seven chambers and two garrets above. The stairs from the bar evidently led down to the cellars. The building was leased in 1696 to John Shelton, citizen and saddler.

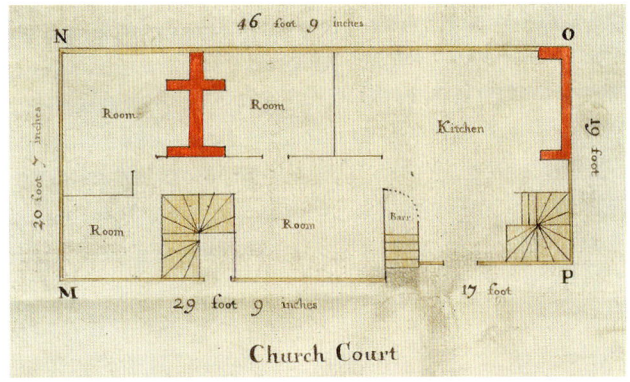

Fig. 211. The Blue Anchor alehouse, Church Court (Duke's Place), 1697. North is to the right.

Plan 102
Alehouse in Fore Street, 1719
Isaac Olley Fig. 212

This alehouse, together with the separate house to the south, was an oblong building with brick external walls and an entirely irregular internal layout. The date of construction, the number and arrangement of upper storeys and how it became so irregular are all unknown. It was dominated by a single 'Drinking Room', twenty-eight feet long, though there were several small rooms which may have been drinking rooms too. The City's lessee in 1719 was John Boover, citizen and poulterer.

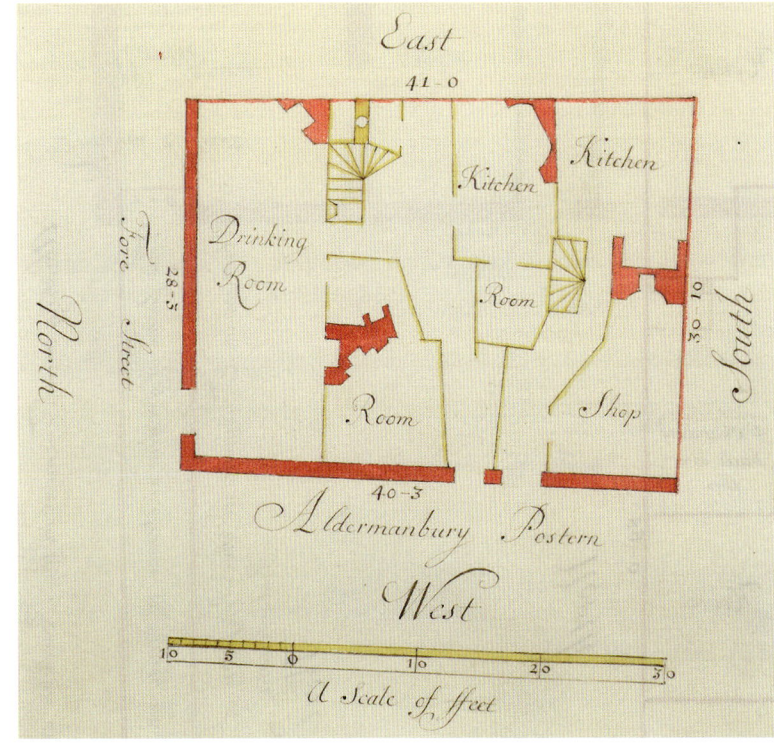

Fig. 212. An alehouse in Fore Street, 1719.

Plan 103
Flying Horse Yard, Houndsditch, 1713
John and Isaac Olley FIG. 213

London depended heavily on its horses, and they tended to be kept on the outskirts of the city where land was cheaper. This property, in Houndsditch and around Flying Horse Yard, near Bishopsgate, contained five stables and ten houses, leased in 1713 to Edward Parratt, citizen and saddler. The stables were livery stables, looking after the horses of people without stables of their own in London.[129] The passage at the south end of the yard led to another part of Flying Horse Yard, which had a different lessee. The plan is in the style the Olleys used for larger properties, giving little information about the individual houses.

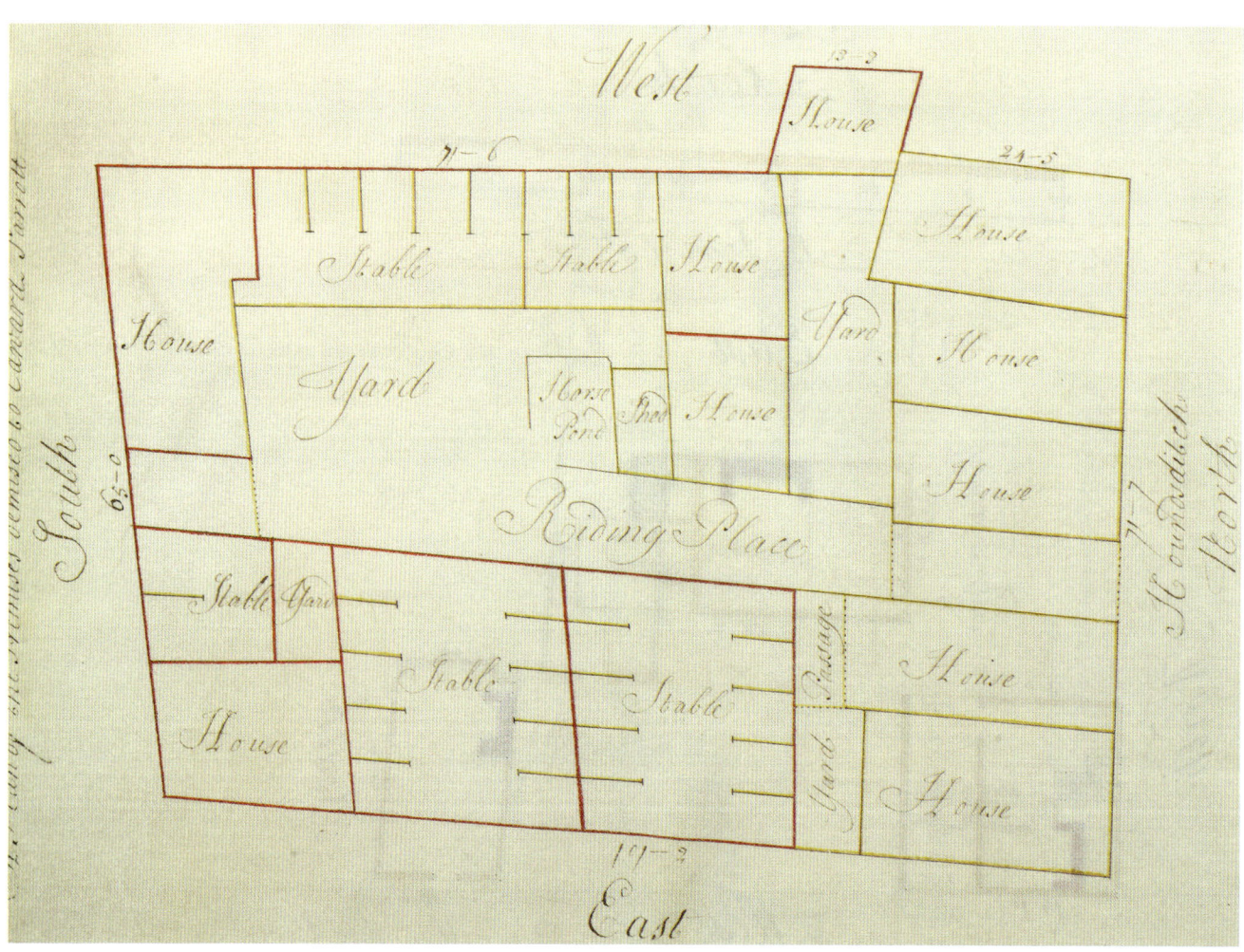

Fig. 213. Part of Flying Horse Yard, Houndsditch, 1713.

Plan 104
Stables in Finsbury Yard, 1715
Isaac Olley FIG. 214

These stables were among several in Finsbury Yard,[130] which was in the angle between Chiswell Street and what is now Finsbury Pavement and was recorded as Finsbury Stables and the Red Lion Inn on Ogilby and Morgan's map of 1676. The City leased those shown here in 1715 to Luke Phillips, described as a gentleman of London.[131] When the parishioners of St Sepulchre petitioned in 1702 against a proposed new hay market in Moorfields, which would damage the parish's own hay market leased from the City, they complained that it would advantage parts of Middlesex, 'especially Finsbury stables which have almost ruin'd the inns of the City'.[132]

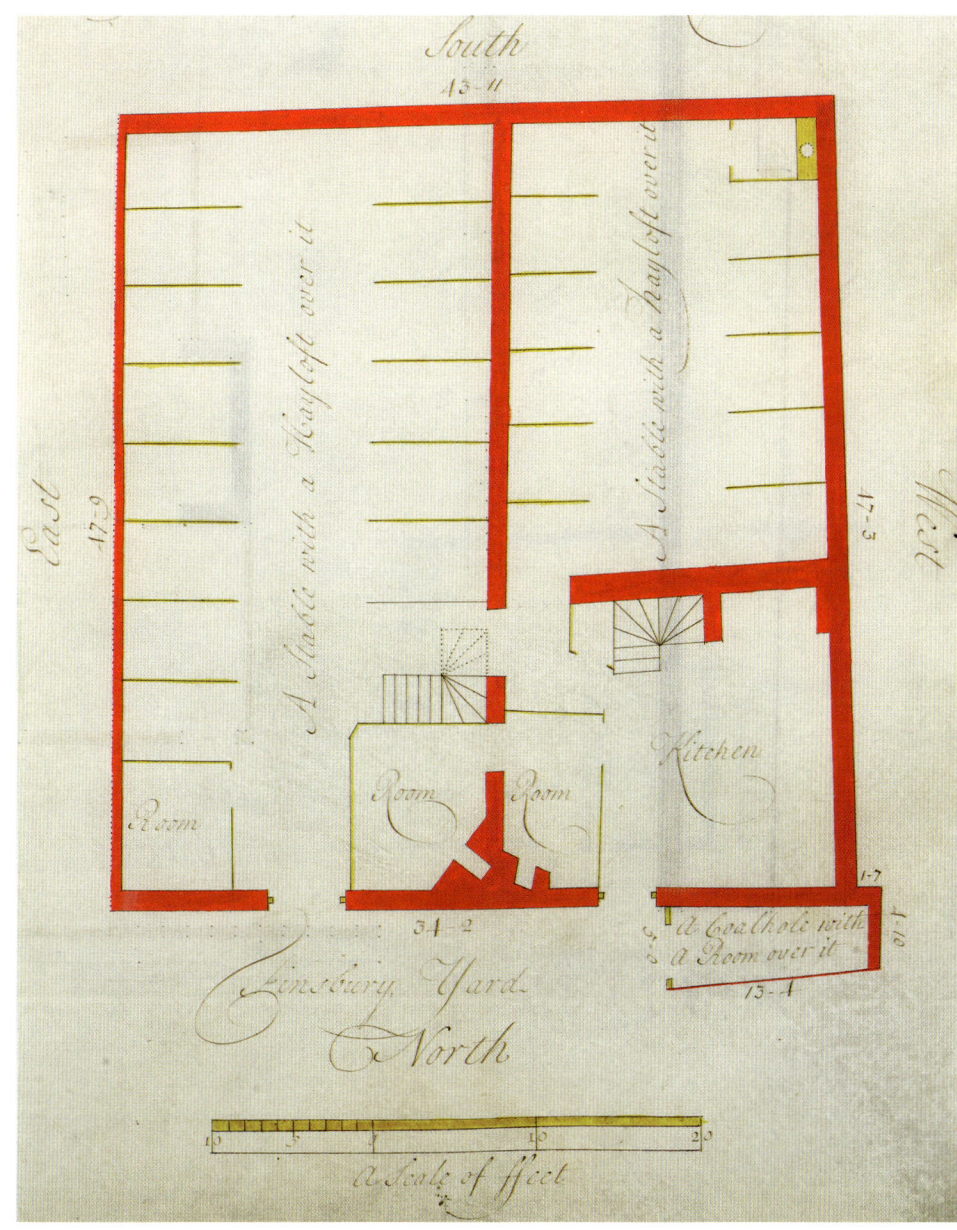

Fig. 214. Stables in Finsbury Yard, 1715.

LIVERY COMPANY HALLS

In the seventeenth century up to three-quarters of adult males living in the City belonged to livery companies. Membership was obtained through apprenticeship, patrimony or purchase, and conveyed not just freedom to work in the City but also London citizenship. Until the 1660s, and in some cases beyond, the companies regulated trade throughout London, but some were becoming dining clubs with charitable functions. An individual's company and trade often differed, especially in the twelve most prestigious companies, but reasonably successful attempts were made in the late seventeenth and early eighteenth centuries to restrict membership of the lesser companies to their trades.[133] Some companies became significant landowners, often by bequest, with some or all of the income designated for charitable purposes such as almshouses. In 1400 only four or five companies had halls, but forty-five did so by 1532.[134] They were often converted from mansions arranged around courtyards, and generally included hall, kitchen, parlour and court room, while the larger ones might also have a great chamber and a gallery.

Plan 105
Tallow Chandlers' Hall, Dowgate Hill, 1678
William Leybourn Fig. 215

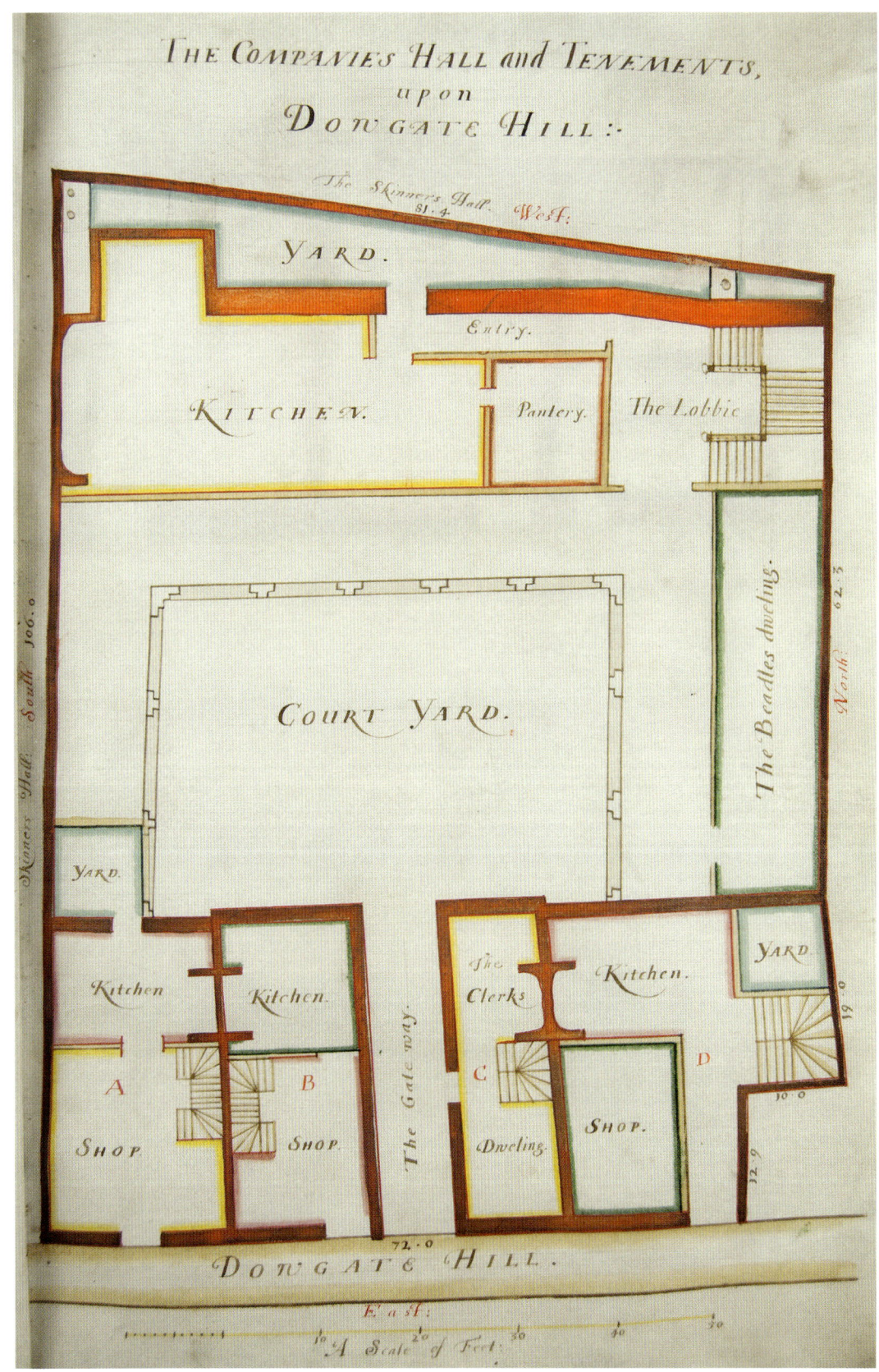

Fig. 215. Tallow Chandlers' Hall, Dowgate Hill, 1678.

The Tallow Chandlers acquired the site of their present Hall in 1476.[135] After the Great Fire they built the Hall which stands today (Fig. 216), on a similar courtyard plan to its predecessor. Work began in 1671, wainscoting was installed in 1673-74, the decoration of the parlour was completed in 1675 and that of the court room in 1676. Of the several designs considered, the one used was almost certainly by the Company's own surveyor, Captain John Caine, as some features, notably the round windows, resembled those of Brewers' Hall, which was definitely by Caine.

As it was largely confined to two sides of a small courtyard, the Hall's rooms were stacked. Above the kitchen wing and the Beadle's house were the hall itself (occupying two storeys) and the parlour respectively, and over the parlour was the court room. Otherwise there were only two rooms over the south side of the courtyard, together with garrets and cellars. The Clerk's house was beside and over the entrance passage. The four houses facing Dowgate Hill were built by Thomas Jones, bricklayer, and William Stanton, carpenter, according to 'a plott or designe' drawn by Stanton.[136] They were all of two-room plan and three and a half storeys. The small yard under the arcade belonging to the southernmost house was granted to its tenant, Richard Drew, citizen and glover, in 1674 as compensation for the Company's building over the south side of the courtyard having obstructed his light.[137]

Having escaped serious war damage, Tallow Chandlers' Hall is now the best example of one of the smaller post-Fire company halls. The Company's plan book remains in the court room where Leybourn presented it on 11 July 1678, more than three centuries ago.

KEY

Hall: Company's common hall over kitchen, pantry, lobby and west side of piazza; garrets above. Parlour over Beadle's dwelling and north side of piazza; court room over that; garrets over that. Two rooms, one over the other, over south side of piazza. Cellars under all the piazzas.

A, B, C, D: Each has cellars; *First storey*, two rooms; *Second storey*, two rooms; *Third storey*, two garrets. First and second storeys have lights east and west; garrets have Lutheran lights. Rooms in C go over the gateway; cellars of B and C each go under half the passage to the Hall. A and C have chimneys on north side; B and D on south side.

Fig. 216. The courtyard of Tallow Chandlers' Hall, seen from the entrance, 1852 (watercolour by T.H. Shepherd).

Plan 106
Armourers' Hall, Coleman Street, 1679
Joseph Titcombe
Fig. 217

This plan shows a pre-Fire company hall. The Armourers' Company bought the site in 1428 and still occupy it today. As new interior walls were constructed of brick in 1537, it is likely that the entire Hall was then of brick. It was just outside the burnt area in 1666 and lost only its windows. Strype described it in 1720 as 'a pretty handsome brick building', and it survived until rebuilt in 1839-41, unfortunately without any drawings being made except of a facade added in 1795.[138] The hall itself was about fifty by twenty-two feet, and was evidently open-roofed, apart from a garret over its west end. The other important rooms were on the first floor: the court room in the north-east corner, partly over the pillars in the courtyard, and a withdrawing room adjoining it on the north side of the courtyard. There was a gallery over the pillars on the south and west sides of the courtyard. When house M adjoining the hall gate was leased in 1680 to John Hurst, citizen and cordwainer, the Company reserved the right to use the room next to the gallery four times a year.[139]

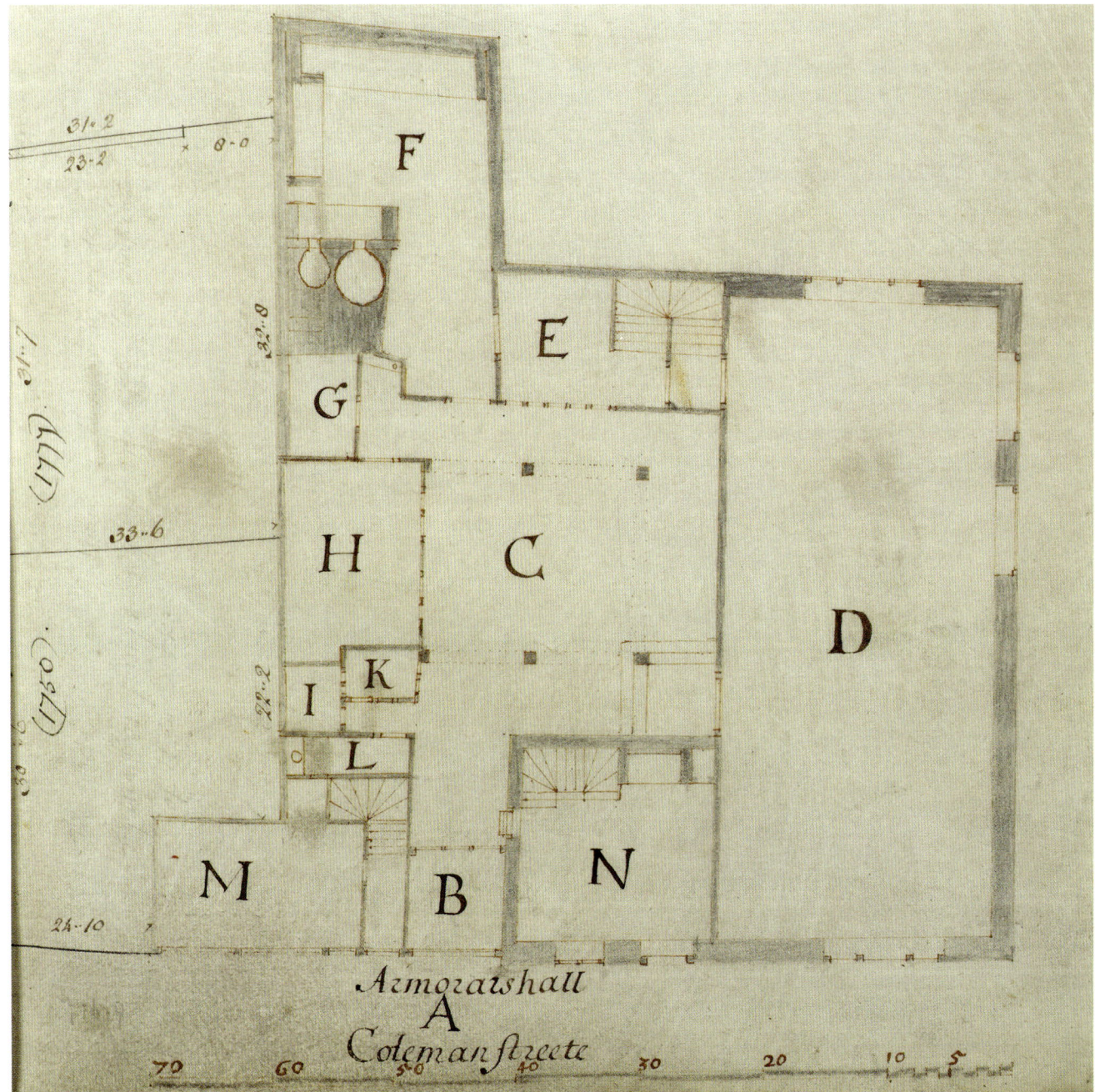

Fig. 217. Armourers' Hall, Coleman Street, 1679. North is to the left. The measurements and dates on the left-hand side are later additions.

KEY

A. Front of Armourers' Hall, Beadle's house on south side of gateway and tenement in Coleman Street on north side of gateway.

B. Passage into courtyard.

C. Courtyard.

D. Great hall.

E. Pantry between kitchen and back stairs leading into hall.

F. Kitchen, containing three chimneys and three ovens.

G. Small cellar for beer; over it a small lumber room.

H. Pastry room floored with board.

I. Small closet.

K. Beadle's study.

L. House of easement.

Passage, courtyard, kitchen, pantry and beer cellar are all paved with Purbeck stone. Hall is floored with boards and wainscoted. In [first] storey, over pantry, front part of kitchen, lumber room and columns on east side of courtyard is the courtroom, wainscoted, with chimney and chimneypiece. On north side of courtyard over the pastry, even with the courtroom, is a withdrawing room, wainscoted, with chimney and chimneypiece. At landing of stairs from hall to courtroom is the armoury. From landing of stairs even with floor of courtroom is a gallery wainscoted that stands on the columns that reach from stairs to northwest corner of courtyard, where there is a private house of easement. From north end of gallery rises a pair of stairs leading to a lead platform covering gallery on south and west sides of courtyard and over withdrawing room on north side of court-

yard, on which platform stand rails and banisters fronting courtyard on south-west and north sides. At south-west corner of gallery is the treasury.

M. Tenement three storeys high and garret but no cellar: *Ground floor*, shop, *First storey*, two rooms, each with chimney, *Second storey*, two rooms, each with chimney; upper floors extend over passage into courtyard and adjoin Beadle's house.

N. Beadle's house, three storeys high besides cellar and garret, one room on each floor, with chimney in each; also another cellar under west end of hall and garret over west end of hall.

Plan 107
Fishmongers' Hall, Thames Street, 1686
William Leybourn

FIG. 220

The Fishmongers' Company has had a Hall on some or all of the present site since 1444.[140] After the Great Fire, it took in land to the east and built a Hall with one of the most impressive facades in London (Fig. 218). The design was by the carpenter Edward Jerman, who died in 1668, apparently from overwork, and was carried out by Thomas Lock, carpenter, sacked in 1674 for 'very ill management'. Building took place largely between 1668 and 1671. As before, there were houses along the Thames Street frontage, all with large shops on the ground floor. Those on the east side were rebuilt only after a tussle with one of the tenants, Isaac Foster, who wished to rebuild exactly what he had had before the Fire, intermixed with other houses. The hall was approached by a passage from Thames Street and then under an open portico and across a courtyard, an arrangement which may have been inspired by Goldsmiths' Hall. Except on the river front, where the hall occupied the full height, there were two and a half storeys and basements. Most of the main rooms were on the same level as the hall, as shown on the plan, but there was a great chamber over the great parlour and a long gallery over the portico and courtroom, as well as the Clerk's house and offices in the northwest corner of the courtyard (not named on the plan) and lodgings for two Beadles over the kitchens. There were stables with their own entry from Thames Street. The slope of the ground allowed warehouses at ground-floor level under the hall and made an external staircase necessary. The design of the river front was modelled on Sir Roger Pratt's houses at Horseheath, Kingston Lacy and Clarendon House, London. As a prestige

Fig. 218. The Thames facade of Fishmongers' Hall, c.1700 (print by Bernard Lens).

Fig. 219. Cross-section of Fishmongers' Hall from the east in 1826, showing, from left to right, the hall, the west wing, the stables and the houses in Thames Street.

building, the riverside block was allowed to encroach on the forty-foot wharf.

Once the Hall was completed, the Company leased out part of it and sometimes nearly the whole of it, for example all but the court room and the Clerk's offices to Nathaniel Herne, merchant, in 1672, with provision for the Company to use it for four feasts a year. Lord Mayors and sheriffs sometimes occupied it during their term of office. The present Hall replaced the one shown by Leybourn in 1831-34.

KEY

A. Fishmongers' Hall.

B, C, D. Cellars; three floors over ground floor and over passage to stable yard.

F, G, H. Ditto; the two back kitchens or sheds have a room or loft over each.

E. Back tenement: cellar; three rooms over the ground room.

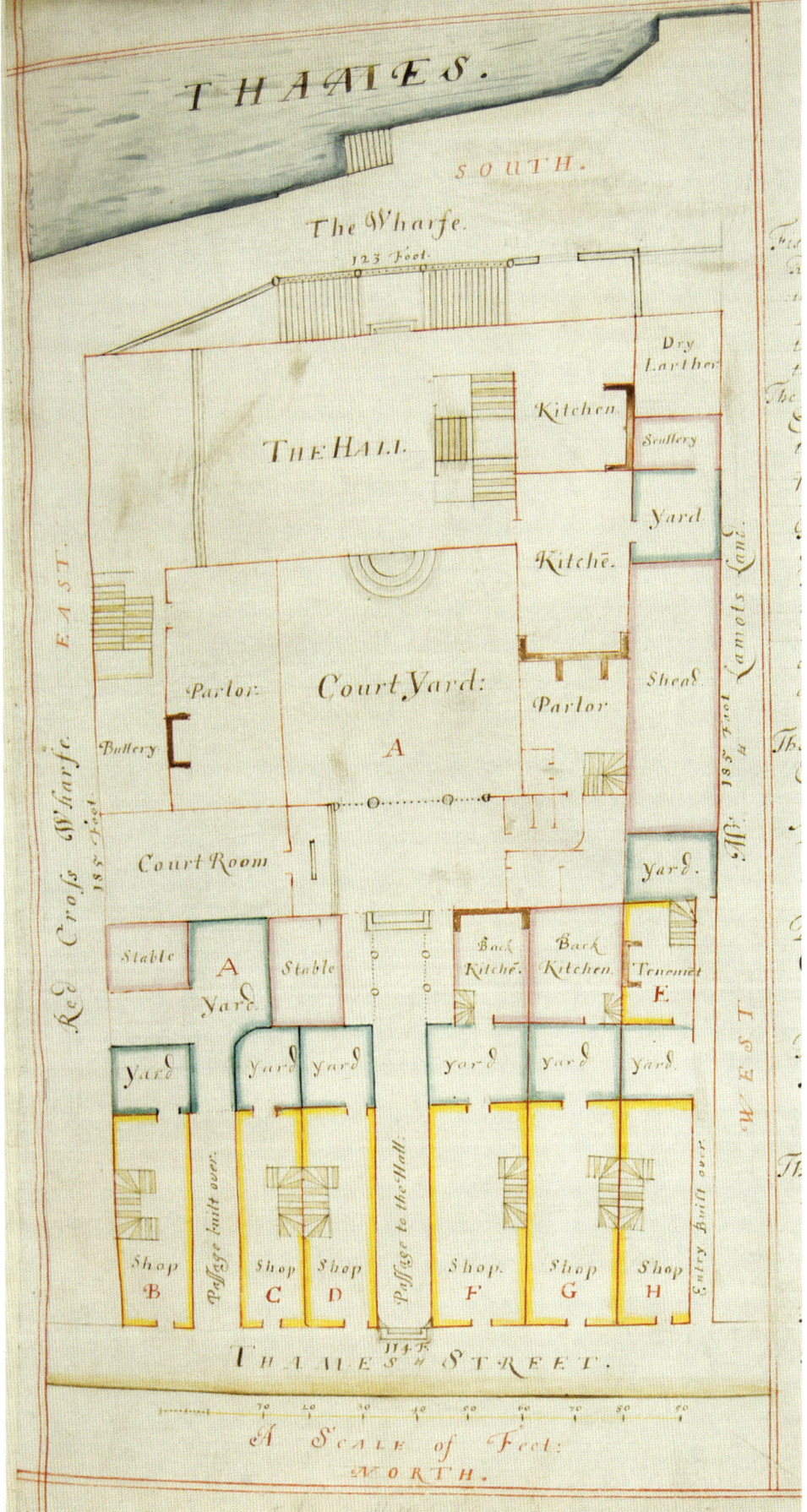

Fig. 220. Fishmongers' Hall, Thames Street, 1686.

Plan 108
Goldsmiths' Hall, Foster Lane, 1692
John Ward
FIG. 221

Goldsmiths' Hall was a major company hall of the 1630s.[141] The site had been in the Goldsmiths' hands since the fourteenth century, and plans were drawn up for rebuilding in 1634. Inigo Jones noticed what was happening 'upon some occasion of passing by', and encouraged the Company to rebuild its Hall larger and to a more regular design. He seems to have recommended as an adviser Nicholas Stone, the King's Master Mason and Master of the Masons' Company, but rather than merely advising, Stone produced his own design, which was approved. The Company decided it needed 'an understandinge and skilfull man well experienced in buildinge to bee a surveyor for the worke', and appointed Stone as that man. Essentially Stone was an architect in the modern sense, producing all the designs, recommending and supervising craftsmen and arbitrating on their payment—one of the earliest examples of such a role outside the royal works. However, Stone told the Goldsmiths that Inigo Jones had taken particular care in advising him. The arrangement of windows in the Foster Lane facade was taken from a work by Serlio of 1619. In 1666 fire swept over the Hall, destroying the roofs, cornice, south wall and some chimney stacks, but most of the walls survived, and it is possible (on stylistic grounds) that the roofs and cornice were rebuilt to the original design, so the Hall shown in later views was essentially the one built by Stone. John Ward provided not just a plan of the Hall but also two exterior views and one interior one (Figs 222, 223). On the plan he shows the hall's black and white floor in detail.

Stone managed to impose a courtyard plan on the Goldsmiths' irregular site. The hall was on the far side of the courtyard, with service rooms to

Fig. 221. Goldsmiths' Hall, Foster Lane, 1692.

Fig. 222. Goldsmiths' Hall, drawn by John Ward in 1692.

Fig. 223. Interior of the hall of Goldsmiths' Hall, looking from the dais end, drawn by John Ward in 1692.

its right; the parlour was to the left of the courtyard, and the great stairs by the hall led up to the great chamber over the parlour. In 1636, while building was under way, the Company decided to have a gallery across the main facade at first-floor level, and one result was the double chimneys in the centre of the facade, enabling the gallery to be heated. House No. 9 on the plan was the Common Assayer's house, and the Goldsmiths' assay workshops later replaced all the houses in the south-east corner.[142] The Hall was superseded by the present building in 1830-35.

Plan 109
Skinners' Hall, Dowgate Hill, *c.*1695
Mr Biggs
FIG. 224

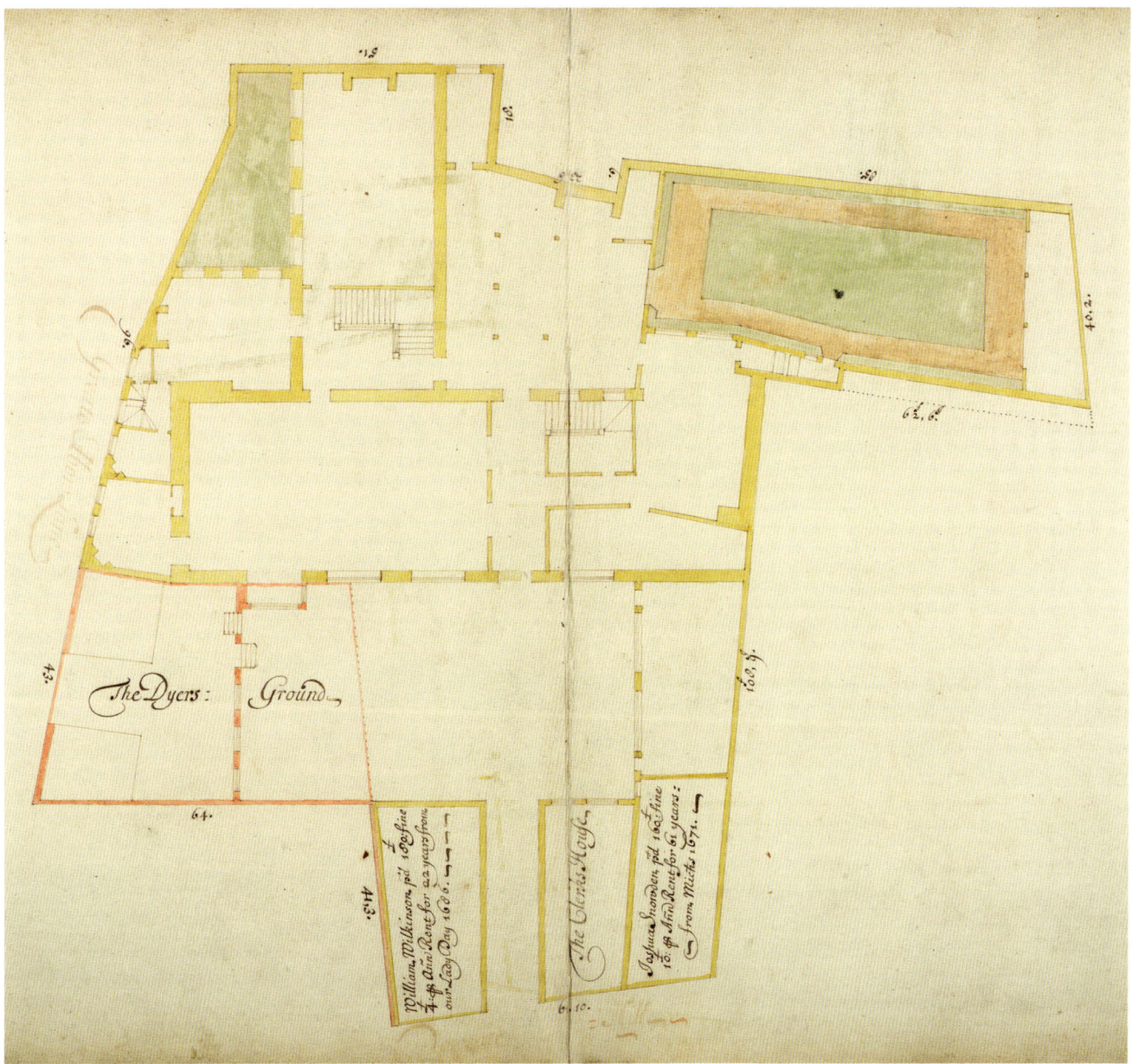

Fig. 224. Skinners' Hall, Dowgate Hill, *c.*1695. North is to the right.

The Skinners may have acquired their present site by 1380, but had certainly done so by 1408. After the Fire, they asked John Oliver, one of the City's surveyors, to 'bring in a moddle for the Hall'. The Hall and the houses facing the street, including the Clerk's house, were rebuilt in 1668-70. The garden was expanded by adding land from Whittington College. The hall was the large room directly opposite the first courtyard (Fig. 225), with the court room beyond it at right angles. The kitchens were between the hall and the garden. The present street facade dates from about 1790, and there have been many other changes, but the hall, court room and staircase survive from the building of *c.*1670.[143] 'Mr Biggs' was probably William Biggs, citizen and carpenter, recorded in lawsuits of 1681 and 1690 acting as a 'measurer' of building work. At the time of his death in 1697 he was living in Thames Street, and was the owner of several houses, which he may well have built, in the City and Whitechapel. The plan book was ordered in 1691 and again in 1694, and payments were made for it from June 1695 to March 1697.[144]

Fig. 225. The entrance to Skinners' Hall from the courtyard and part of the external wall of the hall, 2016.

OFFICIAL BUILDINGS

Plan 110
The Navy Victualling Yard, East Smithfield, 1635   Fig. 226

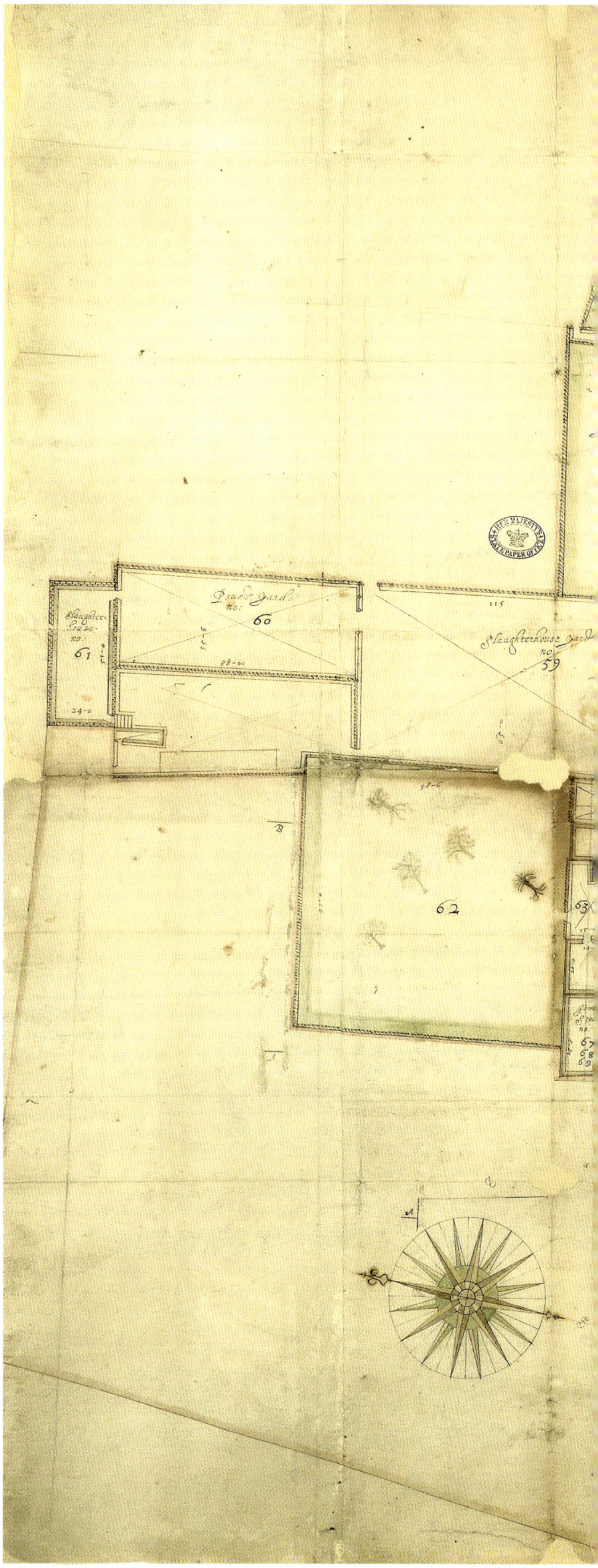

In 1635 the Navy Victualling Yard, just north-east of the Tower in East Smithfield, still preserved much of the outline of a Cistercian monastery.[145] St Mary Graces was founded in 1350 on the site of one of the cemeteries used for victims of the Black Death, and it was suppressed in 1539. In 1560 much of the monastery remained intact, probably including the church. It was then bought by Queen Elizabeth for the newly-established victualling department of the Navy. The site had old monastic buildings which could be converted, and was close to the Thames, to the City and to the meetings of naval officials on Tower Hill. Its new role was baking, meat processing, storage, coopering, administration and (briefly) brewing. There was soon a mixture of new buildings and converted old ones. For example, the monastic refectory south of the church cloister became the bakehouse (No. 43 on the plan). Although the church was quickly demolished, the coopers' yard taking much of its place (No. 34), the south wall of the nave became the south wall of the coopers' yard. The Surveyor of the Victuals, Sir Sampson Darell, lived in the abbot's lodging (Nos. 2-15). Other officials also

PLANS OF BUILDING TYPES 193

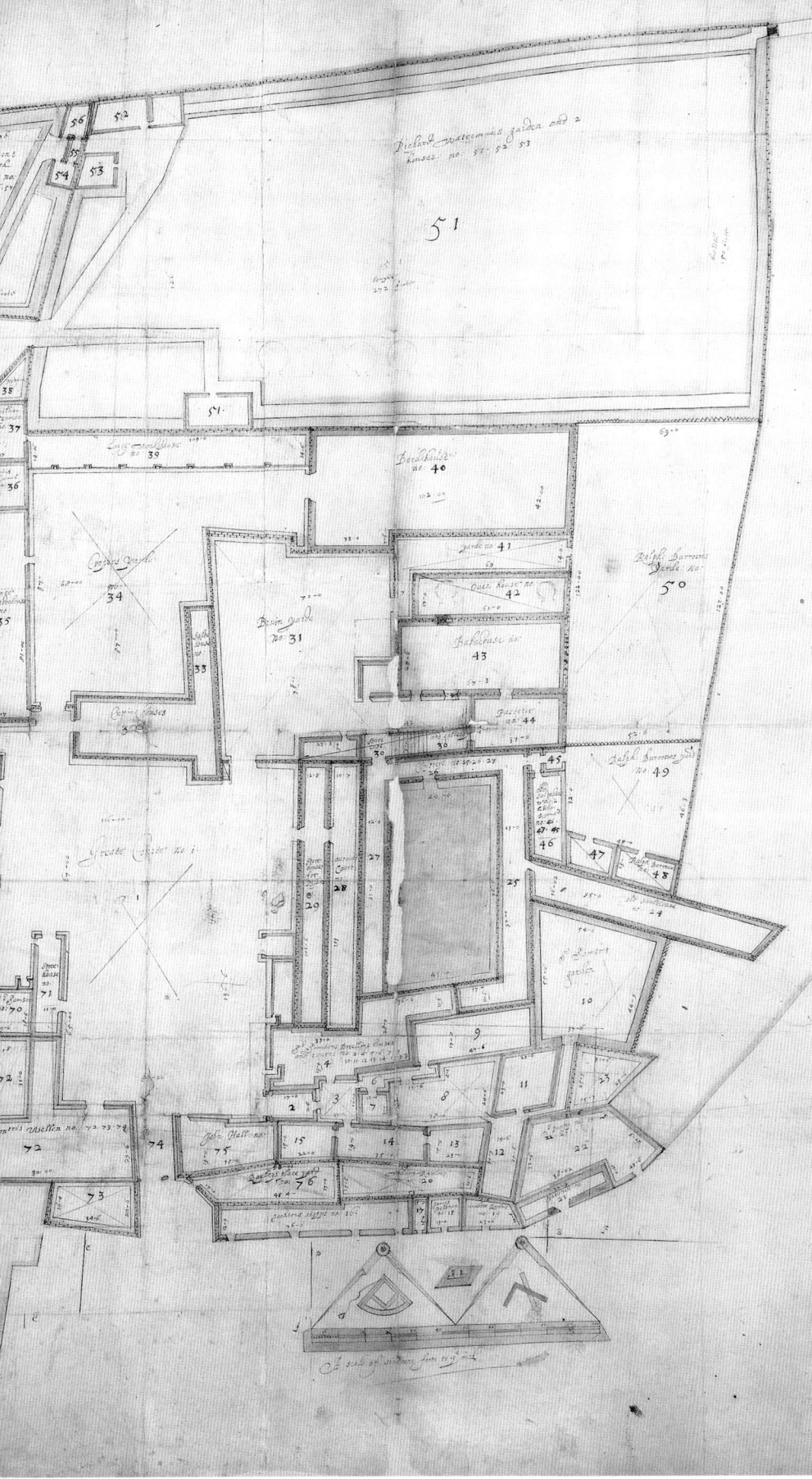

KEY[146]

'occ.' = 'occupied by'

1. Great court.

2-15. Fair dwelling house occ. Sir Sampson Darell, including courts or yards (3 and 8) and garden (10).

16. Four shops occ. Startupp Jackson or assigns.

17. Shop occ. Mr Bonfoy or assigns.

18. Shop occ. James Steedman.

19-20. Shop (19) and yard adjoining (20) occ. Margaret Rawlins widow.

21. Shop occ. [blank] Harsnet.

22-23. Shop, dwelling house and yard occ. Mr Bonfoy.

24. The old salthouse and chambers over it, for bread.

25-27. Cloister with chambers over it, for store.

28. Outer court.

29. Storehouses, with rooms above for biscuit and corn.

30. Staircase and gallery.

31. Bavin yard.

32. Cutting house with chamber above it called the clock-loft.

33. Salthouse.

34. Coopers' yard.

35. Long storehouse.

36. Dwelling house occ. Davy Evance.

37-38. Dwelling house (37) and yard (38) occ. William Newman.

39. Long workhouse for the coopers.

40. Board-house for barrel staves and hoops. Over these last two are garners and other chambers.

(continued overleaf)

Fig. 226. The Navy Victualling Yard, East Smithfield, 1635.

(continuation of the key to Plan 110)

41. Little yard.
42. Four ovens.
43. Bakehouse.
44. Pastry and chamber over it.
45-47. An old salthouse and two other little void rooms, and the great biscuit loft over them.
48-49. Workhouse (48) and yard and garden (49) occ. Ralph Burrowes.
50. Yard and little garden occ. Eliazar Barnes.
51-53. Garden (51) and two dwelling houses (52-53) occ. Richard Waterman.
54-57. Washhouses (54-56) and garden (57) in Sir Sampson Darell's own hands.
58. Garden occ. Mr George Danett.
59. Slaughterhouse yard.
60. Pound yard.
61. Slaughterhouse and chamber above it.
62-64. Orchard and garden (62), yard (63) and fair dwelling house (64) occ. Mr Henry Bludder.
65-66. Dwelling house (65) and yard (66) occ. Mr George Danett.
67-69. Dwelling house (67), yard (68) and shop or workhouse (69) occ. James Steedman.
70. Stable in Sir Sampson Darell's own hands.
71. Storehouse with rooms above for the baker.
72-74. Fair dwelling house with a yard adjoining (72), another yard (73) and gateway or entrance and chamber over it (74) occ. Mrs Wellen.
75-76. Dwelling house called the Baylyes place (75) and yard appertaining (76) occ. John Hall.

Total above, 3 acres, 3 roods, 30 perches.

Item, close of pasture called Well Close in tenure of Sir Sampson Darell or assigns, 9 acres, 0 roods, 34 perches.

---

had houses, such as Henry Bludder, a Deputy Surveyor of the Victuals (Nos. 62-64). The church cloister became the bavin yard (No. 31), but the south-west cloister largely survived; indeed the plan itself refers to it as cloisters (Nos. 25-27). There were shops facing west towards Tower Hill.

The purpose of the plan may have been to assess the need for repairs, as well as the possibility of adding a meeting place for the Navy's officials, houses for those officials and a record repository. It was noted that most of the buildings were 'in great decaie, and unlesse some course be taken to reedifie them, will fall down ere longe, being the ruynes of a decaied monastery'. Plots are edged (not entirely consistently) in grey for buildings, brown for yards and green for gardens; brick seems to be indicated by a double row of bricks.

From 1742 the functions of the Victualling Yard began to be transferred to Deptford, and it closed in 1785. The site was then used as government warehouses until 1805, as the Royal Mint from 1805 to 1971, and subsequently as offices.

Plan 111
The Navy Office, Crutched Friars, 1698
Edmund Dummer

FIGS 227-30

The Navy Board or Office ran the non-operational side of the Navy, from the building and repair of ships to the management of the dockyards and the posting and paying of personnel.[147] From 1654 it occupied half of a mansion in Seething Lane, which provided both offices and dwellings for senior officials. That building, familiar to us from Pepys's diaries, was burnt down in 1673 and the Office moved to temporary premises in Mark Lane. It was decided to enlarge the old site and rebuild there, and an Act providing for the purchase of the extra land was passed in 1673. However, difficulties with owners and lessees and the Government's financial and political problems meant that the new buildings, other than the stables (1678), were not erected until 1682-83. They were built in a Dutch style under the supervision of Sir Christopher Wren, with John Ward as the builder, though the actual designer may have been Robert Hooke.[148] Ward was paid by the grant of a peppercorn lease, with a requirement that he re-let the property to the Navy Office for £560 a year, and the Government did not become the full owner until 1702.

The new Navy Office was beautifully depicted by Edmund Dummer as part of an extraordinary survey of the royal dockyards in 1698, in which every building is shown both in plan and elevation. Dummer (1651-1713) was the son of a Hampshire gentleman farmer. He joined the Navy in 1668 and was Surveyor of the Navy in 1692-99, presumably living in house No. 9 on the plan. He sought to introduce a more rational and

PLANS OF BUILDING TYPES

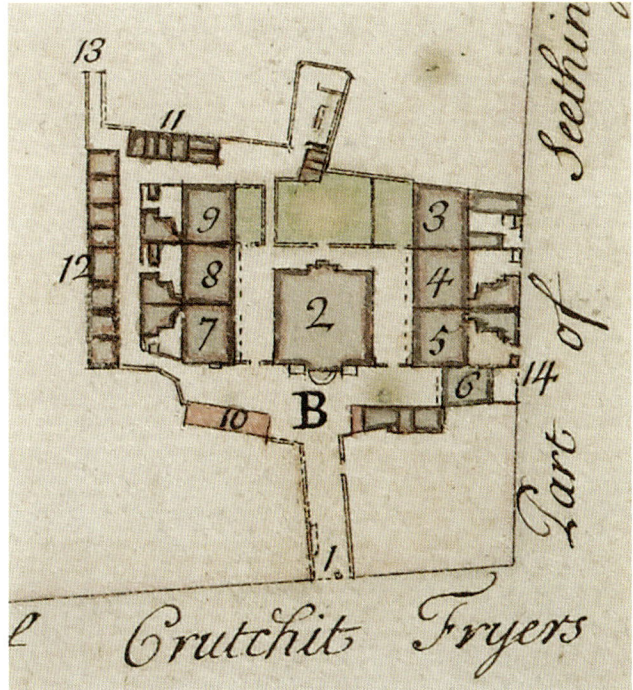

Fig. 227. The Navy Office, 1698. North is at the bottom. Seething Lane is to the right and Crutched Friars at the bottom.

planned approach to shipbuilding and dockyards, assisted by his exceptional skill as an artist, and contributed significantly to the development of the dockyards, though he was criticised for his lack of practical skills. He was dismissed in 1699 on ill-founded charges of corruption. He subsequently founded the first transatlantic mail service by packet boat, as well as building ships and running an ironworks, but died bankrupt in 1713.

The new Navy Office faced Crutched Friars, and included the Navy Office itself and houses for six Navy officials. Each was of three and a half storeys and basement, and on the ground floor had two main rooms together with hall, staircase and kitchen. Off the main courtyard, approached by a separate gate from Seething Lane, was the Ticket Office, where discharged seamen who had been given a ticket in lieu of pay sought to obtain their money. The buildings were valued at £9,244, of which the six officers' dwellings amounted to £5,365. The Navy Office remained here until it moved to the newly-built Somerset House in 1786.[149]

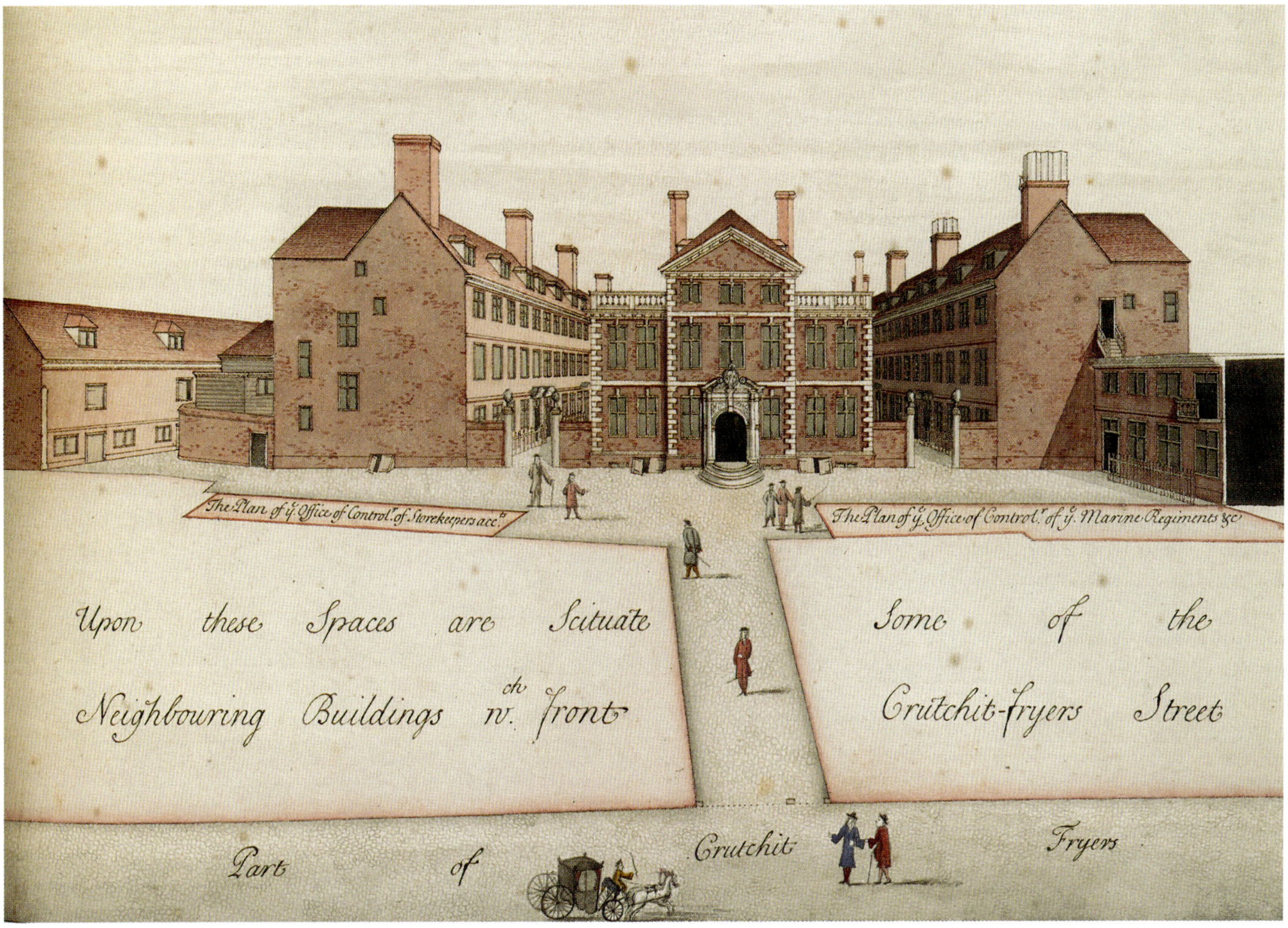

Fig. 228. Edmund Dummer's view of the Navy Office from the north, 1698.

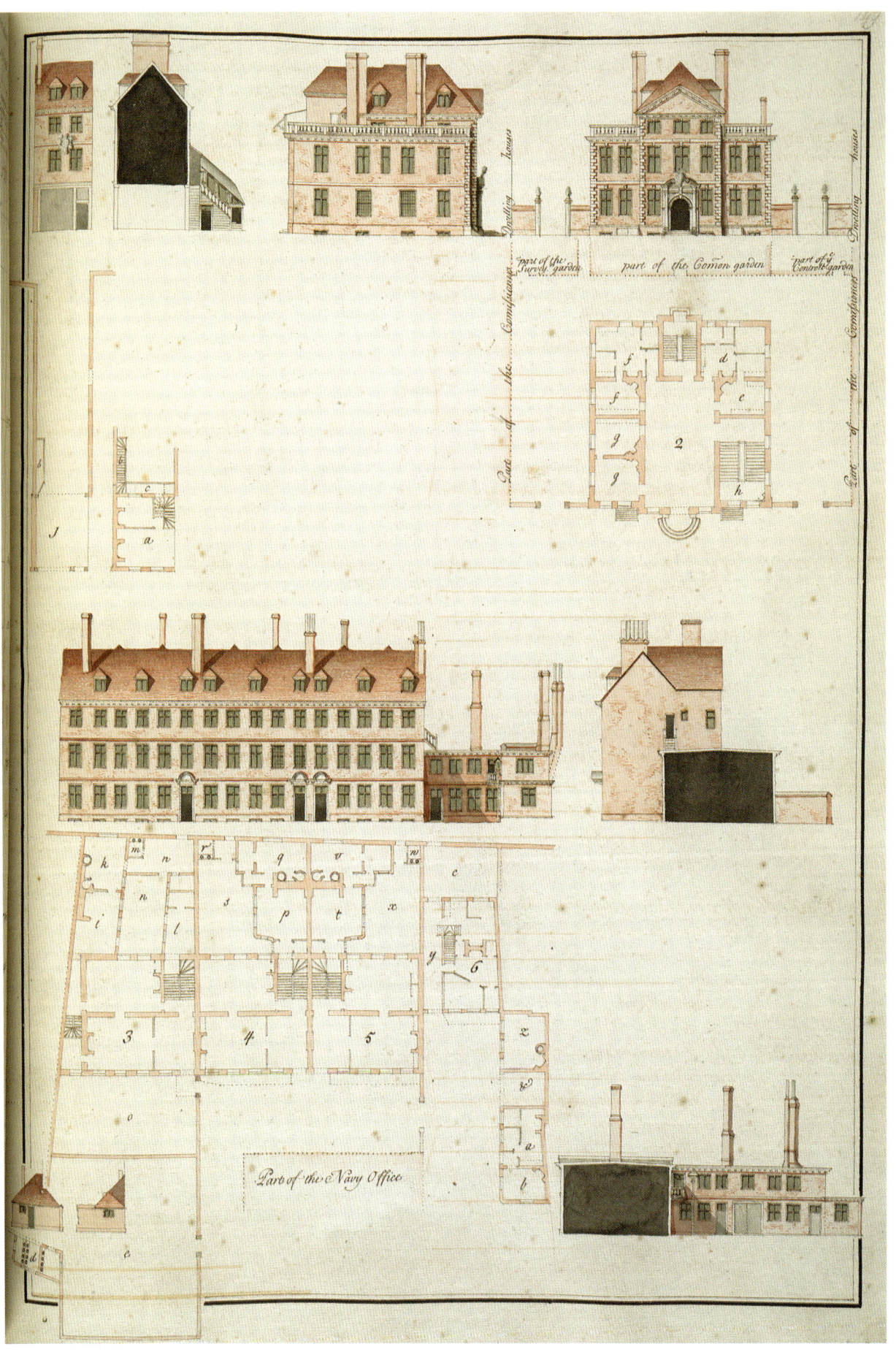

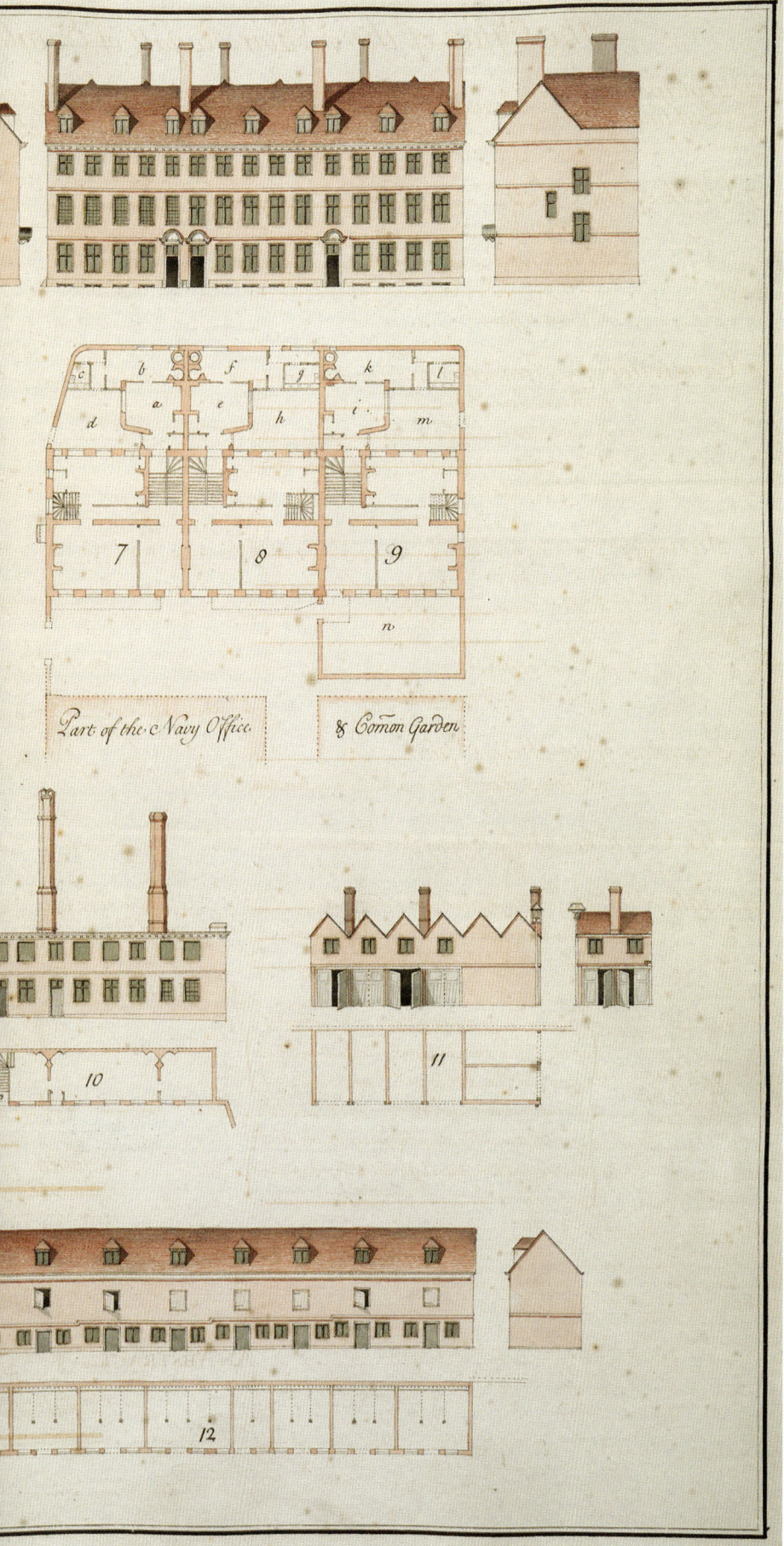

KEY

1. Principal gateway and porter's dwelling. a. Plan of porter's house over gate. b. Porter's watch cabin and stairs over it. c. Balcony etc. at first floor of porter's house.

2. Navy Office Common Hall; also boardroom and a vestibule etc. over it. d, e. Controller of the Navy's office. f. Surveyor's office. g. Controller of the Victualling's office. Over f and g are the Clerk of the Acts' office; over d, the Controller of the Treasurer's Accounts' office; over e, a withdrawing room for persons attending the Board. h. Office for the Marines, under the stairs.

3. Controller of the Navy's dwelling.

4. Controller of the Storekeeper's Accounts' dwelling.

5. Controller of the Victualling Accounts' dwelling.

6. Ticket Office, also second floor and the engine house etc. y. Public passage into Seething Lane. z. The house-keeper's washhouse and engine house. a. Controller of the Marine Regiment's Office. b. New addition to the latter. c. Courtyard behind Ticket Office. d. Three common privies. e. Common garden for drying clothes.

7. Clerk of the Acts' dwelling.

8. Controller of the Treasurer's Accounts' dwelling.

9. Surveyor's dwelling.

10. Controller of the Stores' office. o. Stairs to second storey which is a common store room.

11. Six coach houses with a lodging for servants over each.

12. Eight stables with a hayloft and garret over each; and a horse pond by the common privy with brick walls and timber cabshaw etc.

Key to outbuildings of dwellings: kitchen of one storey 3i, 4p, 5t, 7a, 8e, 9i. Washhouse 3k, 4q, 5v, 7b, 8f, 9k. Privy 3m, 4r, 5w, 7c, 8g, 9l. Court or yard 3n, 4s, 5x, 7d, 8h, 9m. Ante-room and two closets 3l. Garden in front 3o, 9n. Over parts of 7a-c is an added storey.

Figs 229-30. Plans and elevations of the various parts of the Navy Office, 1698.

Plan 112
King's Bench Prison, Borough High Street, Southwark, c.1660

FIG. 231

King's Bench Prison, first recorded in the fourteenth century, stood on the east side of Borough High Street a little north from St George's church (on the north side of Angel Place, now 201-05 Borough High Street).[150] It was rebuilt under Henry VIII, and was one of the largest debtors' prisons, with 393 inmates in 1653. The office of keeper, with entitlement to the profits from the prison, was private property, held under a grant in perpetuity of 1616. It was held from 1633 until his death in 1668 by Sir John Lenthall, brother of the William Lenthall who was Speaker of the House of Commons.[151] This helps to provide the approximate date of the plan, as the note on the orchard ground indicates that Lenthall was paying rent for it. The plan shows the division between the Common Side and the Master's Side, each with its own entrance from the street. The Master's Side allowed more privacy and comfort to those

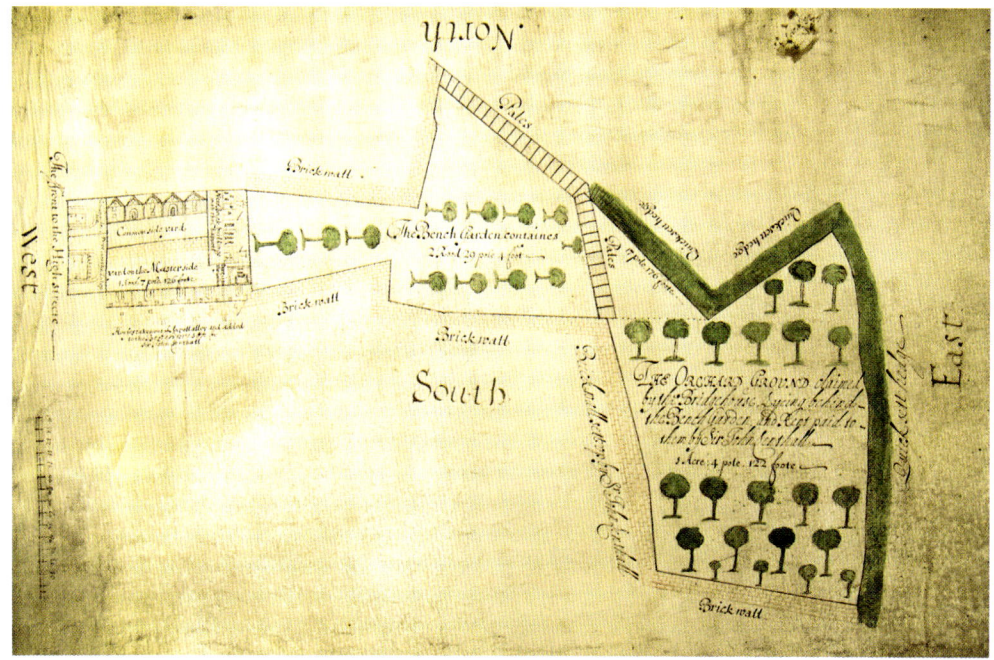

Fig. 231. King's Bench Prison, Southwark, c.1660.

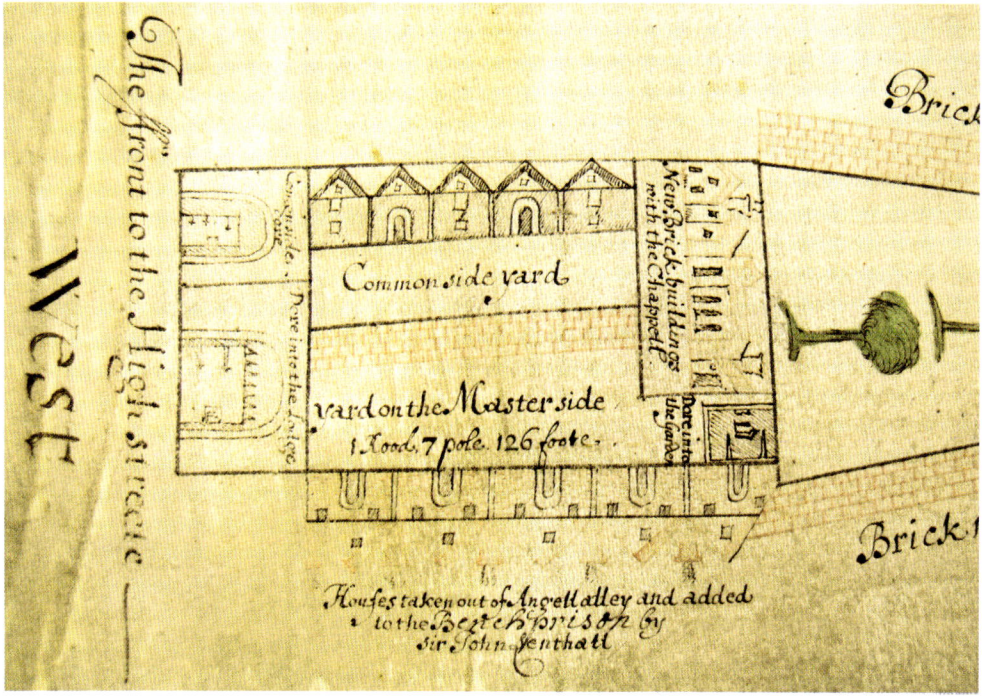

Fig. 232. Detail from Fig. 231, showing the prison itself.

who could pay the fees. Also shown are the new brick range to the east, including the chapel, and the houses to the south added to the prison by Lenthall. The Common Side had to be rebuilt after the Southwark fire of 1689. In 1720 Strype described the prison as 'generally thronged with debtors; a prison wherein great abuses are committed by the marshall or keeper and his underlings', especially the keeper failing to keep the prisoners confined, 'he suffering them for gratuities to go at pleasure where they please'.[152] The prison was moved to a new site in St George's Fields in 1758 and the old prison was demolished in 1761.

Plan 113
Southwark Counter and Sessions House, Southwark, 1686
William Cavell
FIG. 233

This elaborate plan shows among other things the City of London's arms and the Bridge House symbol. It was drawn by William Cavell, whose only other known maps are of estates in Norfolk and Sussex in the 1660s.[153] The site in Borough High Street, just south of what is now the junction with Southwark Street, was occupied from the twelfth century by St Margaret's church. Upon the Dissolution of the Monasteries, St Mary Overy (now Southwark Cathedral) became the parish church for St Margaret's parish, and St Margaret's church was sold. Houses were built there, possibly on the churchyard, and by about 1560 there was a room known as the Court House or

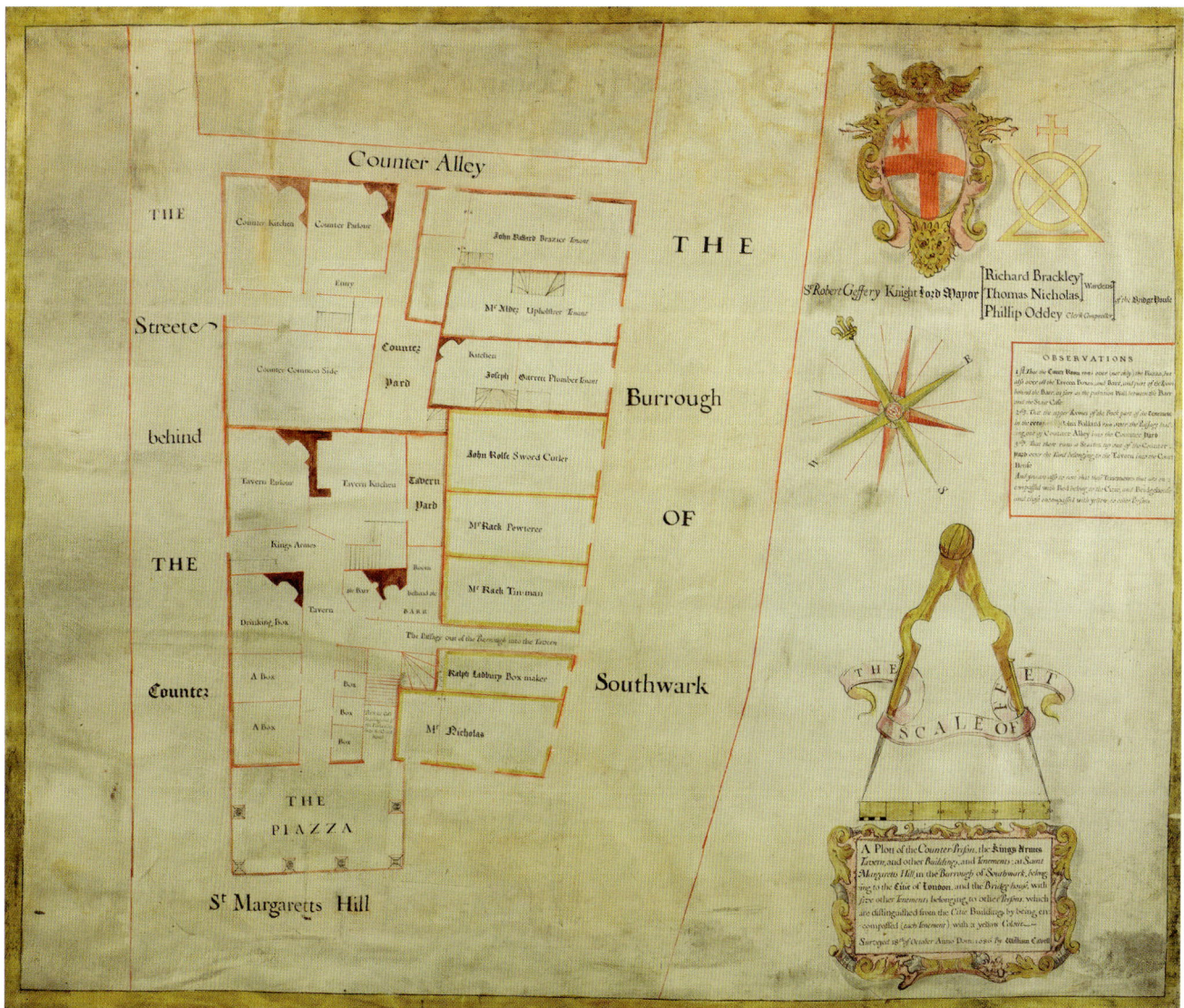

Fig. 233.   Southwark Counter and the Sessions House, 1686.

Sessions Hall, which in 1583 was sold to the Aldermen of the City of London, highlighting the Court of Aldermen's jurisdiction in Southwark. The sale reserved the rights of Surrey's justices of the peace to use the building, and for the Marshalsea Court to be held there. Part of the site became the Compter or Counter prison, possibly in 1608.

The property was destroyed in the Southwark fire of 1676, and rebuilding was completed only in 1685, shortly before the plan was drawn; the court room was still being wainscoted in 1686.[154] The plan's purpose may have been to delineate the rights of the City and of the Bridge House, and both the Lord Mayor and the Bridge House Wardens put their names to it. At the south end of the site, the ground floor was occupied by the King's Arms, with numerous drinking boxes, as well as bar, kitchen and parlour. Above it, stretching from the front of the piazza to a point over the wall between the King's Arms bar and stairs, was the court room (Fig. 234). It had stairs from the piazza, and back stairs over the tavern yard into the Counter yard. The Counter was divided into the Master's Side, with kitchen and parlour,

Fig. 234. The Sessions House seen from the south, c.1750 (watercolour). In the background is the tower of St Saviour (now Southwark Cathedral).

and the Common Side. To the east were houses, only some of which belonged to the Bridge House. They were predominantly occupied by metalworkers.

The Counter moved elsewhere in 1717, and the Sessions House was replaced in 1793 by a Town Hall, which itself disappeared in the mid-nineteenth century. Counter Alley, now Counter Court, still exists.

Plan 114
Royal Mews, Westminster, c.1715
Fig. 235

This plan dates from between 1713 and 1716, and the most likely reason for it is the repairs undertaken in 1715-16, shortly after George I came to the throne.[155] The Mews occupied much of the site of what is now Trafalgar Square and extended back almost to the present Orange Street (Fig. 237). The Mews were under construction in 1273, but the connection was at first with falconry rather than horses. 'Mews' refers to moulting, and the birds were confined at moulting time. In 1531 the Mews were rebuilt as stables, and they were rebuilt again in 1550-56 following a fire. The buildings of the 1550s formed the core of the complex which survived, with many additions and alterations, until 1824-25. Treswell's plan of 1585 shows buildings around three sides of the Great Mews and on the south side of the Little Mews to the east (Fig. 238). Apart from the southern range these largely correspond to the king's stables, hay barns and granary of c.1715. By the latter date, there were many more buildings, many of them in Dunghill Mews to the west or the Green Mews to the north. The first coach-house was added in 1568, for Queen Elizabeth. There were numerous lodgings in c.1715 for equerries, grooms, coachmen and others, many of whom also had stables, and there were workshops for a saddler, a farrier and others. No. 23 was a riding house, and No. 61, by Hedge Lane, was Anne Rochford's 'chocolate house'.[156] The only large house was that of the Master of the Horse adjoining Dunghill Mews, built in about 1661 (No. 56), though Colonel Wentworth, an equerry, also had a relatively large house and garden (No. 36). In the centre of the Great Mews were a horse pond and an equerry's lodging (demolished in 1725). Several of the stables and lodgings were ruinous. In 1686 Wren reckoned that the Mews had accommodation for 300 horses and thirty coaches. The Great Mews and Green Mews were used for parades by the horse guards and horse grenadiers.

In 1773 the Great Mews was said to look like 'a common innyard', apart from the main stables added by William Kent in 1732 between the Great Mews and the Green Mews. In the 1820s new Royal Mews were built on their present site in Buckingham Palace Road and the old ones were cleared in order to create Trafalgar Square.

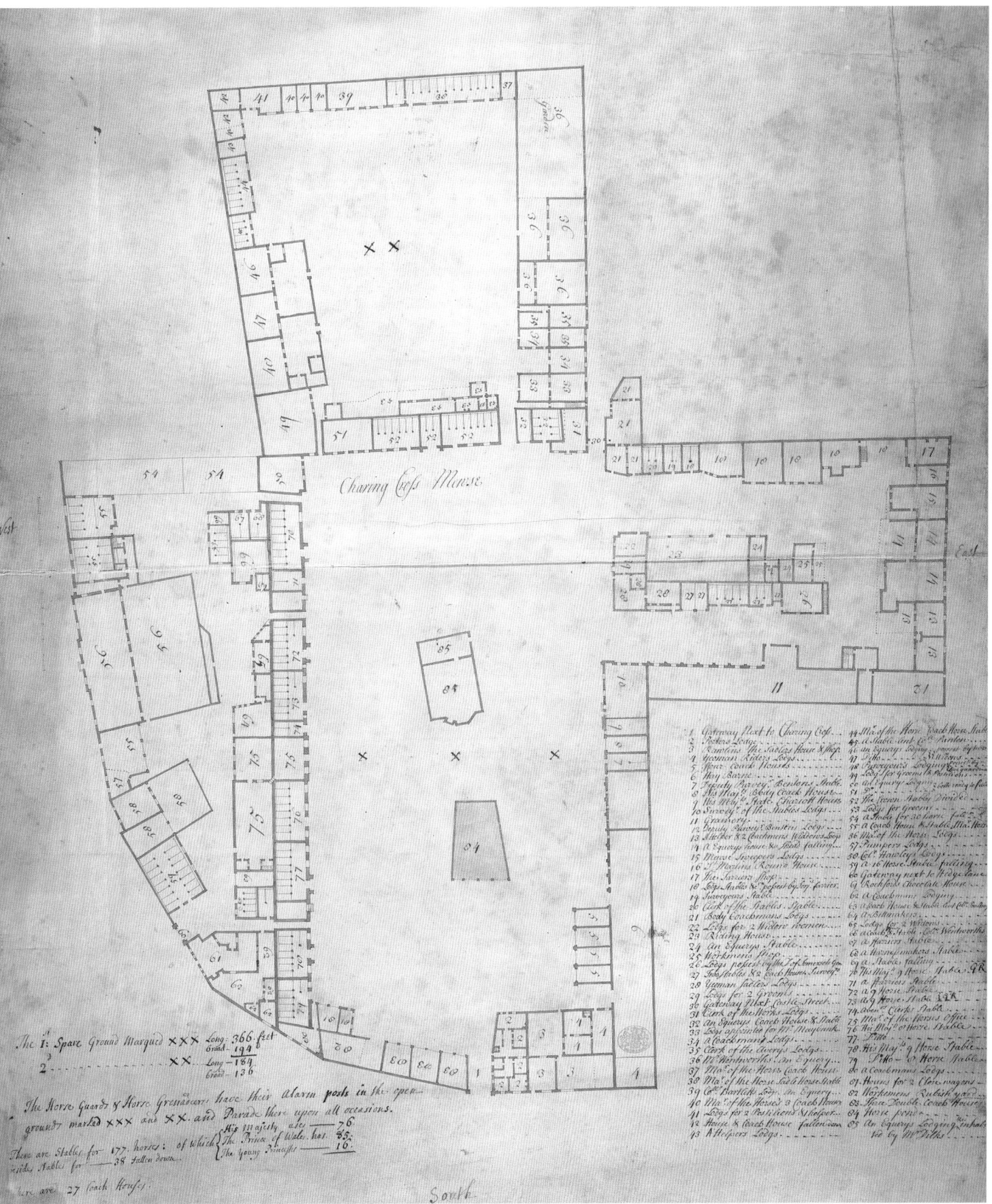

Fig. 235. The Royal Mews, c.1715. North is at the top. For key see overleaf.

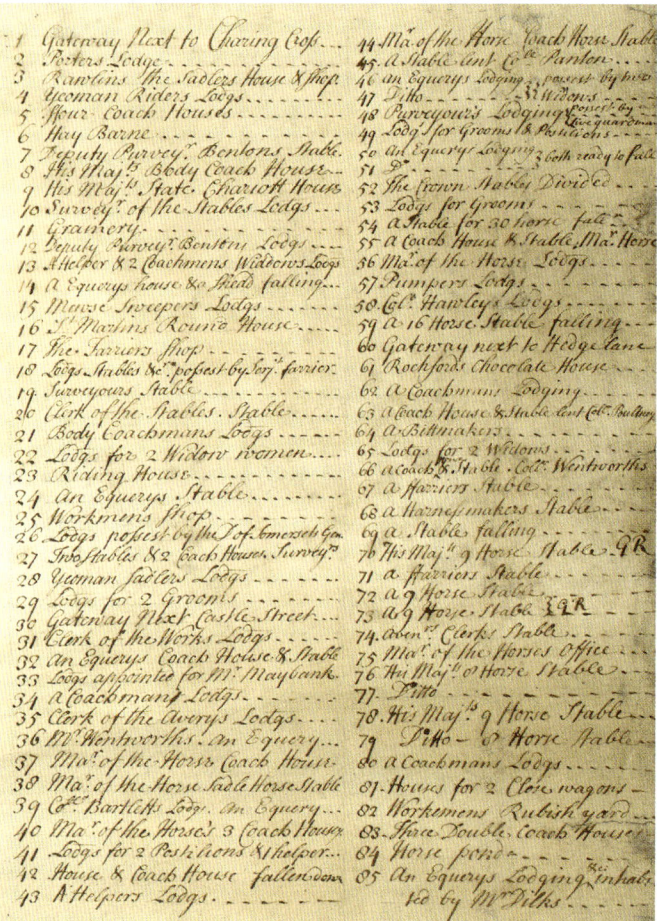

Fig. 236. Key from Fig. 235.

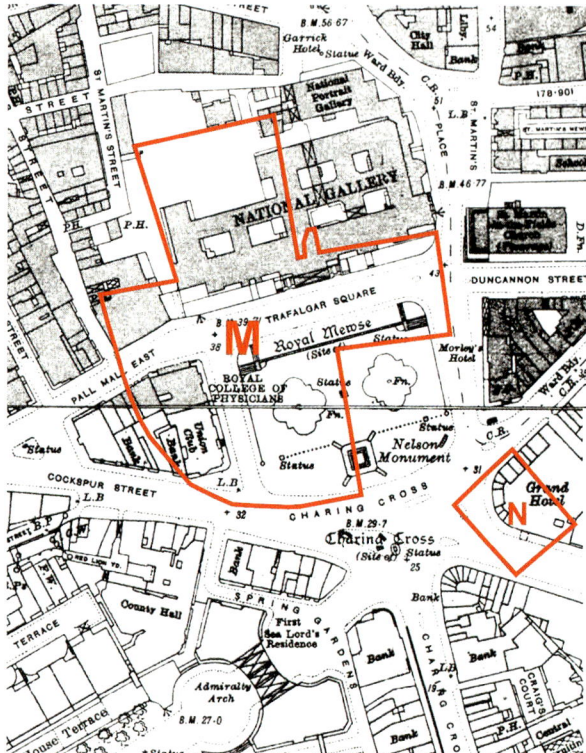

Fig. 237. The approximate site of the Mews ('M') marked on the Ordnance Survey map of 1914-16. The location is based on the c.1715 plan and Horwood's map, which coincide reasonably well except on the east side. 'N' indicates the approximate site of Northampton (later Northumberland) House (see Plan 14).

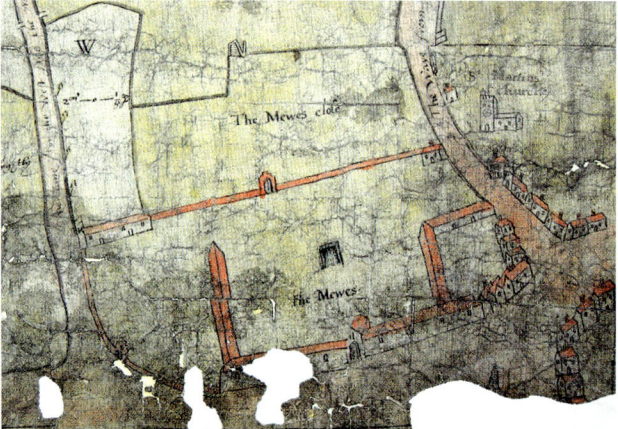

Fig. 238. Detail from Ralph Treswell's plan of land in the parishes of St Martin in the Fields and St Giles in the Fields in 1585, showing the Mews, with St Martin in the Fields to the right.

Fig. 239. The front of the Royal Mews, facing the statue of Charles I—detail from a print by Sutton Nicholls of c.1725. From right to left are the saddler's house and shop, the porter's lodge, the gateway, three coach-houses and a house apparently built since 1715 on the site of a rubbish yard.

Fig. 240. The sixteenth-century range on the east side of the Great Mews in about 1815, when it was being used as a barracks. This is a photograph of a watercolour by William Henry Hunt; the location of the original is unknown. In 1716 most of the range was a hay barn, with coach houses projecting forward and the Surveyor of the Stables' lodging at the left-hand end.

CHURCHES

Plan 115
St Peter upon Cornhill, 1680
Fig. 241

Following the Great Fire, the commissioners for rebuilding approved the reconstruction of St Peter upon Cornhill in 1674, but work did not begin until 1677 and the new church was not roofed until 1680.[157] In September 1680 the churchwardens contracted with Thomas Poultney and Thomas Athew, citizens and joiners, for the pews, benches, screen, pulpit and lining of the pillars, to be completed by 1 April 1681, and to be done in accordance with the 'plotts and scheames' annexed to the contract. The plan of the church has survived within the church-

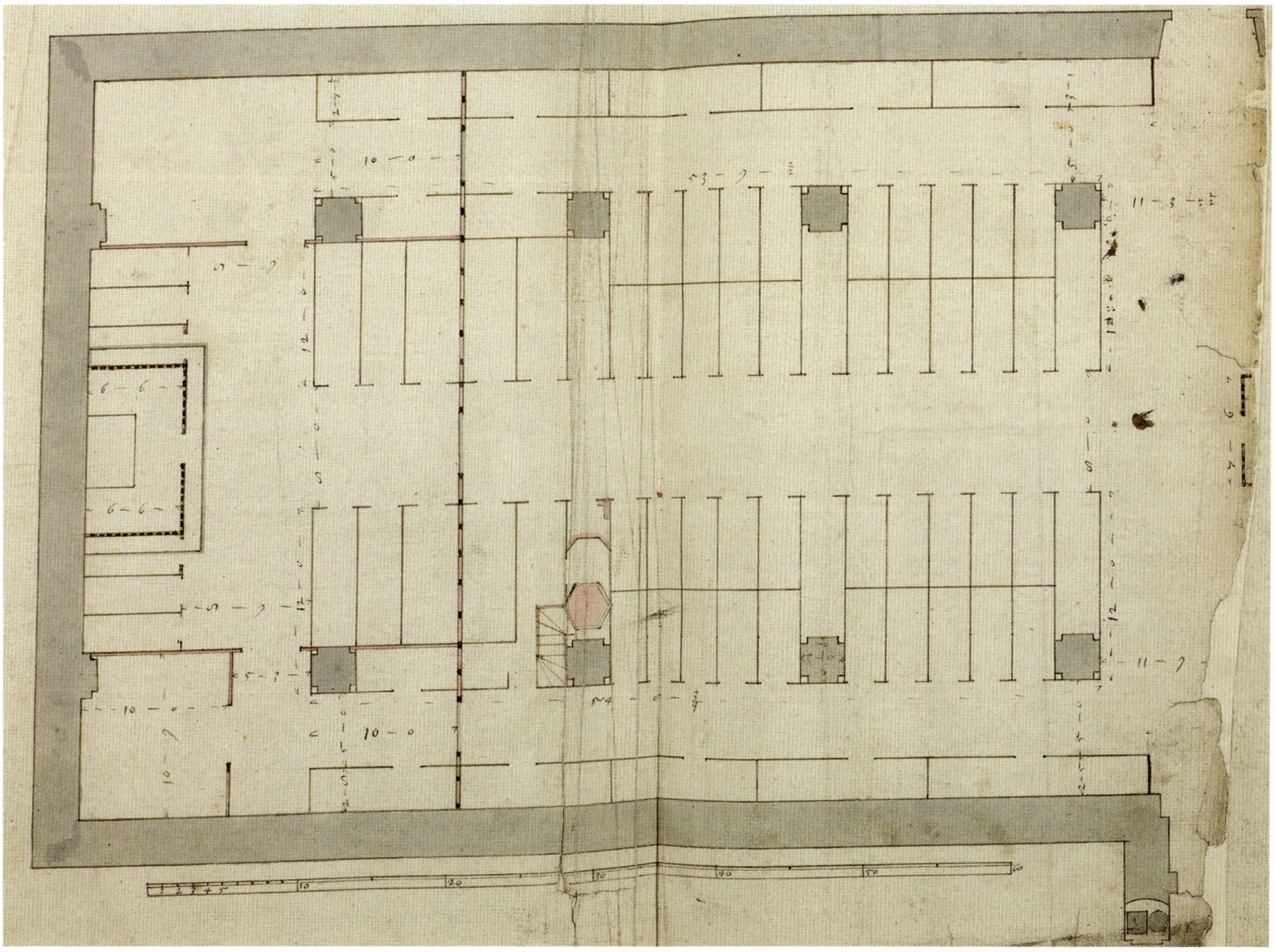

Fig. 241. St Peter upon Cornhill, 1680.

wardens' accounts, though not the 'modell' for the screen and that for the pulpit. Most of the work was to be paid for by the yard, but the pulpit was to cost £30 and the king's arms forming part of the screen £8. St Peter was one of only two Wren churches with a screen, reflecting the insistence of the rector, Dr William Beveridge, on the need to separate nave and chancel. The pews were replaced in 1872 and later removed altogether, but the screen and pulpit (the latter lowered) remain today (Fig. 242).[158]

Fig. 242. The interior of St Peter upon Cornhill, 2016.

Plan 116
Church Entry, Blackfriars, 1702
Mr Williams
Fig. 243

This plan shows no existing church, but includes the site of a church (St Ann Blackfriars) and part of a monastery. The plan is attached to a deed of 1702 which recites an earlier one of 1673 between Thomas Gouge, owner of the rectory or advowson of St Ann, and trustees for the parishioners of St Ann, granting the advowson and associated property to the latter. Disputes had arisen over whether Gouge's grant was valid, and therefore in 1702 Gouge's heirs and the last surviving trustee confirmed the grant. The deed notes that

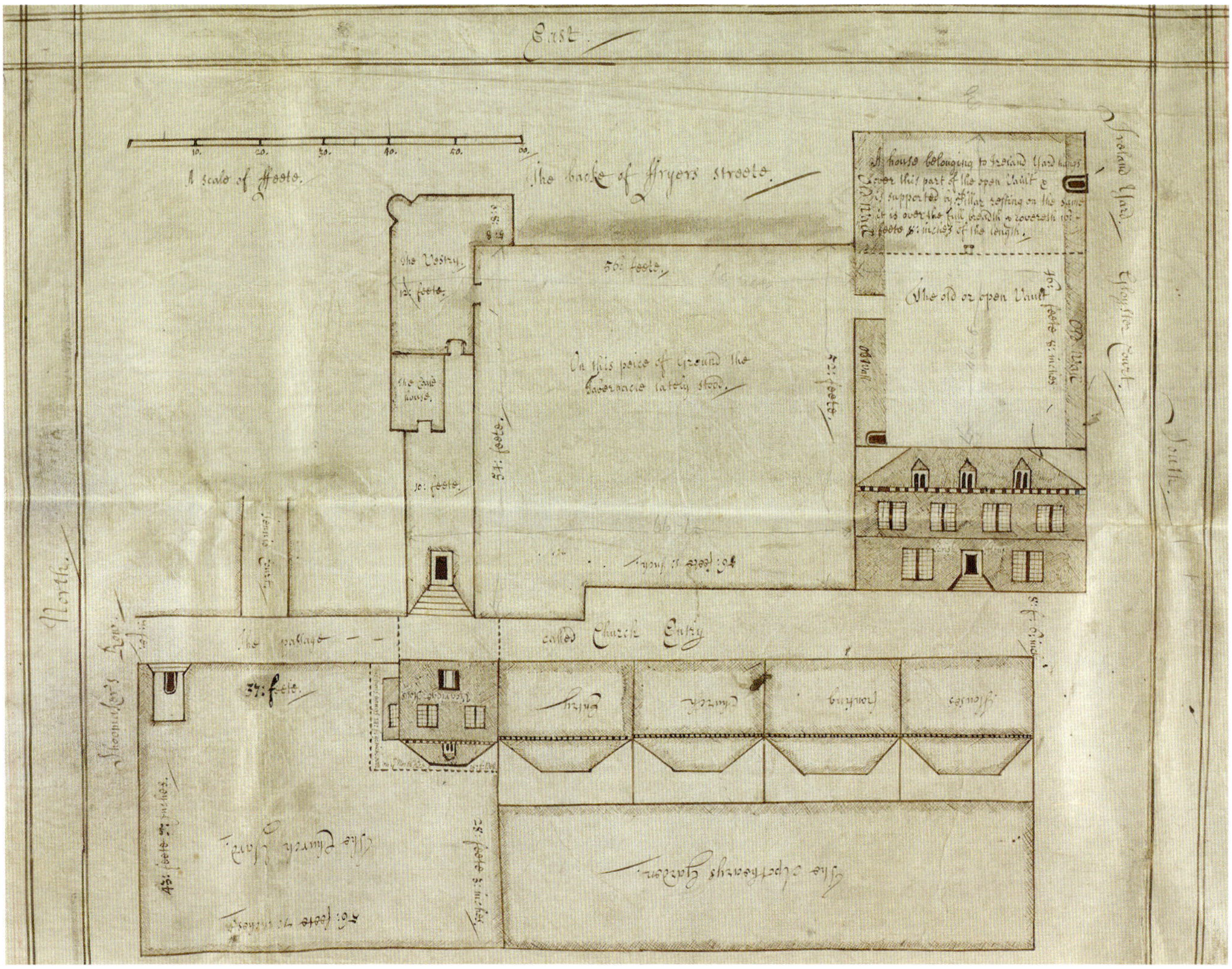

Fig. 243. Church Entry, Blackfriars, 1702.

new streets and buildings had altered the boundaries since 1673, 'so that there was a necessity for the making a new draught chart or ground plott thereof which has been done'. The churchwardens' accounts for 1702 record £1 'Paid Ma: Williams for takeing a draught of ye ground', which is probably this plan, though the surveyor could be Martin, Mark or Master Williams.[159] The plan is pictorial and to scale.[160]

As well as the advowson, four pieces of land were transferred. The largest was the mainly open ground east of Church Entry. This had been the site of St Ann's church,[161] and after the Great Fire the site of the 'tabernacle' serving the united parishes of St Ann and St Andrew by the Wardrobe until (in 1694) the latter had been rebuilt. It contained a vestry house and a coal house. St Ann's churchyard was on the west side of Church Entry. The parishioners could use the former church site as they wished, but the churchyard was to remain as such, and indeed is still an open space today. Adjoining the churchyard was the 'mansion' occupied before the Great Fire by the minister of the parish; it had been rebuilt under a forty-year lease to William Dawes, was occupied in 1702 by James Hubert and was intended to be occupied by the rector of St Andrew's. It overhung both the churchyard and Church Entry, apparently bridging over the latter. Finally, at the south end of Church Entry was a double-fronted house of two and a half storeys, built by the trustees and occupied by Daniel Taylor, a baker.

All the land covered was within the former precinct of Blackfriars, and Church Entry was in origin the east walk of the main cloister and a passage though the monastic church between choir and nave to reach what is now Carter Lane. The two walls behind Daniel Taylor's house marked 'old wall' are therefore of particular interest, especially as the plan refers to the garden between them as 'the old or open vault'. This seems to have been the remains of the house of the Provincial Prior, the head of the Dominican Order in England, built over a vaulted undercroft and partly uncovered in 1900 and subsequently.[162] The plan shows one of the columns of the undercroft still in place, supporting a building above the far end of the vault. These walls had therefore survived both the Dissolution and the Great Fire. The oddly shaped north side of the vestry seems to be the south wall of the choir of the Blackfriars church.

Plans 117-18
St Botolph Aldgate and adjoining shops, 1706 and 1717
Walter Henshaw and Isaac Olley   FIGS 244, 245

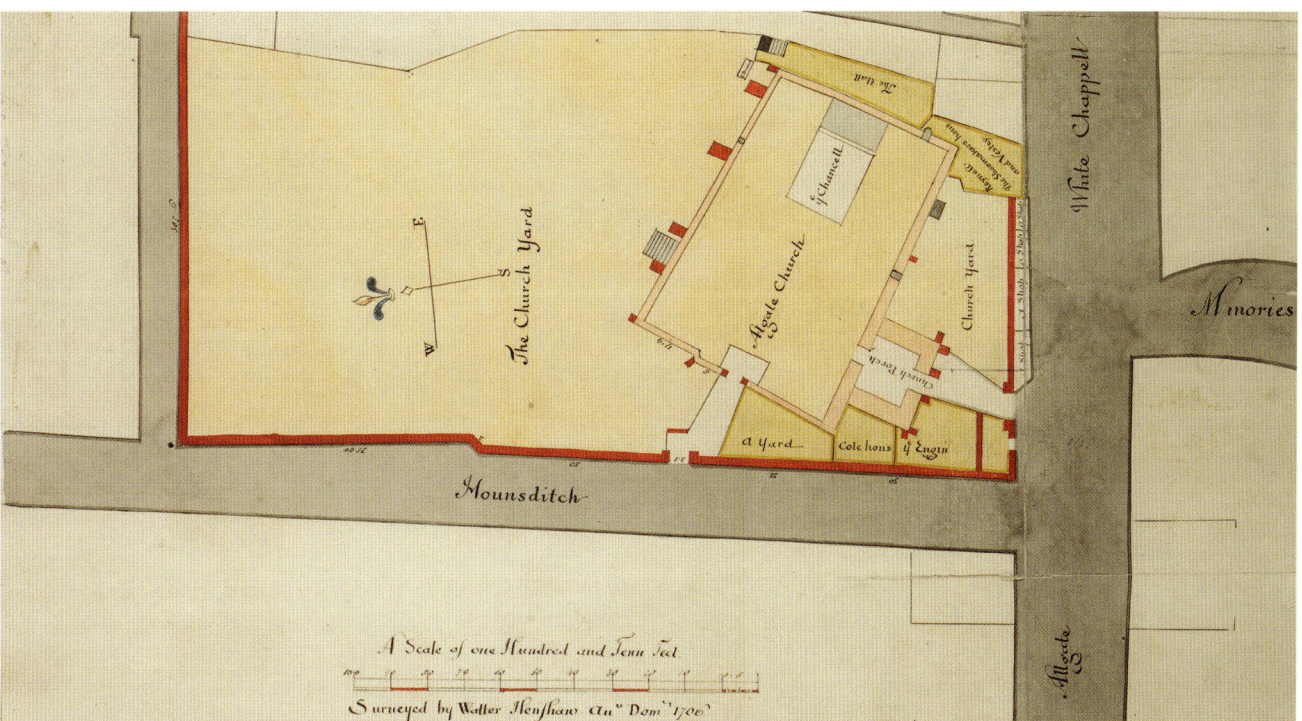

Fig. 244. St Botolph Aldgate, 1706.

The plan of 1706 accompanied a 500-year lease from the owner or 'impropriator' of the rectory of St Botolph Aldgate to the parishioners. It was drawn by Walter Henshaw, clockmaker and mathematical instrument maker, who was a parishioner of St Botolph living at East Smithfield.[163] The lease covered the shop adjoining the chancel and the cellar under it, occupied by Charles Reynolds, shoemaker; the vestry room over Reynolds' shop; the yard behind the shop and the vault under it; and, on the west side of the church, the watchhouse (presumably the building at the front), the engine house, the coal house and the yard adjoining. The opportunity was taken to transfer to the parish the Easter offerings of 2d per inhabitant (collecting which caused 'strife and debate' and which were handed over to the curate anyway), together with the duty of keeping the chancel in repair.[164]

The narrow shops adjoining the churchyard were largely on land formerly part of the street, which was leased by the City to the parish. Before 1616 fruiterers and herb women were allowed to have stalls in the churchyard and the church porch but not to leave things there. In 1616 the parish decided to build shops along the churchyard wall next to Aldgate High Street. There were five shops there in 1654,[165] and in 1717, when the lease from the City was renewed, four shops, with rooms over them (Fig. 245). The lease plan depicts the shops as a mere three feet deep, but they also occupied a strip of the churchyard varying from fifteen to nineteen inches wide, so they were in fact between four and five feet deep.[166] They demonstrate the value of street frontage on a busy thoroughfare. No doubt the shops were rebuilt from time to time, but the eighteenth-century view gives an idea of what they looked like (Fig. 246).

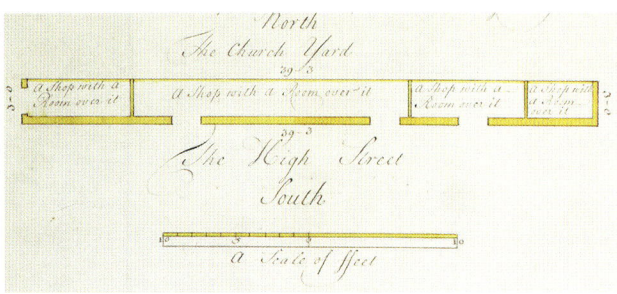

Fig. 245. Shops on the edge of the churchyard of St Botolph Aldgate, 1717.

Fig. 246. Detail from a print showing part of St Botolph Aldgate and the shops shown in Fig. 245, after the building of John Cass's charity school in 1710 (on the left) and before the rebuilding of the church in 1741-44.

OTHER BUILDINGS

Plan 119
Christ's Hospital, c.1660
Fig. 247

This plan shows the ground floor of Christ's Hospital between 1660 and 1666, that is, between the foundation of 'Mr Aldworths schoole' for forty poor boys in 1660 and the Great Fire (see also Plans 20, 26).[167] It is possible that it was drawn just after the Fire, in response to the Governors' demand that the Hospital's officers set out where their houses formerly stood, together with their dimensions, and the somewhat naive character of the plan would be consistent with it having been drawn from memory, though it would have been little use as to dimensions.

When founded in 1552, the Hospital occupied little more than the buildings around the cloister, between Christ Church and London Wall, but other land was soon acquired. The plan shows some of the buildings used by staff and also some let to tenants. Of those named, Mr Parrey was the Hospital's Clerk, George Perkins was the Upper Grammar Master, Shadrach Helmes replaced Perkins as Upper Grammar Master in 1662, and Jonathan Pickes was the Writing Master. The Grammar School was on the east side of the cloister and the 'Maidens Schoole' on the north side. Being a ground plan, no notice is taken of the major buildings above, including the 'wards' or dormitories in the friars' former dormitory on the east side of the cloister, the hall on the west side and probably dormitories in the former Whittington's Library on the north side.

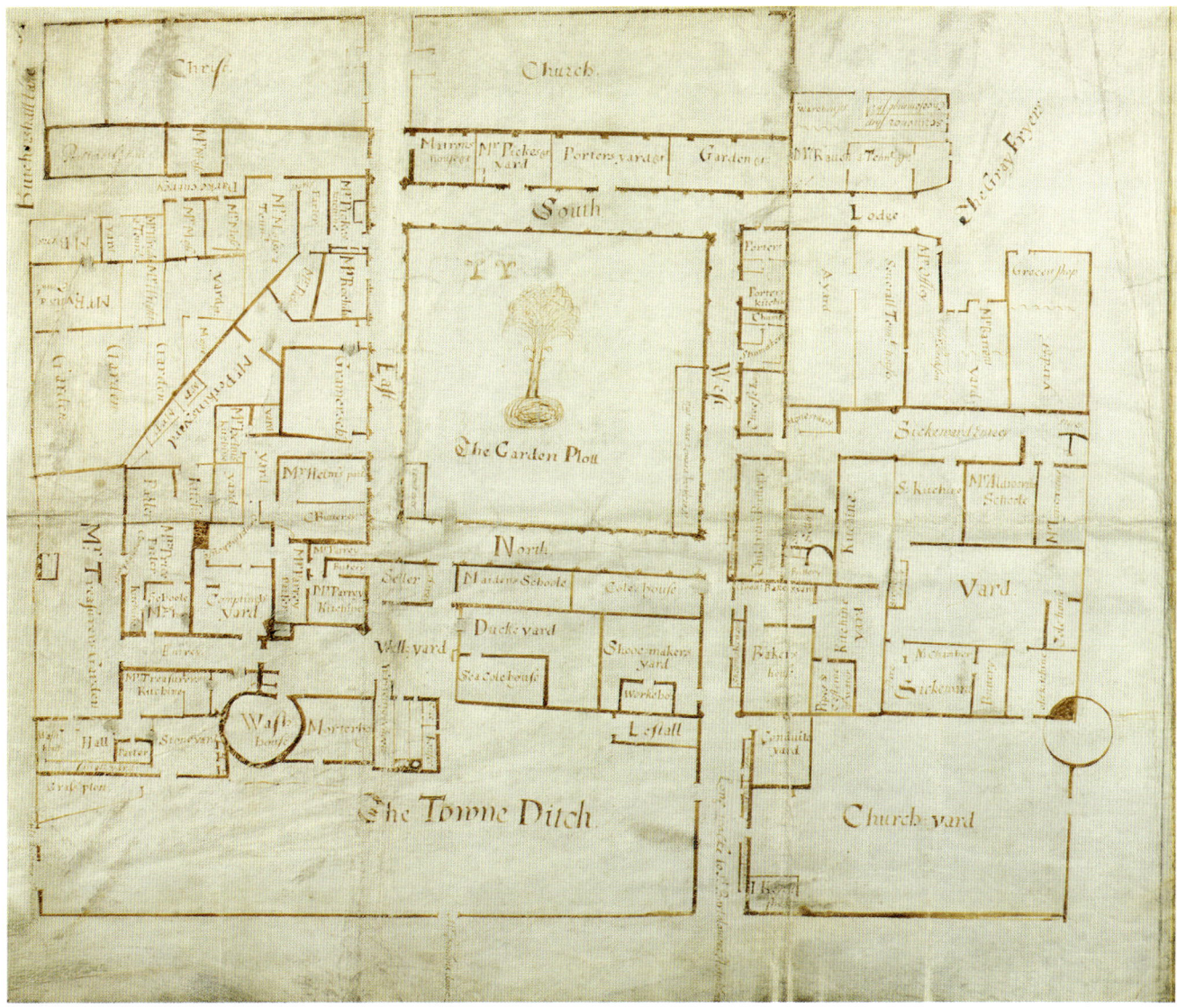

Fig. 247. Christ's Hospital, c.1660. North is at the bottom.

The school eventually filled the whole area between Giltspur Street and Butchers' Hall Lane. In 1902 it moved to Horsham, after which all the buildings on the City site were demolished, and in 1905-11 the General Post Office's King Edward Building was constructed.[168]

Plan 120
Caesar's Buildings, Middle Temple, c.1666 or 1679

FIG. 248

This is in effect a vertical plan, showing the occupancy of different chambers.[169] Caesar's Buildings stood in the middle of what is now Church Court, south of Temple Church, and was so named because it had been built by Sir Julius Caesar, Master of the Rolls, in 1596. It was later replaced by the Lamb Building, and the plan is labelled 'A plott of the anntient Lambs building both ground & inhabitants'. Caesar's Buildings was destroyed in the Great Fire, at the Fire's westward limit, and the plan shows its occupants on the eve of the Fire (two of those listed were not admitted until 1663 and one died in 1666). Caesar's Buildings had earlier belonged to the Inner Temple, but most of the tenants of c.1666 were Middle Templars, and the Middle Temple bore part of the cost of rebuilding. Litigation between the Temples in 1679 over the Middle Temple's refusal to admit to chambers in the successor building the Inner Templars who had been there before the Fire may have given rise to the plan. Since the destruction of the Lamb Building by bombing in 1941 the site has remained open.

Fig. 248. Caesar's Buildings, Middle Temple, c.1666 or 1679.

Plan 121
The Fishmongers', Mercers' and Clothworkers' bargehouses, Vauxhall, 1654
FIG. 249

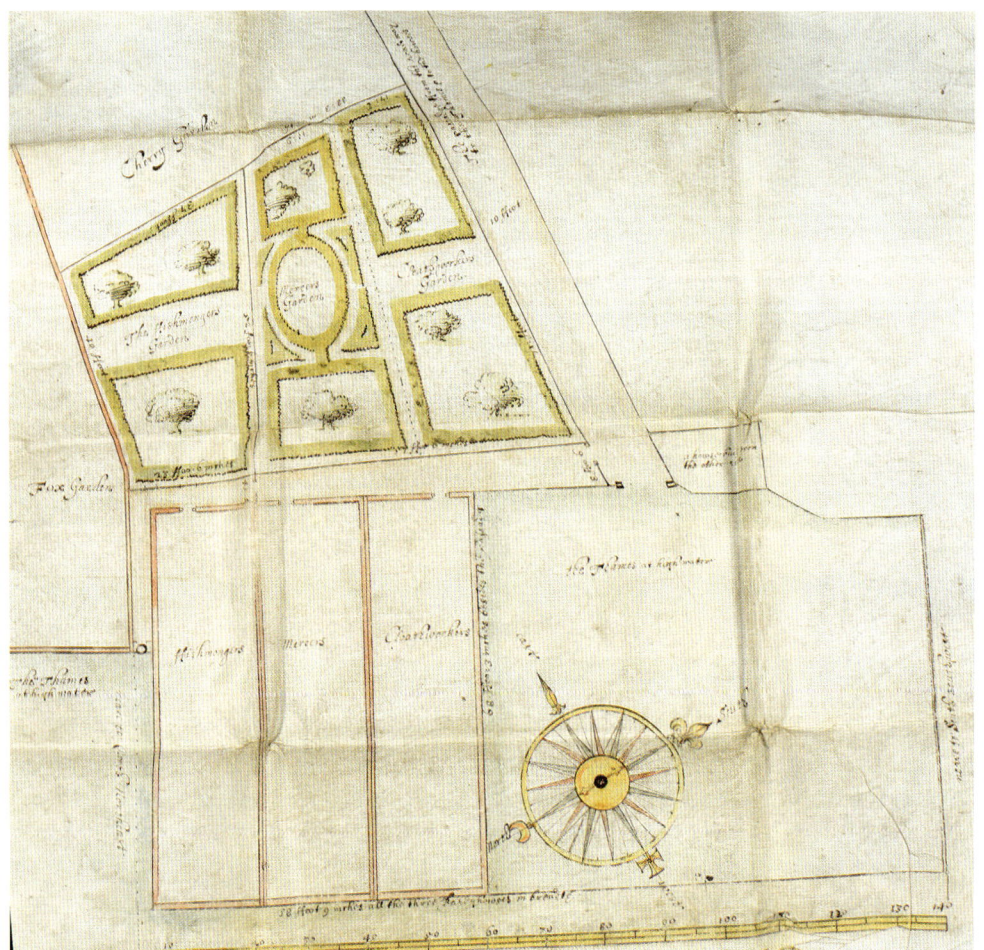

Fig. 249. The Fishmongers', Mercers' and Clothworkers' bargehouses and gardens at Vauxhall, 1654. North is to the left.

In the seventeenth century livery companies began to acquire their own ceremonial barges instead of hiring them when required, and consequently they needed bargehouses. For example, the Mercers built their first barge in 1632 and the Fishmongers in 1634. In 1640 members of the Fishmongers' Company viewed ground in Vauxhall proposed as a site for a bargehouse, and by the time the land was secured in 1643 the Fishmongers, Mercers and Clothworkers were joint lessees and three brick bargehouses were already built. The property was near the present Vauxhall Bridge, on the south-west corner of the site of the MI5 building. There was a tenement over each bargehouse; the Fishmongers let theirs in 1656 to Tobias Pryn, their bargeman.[170] There was also a garden east of the bargehouses, which was divided between the three companies. Unfortunately the land had been leased from the Dean and Chapter of Canterbury, owners of Vauxhall manor, and by 1649, following the Civil Wars, the Dean and Chapter's lands were in the hands of contractors who were selling them. In 1650 the companies refused to match an offer of £450 for the bargehouse site, and they eventually bought it from the new owners for £370, which resulted in the plan of 1654 being drawn in order to be attached to the deed.[171]

In the mid-nineteenth century livery companies began to regard barges as an extravagance, and the Lord Mayor's procession was no longer on the river after 1856. The Clothworkers let their bargehouse to a bargebuilder in 1841, and by 1877 it was a warehouse. The bed of the Mercers' bargehouse was uncovered during an archaeological dig in 1989.[172]

Plan 122
The Skinners' bargehouse, Lambeth, c.1695
Mr Biggs FIG. 250

In 1656 the Goldsmiths' Company leased a site from Thomas Scott for a bargehouse in Lambeth and agreed to share it with the Skinners' Company.[173] Both companies acquired their first barges in that year. The site was just north of Lambeth Palace, and today is under the southernmost part of St Thomas's Hospital. From the second half of the seventeenth century there was a row of bargehouses there, including those of the Goldsmiths and Skinners, stretching about 200 feet (Fig. 251). Two brick bargehouses, costing £232 each, were built for the two companies in 1657-59 under the direction of Edward Jerman, City surveyor, partly on reclaimed land. There were also three cottages: two had a kitchen, a room over part of the bargehouse and a garret; the third, to the south, was shared between the two companies. The Skinners' plan shows bargehouse, cottage, garden and yard. In 1661 the lease had to be renewed with the Archbishop of Canterbury, who had recovered his lands following the Restoration. In 1806 the two companies failed to secure a new lease from the Archbishop, and they established bargehouses at Chelsea instead. The whole row of bargehouses was demolished for St Thomas's Hospital in or about 1868.

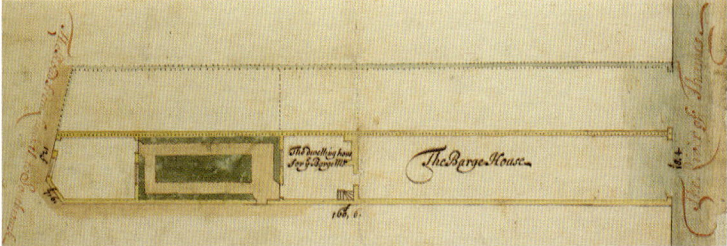

Fig. 250. The Skinners' bargehouse, Lambeth, c.1695. North is at the bottom.

Fig. 251. The bargehouses north of Lambeth Palace in 1829, from Leigh's panorama of the Thames. The former Skinners' and Goldsmiths' bargehouses are the ones sharing a gabled roof immediately to the right of the word 'Houses', the Skinners having the left-hand one.

Plan 123
Dowgate Laystall, 1677
William Leybourn
FIG. 252

In 1671, as part of the post-Fire reforms, the City Corporation began to acquire land for a system of public laystalls to receive 'soyl dirt & dung'. This included street sweepings, rubbish and ash from houses, dung from inns and stables, and oils and other waste from industrial sites and workshops. Laystalls would always be disagreeable neighbours; the plan was to concentrate the nuisance in a few sites and regulate them. Three waterside sites were secured, at Dowgate, Puddle Dock and Whitefriars, and one inland one at Mile End. Leybourn drew plans of them in 1677.[174] The lease of the eastern part of the Dowgate site, which may have continued an existing laystall, was purchased for £650 and incurred rent of £117 a year (the freehold was later bought for £3,000); the lease of the western part, intended as a place for stores, was obtained from William Browne for £1,150 and incurred rent of £50 a year. The accounts refer to the making of 'putt galleries' and the provision of cranes, as well as bricklayers' work.[175] The dirt and soil was laid on the wharf (Fig. 253). The structures coloured brown on the plan, about five feet square and projecting over the water, were presumably for loading vessels.

The three waterside laystalls were leased together in 1688 to Leonard Staples, citizen and dyer, for £400 a year for twenty-one years. He was required to allow anyone to leave soil or dirt without payment, to keep the laystalls fenced and divided, to keep Dowgate Dock and the small dock clean and navigable, to ensure that no more than a specified quantity of soil and dirt was at the laystalls at any one time, and to prosecute anyone except dyers and soapboilers laying soil or dirt at any other City wharf. In fact the City had intended to lease the laystalls to Toby Humfrey, the previous lessee, but Humfrey's partners in the venture suggested that the lease be made to Staples as a trustee because of Humfrey's 'troubles' (unspecified, but probably relating to the lease of the City's markets). Humfrey had a three-tenths share, Samuel Potts, citizen and distiller (involved with Humfrey and others since 1679 in the City's scavage contract) had three-tenths, John Penhallo, a clerk in the Court of Common Pleas, had two-tenths, and William Browne, the merchant who kept the accounts of the scavage partnership and was probably the

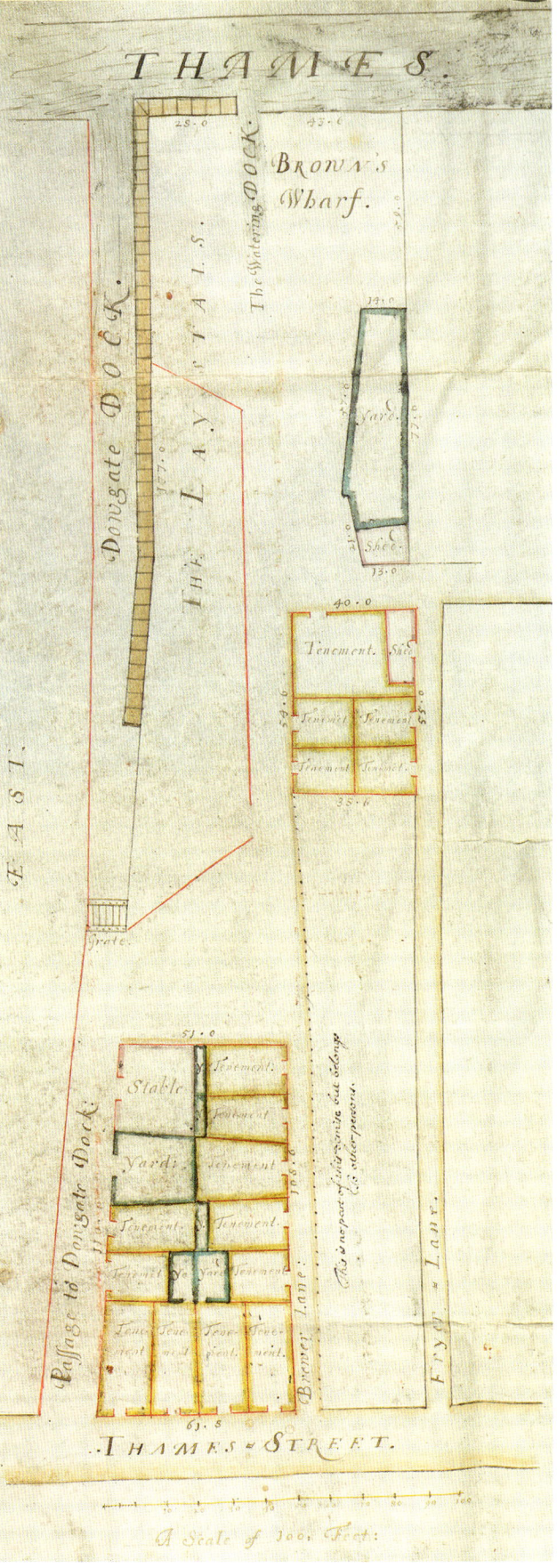

Fig. 252. Dowgate Laystall, 1677.

Fig. 253. Detail from the Bucks' panorama of London in 1749, showing Dowgate Laystall in the centre. To its right are the Cousin Lane brewery (Plan 42), Dowgate Stairs and Steelyard Stairs. There were similar mounds in 1749 at the Puddle Dock and Whitefriars laystalls.

previous lessee of Brown's Wharf, had two-tenths. The profit came from selling the soil and dirt to be spread over market gardens around London, and perhaps also from selling ash to brickmakers, and the partners invested most of their £600 stock in nine lighters and a barge to carry it. Unfortunately the lease said nothing about Staples being only a trustee, and Browne bought him out and claimed the rights under the lease, which resulted in litigation.[176]

The small dock is marked on the plan as 'The Watering Dock', and was used for washing horses. North of it were some back-to-backs. It was noted in 1688 that Leybourn's plan, already eleven years old, did not show an enclosure on Brown's Wharf used for landing hoops and timber, together with four houses built there inhabited 'mostly by poor people'.[177] The wharf by Dowgate was still open land on Horwood's map of 1814, but had been built over by 1855, perhaps reflecting the change around 1850 whereby contractors no longer paid to receive refuse but had to be paid to remove it.[178]

Plan 124
Common house of easement, Queenhithe, 1681
William Leybourn
FIG. 254

This plan records a long-forgotten medieval institution which continued into the eighteenth or nineteenth century: the common house of easement or longhouse at Queenhithe. Public toilets have been documented in almost all late medieval English towns and cities, and at least thirteen have been identified in medieval London, some of them large. The larger ones tended to rely on running water, such as the Thames, the Walbrook and the Fleet, while others, such as the Fenchurch Street one recorded in 1421, relied on deep cesspools. The only one which has been fully researched, the longhouse in Vintry Ward (in modern terms between Southwark Bridge and Cannon Street Station), founded by Richard Whittington in the early fifteenth century, was flushed by the Thames tides and had 128 seats until the Great Fire. The system was still being maintained after the Great Fire, with some new houses of easement being created, usually at markets.[179]

The Queenhithe longhouse was older than the Vintry one. A 'necessary house' at Queenhithe was erected by Matilda, widow of Henry I, in the twelfth century, and was extended towards the river in 1237. In 1314 there was 'a gutter running under certain of the houses ... to receive the rainwater and other water draining from the houses,

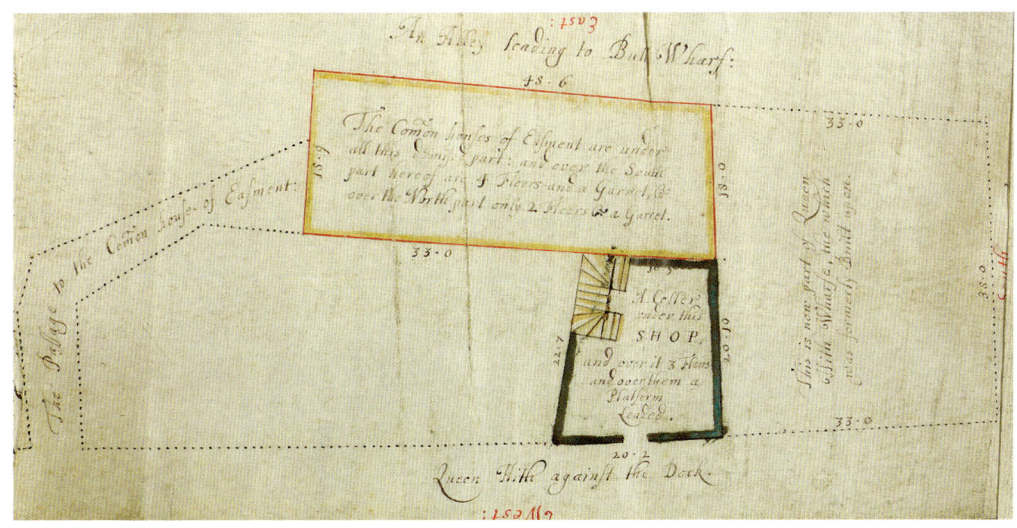

Fig. 254. The common house of easement and other buildings, Queenhithe, 1681.

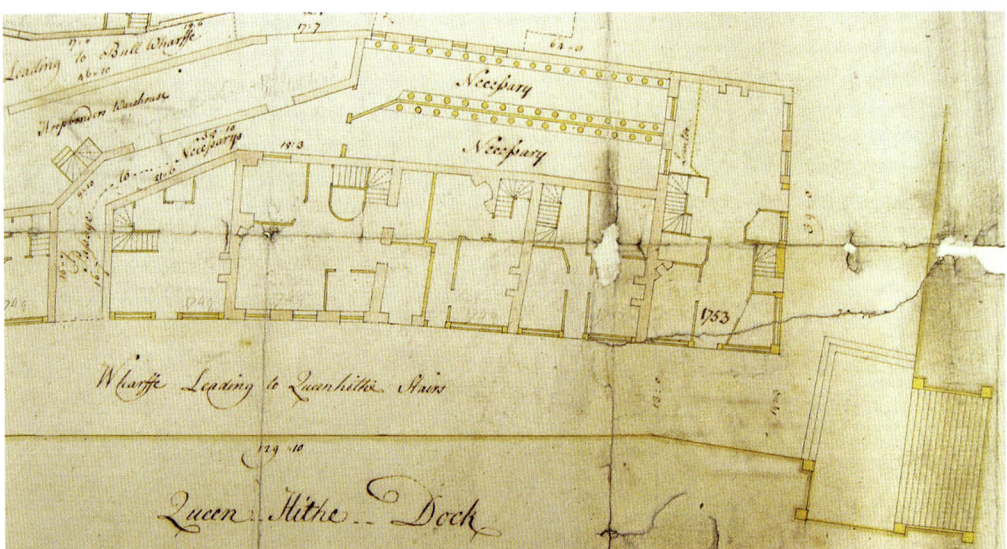

Fig. 255. The Queenhithe house of easement and other buildings, 1747.

gutters and street, so that the flow might cleanse the privy on the Hithe'.[180] In the seventeenth century the Queenhithe longhouse was regarded as having been founded under the will of the former Lord Mayor, Sir John Philpot, of 1389, on ground given by him for the purpose. However, although the longhouse was on Philpot's land, and his will did leave land to the City for the making of conduits and latrines, the bequest may simply have provided for the moving of the longhouse towards the river (following land reclamation on neighbouring sites) or placed the existing longhouse on a more secure basis.[181] Until the Fire the longhouse was sixty-eight feet long and eighteen feet wide, and had eighty seats, of which forty were for men and forty for women, arranged in four rows. Over it were five chambers and five garrets belonging to the two houses adjoining. Its outlet to the Thames can be seen clearly on the Copperplate Map of c.1555.[182]

After the Fire the City agreed to pay for rebuilding the longhouse. Bartholomew Fish, citizen and fletcher, the occupant of the City's ground as a sub-tenant, rebuilt it in 1671-72 together with the rooms above, though in 1673 it was described as unfinished; plastering work was paid for in 1674. The forty-foot wharf had taken away about twenty feet of the longhouse's site, and in 1672 a committee chaired by Alderman Sir John Lawrence concluded that Fish could use twenty-two feet of the longhouse as a shop, leaving the rest for public use. Something similar happened to the Vintry longhouse, which was reduced after the Fire from 128 seats to twelve. But the Queenhithe longhouse was defended by the City Corporation and the parish of St Michael Queenhithe, which took the matter to the Fire Court, and the Court ruled against the proposed shortening.[183] The market at Queenhithe was presumably why the longhouse there remained important. Fish's rebuilding probably followed the medieval arrangement, and is shown in detail on a plan of 1747 (Fig. 255). There were separate compartments for men and women, with thirty-three seats in one and fifteen in the other, unless one row has simply been omitted from the plan.[184] Cleaning was probably organised by the ward scavengers.[185]

As for the adjoining houses, there were two before the Fire, one known as the Saracen's Head, 'being the auncient Tidehouse', and the other the Adam and Eve, both with three and a half storeys, but the forty-foot wharf left room for only one house. Bartholomew Fish insisted that he as occupant should rebuild rather than the City's lessee, 'in regard hee hath bin an ancient inhabitant upon the place, and that his livelyhood wholly dependeth upon his continuing there', and the Fire Court accepted his case; indeed Fish was already using sheds he had put up there, some of which he let out. The new house had three storeys without garrets. Over the longhouse were four and a half storeys at one end and two and a half at the other, with a total of nineteen or so rooms.[186]

By 1747 part of the forty-foot wharf had been built over, reducing the light to the longhouse from the south. The property, including 'the Boghouses', was to be rebuilt under a lease of 1750, but even then it was provided that ground should be reserved for new boghouses. The Vintry longhouse in its reduced form survived until at least 1851, but whether the Queenhithe one was replaced as intended in 1750 and when it finally disappeared is not known.[187]

PLANS OF HOUSES

MANSIONS

Plan 125
Greyfriars Court, 1663 or earlier
Fig. 256

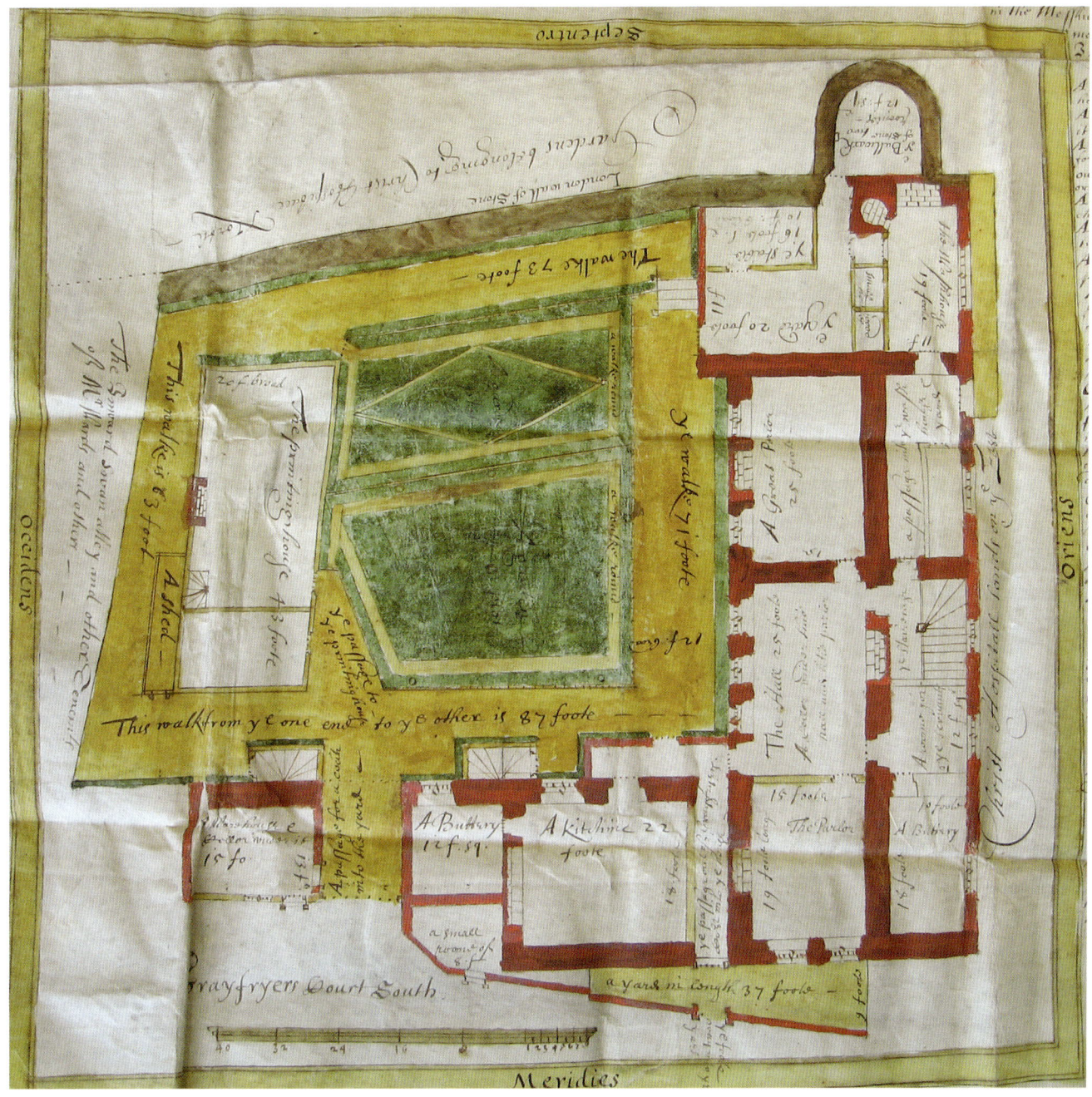

Fig. 256.   The mansion in Greyfriars Court, 1663 or earlier. North is at the top.

KEY, Fig. 256

East. Cellar under hall and little parlour; little parlour and over it a chamber; buttery and room for the servants; over them two rooms or chambers; hall and over it a fair chamber with a balcony; great parlour and over it two fair chambers; chamber over passage; coal house; two yards not in the plot; washhouse, stable and other small rooms; in the bulwark two rooms.

South. Yard paved with freestone and passage into the house; kitchen over [over against?] it and buttery next adjoining; two chambers; over the passage for a coach, a small room; warehouse, and cellar under it; room over the warehouse with two small garrets.

West. Building now used for a printing house, containing lower room and over it another room of same length and breadth; over it three garrets; on west and south end, a shed. Large garret over east part of house the whole length.

This plan shows a mansion created out of former monastic buildings. It stood west of Christ's Hospital just inside the City wall, in the area which became known as Greyfriars Court, and had a large enclosed garden (marked as 'Boltons garden now Mallowes' on Plan 20). Christ's Hospital purchased it in 1583, with the whole of the Greyfriars' little cloister.[1] The plan was once attached to a lease, but the lease has not been found.[2] The Hospital's accounts record £2 paid in October 1663 to William Conyers, bricklayer, for drawing a plan of the capital messuage in Greyfriars Court lately granted to Lady Whitmore, which was this house.[3] However, Conyers was one of two surveyors drawing plans for Christ's Hospital in 1667 (neither of whom signed their work), and the lettering on the Greyfriars plan corresponds to neither of the two styles then being used on those plans, so it may have been drawn by someone else for an earlier lease.[4]

The mansion occupied the Greyfriars' thirteenth-century infirmary and the west walk of the little cloister, together with the fourteenth-century hospice on the south side of the garden, though these had no doubt been much altered; when Sir William Bird, Dean of the Arches, negotiated a new lease in 1619 he offered to spend money to make the house more habitable.[5] Walls about three and a half feet thick suggest a medieval stone building, while the red colouring of the walls could indicate that it had been refaced in brick. The house was entered from a yard off Greyfriars Court and a passage, from which the hall and then the stairs could be reached. The main rooms were in the garden front—great parlour, hall and little parlour, twenty-five, twenty-five and nineteen feet long respectively. The kitchen was west of the passage. On the first floor were nine chambers, including what was probably the great chamber (with a balcony) over the hall, and there was a garret the length of the east part of the house. James Fletcher, the occupant in 1666, was assessed at seventeen hearths.[6] The most surprising building is the printing house in the garden, of two and a half storeys, which does not seem to be connected with any known printer.[7]

In 1629 the lease was acquired by Alderman William Acton. Acton was nominated by Charles I as Lord Mayor in 1640, but failed to be elected because of his Royalist views. He died in 1650/51. His daughter and heiress, Elizabeth, married Sir Thomas Whitmore, and obtained a new lease in 1663, despite much complaining about the £20 annual rent; Whitmore said it 'was a great rent, and that the said Lady would rather lessen the same than augment it'. When he complained again in 1667 the Hospital pointed out that before the Fire he had sub-let the mansion for £60 a year and a £120 fine. Whitmore secured a new lease in 1669 and assigned it to Andrew MacDowgall, who rebuilt the premises on a different plan, without a mansion.[8] The site was later absorbed into Christ's Hospital.

Plan 126
Peter Du Cane's house, Pancras Lane, 1671
John Daynes
FIG. 257

This plan provides the best example of a merchant's house combining the domestic and the commercial. Its style, including the writing, the blue border and the lack of any indication of staircases (other than in words) indicate that it was by John Daynes, who drew plans for Christ's Hospital in 1668-71.[9] The Hospital bought this land on the south side of Pancras Lane in 1602, and it is shown on a plan of about 1611 by Treswell.[10] Peter Du Cane, or Du Quesne, who obtained the lease of most of the site in 1650, was a merchant and the grandson of a Protestant refugee from Flanders; he was himself born in

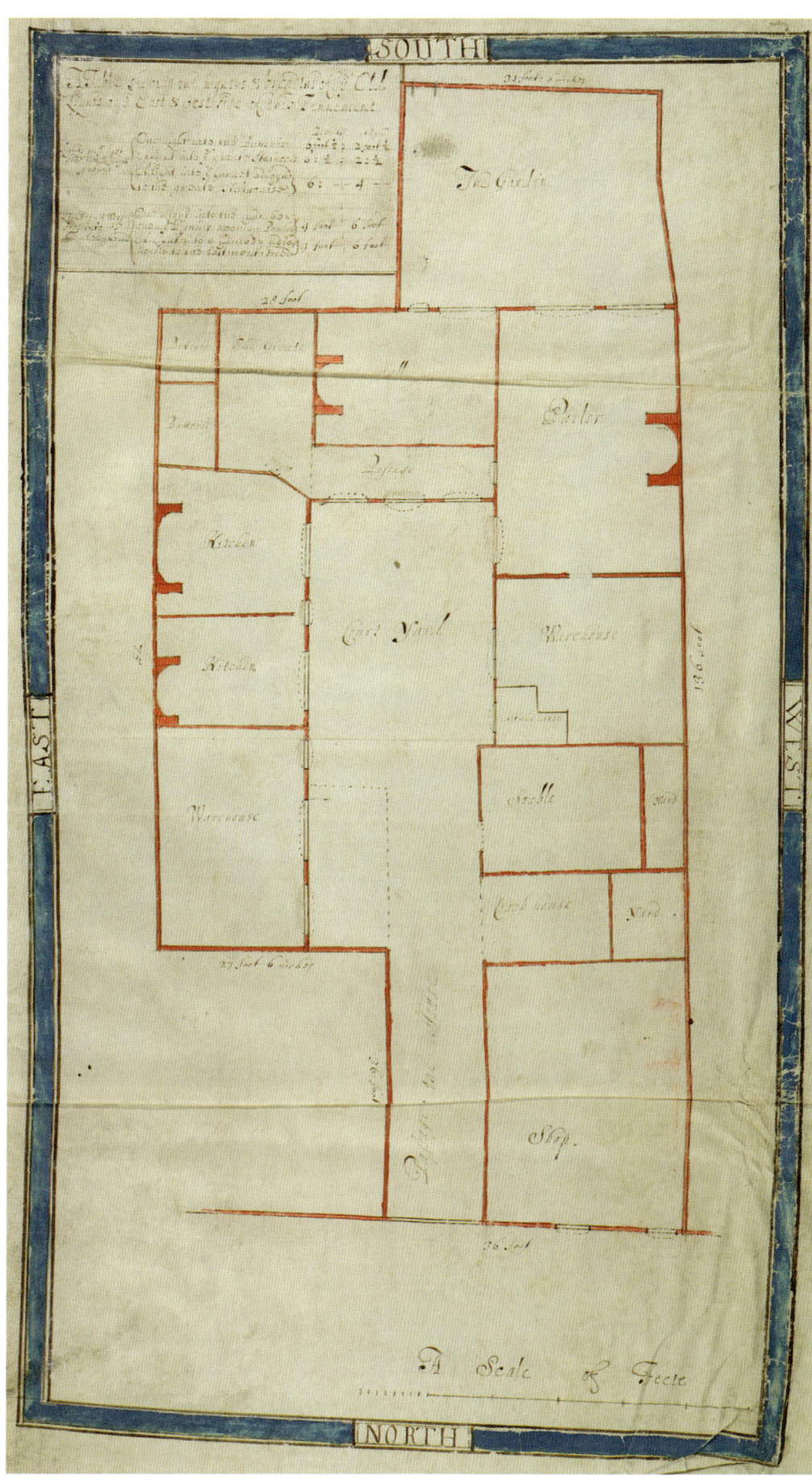

Fig. 257. Peter Du Cane's house, Pancras Lane, 1671.

France. In 1662 his premises included three large warehouses, a large dining room and a great chamber and were described as a capital messuage. After the Fire Du Cane added the smaller property facing the street in the north-west corner and rebuilt the whole site as shown here, being rewarded in 1671 with an eighty-year lease. The layout followed fairly closely the pre-Fire one, but with a larger courtyard and with the outer boundaries straightened.[11] The ground floor included two warehouses, hall, parlour, kitchen and two staircases, including 'The greate stairecaise' (towards the top left). Ogilby and Morgan's map and later plans suggest that the upper floors extended around three sides of the courtyard in a U shape (Fig. 258).

Du Cane died in 1672. He was succeeded by his son of the same name, also a merchant, who died in 1714. It was this Peter who built up the family's estate at Balham and Clapham.[12] Later plans suggest gradual changes to the house. By about 1810 there had been a remodelling of the west range, including a new staircase, with the whole of the ground floor now given over to warehousing. By 1842 the east wing had been remodelled, and the entire ground floor was used as offices and warehouses. The garden shown by Daynes still existed in 1842. In the 1860s the property was taken by the Metropolitan Board of Works in order to create Queen Victoria Street, which clipped one corner of the site.[13]

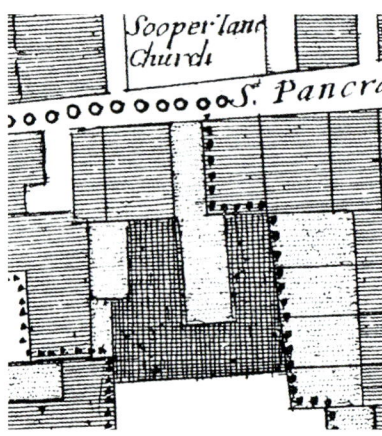

Fig. 258. Detail from Ogilby and Morgan's map of 1676 showing Du Cane's house.

Plan 127
St Paul's Deanery, 1677
William Leybourn
FIG. 259

The Deanery of St Paul's is the last of the City's seventeenth-century mansions (Fig. 260).[14] It was built by Israel Knowles, carpenter, and Thomas Warren, bricklayer, in about 1670-73. The cost was £2,792, including £578 for the coachhouse, stables and scullery (perhaps the building projecting at the back). The Dean was then William Sancroft, who became Archbishop of Canterbury in 1678. Leybourn surveyed the mansion in 1677, together with the Dean's other property adjoining. He drew it in what for him was unusual detail, even showing the windows, though on this version of the plan he omitted the main staircase in the front room furthest on the right. The room at the back on the right seems to have been the kitchen, as it contained an oven. The coachhouse and stables, with hayloft over, are A2, the stable yard is A3 and the garden A5. Of particular interest are the four tiny shops in the Deanery's forecourt, only about six by

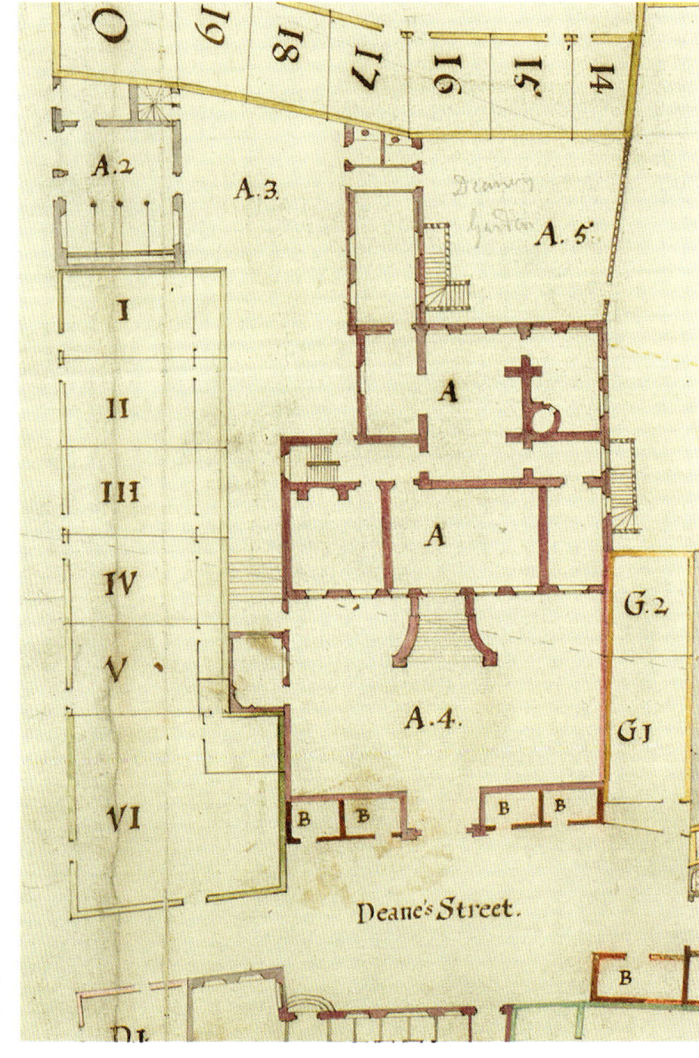

Fig. 259. St Paul's Deanery, 1677. North is to the right.

Fig. 260.   St Paul's Deanery, 2013.

ten feet and now long gone. In 1677 they had been let to William Sancroft, grocer, presumably a relative of the Dean.

Leybourn's elevation or 'upright' (Fig. 261) is curious, as there is no evidence even on his own plans of the windows being irregularly spaced. That makes it hard to know whether there really was a shell porch at first, as opposed to the current flat-headed porch.

Plan 128
Thomas Papillon's house, Fenchurch Street, 1686
William Leybourn
FIG. 262

This plan shows another mansion of the post-Fire period, on land belonging to the Fishmongers' Company. The 'great messuage' previously on the site was known as the Leaden Porch and survived the Great Fire. A list of fixtures in 1648 indicates that it was at the narrow, front part of the site, and that the back part of the site was then a garden. The ground floor consisted of warehouses either side of a central passage, great and little parlours, kitchen, two butteries and beer room; on the first floor were eight chambers, and above them at least four garrets. There were eleven hearths. There was a porch covered with lead, which had evidently given the house its name.[15]

Thomas Papillon (Fig. 263) occupied the house from 1652 and acquired the lease, with seven years to run, in 1672. Papillon was a merchant, and was both extremely wealthy and politically important, as a Member of Parliament and a leader of the City whigs. In 1701 he had a fortune of £20,000. He argued in 1672 that the house 'was old and must needs be new built', and requested a ninety-nine year lease; the Fishmongers' Com-

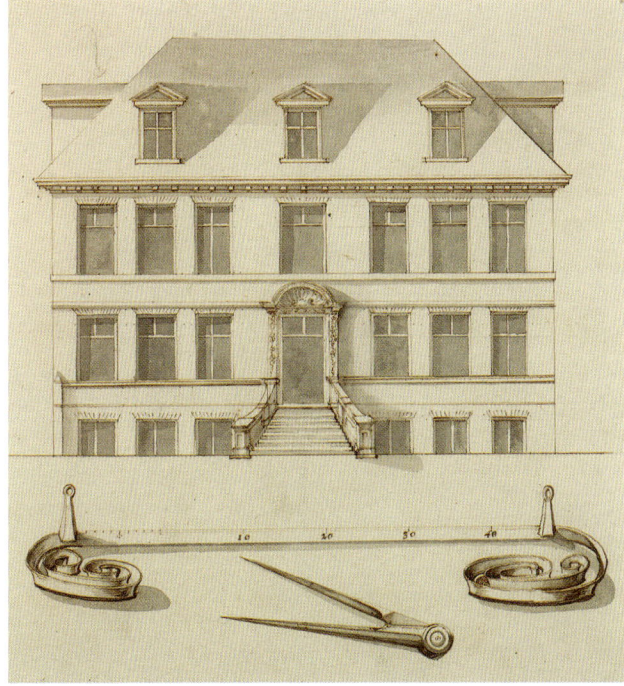

Fig. 261.   Leybourn's elevation of St Paul's Deanery, 1677.

pany offered twenty-one or thirty-one years, and they compromised in 1673 on seventy-two years. Papillon paid £250, and was required to spend at least £1,000 building one or at most two substantial houses on the site.[16] Papillon's is the house depicted by Leybourn. Papillon changed the layout: he built on the former garden and turned the former house site into stables and a coach-house. The prodigal use of the street frontage as stables rather than shops reflected the fact that this was the house's only street access, apart from the narrow passage through White's Court. Ogilby and Morgan's map shows the house as U-shaped, stretching from kitchen to great hall (Fig. 264). The great hall, about sixty by twenty-six feet, is the most surprising feature, but it was probably just a very large single-storey room, and there were certainly first-floor rooms over it in 1745.

Leybourn gives minimal information about upper storeys, referring to 'two floors of rooms over the ground floor; and a platform over the north part'. The house is better understood from the list of fixtures of 1745. It had three and a half storeys, and at the back it had seven bays. Between about 1725 and 1745 the great hall had been divided into a warehouse at the front and the 'largest parlour' behind; the hall next to it was now described as a parlour. On the first floor were five rooms (two at the front and three at the

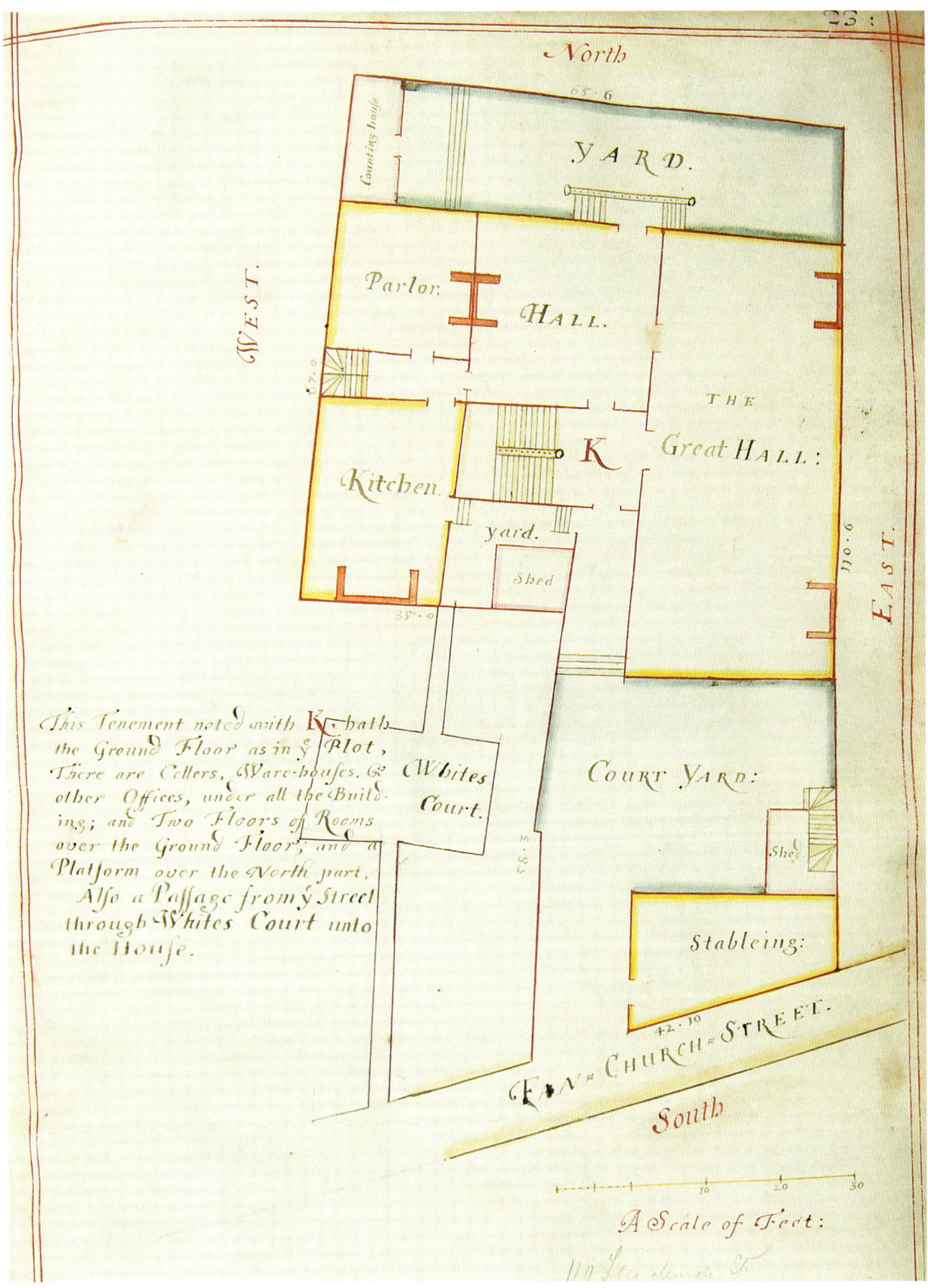

Fig. 262. Thomas Papillon's house, Fenchurch Street, 1686.

Fig. 263. Thomas Papillon (1623-1702), painted by Sir Godfrey Kneller in 1698.

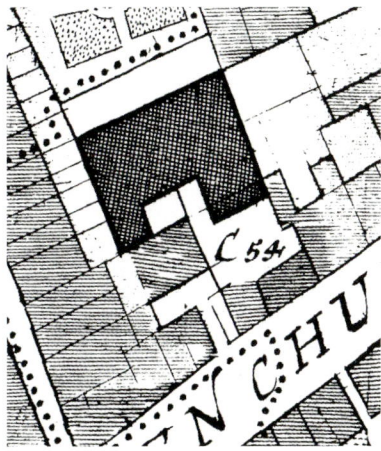

Fig. 264. Detail from Ogilby and Morgan's map of 1676 showing Papillon's house.

back) and closets and lobbies; on the second floor were six rooms, including a study among the back four rooms and a warehouse at the front on the east side; over them were garrets. In the 'middle part' of the house were leads enclosed with rails and banisters. All the windows looked into the three yards. There were marble chimneypieces in the three parlours and four of the first-floor rooms, and much wainscoting and many carved panels over doors. Water was obtained by means of a 'water engine' in the front yard, pumping water (probably piped) to a cistern under the roof, and by lead pipes bringing rainwater from the top of the house to a wooden trunk in the little yard by the kitchen. There were privies in a garret, in a first-floor room and under the stairs.[17] By the street there were two storeys of workrooms over the coachhouse and the gateway.

Papillon's son sub-let the house in 1706 to William Fisher, a merchant, and in 1733 to Christopher Lethieullier, esquire. The emphasis gradually shifted towards warehousing and workshops and away from grand living. The lease was granted successively to packers, who packed bales for shipment overseas (1745-88), a cabinet maker (1812) and upholsterers (1830-72). The upholsterers, and probably the others too, occupied the premises themselves. Successive leases indicate little change in the ground plan between 1686 and the 1870s. The lease of 1872 refers to the lessee's expense in pulling down part of the building and altering the rest, and the accompanying plan indicates that at least the western part of Papillon's mansion and the main staircase had been rebuilt. By 1895 all trace of Papillon's building had gone.[18] The site is now 110 Fenchurch Street.

Plan 129
George Jeffreys' house, Aldermanbury, 1701
John Olley
FIG. 265

This mansion stood in a courtyard off Aldermanbury, close to the Guildhall.[19] It was built at the City's charge in 1671-73 by Thomas Fitch, carpenter, and John Fitch, bricklayer.[20] In 1672 the City leased it 'out of special favour' to George Jeffreys (Fig. 266), then the City's recently-elected Common Serjeant and later the notorious 'Hanging Judge'. Jeffreys then spent large sums improving it. He ceased to be a City officer in 1680, but it remained his London home as Lord Chief Justice of England until 1685.

The house was approached by a passage between shops, not quite opposite what was evidently a grand entrance to a large hall. It had three and a half storeys and cellars. The front of the house had seven bays facing the yard, and the back was nine bays wide. Schedules of fixtures of 1685, 1701 and 1714 provide information about its interior. The ground floor is shown on the plan, including the 'dineing roome', about twenty-eight by nineteen feet, always referred to in the schedules as the 'great parlor'. Above were, on the south side, a room and a withdrawing room; in the centre a room 'fronting the stairs', evidently over the front part of the hall; and on the north side four rooms. On the second storey only three rooms are mentioned: one fronting the stairs, one over the withdrawing room and one even with the latter. At the top were six garrets. There were wooden chimneypieces rather than marble ones. Bassishaw Alley, or Church Alley, abutted the north and east sides of the site, so the stables could be in the back yard. There was a 'pissing cisterne' (continuously running) in the front yard and a pump at the back.

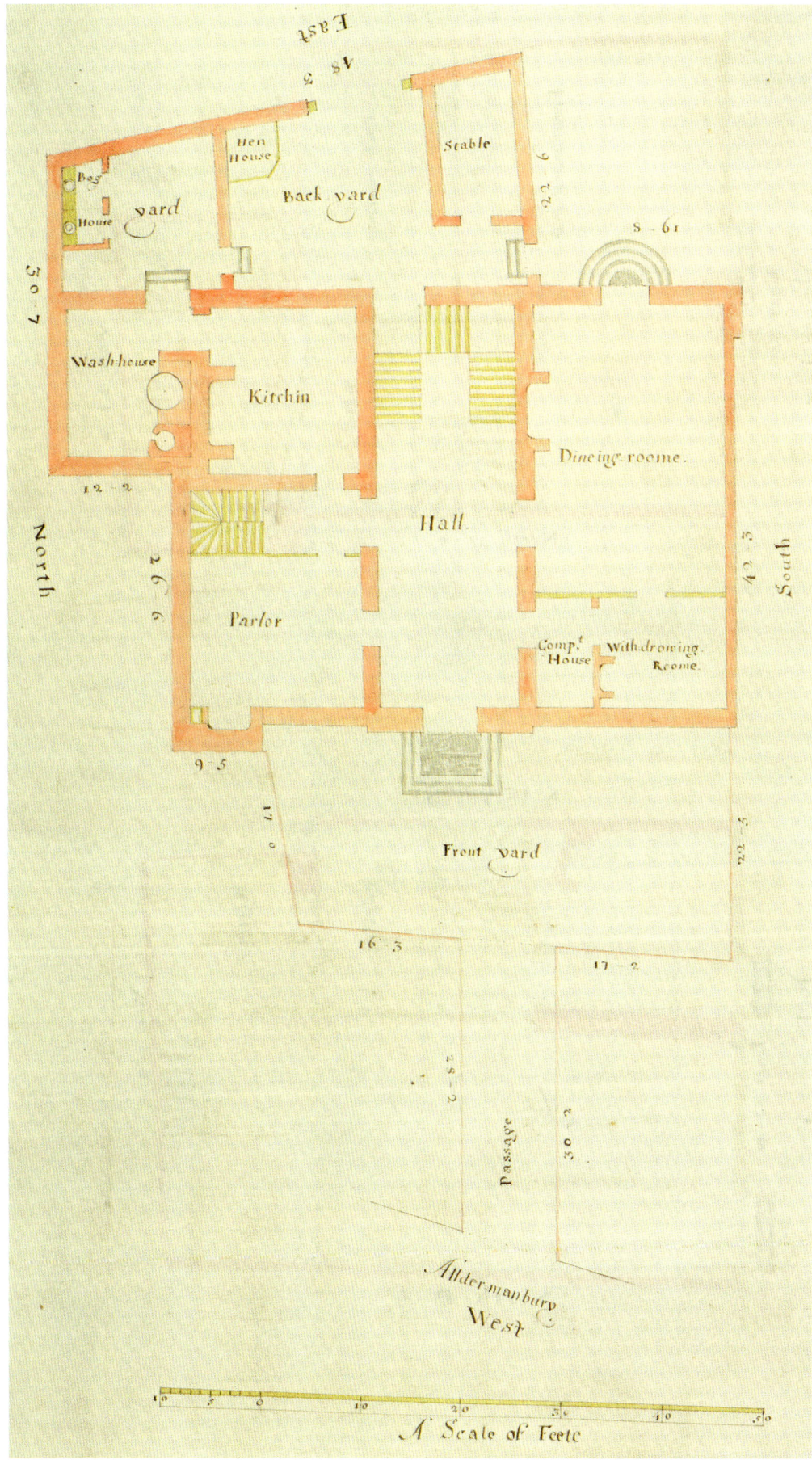

Fig. 265. George Jeffreys' house, Aldermanbury, 1701.

Fig. 266. George Jeffreys (1648-89) – portrait of c.1679, attributed to William Wolfgang Claret.

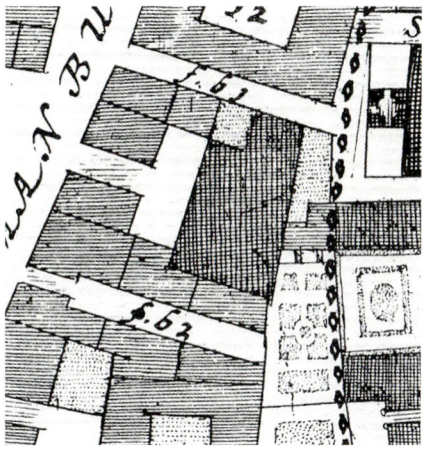

Fig. 267. Detail from Ogilby and Morgan's map of 1676 showing Jeffreys' house, including its garden.

The plan shows what seems to be a semi-circle of steps leading into a garden, but no garden. That was because the garden was not City property and was leased separately. It can be seen south-east of the house on Ogilby and Morgan's map (Fig. 267). It was approached from the dining room by 'two folding doors into the garden with glasse in them'. The house is shown on the ward map of 1858, but had gone by 1873.[21]

Plan 130
The Deanery, Westminster Abbey, 1715
William Dickinson
FIGS 268-70

This set of plans shows one of London's most remarkable medieval survivals—the Abbot's House, later the Deanery, of Westminster Abbey (Fig. 271),[22] standing just south of the Abbey's west towers. It was rebuilt by Abbot Litlyngton between 1362 and 1386. He added rooms over the entrance to the Abbey's cloister (1362-65), the great chamber or Jerusalem Chamber jutting out in front of the Abbey's west facade (1371-72), the Abbot's Hall (nearly complete in 1376) and two-storey galleries around the north and east sides of the courtyard (1383-84). The kitchen, hall and Jerusalem Chamber formed a single main range. Litlyngton's buildings still stand, except the galleries. There were gardens west of the house and between the east gallery and the cloisters. John Islip, Abbot from 1500 to 1532, added two-storey chambers on the north side of the courtyard, including the Jericho Parlour (marked 'Organ Roome' on the plan).

In Elizabeth's reign the house became the Deanery. She provided in 1560 that the scholars of the recently-established Westminster School should dine in the Dean's hall (the 'Queen's Scholars Hall' on the plan), which they still do. In 1650, during the Interregnum, part of the Deanery was leased to John Bradshaw (1602-59), who had presided at the trial of Charles I and was President of the Council of State in 1649-52. The lease excluded the hall and kitchen but included the lodgings of Nicholas Pay and John Humphries over the south-west part of the cloister. Bradshaw noted that his part of the Deanery 'containes onely a hall or parlor, a gallerie a kitchen a dineing chamber and withdrawing roome adioyning to it, the Tower chamber, some three lodging chambers a studie, with some other odd roomes not worth the mencioning, all of which are exceeding smokie, ly at such a distance as that they have noe dependance one upon another; the quiet of them is perpetually disturbed by the scholars and otherwise'; Pay's lodging consisted only of '4 little smokie roomes and twoe closets', though that of Humphries was larger. Bradshaw remedied this situation by rebuilding or remodelling the buildings over the cloister and south of the courtyard (Fig. 272), and had spent £760 by 1654. Entry was from the east side of the courtyard to a lobby, and the great stairs led from there to the 'Great Dining Roome' over the new kitchen. These, together with 'my Ladys bedchamber' and rooms above were additions by Bradshaw; the nearby high dining room and drawing room (described in 1743 as the Deanery's two best rooms) seem to have used existing structures. Bradshaw also added a room within the Abbey's south-west tower, but the room had gone by 1715. In 1664 the house had twenty-eight hearths.[23]

Most subsequent changes have been small-scale. Dean Sprat in 1683-84 added the room

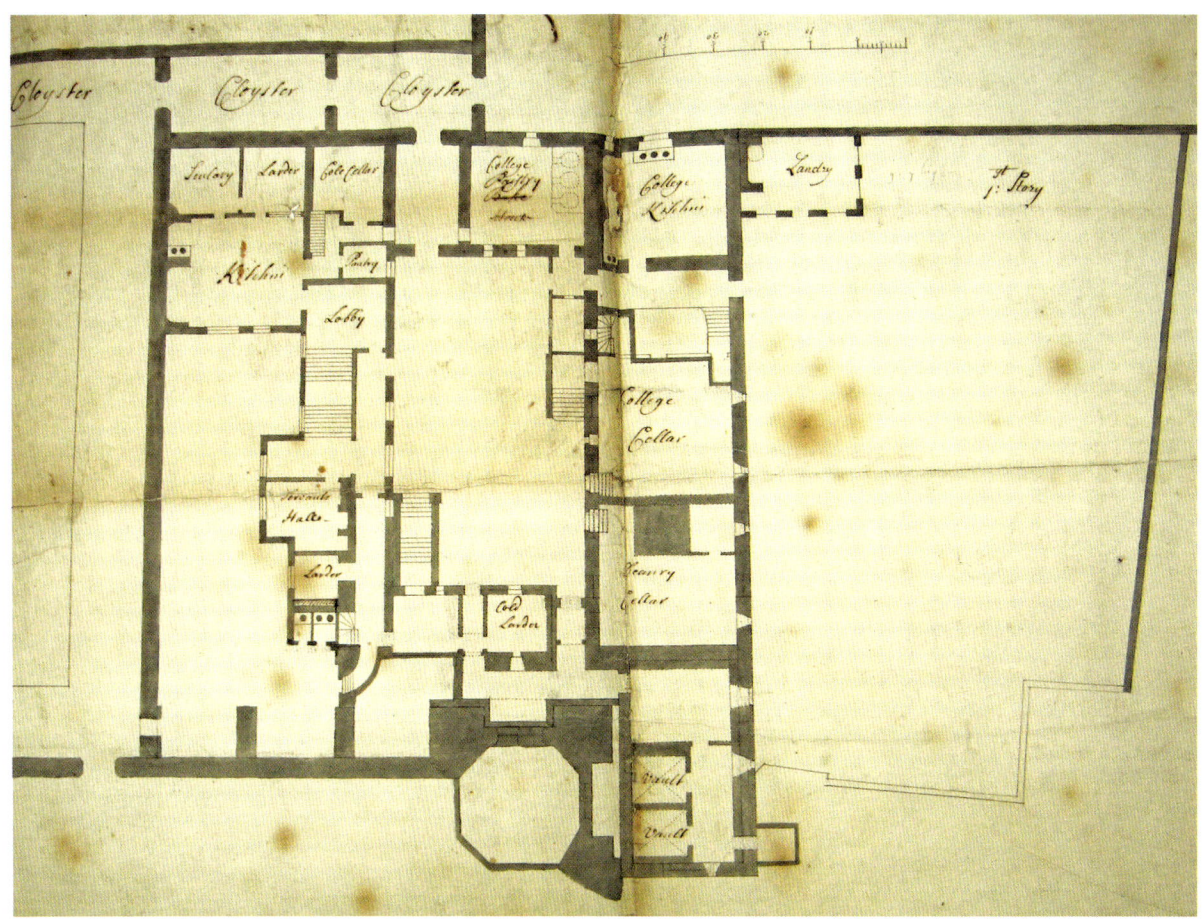
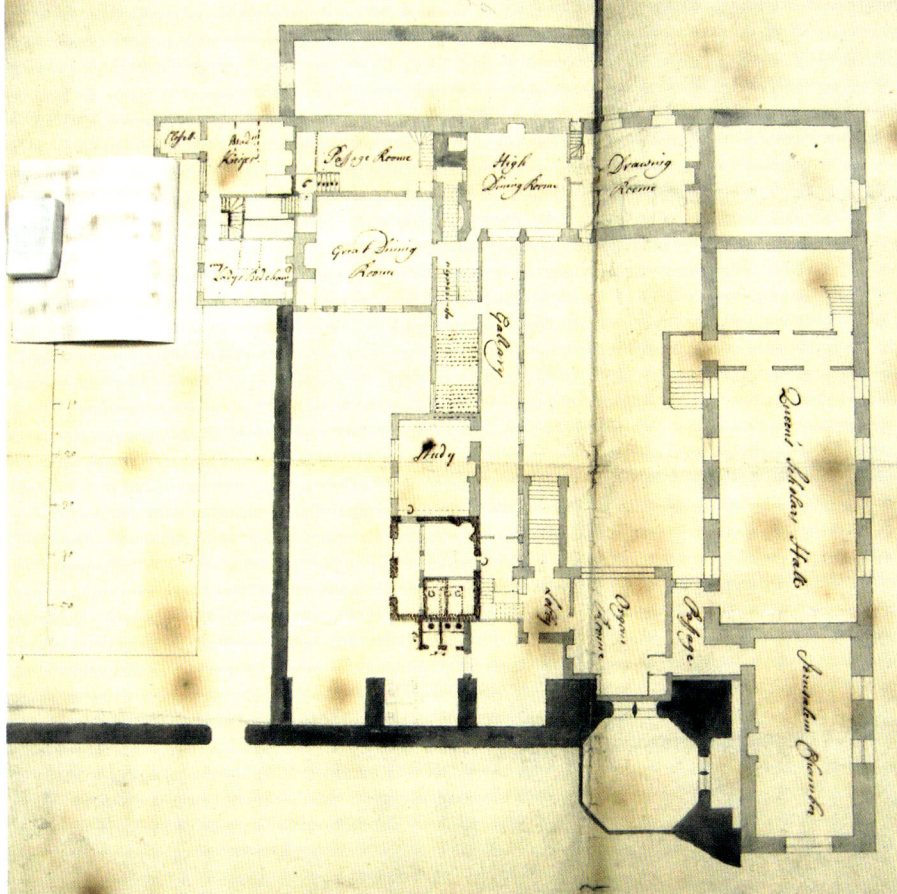

Fig. 268-70. The basement (top), ground floor (left) and first floor (above right) of the Deanery, Westminster Abbey, 1715. North is at the bottom.

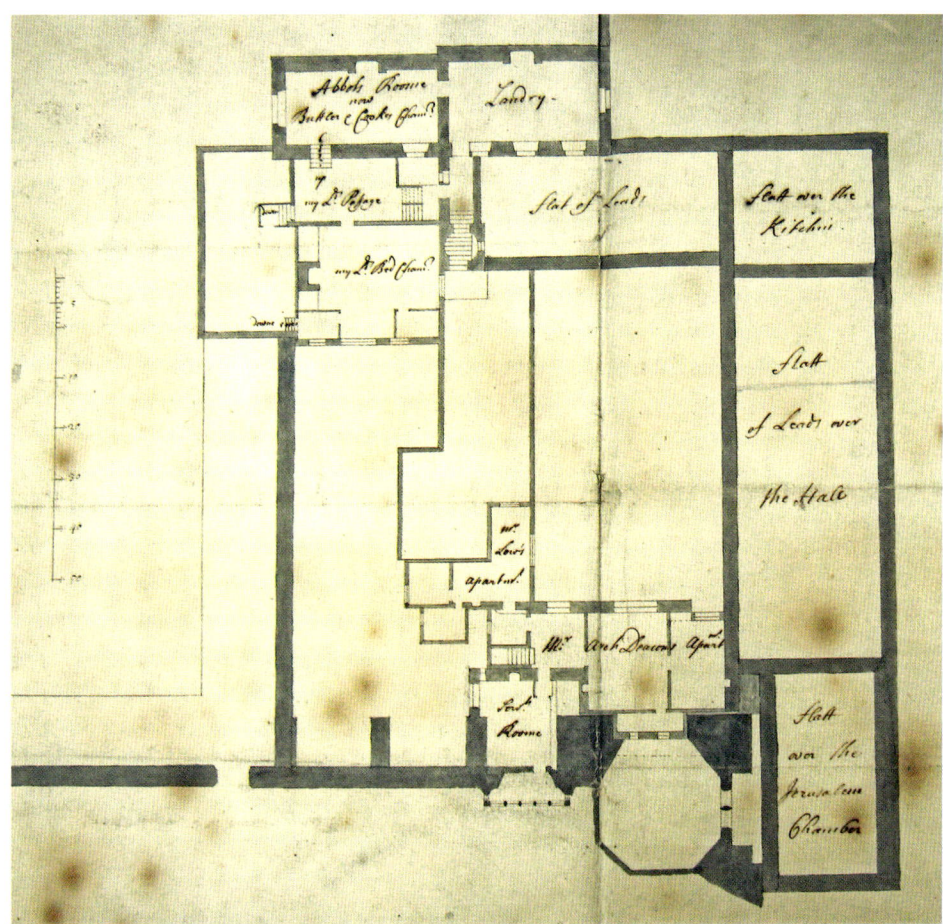

Fig. 271. The courtyard of the Deanery, with the hall on the left and the south-west tower beyond, 2010.

Fig. 272. The Deanery seen from the cloister of Westminster Abbey to the east, c.1900, showing the part not rebuilt after the Second World War.

marked 'Study' on the first-floor plan, probably with the smaller room to its north. Dean Atterbury made changes in 1713-18, and this gave rise to the plans, drawn by William Dickinson, surveyor to the Dean and Chapter. They are much more detailed than the rather sketchy plans usually drawn for the Dean and Chapter. Proposed changes marked on them are a new room north of the study and alterations to the east part of the house over the cloister (marked on a flap which is folded back on Fig. 269); the latter may not have been carried out. In the late eighteenth century the gallery (not shown on the plan) which linked the Jerusalem Chamber to the great gatehouse at the entrance to Dean's Yard disappeared. Second World War bombing destroyed Bradshaw's additions over the cloister, and these were not rebuilt.

OTHER LARGE HOUSES

Plan 131
Austin Friars, 1672
FIG. 273

Plans on Drapers' Company leases were usually only plot outlines. This rare example of a plan showing all floors was undoubtedly drawn because the house was intermixed with Drapers' Hall, having a different outline in each storey. In part it was the successor to Isaac Jones's house in c.1620 (see Plan 24), on the corner in Austin Friars. After the Great Fire the Drapers bought out the tenant in order to enlarge their Hall, and following the enlargement they had spare rooms —a warehouse under part of the hall and rooms 'parte over the kitchen and over the larders or

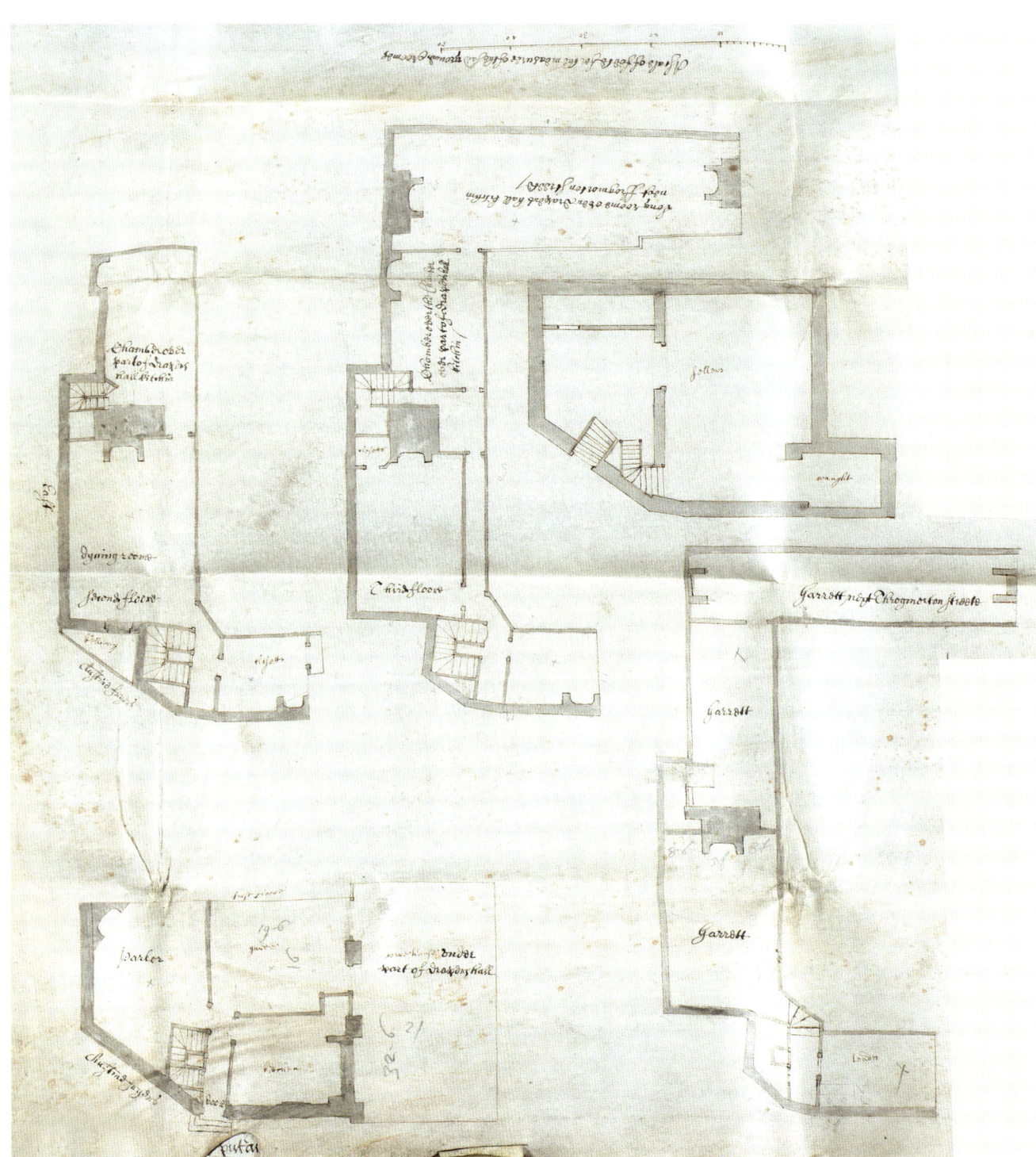

Fig. 273. A house in Austin Friars, 1672.

buttries lying over parte of the said kitchen and ovens'. In 1670 they leased to Thomas Cartwright, the mason who had rebuilt the Hall, those rooms 'already in parte built', which he was to finish, and the remaining ground of the former Jones house, which he was to build on. More specifically, he was to build on the east side of the yard 'on the old foundations' and not further westward (presumably to protect the light to the hall) or higher than the building to the south over the Drapers' kitchen and ovens. He was to build north of the yard, but no higher than the window at the north-east corner of the hall.[24] By the time the lease was granted in 1672 the house was already let out.

The house was entered from the corner of Austin Friars, with a staircase squeezed in just inside. On the ground floor (marked as the first floor here) there were parlour and kitchen, together with the warehouse and yard. The warehouse was not only under the Drapers' hall but also partly over one of their cellars. On the first floor the house did not extend over the warehouse, but in the other direction it advanced towards Throgmorton Street, with a chamber, a dining room and a closet. The second and garret storeys included the Throgmorton Street frontage (Fig. 274), with a 'long roome' on the second floor, and there was access to the leads at its north end. In 1772 the house was destroyed by the fire which consumed much of Drapers' Hall. It was rebuilt in a simpler form, on a footprint not much larger than the ground floor of Cartwright's house, subsequently becoming 29 Austin Friars.[25]

Fig. 274. The facade of Drapers' Hall in Throgmorton Street before the fire of 1772. The house in Fig. 273 included the second floor and garrets on the right-hand side.

Plan 132
Abchurch Lane, 1678
Mr Scarborow
FIG. 275

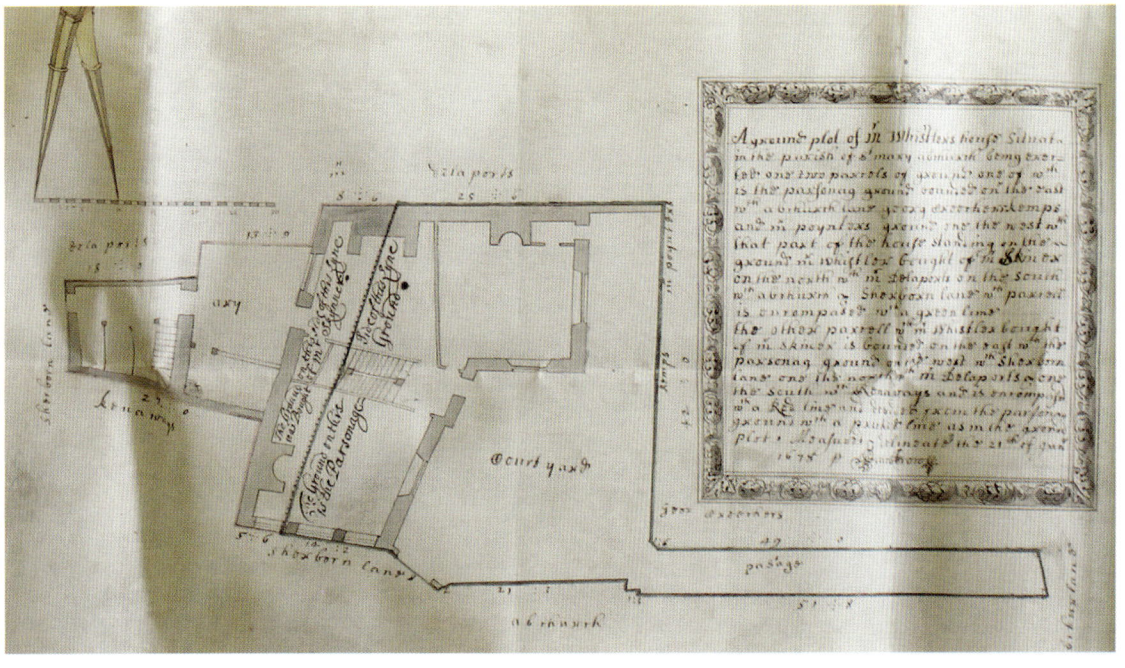

Fig. 275. A house between Abchurch Lane and Sherborne Lane, 1678. North is at the top.

This plan provides an example of change after the Great Fire, and of squeezing a large house onto a cramped and irregular site. There was a specific reason for a plan: two plots belonging to different owners had been used for a single house and the property boundary was no longer visible on the ground. Before the Fire, the eastern part of the site (edged in green on the plan) was the parsonage house of St Mary Abchurch, immediately north of the church, while the western part (edged faintly in red) was occupied by two tenements. Henry Whistler, described as a gentleman of London but possibly the merchant of that name engaged in the slave trade, built a house on the two sites in or about 1672, purchasing the western part in 1675 and leasing the eastern part from the rector of St Mary Abchurch for forty years in 1678.[26] Whistler's house was approached by a long passage from Abchurch Lane leading to a courtyard. The house had three rooms on a floor, and behind it were a yard or 'ary' and a three-stall stable with rooms over. When the lease of the eastern part expired in 1718 the then rector of St Mary Abchurch purchased the western part, and the church's rectory house still occupied the combined site in the 1850s.[27] Nothing is known about Mr Scarborow or Scarborough. The plan survives among the archives of Corpus Christi, Cambridge, which owned the rectory of St Mary Abchurch from 1568.

Plan 133
Little Britain, 1681   Fig. 276

This plan shows part of what had been Sir Thomas Bodley's house, belonging to St Bartholomew's Hospital (see Plan 16). The lease of that house was jointly purchased in 1666 by Richard Nelmes and William Allington, both described as esquires though Allington was a citizen and fishmonger. They divided the house

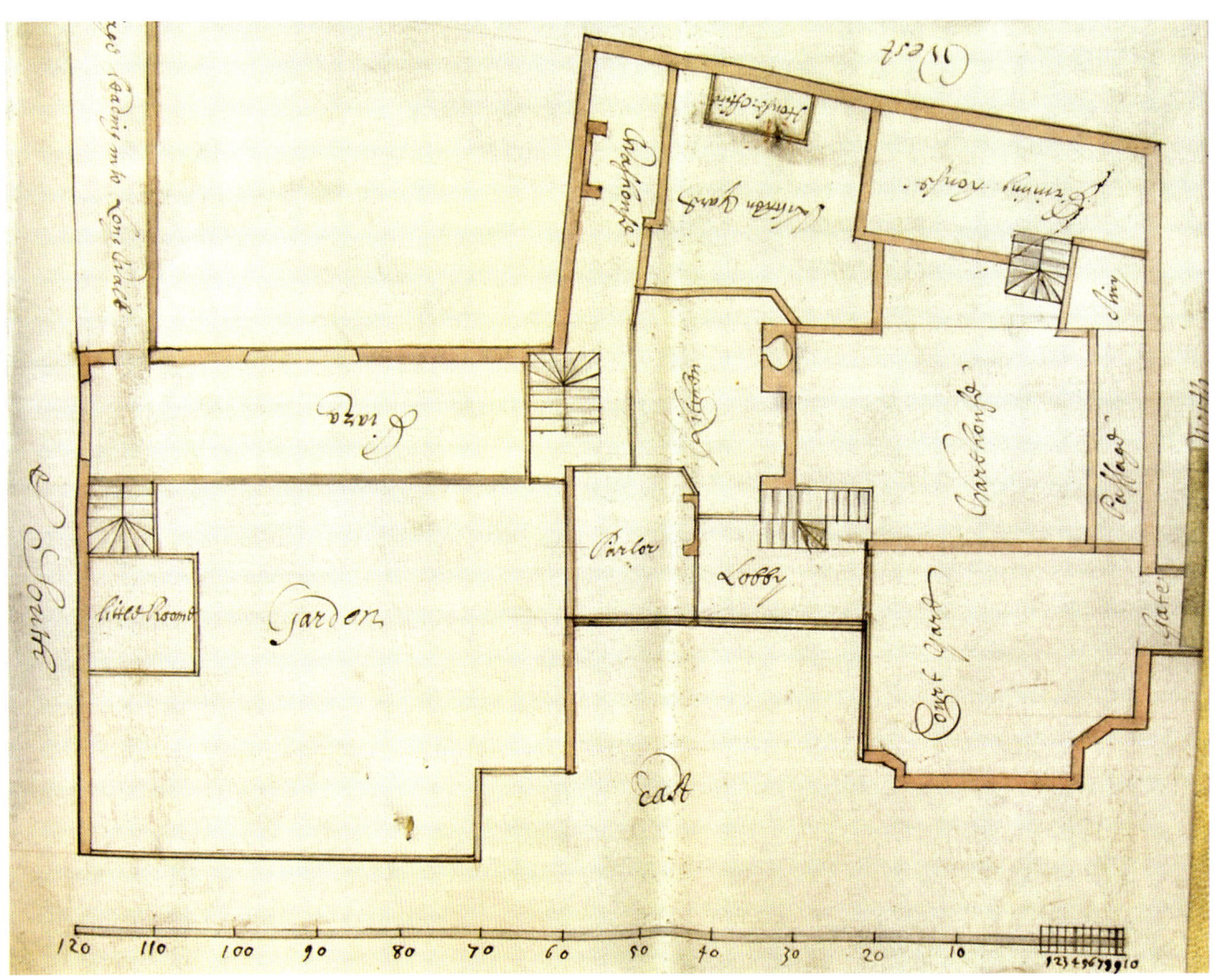

Fig. 276.   A house in Little Britain, 1681. North is to the right.

into two: Nelmes occupied the western half and Allington the eastern half, not without litigation between them. Use of the gateway was shared, and the garden was divided by a fence. Each half had eleven hearths in 1674. Nelmes sold his part in 1676 to Roger Norton, citizen and stationer and a Governor of the Hospital, and Norton stated in the following year that he had had to rebuild the greater part of it and repair the rest, costing £700.[28]

The plan shows Norton's reconstruction. He had built on most of the yard and the site of the former stables. His lobby and the adjoining parlour probably occupied the screens passage or its site, and the kitchen had perhaps survived from the old mansion; the mansion's hall evidently belonged to Allington's part of the property. At the back, the 'Piaza' is clearly Bodley's gallery, and the 'little roome' is probably the 'tarrys room' of 1655. Much of Norton's ground floor was occupied by a warehouse and a printing house, twenty-nine feet long, and the plan provides a glimpse of the establishment of an important printer and publisher. Norton was the fourth generation of printers in his family and the grandson of the King's Printer from 1596 to 1635. He succeeded his father in 1662, and in 1668 had three presses, one apprentice and seven workmen. He lived in the house in Little Britain until at least 1690.[29] It disappeared when the present Hospital courtyard was built.

Plan 134
Mitre Court, Duke's Place, 1697
John Olley FIG. 277

These houses were between the Mitre Tavern on the south side (Plan 100) and St James Duke's Place on the east side. When the lease was granted to John Shelton, citizen and saddler, in 1696, he had already rebuilt the house adjoining the Mitre, to the right here, and the lease required him to rebuild the 'ruinous' house to the left in a similar manner.[30] (The plan seems to show three houses rather than two.) The rebuilt house had brick side walls, but, surprisingly for the 1690s, timber front and back walls. It had three rooms on the ground floor and a spacious staircase. The plan is dated more than a year after the lease, indicating that the lease was not sealed until some time after the ostensible date, but the timber construction of the house to the left suggests that it had not yet been rebuilt.

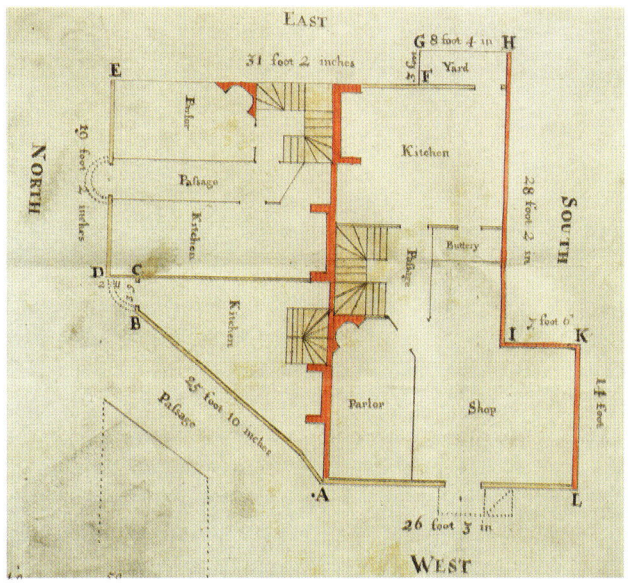

Fig. 277. Houses in Mitre Court, Duke's Place, 1697.

Plan 135
Weighhouse Yard, Cornhill, 1700
John Olley
FIG. 278

Before the Fire, the Weighhouse property on Cornhill included the room where imported goods were weighed and several tenements.[31] After the Fire there was a new Weighhouse in Eastcheap instead. The Cornhill property was rebuilt at the City's charge in 1671-72 by John Fitch, bricklayer, as a single 'great messuage' with four and a half storeys and cellars.[32] Its hall was approached by five stone steps from the yard. Above the ground floor were dining room and two chambers on the first floor; three chambers on the second (one of them a 'great room' in 1719); three or four chambers (the lease and its schedule disagree) on the third; and four garrets (unheated). The dining room was over the hall and warehouse, and if it extended the full length was just over forty-three feet long; it had both a marble chimneypiece and a painted one. (In 1719 it was called 'the great room over the hall'.) The staircase had 'carved fflower potts on the top and pendants below upon all the posts of the stairs'. In the garrets were a privy with a pipe into the cellar and lead pipes for

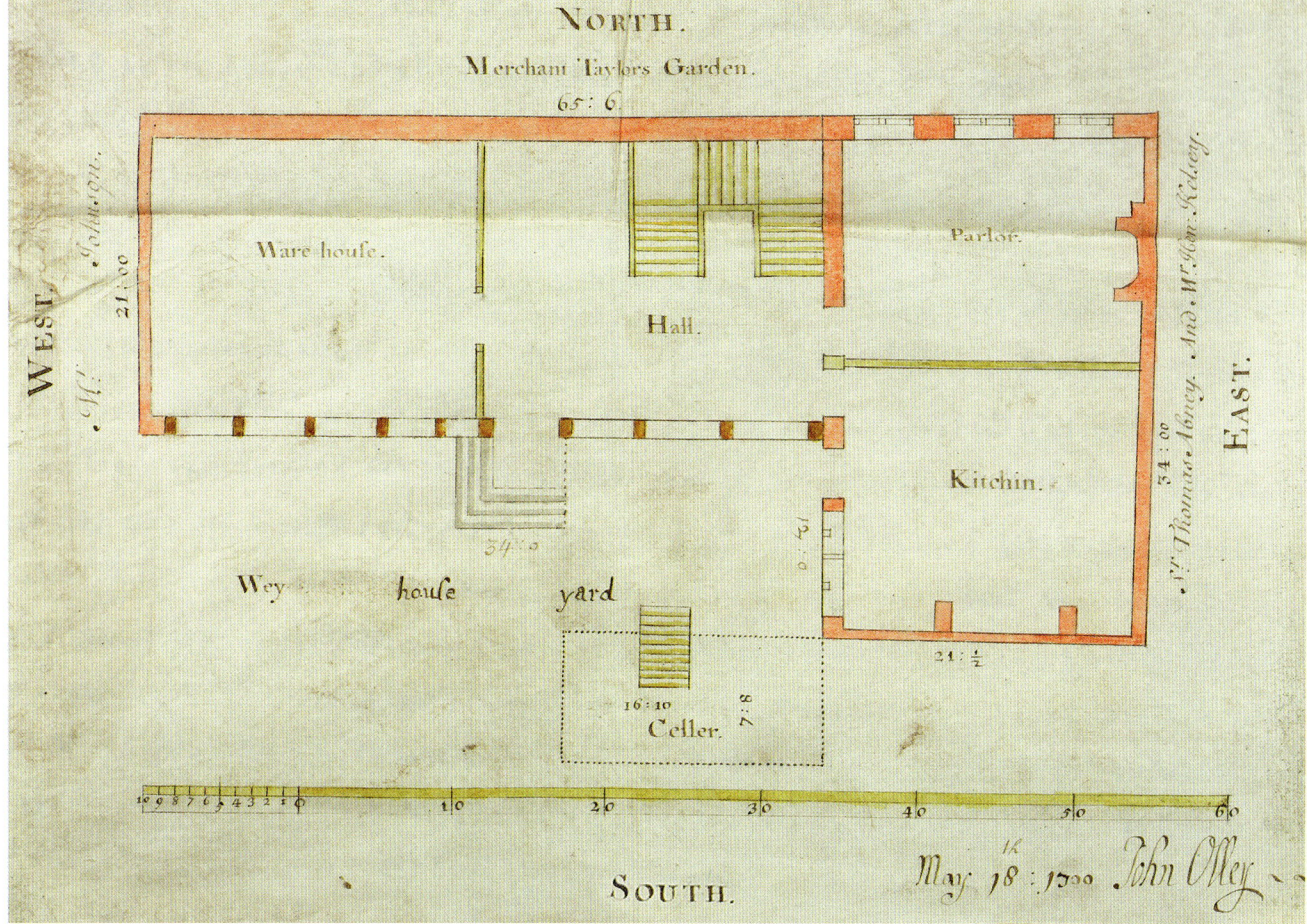

Fig. 278.   A house in Weighouse Yard, Cornhill, 1700.

water. Tax was levied on thirteen hearths in 1674,[33] corresponding to the chimneypieces mentioned in the schedule of the previous year. By 1719 the hall and warehouse had been thrown together (labelled as 'Hall'), the kitchen had become a warehouse and one of the first-floor chambers had become the kitchen. The nineteenth-century map (Fig. 279) explains the arrangement of windows. It was noted in 1693 that the house had been 'considerably darkned by new buildings' in the previous twenty years,[34] and the occupant paid £5 a year to the Merchant Taylors' Company for the lights towards its garden at the back.

The City's lessees were Richard Williams, citizen and clothworker, in 1673, Lewis Wilson, citizen and vintner, in 1700 and Gilbert Page, citizen and barber surgeon, in 1719; Williams and Page were the occupants in 1674 and 1719 respectively. The house was known in the eighteenth century as Sun Hall. It was damaged in the Cornhill fire of 1765.[35] Weighouse Yard still exists, now called Sun Court.

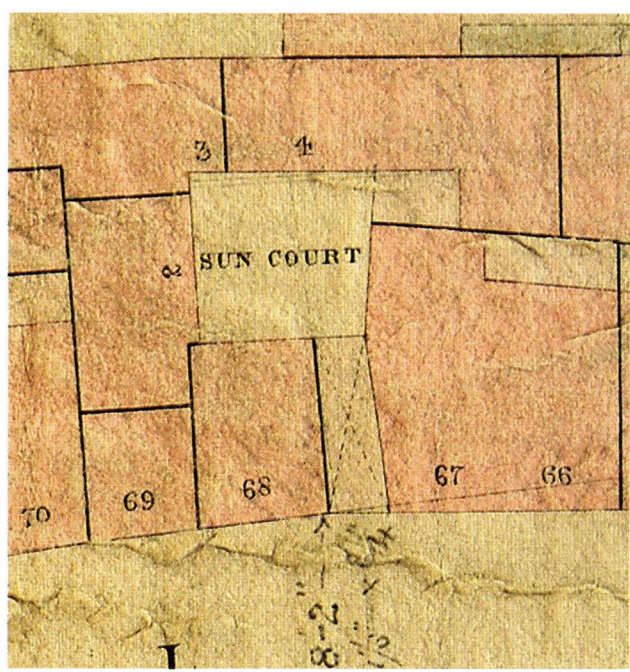

Fig. 279.   Detail from a map of 1858 showing the house in Weighouse Yard—then 4 Sun Court. North is at the top. The street at the bottom is Cornhill.

Plans 136-37
Mincing Lane, 1701 and 1721
John and Isaac Olley
FIGS 280-81

Warehouses in the City were most heavily concentrated in the area just north of the Legal Quays, reflecting the needs of the Port of London's import-export trades.[36] These two adjoining houses illustrate what this meant in practice, though not all warehouses formed part of dwellings. They were on the west side of Mincing Lane at its south end (later No. 17). After the Fire, Anthony Selby, citizen and draper, bought the site for £450 and more than covered the interest on that sum by letting out the surviving vaults. He then began building four houses with fronts up to five feet beyond the newly staked-out building line, and resisted all attempts to restrain him. The case reached the Court of Aldermen, the Privy Council, the House of Commons and the Court of Exchequer. The front parts were demolished by City workmen in 1668, at which point it was noted that the back parts were all of timber. Subsequently the City ended the controversy by purchasing the land and partly-finished buildings from Selby for £2,070 and spent £610 completing them, the work being done by John Fitch, bricklayer. They were subsequently let out as two houses, but their origins as four are clear on the plans.[37]

Each house was about thirty-five feet wide. The northern one was leased in 1701 to John Provost, merchant, and in 1721 to James Noke, also a merchant. A schedule of fixtures of 1722 supplements the plan of the previous year. The ground floor on one side was entirely given over to a large warehouse, with folding doors to the street; the room at the front on the other side was the hall, paved with stone and black marble, while the room at the back marked 'washhouse' on the plan was described in the schedule as the kitchen. On the first floor were rooms over the hall, warehouse and kitchen, and a little room and a pantry. The second floor had four rooms. Above them were three garrets and, at the back, the leads, with banisters around them and a privy. Nine closets were scattered about. Much of the house was wainscoted. Since 1701 the buttery had become known as the pantry and the counting house had become known as the hall. The 1701 lease records

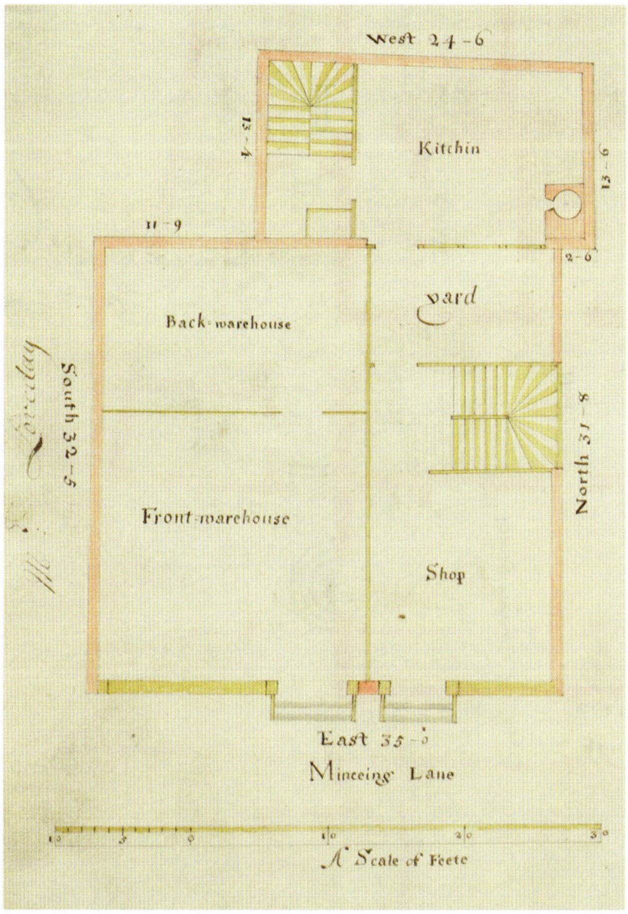

Fig. 280. A house in Mincing Lane, 1701.

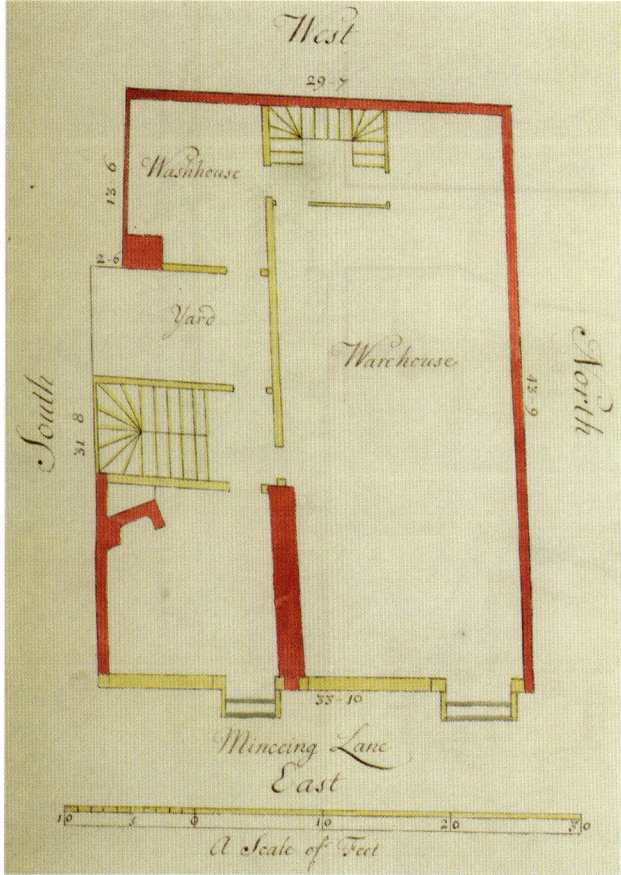

Fig. 281. A house in Mincing Lane, adjoining the one shown in Fig. 280, 1721.

two vaults and a cellar, together with another vault in the street in front of this house and its neighbour to the south, which was presumably a pre-Fire one extending to the old building line.[38]

The southern house, described as the smaller of the two, was leased in 1701 and 1712 to Thomas Loveday, citizen and turner, a member of the City Lands Committee and purchaser of the office of Cornmeter[39] in 1705. It too was double-fronted, with one side given over to warehouses. On the upper floors were seven chambers, three closets, three garrets and leads on the back building with rails and banisters. Like Noke's house it had two vaults and a cellar. Both plans record the fronts of the houses as timber. In 1720 Strype described Mincing Lane as 'garnished with very good houses, which for the generality are taken up by merchants, and persons of repute'.[40]

Plan 138
The keeper's house at Wood Street Compter, 1707
John Olley   Fig. 282

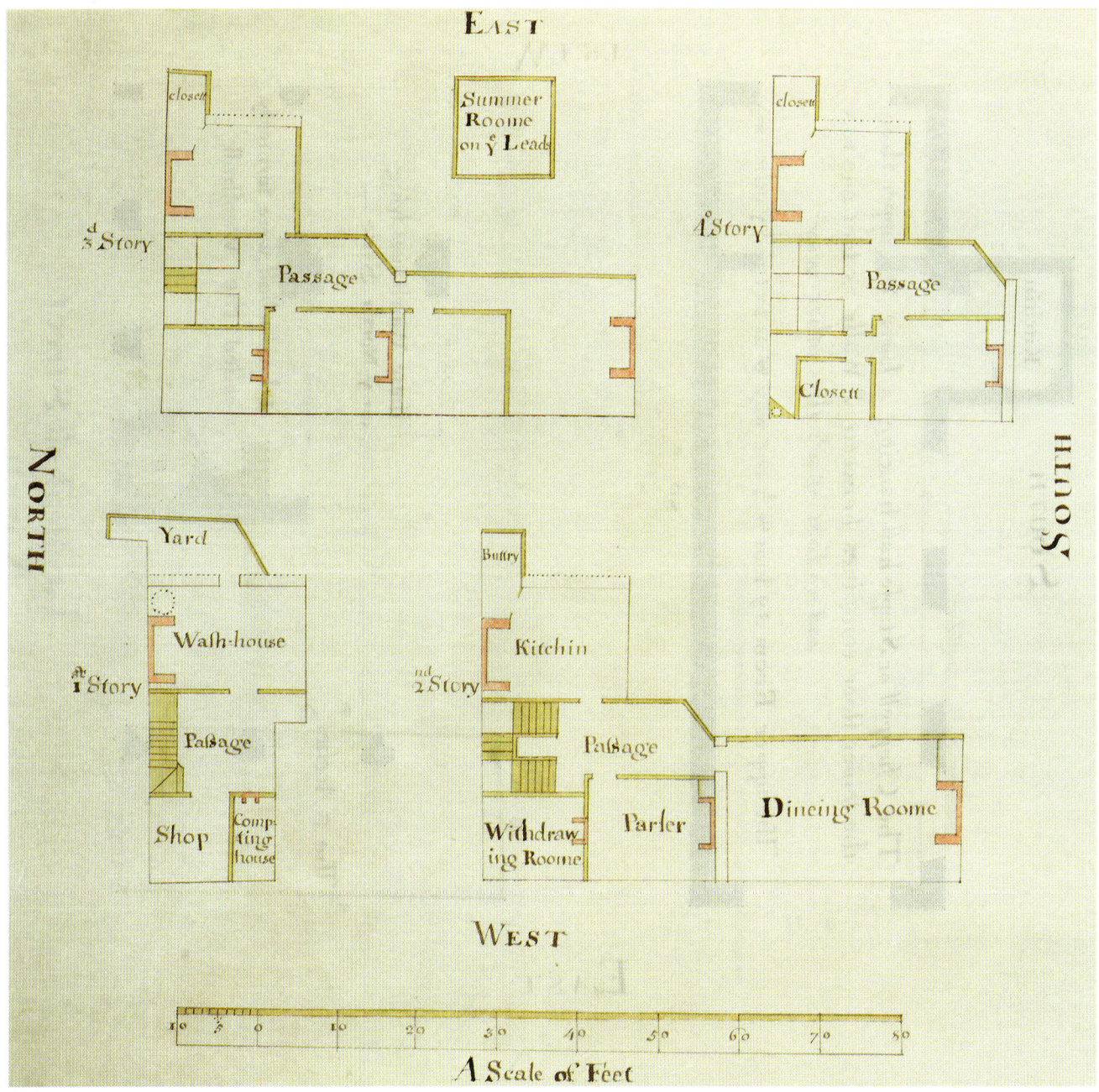

Fig. 282. The keeper's house at Wood Street Compter, 1707.

This is the only plan for a City Lands lease before 1720 showing all storeys of a building, probably reflecting the fact that there had been litigation with a previous keeper over exactly what was included in the lease.[41] The Compter, or prison, stood on the east side of Wood Street, about two-thirds of the way from Cheapside towards what is now Gresham Street. It had existed since 1555, mainly for debtors. It was rebuilt after the Fire and bore the date 1670 above the entrance, though much of the work seems to have been done in 1671. John Oliver was given a pair of silver candlesticks in 1672 for building it.[42]

A later plan indicates the Compter's layout and the location of the keeper's house within it (Fig. 283).[43] The ground floor of the keeper's house ('1st Story' on the plan) was to the left of the gateway; the first and second floors extended across the gateway to the other end of the building, but did not occupy the whole of it; and the third floor consisted only of the left hand part—there may have been no right hand part at this level, as the view of 1793 shows only bricked-up window openings (Fig. 284). On the first floor, the two windows on the left lit the withdrawing room, the four on the right the dining room and those between the parlour. The 'summer roome on ye leads', built of wood, had probably gone by 1793. Of the rooms not included in the keeper's house, those on the ground floor to the right of the passage were 'the office where the secondaries, clerkesitters &c. are and the roomes behind where the Mr. Keepers bookekeepers and doorekeepers sitt and keepe their offices', and the upper rooms, at least on the second floor, were used to accommodate sick prisoners.[44]

Olley's treatment of the external walls is unusual. These, being of brick, would normally have been shown in red, whereas what appear at first sight to be external walls are indicated either by a thin line or by a thicker line in yellow denoting timber. The thick yellow lines in fact mark internal walls, except those of the small extension at the back, and the reason for the thin lines was presumably that the City maintained the outer walls throughout the site, which were therefore of no concern to the tenant.

The office of keeper was a profitable one, acquired by purchase until 1766, and Stephen Ashton and Samuel Whincop, lessees in 1700 and 1707 respectively, were both described as gentlemen.[45] They were accordingly well housed. The shop, the stairs, all the first floor rooms except the kitchen, and parts of the second floor were wainscoted. The unlabelled rooms were presumably chambers and closets; those on the third floor ('4th Story' on the plan) were described as two chambers and two closets. There was a privy in the cellar and one on the third floor, from which there was 'a leaden pipe to carry the soile into the cellar'. In the cellars was 'a leaden pipe and cock', and there was a lead cistern in the yard with three pipes from it, one leading to the cistern in the kitchen, where there was a pump.

The prisoners were moved elsewhere in 1791 and the Compter was demolished in 1816.[46]

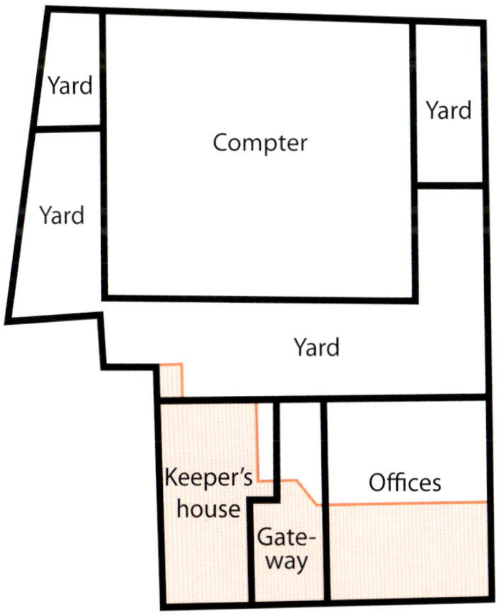

Fig. 283. A plan of Wood Street Compter, based on one of 1730. Wood Street is at the bottom. The pink shading indicates the part of the first floor occupied by the keeper's house.

Fig. 284. The street facade of Wood Street Compter, including the keeper's house, shortly after it went out of use, 1793 (print by J. T. Smith).

Plan 139
The Minories, 1712
John and Isaac Olley Fig. 285

This substantial brick house and the smaller one facing the street dated from about 1647. In that year Richard Banks, freemason, secured from the City a new forty-one-year lease, later extended to sixty-one years, of this and adjoining land on condition that he replace the two existing tenements with five new ones. By 1712 there were six houses. The irregular shape of the plot reflected the fact that Banks's rectangular site was divided in 1712-13 into three, each with two houses, including the two shown here. The new lessee of this plot in 1712 was Peter Monger, described in the lease as an Alderman's deputy but in fact a brewer in the Minories. Part of the property, presumably the smaller house, was sub-let to Richard Banks.[47] The larger house, with a facade fifty feet long, had rooms either side of a central hall and staircase which extended the full depth of the house. The house was entered from the south through the brewhouse yard because Monger also held the property in that direction, including the Phoenix Brewhouse. The latter had been constructed under a building lease of 1681.[48]

Plan 140
Houndsditch, 1712
John or Isaac Olley Fig. 286

Until at least 1680 this property had two similar timber houses at the front, each with shop and kitchen on the ground floor, two chambers over, two garrets and a cellar.[49] Behind the right-hand one was a brick building of two and a half storeys, apparently erected in 1634. By 1712 the right-hand property had enlarged its shop, moved its kitchen into the back building and acquired an extra room behind the left-hand house, though it seems also to have surrendered some space to enable the latter's kitchen to be enlarged. It had a triangular garden extending to a bastion of London Wall (the one shown on Plan 65). The lessees were Richard Stoakes of Wapping, mariner, and his wife Maria in 1652 (they occupied one of the houses), John Howard of Stepney, mariner, and his wife Ann in 1680 (they sub-let the houses to two widows) and their daughter Ann Howard in 1712. In 1711 the viewers of the property thought it should be rebuilt, and that the boundary with the next property towards Aldgate should then be straightened.[50]

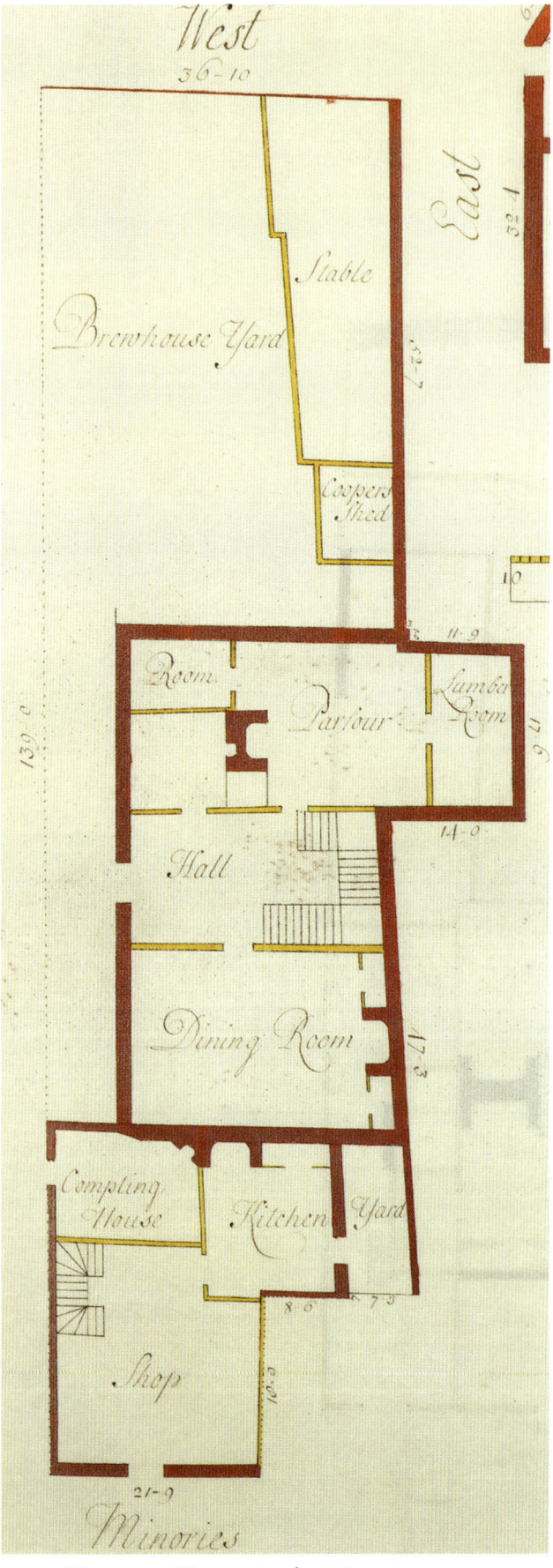

Fig. 285. Houses in the Minories, 1712.

Plan 141
Bishopsgate, 1712
John and Isaac Olley
Fig. 287

This substantial timber house, known as the Carp and King, was on the east side of Bishopsgate Street just outside Bishopsgate, abutting north and east on Flying Horse Inn and south on the house shown on Plan 166. It was said to be an old house continually needing repair. In 1712 it was leased to Edward Courthope, citizen and goldsmith, who was already occupying it.[51]

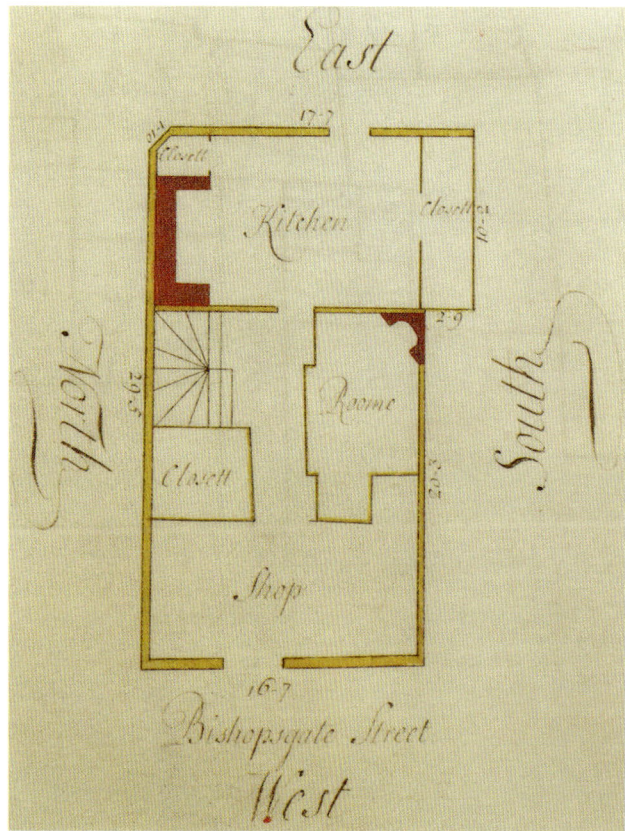

Fig. 287. A house in Bishopsgate Street, 1712.

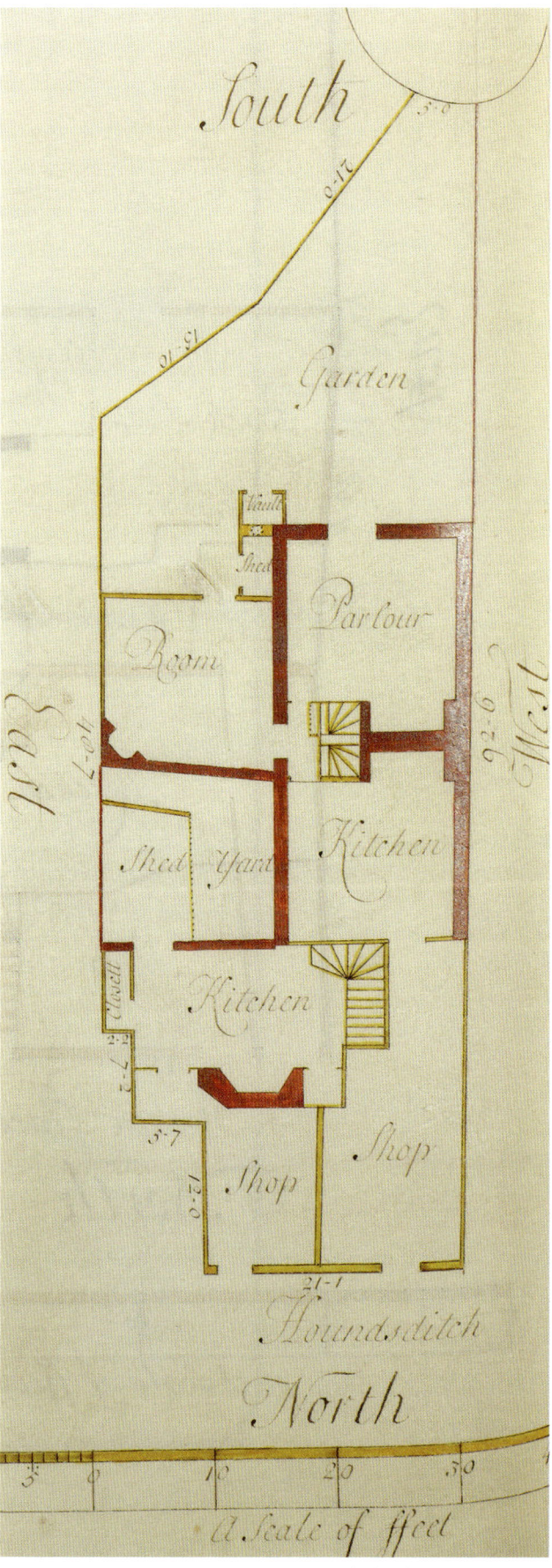

Fig. 286. Houses in Houndsditch, 1712.

TWO-ROOM PLAN HOUSES

Plan 142
Holborn Hill, 1640
Richard Ryder
FIG. 288

This long, narrow property known as the Rainbow, on the south side of Holborn Hill, a few doors east from Shoe Lane, was in part only nine feet wide. It was bequeathed to the Clothworkers' Company by Samuel Lese, citizen and clothworker, who lived there until his death in 1634.[52] By 1640 William Cox, citizen and haberdasher,

KEY

Forehouse: little cellar 7 by 7 feet under the entry; *First storey*, over the shop, chamber backward with chimney, 9½ feet by 17 feet 1 inch; little buttery at the stairs head; little kitchen with chimney, 7 feet 2 inches by 13½ feet; chamber forward next the street with chimney, 11 feet 1 inch by 13 feet 1 inch; *Second storey*, garret forward, 15 feet 3 inches by 15 feet; middle garret, 9 by 9 feet; back garret, 10 by 6 feet.

Backward: *First storey*, chamber with chimney, part over parlour and part over kitchen, 17 feet 7 inches by 9½ feet (from window to door) or 8 feet 9 inches (from door to door of next room); chamber with chimney over part of kitchen, 10 feet by 9 feet 2 inches; *Second storey*, garret, 18 by 12 feet.

Little back tenement: cellar, 9 by 8 feet; *First storey*, chamber with chimney, 9 by 8½ feet; *Second storey*, chamber, 9 by 8½ feet.

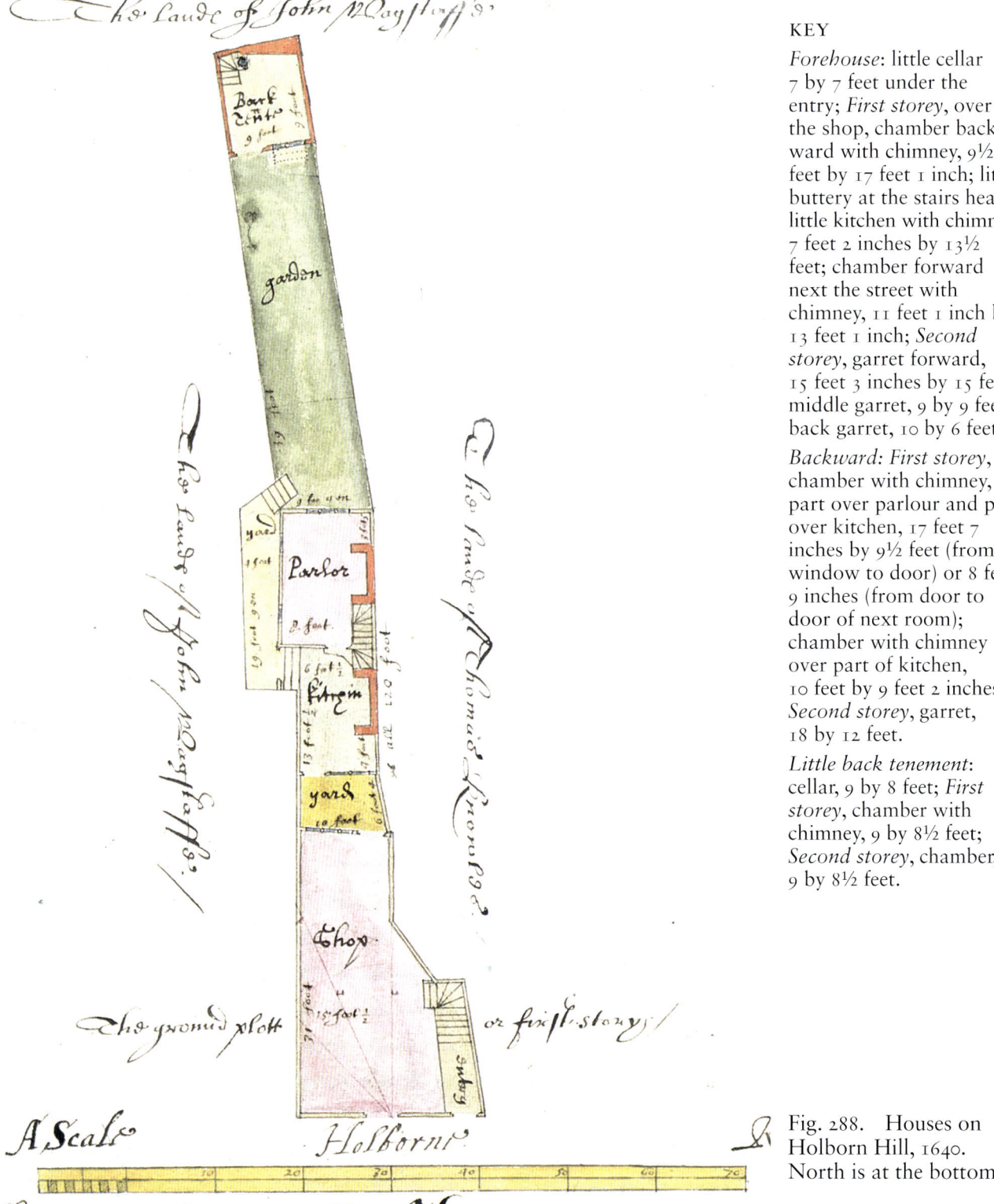

Fig. 288. Houses on Holborn Hill, 1640. North is at the bottom.

was lessee of the whole property.[53] It comprised houses of three-room, two-room and one-room plan. The front house, of two and a half storeys, had shop and entry on the ground floor, two chambers, buttery and small kitchen on the first floor and three garrets. The middle house, also of two and a half storeys, had parlour and kitchen, two chambers above and a garret. It could apparently be accessed only through the shop, but was separately occupied in 1634 and was described as a little tenement in 1676. The back tenement, just nine feet square, had three rooms, one over the other. Both the plan and the leases indicate that it was brick-built. Its only access seems to have been through the other two houses. Between 1676 and 1683 the middle house was demolished, and in 1683 the property was let on a building lease.[54] Richard Ryder was probably the carpenter of that name who built in Covent Garden and was employed by the first Earl of Salisbury.[55]

Plan 143
Houndsditch, 1667
FIG. 289

These two houses on the east side of Houndsditch had been donated to Christ's Hospital in 1593.[56] When surveyed by Ralph Treswell in 1607, each contained shop and kitchen, two chambers over and a garret, with the first floors jettied out two or two and a half feet.[57] By 1667 the sites were more intensively used. The yard of the left-hand dwelling now contained a buttery and a washhouse, and at the end of the yard a kitchen and a shed with its own fireplace, both accessed from the property to the north. The right-hand dwelling had been remodelled, with both shop and kitchen being extended and the stairs being moved. Instead of a shed, there was a washhouse with an oven and external stairs. By 1672 the houses were said to be ruinous, and a lease of 1673 provided for their rebuilding. The rebuilt houses had an extra storey, containing two chambers. They in turn were destroyed by fire in 1714. Two men were drawing plans for Christ's Hospital in 1667 — William Conyers, bricklayer, and Joseph Hutchinson, carpenter — but which of them drew this plan is unknown.[58]

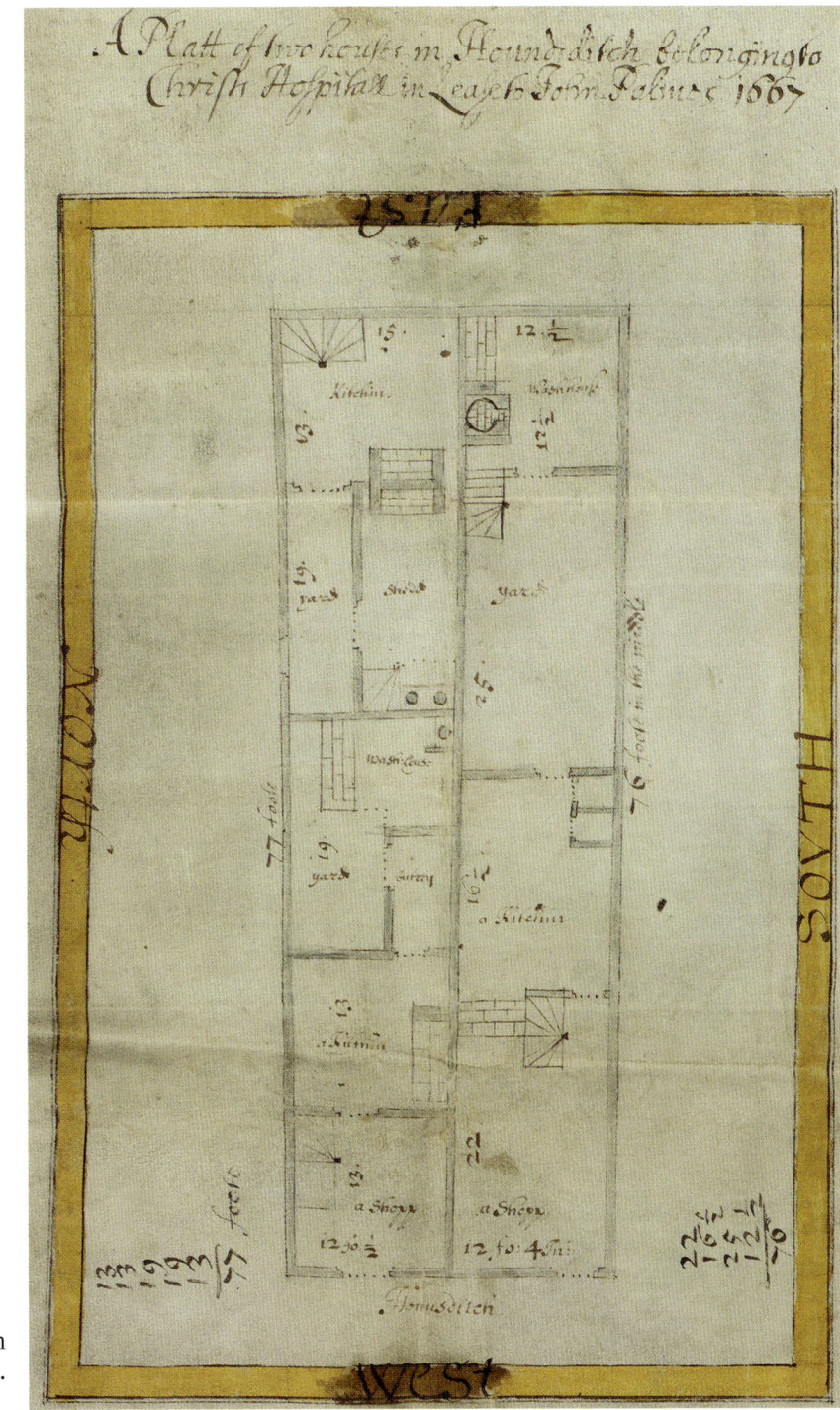

Fig. 289. Houses in Houndsditch, 1667.

Plan 144
Grange Road, Bermondsey, 1682
Nathaniel Hanwell
Fig. 290

This property, given to St Thomas's Hospital by John Wright, was west of the junction of what are now Tower Bridge Road and Decima Street, facing the latter, though the north-east corner had been taken into the roadway by 1794.[59] The plan was by Nathaniel Hanwell, a carpenter, who drew plans for St Thomas's in 1681-82 and apparently did carpentry work for it too. In January 1684 he was paid £1.10s.0d 'for making three drafts of the lands in Bermonsey of Mr. Wright's guift'.[60] The plan is finely drawn, with the four-light and two-light windows carefully depicted. The three houses were part of a larger group (at least some of them of brick) built by Thomas Miller, citizen and leatherseller, around 1620. These three were bought in 1664 by John Wright, citizen and merchant taylor, and were left by him to St Thomas's on his death in 1674.[61] There were three-room, two-room and one-room plan houses. Two were lobby-entry houses, in one case entered from the back. In 1668 William Shewin's and John Dudwick's houses together had ten rooms, suggesting that the larger house at least had two and a half storeys. It also had a great shed covered with pantiles and divided into buttery, washhouse and coal house, which was probably the shed to the right of Shewin's front door. The garden and orchard behind were large. Shewin was a pinmaker.[62] The two-room plan house also had two and a half storeys.[63] Its occupant, Elizabeth Smith, was a tanner, and carried on her trade at the back of the property (see Plan 83). In 1737 Smith's house was to have a new roof and one of the other houses was to be rebuilt.[64]

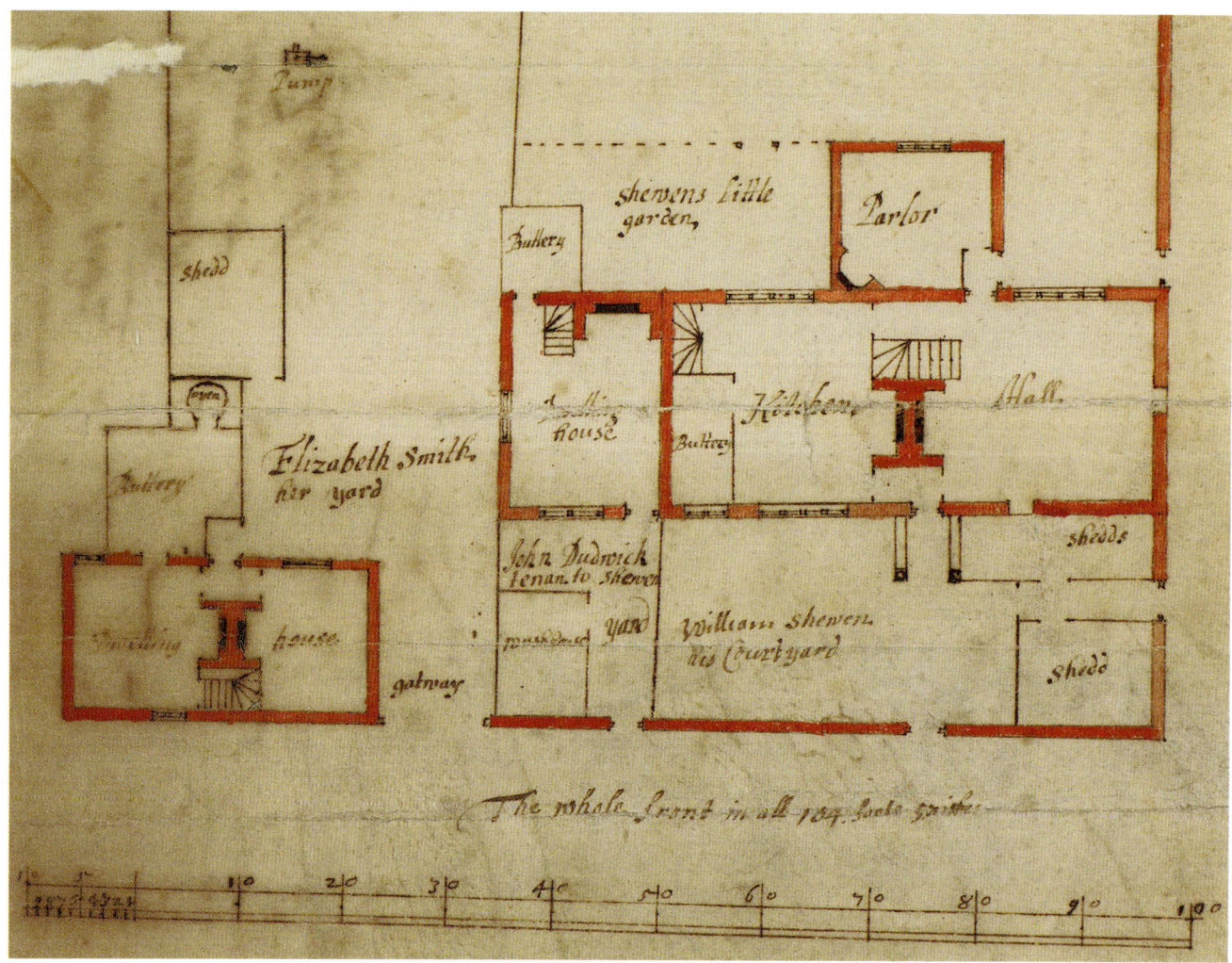

Fig. 290. Part of the plan of houses in Grange Road, Bermondsey, 1682.
North is at the bottom.

Plan 145
Whitefriars, 1683
William Leybourn Fig. 291

This plan provides an interesting example of planning on a constricted site. The row of five houses on land belonging to the Clothworkers' Company replaced a single house and garden after the Fire (Fowkes's on Plan 27). They were probably built by Sir Denis Gauden, Navy victualler and in 1667-68 Master of the Clothworkers' Company, who held the land after the Fire, though the fifty-one-year lease granted in 1683 was to William Phillips, citizen and clothworker. Despite the narrowness of the site, Gauden contrived to build three houses of two-room plan by placing two of one-room plan between them and providing light from yards at the back of the latter. Even the one-room plan houses had tiny yards. Each parlour had an entrance separate from the rest of the house, which would have made subdivision easier, whether or not this was intended. The passage was later known as Glasshouse Alley, and survived until the most recent rebuilding.[65] The site is just northeast of the corner of Tudor and Bouverie Streets.

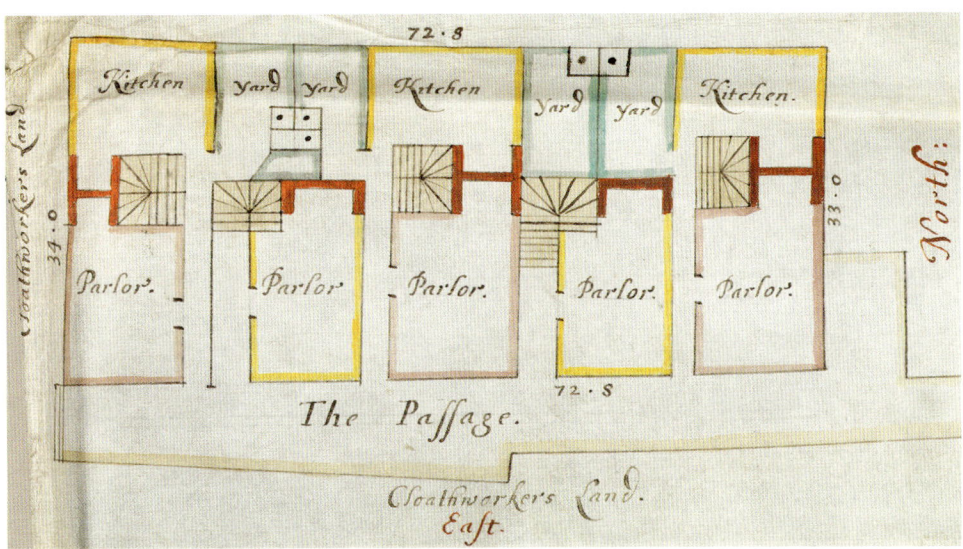

Fig. 291. Houses in Whitefriars, 1683.

Plan 146
The Round Woolstaple, Westminster, 1683
Isaac Rowe Figs 292-95

This set of plans was drawn for Christ's Hospital in connection with the re-letting of the houses, though it was not included in the leases.[66] It probably covered all floors because, although the tenancies were for distinct houses, sub-letting between two of the tenants had complicated matters. The Hospital's property in the Round Woolstaple had been surveyed as a whole by Ralph Treswell in about 1607, whereas here just the four houses in the north-west corner are depicted. William Furnis's house in 1683 is recognisably the one shown by Treswell, only slightly altered on the ground floor, and Henry Gerrard's room in the north-west corner still has what looks like the large fireplace drawn by Treswell, but otherwise the houses had been rebuilt or remodelled, at least on the ground floor. Gerrard's lease of 1660 refers to a plot in the great book of survey, presumably Treswell's, whereas in 1683 Furnis's is the only one of the three leases which refers to the survey book; Gerrard's states that the premises are described in a plan at the Hospital, and John Heard's that measurements are to be found in a view book at the Hospital.

All the houses, both in 1607 and 1683, were of three and a half storeys. Gerrard held two houses, and occupied the ground floors of both, but sub-let most of the upper rooms to Heard. Gerrard was a citizen and salter of London, but by trade a cheesemonger. Heard, a butcher, had a two-room plan house including a shop, together with most of the upper rooms of Gerrard's houses. Furnis, a grocer, also had a two-room plan house including a shop. In his case the plan and description differ in that the latter refers to a single room on both the second and top floors, whereas the plan shows two rooms on each floor.[67] The site is now at the south end of Parliament Street on the west side, partly under the south-east corner of the Government Offices and partly under the pavement.

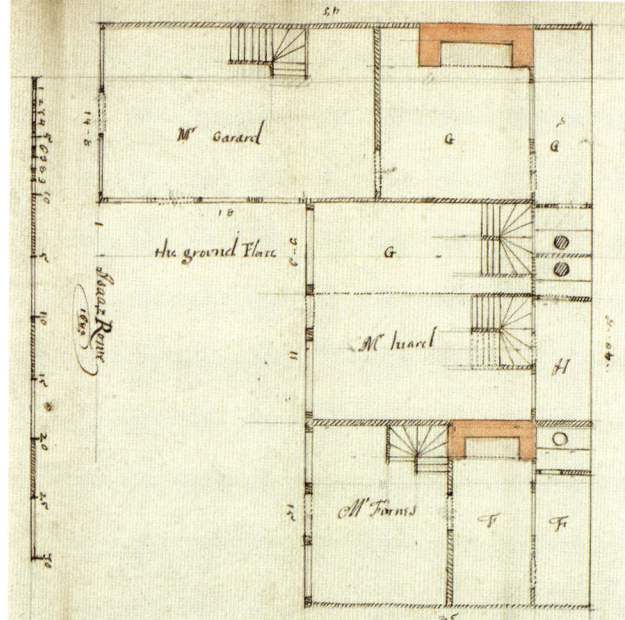
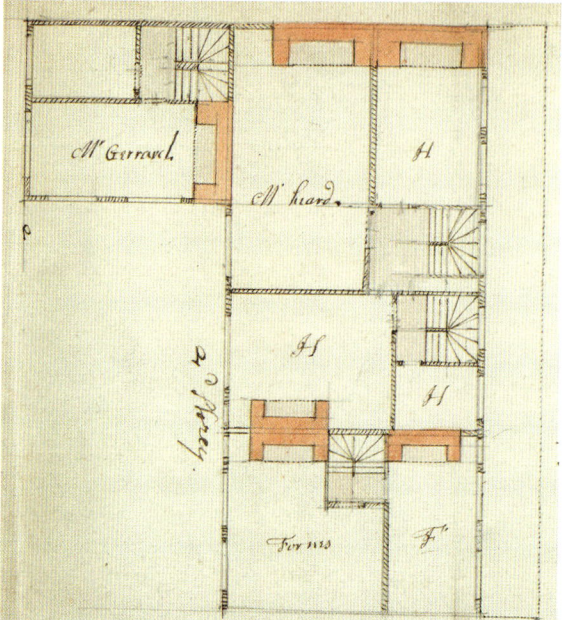
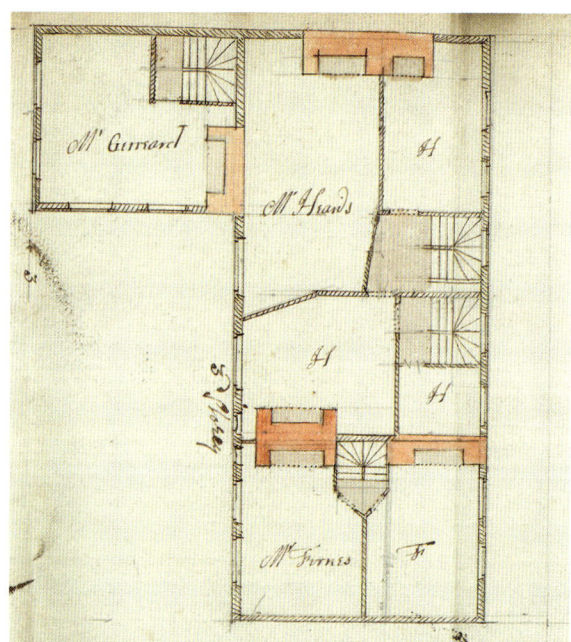
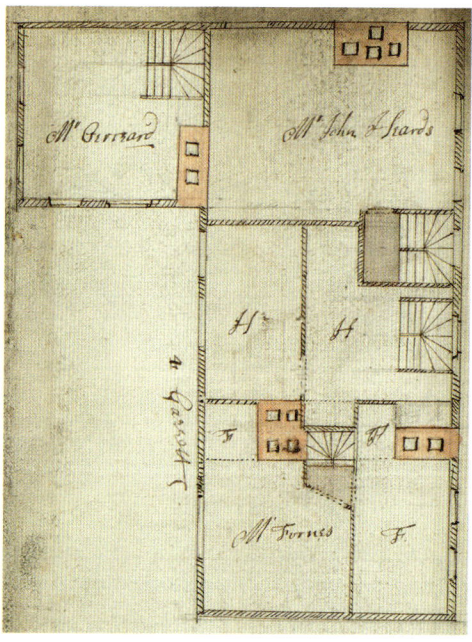

Figs 292–95. Houses in the Round Woolstaple, Westminster, 1683, showing the ground floor (top left), first floor (top right), second floor (above left) and third floor (above right). North is to the right.

KEY[68]

Henry Gerrard 1660: messuage previously two: (1) corner house now used by a potter: cellar, shop, entry, kitchen behind shop, hall, chamber over hall, chamber over last mentioned, garret; (2) other house northward: shop, entry, kitchen, yard, chamber over kitchen occupied by Gabriel Clinkard, chamber over his own kitchen, chamber next the street, two other chambers over said chambers, garret.

John Heard 1680 and 1683: *Ground floor*, shop, room behind shop (formerly kitchen), little yard; *First storey*, chamber over shop, little room; *Second storey*, fair chamber, little room [latter in 1680 only]; *Third storey*, two garrets.

William Furnis 1683: *Ground floor*, shop, kitchen, both 20 feet 2 inches by 14 feet 11 inches, little yard 14½ by 5 feet; *First storey*, chamber over part of shop 12 by 14½ feet, back chamber over kitchen 9 by 14½ feet; *Second storey*, chamber over all 22½ by 14½ feet including staircase; *Third storey*, garret over all 24 by 18 feet including stairs.

Plan 147
Tothill Street and
Carteret Street,
Westminster, 1702
John Hobbs
Fig. 296

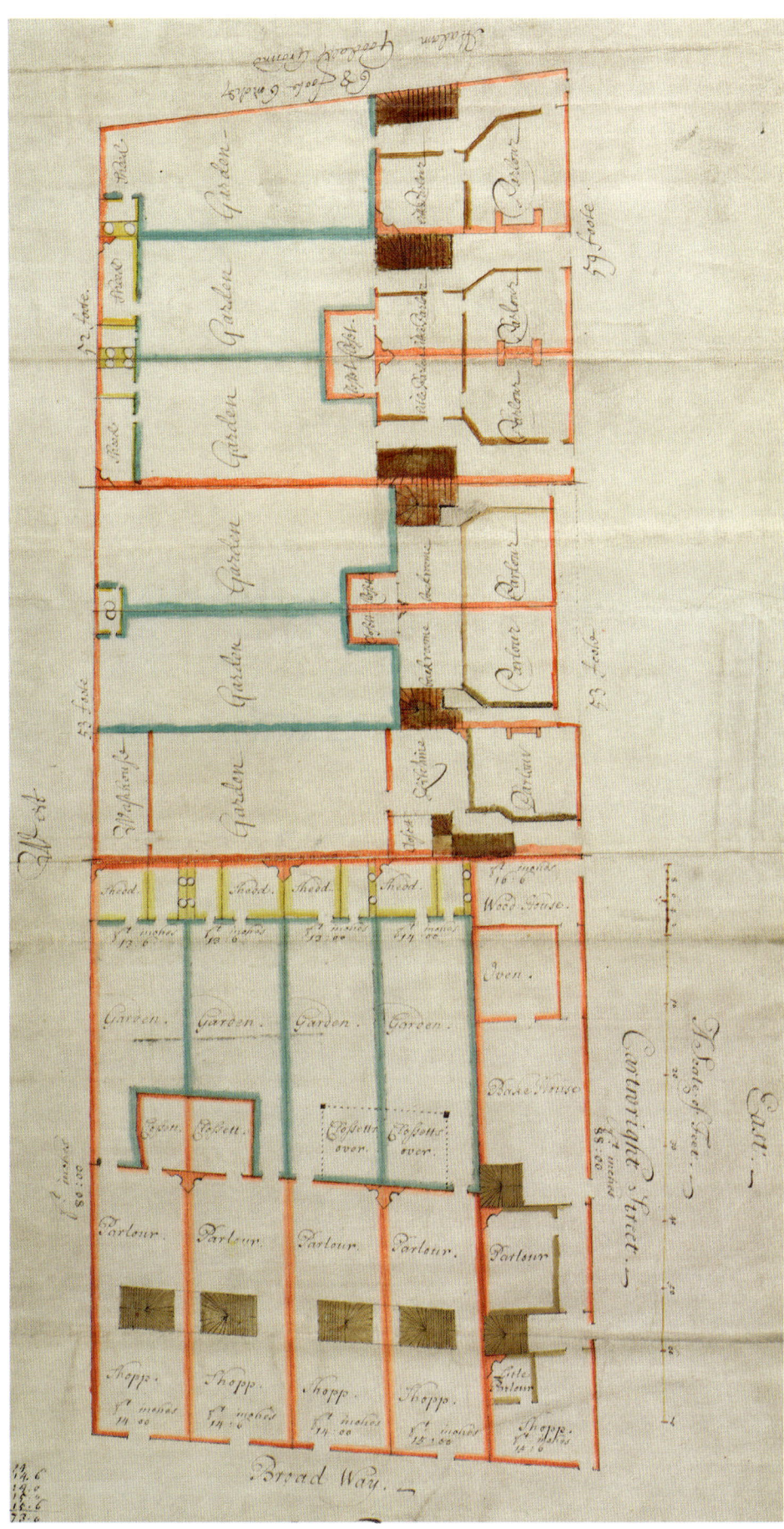

Fig. 296. Houses in Tothill Street and Carteret Street, Westminster, 1702. North is at the top.

This plan marks the completion of a rebuilding scheme on Christ's Hospital land in Tothill Street.[69] It was drawn by John Hobbs,[70] who is recorded from 1686 to 1702 surveying estates in and near London, including some of Christ's Hospital's rural properties in 1686 and 1695 and its London properties in 1698-1702.[71] Until the 1690s there were six houses here facing Tothill Street opposite Broadway, with long gardens. The Hospital's viewers recommended in 1697 that they be rebuilt, and that the new houses face Carteret Street, 'ranging with the houses already built in Carteret streete'. Carteret Street had been created in the mid-1680s as part of Sir Edward Carteret's development of Park Street (now the eastern part of Queen Anne's Gate), for which Carteret Street was at first the only access.[72] In 1697 the middle four Tothill Street properties were held by Giles Clarke and his son Rupert Clarke, described as a gentleman of Lyon's Inn,[73] and Giles Clarke made proposals for building four brick houses in Tothill Street and six or seven in Carteret Street in place of most of the existing houses. He added that 'you know they stand in a place of little trade & amongst people that cannot pay great rents', and that the new houses must be built accordingly.

In May 1699 the Clarkes proposed to rebuild the entire site, including the two houses in Tothill Street to east and west, and presented 'a plat or designe' of their proposal. The Hospital agreed to grant a forty-one year lease. The Clarkes were to make 'two intire fronts' in Tothill Street and Carteret Street, and their builder Mr Hodges (also referred to as 'Mr Hodge the carpenter') was advised of the dimensions of the timber to be used. In August the two houses under construction were viewed and found to be good; indeed the Hospital later described the new houses as 'extraordinary well built'. By September 1702 all eleven had been completed and, after negotiation over the term, Rupert Clarke was granted a fifty-one year lease, to which Plan 147 was attached.

The Tothill Street houses, fourteen or fifteen feet wide, were of two-room plan with back extensions. They had central stairs, and consisted on the ground floor of shop, parlour and in two cases closet; two had closets at an upper level, presumably on posts. On the corner of Tothill Street was a bakery, with bakehouse, oven and wood house. The Carteret Street houses were wider—seventeen to twenty feet—and formed two pairs and two single houses, all with back staircases. The paired houses otherwise had similar plans to the Tothill Street ones, the ground floor rooms being parlour, back room or little parlour and closet. Why the houses in the two streets differed was probably not because back stairs were less suitable for shop-houses but because they were less suitable for narrow houses. By 1838 the Tothill Street houses had been rebuilt.[74]

Plan 148
Crutched Friars, 1711
John Smith
FIG. 297

In 1596 the Clothworkers' Company acquired five houses on the north side of Crutched Friars, west of Northumberland Alley, under the will of Thomasine Evans.[75] The one shown here, largely timber-built, was let to Robert Wood, citizen and farrier, in 1711. The lease mentions a 'little parlour backwards', which seems to be the 'little room in the yard'; there were two rooms over the shop and kitchen, two more rooms above them, and three garrets, together with a cellar. Judging by the measurements it was the second house west from Northumberland Alley.

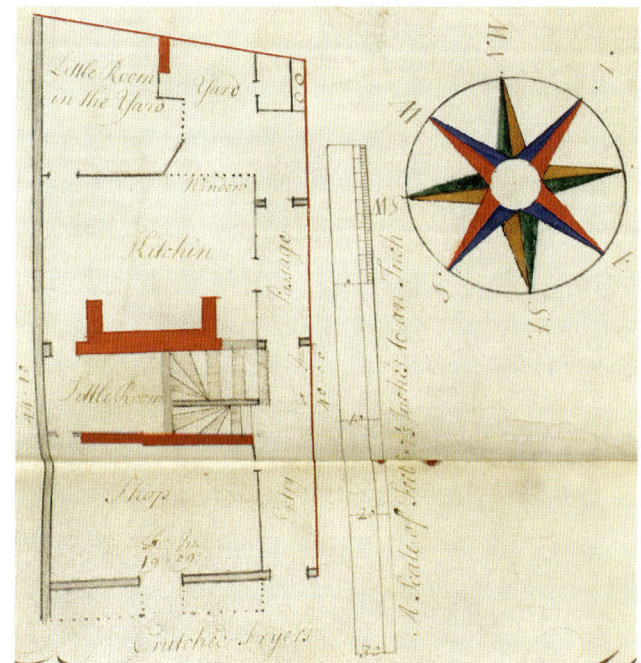

Fig. 297. A house in Crutched Friars, 1711.

Plan 149
Newgate Street, 1716
Fig. 298

This post-Fire brick house belonging to St Bartholomew's Hospital was unusual in having a dining room and a kitchen on the ground floor, though there might not be much difference in practice between rooms described as dining room and parlour. It had the rear staircase plan. Oddly, no door to the street is shown, nor access from the dining room to the rest of the house. The occupant in 1716 was John Savage. The new lessee in that year, Charles Baron, citizen and clothworker, was required to rebuild 'the fore front' of the house within five years. The house presumably stood on the Hospital's property in the area of the former Greyfriars gatehouse (Plan 20).

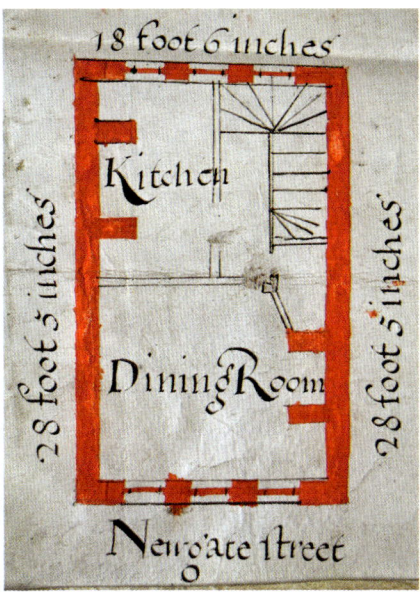

Fig. 298. A house in Newgate Street, 1716.

Plan 150
High Holborn, 1717
Fig. 299

The probable reason for this plan, drawn for a lease granted by a private individual, was that a neighbouring property belonging to the same owner had access to a shared privy and the access needed to be defined clearly. Text underneath the plan gives the dimensions of the two houses and states that the privy marked J is shared by the Golden Cock and William Thompson's house next door and that Thompson has access to it by the passage marked 1, 2 and 3. Both houses shown had central stairs and central chimneys. Neither the plan nor the lease identify which side of High Holborn they were on. The most likely site, given the plan's reference to 'The Brewhouse Passage', is the south side opposite Red Lion Street, where Rocque's map of the 1740s shows the Union Brewhouse. The owner of the property in 1717 was Gilbert Urwin of Clifford's Inn; the lessee was John Driver, carpenter, who occupied the house called the Golden Cock; and the other occupant, at the Three Horseshoes, was Robert Tucker.

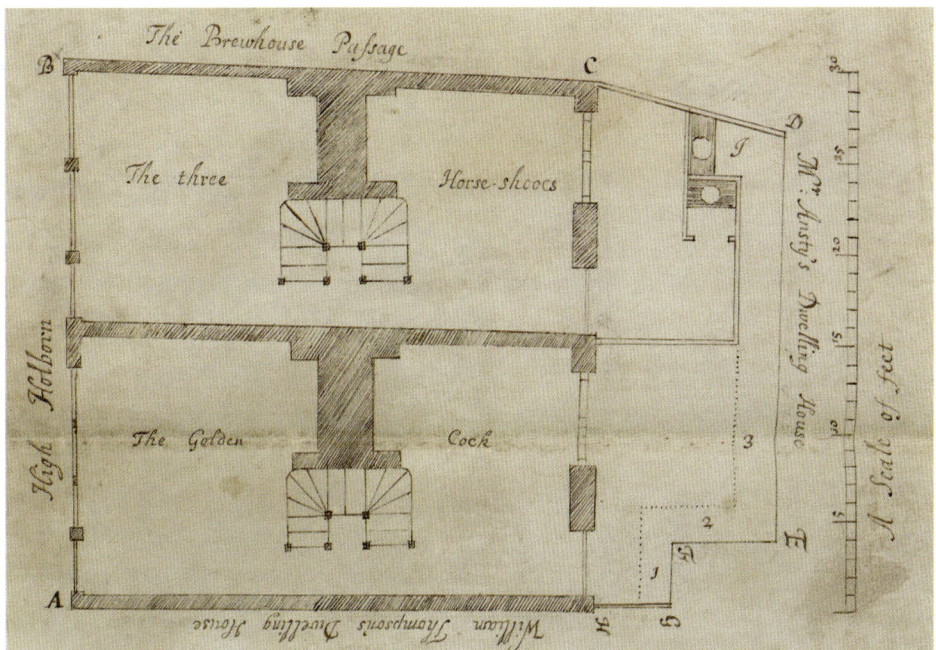

Fig. 299. Houses in High Holborn, 1717.

CITY LANDS HOUSES OF TWO-ROOM PLAN

All these properties belonged to the City, and all the plans except the first are from the plan books compiled by John and Isaac Olley. They are arranged here as follows: four with central stairs, two with both central stairs and central chimneys, two with rear stairs, eight with irregular plans (at least as regards their staircases), and one with its long side facing the street.

Plan 151
Fore Street, 1696
John Olley
Fig. 300

These two timber and brick houses were described as old messuages, but may have dated only from 1654, as the lease made in that year to Richard Middleton, citizen and freemason, was still unexpired in 1696, suggesting a building lease. On taking a new lease in 1696 Roger Poston, citizen and merchant taylor, undertook to replace them with two new houses of the second sort specified in the Rebuilding Act (three and a half storeys). They were at the west end of Fore Street backing on to the White Horse Inn.

Plan 152
Mark Lane, 1701
John Olley
Fig. 301

This property on the east side of Mark Lane, just south of Blanch Appleton (see Plan 169),[76] was a mixture of brick and timber, and most or all of it must have pre-dated the Fire. In 1699 it was described as two front tenements (one ruinous) and several small tenements behind, and there were five occupants. They included Margaret Russell, who held only the brick washhouse (with its own fireplace); it seems to have been used as

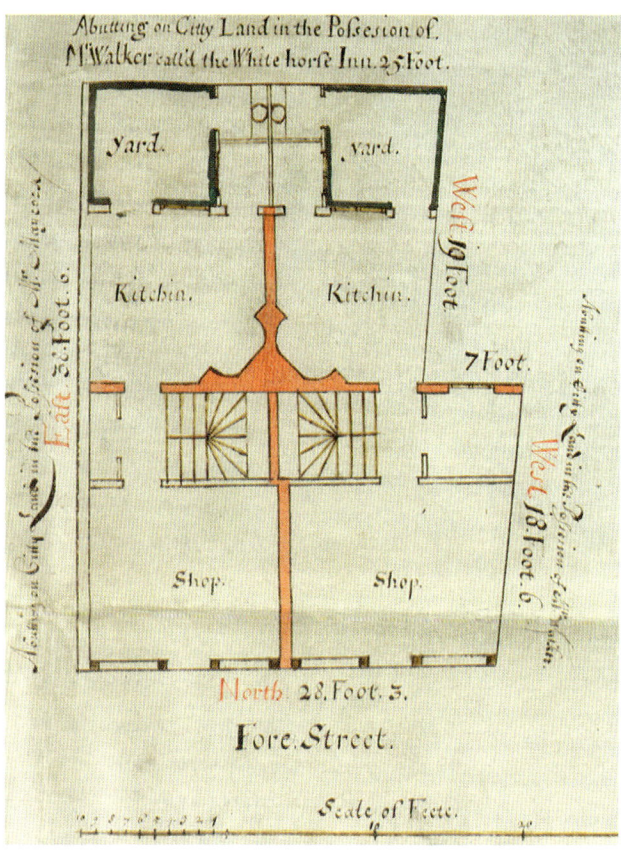

Fig. 300. Houses in Fore Street, 1696.

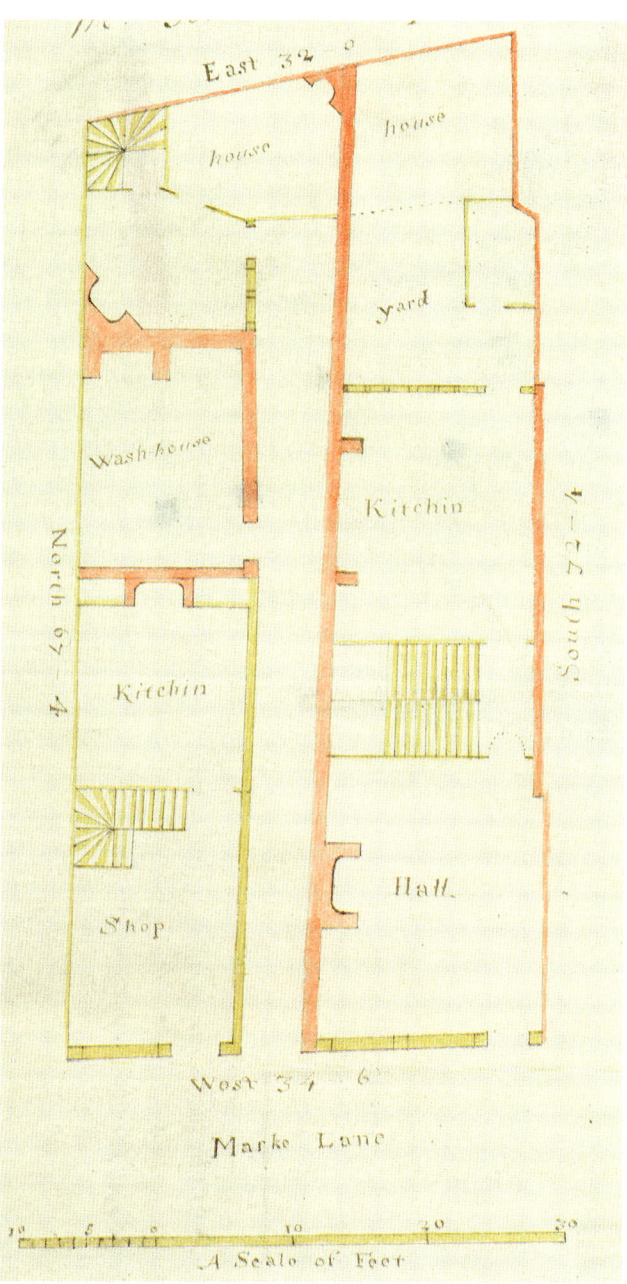

Fig. 301. Houses in Mark Lane, 1701.

part of the next-door property, leased by Russell, the water from which drained through this house into the street by 'ancient watercourses'. On the right-hand side was a single large house of two-room plan with a central staircase and a ground-floor hall. Behind it was a yard and a 'house' apparently with no independent access. The two houses on the left-hand side were both of two-room plan at ground level. The premises were leased in 1700 to John Foltrop, citizen and carpenter, who was required to spend at least £1,000 rebuilding them, and who built three new houses.[77] Foltrop was an important master builder involved in developments in many parts of London from the 1680s, especially City projects such as rebuilding the houses on London Bridge and Emanuel Hospital; he was City Carpenter at least from 1687 to 1690. He died in 1724.[78]

Plan 153
Grocers' Alley, 1711
John Olley
FIG. 302

This brick house was one of a pair built after the Great Fire, at the far end of Grocers' Alley on the east side.[79] It had three and a half storeys and a cellar, and two rooms on each floor. There were two bays at the front, with sash windows up to the first floor and casement windows above, and a shell porch over the front door. Back rooms also had two windows on each floor, presumably looking into the yard, as the three windows to the staircase must have done too; the staircase also had a 'skylight' over it in the garret storey. The version of the plan attached to the lease shows a wooden partition between the passage by the stairs and the kitchen. The ground-floor hall was evidently a working area, as the fixtures included a wainscot writing desk, an enclosed office with a desk and an arched partition with its own sash window. The ground floor must have been slightly raised, as the cellar had windows at front and back; it contained an oven and a privy. The other privy was in the back garret, with a 'leaden ffunnell' connecting it to the lower one. Many of the chimneypieces had Dutch tiles, as well as pictures over them, and there was much wainscoting. In the yard was a cistern. The City's lessees were Edward Shaler, gentleman, in 1679 and Anne Bower, widow, in 1711. In 1720 Grocers' Alley was said to be largely occupied by sponging houses, accommodating people who would otherwise have been in Poultry Compter next door.[80] It is now called Grocers' Hall Court.

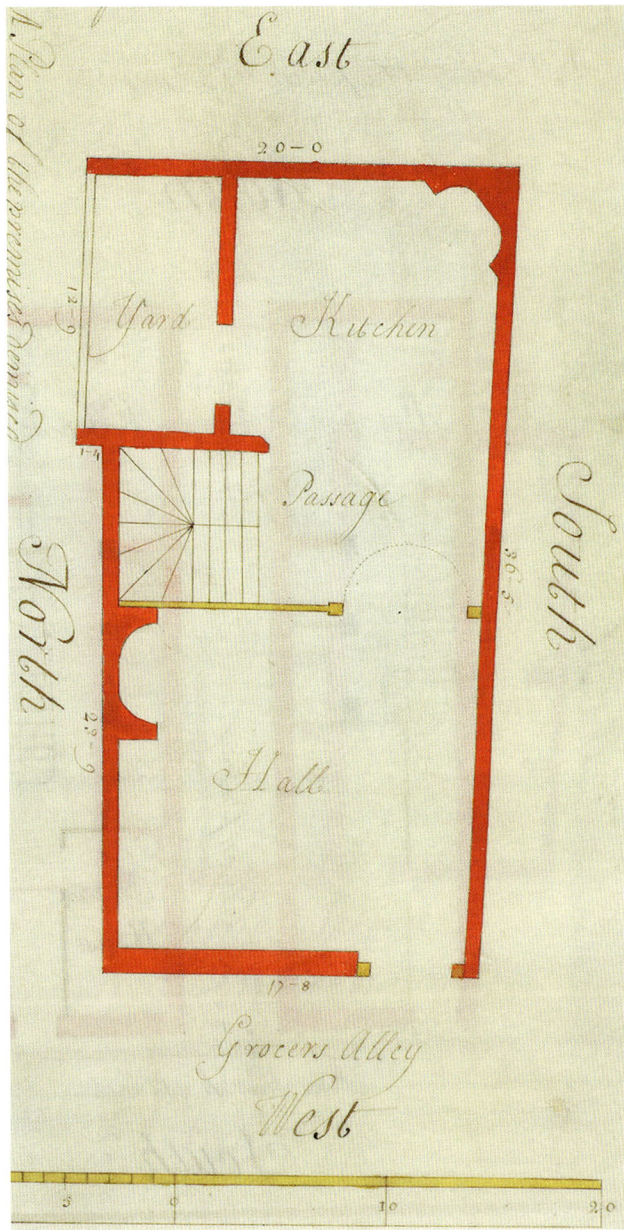

Fig. 302. A house in Grocers' Alley, 1711.

Plan 154
Pudding Lane, 1719
Isaac Olley
FIG. 303

This house is of particular interest as the site of Thomas Farriner's bakehouse, where the Great Fire began. The southern part of the yard shown on the plan was described in 1679 as having been 'the bakers yard whear he laid his bavins',[81] and, as the inscription on the Monument states that it is 202 feet from where the Fire broke out (indicating that Farriner's oven was at the back of the site), the oven is most likely to have been east of that yard, where the washhouse was in 1719.[82] When a

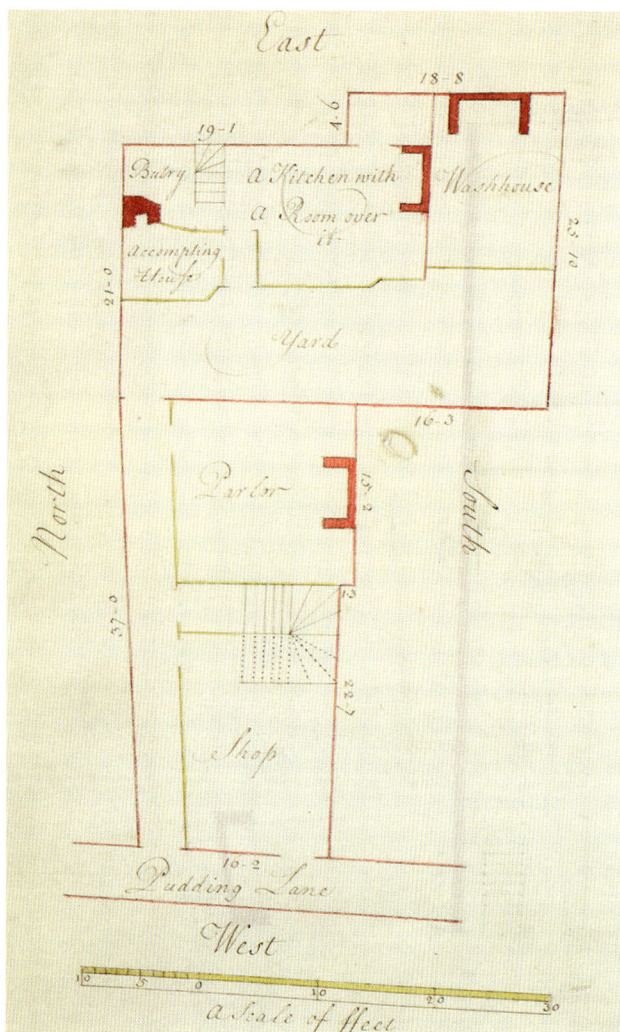

Fig. 303. A house in Pudding Lane, 1719.

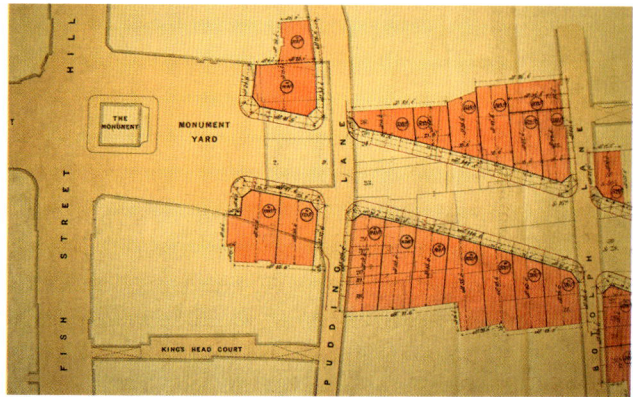

Fig. 304. The plan approved for Monument Street in 1886, showing the exact site of 23 Pudding Lane.

The stone, erected in 1681, stated that 'Here ... Hell broke loose upon this Protestant city, from the malicious hearts of barbarous papists'.[86] It was removed in about 1750 and is now in the Museum of London. The site is where Monument Street now meets the east side of Pudding Lane (Fig. 304).

Plan 155
Basinghall Postern, 1706
John Olley Fig. 305

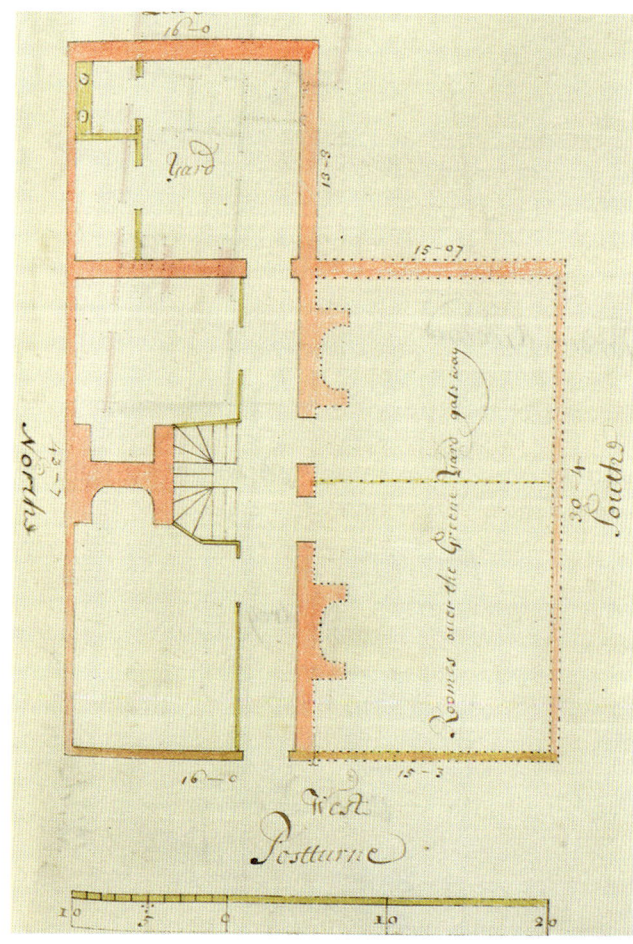

Fig. 305. A house in Basinghall Postern, 1706.

lease of the vacant site was requested in 1674, nothing was done because 'there was a supposicon that it ought perpetually to ly wast'.[83] The site, later 23 Pudding Lane, is empty on Ogilby and Morgan's map. Subsequently it was realised that neither an Act of Parliament nor an order of the Court of Aldermen forbade rebuilding, and the house on the plan was built in 1680 by Daniel Harris, citizen and cooper, whom the City Lands Committee required to build 'according to the plot here presented'. He was also required to attach a stone commemorating the Great Fire, which was to mention 'ye papists fireing this City'.[84] The house was of two-room plan with central staircase, and had four and a half storeys and a cellar. The first floor consisted of dining room and chamber. In the yard at the back were a kitchen with one floor over, counting house, buttery and washhouse. In 1708 it was occupied by Joseph Wilson, a wine cooper, and in 1719 the lessee and occupant was Samuel Wilson, a merchant.[85]

This building, just outside the area burnt in 1666, was partly over the gateway leading into the City's Green Yard, in what became known as Basinghall Postern, between Fore Street and London Wall. It had a central chimney stack and central stairs. It consisted of two cellars; on the ground floor, parlour, kitchen, buttery, yard and privy; on the first floor, two rooms; on the second floor four rooms, of which two were over the gateway; and four garrets. John Olley obtained the lease in 1706, promising to live there 'for the more commodious service of the City in this station'. Basinghall Postern was described as a new street in 1681, and had at one end a passage through the Wall made in 1655, which was probably when the street was created.[87]

Plan 156
Basinghall Postern, 1718
Isaac Olley
Fig. 306

This largely brick house backed on to the City's Green Yard immediately north of London Wall, and was probably part of the same development as the house on Plan 155. It was leased in 1718 to Francis Albone, a chemist.[88]

Plan 157
Tower Hill, c.1707
John Olley
Fig. 307

This house had a generous width of just over twenty feet and the classic rear staircase plan. It was brick at the front and timber at the back; the materials used for the side walls are unknown, as the plan does not show them, presumably because they were excluded from the lease for some reason. No lease has been found, and the exact location is uncertain, but the irregular shape of the plot matches ones shown on later maps on the west side and towards the north end of Great Tower Hill (now Trinity Square).[89]

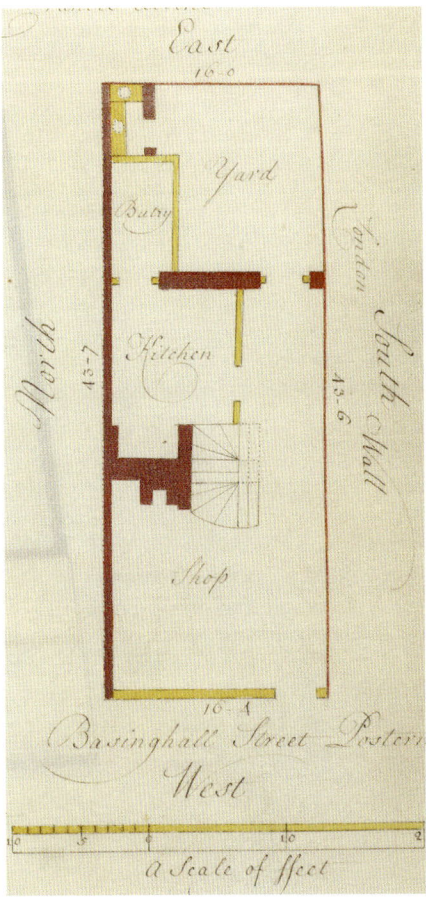

Fig. 306. A house in Basinghall Postern, 1718.

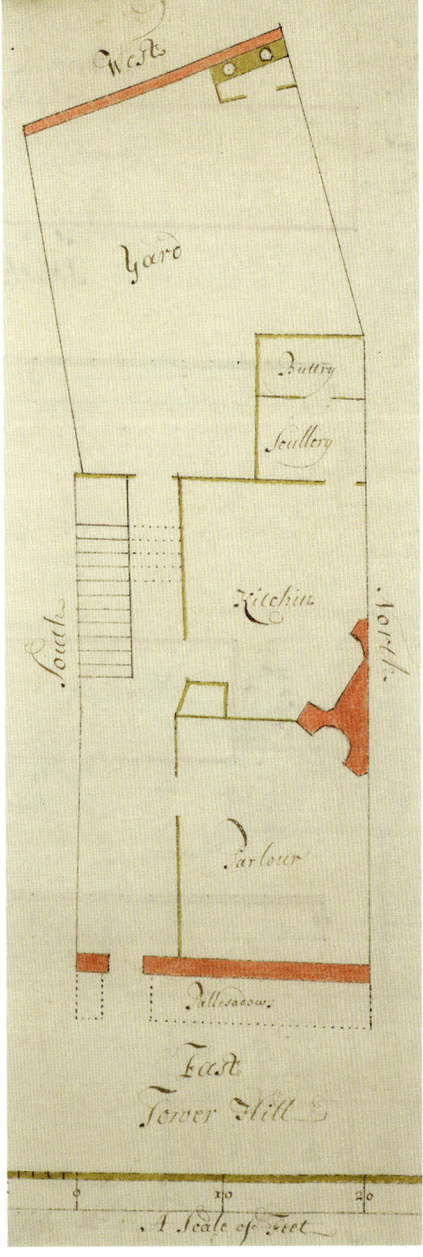

Fig. 307. A house on Tower Hill, c.1707.

Plan 158
Fenchurch Street, 1713
Isaac Olley
Fig. 308

This largely timber house was of the rear staircase type, though not in a very regular form. The shop, kitchen and stairs were all entered by the passage rather than directly from the street or through the shop. The property was leased in 1713 to Sarah Rawlins, widow, who was living there. As it was on the north side of Fenchurch Street in St Katherine Coleman parish and abutted east but not west on other City land, it was apparently the western part of the group of City properties which were redeveloped in 1734 as Fenchurch Buildings (a little east from Billiter Street).[90]

Plan 159
Duke's Place, 1705
John Olley
Fig. 309

This timber house was on the south side of Duke's Place, backing on to the churchyard of St James Duke's Place, and therefore probably in the part of Duke's Place known as Shoemakers' Row. It was unusual in having a front staircase. The schedule of fixtures indicates that it had four and a half storeys and cellar, apparently with one room on each of the first and second floors and two on the third and the garret floors. The curving chimney in the kitchen was decorated with Dutch tiles. There was a privy with a lead pipe on the third floor. Both the stairs and the 'jetty' intruded into the next-door property. The lessee and occupant in 1705 was Jonathan Evans, tailor.[91]

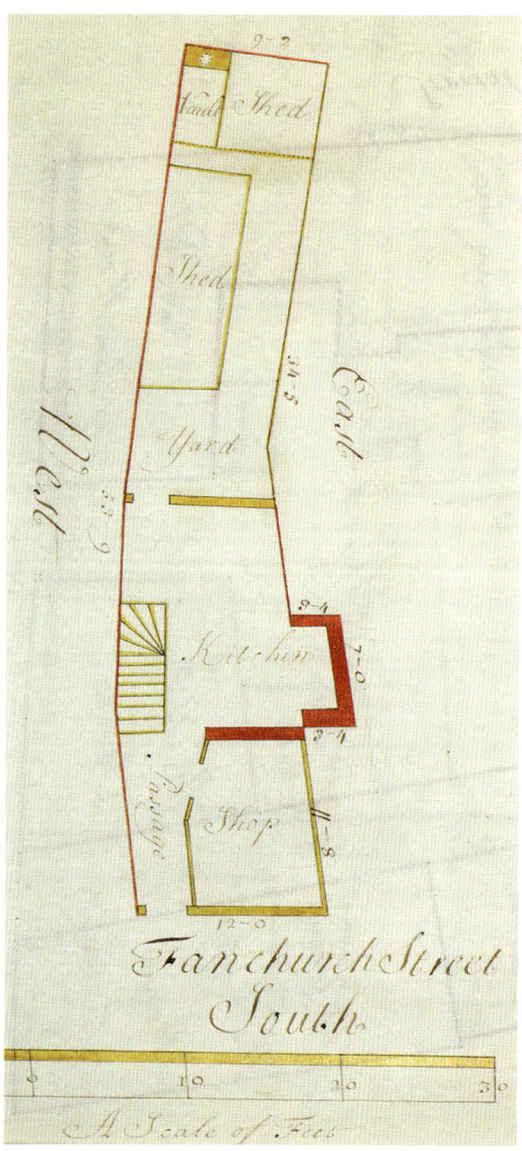

Fig. 308. A house in Fenchurch Street, 1713.

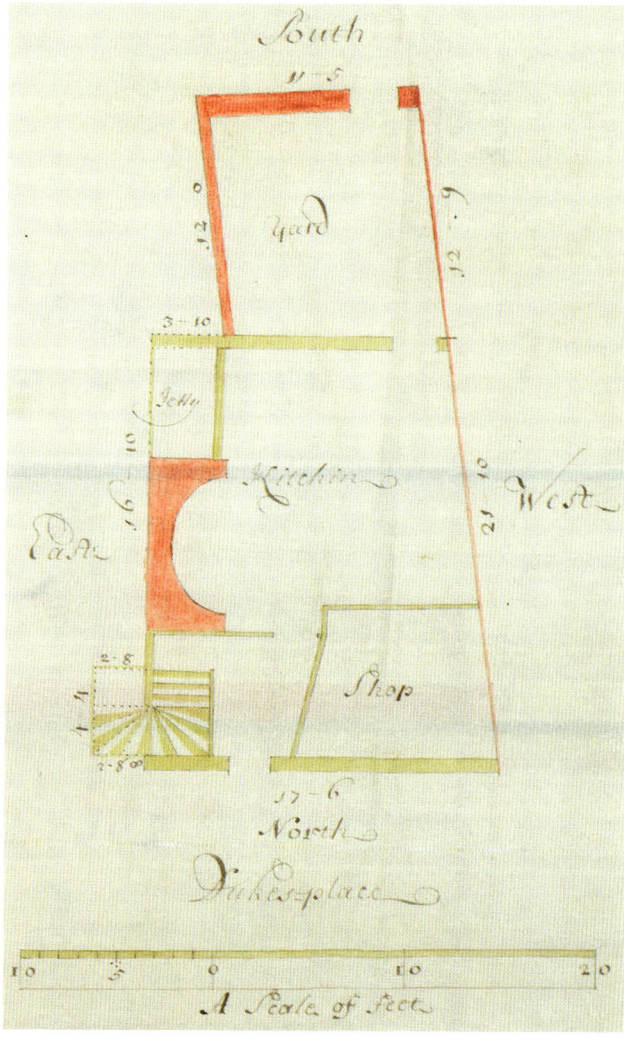

Fig. 309. A house in Duke's Place, 1705.

Plan 160
Fenchurch Street, 1710
John Olley
FIG. 310

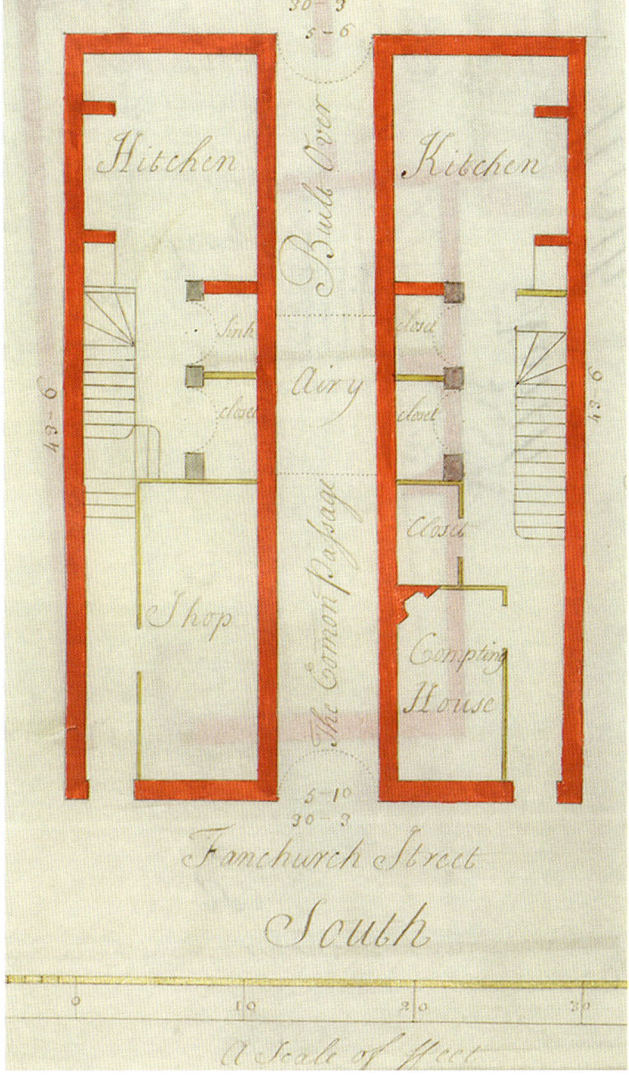

Fig. 310. Houses in Fenchurch Street, 1710.

These two brick dwellings were on the north side of Fenchurch Street (Fig. 311; see Fig. 102 for the location). They were not quite within the area shown by Ogilby and Morgan as having been destroyed by the Great Fire, but nevertheless had been rebuilt by 1671 by Francis Drinkwater. In that year they were occupied by John Barnett, draper, and John Finch, grocer. The property was let in 1710 to Thomas Welham, described as a gentleman.[92] In 1710 the ground floor of the right-hand property seems to have been largely commercial, with a counting house and several closets. The passage led to a mansion described in 1682 as 'lately new built', and which served from 1696 to the 1790s as the headquarters of the Hudson's Bay Company (accessed later from Culver Court).[93]

Fig. 311. The north side of Fenchurch Street, just west of Ironmongers' Hall, *c.*1750 (detail from a print by Thomas Bowles after John Donowell). The gabled building above the coach is the houses of Fig. 310, evidently with the ground floor altered since 1710. The plain building to their right straddled Culver Court, and to its right was part of John Smith's development at Clothworkers' Court (see Plan 41).

Plan 161
Houndsditch, 1712
John or Isaac Olley
Fig. 312

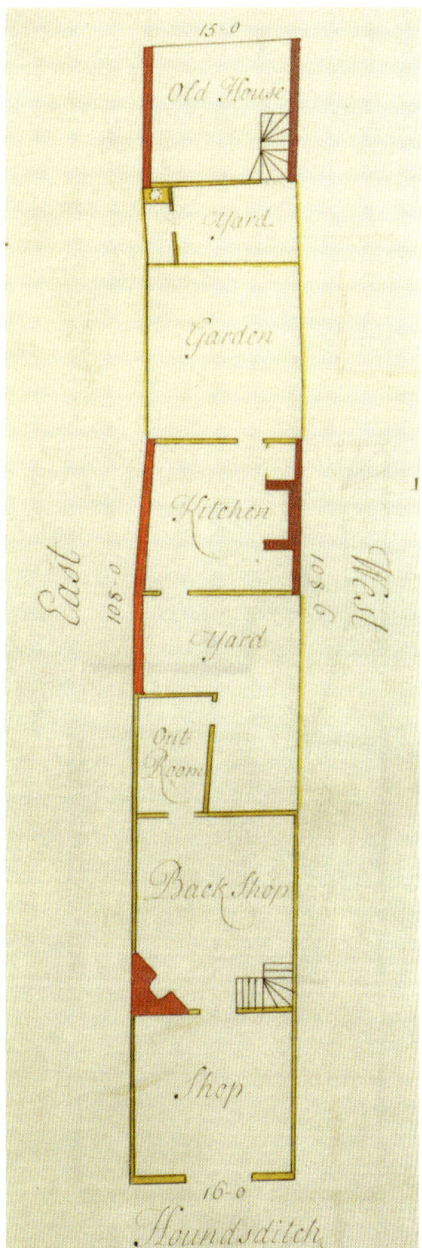

Fig. 312. A house in Houndsditch, 1712.

This timber house had a two-room plan but also a detached kitchen. In 1652 it had been let to Joseph Hendrick for sixty-one years, which almost certainly means that the house was then rebuilt under a building lease. The 'old house' at the back apparently had no independent means of access, and was described in 1711 as 'some rooms backwards'. The lessee in 1712 was William Warren, citizen and draper, who was occupying the property.[94]

Plan 162
Shoemakers' Row, 1712
John or Isaac Olley
Fig. 313

This timber house was in the part of Duke's Place known as Shoemakers' Row, and had somewhat more than a two-room plan. The ground floor had a shop (separately accessed from the street) and a kitchen and a back shop, together with two staircases, one of which provided separate access from the street to the upper floors. It was leased in 1712 to John Rowton, citizen and cordwainer.[95]

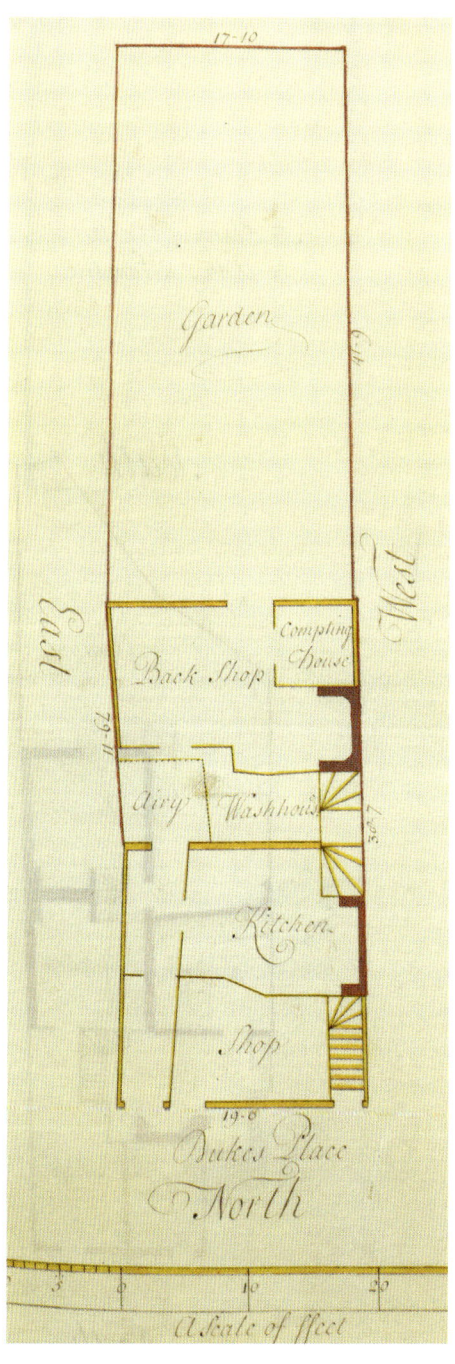

Fig. 313. A house in Shoemakers' Row, also known as Duke's Place, 1712.

Plan 163
Aldgate High Street, *c.*1715
Isaac Olley
FIG. 314

This timber house on the north side of Aldgate High Street was leased in about 1715 to John Hill.

Plan 164
Hart Street, London Wall, 1717
Isaac Olley
FIG. 315

These three houses were bounded by London Wall to the north and Cripplegate to the east. The site was just outside the area burnt in the Great Fire, but Thomas Jackson, citizen and draper, who leased it in 1717, claimed in the previous year that he had had to rebuild the houses because of decay caused by a sewer running underneath. Two of the three were of two-room plan. The right-hand one had a central chimney stack and central stairs, but not next to each other. The left-hand one had front stairs.[96]

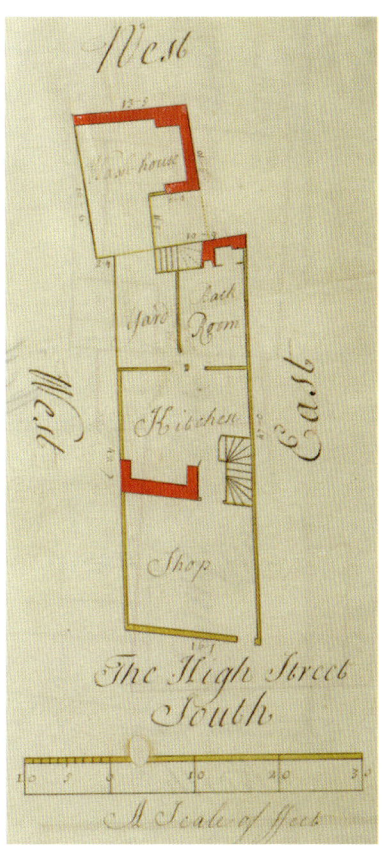

Fig. 314. A house in Aldgate High Street, *c.*1715.

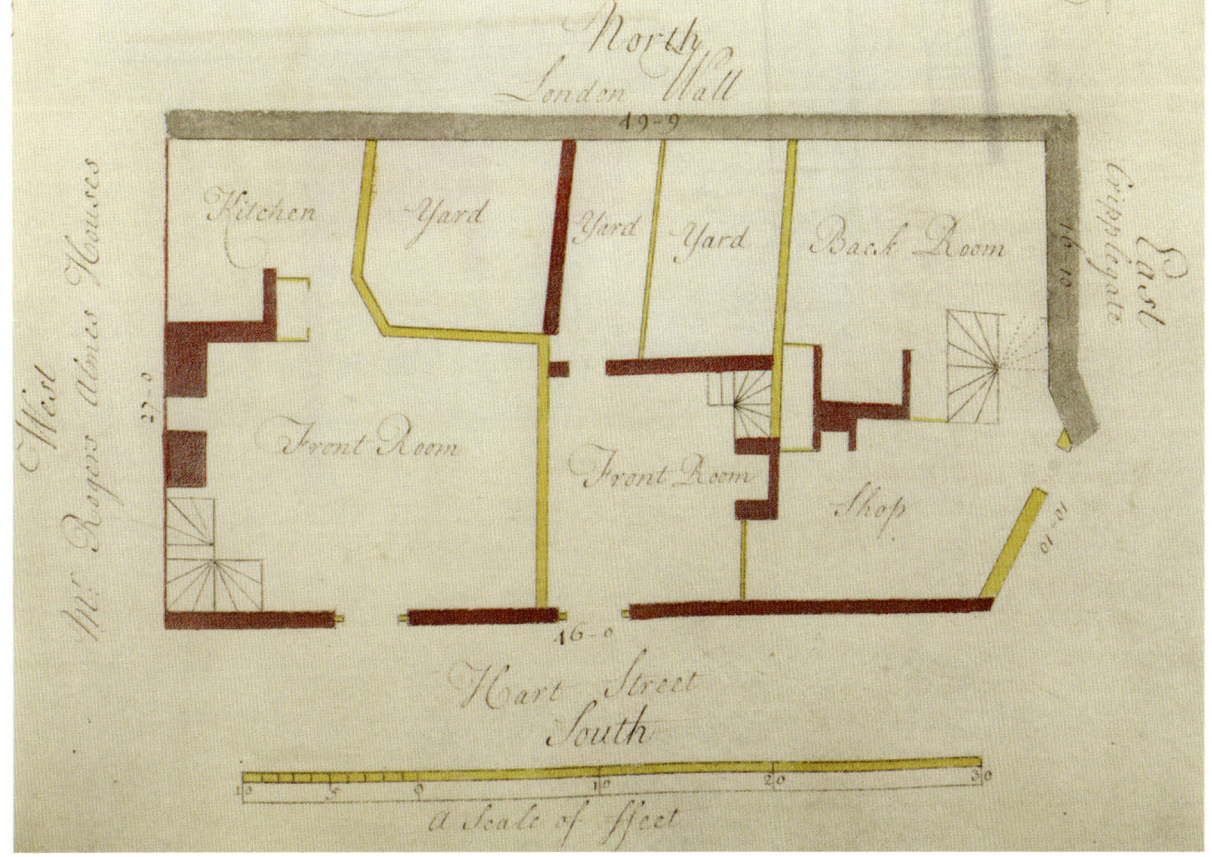

Fig. 315. Houses in Hart Street, London Wall, 1717.

Plan 165
Aldermanbury Postern, 1717
Isaac Olley
Fig. 316

Aldermanbury Postern was a short continuation of Aldermanbury between London Wall and Fore Street, using a passage through the Wall opened in 1655. Part of London Wall is shown, and this identifies the house as the second from the Wall. The house had a central chimney stack and central stairs, and sacrificed much of its ground floor to provide access to the garden and shed at the back. It was leased in 1717 to its occupant, Charles Butler, citizen and feltmaker.[97]

Plan 166
Bishopsgate Street, 1718
Isaac Olley
Fig. 317

The ground floor of this timber house, just outside Bishopsgate, was shared by a large shop and a small one, with eighteen feet of frontage between them. It was described in 1718 as the Horseshoe Alehouse, occupied by Sarah Whitwang, and a shop adjoining. Whitwang tried to obtain the lease in that year, but it went instead to John Vincent, citizen and combmaker, who offered more.[98]

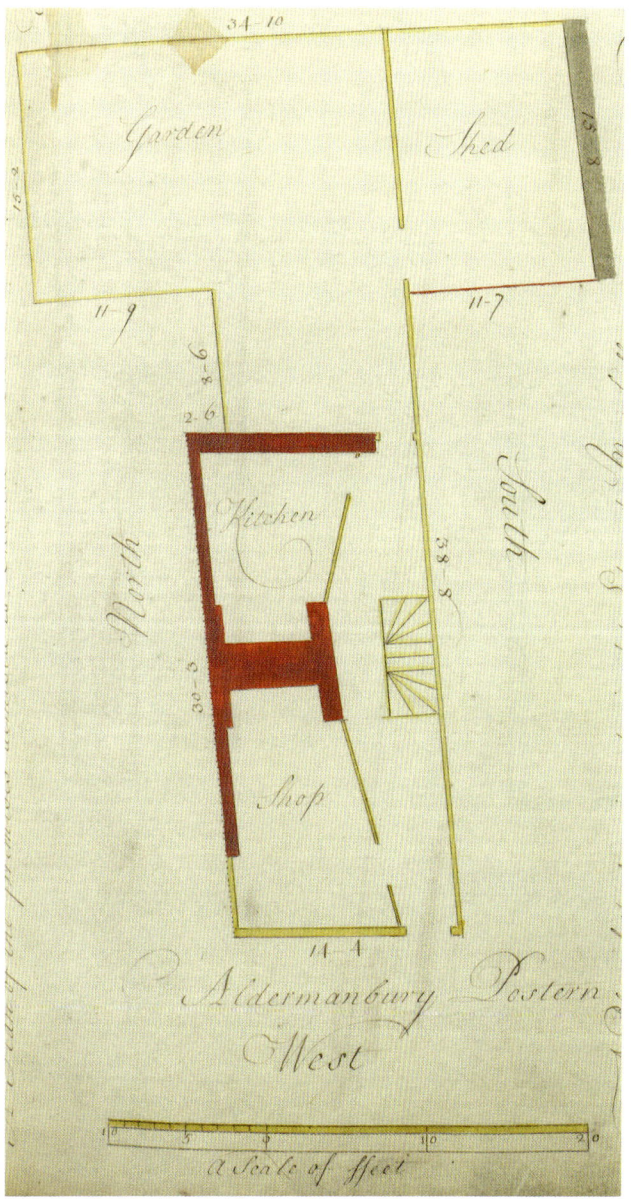

Fig. 316. A house in Aldermanbury Postern, 1717.

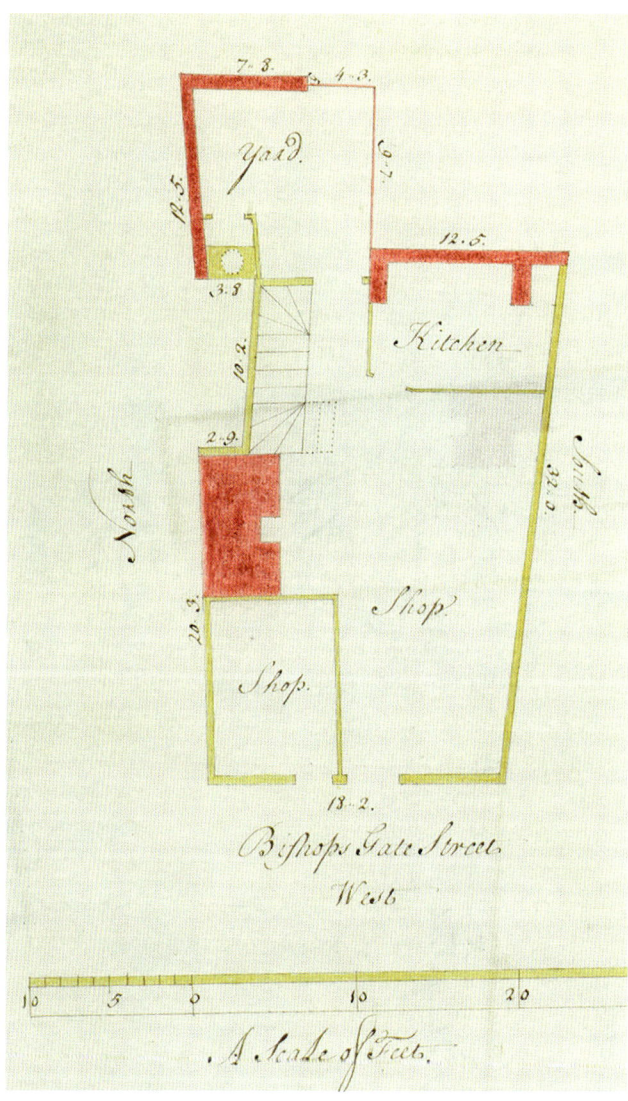

Fig. 317. A house in Bishopsgate Street, 1718.

Plan 167
Wormwood Street, 1721
Isaac Olley

FIG. 318

This house was built partly over London Wall, with stairs apparently hacked out of the Wall. It had three and a half storeys, with kitchen and dining room on the first floor, two chambers above and two garrets at the top. In 1721 it was let to William Collins, citizen and innholder.[99]

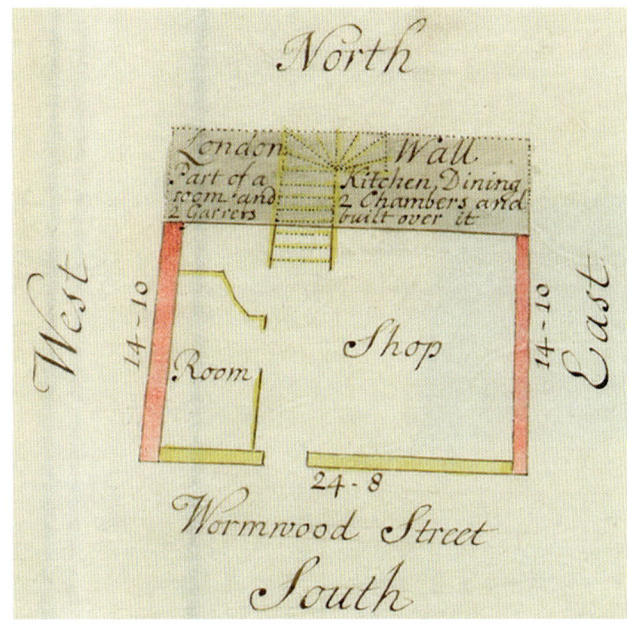

FIG. 318. A house in Wormwood Street, 1721.

Plan 168
Creechurch Lane, 1714
Isaac Olley

FIG. 319

This house, of timber but with brick end walls, was on the west side of Creechurch Lane. It was entered on its long side, and had fireplaces in the end walls rather than centrally placed. In 1652 the property was leased for sixty-one years, which probably indicates a building lease. The lessee in 1714 was Sarah Crippes of Enfield, widow, and her tenant was Jacob Mazahod, merchant.[100]

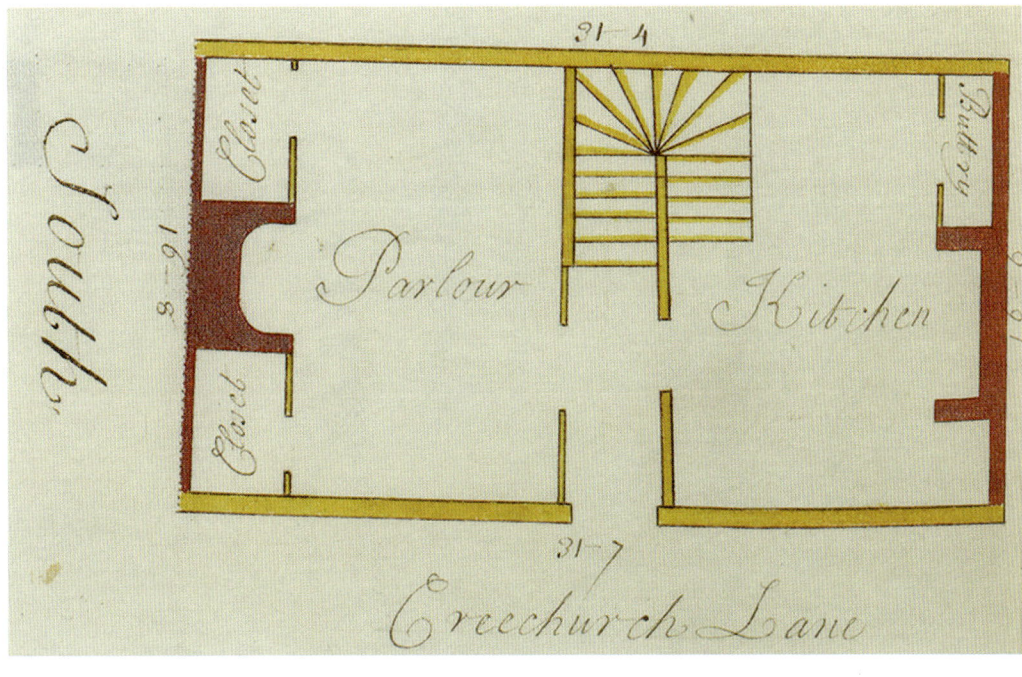

Fig. 319. A house in Creechurch Lane, 1714.

ONE-ROOM PLAN HOUSES

Plan 169
Burnt Yard, Blanch Appleton, 1640
Fig. 320

Blanch Appleton, east of Mark Lane and south of Fenchurch Street, seems originally to have been an Anglo-Saxon soke (or local jurisdiction), and was later a manor outside the City's authority. By the reign of Edward IV it was held by the City. In 1635 there were said to be thirty-six houses there and four or five gardens, and in 1719 about forty-seven houses.[101] Most of them were around a courtyard called Blanch Appleton, but the houses on the plan were further south in the alley described on Ogilby and Morgan's map as Burnt Yard, in modern terms between Mark Lane and London Street; in 1702 it was known as Cabidge (or Cabbage) Court.[102] In 1640 the City leased the site for forty-one years to William Devonshire, citizen and turner, who had already rebuilt four of the houses. He was required to spend a further £300 rebuilding the other four, 'being ruinous', in brick or stone.

The plan depicts eight similar houses, and when a new lease was drawn up in 1679 the layout of the site was almost identical,[103] which suggests that what was attached to the lease of 1640 was Devonshire's building plan with the eight houses as intended rather than what was actually standing on the site. The City rarely bothered with plans on its leases in this period, and what it was most interested in was boundaries, so a building plan, readily available, would have met its needs. All eight houses were of one-room plan, and the lease of 1679 states that each had four floors and a cellar. The smallest was about fifteen by twelve feet. All had light at the back or side as well as the front. The staircases were all at the front, with the fireplace adjoining. By 1679 five houses had sheds and there was a pump in the yard. The whole of Blanch Appleton, including the former Burnt Yard, was rebuilt under a lease of 1720.[104]

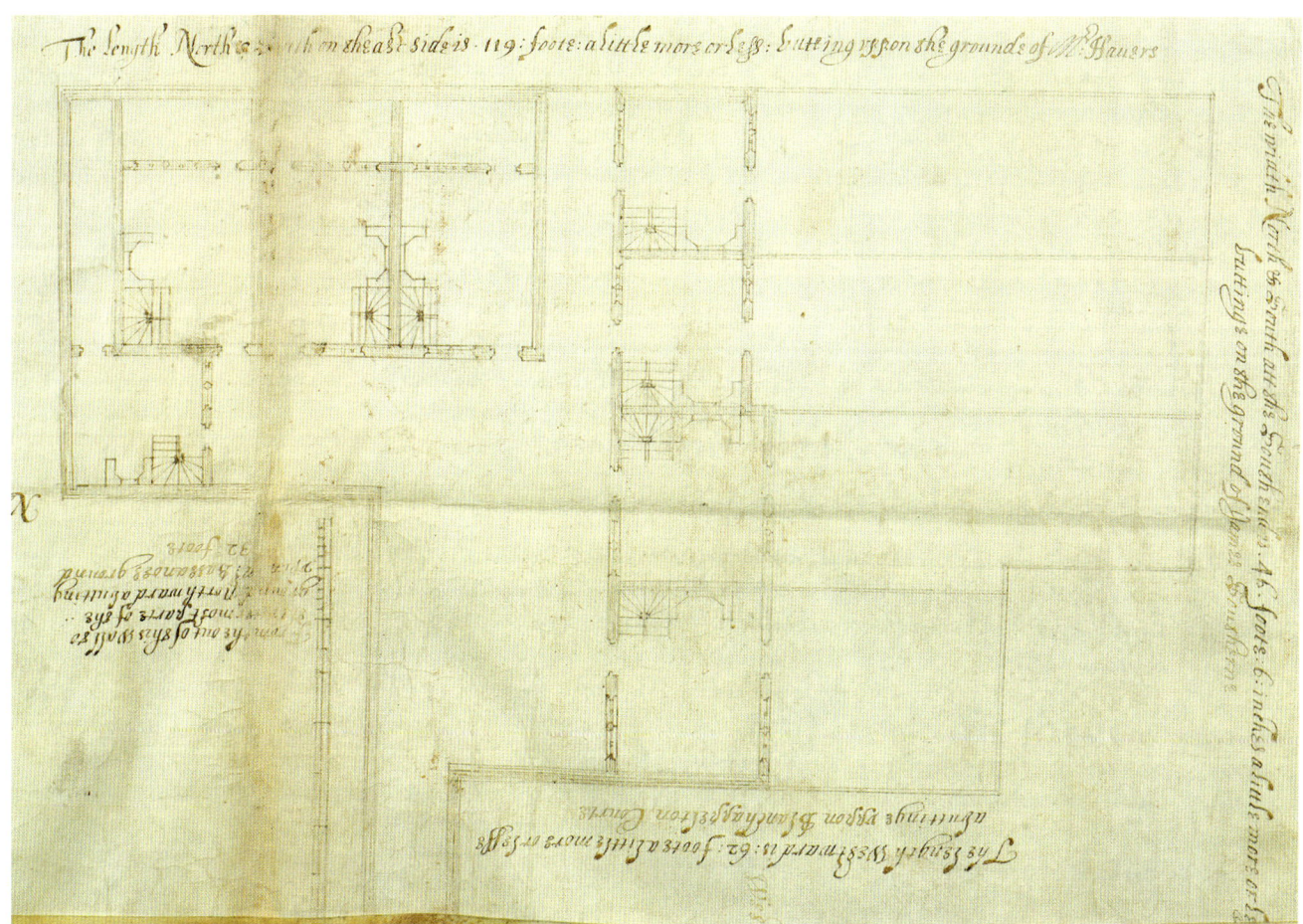

Fig. 320. Houses in Burnt Yard, Blanch Appleton, 1640. North is to the left.

Plan 170
Dowgate Hill, 1678
William Leybourn
FIG. 321

This plan provides an example of houses squeezed into shallow plots. The three properties, on the east side of Dowgate Hill opposite the Tallow Chandlers' gateway, were acquired by the Tallow Chandlers' Company in 1624 under the will of Matthew Kempton. They were rebuilt after the Fire by Henry Worster, citizen and draper.[105] Leybourn's descriptions make clear the importance of light, which was the main reason for the tiny yards behind two of the houses. The site is now part of Cannon Street Station.

KEY

A, B. Each has: *First storey*, one room, lights west to street and east to yard; *Second storey*, ditto; *Third storey*, garret, with Lutheran light towards street; cellar.

C. Corner tenement: *First storey*, Fair room with closet over shop and kitchen, with lights south and west towards street; *Second storey*, ditto; *Third storey*, ditto; platform over all, leaded; cellar under shop and kitchen.

Fig. 321. Houses in Dowgate Hill, 1678. North is to the left.

Plans 171-72
Fore Street, 1682 and 1719
William Leybourn and Isaac Olley
FIGS 322-23

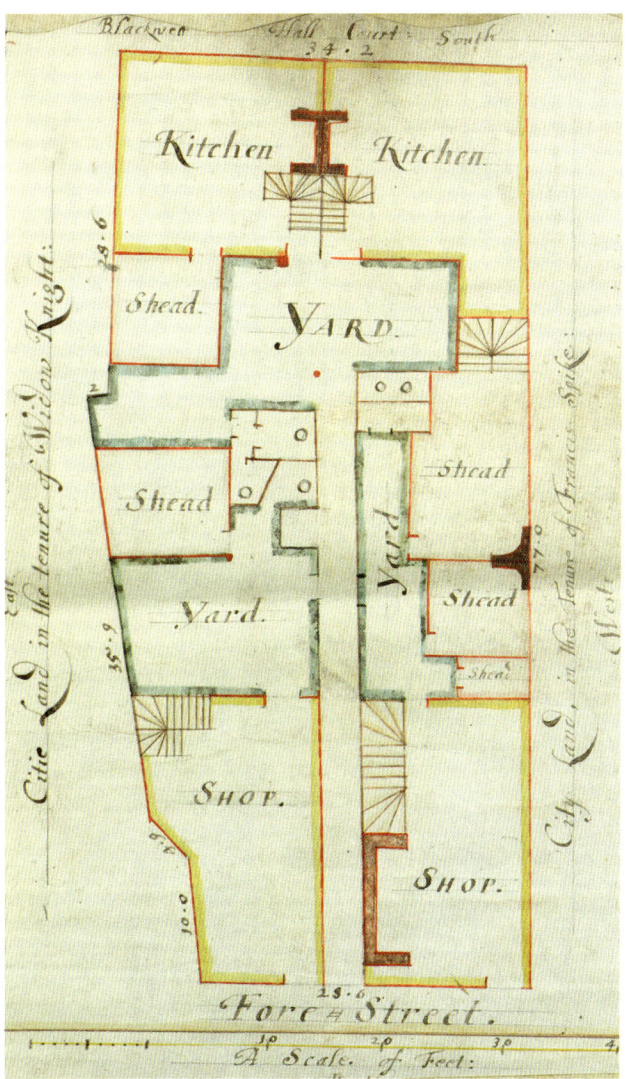

Fig. 322.   Houses in Fore Street, 1682.

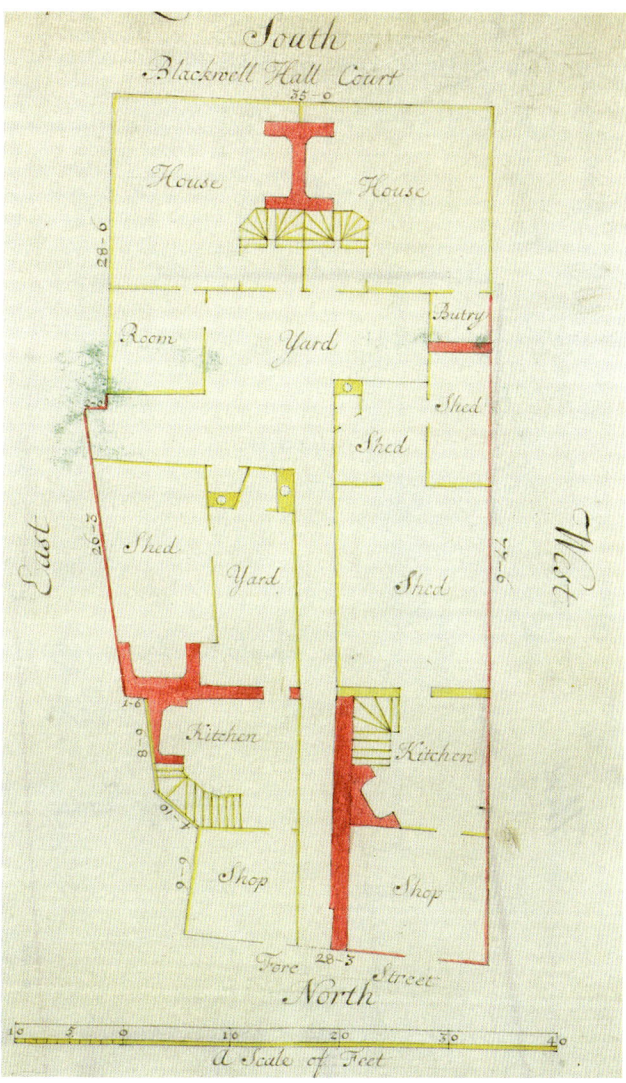

Fig. 323.   Houses in Fore Street, 1719.

These plans provide an opportunity to compare how Leybourn and Isaac Olley dealt with the same site. The property was on the south side of Fore Street a little west of Aldermanbury Postern, backing on to Blackwell Hall Court. The lease of 1682 provided for William Stanton, citizen and dyer, to rebuild the front two houses. The right-hand one then had three floors over the shop and one floor over the sheds at the back (apparently with its own staircase), together with a cellar. The other consisted of cellar, shop and three rooms above, with yard and shed at the back. The two back houses each had cellar, kitchen and two rooms over. Each house seems to have had at least one privy of its own. By 1719, when the lessee was Thomas Jackson, citizen and draper, the rebuilt front houses each had a shop and a kitchen on the ground floor, both small.[106] The left-hand one seems to have been timber-built.

Plan 173
Haberdashers' Square, 1691   FIG. 324

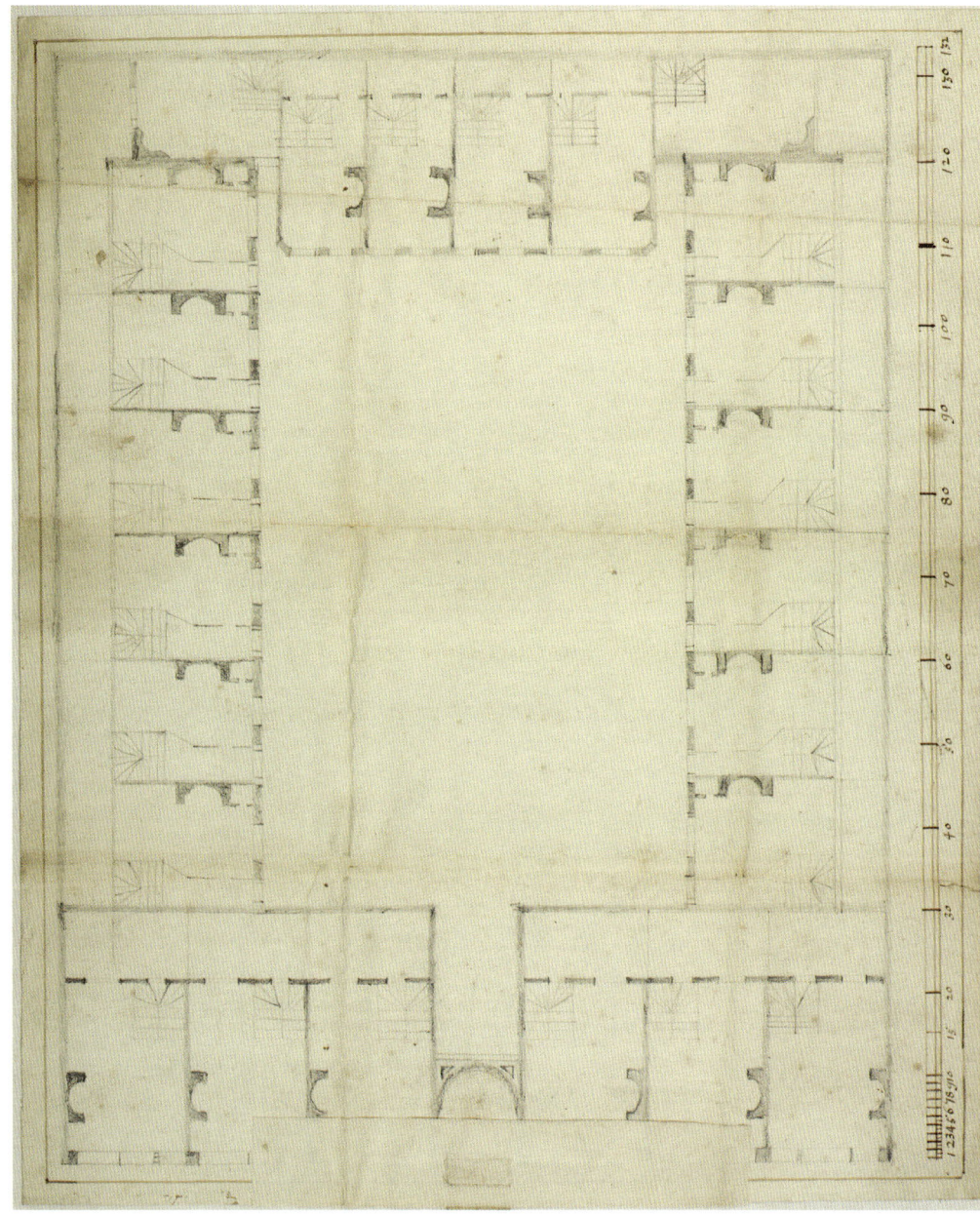

Fig. 324.
Haberdashers' Square,
1691. North is to the
right.

This plan records what was for the fringes of the City an unusually regular development.[107] The land was towards the north end of Grub Street (now Milton Street) on the west side, and was bequeathed to the Haberdashers' Company by Roger Jeston, a haberdasher of Lambeth, in 1622.[108] Until 1690 there were two alleys there, known as Paviors Court and Robin Hood Court, with houses and gardens between them (Fig. 325). In March 1690 the Company agreed with Edmund Paybody, one of its members, that he would rebuild the property. The plan shows Paybody's proposal, and was attached to the formal agreement of March 1691. It is in pencil rather than ink (except the scale), and on paper rather than vellum.

Paybody's plan was for twenty-four houses around a courtyard, which was to be created by removing the houses and gardens between the two alleys. He was to build six houses by Christmas 1690 and the rest within five years. The front houses were to be second-rate houses, and therefore to have three and a half storeys; the others had two and a half storeys. House widths in the courtyard varied from eleven to fifteen and a half feet. The agreement specified that the front walls

Fig. 325. Detail from Ogilby and Morgan's map of 1676 showing Paviors Court and Robin Hood Court (b.93 and b.94). The buildings between them were removed in 1690 to form Haberdashers' Square.

were to be two bricks thick in the ground floor and one and a half bricks thick above, and that all upper rooms were to be eight foot six inches high. The four leases granted to Paybody in April 1691 (one for each side) record that he had already built the six houses on the north side, two on the east and one on the west.[109] Plans of 1757 and 1761 indicate that the northern and southern houses were built exactly as planned, but that there were minor changes to the eastern and western ones, the most important of which was that the four houses in the middle of the west side

Fig. 326. Haberdashers' Square in 1887, looking west from the entrance (watercolour by John Crowther). By that time the north side of the Square (on the right) had been rebuilt, but the houses of c.1690 remained on the south and west sides. The tall building in the background was part of the Chiswell Street brewery.

were set against the back wall rather than having small yards behind them.[110]

Strype described Haberdashers' Square in 1720 as 'very genteel, with new well built houses', whereas in 1867 it was described as 'a squalid quadrangle'. The north side was rebuilt in about 1800, and the front houses facing Milton Street under a building lease of 1830, but those on the west and south sides were still standing in the 1880s (Fig. 326).[111]

Plans 174-75
Barnham Street, Southwark, 1699
John Hobbs
FIGS 327-28

Back-to-backs were not common in the London area, but they certainly existed, sometimes, as here, where plots were large enough for different layouts to have been possible. These ones were on land known as Oatmeal Yard and Glue Yard, north of Crucifix Lane. In 1698 Robert Burt, citizen and cordwainer of London but by trade a carpenter of St Olave, Southwark, agreed with Christ's Hospital that he would develop four plots according to the 'plat or designe' he provided (which has not survived). Two of the plots are shown here; north of them was another containing four houses and a wheelwright's yard, and on the opposite side of Barnham Street was one containing three houses. Burt was to construct a 'passage' twenty feet wide, marked on the plans as Barnham Street, extending the existing Dog and Bear Alley southwards to Crucifix Lane. Once Burt had built enough houses to secure the ground rent (£20 a year), he was to have four leases lasting fifty-one years, and these were granted in 1699.[112] The lease plans must largely show the pre-existing houses together with some new ones built by Burt. The notes in pencil saying '5 houses built' (on the large yard by Barnham Street) and 'Liberty to be taken down' (written against the back-to-backs opposite that yard) probably relate to Burt's activities. The back-to-backs were of varying sizes, from sixteen by twelve feet to nineteen by seventeen feet. Who used the stables is unknown. The attribution of the plans to John Hobbs is based on similarity in style and writing to the Tothill Street plan (Plan 147) and the fact that he was the only surveyor recorded drawing plans for Christ's Hospital in this period. The premises were redeveloped again in about 1810.[113] Barnham Street still exists, but the site is now under the railway tracks leading into London Bridge Station.

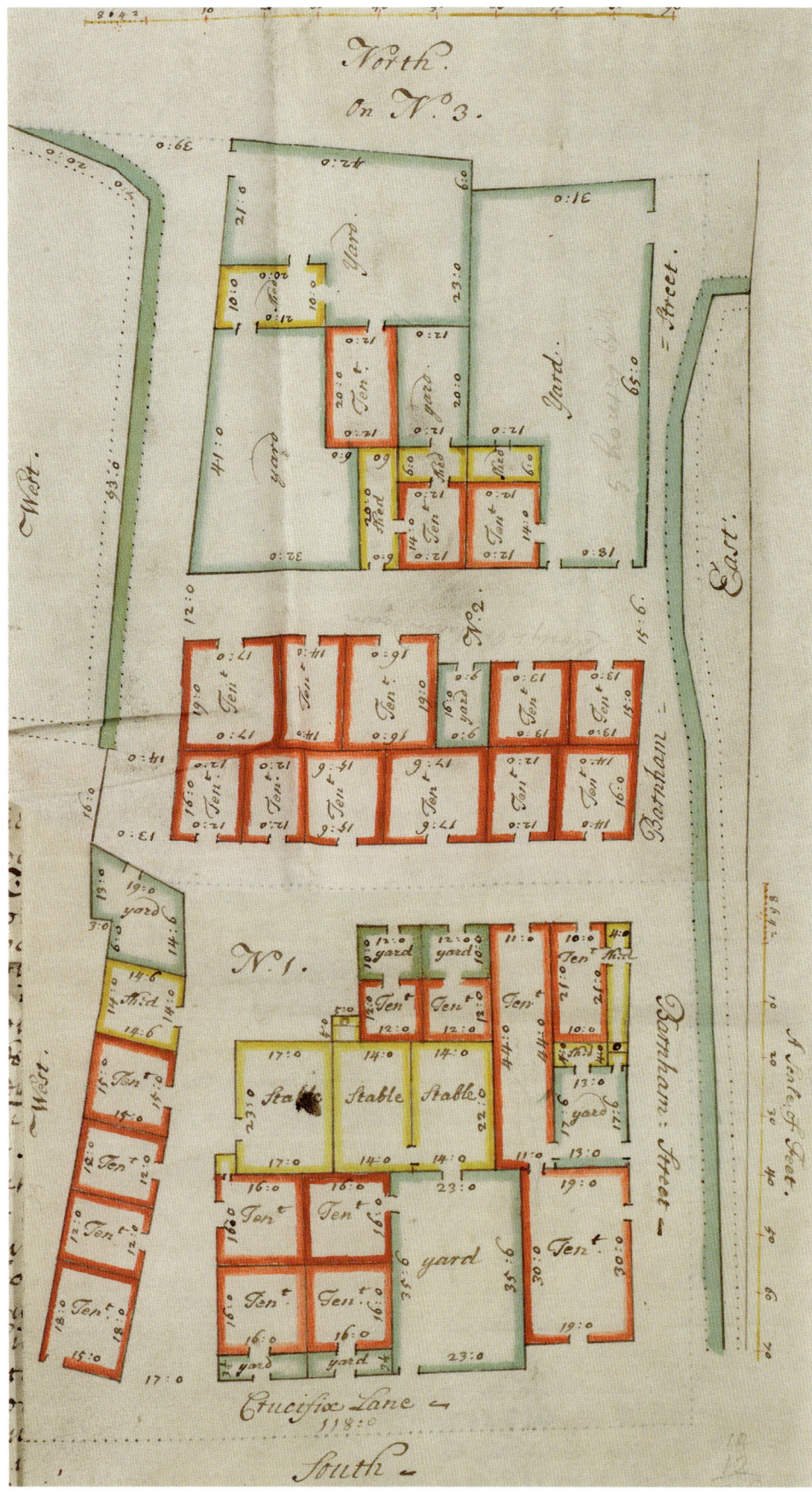

Fig. 327-28. Property in Barnham Street, Southwark, 1699 (assembled digitally from two separate lease plans).

Plan 176
Rose Alley, 1700
John Olley FIG. 329

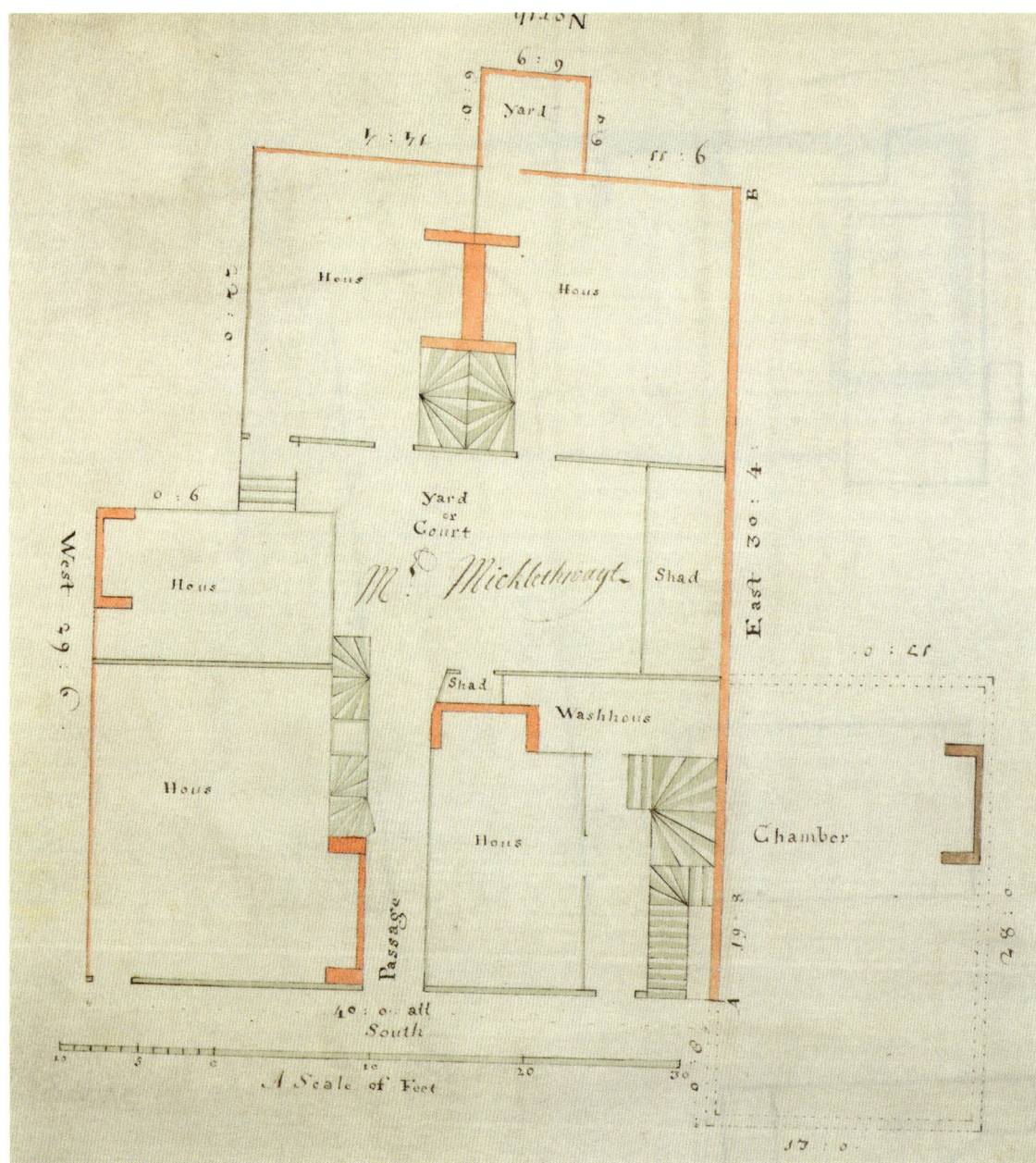

Fig. 329. Houses off Rose Alley, 1700. North is at the top.

This property, with five timber houses, belonged to the City. It was just north of the churchyard of St Katherine Cree, on the north side of Rose Alley, off Creechurch Lane. The site had already been built up by the 1580s: the plan drawn then of the former Holy Trinity Aldgate shows an area labelled 'Tenyments' west of the former nave and adjoining that churchyard (Plan 9). All five houses were of one-room plan, and the placing of the staircases suggests that some of the upper storeys may have been in separate occupation, as they were in 1718. The lease included a large room at first-floor level to the east, indicated by dotted lines and probably accessed by the staircase at the front (on Plan 9 the room's location was approximately in the angle between the porch of the priory church and the western end of the nave wall). When the existing lessee failed to offer enough for a new lease in 1699 the City turned to the occupants. One of them, Thomas Micklethwait, citizen and merchant taylor, offered £7 and no fine, but because this was too little '& because hee is in a low condicon', the City rejected his proposal. Eventually Micklethwait was persuaded to pay £12 a year and obtained a lease. When it was to be renewed in 1718, his wife stated that it would not suit his 'conveniency' to pay a fine or give security for the rent; a rent of £15 a year was agreed. The houses were then 'all lett to inmates', at £43.12s.0d per year. The plan of 1718 shows little change since 1700, though the shed on the east side had been replaced by a yard and two privies.[114] Mitre Street was driven through the site in the early nineteenth century.

Plan 177
Dolphin Court, Ratcliff, 1703
John Olley   Fig. 330

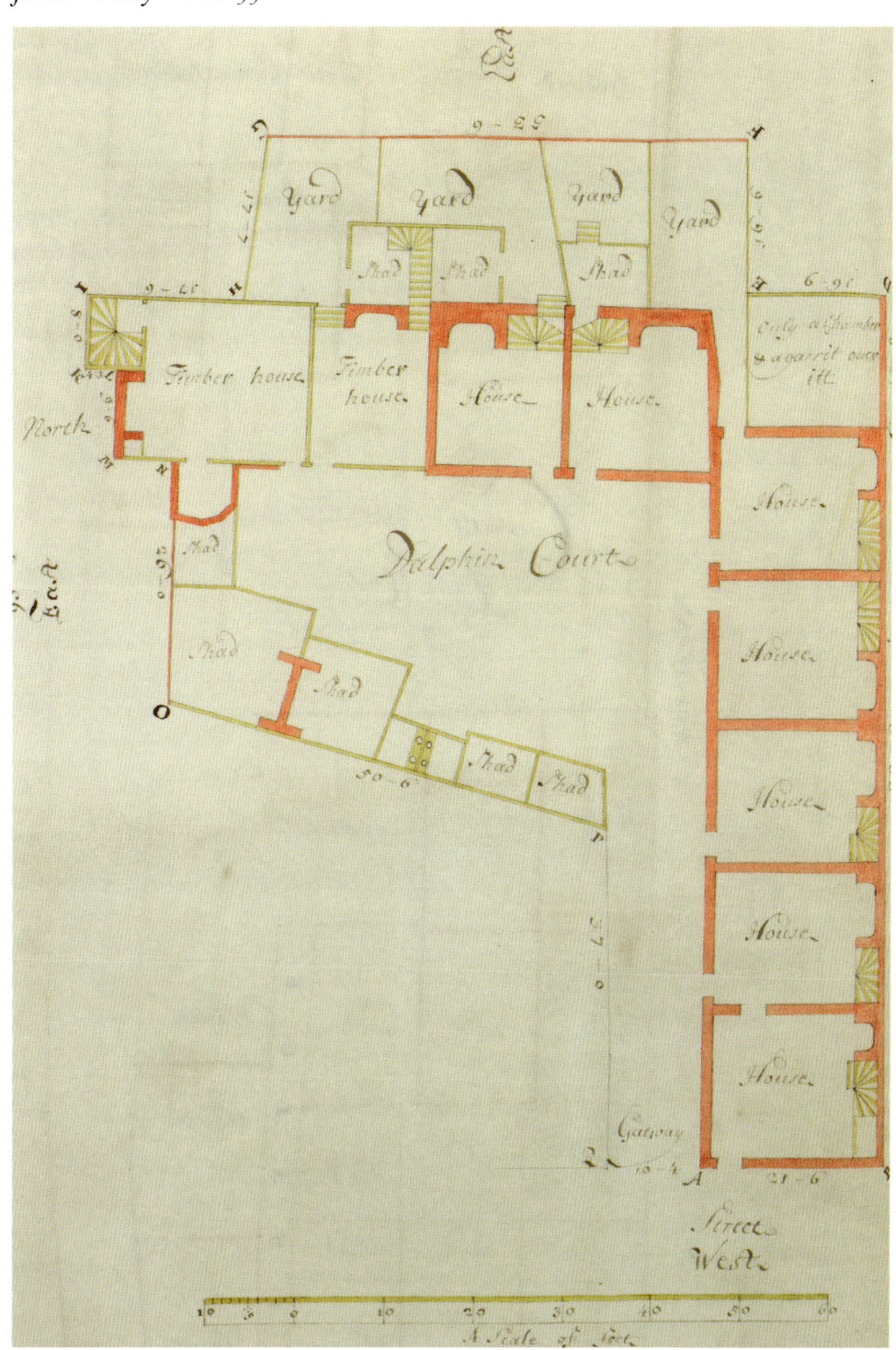

Fig. 330. Dolphin Court, Ratcliff, 1703.

Dolphin Court was on the east side of what is now Butcher Row, near its junction with the present Cable Street, and provides an example of small houses in a riverside settlement.[115] In 1703 it had seven brick houses and two timber ones, all of one-room plan, except that the one in the south-east corner also had a chamber next to it with a garret over. The two nearest the street had an interconnecting door. The houses were mostly around sixteen feet wide and twenty feet deep. They probably had two and a half storeys, as that was typical for small East End houses at this time.[116] There were enough sheds for each house to have one, and there were four privies in common.

The site had been purchased by the City in 1616.[117] In 1640, Colonel Francis Zacharie, a brewer in Limehouse,[118] was granted a sixty-year lease of Dolphin Court, paying £16 a year, on condition that he rebuild the tenements there in accordance with the King's proclamations, and therefore of brick, within six years. The brick houses therefore dated from the 1640s, though the survival of two timber ones indicates that Zacharie never quite finished. His lease was transferred in 1644 to Richard Rookes, later described as a gentleman, and was renewed so as to continue until 1705. By 1703 it was held by Elizabeth Holland, widow, of Ratcliff, who sought a new lease, and argued that the rent of £16 a year was too high. The rack rents payable to her were £36, from which the City's rent and 'water money' totalling £20 had to be deducted, leaving only £16, which she said was too little, 'when too often her overplus of rent will not defray her charges of repairs emtying vaults los of tenants and the great charge of repairing a common sewer, and all inhabited by seafaring men which sometimes do not pay their rent in three years and sometimes never pay'. The City successfully insisted on the £16.[119] Dolphin Court is marked on Rocque's map of the 1740s, but had gone by the time of Horwood's map. Anything from 1703 which survived until 1794 would have been destroyed by the major fire in Ratcliff in that year.[120]

Plan 178
Great Swordbearers Alley, Finsbury, 1712
John or Isaac Olley Fig. 331

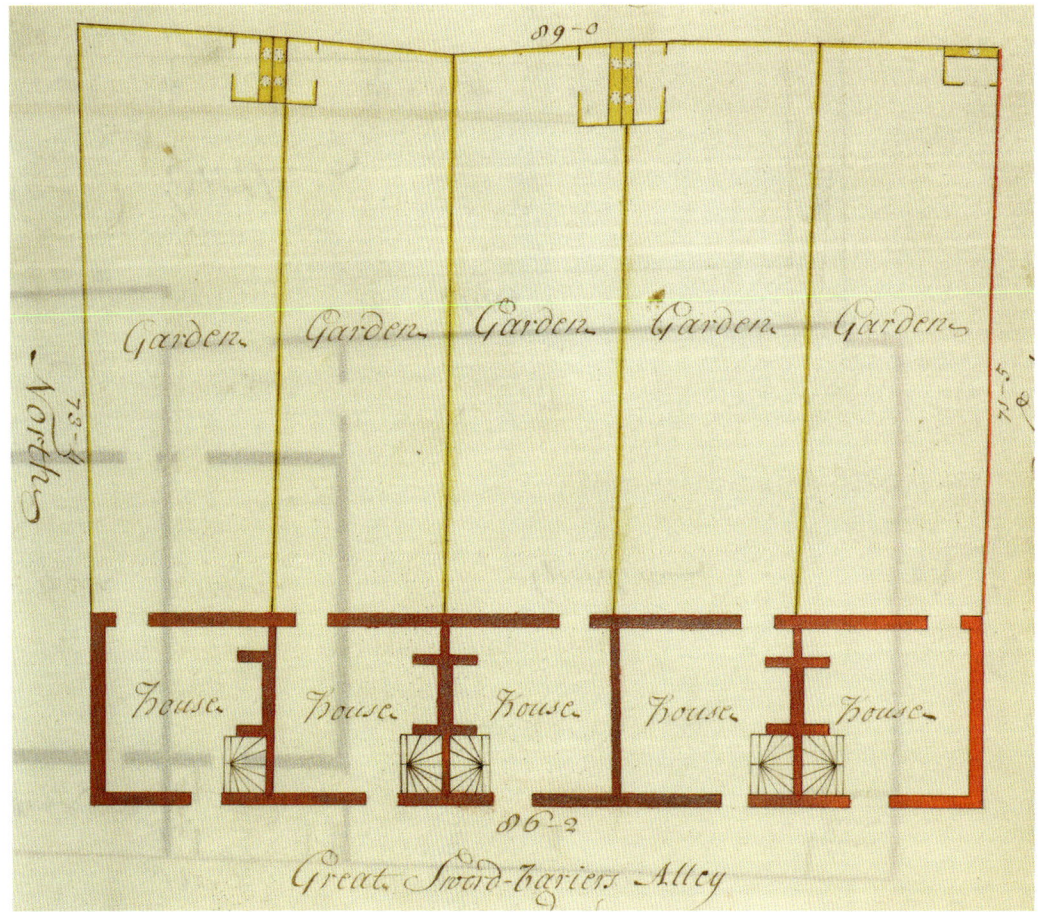

Fig. 331. Houses in Great Swordbearers Alley, Finsbury, 1712.

The City leased this land in 1642 to William Dickenson, citizen and girdler, for fifty-one years. The length of the term suggests that it was a building lease and that the five brick houses were built about that time. It was probably the property consisting of an old tenement and gardens which was leased to John Wright in 1641 on condition that he rebuild the tenement, and which was conveyed at Wright's request to Dickenson the following year. New twenty-one year leases were granted in 1691 to William Boughey, citizen and baker, in 1712 to John Shaler, citizen and merchant taylor, who lost it five years later having failed to pay any rent, and in 1717 to William Westbrook, citizen and goldsmith. Shaler claimed that 'the tenants are very uncertain and what are lett are lett to tenants at will'.[121] The houses seem to be those shown on Ogilby and Morgan's map with gardens half-way along the Alley. The Alley is now called Lamb's Passage.

Plan 179
Thames Street, 1714
Isaac Olley
Fig. 332

These four post-Fire houses were on the south side of Thames Street west of the passage to Broken Wharf. Three of them were of one-room plan and one was an alehouse. They were leased in 1714 to James Browne, citizen and tyler and bricklayer.[122]

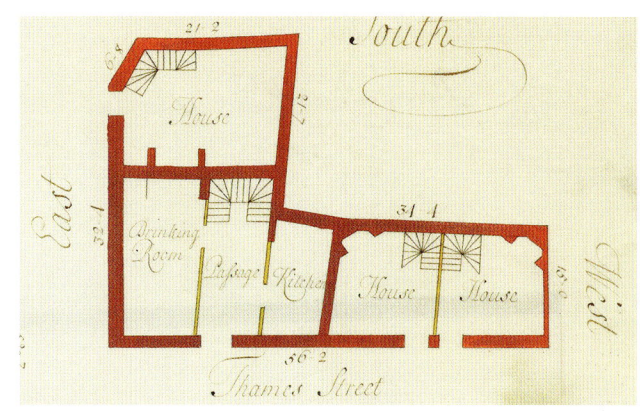

Fig. 332. Houses in Thames Street, 1714.

Plan 180
Shoemakers' Row, 1714
Isaac Olley
Fig. 333

These largely brick houses were in, and partly over, the passage between Shoemakers' Row and the church of St James, Duke's Place, and backed onto the latter's churchyard. Though basically of one-room plan, they had butteries and in one case a washhouse as well as kitchens on the ground floor, and were of unusual depth—just over thirty-one feet. The lease describes them as three houses, and the staircase at the front of the right-hand house evidently led to a separate dwelling. All three were leased in 1714 to Mary Wych, a widow.[123]

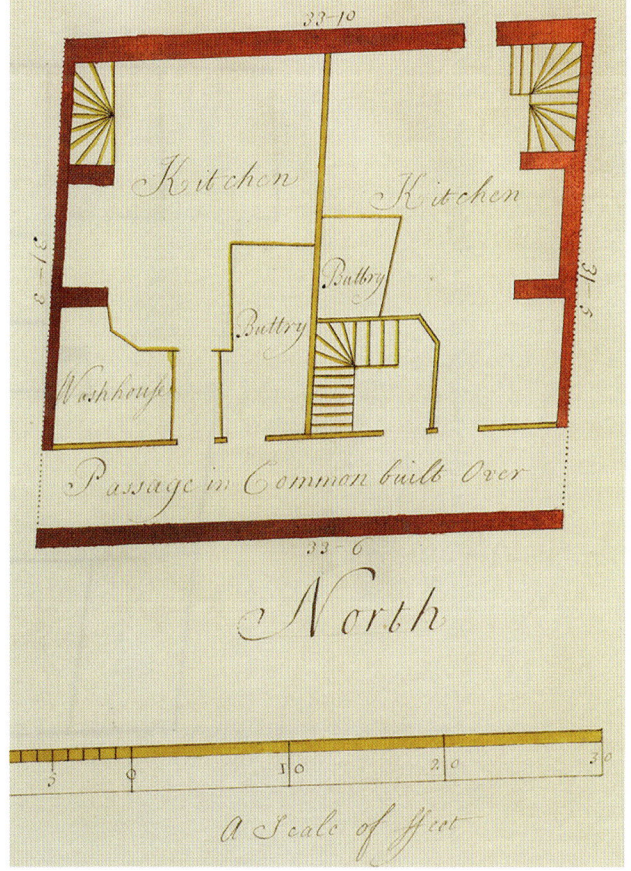

Fig. 333. Houses in Shoemakers' Row, 1714.

Plan 181
Fore Street, 1715
Isaac Olley

Fig. 334

This house was in the short street outside Cripplegate later known as Cripplegate Buildings but apparently regarded in 1715 as part of Fore Street.[124] It was just eight feet from front to back. The City leased it in 1715 to Gamaliel Lewing, citizen and carpenter.[125] The words 'Light purchas'd' indicate that the right to open a window or windows to the east had been bought, making it possible to light the staircase.

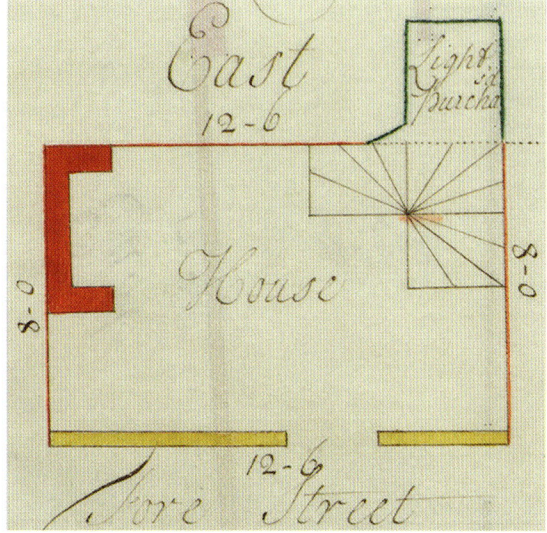

Fig. 334. A house in Fore Street, 1715.

Plan 182
Broad Court, Duke's Place, 1715
Isaac Olley

Fig. 335

These two timber houses were on the west side of Broad Court, and were about fifteen by twenty-one feet. They were leased in 1715 to John Hardy, citizen and pewterer, who was occupying one of them.[126]

Fig. 335. Houses in Broad Court, Duke's Place, 1715.

Plan 183
Fore Street, 1718
Isaac Olley

Fig. 336

These three houses, two of them brick-built, were on the south side of Fore Street backing onto the City's Green Yard, about half-way between Moorgate and Moor Lane (strictly in the part of the street known as the Postern). Two of them were unusually large. One of these had ground at the back which had been taken out of the Green Yard by Samuel Cox, distiller, and had been used as a stable and then a stillhouse. The property was leased in 1718 to Cox.[127]

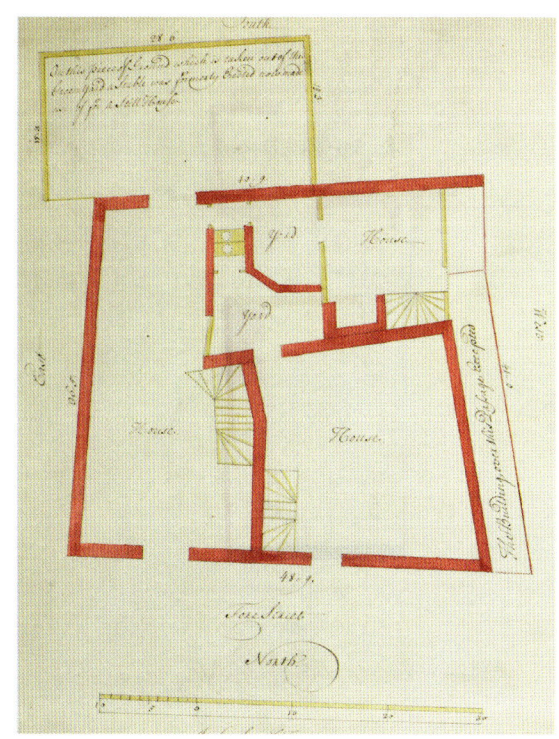

Fig. 336. Houses in Fore Street, 1718.

Plan 184
Lime Street, 1719
Isaac Olley

FIG. 337

These two houses, partly brick and partly timber, were west of the passage from Leadenhall Market to Lime Street. They were leased in 1719 to William Lawrence, citizen and joiner.[128]

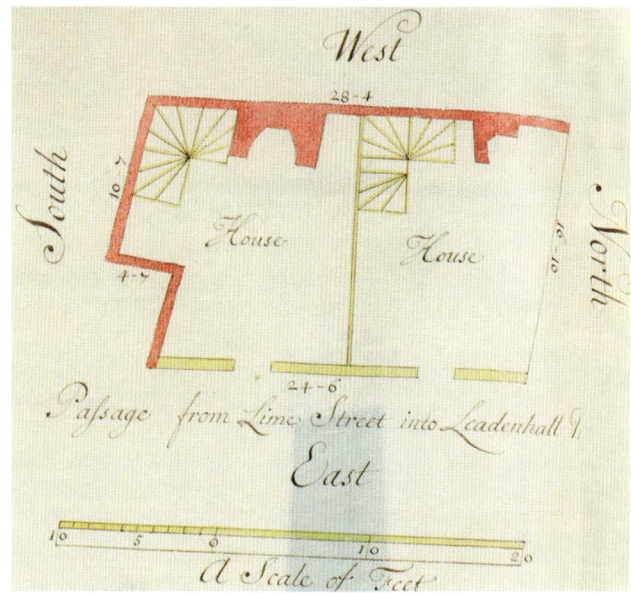

Fig. 337. Houses in Lime Street, 1719.

Plan 185
Camomile Street, 1719
Isaac Olley

FIG. 338

Five of these six houses built against the inner side of London Wall in Camomile Street were of one-room plan. They were evidently pre-Fire houses, constructed of timber, apart from the brick walls to east and west, the fireplaces and of course London Wall at their back. Three of the one-room plan houses had staircases which could be entered from the street without passing through the ground-floor room, and the position of one of them suggests that the relationship of the different floors was not always straightforward. The City leased the six houses to Matthew Woodward, cornchandler, in 1719, on condition that he spend £700 rebuilding them. Woodward had asked to be allowed to take down the Wall, as his father had done in the same street, and to have lights into Flying Horse Yard on the other side of the Wall, but the lease forbade him to make any doorways through the Wall and retained the right to block the light to any windows made at the back of the premises, indicating the City's determination to protect its property rights north of the Wall.[129]

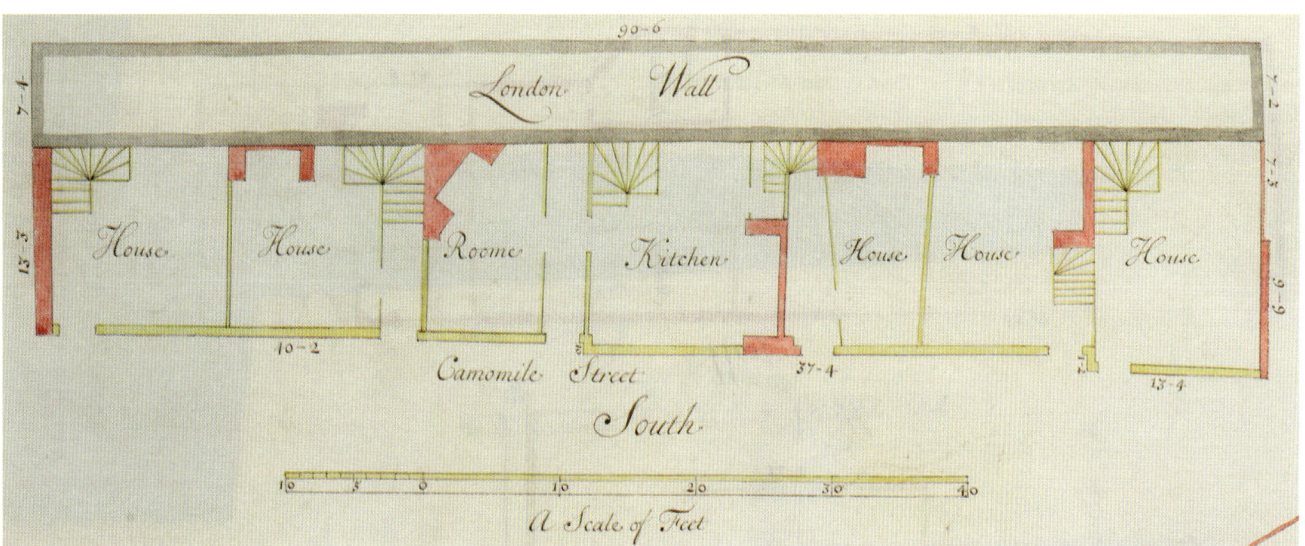

Fig. 338. Houses in Camomile Street, 1719.

ALMSHOUSES

The plans show two different types of almshouse: one or one and a half storey almshouses around a courtyard, the type most familiar today (Plans 186, 188), and what might be called stacked almshouses, with up to four storeys separately occupied, usually on cramped sites (Plans 27, 36, 72, 187).[130] In the eighteenth century almshouses began to be moved out of the central parts of the City to places where land was less valuable.

Plan 186
The Skinners' Almshouses, Mile End, *c.*1695
Mr Biggs
Fig. 339

In 1682 the Skinners' Company considered replacing its existing almshouse at St Helen's with a new one outside the City.[131] It approved a 'modell or scheme' for the new building, 'haveing well weighed the uniformity, proporcon and design of the same', and in early 1683 bought land at Mile End Green for the purpose. By 1684, apparently because of financial problems, it was seeking to sell the land again. Then, in 1685, Lewis Newberry, citizen and skinner, bequeathed most of his estate to build and endow small houses for six poor widows whose husbands had been free of the Skinners' Company. His executor agreed to buy the land at Mile End Green for this purpose. Building was in progress in 1687, and the chapel was being built in 1691, by which time the almshouses were already occupied. The building cost £1,084, and £1,851 left from Newberry's estate provided the endowment.

Despite Newberry's will, there were always twelve places rather than six, and the twelve single-storey, single-room dwellings lined two sides of a narrow court (Fig. 340). At the far end was a three-storey building, with a warehouse or laundry in the basement, a room above used as the chapel, and above that the original chapel, which had been found inconvenient because of the steep and narrow stairs. Behind it was a garden. The Skinners' Mile End and St Helen's almshouses were replaced in 1891-95 by a single larger building at Palmers Green, now known as Pellipar Close.[132]

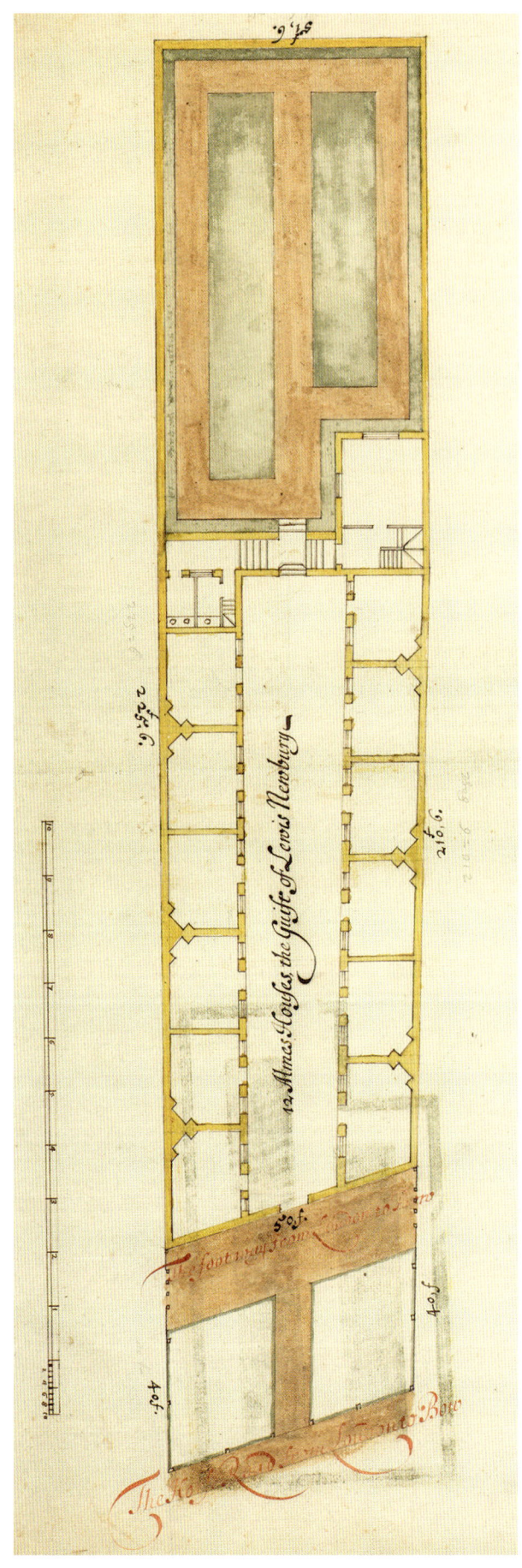

Fig. 339. The Skinners' Almshouses, Mile End, *c.*1695. North is at the top.

Fig. 340. The Skinners' Almshouses, 1883 (watercolour by John Crowther).

Plan 187
Lawrence Camp's almshouses, Wormwood Street, 1697
John Olley
Fig. 341

These almshouses were provided by Lawrence Camp, citizen and draper, shortly before 1611, when they were described as 'latelie erected'. Camp left an annuity of £20 from his property in the parish of St Andrew Undershaft for various charitable purposes, of which £10.8s.0d was to be used to pay 2s.8d to each of the six men or women in the almshouses every fourth Saturday. The almshouses were run by the parish of Allhallows London Wall, which was evidently responsible for repairs. Camp's heirs were entitled to nominate a person or couple to one of the almshouse places, though in that case they had to pay the maintenance themselves.[133]

The almshouses were of brick, like Camp's other almshouses at Barnet (Fig. 342), and comprised six houses, each with lower and upper room, together with a vault containing privies and a shop at the east end. The downstairs rooms were about eight feet wide and fourteen feet deep, and the upstairs ones were about two feet wider. They were at some stage divided into separate upper and lower almshouses, and in about 1672 they contained ten women (only one having two rooms) and one man. Only six of the occupants received Camp's monthly allowance, and even these needed additional help from the parish. In 1710 the parish decided that two women should not have more than one room between them unless they had children.[134]

The almshouses were on land leased from the City, and the annuity was to cease if the lease expired without being renewed for a further forty-one years at the old rent. The renewal in 1697 was probably the second, and cost the parish £50 as a fine and a further £16.9s.0d in fees and costs, including £1.10s.0d to John Olley for drawing the plan. In 1736, Allhallows vestry noted that the lease was due for renewal again and decided not to renew it. At the same meeting they agreed to set up a parish workhouse, and they shortly afterwards leased a house in Hoxton for that purpose.[135] The almshouses were re-let by the City to an individual, without any reference to rebuilding, and were presumably let out as houses. By 1820 no-one alive could remember them. They are shown on Leybourn's plan of London Wall in 1676, which places them at 33 Wormwood Street (now part of Broad Street House), slightly east of what is now the northern corner of Wormwood Street and Old Broad Street.[136]

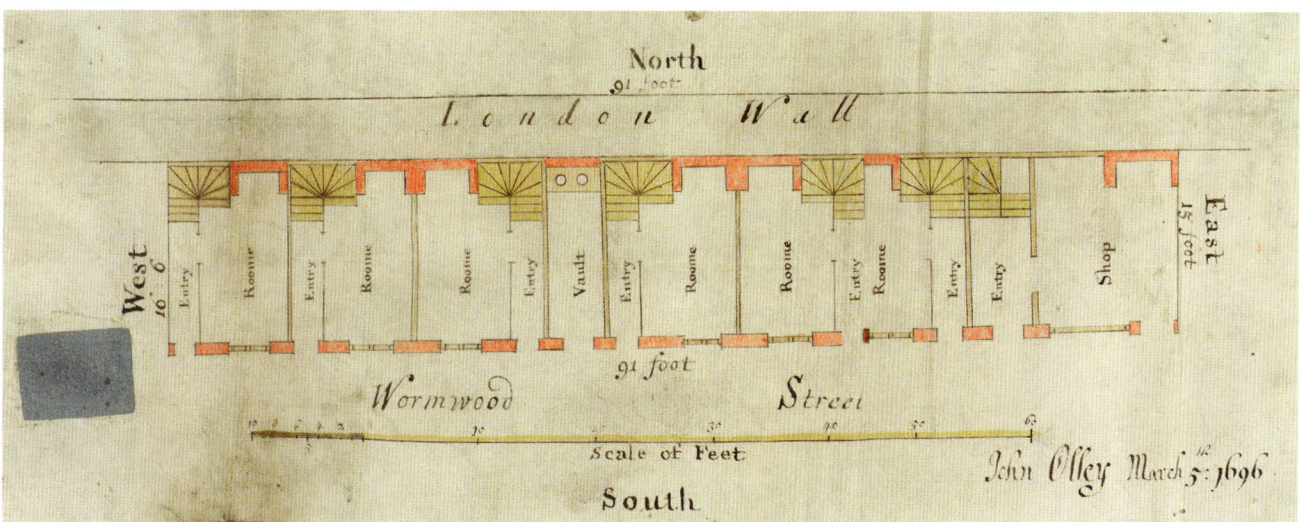

Fig. 341. Lawrence Camp's almshouses, Wormwood Street, 1697.

Fig. 342. Lawrence Camp's almshouses at Friern Barnet. The Wormwood Street almshouses were probably similar, though they apparently had only lower and upper rooms without garrets.

Plan 188
Emanuel Hospital, Buckingham Gate, c.1698
John Olley   Fig. 343

Emanuel Hospital was founded under the will of Anne, Lady Dacre, of 1595.[137] It was to house twenty poor men and women and twenty poor children, who were to be from Westminster, Chelsea or Hayes, places with which the Dacres were connected. To establish and maintain it she provided £300 and the revenues from Brandesburton manor in Yorkshire, which was to be let for 100 years for £100 a year. A generous three or

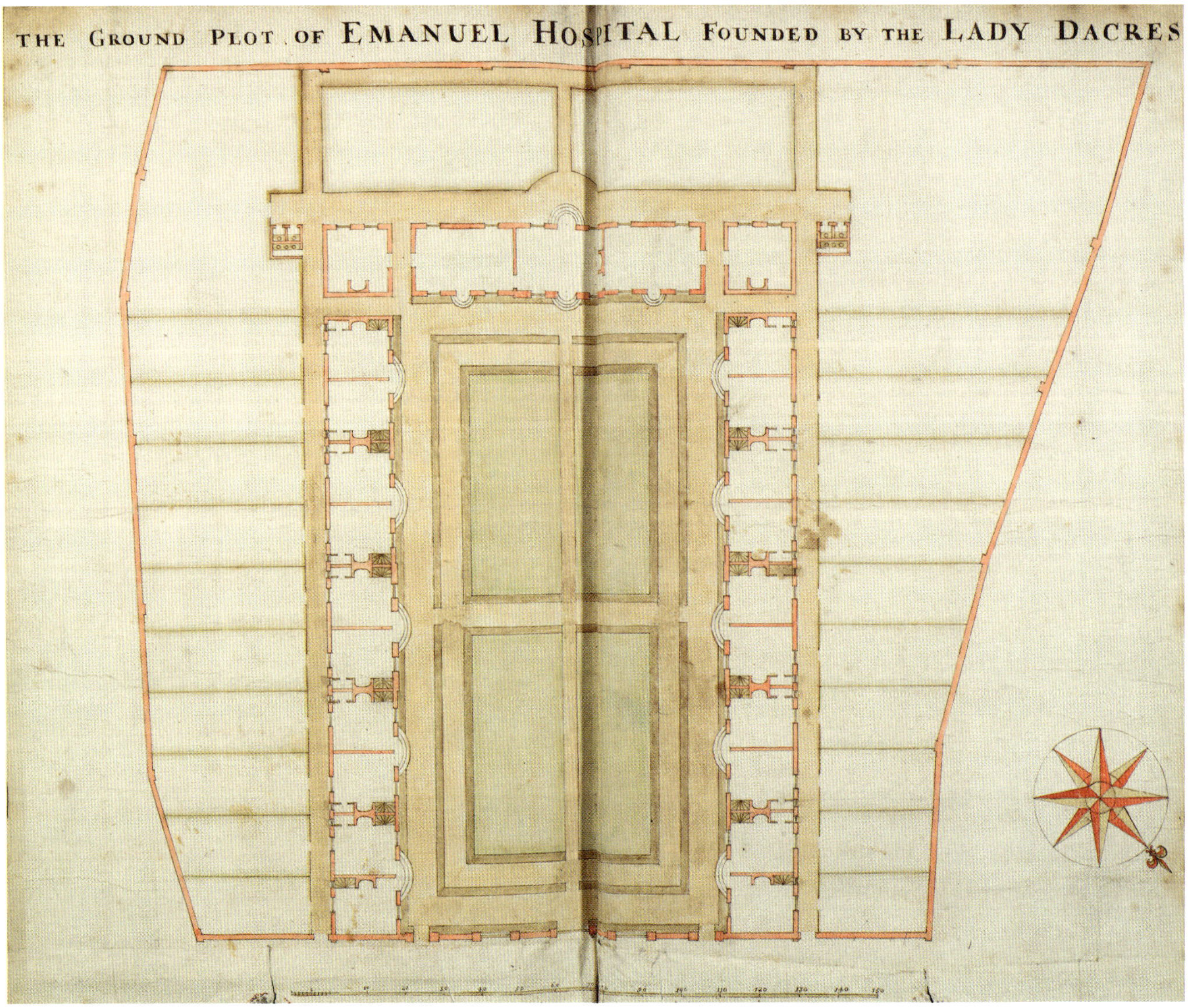

Fig. 343. Emanuel Hospital, c.1698.

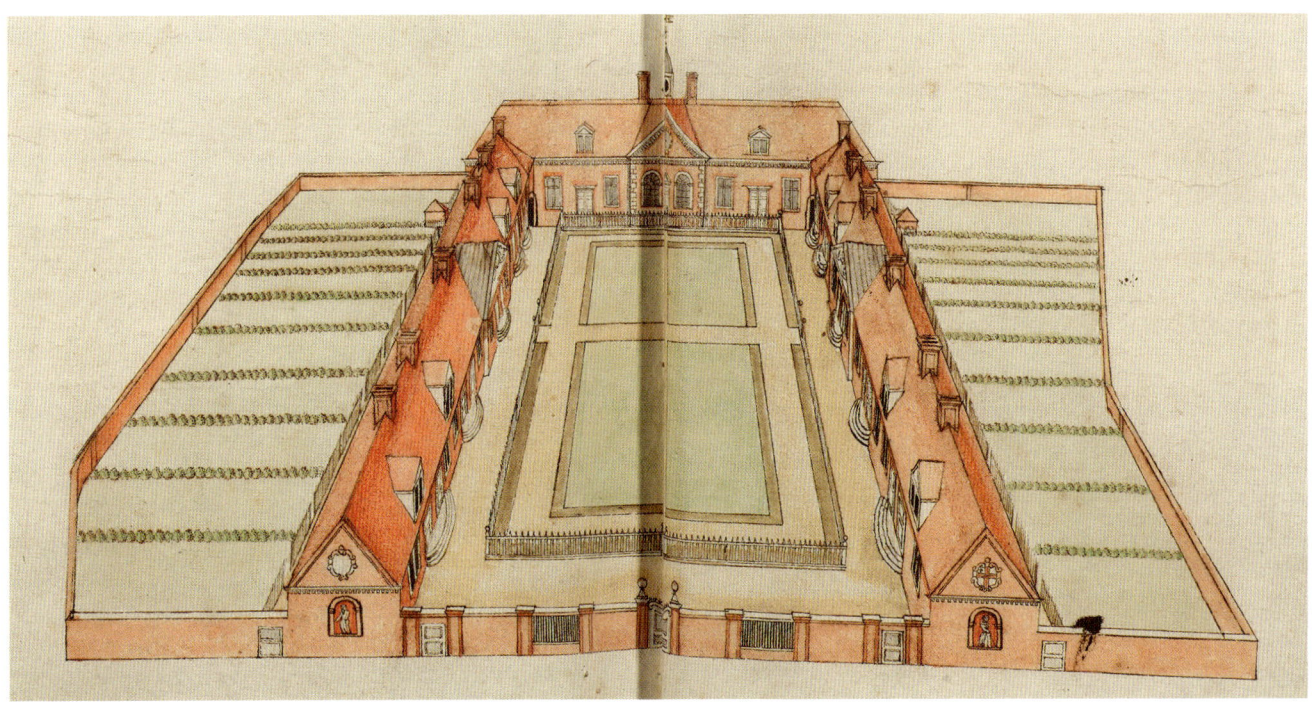

Figs 344-45. Drawings of the planned Emanuel Hospital by John Olley, c.1698.

Fig. 346. Emanuel Hospital in 1850 (watercolour by T.H. Shepherd).

four acre site was secured on the west side of what is now Buckingham Gate, where St James's Court now stands. By 1602 the Hospital had been built, consisting of twenty brick almshouses and a chapel around four sides of a courtyard.[138] Few poor children were accommodated, and the aim seems to have been to train them in a craft rather than to provide a school. Married couples were allowed, though only the husband or wife actually admitted received a pension. The Hospital was to be administered by the City of London after the last of the executors of Lady Dacre's will had died, which happened in 1623. Day-to-day management was by a Warden and Sub-Warden, elected from among the almsfolk.

Brandesburton was re-let in 1695 for £360 a year instead of £100, and this provided the funds for rebuilding. John Olley, as the City's Clerk of the Works, drew the plans and elevations reproduced here (Figs 343-45), probably in 1698, and supervised the work; he was paid for 'his severall draughts, surveying and attendance'. In 1701 he certified that the Hospital had been rebuilt in accordance with his draught, at a cost of £1,776. The twenty brick houses, of one and a half storeys, formed two sides of the courtyard, and the chapel and two other rooms formed the third; the fourth was open (Fig. 346).

NEW RESIDENTIAL DEVELOPMENTS

Much of the West End was developed in the period covered here, together with other wholly residential streets, such as those which replaced the Strand mansions. The process did not generate many detailed plans of buildings. A plan showing the outline of plots might be needed at the start, or to help in collecting rents, but it was rarely thought worthwhile to include details of the buildings. Only limited attempts were made to regulate the design of houses in this period, and, once built, the houses were usually of regular shapes and clearly distinct from their neighbours, without the complications which sometimes caused plans to be drawn elsewhere. The plans in this section are therefore exceptional, and mostly reflect the desire of particular landlords to control what their builders constructed. Most of them show houses of two-room plan, but with relatively generous dimensions. Like other building plans, none of them indicates the uses of rooms. Until at least the 1720s the best rooms were usually on the ground floor.[139]

Plans 189-91
Salisbury Street, c.1672, and Cecil Street, c.1693
FIGS 347, 349, 350

The first of these plans (Fig. 347) is labelled 'Plotts of Salisbury house ground & ye proposed changes'. 'The streatte outt of ye Strand' is bounded by 'the Chinge' on one side, and there is also 'The streatt outt of ye Derham Yarde'. It therefore shows the proposed Salisbury Street, between Durham Yard to the west and the Middle Exchange to the east.[140] The site had been occupied by Little Salisbury House, built in 1611-13 by Sir Robert Cecil, first Earl of Salisbury. By 1670 the Cecils were thinking about redeveloping the site, and the following year the King gave the third Earl his approval, 'so he is full of designs, & we are advising the best way to advantage ourselves'. The plan seems to have been one result of that process, as it differed from what was actually built. When the patent permitting building was granted in 1673, the plan attached to it showed only an extension of the Middle Exchange and a single new street between the Strand and the Thames, without the houses facing the river either side of the Exchange, and this is what is shown on Morgan's map of 1682 (Fig. 348).[141]

A school was eventually added in 1736, behind the chapel. It became a boys-only school in 1873, as part of a reorganisation of Westminster's charity schools, and moved in 1883 to Wandsworth, where it remains today. In 1894 the Hospital was sold and demolished, after three centuries of providing accommodation for the poor, though Lady Dacre's charity continued to provide out-payments to the poor of Westminster, Chelsea and Hayes.

The plan shows not just the plots in the proposed layout but also the buildings intended. The site was narrow, with plot depths of about thirty-nine feet on the east side (later reduced by three feet to protect the light of the Middle Exchange)[142] and only twenty-nine to thirty-two feet on the west. On the east side this allowed for small yards, whereas on the west side only every third house was to have a yard, allowing light to itself and its neighbours either side but reducing the house to one-room plan. On the other hand the upper storeys on the west side could be built over Ivy Lane at the back. The pairs of black dots evidently indicate fireplaces, and enough staircases are shown to indicate what was intended for most of the different types of house; windows are also indicated. Some of the houses facing the Thames were to have central chimney stacks, whereas elsewhere the chimneys were in side or back walls. The internal division into rooms is not shown, except in so far as it is indicated by the staircases and fireplaces.

As built there were six houses in the Strand and twenty-nine in Salisbury Street, together with a wharf at the south end.[143] The building leases and agreements of 1673-74 required that the houses in the new street be 'substantiall uniforme brick houses', mostly eighteen feet wide, in a continuous line and without jettying. They were to be of the second sort specified in the Rebuilding Act and therefore of three and a half storeys. The windows in each storey of each house were to be of

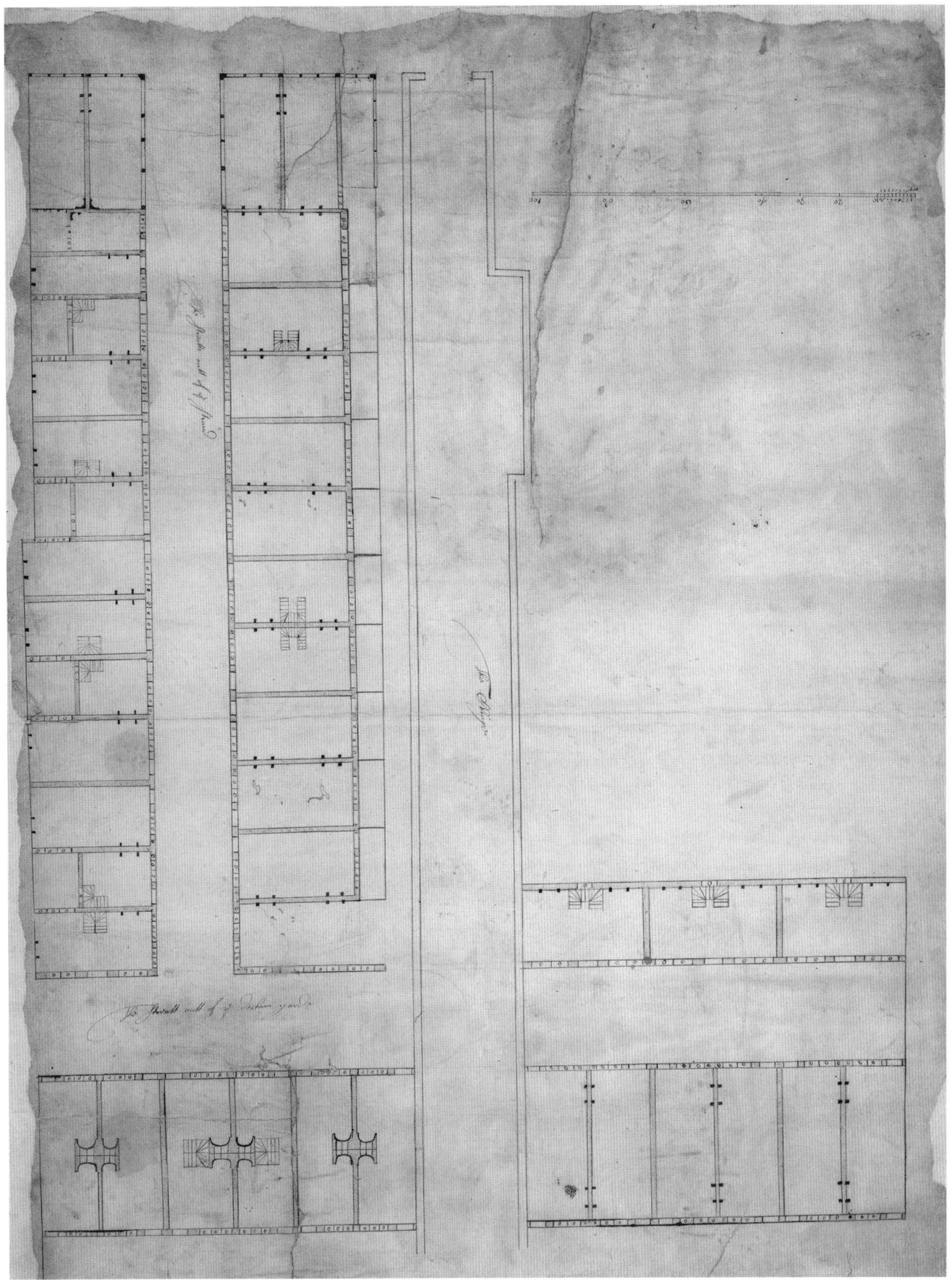

Fig. 347. Proposed houses in Salisbury Street and the Strand, c.1672. North is at the top.

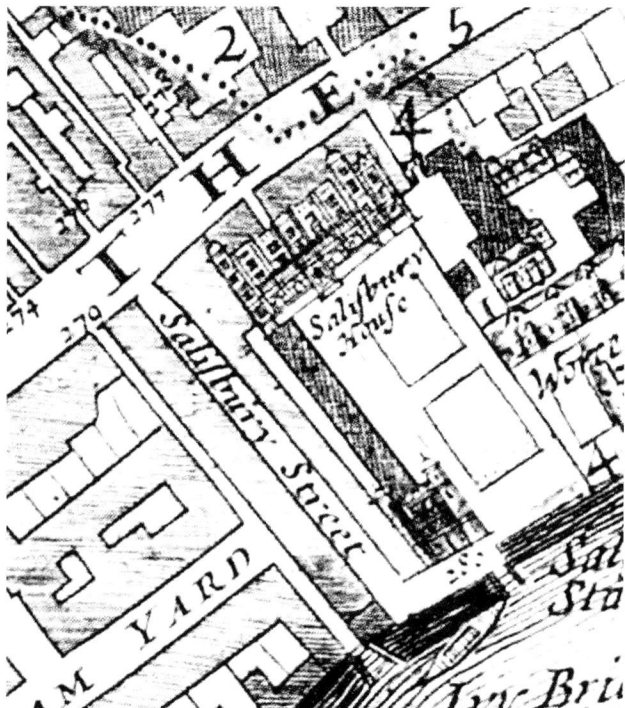

Fig. 348. Detail from Morgan's map of 1682, showing from left to right Salisbury Street, the Middle Exchange and Great Salisbury House, all between the Thames and the Strand. The Middle Exchange was in the long narrow building extending from 'Salisbury House' to the Thames, over the long gallery of Great Salisbury House.

the same height, and all the windows were to be directly over one another. Materials were specified (there must be no loam or rubbish in the bricks). Lessees were to pave their part of the street to the middle, and to share the cost of the drains. One of the building agreements required that the houses be built 'according to a moddell or draught thereof agreed uppon'. Leases were for forty years. The lessees were the usual mixture of developers and builders: Ralph Crowther, goldsmith (two houses), Robert Cordell, merchant (five houses), Robert St Hill, gentleman (three houses), Henry Angell, carpenter (sixteen houses) and others.[144] Not everyone did what they promised: Cordell built six narrower houses, about fifteen feet wide, instead of the five of eighteen feet agreed on; he also lost four feet of his frontage because the Strand houses were built first and took some of his land.[145] The building process seems otherwise to have been fairly trouble-free, but, according to Strype, the street was 'better built than inhabited': 'being too narrow, and withal the descent to the Thames too uneasy, it was not so well inhabited as was expected'.[146]

The second plan (Fig. 349) shows twenty-six houses, including their internal layouts. Twenty houses face each other across a new street, each eighteen to nineteen feet wide and of two-room plan with central stairs. There is a wharf at one end. The street and houses together are too wide to be Salisbury Street, whereas the south, east and north sides match the shape of Cecil Street on the 1871 Ordnance Survey map. The west side, however, does not extend far enough west, by fourteen or fifteen feet. There is also a less detailed plan (Fig. 350), which includes that ground to the west and corresponds closely to Cecil Street as built. Statements in a Chancery suit by John Hodge, the builder of Cecil Street, and Ebenezer Sadler, receiver-general to the fourth Earl of Salisbury, provide the likely context.

In 1693, when almost all the Strand mansions had gone and the Middle Exchange was languishing, the Earl decided to redevelop the Exchange and Great Salisbury House (Plan 13). He instructed Sadler to consult persons skilled in building 'and to gett draughts and modells of such intended buildings'. Sadler had the property viewed by Nicholas Barbon, the most prolific builder of the period, and Joseph Avis, carpenter and surveyor to the Earl, 'and shewed them the modell by which [Hodge] did afterwards undertake the said building and allsoe one other modell made by Richard Rossington ... who was allsoe a great builder'.[147] Rossington was the developer of much of the Gray's Inn Road area, Wild House in Covent Garden and Park Place, St James's Street.[148] His scheme included keeping some of the existing buildings, including part of the Exchange.[149] The likelihood is therefore that Fig. 349, showing a slightly smaller site excluding the Exchange, was Rossington's, whereas Fig. 350, from an unknown source, was the one implemented.

Barbon and Avis thought the scheme later implemented by Hodge 'the properest modell', but considered £400 a year the maximum possible ground rent. The Earl, however, insisted on £600 a year, and instructed Sadler to find 'the best chapman' willing to provide it. Sadler found a local carpenter—John Hodge of St Clement Danes parish, who was to be ruined as a result. As agreed in 1694, shortly before the Earl's death, Hodge was by March 1696 to build eight houses facing the Strand and a new street lined with houses between the Strand and the Thames, 'according to a platform annexed to ye said lease', yielding the £600.[150] Including the whole site of the Exchange

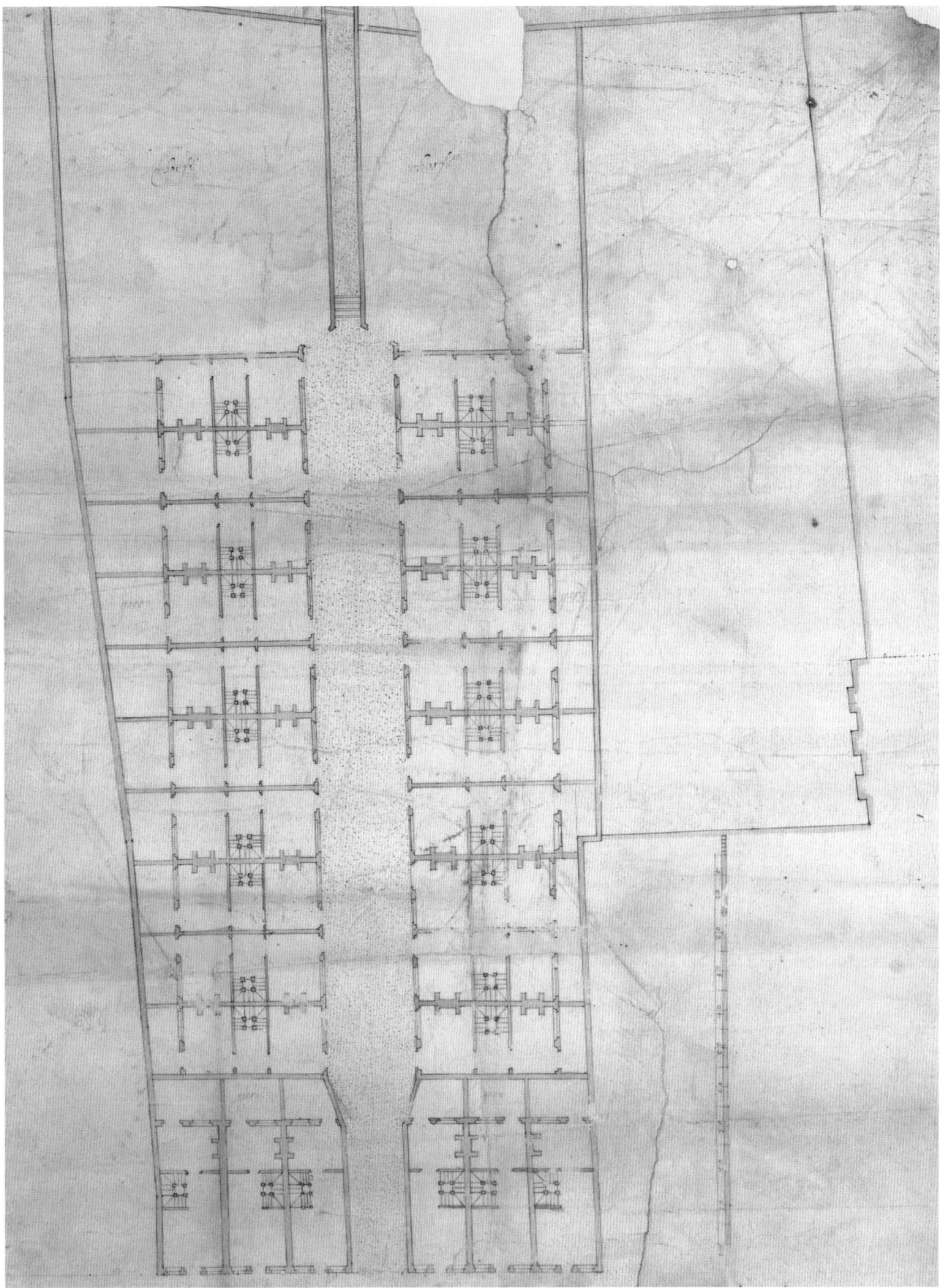

Fig. 349. Proposed houses in Cecil Street and the Strand, c.1693. North is at the bottom.

Fig. 350. Proposed houses in Cecil Street and the Strand, c.1693. North is to the left.

meant that there could be eight houses in the Strand instead of six, and that the new street could be about thirty-eight feet wide instead of twenty-three feet wide, lined by plots of similar depth and width to those on Rossington's plan. Although what was built corresponded closely to the less detailed plan (Fig. 350), the twelve houses on each side became instead thirteen houses on the east side and eleven on the west.[151]

Hodge was soon in difficulties, exacerbated by war with France, which pushed up the cost of building materials, and by the recoinage of 1696, which made money scarce. Sadler referred to 'the greate ground rent and the high taxes and scarcity of mony frighting all builders from joyneing with him or building under him', as well as the great cost of building, 'most of it being two storeys under ground', which seems to be a reference to the embanking of the street near the Thames, visible in Fig. 351. Leases of eight houses (five of them in the Strand) were granted in February-May 1696, and by selling or mortgaging these Hodge raised the funds to complete the eight houses and three more and to construct the foundations and first storeys of another nine. Then his money ran out again and Sadler had to lend him funds to continue. By June 1698, seventeen more leases had been granted to Hodge, and were either assigned to building craftsmen in return for work done on the houses or mortgaged to Sadler. Also, in 1697 the son of Hodge's timber merchant, who had guaranteed that Hodge would complete the scheme, was prevailed on to build seven of the houses. By 1700 the development seems to have been largely completed, but Hodge owed the Earl £5,479, and Hodge and Sadler estimated the loss at £100 per house. The Earl had achieved £613.18s.0d in ground rents, but presumably never recovered most of the money lent. Hodge may have been the carpenter who later built in Tothill and Carteret Streets (Plan 147). Strype described Cecil Street in 1720 as 'having very good houses fit for persons of repute; and will be better ordered than Salisbury Street was'.[152]

Salisbury Street was rebuilt in 1765-69. Both streets disappeared after the Cecils sold them in 1888. Their site is now occupied by Shell-Mex House.[153]

Fig. 351. Detail from the Bucks' panorama of 1749. 23 is Ivy Bridge; 24 is Salisbury Stairs. The narrowness of Salisbury Street is clear, as is the way the river end of Cecil Street has been built up to reduce the gradient. The large riverside house between the two streets was a later addition occupying a former wharf.

Fig. 352. A glimpse of houses built by Hodge on the east side of Cecil Street, drawn when one of the Strand houses had been demolished, 1857 (detail from a watercolour by John Wykeham Archer).

Plans 192-95
Arlington Street, 1682 and 1687
FIGS 353-56

Until 1682 St James's Park, or that part of it now called Green Park, still extended as far as the northern part of St James's Street. In 1682 Charles II granted to Henry Bennet, Earl of Arlington, a large block of park land bounded on the north by Piccadilly, on the east by St James's Street, on the south by new buildings in what is now Park Place and on the west by the park, together with permission to build on it (Fig. 357). Arlington immediately sold the land for £10,000 to Johnshall Crosse and William Pym, both described as gentlemen of Clerkenwell, who proceeded rapidly to develop it.[154] Pym had previously been involved in financing the development of Soho Fields, from 1677, and was the only one of the four men primarily responsible for that development not to be ruined by it. At the time of his death in 1716 he owned land in four counties. Johnshall Crosse was his brother-in-law.[155]

Crosse and Pym laid out Arlington and Bennet Streets. Arlington Street was to one side of the site, and the plots west of Arlington Street were exceptionally long, probably because the licence to build stipulated that there should be no build-ing further west than the east corner of the Duchess of Cleveland's garden (a condition almost immediately breached by Richard Frith).[156] The houses west of Arlington Street seem to have been built fairly quickly. The surviving evidence relates largely to the east side, which long remained in the hands of the Pym family. The twelve plots let out in 1682-83 were mostly seventy feet long but were of varying widths, presumably reflecting the offers made. Four were wide, from thirty-nine feet to forty-three feet five inches, suitable for five-bay houses, while the others ranged from twenty to thirty feet, allowing three or four bays. Rents and length of term also varied, the latter from forty-five and a half years to ninety-nine years for the large house in Fig. 355. As was usual in this period, there was no attempt to create anything approaching a uniform terrace, but the number and height of storeys and the facades were to be 'uniforme and alike with the houses on the west side' or, in the case of two of the larger houses, uniform with those houses 'as they are or shall be built beautify'd and finish'd'. This seems to have meant three and a half storeys with cellars. Each lessee was required to pave the street to the middle and to pave the ten feet nearest the house with portland stone (creating what we would call the pavement).[157]

The leases each include a small plan, in varying styles, evidently drawn by or for the individual lessees and presumably required by Pym and Crosse to ensure that what was proposed was suitable. The internal planning varied from house to house. Fig. 355 shows one of the wider houses, and the other for which a plan survives (drawn by the same hand) differed only in dividing one of the large rooms. The grander of the two staircases probably ascended no further than the first floor. One of the thirty-feet wide houses, also drawn by the same hand, differed in having a narrower hall and only one staircase. Most of the narrower houses had two rooms on the ground floor and a staircase to one side at the back, sometimes with a closet wing or back extension, in one case extending to the back of the plot with back stairs in the furthest corner. Three had central staircases, though none had central chimneys. Only Richard Glaspole, carpenter, and possibly John Webley, followed the convention of red for brick and yellow or brown for timber (Fig. 356). Some showed staircases in simplified form.

The lessees were as usual a mixture of carpenters and bricklayers on the one hand and wealthy

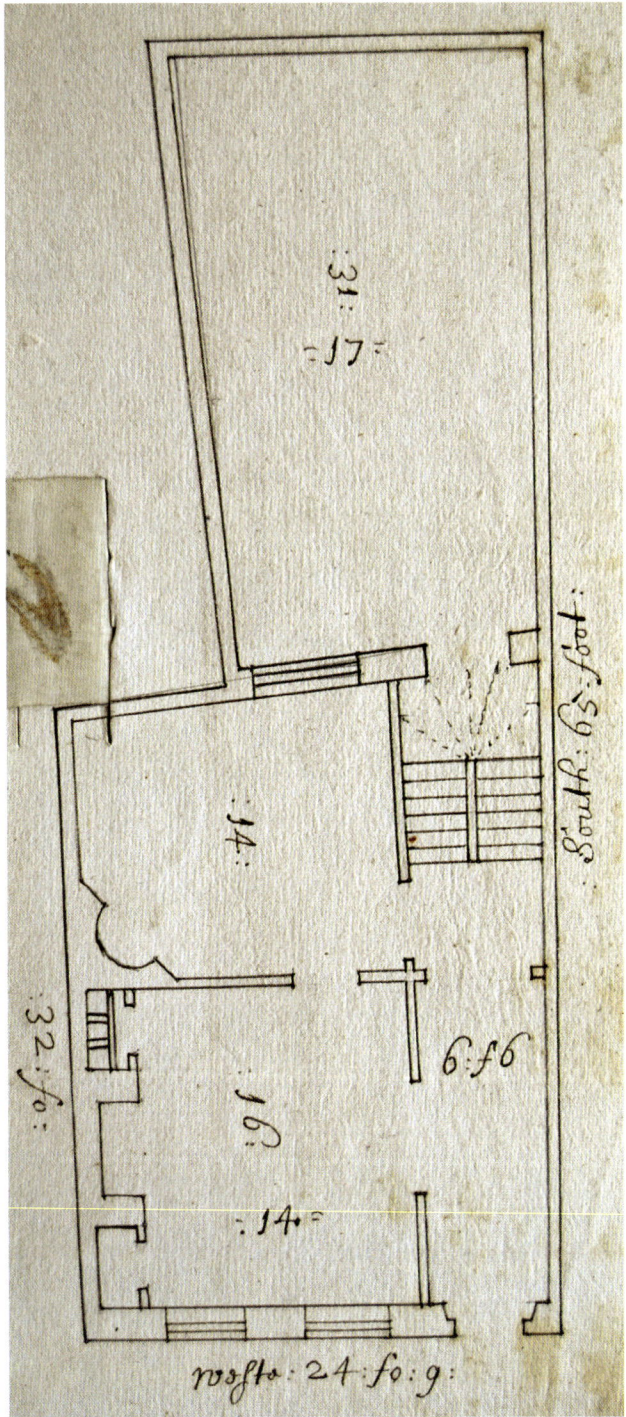

Fig. 353. No. 2 Arlington Street, as proposed by Matthew Frith, bricklayer, 1682. North is to the left.

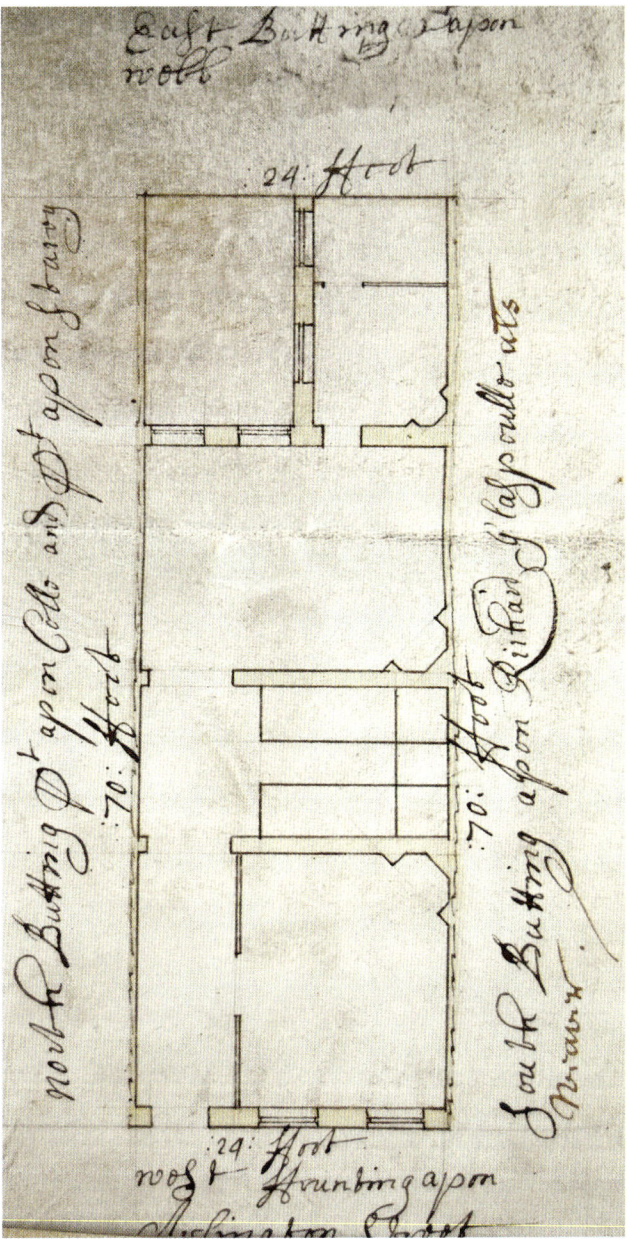

Fig. 354. No. 9 Arlington Street, as proposed by William Marchant of St Martin in the Fields, woodmonger, 1682. North is to the left.

people, who may have been building for their own occupation or just speculating, on the other. For example, Matthew Frith, a bricklayer and the brother of Richard Frith,[158] took three plots, as well as two in Piccadilly, while the takers for the wider plots were James Whitehall of Furnival's Inn, an attorney, John Malcher of Clifford's Inn, Benjamin Coles, citizen and dyer, and Edmond Card, gentleman.

Development did not run smoothly. Although Matthew Frith started building what became 2 Arlington Street, by 1686 he had abandoned it and absconded; worse, he had transferred his lease to a merchant, raising the possibility of litigation if Pym and Crosse sought to finish the house. The same applied to one of the Piccadilly houses, which had been so badly built that part of it had fallen down by 1689. Other lessees apparently abandoned their leases, and in partic-

PLANS OF HOUSES

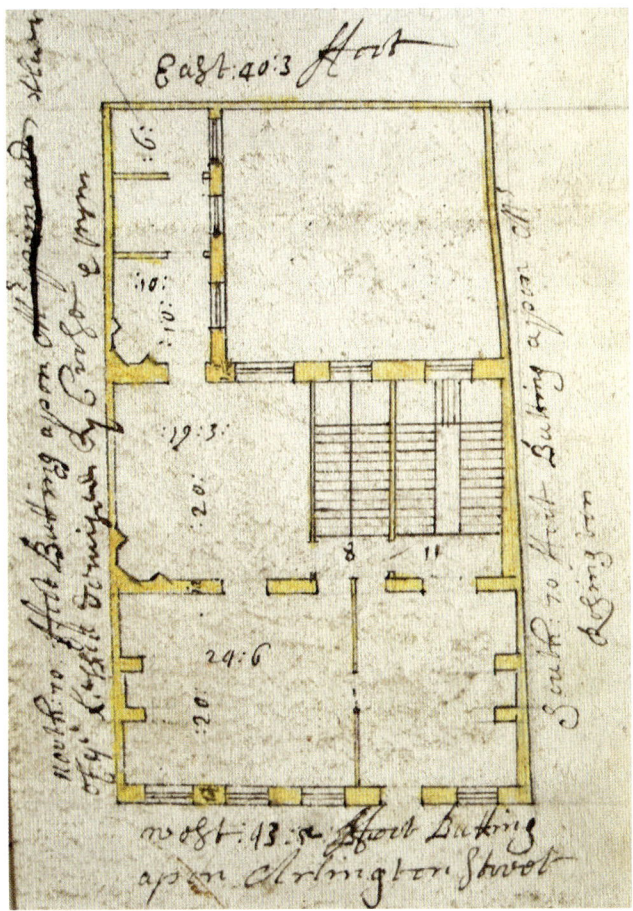

Fig. 355. A house at the south end of Arlington Street, as proposed by Edmond Card, gentleman, 1682 (burnt down in 1689). North is to the left.

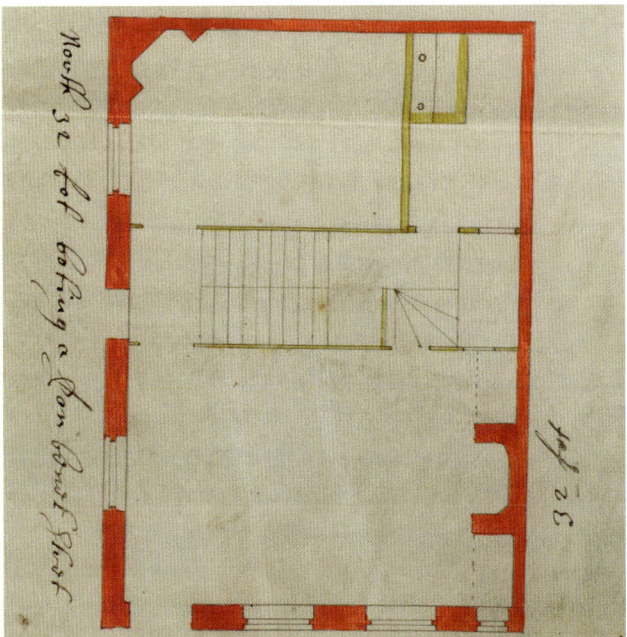

Fig. 356. A house on the south corner of Arlington and Bennet Streets (later 6 Bennet Street, the Blue Posts), as proposed by Richard Glaspole, carpenter and Richard Stacey, bricklayer, 1687.

Fig. 357. Detail from Horwood's map of 1813 showing Arlington Street, with the plot granted to the Earl of Arlington in 1682 edged in red. Piccadilly is at the top and St James's Street to the right.

ular only two of the four wider houses were built. The plots taken by Malcher and Coles were divided and re-let in 1687-88. And when one of the wider houses actually built burnt down in 1689, together with its three neighbours, its site was divided into smaller plots.[159] Evidently a width of about twenty feet was best for this location. In the rate list of 1691 there seem to be only five houses completed on the east side of the street. And what was built was apparently of poor quality: Roger North referred to 'the high buildings in Arlington-street, which were scarce covered in before all the windows were wrymouthed, the fascias turned SS, and divers stacks of chimnies sunk right down, drawing roof and floors with them'.[160] Nevertheless, Arlington Street soon became fashionable, with several titled owners by 1691. Horace Walpole described it as 'the ministerial street' because so many government ministers lived there, and this applied to some extent to the eastern houses as well as the western ones. Sir Robert Walpole moved from No. 17 on the west to No. 5 on the east in 1742 and died there three years later, and Charles James Fox lived at No. 9 on the east side in 1804-06.[161] None of the original houses is known to survive.

Plan 196
Charterhouse Yard, 1703
Fig. 358

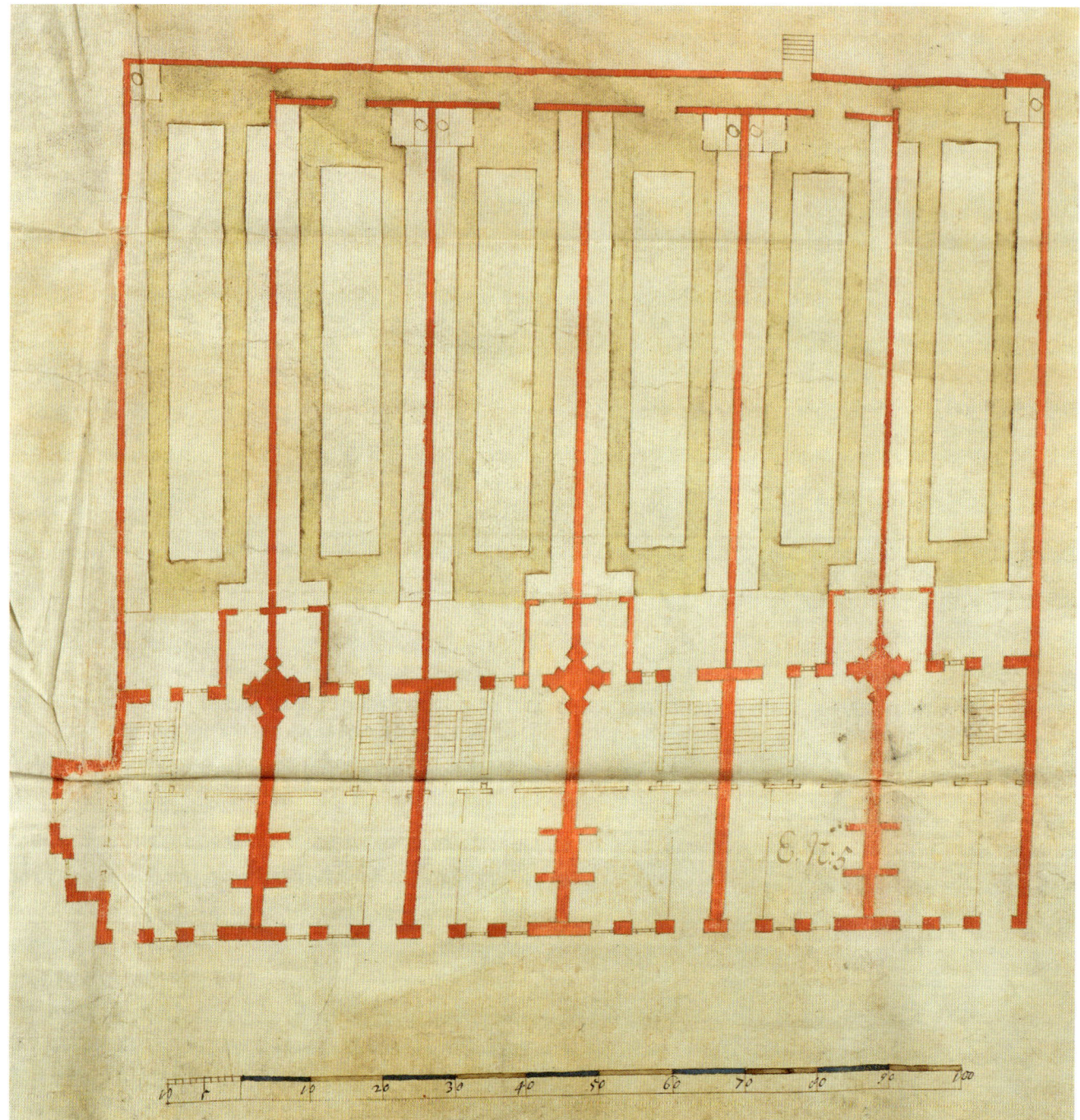

Fig. 358. Houses in Charterhouse Yard, 1703. North is at the bottom.

Charterhouse Yard (now Square) was almost entirely rebuilt in 1688-1705, erasing its previously aristocratic character.[162] This plan records a development on the south side of the Yard in 1703-05, on land belonging to Sir Rowland Winn, baronet, of Nostell Priory, Yorkshire. Richard Boulton and George Willson, both citizen and carpenter, replaced three old houses there by six new ones. The houses were each twenty-one feet wide, with three and a half storeys and three bays (Fig. 359), and had the rear staircase plan, including small wings at the back containing closets.

Fig. 359. The south side of Charterhouse Yard in about 1728 (print of c.1725 by Sutton Nicholls). The six houses of Fig. 358 are in the centre.

The lease containing this copy of the plan related only to the house marked as No. 5, then under construction, and included a commitment to complete it and detailed provisions about the materials to be used. The street outside was to be paved to a width of five feet with purbeck stone and protected by posts. In 1715 the Yard itself was enclosed by a dwarf wall and railings, becoming the equivalent of a West End square. Boulton and Willson's houses were destroyed after the site was purchased for the Metropolitan Railway in 1864-65.

Plan 197
Frith Street, 1718
FIG. 360

This plan and elevation are from a building agreement relating to five houses at 6-10 Frith Street, Soho.[163] Inclusion of an elevation is unique for the period covered here (Fig. 361).[164] The site was previously occupied by outbuildings of Monmouth House, which faced Soho Square and remained unfinished after the execution of the Duke of Monmouth in 1685. In 1717 Sir James Bateman acquired the lease of Monmouth House and remodelled it, as well as adding houses on the Frith Street frontage. His builder in Frith Street was William Thomas of Soho, to whom he lent £2,000 for the purpose. Under the first agreement, of September 1717, there were to be one wide house and four narrower ones;[165] under the second, of January 1718, to which the plan and elevation reproduced here belong, a second wide house was introduced by reducing the width of two of the others, so that there were two of thirty-two to thirty-three feet and three of eighteen to twenty-four feet. The empty houses were insured against fire in July 1718 and some of them were occupied in October 1718.

Nos. 8 to 10 have been demolished (though the pilaster between Nos. 9 and 10 remains), and while Nos. 6 and 7 still stand their facades have been rebuilt. Fortunately there is enough evidence to determine that the ground plan and elevation

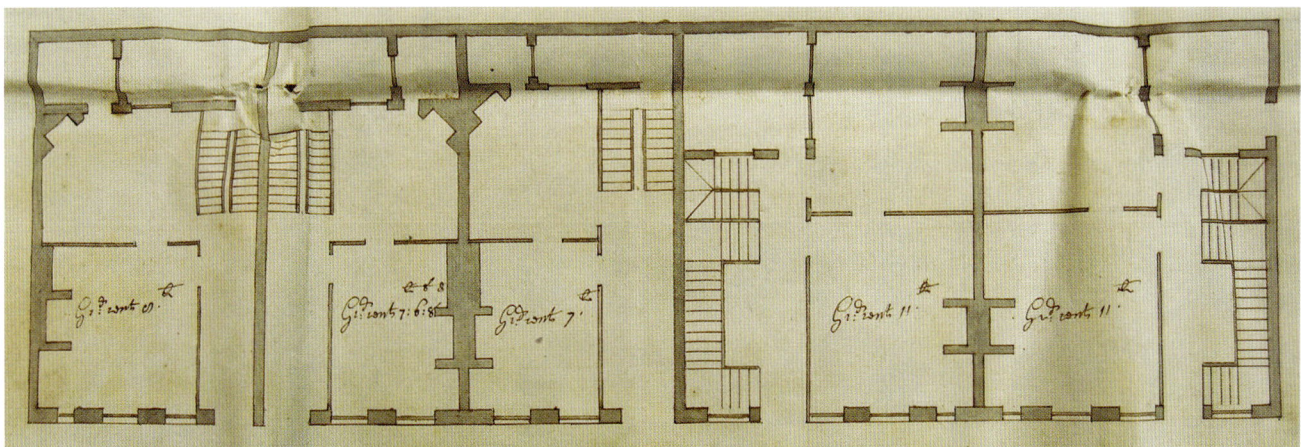

Fig. 360. Proposed houses at Nos. 6-10 Frith Street, 1718. North is to the left.

Fig. 361.   Proposed elevation of Nos. 6-10 Frith Street, 1718.

Fig. 362. A later drawing of the staircase at No. 9 Frith Street.

room plan, but they had front and back stairs and a yard at the side, so the two rooms could occupy the full depth of the site. The front stairs extended only up to the first floor. The design was a mixture of old and new. The half-windows were an old-fashioned aspect of the design (see Plans 28, 41), and fourth storeys were also rare by this time. The most advanced aspect was the attempt to disguise the varying widths of the houses behind a uniform facade, with pilasters between groups and at the ends rather than separating each house. Also unusual were the horizontal raised panels of the fourth storey, though these may not have been built. The houses had well-to-do occupants in the eighteenth-century, but by 1830 had become lodging houses.

were largely followed. No. 9, for example, had a spacious hall with a staircase around three sides of it (Fig. 362), as in the plan. Numbers of storeys and bays were as in the plan and elevation, but the brickwork above the windows was curved rather than flat, the windows of the three lower storeys were set in shallow recesses continuing across all three storeys, the bandcourses above the ground storey were carried across the pilasters, and the fourth storey seems to have been built without the long horizontal panels (Fig. 363).

The three smaller houses had the two-room plan with closet wings at the back, together with rear staircases and chimneys in the side walls or corners. The two larger houses also had the two-

Fig. 363. Nos. 6-8 Frith Street in 1910, before the rebuilding of the facade.

APPENDICES

APPENDIX 1

Document references, scales and dimensions

Sources: abbreviations are listed on p. 294. An asterisk indicates that only part of the plan or a detail or details is included; # indicates that the plan or group of plans shows more than one storey but only one storey has been included.

Scale: 96 in the table indicates 1:96 (eight feet or 96 inches to the inch). Only six plans here state the scale (Plans 8, 12, 15, 17, 18, 110, and 148). In all other cases the scale bar or stated distances have been measured. Where this produces a figure within 2% of a number of feet to the inch the figure has been corrected (e.g. 1:119 and 1:121 to 1:120 or 10 feet to the inch); otherwise it has been left as measured.

'N' indicates not to scale; '?' indicates uncertainty about whether a plan is to scale; 'nn' indicates either scale or dimensions not known.

Dimensions: these are in millimetres, with the measurement from top to bottom first and then side to side. Measurements relate to the page rather than the border, unless a plan with a border forms only part of a page. All such measurements are approximate: often one or more edges is concealed within a lease, or the plan is not a regular shape. Where only details have been printed in this book, the measurements are given in round brackets (unless the detail is a tiny part of the whole) and relate to the whole plan. Where a plan forms part of a page but has no border, measurements are given in square brackets and indicate the size of the plan with a small margin around it.

Plan No.	Place	Source	Scale (1:)	Size (mm)
1	Charterhouse etc.	Sutton's Hospital*	N	(2990 × 520)
2	Charterhouse etc.	Sutton's Hospital*	N	–
3	Cheapside	LMA, H01/ST/E/067/001/034	N	78 × 171
4	Fleet Lane	LMA, H01/ST/E/067/001/032	N	310 × 350
5	Steelyard	TNA, MPF 1/23	?	560 × 410
6	Cecil House	Burghley Estate, M358	192	483 × 737
7	Nonsuch House	LMA, COL/CCS/PL/01/202/23	48	365 × 570
8	Cursitors' Hall	TNA, MPA 1/71	84	90 × 149, 320 × 430, 160 × 216
9	Holy Trinity Aldgate	HH, CPM I 10 #	N	570 × 538
10	Hermitage	TNA, MPB 1/4/2*	840	(680 × 535)
11	Hermitage	Museum of London, PLA 855	?	1020 × 580
12	The Erber	DC, A XIII 16S	120	612 × 945
13	Great Salisbury House	Bodleian Library, Gough Drawings, A3, f. 79r #	144	372 × 296
14	Northampton House	RIBA Drawings Collection, SC 229 I/12	480	385 × 135
15	Whitehall	TNA, MPB 1/12	125	535 × 920 (max)
16	Petty France	SBH, HC 20*	N	387 × 472
17	West Smithfield	CC, CL/G/7/1, f. 31	96	495 × 368
18	Fenchurch Street	CC, CL/G/7/1, f. 12*	144	(495 × 368)
19	St Bartholomew's	SBH, HC 19, f. 52	648	280 × 420
20	Greyfriars	SBH, HC 19, f. 59	444	410 × 510
21	St Bartholomew the Less	SBH, HC 19, f. 51	?	280 × 420

Plan No.	Place	Source	Scale (1:)	Size (mm)
22	Cheapside	Eton College, 16/WB/44	86	435 × 320 (each)
23	Glaziers' Hall	GL, Fishmongers' plans, Fo. IV, No. 106a	93	267 × 330
24	Throgmorton Street	DC, A XII.121*	192	(830 × 700)
25	St Paul's Cathedral	All Souls College, Oxford, AS II.1	1056	527 × 803
26	Christ's Hospital	LMA, CLC/210/H/049/MS22637/001	240	640 × 432
27	Whitefriars	CC, CL/G/7/1, f. 42	96	495 × 368
28	Nevill's Alley	Bodleian Library, Gough Maps 21, f. 28	72	448 × 595
29	Tower Street	SBH, uncatalogued leases, box 2, No. 1808	129	240 × 350
30	Stationers' Hall area	Stationers' Company, plan book 1674, p. 4	nn	nn
31	Stationers' Hall area	Stationers' Company, plan book 1674, p. 22	nn	nn
32	Stationers' Hall area	Stationers' Company, plan book 1674, p. 36	nn	nn
33	Stationers' Hall area	Stationers' Company, plan book 1674, p. 42	nn	nn
34	Chandlers' Rents	Tallow Chandlers' Company, plan book 1678, plan 7	120	478 × 300
35	Bottle Alley	GL, MS 12104, f. 5	120	500 × 250
36	Old Jewry	GL, MS 12104, f. 8	120	450 × 250
37	Billiter Lane	Fishmongers' Company, plan book, f. 12	148	465 × 340
38	Leadenhall Street	Fishmongers' Company, plan book, f. 10	147	465 × 340
39	Thames Street	Fishmongers' Company, plan book, f. 6	147	425 × 200
40	Ludgate Hill	Medway Archives, DRc/EP/26	84	565 × 705
41	Clothworkers' Court	CC, Estate/8/1C/2	144	400 × 640
42	Cousin Lane	CCLD, 41.16	240	385 × 97
43	Goldsmiths' Alley	GC, deeds B IV 106(vi)	120	300 × 590
44	Goldsmiths' Alley	GC, Ward's plans, No. 17*	160	(1475 × 1170)
45	Primrose Alley	GC, Ward's plans, No. 14	160	657 × 1543
46	Maiden Lane	GC, Ward's plans, No. 7*	160	(640 × 785)
47	Bishopsgate Street	LMA, COL/CCS/PL/203/39	120	380 × 265
48	Houndsditch	CLPB, B3	72	[350 × 170]
49	Houndsditch	CLPB, B22	96	[290 × 150]
50	Houndsditch	CLPB, A81	120	[270 × 190]
51	Houndsditch	CLPB, A82	120	[280 × 200]
52	Houndsditch	CLPB, B23	96	[320 × 200]
53	Houndsditch	CLPB, A76*	120	[(440 × 260)]
54	Bull and Mouth Street	LMA, CLC/210/H/005A/MS22634/007A	180	625 × 800
55	Leadenhall Street	RBT, E01/02/014	84	638 × 497
56	Rose Street	TNA, MPF 1/288	116	470 × 666
57	Wapping Street	LMA, CLC/275/MS33360/005, No. 84	240	390 × 275
58	Blackman Street	Society of Antiquaries, Surrey red portfolios, S-Z, f. 22	192	385 × 545
59	Millbank	Westminster Abbey Archives, WAM(P)652	192	700 × 795
60	East Lane	SLSL, West Box D, No. 411	300	495 × 770
61	Bermondsey Wall	SLSL, West Box D, No. 411	300	270 × 390
62	London Bridge	LMA, SC/GL/PR/LA/361/LON/1/q6886938	148	510 × 1250

APPENDICES

Plan No.	Place	Source	Scale (1:)	Size (mm)
63	London Wall gates	LMA, COL/PL/02/G/006*	120	(330 × 560)
64	Poor Jewry Lane	CCLD, 64.22*	120	(250 × 355)
65	Shoemakers' Row	CCLD, 34.18	72	240 × 325
66	Windsor Court	CLPB, A66	120	[240 × 220]
67	Shoemakers' Row	CLPB, B6*	72	[(190 × 420)]
68	Bull and Mouth Street	CLPB, B43	96	[270 × 180]
69	Coleman Street	CLPB, B38	48	[160 × 460]
70	Botolph Wharf	CCLD, 36.27	148	340 × 495
71	Porter's Key	Fishmongers' Company, plan book, f. 3	168	465 × 340
72	Dyers' Hall Wharf	GL, MS 32588/4, No. 71/73	240	465 × 170
73	Steelyard	TNA, RAIL 635/102	264	485 × 365
74	Steelyard	TNA, RAIL 635/102 #	252	(632 × 732)
75	Bermondsey wharves	HH, CPM Supp 51a	?	290 × 357
76	Battle Mills	LMA, COL/CCS/PL/01/202/47*	192	(850 × 280)
77	Morgan's Lane	Magdalen College, Oxford, MP/1/86	240	1060 × 390
78	Bridge House Brewhouse	CCLD, COL/CCS/RM11/04006	168	430 × 400
79	Peacock Brewhouse	Fishmongers' Company, plan book, f. 18	123	465 × 340
80	Pye Corner brewhouse	LMA, CLC/B/169/MS39246, lease of 1718	240	240 × 290
81	Pye Corner brewhouse	LMA, CLC/B/169/MS39246, lease of 1718	240	255 × 285
82	Whiting ground	HH, CPM Supp 53	960	579 × 417
83	Grange Road	LMA, H01/ST/E/067/011, No. 22	187	430 × 168
84	Coleman Alley	CLPB, A95	180	[750 × 400]
85	Grub Street	CCLD, 56.1	120	730 × 167
86	Old Bethlehem	CLPB, B41	120	[360 × 180]
87	Houndsditch	CLPB, A81*	120	[(290 × 230)]
88	Perpoole Lane	LMA, LCC/CL/GEN/08/C/82/897	84	200 × 200
89	Leadenhall Market	CCLD, COL/CCS/RM10/15336 (40.001)	528	310 × 255
90	Beef Market, Leadenhall	LMA, COL/PL/01/092/C	144	590 × 400
91	Greenyard, Leadenhall	CLPB, A7	72	[180 × 310]
92	Smithfield sheep pens	CCLD, 39.12	248	280 × 440
93	Meal Market	COL/CC/CLC/01/001, f. 64v	144	435 × 260
94	Star Inn	GL, CLC/L/FE/H/003	96	462 × 400 (max)
95	Star Inn	Fishmongers' Company, plan book, f. 21	120	465 × 340
96	Cross Keys Inn	Bodleian Library, MS Charters London a.2, f. 18	180	301 × 294
97	Catherine Wheel Inn	LMA, H01/ST/E/067/011, No. 28	192	485 × 140
98	Boar's Head Inn	Magdalen College, Oxford, MP/1/87a	120	604 × 150
99	Horn Tavern	GC, Ward's plans, No. 20*	160	–
100	Mitre Tavern	CLPB, B44	96	(220 × 405)
101	Blue Anchor	CCLD, 56.2 (part is Plan 134)	96	[(350 × 220)]
102	Fore Street	CLPB, B34	96	[240 × 210]
103	Flying Horse Yard	CLPB, A116	120	[260 × 370]
104	Finsbury Yard	CLPB, B6	72	[320 × 280]

Plan No.	Place	Source	Scale (1:)	Size (mm)
105	Tallow Chandlers' Hall	Tallow Chandlers' Company, plan book, plan 1	92	477 × 300
106	Armourers' Hall	GL, MS 12104, f. 3	120	(230 × 250)
107	Fishmongers' Hall	Fishmongers' Company, plan book, f.1	192	465 × 340
108	Goldsmiths' Hall	GC, Ward's plans, No. 3	96	640 × 780
109	Skinners' Hall	GL, MS 30995/1, f. 1	120	705 × 500
110	Navy Victualling Yard	TNA, MR 1/106	192	900 × 980
111	Navy Office	BL, Kings MS 43, ff. 147-50	240	513 × 355 (page)
112	King's Bench Prison	TNA, MPE 1/1090	480	(387 × 572)
113	Southwark Counter	LMA, COL/CCS/PL/01/049A	96	565 × 680
114	Royal Mews	BL, Maps K.Top.24.15.1.a	312	800 × 620
115	St Peter upon Cornhill	LMA, P69/PET1/B/001/MS04165/001, p. 492	77	300 × 370
116	Church Entry	LMA, P69/ANN/D/033A/MS09258	129	370 × 480
117	St Botolph Aldgate	LMA, P69/BOT2/D/001/MS02630, f. 59	240	450 × 248
118	St Botolph Aldgate	CLPB, B20	48	[150 × 330]
119	Christ's Hospital	LMA, CLC/210/H/181	N	370 × 570
120	Caesar's Buildings	Middle Temple	–	[250 × 300]
121	Fishmongers' bargehouse	CC, Estate 29/1A/6	112	460 × 485
122	Skinners' bargehouse	GL, MS 30995/2, f. 13	120	490 × 355
123	Dowgate	CCLD, 38.10	246	660 × 230
124	Queenhithe	CCLD, 49.6	120	153 × 310
125	Greyfriars Court	Nomura International plc	nn	nn
126	Pancras Lane	LMA, E/DCA/135	96	540 × 310
127	St Paul's Deanery	LMA, CLC/313/L/F/019/MS12193*	192	(400 × 720)
128	Fenchurch Street	Fishmongers' Company, plan book, f. 23	120	465 × 340
129	Aldermanbury	CLPB, A9	96	[480 × 250]
130	Westminster Deanery	Westminster Abbey Archives, WAM 52239 to 52241	163	380 × 490 (each)
131	Austin Friars	DC, A.I.44	96	565 × 420/475
132	Abchurch Lane	Corpus Christi, Cambridge, CCCC 09L/H11	126	225 × 368
133	Little Britain	SBH, uncatalogued leases, box 1, 1681 lease to Norton	168	320 × 260
134	Mitre Court	CCLD, 56.2 (part is Plan 101)	96	(220 × 405)
135	Weighhouse Yard	CCLD, 41.21	96	195 × 355
136	Mincing Lane	CLPB, A10	72	[270 × 200]
137	Mincing Lane	CLPB, B43	72	[300 × 210]
138	Wood Street	CLPB, A41	120	[320 × 350]
139	Minories	CLPB, A75	120	[480 × 170]
140	Houndsditch	CLPB, A70	120	[370 × 150]
141	Bishopsgate	CLPB, A66	79	[230 × 220]
142	Holborn Hill	CC, CL/G/7/1, f. 39	149	[275 × 145]
143	Houndsditch	LMA, CLC/210/G/BLC/002/MS13443/001	103	385 × 294
144	Grange Road	LMA, H01/ST/E/114/018*	180	(450 × 250)
145	Whitefriars	CC, Estate/25/1C/8	96	188 × 281

APPENDICES

Plan No.	Place	Source	Scale (1:)	Size (mm)
146	Round Woolstaple	LMA, CLC/210/G/BCA/126A/MS22635/021	96	170 × 195 (each)
147	Tothill Street	LMA, CLC/210/G/BCA/097/MS13071	116	560 × 290
148	Crutched Friars	CC, CL/G/Charity/Evans/G/C/1/13	82	312 × 245
149	Newgate Street	SBH, uncatalogued leases, box 19, 1716 lease to Baron	92	165 × 165
150	High Holborn	LMA, HB/D/117	84	220 × 180
151	Fore Street	CCLD, 67.4*	81	(250 × 270)
152	Mark Lane	CLPB, A8	120	[250 × 120]
153	Grocers' Alley	CLPB, A50	55	[330 × 170]
154	Pudding Lane	CLPB, B33	96	[290 × 170]
155	Basinghall Postern	CLPB, A35	72	[290 × 150]
156	Basinghall Postern	CLPB, B25	72	[290 × 140]
157	Tower Hill	CLPB, A37	72	[360 × 190]
158	Fenchurch Street	CLPB, A124	72	[350 × 190]
159	Duke's Place	CLPB, A22	72	[240 × 150]
160	Fenchurch Street	CLPB, A49	72	[320 × 220]
161	Houndsditch	CLPB, A80	120	[420 × 150]
162	Shoemakers' Row	CLPB, A69	79	[440 × 170]
163	Aldgate High Street	CLPB, A149	96	[330 × 150]
164	Hart Street	CLPB, B25	69	[290 × 220]
165	Aldermanbury Postern	CLPB, B21	72	[320 × 190]
166	Bishopsgate Street	CLPB, B27	79	[290 × 200]
167	Wormwood Street	CLPB, B44	120	[200 × 140]
168	Creechurch Lane	CLPB, A130	72	[240 × 150]
169	Burnt Yard	CCLD, E.9	120	390 × 250
170	Dowgate Hill	Tallow Chandlers' Company, 1678 plan book, plan 2	54	260 × 300
171	Fore Street	CCLD, 56.24	92	185 × 290
172	Fore Street	CLPB, B46	96	[320 × 190]
173	Haberdashers' Square	GL, Haberdashers' deeds 1996/14, Box 1/15, No. 2	96	450 × 376
174	Barnham Street	LMA, CLC/210/G/BBH/001/MS12918/003, 1699 lease	222	190 × 305
175	Barnham Street	LMA, CLC/210/G/BBH/001/MS12918/003, 1699 lease	222	190 × 190
176	Rose Alley	CLPB, A4	72	[300 × 280]
177	Dolphin Court	CLPB, A20	120	[400 × 240]
178	Great Swordbearers Alley	CLPB, A88	120	[310 × 260]
179	Thames Street	CLPB, A75	120	[220 × 200]
180	Shoemakers' Row	CLPB, A134	72	[280 × 230]
181	Fore Street	CLPB, B1	48	[180 × 160]
182	Broad Court	CLPB, A137	48	[270 × 250]
183	Fore Street	CLPB, B28	48	[260 × 180]
184	Lime Street	CLPB, B38	72	[170 × 190]

Plan No.	Place	Source	Scale (1:)	Size (mm)
185	Camomile Street	CLPB, B37	72	[180 × 460]
186	Skinners' Almshouses	GL, MS 30995/1, f. 17	138	500 × 705
187	Camp's almshouses	CCLD, 58.32	96	140 × 380
188	Emanuel Hospital	LMA, COL/CA/01/01/110, pp. 613-14	186	260 × 425
189	Salisbury Street	HH, London plans No. 12 (CPM Supp 84)	144	530 × 755
190	Cecil Street	HH, London plans No. 13 (General 63/5)	186	545 × 425
191	Cecil Street	HH, London plans No. 17	252	260 × 530
192	Arlington Street	LMA, E/PYM/580	252	130 × 78
193	Arlington Street	LMA, E/PYM/593	148	220 × 115
194	Arlington Street	LMA, E/PYM/597	72	205 × 115
195	Arlington Street	LMA, E/PYM/591	72	170 × 150
196	Charterhouse Yard	LMA, CLC/522/MS10500	123	440 × 400
197	Frith Street	Northamptonshire Record Office, BH(K)1104	93	280 × 435

APPENDIX 2

Payments for London plans, 1587-1721

The table covers all known payments rather than just those for plans in this book. An asterisk indicates a plan not known to exist. Plan numbers are those of plans in this book. Dates are those of payment, not necessarily of the surveying. Payments to Leybourn for surveying ground without buildings in 1676-77 and 1683 were 5s., 10s. (four times) and £1 (four times) (LMA, COL/SJ/09/017).

Ref	Year	Surveyor	Plan	Client	Sum (£.s.d)
1	1587	Arthur Gregory	London Bridge*	Bridge House	4.0.0
2	1596	Unknown	The Erber, Dowgate Hill (Plan 12)	Drapers' Company	3.6.8
3	1612	Ralph Treswell	Plan book (30 plans) (Plans 17-18)	Clothworkers' Company	35.0.0
4	1616	Edward Mansell	Former Greyfriars*	St Batholomew's Hospital	6.13.4
5	1630	Adam Bowen	Queenhithe*	Fishmongers' Company	2.0.0
6	1633	Adam Bowen	Houses at St Katherine's*	Fishmongers' Company	2.5.0
7	1633	Joseph Darvoll	London Bridge;* house in Gracechurch Street (2 copies)	Bridge House	2.0.0
8	1654	Joseph Darvoll	Brewery (2 copies) (Plan 78)	Bridge House	0.13.0
9	1655-56	Richard Daynes	Slaughterhouses, Pincock Lane*	Christ's Hospital	2.0.0
10	1663	William Conyers	Mansion, Greyfriars Court (Plan 125)	Christ's Hospital	2.0.0
11	1663	William Conyers	Red Bull, Southwark*	Christ's Hospital	1.0.0
12	1663	William Conyers	5 houses, Trinity Lane ('rough plans')*	Christ's Hospital	0.15.0
13	1664	Richard Daynes	Nag's Head, Islington*	Christ's Hospital	3.9.0
14	1664	Richard Daynes	House, Fenchurch Street (4 copies)*	Christ's Hospital	2.15.0
15	1667	William Conyers	6 plans*	Christ's Hospital	3.0.0
16	1667	Joseph Hutchinson	Plan of house*	Christ's Hospital	0.10.0
17	1673	William Leybourn	Old Street*	Ironmongers' Company	5.0.0

Ref	Year	Surveyor	Plan	Client	Sum (£.s.d)
18	1675	William Leybourn	Houses at Shoreditch*	Christ's Hospital	2.10.0
19	1676	John Saxton	Blowbladder Street (and copies)	Christ's Hospital	1.0.0
20	1677	John Saxton	8 houses, Blue Anchor Alley (2 copies)	Christ's Hospital	0.10.0
21	1677	William Leybourn	City markets (6 plans) (Plan 90)	City	32.0.0
22	1677	William Leybourn	City laystalls (3 plans) (Plan 123)	City	4.0.0
23	1678	William Leybourn	Plan book (11 plans) (Plans 34, 105, 170)	Tallow Chandlers' Company	10.0.0
24	1679	Joseph Titcombe	Plan book (6 plans) (Plans 35, 36, 106)	Armourers' Company	12.0.0
25	1679	John Saxton	Ground in Coleman Street (2 plans)	Christ's Hospital	0.10.0
26	1680	William Leybourn	Houses etc. in Town Ditch	Christ's Hospital	3.0.0
27	1680	William Leybourn	4 houses in Borough*	Christ's Hospital	0.10.0
28	1680	William Leybourn	St Bennet's Hill (2 copies)*	Christ's Hospital	0.10.0
29	1680	William Leybourn	Near Pye Corner (2 copies)	Christ's Hospital	0.10.0
30	1680	William Leybourn	Silver Street (2 copies)	Christ's Hospital	0.10.0
31	1681	Nathaniel Hanwell	Houses by Hospital (4 copies)*	St Thomas's Hospital	5.0.0
32	1682	Mr Handy	Houses in Kent Street*	St Thomas's Hospital	0.10.0
33	1683	William Leybourn	New buildings, Little Tower Hill*	City	1.10.0
34	1684	Nathaniel Hanwell	3 houses in Bermondsey (3 copies) (Plan 144)	St Thomas's Hospital	1.10.0
35	1686-87	William Leybourn	Plan book (24 pages, c.32 plans) (Plans 37-39, 71, 79, 95, 107, 128)	Fishmongers' Company	34.0.0
36	1688	William Leybourn	Ratcliff and Limehouse*	City	25.0.0
37	1688	William Leybourn	Houses in Fenchurch Street, etc.	Clothworkers' Company	2.0.0
38	1691	Unknown	5 houses in East Smithfield*	Clothworkers' Company	0.12.6
39	1693	John Ward	Plan book (10 plans and 8 copies) (Plans 44-46, 99, 108)	Goldsmiths' Company	130.0.0
40	1697	Mr Biggs	Plan book (3 plans, 32 outlines) (Plans 109, 122, 186)	Skinners' Company	40.0.0
41	1697	John Olley	6 almshouses and shop, Wormwood Street (Plan 187)	City/Allhallows London Wall	1.10.0
42	1702	Mr Williams	Houses etc., Blackfriars (Plan 116)	St Ann Blackfriars	1.0.0
43	1702	John Hobbs	11 houses in Tothill Street (and copies) (Plan 147)	Christ's Hospital	4.12.6
44	1710	Mr Gould	Lime Street*	Fishmongers' Company	3.3.0
45	1717	Heber Lands	Bull and Mouth Street (Plan 54)	Christ's Hospital	25.0.0
46	1717/18	Heber Lands	Long Acre*	Christ's Hospital	18.0.0
47	1721	James Gould	Plan book (5 plans)	Dyers' Company	21.0.0

Notes (numbers relate to references above)

3. Payment also covered several rural surveys.

4. Original plan, of which copy by Llewellyn survives (Plan 20).

7. Darvoll's plan was copied by Thomas Sterne for 8s. (Plan 62). The Gracechurch Street plan is probably the plot outline now attached to a lease of 1667 (COL/CCS/RM11/06257 – 293.2).

31. Four drafts of houses as they were and as they could be rebuilt.

39. Included three views of Goldsmiths' Hall; payment said to cover 'all other his services'.

40. £40 money or a bill for £50; the Company's clerk received £65 and the upper beadle £10 for assisting.

43. Several copies at different stages.

Sources (numbers relate to references above)

1. LMA, CLA/007/FN/02/010, p. 386.
2. DC, Accounts 1595-96, p. 18.
3. Schofield, p. 4.
4. SBH, HB1/4, f. 52v.
5. GL, MS 5570/2, p. 799.
6. GL, MS 5570/3, p. 68.
7-8. LMA, CLA/007/FN/03/016, 25 May 1633, and 017, 17 June 1654.
9-15. LMA, MS 12819/8-9, 1655/56 to 1666/67.
16. LMA, MS 12819/10, 1667/68, 3 August 1667.
17. GL, MS 16967/6, p. 154.
18-20. LMA, MS 12819/10, 1675/76, 30 October 1675, 1676/77, 18 October 1676, 2 June 1677.
21. Betty R. Masters, *The Public Markets of the City of London surveyed by William Leybourn in 1677* (LTS No. 117, 1974), p. 11.
22. LMA, COL/SJ/09/017 (Misc.MSS.160.15).
23. GL, MS 6153/5, f.27v.
24. GL, MS 12071/4, f. 26v.
25-30. LMA, MS 12819/10, 1678-79, 31 May 1679, 1679-80, 20 February 1679/80, 20 May 1680.
31. LMA, H01/ST/D/07/003, 26 August 1681.
32. LMA, H01/ST/D/06/001, 14 September 1682.
33. LMA, COL/SJ/09/017 (Misc.MSS.160.15).
34. LMA, H01/ST/D/07/003, 18 January 1683/84.
35. GL, MS 5570/5, p. 625.
36. LMA, COL/SJ/09/017 (Misc.MSS.160.15).
37-38. CC, Accounts.
39. GC, Court book, 1688-1708, f. 80.
40. GL, MS 30708/6, pp. 344, 390, 412.
41. LMA, P69/ALH5/B/003/MS05090/003, pp. 209-10.
42. LMA, P69/ANN/B/021/MS01061/017, 30 May 1702.
43. LMA, MS 12819/12, 1701/02, p. 178.
44. GL, MS 5570/6, p. 187.
45-46. LMA, MS 12819/13, 1717-18, p. 31.
47. GL, MS 8164/2, p. 413.

APPENDIX 3

Fines and rents

This appendix consists mainly of information from leases to which the relevant plans were attached. In other cases such information, drawn from other documents usually of different years, is included here only selectively.

Date: an asterisk against the year indicates that the information is not from the same year as the plan, or the previous or subsequent year.

Premises: '#' indicates that the information relates to only part of the property shown on the plan.

Term: '(BL)' indicates a building lease. Building leases were sometimes for only partial rebuilding.

Fine: 'R' indicates that the lessee was also required to spend money on repairs or rebuilding, with the amount in pounds if specified.

Actual value: this is either the actual rent then being levied from sub-tenants or the annual value estimated by the landowner at the time.

Fines and rents might be affected by the fact that the term was to start in a future year (e.g. after an existing lease expired), or that an existing lease with unexpired years was to be surrendered in return for a new one, or that the lessee was to spend a stated sum on repairs.

The source is the plan and associated information (usually the lease to which the plan is attached) or, in the case of City Lands, the City Lands journals (CLJ, 002 to 008, indexed in LMA, COL/CC/CLC/01/162 and 163), unless a source is indicated below. The source given below is asterisked if it is wholly or partly for actual rents.

Plan No.	Location	Date	Premises	Term (years)	Fine (£)	Rent (£ or £.s.d)	Actual value (£ or £.s.d)
3	Cheapside	1542*	House	70	0	5.6.8	
4	Fleet Lane	1542	2½ houses	41	0	1.13.0	
7	Nonsuch House	1579*	East part#	31	200	10	
		1579*	West part#	41	200	10	
12	The Erber	1580*	Mansion and houses	80 (BL)	200	26.3.4	
18	Fenchurch Street	1601*	House (Sutton)#	21	30	4	
		1602*	House (Yeoman)#	23	15	2	
22	Cheapside	1618	3 houses, 3 shops	40	0	13.6.8	
23	Glaziers' Hall	1618	Company hall	35	100	20	
24	Throgmorton Street	1620	Mansion (Sir W. Garway)#	36	0	9	

APPENDICES

Plan No.	Location	Date	Premises	Term (years)	Fine (£)	Rent (£ or £.s.d)	Actual value (£ or £.s.d)
27	Whitefriars	1657	House (Mayes)#	41 (BL)	0	14	
		1660*	House (Fowkes)#	34.5	0+R72	16	
29	Tower Street	1671	7 houses	79.5 (BL)	0	30	
34	Chandlers' Rents	1671*	17 houses	60 (BL)	10	30	
37	Billiter Lane	1651*	2 houses (Turges)#	21	700	7.8.0	120
		1669*	2 houses (Turges)#	26	800	7.8.0	
		1651*	3 houses (Middleton)#	24	400	6	80
		1673*	3 houses (Middleton)#	27	300	6	
38	Leadenhall Street	1669*	House (west plot)#	31	340	3	
		1699*	2 houses (middle plot)#	31	700	5	
		1697*	2 houses (east plot)#	31	300	5	
39	Thames Street	1667*	2 houses and dyehouse#	51 (BL)	0	20	
	Black Raven Alley	1671*	6 houses#	61 (BL)	0	20	
41	Clothworkers' Court	1690	Mansion site etc.	61 (BL)	380	200	
42	Cousin Lane	1692	Brewhouse, wharf etc.	41 (BL)	0	55	
43	Goldsmiths' Alley	1687	15 houses	41	900	4	
46	Maiden Lane	1691	Mansion and 6 houses#	48	300+R	18.10.0	
47	Bishopsgate Street	1698	8 houses	21	500	40	153
49	Houndsditch	1717	2 houses	21	60	10	23
50	Houndsditch	1712	2 houses	21	100+R250	9	22.10.0
51	Houndsditch	1712	7 houses	21	125	10	61
52	Houndsditch	1718	4 houses	61 (BL)	53.15.0	20	54
53	Houndsditch	1712	3 houses and stables	21	150	10	56
55	Leadenhall Street	1718	5 houses D on plan#	31	0	45	
		1718	House B on plan#	31	0	16	
		1719	2 houses A on plan#	31	0	28	
		1719	House L on plan#	31	0	19	
		1720	House K on plan#	31	0	7	
		1721*	House I on plan (next to H) #	31	0	3	
		1721*	2 houses G on plan#	21	0	16	
		1722*	House F on plan#	21	0	7	
57	Wapping Street	1676	c. 5 houses and timber yard	30 (BL)	0	8	
65	Shoemakers' Row	1699	Bastion	61 (BL)	10	3	
66	Windsor Court	1712	Bastion	21	0	4	7
67	Shoemakers' Row	1716	Bastion and shops	21	75	5	
70	Botolph Wharf	1680	Wharf etc.	60 (BL)	0	30	
71	Porter's Key	1670*	Wharf and 10 houses	46 (BL)	600	112	
77	Morgan's Lane	1679*	Mills, wharf etc.	40	?	24.3.4	
78	Bridge House Brewhouse	1653	Brewhouse and 10 acres	61	80	111.6.8	
79	Peacock Brewhouse	1681*	Brewhouse	28	520	5	

Plan No.	Location	Date	Premises	Term (years)	Fine (£)	Rent (£ or £.s.d)	Actual value (£ or £.s.d)
80-81	Pye Corner brewhouse	1718	Brewhouse (both parts)	28-29	200+R250	20	
83	Grange Road	1683	House and tannery	31	50	8	
84	Coleman Alley	1713	33 houses	61 (BL)	120	10	198
85	Grub Street	1715	2 houses and long shed	21	14	2	6
86	Old Bethlehem	1720	2 houses and foundries	21	210	7	
87	Houndsditch	1712	4 houses (inc. 1 not shown)	21	100+R250	10	
91	Leadenhall Market	1700	2 houses	48	200	3	
92	Smithfield sheep pens	1682	Market and 6 houses	32	0	103.6.8	
94	Star Inn	1645*	Inn	31 (BL)	550	12	84
95	Star Inn	1669*	Inn and 4 houses#	91 (BL)	300	16	
97	Catherine Wheel Inn	1686	Inn and 5 houses	21	300	25	
98	Boar's Head Inn	1674*	Inn and 2 houses	40	?	7	
99	Horn Tavern	1672*	Tavern	55 (BL)	0	6.13.4	
100	Mitre Tavern	1721	Tavern	21	140	15	56
101	Blue Anchor	1697	(See Plan 134 below)				
102	Fore Street	1719	Alehouse and house	21	120	8	
103	Flying Horse Yard	1713	Stables and 10 houses	21	250+R300	22	
104	Finsbury Yard	1715	Stables and house	21	80+R40	10	
118	St Botolph Aldgate	1717	4 small shops	21	10	1	31
124	Queenhithe	1681	House	60 (BL)	0	8	
125	Greyfriars Court	1663	Mansion	21	260	20	60 + fine
126	Pancras Lane	1671	Mansion	80 (BL)	0	25.16.8	
128	Fenchurch Street	1673*	Mansion	72 (BL)	250	8.6.8	
129	Aldermanbury	1701	Mansion	11	0	65	
131	Austin Friars	1672	House	70 (BL)	250	5	
132	Abchurch Lane	1678	House (parish's part)#	40	?	5	
133	Little Britain	1681	House	51 (BL)	0	4	
134	Mitre Court	1696	3 houses (inc. Plan 101 above)	41 (BL)	0	22	
135	Weighhouse Yard	1700	House	21	157.10.0	100	
136	Mincing Lane	1701	House	21	200	20	
137	Mincing Lane	1721	House	21	100+R100	40	
138	Wood Street	1707	House	21	0	50	
139	Minories	1712	2 houses	21	200	10	
140	Houndsditch	1712	2 houses	21	100	9	34
141	Bishopsgate	1712	House	21	120	10	24
144	Grange Road	1668*	2 houses (Shewen)#	29.5	0	15	
145	Whitefriars	1683	5 houses	51 (BL)	0	14	

APPENDICES

Plan No.	Location	Date	Premises	Term (years)	Fine (£)	Rent (£ or £.s.d)	Actual value (£ or £.s.d)
146	Round Woolstaple	1683	House (Heard)#	21	70	6.13.4	
		1683	House (Furnis)#	21	70	6.13.4	
147	Tothill Street	1702	11 houses	51 (BL)	70	10	
148	Crutched Friars	1711	House	21	50	6	
149	Newgate Street	1716	House	25	200+R	10	
150	High Holborn	1718	2 houses	50	0	20	
151	Fore Street	1696	3 houses (inc. 1 not shown)	51 (BL)	65	0	
152	Mark Lane	1701	4 houses	61 (BL)	170	12	
153	Grocers' Alley	1711	House	21	50	20	
154	Pudding Lane	1719	House	21	250	21	55
155	Basinghall Postern	1706	House	21	0	12	
156	Basinghall Postern	1718	House	21	60+R50	6	18
158	Fenchurch Street	1713	House	21	10	6	12
159	Duke's Place	1705	House	9	R25	8	
160	Fenchurch Street	1710	2 houses	21	300	4	44
161	Houndsditch	1712	House	21	50+R70	4	19
162	Shoemakers' Row	1712	House	21	25.5.0	7	
164	Hart Street	1717	3 houses	21	125+R50	5	
165	Aldermanbury Postern	1717	House	21	25+R40	5	12
166	Bishopsgate Street	1718	House and shop	21	120	12	32
167	Wormwood Street	1721	House	21	70	4	
168	Creechurch Lane	1714	House	21	65+R20	5	
169	Burnt Yard	1640	8 houses	41 (BL)	10	7	
170	Dowgate Hill	1670*	3 houses	71 (BL)	0	13.6.8	
171	Fore Street	1682	4 houses	41 (BL)	70	3	
173	Haberdashers' Square	1691	24 houses	61 (BL)	0	52	
174-75	Barnham Street	1699	34 houses (inc. 7 not shown)	51 (BL)	0	20	
176	Rose Alley	1700	5 houses	21	0	12	
177	Dolphin Court	1703	9 houses	21	0	16	36
178	Great Swordbearers Alley	1712	5 houses	21	100	5	33
179	Thames Street	1713	4 houses	21	125	10	
180	Shoemakers' Row	1714	3 houses	21	20	7.1.10	20
181	Fore Street	1715	House	21	40	2	
182	Broad Court	1715	2 houses	21	40	4	11
183	Fore Street	1718	3 houses and workshop	21	250+R250	10	43
184	Lime Street	1719	2 houses	21	40	5	
185	Camomile Street	1719	6 houses	61 (BL)	160	8	52.10.0

Plan No.	Location	Date	Premises	Term (years)	Fine (£)	Rent (£ or £.s.d)	Actual value (£ or £.s.d)
187	Camp's almshouses	1697	Almshouses	41	50	1.6.8	
192	Arlington Street	1682	House	51 (BL)	0	15	
193	Arlington Street	1682	House	51 (BL)	0	12	
194	Arlington Street	1682	House	99 (BL)	0	14	
195	Arlington Street	1687	House	45 (BL)	0	5.10.0	
196	Charterhouse Yard	1703	House#	55 (BL)	0	10	
197	Frith Street	1718	5 houses	60 (BL)	0	11.9.8	

Notes (numbers relate to plans)

37. Middleton lease of 1673 was from 1677. Five years of old lease surrendered for new Turges lease of 1669.

42. The City paid £800 and £38 a year for its leasehold interest in this land (GL, MS 184/4, ff. 47-48).

47. The £153 was from a mixture of tenants at will, leases without entry fine and leases with entry fine.

57. The 30 years were extra years from 1715.

70. Lease was from 1672; responded to a Fire Court decree.

78. Lease with 21 unexpired years surrendered.

79. Lease was from 1685.

85. Back tenement untenanted in 1714, so no rent being paid.

91. Lease was from 1705.

94. The building lease of 1640 was surrendered, and the 31 years was to start in 1651. Actual rent is value estimated in 1639 once the rebuilding was complete.

118. The figures are what the parish offered; nothing more is recorded.

124. Lease was from 1672.

125. Lease was from 1669. Valued at £60 p.a. in 1663; subsequently sub-let for a fine of £120 and rent of £60 p.a.

128. Six years of old lease surrendered. In 1678 the lessee was offered the additional 27 years he wanted (making 99) for £200 (GL, MS 5570/5, p. 443).

129. No fine probably because a lease of 1697 was surrendered.

133. Lease of 1668 surrendered.

151. Lease included a third one-room plan house in Fore Street.

155. Lease was from 1698.

Sources (asterisked if for actual rents)

7. LMA, CLA/017/EM/05/01/001, f. 18.
12. DC, minute book 1574-84, f. 142v.
18. CC, catalogue entry for Estate/4/1C/14 and 15.
23. GL, MS 5570/2, pp. 275, 281.
24. DC, A.II.4.
27. CC, catalogue entry for Estate/25/1C/4 and 5.
34. GL, MS 6165/1.
37. GL, MS 5570/4, pp. 227*, 262, 263, 398; GL, MS 5570/5, pp. 9, 172, 311.
38. GL, MS 6955/1, Nos. 882, 888, 892.
39. GL, MS 6931/3, No. 282; GL, MS 5570/5, p. 225.
46. GC, No. 1930, B393.
47. LMA, COL/CC/BHC/01/004, pp. 36-37*.

55. RBT, E1/1/2, ff. 200, 203, 205, 208, 210, 213, 214, 221.
71. GL, MS 5570/5, p. 188.
77. MCO, Surrey leases, bundle 1, 1679 lease.
79. GL, MS 5570/5, p. 517.
94. GL, MS 6945/1, No. 532; GL, MS 5570/3, p. 383*.
95. GL, MS 6945/1, No. 535.
98. MCO, Lease books, vol. R, p. 132.
99. GC, B IV, 135 (i).
125. LMA, MS 12806/6, pp. 143, 309-10*.
128. GL, MS 6956, No. 951.
144. LMA, H01/ST/E/067/006, No. 29.
146. LMA, CLC/210/G/BCA/047/MS13021 and 13021A.
170. GL, MS 6165/1.

APPENDIX 4

Sources of pre-1720 plans

The purpose of this appendix is to indicate what plans are available and how to find them. It ignores mere plot outlines, but is more inclusive than the rest of this book. Royal palaces are also omitted. Where references would otherwise be needed below, plans in this book are referred to by their Plan number here; document references for these can be found in Appendix 1.

Plan books and loose plans tend to be well catalogued, but deeds and leases have rarely been catalogued in enough detail to identify plans. For plans not identified in catalogues, I have done no more than sample the deeds and leases for properties which are especially interesting or which were drawn up for institutions which tended to include plans. For the City the indispensable list of sources is Derek Keene and Vanessa Harding, *A Survey of Documentary Sources for Property Holding in London before the Great Fire* (London Record Society, vol. 22, 1985), though the locations of documents have often changed subsequently; it includes plan books made after the Great Fire.

BODLEIAN LIBRARY

See Map List 3, Nigel James (comp.), *A Selected List of Estate and Parish Maps up to 1850 in the Bodleian Library Oxford* (2004, updated 2007) (http://lgdata.s3-website-us-east-1.amazonaws.com/docs/999/424860/estate_maps_list.pdf.). All floors of Great Salisbury House *c.*1601 (Gough Drawings, A3, ff. 77-80; Plan 13); Cross Keys Inn, Whitecross Street 1667 (Plan 96); Nevill's Alley 1670 (Plan 28), houses in Broad Street 1671 (MS Ch London a.2, f. 68); house in Copthall Court 1671 (MS DD Harcourt c311 (2)); Press Yard, Newgate Gaol 1702 (MS Ch London a.1, f. 55); house for Baron Shutte 1705 (Gough Maps 22, f. 72v); house in Pall Mall 1719 (ditto); proposed extension of Leadenhall Market 1720 (Gough Maps 21, f. 27); St Stephen Walbrook 1720 (Gough Maps 20, f. 49r); house in Bond Street (Gough Drawings a.3, f. 6).

BRITISH LIBRARY

Navy Office 1698 (Plan 111); Royal Mews *c.*1715 (Plan 114). The Crace Collection of maps is online, albeit incompletely as yet, but includes few detailed pre-1720 plans. Only plot outlines were found among the East India Company deeds at IOR/L/L/2.

BURGHLEY HOUSE

Cecil House *c.*1565 (Plan 6).

CAMBRIDGE COLLEGES

House adjoining St Mary Abchurch 1678, 1718 (Plan 132; Corpus Christi, 09L/H15b); Addle Hill *c.*1700 (St John's, MPS861/1); Ludgate Hill and Blackfriars Lane post-Fire (Trinity, 43 Ludgate Hill, 26a); house in Blackfriars Lane 1717 (ibid., 27). Some plans are listed on the Janus database (janus.lib.cam.ac.uk).

CANTERBURY CATHEDRAL ARCHIVES

Tenter Alley, Southwark *c.*1680 (BB/52/5), Flower de Luce Court, Southwark 1698 (BB/52/8).

CHARTERHOUSE, SUTTON'S HOSPITAL IN

Water supply to Charterhouse *c.*1450 (Plan 1), *c.*1511 (Plan 2), early seventeenth century.

CLOTHWORKERS' COMPANY

The many lease plans are listed in the online catalogue, covering all the Company's properties. So are the non-Treswell plans added after 1612 to the Treswell plan book. See Schofield for Treswell's plans of 1612.

COLLEGE OF ARMS

North and west wings of College, all floors, 1673: see *SOL, The College of Arms* (Monograph 16, 1963), pp. 14, 16, 17, plates 30-34.

COMPTROLLER'S CITY LANDS DEEDS

These cover the extensive estates of the City and the Bridge House, with plans routinely from 1676 and occasionally earlier to the present. The easiest means of access to those from 1700-23 is through the two volumes of plans at LMA (CLA/008/EM/03/018 and 019), containing indexes of places and persons, but the information in the leases is often needed to make sense of them. The leases themselves have been retained by the City Corporation, and permission is needed to examine them. Three different ways may be needed to identify relevant leases: (i) City Lands leases for places within the City are card indexed by place; ask at LMA for Corporation of London RO card indexes, City Lands deeds, places, and the letter of the alphabet required; the card index indicates whether each lease has a plan, and extends before and after 1700-23. (ii) City Lands leases for places outside the City are not included in the index by place, but the lessees are included in the card index of names of lessees; ask at LMA for Corporation of London RO card indexes, City Lands deeds, names, and the letter of the alphabet required; this index too extends before and after 1700-23, as well as beyond the City, but does not indicate whether the leases have plans. (iii) For Bridge House leases there is an index of places and lessees held by the City Corporation (not specifying whether leases include plans), but public access to this is not permitted. The Bridge House rentals (LMA, CLA/007/FN/02/001 onwards) indicate who the lessees were. There are also leases for the City's Conduit Mead estate, but the two pre-1720 ones examined had only plot outlines.

DRAPERS' COMPANY

The Erber 1596 (Plan 12); Throgmorton Street and Austin Friars *c.*1620 (Plan 24); house in Austin Friars 1672 (Plan 131); some rough plans 1656-92 (a51); elevation of house in St Mildred Poultry parish 1720 (I.609.1). Plan book of 1698 consists of plot outlines.

Dyers' Company
Plan book of 1721 for Dyers' Hall Wharf, Dowgate Hill, Black Boy Alley, Thames Street, Holborn. Leases are at Guildhall Library; plans in these are largely plot outlines, except Dyers' Hall Wharf 1716 (Plan 72).

Eton College
Houses in Cheapside and Bread Street c.1617 (Plan 22).

Fishmongers' Company
Plan book of 1686 for Fishmongers' Hall, Thames Street, Porter's Key, High Timber Street, Labour in Vain Hill, Five Foot Lane, Billiter Lane, Leadenhall Street, Bread Street, Friday Street, Lime Street, George Alley off Aldgate, Gracechurch Street, Lombard Street, New Fish Street Hill, Crooked Lane, Aldersgate Street, Great Wood Street, Barbican, Whitecross Street, Fore Street, Pudding Lane, St Olave Southwark, Old Change, Old Fish Street, Fenchurch Street. Other documents are at Guildhall Library, including leases (no pre-1720 plans found in those consulted) and loose plans (mostly listed but not yet in the LMA catalogue); the latter include Glaziers' Hall 1618 (Plan 23); Star Inn c.1639 (Plan 94).

Goldsmiths' Company
Ward's plans of 1692 for Goldsmiths' Hall, Foster Lane, Carey Street, Gutter Lane, Maiden Lane, Noble Street, Lillypot Lane, Staining Lane, Goldsmith Street, Wood Street, Silver Street, Mugwell Street, Bread Street, Trinity Lane, Bow Lane, Budge Row, Cheapside, Cornhill, Poultry, Scalding Alley, Lombard Street, Ludgate, Bowyer Row, Fenchurch Street, Birchin Lane, Old Fish Street, Carter Lane, Bishopsgate Street, Primrose Alley, Walnut Tree Yard, Acorn Alley, Jewin Street, Red Cross Alley and Street, Crowder's Well Alley, Bullhead Court, Goldsmiths' Alley, New Street area, Fleet Street. A few leases include plans, e.g. Goldsmiths' Alley 1687 (plan 43).

Guildhall Library
(1) Armourers' Company: plan book of 1679 (MS 12104) for Armourers' Hall, Thames Street/Trig Lane, Bottle Alley, Thames Street (opposite Custom House), Goose Alley (Fleet Ditch), Old Jewry.

(2) Haberdashers' Company: Haberdashers' Square 1691 (Plan 173). List of deeds available.

(3) Merchant Taylors' Company: plan books of c.1670 (MS 34216) and 1694/95 (MS 34217) provide slightly more than plot outlines. Only plot outlines were found in leases consulted in MS 34100 (listed in MS 34102).

(4) Skinners' Company: plan book of c.1695 (MS 30995/1 and 2) for Skinners' Hall, the Skinners' bargehouse and the Mile End almshouses (otherwise only plot outlines).

(5) Vintners' Company: Garlick Hill 1681 and 1714 (MS 15513 and 15462); off Maiden Lane 1682 (MS 15468). See the detailed list of Vintners' records (MS 33963/1-3).

(6) Other: 62-64 Mark Lane 1675 and 1715 (MS 15177/2/1 and 2/2).

Hatfield House
Proposed exchange in Cornhill c.1537 (CPM I 9); ground and first floors of Holy Trinity Aldgate c.1585 (Plan 9; CPM I 19); several of Bermondsey, Britain's Bourse and the Salisbury House site, including Salisbury and Cecil Streets.

Lincoln's Inn
24 Newgate Street 1667 (D1c13); 11 New Square 1705 (D1e10/1-26).

London Metropolitan Archives
Some plans are referred to in the online catalogue, but cataloguing of deeds and leases is rarely detailed enough to indicate whether plans are present.

(1) City Lands and the Bridge House. Loose plans individually catalogued (COL/CCS/PL or COL/PL). Also London Wall 1676 (Plan 63); City markets 1677 (Plan 90); Meal Market 1700 (Plan 93). For Comptroller's City Lands deeds see separate item.

(2) Christ's Hospital. Leases often include plans, only occasionally mentioned in the catalogue. Some separate plans, of which some are catalogued and others are being catalogued. See Schofield for Treswell's plans of 1607-11.

(3) St Thomas's Hospital. Lease plans and a few separate ones, the latter individually listed in the catalogue, including the Hospital 1697 (H01/ST/A/114/001). The leases fall into three categories: those separately listed in the catalogue (not indicating whether they contain plans; none of those examined did so); those in boxes arranged chronologically (catalogued in H01/ST/INDEX/003, identifying the many plans); and those in three boxes arranged similarly (catalogued in H01/ST/INDEX/004; only one detailed plan found). The NRA list of St Thomas's leases on the shelves at LMA (arranged by county and parish) sometimes ignores plans.

(4) Nomura (CLC/B/169). Leases with plans for the Christ's Hospital area, originally granted by the Hospital. The catalogue indicates some plans but not others.

(5) Bridewell Hospital. Some leases have plans, e.g. Dorset Gardens 1677 (COL/275/MS33224/003, No. 15) and many in Wapping; the catalogue does not identify them.

(6) Dean and Chapter of St Paul's. Plan book for Dean Street, Carter Lane, Schalop Court, Creed Lane (Plan 127).

(7) Miscellaneous plans digitised in Collage (collage.cityoflondon.gov.uk) and searchable there.

(8) Other: including Austin Friars churchyard 17th century (CLC/180/MS07418); Sun Tavern, Fleet Street 1670 (P69/CR1/D/007/MS04447); St Peter Cornhill 1680 (Plan 115); Park Place, St James's Street 1682 (BRA/432/005); Arlington Street, Bennet Street and Piccadilly 1680s (E/PYM/414, 557, 579-81, 586-87, 590-97, 603, 614, 641-42); Billingsgate Dock 1697 (SC/GL/PR/372/LOW-LUD); Emanuel Hospital c.1698 (Plan 188); upper part of Founders' Hall 1700 (CLC/182/MS05896); Church Entry 1702 (Plan 116); Charterhouse Yard 1703 (Plan 196); St Botolph Aldgate (Plan 117); Borough High Street 1712 (E/HOD/058); High Holborn 1717 (Plan 150); Perpoole Lane 1719 (Plan 88).

Medway Archives
Ludgate Hill and Fleet Ditch 1689 (Plan 40).

MIDDLE TEMPLE
Caesar's Buildings c.1666/79 (Plan 120); two sets of chambers 1713.

MUSEUM OF LONDON
Hermitage c.1605 (Plan 11); Hare Street/St John Street 1671 (80.389 6D).

NOMURA INTERNATIONAL PLC
Mansion at Greyfriars 1663? (Plan 125); Aldersgate Street 1667.

NORTHAMPTONSHIRE RECORD OFFICE
Frith Street (Plan 197).

OXFORD COLLEGES
St Paul's Cathedral 1633 or earlier (Plan 25); Morgan's Lane 1684 (Plan 77); Boar's Head Inn (Plan 98); Chancery Lane 1684 (Magdalen, MP/1/39); the Strand and Holywell Lane 1684 (Magdalen, MP/1/45); Mugwell and Silver Streets 1691 (New College, 2369); Petty Wales (New College, 4666 and 3578 f. 348). For All Souls, see Anthony Geraghty, *The Architectural Drawings of Christopher Wren at All Souls College, Oxford: a Complete Catalogue* (2007).

RIBA DRAWINGS COLLECTION
See Mark Girouard, 'The Smythson Collection of the Royal Institute of British Architects', *Architectural History*, vol. 5 (1962), pp. 21-184. Also proposed house in Cheapside 1668 (TiJ/1/1/1).

ROCHESTER BRIDGE TRUST
The plans of the Trust's estate in Leadenhall Street are on the internet: http://www.rbt.org.uk/estate/London/images.htm.

ROYAL ACADEMY
Burlington House 1665-68: see *SOL*, vols 31-32, *St James Westminster*, part 2 (1963), plates 40-41.

ST BARTHOLOMEW'S HOSPITAL
Nine of the ten plans by Llewellyn are in HC 19; the other is in HC 22 (f. 50), together with plans of Turks Head Court (Golden Lane), Purse Court (corner of Moor Lane and Fore Street), the way from Goswell Street towards Islington c.1630, houses north of St Nicholas Shambles 1662, a house in Cow Lane and several undated plans by Heber Lands. Also Limehouse 1588 (HC 21/4); Petty France/Little Britain c.1610 (Plan 16). Most of the Hospital's seventeenth- and eighteenth-century leases are uncatalogued, but see H1/2088 for West Smithfield 1692. Plans in uncatalogued leases include Tower Street and Harp Lane 1671 (Plan 29), Knightrider Street 1671 (box 3), Little Britain 1681 (Plan 133), Old Street 1682 (box 9), the Long Walk 1710 (boxes 9, 19), White Lion Court, Barbican 1712 (box 19), Limehouse Street 1713 (box 19), Duck Lane 1713 (box 19), Newgate Street 1716 (Plan 149), and probably others.

SALTERS' COMPANY
Plan book of 1709 includes Salters' Hall, Whistlers Court, Gracechurch Street, Lombard Street, Cheapside, Red Lion Court, Bread Street, Watling Street, Friday Street, Fell Street, Mugwell Street, Hart Street, Newgate Street, Fore Street, Whitecross Street, Moor Square, Carr Square. Loose plan of Moor Lane 1674.

SOCIETY OF ANTIQUARIES
Blackman Street c.1678 (Plan 58).

STATIONERS' COMPANY
Plan book of 1674 and some plans on leases, relating to Ave Maria Lane and Stationers' Court, Milk Street and Fryer Alley, and the Dark House (parish of St Mary at Hill). All are in the microfilm edition of the Company's records, *Records of the Stationers' Company 1554-1920* (see reels 74 and 110-111); copy at British Library, Manuscripts Department, Microfilm 985/1-96, Microfilm 992/1-19.

SOUTHWARK LOCAL HISTORY LIBRARY
East Lane, Salisbury Lane and Bermondsey Wall 1711 (Plans 60-61).

TALLOW CHANDLERS' COMPANY
Plan book of 1678 for Tallow Chandlers' Hall, Dowgate Hill, Minories, Bishopsgate Street, Newgate Street, Chandlers' Rents, Golden Lane, Old Street, St Olave Street (Southwark) and Bankside (Southwark).

THE NATIONAL ARCHIVES
Plans are usually listed in the online catalogue. Mansion in Cornhill early 16th century (MPI 1/68/2); Steelyard sixteenth century (Plan 5); Cursitors' Hall c.1578 (Plan 8); Hermitage c.1590 (Plan 10); houses in Whitehall (Plan 15); Navy Victualling Yard 1623 and 1635 (MPE 1/564; Plan 110); Durham House 1626 (SP 16/21, No. 64); Rose Street 1638 (Plan 56); property in the Minories (MPE 1/479); St Paul's Convocation House c.1657 (MPF 1/230); King's Bench Prison c.1660 (Plan 112); artillery ground near Leicester House 1661 (MPE 1/1083); George Inn, Southwark 1671 (C 108/129, No. 19); house in Whitehall c.1675 (MPE 1/564); Custom House 1675 and 1717 (C 66/3168, No. 16; T 1/217, f. 120); Steelyard 1680/1 and c.1714 (Plans 73-74); house in Old Queen Street/Dartmouth Street area 1690 (WORK 30/6465/4); Royal Mews c.1690 and c.1720 (MPE 1/560, WORK 30/455); Savoy Hospital c.1700 (MPE 1/478); Marlborough House 1709 (MPE 1/485); Hyde Park Corner 1717 (MPE 1/316).

TOWER HAMLETS LOCAL HISTORY LIBRARY
House at corner of King Street and Old Gravel Lane, including elevation, c.1708 (TH 2830); house between Wapping Street and the Thames (TH 4194). Only the earlier part of the card index of deeds specifies whether they have plans. A separate list of plans on deeds, covering TH 4592-8179, includes nothing pre-nineteenth century.

WESTMINSTER ABBEY MUNIMENTS
There are card indexes of loose plans. Only a few provide more than plot outlines, including Millbank 1696 (Plan 59); Cross Keys Inn in Wood Street 1714 (WAM (P) 496); the Deanery (Plan 130); brewery in Peter Street 1719 (WAM 52505).

WESTMINSTER CITY ARCHIVES
Harrow Alley and Spur Alley, off the Strand, 1621 (1815).

YORK MINSTER LIBRARY
Serjeants' Inn, Fleet Street 1657.

LIST OF ABBREVIATIONS

Bendall	Sarah Bendall, *Dictionary of Land Surveyors and Local Map-makers of Great Britain and Ireland 1530-1850* (2nd edn, 1997), 2 vols	Holder	Nick Holder, 'The medieval friaries of London' (Royal Holloway, London, DPhil, 2011)
BL	British Library	*LAMAS*	*Transactions of the London & Middlesex Archaeological Society*
CC	Clothworkers' Company	LMA	London Metropolitan Archives
CLPB, A	Plans of City Lands properties, 1701-13, LMA, CLA/008/EM/03/018 (abbreviation followed by page number)	*LTR*	*London Topographical Record*
		LTS	London Topographical Society
		McKellar	Elizabeth McKellar, *The Birth of Modern London* (1999)
CLPB, B	Plans of City Lands properties, 1713-23, LMA, CLA/008/EM/03/019 (abbreviation followed by folio number)	MCO	Magdalen College, Oxford
		RBT	Rochester Bridge Trust
		SBH	St Bartholomew's Hospital
CCLD	City Corporation, Comptroller's City Lands deeds (e.g. COL/CCS/RM16/058/032 becomes CCLD, 58.32, taking the last two numbers from the full reference); for Bridge House leases and the Leadenhall plan of 1698, the abbreviation is instead followed by the full reference	Schofield	John Schofield (ed.), *The London Surveys of Ralph Treswell* (LTS No. 135, 1987)
		SLHL	Southwark Local History Library
		SMLH	John Schofield, *Medieval London Houses* (1995)
		SOL	*Survey of London*
		Stow	C.L. Kingsford (ed.), *A Survey of London by John Stow* (1908), 2 vols
CLJ	Journals of the City Lands Committee, LMA, COL/CC/CLC/01/001 to 009, 019, 020, 022, 034 (abbreviation followed by item number and folio number, e.g. CLJ, 001, f. 1)	Strype	John Strype, *A Survey of the Cities of London and Westminster* (1720)
		TNA	The National Archives
		Woodhead	J.R. Woodhead, *The Rulers of London 1660-1689* (1965)
DC	Drapers' Company		
GC	Goldsmiths' Company		
GL	Guildhall Library, London		
HH	Hatfield House		
Hearth tax	Matthew Davies *et al* (eds), *London and Middlesex 1666 Hearth Tax* (British Record Society hearth tax series, vol. 9, 2014), 2 vols		

Shortened references are given for LMA documents which are on microfilm arranged by the old Guildhall Library MS references. No footnotes are given where the information is from the same document as the plan (e.g. in the lease to which the plan is attached).

NOTES

Notes to the 'Introduction', pages 1-36

1 See Schofield.
2 See text for Plans 105, 147, 174-75; GL, MS 6153/4, f. 3v. For discussion, see McKellar, pp. 120-23.
3 Examples of these are St Paul's Cathedral before the Fire and Powis House.
4 Craig Spence, *London in the 1690s: A Social Atlas* (2000), p. 65. Spence's 'Eastern parishes' and 'Middlesex within the Bills' have been excluded for this purpose.
5 A. L. Beier, 'Engine of manufacture: the trades of London', in A. L. Beier and Roger Finlay (eds), *London 1500-1700: The Making of the Metropolis* (1986), pp. 155-56.
6 William C. Baer, 'Landlords and tenants in London, 1550-1700', *Urban History Review*, vol. 38 (2011), pp. 245, 252.
7 Peter Earle, *The Making of the English Middle Class* (1991 edn), pp. 17-18; Jan de Vries, *European Urbanization 1500-1800* (1984), p. 270.
8 P. D. A. Harvey, *Maps in Tudor England* (1993), p. 79; R. A. Skelton and P. D. A. Harvey (eds), *Local Maps and Plans from Medieval England* (1986), p. 6.
9 John H. Harvey, 'Four fifteenth-century London plans', *LTR*, vol. 20 (1952), pp. 1-8; Skelton and Harvey, *Local Maps and Plans*, pp. 260-61.
10 Harvey, *Maps in Tudor England*, pp. 104, 107. For other pre-Fire examples, see East Sussex Record Office, DAN/1719, 1721; GL, Haberdashers' deeds, MS 1996/5, 1/9, No. 15.2; LMA, E/BER/CG/T/003/010, 1659 lease; GL, MS 24972, bundle 6, 1638 abstract; CCLD, F.1.
11 *Survey of Building Sites in the City of London after the Great Fire of 1666*, vols 1-5 (LTS Nos. 97-99, 101, 103, 1963-67).
12 e.g. *A Survey of Hatton Garden by Abraham Arlidge 1694* (LTS No. 128, 1983); GL, MS 30995/1 and 2; TNA, C 105/21; Peter Barber, *London: A History in Maps* (LTS No. 173, 2012), pp. 68, 70.
13 Peter Barber, 'Mapmaking in England, ca.1470-1650', in David Woodward (ed.), *The History of Cartography*, vol. 3, *Cartography in the Renaissance*, part 2 (2007), pp. 1600-08.
14 There is an early sixteenth-century plan of a large mansion described as being beside the Stocks end (i.e. the west end) of Cornhill and belonging to the Charterhouse (TNA, MPI 1/68/2), probably on the site of the Royal Exchange, but the date, exact location and purpose are all unknown.
15 Harvey, *Maps in Tudor England*, p. 98; Anthony Gerbine and Stephen Johnson, *Compass and Rule: Architecture as Mathematical Practice in England 1500-1750* (2009), p. 29.
16 Derek Keene, 'Not the Royal Exchange', *LTR*, vol. 31 (2015), pp. 107-08, 111, 114.
17 Harvey, *Maps in Tudor England*, pp. 31, 69, 72-74, 95-101; Gerbine and Stephens, *Compass and Rule*, pp. 39-42; L.R. Shelby, *John Rogers, Tudor Military Engineer* (1967), p. 146 and plates. See also P. D. A. Harvey, *Manors and Maps in Rural England, from the Tenth Century to the Seventeenth* (2010), XV, p. 2, XVII, p. 3.
18 Harvey, *Maps in Tudor England*, pp. 69-74.
19 David Pannett, 'The manuscript maps of Warwickshire 1597-1880', *Warwickshire History*, vol. 6 (1984-85), p. 74; Vestry House Museum, Walthamstow, map of High Hall manor 1699; West Sussex Record Office, Petworth 3580 and 3581 (from 1706).
20 This conclusion is not affected by the fact that Plan 12 may be a later copy.
21 P. D. A. Harvey, 'Estate surveyors and the spread of the scale-map in England, 1550-80', in Harvey, *Manors and Maps*, pp. 1-2.
22 e.g. a brewery at Chatham in 1688 (Medway Archives, U1191/P1).
23 Arata Ide, 'Corpus Christi College, Cambridge in 1577: reading the social space in Sir Nicholas Bacon's college plan', *Transactions of the Cambridge Bibliographical Society*, vol. 15 (2013), pp. 281, 290, plates. For other Cambridge plans, see Robert and John Willis, *The Architectural History of the University of Cambridge* (1886), vol. 1, pp. 81-82, 291, vol. 2, pp. 255, 466, vol. 3, pp. 4, 319-20. I am grateful to Elisabeth Leedham-Green for these references.
24 Personal communication from Roger Leech; see Roger H. Leech, *The Town House in Medieval and Early Modern Bristol* (2014). For the outline, of 1649, see Roger Leech, *The Topography of Medieval and Early Modern Bristol*, part 1 (Bristol Record Society, vol. 48, 1997), Fig. 14.
25 Schofield, pp. 2-4.
26 Barber, 'Mapmaking', p. 1643n.
27 e.g. Cheapside Gazetteer, 11/8A 1-5 at http://www.british-history.ac.uk/no-series/london-gazetteer-pre-fire/pp48-78#h3-0 008. I owe this point (and the reference) to Vanessa Harding.
28 GL, MS 34010/8, p. 260; GL, MS 34216.
29 GL, MS 7353/2, f. 15r; GL, MS 7528. The latter comprises plans marked 'No. 1' and 'No. 8'.
30 GL, MS 34216; GL, MS 34217; GL, MS 30995/1-2; DC, plan book 1698.
31 For the rising numbers of rural estate maps and surveyors, see Bendall, vol. 1, p. 11; A. Sarah Bendall, *Maps, Land and Society* (1992), p. 30; A. Stuart Mason, *An Upstart Art: Early Mapping in Essex* (typescript, c.1996, copy in British Library), passim; F. Hull (ed.), *Catalogue of Estate Maps 1590-1840 in the Kent County Archives Office* (1973), pp. 1-52.
32 LMA, COL/CC/CLC/03/003, f. 33r.
33 LMA, COL/CC/BHC/05/001, p. 271.
34 LMA, COL/CC/CLC/03/003, f. 33r.
35 Based on Derek Keene and Vanessa Harding, *A Survey of Documentary Sources for Property Holding in London before the Great Fire* (London Record Society, vol. 22, 1985), pp. 12-36.
36 CC, minute book 1683-1712, p. 247.

37 GL, MS 16967/6, pp. 59, 60, 62, 75, 113, 119, 154. Only the written description survives (GL, MS 17254).
38 LMA, P69/MTN2/B/007/MS00958, ff. 1-9. See also LMA, P69/EDK/B/011/MS04266/001, pp. 148, 200-01; LMA, Collage 27210.
39 Harvey, *Maps in Tudor England*, pp. 104, 107.
40 LMA, COL/CC/CLC/04/02, No. 397. There are examples of Christ's Hospital referring for dimensions and abuttals to Treswell's plan book or to a plan held by the Hospital rather than appended to the lease (Plan 146).
41 LMA, COL/CC/CLC/03/003, f. 33.
42 In the City's case, at least 27 of John Olley's plans from the 1690s are dated, but only nine were drawn significantly before the date of the lease, and nine were drawn after that date.
43 LMA, COL/CC/CLC/03/005, p. 49. The one outcome was the plan of City lands in Ratcliff and Limehouse, which has not survived (ibid., pp. 182, 214; LMA, COL/CC/CLC/03/006, p. 59).
44 See also p. 291 above (College of Arms). There are also two which show the first floor as well as the ground floor, but not the floors above: see Plans 9, 74.
45 GL, MS 5570/5, p. 123.
46 Above, p. 6; LMA, COL/CC/CLC/03/007, f. 40r.
47 CLJ, 001, f. 57v.
48 'Thomas Penson pinxit' is written on the Fishmongers' title page. For Penson, see C.D. van Strien, 'Thomas Penson: precursor of the sentimental traveller', in Z.R.W.M. von Martels (ed.), *Travel Fact and Travel Fiction* (1994), p. 194.
49 GL, MS 6153/5, f. 27v.
50 McKellar, pp. 123-35. See also Gerbine and Johnson, *Compass and Rule*.
51 GL, MS 5570/3, p. 506; CC, minute book 1639-49, ff. 17r, 31r; LMA, H01/ST/D/07/003, 26 August 1681. See also GL, MS 5570/2, p. 832.
52 e.g. LMA, CLC/210/G/BBH/001/MS12918/003, 1674 lease; Plans 3, 169. For the City, see LMA, COL/CC/CLC/03/005, pp. 67, 71, 214.
53 The only suggestion that the written word was considered superior to the plan is from a witness on behalf of the notoriously unscrupulous Nicholas Barbon (McKellar, p. 131).
54 e.g. 'Shere Lane, Little Lincoln's Inn Fields: a building agreement of 1675', *LTR*, vol. 18 (1942), pp. 34-40; BL, Eg Ch 325.
55 LMA, CLA/007/FN/02/010, p. 386, 18 November and 9 December; John Cooper, *The Queen's Agent: Francis Walsingham at the Court of Elizabeth I* (2011), pp. 168, 201, 301.
56 Anna Keay, *The Elizabethan Tower of London: The Haiward and Gascoyne Plan of 1597* (LTS No. 158, 2001), pp. 12-13.
57 Philip E. Jones, 'The estates of the Corporation of London', *Guildhall Miscellany*, vol. 1, No. 7 (1956), p. 3; Carl Moreland and David Bannister, *Antique Maps* (1989), pp. 65, 71.
58 Bendall, vol. 2, p. 339.
59 Westminster City Archives, 1815; Bendall, vol. 2, p. 396.
60 GL, MS 5570/2, p. 799; GL, MS 5570/3, pp. 62, 68; Martin Devereux, Stacey Gee and Matthew Payne, *Lords of All They Survey: Estate Maps at Guildhall Library* (2004), pp. 36-37; LMA, CLA/007/FN/03/016, 11 June 1631, and 017, 9 March 1644; LMA, catalogue entries for H01/ST/E/103/003, 114/002, 115/025 and 115/063; Ian Doolittle, *The Mercers' Company 1579-1959* (1994), plate VIII; Bendall, vol. 2, p. 55.
61 Schofield, pp. 1-2; Dorian Gerhold, 'New light on Ralph Treswell senior and junior', *LTR*, vol. 31 (2015), pp. 45-49.
62 Ibid.

63 SBH, HC 19, ff. 51-9; SBH, HC 22, f. 50. All except the plan of St Bartholomew the Less and the second Hosier Lane plan were published as LTS Nos. 84, 87 and 88 (1950-51, 1953-54, 1955). The suggestion that the plans were by Ralph Treswell is unfounded (Peter Whitfield, *London: A Life in Maps* (2006), p. 41).
64 Tony Campbell, 'Atlas pioneer', *Geographical Magazine* (December 1975), pp. 162-67.
65 SBH, HA 1/4, f. 94r.
66 SBH, HB 1/3, f. 458r; SBH, HB 1/4, f. 28r. In 1626 Bridge House paid Jordan 8s. 'for composeinge the modell of a parte of London Bridge set up in ye hall' (LMA, CLA/007/FN/03/015, 29 April 1626). For architectural models 1568-1638, see Malcolm Airs, *The Tudor and Jacobean Country House: A Building History* (1995), pp. 86-87; McKellar, p. 121.
67 SBH, HB 1/3, f. 545r.
68 SBH, HB 1/4, f. 52v and 10th page of discharge 1620-21. From 1617 to 1620 the Hospital's accounts are less informative than before and after.
69 Michael Treadwell, 'Lists of master printers: the size of the London printing trade, 1637-1723', in Robin Myers and Michael Harris (eds), *Aspects of Printing from 1700* (1987), p. 158; C.E. Kenney, 'William Leybourn, 1626-1716', *The Library*, 5th ser., vol. 5 (1950-51), pp. 159-62.
70 A.W. Richeson, *English Land Measuring to 1800: Instruments and Practice* (1966), pp. 113-14, 118. The possible exception was John Love.
71 Kenney, 'William Leybourn', pp. 159-60; Treadwell, 'Lists of master printers', p. 159. The Southall dwelling had three hearths (TNA, E 179/143/370).
72 Introduction by Ralph Hyde in *A to Z of Restoration London* (LTS No. 145, 1992), pp. v, vii, ix; Wiltshire Record Office, 490/560/1; CC, CL/G/7/1, f. 43r; CC, Estate/5/4A/1; GL, MS 17254; GL, MS 16967/6, pp. 75, 119, 154.
73 LMA, COL/CC/CLC/07/03, pp. 73, 187-88; TNA, C 24/1109, No. 93.
74 GL, MS 5570/5, pp. 397, 621.
75 CCLD, *passim*. See also LMA, COL/CC/CLC/07/03, pp. 73, 187-88; Betty Masters, *The Public Markets of the City of London Surveyed by William Leybourn in 1677* (LTS No. 117, 1974), pp. 9-10.
76 LMA, H01/ST/E/067/011 and 012.
77 LMA, MS 12819/10, 1675-76, 1679-80.
78 An agreement was made in May 1680, the intended book to include plots already made, and the Beadle was ordered to accompany Leybourn, but subsequently there is only a summons in February 1681 for Leybourn to attend the court and an order to him in 1682 to plot the Company's land in Pope's Head Alley (GL, MS 34010/10, pp. 50, 52, 67, 76, 102, 204). The plan book labelled on the binding as of 1680 (GL, MS 34216) is not in Leybourn's style and is probably the book made by John Oliver and others in 1668-71 (GL, MS 34010/8, pp. 198, 206, 214, 247, 260, 383).
79 LMA, CLA/007/FN/03/020, 3 July, 16 October 1680, 8 January, 21 May, 30 July 1681, 10 February, 31 March 1683, 13 and 20 September 1684; LMA, COL/CCS/PL/01/51B.
80 RBT, E21/05/013.
81 See Bendall, vol. 2, pp. 317-18.
82 Kenney, 'William Leybourn', pp. 166, 168, 169.
83 William Leybourn, *Pleasure with Profit* (1694), advertisement.
84 MCO, MP/1/39, 45, 86 and 87a; LMA, CLC/313/L/F/019/MS12193; LMA, COL/PL/02/G/006.
85 Twenty depositions in TNA, class C 24, give a range of

possible birth dates from 1655 to 1659. Date of death from TNA, C 11/982/8, answer.
86 TNA, C 24/1101, No. 33; TNA, C 24/1317, No. 1; TNA, C 24/1315, Fleet v. Ashton; TNA, C 11/982/8, answer (schedule).
87 TNA, C 24/1106, No. 4; TNA, C 24/1210, Nicholl v. Bearcroft; TNA, C 24/1262, No. 26; TNA, C 24/1299, No. 21; TNA, C 24/1320, No. 82; TNA, C 24/1347, No. 51.
88 TNA, C 24/1284, No. 9; TNA, C 24/1340, No. 56.
89 TNA, C 11/2285/94; TNA, C 11/2368/2; TNA, C 24/1253, No. 40; TNA, C 24/1331, No. 97; Cliff Webb, *London Apprentices*, vol. 10, *Basketmakers' Company*, pp. 5, 18, 17, 18, 23, 25.
90 Howard Colvin, *A Biographical Dictionary of British Architects 1600-1840* (1995 edn), p. 1150; LMA, COL/CC/CLC/03/009, f. 163.
91 CLJ, 003, f. 230r.
92 LMA, COL/CC/CLC/03/007, pp. 77, 198, and 008, p. 31; Plan 64.
93 CLJ, 003, ff. 95v, 98r.
94 CLJ, 001, f. 57v, 005, ff. 118r, 202r, 254v, 292r.
95 LMA, CLA/008/EM/03/018 and 019. CCLD provide the dates.
96 TNA, C 24/1299, No. 21.
97 LMA, P69/ALH5/B/003/MS05090/003, pp. 209-10.
98 Colvin, *Biographical Dictionary*, pp. 715-16.
99 TNA, C 24/1331, No. 97. See McKellar, pp. 95, 106.
100 TNA, C 24/1335, No. 53.
101 CLJ, 001, f. 162v, 002, f. 15r; TNA, C 5/597/93; TNA, C 11/982/8, answer (schedule); TNA, C 11/2368/2.
102 TNA, C 11/2031/15; TNA, C 11/982/8, answer (schedule); TNA, C 11/2285/94.
103 TNA, C 11/982/8, answer (schedule).
104 TNA, C 24/1325, No. 15; TNA, C 24/1390, No. 17; TNA, PROB 11/595/186; Colvin, *Biographical Dictionary*, p. 1150; CCLD; LMA, COL/OF/02/036; CLJ, 005, ff. 118r, 202r, 254v, 292r, 006, 110r. Isaac may have assisted from as early as 1702, when the writing on John's plans changes from his somewhat square style to one similar to Isaac's more flowing style.
105 CC, minute book 1683-1712, p. 247; CC, Estate/15/1C/1; CC, Charity/Heron/G/C/1/14; CC, Estate/10/1C/21; CC, CL/G/Charity/Evans/G/C/1/12 and 13; CC, Estate/15/1C/3.
106 Somerset Record Office, catalogue entry for T\PH\bm/32; TNA, catalogue entry for Lambeth Palace Library, TD 98; CC, CL/G/Charity/Hobby/G/C/1/8.
107 John Ward, *A Compendium of Algebra* (1695); John Ward, *The Young Mathematician's Guide* (1707), preface.
108 Benjamin Wardhaugh, 'Consuming mathematics: John Ward's *Young Mathematician's Guide* (1707) and its owners', *Journal for Eighteenth-Century Studies*, vol. 38 (2015), pp. 65, 79.
109 GC, Court minute book 10 (1688-1708), f. 80.
110 John Darling, *The Carpenters Rule made Easie* (1694, 1709, 1727, 1738). He was almost certainly 'Eber Land', son of John Land, barber chirurgeon, christened at St Giles Cripplegate in 1672. Land tax was paid in Castle Baynard ward by Lands 1721-22, Eben Lands 1723 and 1730-33, Ebeneser Lands 1724-29 and Heber Lands 1734-36 (Ancestry, London land tax).
111 Bendall, *Maps, Land and Society*, pp. 1-2; GL, Fishmongers' uncatalogued plans, Box 2, No. V (maps of Willesden and Neasden, 1716). I am not persuaded that he was the same as Helier Lands, military engineer (Bendall, vol. 2, p. 303).
112 LMA, CLC/B/169/MS39229; LMA, CLC/210/G/BNB/003/MS13506; BL, Add MS 17939B; SBH, catalogue entries for HC/22/39 and 40; CCLD, 66.15; RBT, E21/04/009 and 024; GL, MS 30995/2, between f. 5 and f. 6; MCO, MP/1/41.
113 CC, CL/G/Charity/Holligrave/G/C/24; CC, Estate/31/3A/12; CC, Estate/16/1C/7.
114 Bendall, vol. 2, p. 19; TNA, catalogue entry for PROB 18/57/49.
115 TNA, C 24/1168, No. 32; TNA, C 24/1189, No. 5; TNA, C 24/1220, No. 107; Bendall, vol. 2, p. 242.
116 LMA, Collage 5244; Museum of London, 80.389 6D. See Robert Latham and William Matthews (eds), *The Diary of Samuel Pepys*, vol. 10 (*Companion*) (1983), p. 34.
117 Simon Thurley, *The Whitehall Palace Plan of 1670* (LTS No. 153, 1998), p. 7.
118 E.G.R. Taylor, *The Mathematical Practitioners of Tudor and Stuart England* (1954), pp. 294-95; LMA, CLC/210/G/BCG/006A/MS22634/9; Ward, *Young Mathematician's Guide* (1707), p. 369.
119 TNA, C 24/1014, No. 12; TNA, PROB 11/425/266. Titcombe is sometimes referred to as Fitcombe because of the way his name is written on the title page of the Armourers' plan book, but the statement there that he was a Company member and a City viewer and the references to him in the Armourers' minutes make it certain that he was Titcombe.
120 Cliff Webb, *London Apprentices*, vol. 22, *Armourers' and Brasiers' Company c1610-1800* (1998), p. 58; TNA, PROB 11/425/266; TNA, C 24/1014, No. 12.
121 TNA, C 5/447/9; McKellar, pp. 127-28; GL, MS 184/4, f. 46v.
122 LMA, COL/CC/CLC/07/002, f. 5v; GL, MS 12104; LMA, COL/SJ/27/467.
123 GL, MS 12071/4, ff. 24r, 26r, 30v; TNA, C 24/1014, No. 12.
124 Woodhead, p. 163; GL, MS 12071/4, ff. 22v, 26v, 42r, 62r.
125 TNA, C 24/1022, No. 84; Bower Marsh, *Records of the Worshipful Company of Carpenters*, vol. 1 (1913), pp. 81, 111, 159.
126 LMA, H01/ST/D/07/003, 26 August 1681, 28 September 1682, 18 January 1684.
127 LMA, MS 12819/8 to 12.
128 TNA, C 24/961, No. 32.
129 TNA, C 24/996, No. 31.
130 *LTR*, vol. 10 (1916), plate opposite p. 3; New College, Oxford, 4666.
131 TNA, C 24/996, No. 31.
132 GL, MS 30708/5, pp. 292, 321, 391, 438; GL, MS 30708/6, p. 77; CCLD, 66.13.
133 RBT, E 21/12/007.
134 Bodleian Library, MS DD Harcourt c311 (2); LMA, CLC/210/G/BSK/018/MS13886; Colvin, *Biographical Dictionary*, p. 836; McKellar, pp. 132-33; TNA, C 24/987, No. 84.
135 Salters' Company, plan book 1709; Salters' Company, minute book 1685-1721, 12 May, 6 July 1709; Priscilla Metcalf, *The Halls of the Fishmongers' Company* (1977), p. 99; Dyers' Company, plan book 1721; GL, MS 8164/2, pp. 306, 413; Bendall, *Maps, Land and Society*, p. 224; Bendall, vol. 2, p. 208; Colvin, *Biographical Dictionary*, p. 419.
136 Ibid., pp. 302-03.
137 TNA, C 24/1349, No. 52; Tony Campbell, 'The Drapers' Company and its school of seventeenth century chart-makers', in Helen Wallis and Sarah Tyacke (eds), *My Head is a Map: Essays and Memoirs in Honour of R.V. Tooley* (1973), pp. 81-106; Bendall, vol. 2, p. 189; Plans 60, 61; BL, Add Ch 76643. Friend's address was East Lane in November 1715 but Leadenhall Street in February 1716 (TNA, C 24/1349, Nos. 52 and 91).

138 John Holwell, *A Sure Guide to the Practical Surveyor* (1678), 2nd part; D. J. Bryden, 'The surveyor's task', in Philippa Glanville, *London in Maps* (1972), pp. 63-65; Bendall, *Maps, Land and Society*, pp.129-38.
139 BL, Sloane MS 3254A.
140 See Leech, *Town House*, pp. 60-62 for partable walls.
141 GL, MS 30708/6, pp. 309, 344, 390, 412; GL, MS 34101/10, p. 76.
142 GC, Court minute book 1736-42, f. 111.
143 GL, MS 6153/5, f. 30v; GL, MS 16967/6, p. 154. See also GL, MS 5570/2, p. 799; LMA, H01/ST/E/068/004/27.
144 TNA, C 24/1144, No. 60; LMA, CLA/007/FN/03/020, 10 February, 31 March 1683, 13 and 20 September 1684.
145 LMA, COL/CC/CLC/04/02, No. 397.
146 GL, MS 34010/10, p. 52.
147 Rebuilding Act 1667, s. V.
148 e.g. Leybourn might use two different types of capital letter on the same plan (CC, CL/G/7/1, f. 43r).
149 I owe this point to Peter Barber.
150 GL, MS 5570/5, pp. 397, 621, 625.
151 GL, MS 34010/10, p. 52; LMA, COL/CC/CLC/03/005, p. 65.
152 LMA, MS 12819/8 to 12.
153 GL, MS 5570/5, p. 146.
154 LMA, P69/ALH5/B/003/MS05090/003, pp. 209-10.
155 SMLH, p. 1; Schofield, p. 28; Thurley, *Royal Palaces*, pp. 41, 54-55, 81; Plans 106, 188 below.
156 C.C. Knowles and P.H. Pitt, *The History of Building Regulation in London* (1972), pp. 19-31.
157 M.J. Power, 'The East and West in early-modern London', in E.W. Ives et al, *Wealth and Power in Tudor England* (1978), pp. 170-71. See also Roger H. Leech, 'The prospect from Rugman's Row: the row house in late sixteenth- and early seventeenth-century London', *Archaeological Journal*, vol. 153 (1996), pp. 225-30.
158 LMA, CLA/008/EM/02/01/002, f. 181v.
159 For other timber buildings of the 1650s, see Peter Guillery, *The Small House in Eighteenth-Century London* (2004), p. 41.
160 McKellar, pp. 85, 159.
161 Guillery, *Small House*, pp. 41, 127, 146. There are also late seventeenth century timber houses in Middle Temple Lane.
162 e.g. Hampshire RO, 148M71/9/2/27; DC, minute book 1667-1705, f. 12v.
163 Metcalf, *Halls of the Fishmongers' Company*, p. 62.
164 LMA, H01/ST/E/067/018, No. 8. See Dan Cruickshank and Neil Burton, *Life in the Georgian City* (1990), p. 60.
165 Guillery, *Small House*, pp. 34-35; William Baer, 'Housing for the lesser sort in Stuart London: findings from certificates, and returns of divided houses', *London Journal*, vol. 33 (2008), p. 75; Peter Guillery, 'Houses in London's suburbs', in Hearth tax, p. 144; Power, 'East and West in early-modern London', p. 172.
166 TNA, SP 29/194, No. 94. The high streets were Temple Bar-St Paul's Churchyard-Cheapside-Aldgate, Newgate-Cheapside, the new street Guildhall-Cheapside, Lombard Street, Fenchurch Street, London Bridge-Gracechurch Street-Bishopsgate.
167 *Records of the Worshipful Company of Stationers*, reel 74 (BL, Microfilm 985/74).
168 Schofield, pp. 11, 15.
169 Schofield, p. 15.
170 See also CLPB, A39 for a development of the 1640s by Francis Zacharie in Rose Lane and White Horse Street in Stepney (LMA, COL/CHD/CT/01/023, p. 76; LMA, CLA/008/EM/02/01/002, ff. 86v, 101r-v; CLJ, 003, f. 94r).
171 Schofield, p. 15.
172 Guillery, *Small House*, pp. 61-66. For plan types, see Neil Burton and Peter Guillery, *Behind the Facade: London House Plans, 1660-1840* (2006), especially pp. 14-22.
173 See also Plans 27, 52, 79-81, 105; CLPB, A130; LMA, CLC/180/MS07418.
174 John Bennell, 'Shop and office in medieval and Tudor London', *LAMAS*, vol. 40 (1989), p. 198.
175 GC, 1725, B393, entry for Ward's plan 8, No. 31; Plans 30-33. The Rebuilding Act of 1667 provided that the first floor over the cellar should not be more than eighteen inches above street level (s. XII).
176 Cruickshank and Burton, *Life in the Georgian City*, p. 52.
177 Earle, *Making of the English Middle Class*, p. 297.
178 SMLH, p. 88.
179 Leech, *Town House*, pp. 109-12, 117, 122.
180 See Leech, *Town House*, pp. 281-93.
181 Schofield, pp. 18-19; D. Portman, *Exeter Houses 1400-1700* (1966), p. 35; Ursula Priestley and P. J. Corfield, 'Rooms and room use in Norwich housing, 1580-1730', *Post-Medieval Archaeology*, vol. 16 (1982), p. 103; Cruickshank and Burton, *Life in the Georgian City*, p. 54.
182 GC, 1725, B393, entries for Ward's plan 7, No. 39 (i.e. house 15 on Plan 108).
183 GC, 1725, B393.
184 *Records of the Worshipful Company of Stationers*, reel 111 (BL, Microfilm 992/15), Box 19; Earle, *Making of the English Middle Class*, p. 292.
185 SMLH, p. 81; Lena Cowen Orlin, *Locating Privacy in Tudor London* (2007), pp. 296-326.
186 Only the third room on the first and second floors of the largest of the Stationers' houses in Ave Maria Lane and, among the Armourers' properties, one first-floor room and one third-floor room.
187 SMLH, pp. 86-87; Orlin, *Locating Privacy*, pp. 161-62.
188 Schofield, pp. 22-24; SMLH, p. 3.
189 Cruickshank and Burton, *Life in the Georgian City*, pp. 194-95.
190 Baer, 'Landlords and tenants', p. 254.
191 LMA, CLA/008/EM/02/01/002, f. 34v.
192 Appendix 3; MCO, Surrey leases, bundles 1 to 4; MCO, lease books, vols P-S.
193 Baer, 'Landlords and tenants', p. 240n.
194 See LTS Newsletter 76 (May 2013), pp. 9-11, for length of leases.
195 e.g. Hampshire Record Office, 148M71/9/27; Derek Keene and Vanessa Harding, *Historical Gazetteer of London before the Great Fire: Cheapside* (1987), pp. 713-23; above, p. 20.
196 Walter George Bell, *The Great Fire of London in 1666* (1923), pp. 223-24, 282-83; Stephen Porter, *The Great Fire of London* (1996), pp. 127-28. Bell's case for a fall from 13,200 houses in the burnt area (the number estimated after the Fire) to between 8,000 and 9,000 was based on the incorrect assumption that the numbers of payments to the surveyors for staking out foundations provide a complete record of the number of foundations laid (see T.F. Reddaway, *The Rebuilding of London after the Great Fire* (1940), p. 279n; Peter W. M. Blayney, *The Bookshops in Paul's Cross Churchyard* (Occasional Papers of the Bibliographical Society, No. 5, 1990), pp. 7-8). Defoe believed the number of houses had increased (quoted in McKellar, pp. 176-77).

197 See also Strype, book 3, p. 121; Philip E. Jones (ed.), *The Fire Court*, vol. 1 (1966), pp. 130-31.
198 E. A. Wrigley, 'A simple model of London's importance in changing English society and economy, 1650-1750', *Past and Present*, vol. 37 (1967), p. 44. But see also Spence, *London in the 1690s*, p. 65; Roger Finlay and Beatrice Shearer, 'Population growth and suburban expansion', in Beier and Finlay, *London 1500-1700*, pp. 37-59; Vanessa Harding, 'The population of London, 1550-1700: a review of the published evidence', *London Journal*, vol. 15 (1990), pp. 111-28; L. D. Schwarz, *London in the Age of Industrialisation* (1992), pp. 125-28. The figures for 1700 and 1750 are the least certain, and those given here may be too high.
199 GL, MS 30708/6, p. 309.
200 e.g. Tallow Chandlers' Company, plan book 1678.
201 COL/WD/03/001 to 031.
202 CCLD, dated lease plans by John Olley in the 1690s.
203 M. J. Power, 'The social topography of Restoration London', in Beier and Finlay, *London 1500-1700*, pp. 205, 214.

Notes to 'Early Plans, c.1450-1630', pages 37-84

1 Entry based mainly on Philip Temple, *The Charterhouse* (SOL monograph, 2010); Sir William St John Hope, *The History of the London Charterhouse* (1935), pp. 107-32. See also M.D. Knowles, 'Clerkenwell and Islington, Middlesex', in R.A. Skelton and P.D.A. Harvey (eds), *Local Maps and Plans from Medieval England* (1986), pp. 221-28.
2 P. D. A. Harvey, *The History of Topographical Maps* (1980), pp. 90, 97.
3 Hope, *History*, pp. 113, 116, 129, 132.
4 For buildings shown on the plan, see *SOL*, vol. 47, *Northern Clerkenwell and Pentonville* (2008), pp. 1, 281.
5 Stephen Porter, 'The Charterhouse water supply', unpublished paper.
6 Robert Somerville, *The Savoy – Manor: Hospital: Chapel* (1960), pp. 25, 35, 236-37.
7 LMA, H01/ST/E/015/B, f. 134v.
8 LMA, P69/MIC4/C/003/MS00814/001 to 010.
9 E. A. Gee, 'Oxford carpenters, 1370-1530', *Oxoniensa*, vols 17-18 (1952-53), pp. 134-36; H. M. Colvin, *The History of the King's Works*, vol. 3, 1485-1660, part 1 (1975), p. 408.
10 e.g. Plans 169, 192-95; LMA, CLC/210/G/BBH/001/MS12918/003, lease of 1673.
11 The Savoy Hospital owned property both west and east of that covered by the plan, and in 1846 St Thomas's Hospital, which had acquired the Savoy lands, held Nos. 17-27 Fleet Lane (LMA, P69/SEP/C/036/MS03133/001), which was roughly the eastern third of Fleet Lane's south side.
12 Entry based mainly on Derek Keene, 'New discoveries at the Hanseatic Steelyard in London', *Hansische Geschichtsblätter*, vol. 107 (1989), pp. 15-25; illustrations in T. G. Werner, 'Der Stalhof der deutschen Hanse in London in wirtschafts und kunsthistorischen bildwerken', *Scripta Mercaturae* 2/1973; Philip Norman, 'Notes on the later history of the Steelyard in London', *Archaeologia*, vol. 61 (1909), pp. 389-426.
13 See text for Plans 73-74. Counsel's opinion in the 1670s was that the property might be seized if rebuilt 'otherwise than it was in antient time' (TNA, C 118/412, Almaine merchants v. Jacobsen, No. 23).
14 This assumes that Allhallows Lane was straightened after the Fire.
15 The plan first appeared in J. M. Lappenberg, *Urkundliche geschichte des Hansischen Stahlhofes zu London* (1851), plan II, as a reproduction of a printed plan stated to have been copied by 'Lieut G' from a work by Hollar of 1667. A manuscript version, published in Werner, 'Stalhof', Fig. 76 (and then in British Railways' archive), bears a note stating 'Original printed plan lent to Dr Lappenberg 24 March 1843'. The date indicates that the loan was made in Germany, whereas, as the note is in English and the plan has the key in both English and German, the manuscript copy was presumably made after the 1853 sale of the site (see Plans 73-74), perhaps from Lappenberg's book. If dated 1667, the plan must have related to the pre-Fire Steelyard. The plan misplaces the hall, which archaeology has shown did not adjoin Cousin Lane, and it has an implausibly large Rhenish winehouse and an implausibly regular layout, with Windgoose Lane in the wrong place.
16 In 1663, of the houses described as outside the Steelyard, those in Thames Street and Allhallows Lane had occupants with English names, whereas those of houses in Windgoose Alley mostly had occupants with German names, as did the chambers and warehouses within the Steelyard (TNA, C 118/412, Almaine merchants v. Jacobsen, No. 51).
17 Derek Keene and Ian W. Archer (eds), *The Singularities of London, 1578* (LTS No. 175, 2014), pp. 94-95, 161-62.
18 Tony Dyson, *The Medieval London Waterfront* (1987), pp. 19-20.
19 Entry based mainly on Jill Husselby and Paula Henderson, 'Location, location, location! Cecil House in the Strand', *Architectural History*, vol. 45 (2002), pp. 159-93.
20 Ibid., pp. 168-69; Mark Girouard, *Elizabethan Architecture: its Rise and Fall, 1540-1640* (2009), p. 39.
21 P. D. A. Harvey, *Maps in Tudor England* (1993), p. 97.
22 Stow, vol. 1, p. 60.
23 The earliest reference I have found for these is [Edward Hatton], *A New View of London* (1708), vol. 2, p. 790.
24 LMA, CLA/007/EM/05/01/001, f. 18.
25 LMA, CLA/007/FN/03/016, 9 January 1629, and 017, 27 December 1645, 6 May-20 October 1646.
26 CCLD, COL/CCS/RM11/02805.
27 CCLD, COL/CCS/RM11/02795; CCLD, COL/CCS/RM11/02679. The description of the eastern house is from a lease of 1713, but clearly pre-dates the changes made in 1685, and was probably copied from the lease of 1653 to Samuel Wilmot or Williamot (which has not survived), just as the obsolete description in the lease of the western house in 1714 (CCLD, COL/CCS/RM11/02783) was copied from that of 1653.
28 LMA, COL/CC/BHC/01/013, pp. 178, 181-82, 197; LMA, CLA/007/FN/02/028, 1684-85, 27 June, 4 July, 1685-86, 7 and 14 November, March.
29 LMA, CLA/007/FN/02/044, 1756-57 and 1757-58; LMA, CLA/007/EM/04/011, p. 96; Richard Thompson, *Chronicles of London Bridge* (1827), p. 393.
30 TNA, C 220/15, part 3, No. 13; Stow, vol. 2, p. 88.
31 TNA, C 207/27, No. 15.
32 W. J. Jones, *The Elizabethan Court of Chancery* (1967), p. 159.
33 John Summerson, 'Three Elizabethan architects', *Bulletin of the John Rylands Library, Manchester*, vol. 40 (1957), pp. 209-15; John Schofield and Richard Lea, *Holy Trinity Priory,*

Aldgate, City of London (MOLAS monograph 24, 2005), p. 21; Colvin, *History of the King's Works*, vol. 3, *1485-1660*, part 1, p. 71n; Anthony Gerbine and Stephen Johnson, *Compass and Rule: Architecture as Mathematical Practice in England 1500-1750* (2009), pp. 55-60.

34   TNA, C 207/27, No. 19.

35   Christopher Kitching, 'The Cursitors' Office (1573-1813) and the Corporation of the Cursitors of Chancery', *Journal of the Society of Archivists*, vol. 7 (1982), pp. 78, 80.

36   Entry based on Schofield and Lea, *Holy Trinity Priory, Aldgate*.

37   Kenneth C. Reid, 'The water-mills of London', *LAMAS*, vol. 17 (1954), p. 230; Marjorie B. Honeybourne, 'Two plans of the precinct and adjoining property of St. Mary Graces', *LAMAS*, vol. 12 (1933), p. 202; C.L. Kingsford, 'Historical notes on medieaval London houses', *LTR*, vol. 10 (1916), pp. 101-02; Marjorie B. Honeybourne, 'The Abbey of St. Mary Graces, Tower Hill', *LAMAS*, vol. 17 (1954), p. 22.

38   A re-drawing of the plan was published as LTS No. 61 (1929). See Honeybourne, 'Two plans', pp. 199-204.

39   Ibid., p. 203; Honeybourne, 'Abbey of St. Mary Graces', p. 22.

40   Ibid., p. 21.

41   Museum of London, PLA archive, Deeds for Crash Mills, bill of Robert Cheslin.

42   TNA, C 3/113/73.

43   Museum of London, PLA archive, Deeds for Crash Mills, 1609 grant to Ferrers; TNA, E 134/11JasI/East10.

44   Museum of London, PLA archive, Deeds for Crash Mills, 1644 deed.

45   A. H. Johnson, *The History of the Worshipful Company of the Drapers of London*, vol. 2, *1509-1603* (1915), pp. 84-85, 210, 232; W. Archer-Thomson, *Drapers' Company: History of the Company's Properties and Trusts* (1939-40), vol. 1, pp. 124, 128; SMLH, p. 179; Stow, vol. 2, p. 318.

46   Stow, vol. 1, p. 231; DC, minute book 1574-84, f.142v.

47   DC, minute book 1584-94, pp. 348, 355; Johnson, *History*, p. 232.

48   Johnson, *History*, pp. 209, 210; TNA, E 178/1382.

49   DC, Warden's accounts, 1595-96, p. 18; DC, minute book 1594-1603, ff. 10r, 13v.

50   I owe the suggestion that it was redrawn to Peter Barber.

51   Archer-Thomson, *Drapers' Company*, vol. 1, p. 122. For the Checker: DC, C36/1; DC, C43/1 (with plan). Johnson, *History*, p. 478, places the Checker at 31-32 Dowgate Hill (and therefore within the area covered by the plan), but it was certainly not there in the seventeenth century.

52   DC, C31/1-2; DC, minute book 1640-67, f. 209r.

53   DC, minute book 1640-67, ff. 193v, 195v, 209r, 210r; DC, C37.

54   TNA, C 6/348/16.

55   Johnson, *History*, vol. 4, p. 478.

56   Entry based on Manolo Guerci, 'Salisbury House in London: the Strand palace of Sir Robert Cecil', *Architectural History*, vol. 52 (2009), pp. 31-78.

57   Entry based mainly on Manolo Guerci, 'The construction of Northumberland House and the patronage of its original builder, Lord Henry Howard, 1603-14', *The Antiquaries Journal*, vol. 90 (2010), pp. 341-400.

58   Howard Colvin, *A Biographical Dictionary of British Architects 1600-1840* (1995 edn), pp. 903-04.

59   Hearth tax, p. 1177.

60   Manolo Guerci, 'From Northampton to Northumberland: the Strand palace during the Suffolk ownership and the transformations of Algernon Percy, tenth Earl of Northumberland, 1614-68', *The Antiquaries Journal*, vol. 94 (2014), pp. 221, 223, 246-47.

61   Marjorie B. Honeybourne, 'Charing Cross riverside', *LTR*, vol. 21 (1958), pp. 44-78; *SOL*, vol. 16, *Charing Cross* (1935), pp. 226, 240-43; Gervase Rosser and Simon Thurley, 'Whitehall Palace and King Street, Westminster', *LTR*, vol. 26 (1990), pp. 72-73. The street numbers used here are from the *SOL*.

62   TNA, E 134/8JasI/Mich8; TNA, E 178/4186.

63   TNA, E 112/96, No. 656; TNA, E 133/148/6; *SOL*, vol. 16, pp. 241-42.

64   TNA, E 133/148/6.

65   *SOL*, vol. 16, pp. 241-42.

66   Ibid., pp. 232, 242.

67   SBH, uncatalogued leases, box 2, No. 1730; Hearth tax, p. 826.

68   Sir D'Arcy Power, 'Sir Thomas Bodley's London house', *The Bodleian Quarterly Record*, vol. 8, No. 90 (1936), p. 2; SBH, HB 1/6; SBH, uncatalogued leases, box 2, No. 1730.

69   Entry based mainly on Schofield, pp. 132-34, which includes the description.

70   http://www.clothworkersproperty.org/ (accessed 21 July 2014).

71   Entry based mainly on Schofield, pp. 72-73, which includes the description.

72   www.clothworkersproperty.org/properties/fenchurch-street; Ogilby and Morgan's map.

73   SBH, HB/1/3, ff. 458r, 545r; SBH, HB/1/4, f. 28r. For Llewellyn's role, see the Introduction.

74   SBH, HC 19, f. 55.

75   TNA, E 179/252/23.

76   SBH, HB 1/4, f. 52v.

77   Marjorie B. Honeybourne, 'The precinct of the Greyfriars', *LTR*, vol. 16 (1932), pp. 11-12; Holder, p. 306.

78   TNA, C 3/280/43; SBH, H2/3, ff. 119-21; above, pp. 10-11.

79   See Holder, pp. 77-109.

80   E. H. Pearce, *Annals of Christ's Hospital* (1901), pp. 50, 64.

81   Thomas Bayly, *Herba parietis* (1650), title page, reprinted in Felix Barker and Peter Jackson, *The History of London in Maps* (1990), p. 70.

82   Norman Moore, *The History of St. Bartholomew's Hospital*, vol. 2 (1918), pp. 27, 155; Gwenneth Whitteridge, 'The parish church of St. Bartholomew the Less', *Saint Bartholomew's Hospital Journal*, vol. 55 (December 1951), p. 261.

83   See pp. 10-11 above.

84   Whitteridge, 'Parish church', pp. 261-64.

85   Entry based mainly on Noel Blakiston, 'Milton's birthplace', *LTR*, vol. 19 (1947), pp. 1-12; Eton College, typescript list of estate records, vol. 16 (London), WB/4-7. The College accounts record only 15s.4d for Messrs Wever and Collins, the compilers of the written survey, riding to London to view the premises (Eton College, 62/8, p. 681). Blakiston, 'Milton's birthplace', includes the written description in full.

86   See also Kenneth Rogers, 'Bread Street: Its ancient signs and houses', *LTR*, vol. 16 (1932), pp. 54-55.

87   *History of Parliament, The House of Commons, 1604-29* (2010), vol. 4, pp. 690-93; B. Woodd Smith, 'Sir Baptist Hicks', *Middlesex County Records*, vol. 4, *1667-88* (1892), pp. 329-49.

88   Quoted in Blakiston, 'Milton's birthplace', p. 3.

89   Stow, vol. 2, p. 5.

90   Priscilla Metcalf, *The Halls of the Fishmongers' Company* (1977), pp. 12-13; GL, MS 5758/6; GL, MS 5570/2, pp. 275, 281.

91   GL, MS 5570/4, pp. 269, 288, 316, 377; GL, MS 6927/2, Nos. 150-51.

92 DC, minute book 1603-40, ff. 138r, 161r. DC, Warden's accounts 1619/20, record £203.7s.4d spent by the Company's 'renter' on its affairs, as set out in a separate account now lost.
93 Holder, pp. 162-69, 432-34; DC, minute book 1543-53, pp. 759-62. For alterations, see Lena Cowen Orlin, *Locating Privacy in Tudor London* (2007), pp. 117-19.
94 DC, minute book 1543-53, pp. 759-62; DC, A.II.4.
95 Orlin, *Locating Privacy*, p. 135; DC, notes on Garway family.
96 DC, A.I.11. In the sixteenth century there was some shared use of the ladies' gallery (Orlin, *Locating Privacy*, pp. 132, 151), though the description of 1543 assigns the ladies' gallery to the Drapers and the great chamber to the mansion (DC, minute book 1543-53, pp. 759-62).
97 DC, A.II.16/1; Woodhead, p. 169; Hearth tax, p. 1763.
98 DC, a583; DC, minute book 1603-40, ff. 123r, 124r, 125r, 156r, 157-58; DC, A.II.5; Hearth tax, p. 1763. Garway's rebuilding required the demolition of a small house on part of the site, which does not appear on the *c*.1620 plan.
99 Holder, pp. 158, 160-62, 429; Hearth tax, p. 1763; DC, a583.
100 DC, minute book 1667-1705, ff. 1v, 12v, 29r, 31r.
101 The description is sometimes ambiguous, in the absence of punctuation, and many assumptions have been made here. Mr Williams's and Mr Garway's houses are also described on the plan.
102 DC, Warden's accounts 1617-18.
103 Entry based on John Schofield, *St Pauls' Cathedral before Wren* (2011). See also Peter W. M. Blayney, *The Bookshops in Paul's Cross Churchyard* (Occasional Papers of the Bibliographical Society, No. 5, 1990).

Notes to 'Plans of Areas', pages 85-134

1 One of these is to similar effect and has the same key letters as Plan 26, suggesting a similar date (LMA, Collage 215756); the other can be dated to 1653-60 from its reference to 'Mr George Perkins Gramer Mr' (E.H. Pearce, *Annals of Christ's Hospital* (1901), p. 71) and has more differences in what it shows (LMA, CLC/B/169/MS39255).
2 Pearce, *Annals*, p. 147.
3 Holder, pp. 128-29, 135-36; Schofield, pp. 129-30.
4 CC, minute book 1649-65, ff. 50v, 135r, 232v; CC, Estate/25/1C/3 and 4; CC, catalogue entries for Estate/25/1C/5 and 6 and Estate/25/1A/7 to 11; Hearth tax, p. 767; Holder, pp. 123, 406. The Company considered acquiring further ground on the north side in 1657 (CC, minute book 1649-65, f. 92v), but the 1654 purchase was the Company's only one at Whitefriars apart from the almshouse site (CC, CL/G/7/10).
5 CC, catalogue entry for Estate/25/1C/7.
6 CC, catalogue entries for CLG/G/Charity/Kent, and Estate/25/1A and 1C.
7 Entry based on Dorian Gerhold, 'John Coffyn and Nevill's Court', *LTR*, vol. 31 (2015), pp. 121-40.
8 Cyprian Blagden, *The Stationers' Company: A History, 1403-1959* (1960), pp. 212-13.
9 Ibid., pp. 219-20; *Records of the Worshipful Company of Stationers* (microfilm), reel 56, minutes 1669-74.
10 Some material is omitted.
11 Key opposite; *Records of the Worshipful Company of Stationers*, reel 111, box 16, 1699 leases.
12 Ibid., box 19, 1709 lease.
13 Strype, book 3, p. 194; Blagden, *Stationers' Company*, pp. 226, 228.
14 Gordon Phillips, *The Tallow Chandlers' Company: Seven Centuries of Light* (1999), pp. 222-23; GL, MS 6165/1; GL, MS 6153/4, ff. 20v, 45v, 51v, 53v. For Gamon, see McKellar, p. 67.
15 Tallow Chandlers' Company, 1790 plan book (with later note about the 1864 sale).
16 Elizabeth Glover, *Men of Metal: History of the Armourers and Brasiers of the City of London* (2008), pp. 63-64, 88, 252; GL, MS 12103, part 2, p. 1; Stow, vol. 1, p. 165.
17 TNA, E 179/252/23.
18 GL, MS 12098/2.
19 Strype, book 2, p. 108; Glover, *Men of Metal*, p. 178; GL, MS 12130/1, No. 25.
20 The number of storeys is not given for E.
21 Glover, *Men of Metal*, pp. 52, 88; Stow, vol. 1, p. 278; GL, MS 12093/1, pp. 1, 166
22 Philip E. Jones (ed.), *The Fire Court*, vol. 2 (1970), pp. 86-87; GL, MS 12098/2, rental of 1670; GL, MS 12071/4, f. 27v.
23 GL, MS 12071/4, f. 31v.
24 Glover, *Men of Metal*, pp. 134, 144, 150-51; GL, MS 12104, plan of 1791; GL, MS 12093/1, pp. 166, 168.
25 *City of London Livery Companies' Commission* (C.4073 I, 1884), vol. 2, p. 263.
26 GL, MS 5563/1, pp. 9, 353; GL, MS 5570/1, p. 524; GL, MS 5570/3, p. 266; GL, MS 5570/4, pp. 226-27, 398, 997, 1008; GL, MS 5570/5, pp. 9, 138, 172, 734, 741; LMA, COL/CHD/LA/03/025/009/035; LMA, COL/CHD/LA/03/011/016; TNA, PROB 11/415/458. For Owfeild (or Oldfield), see TNA, PROB 11/112/508; TNA, C 142/660/30; TNA, catalogue entry for C 2/Eliz/D4/28.
27 GL, MS 5563/1, p. 353; GL, MS 5570/1, pp. 525, 528-29, 581, 583; GL, MS 5570/2, pp. 1, 9, 46; GL, MS 5570/4, pp. 227, 250, 263; GL, MS 5570/5, pp. 297, 311; TNA, PROB 11/307/64; TNA, PROB 11/376/173; TNA, PROB 11/386/151.
28 GL, MS 5570/5, pp. 792-93, 797, 803, 807; GL, MS 5860/1, No. 15.
29 Stow, vol. 1, p. 138.
30 GL, MS 5570/1, pp. 523-24, 563-64; GL, MS 5563/1, pp. 9, 353.
31 GL, MS 5570/4, pp. 225-26; GL, MS 6955/1, Nos. 887, 889.
32 TNA, E 179/252/23; LMA, COL/CHD/LA/03/011/016.
33 GL, MS 5570/4, pp. 225-28, 253, 274, 842; GL, MS 6955/1, Nos. 887 to 892; GL, MS 5570/5, pp. 18, 523, 601, 880; Fig. 104. A vault under part of one of Cressey's cellars was used with Boone's house.
34 GL, MS 5570/4, p. 665; GL, MS 5570/5, pp. 202, 748; LMA, COL/CHD/LA/03/011/016.
35 GL, MS 6955/1, No. 882, interpreted with the help of lists of 1734 and 1816 – GL, MS 6955/1, No. 883; GL, MS 6955/2, No. 905.
36 GL, MS 6955/1, No. 892.
37 *City of London Livery Companies' Commission* (C.4073 I, 1884), vol. 2, pp. 215, 264; GL, MS 5563/1, pp. 14, 358; GL, MS 5570/3, p. 916; GL, MS 5570/5, p. 68; GL, MS 6931/3, Nos. 274 and 282; Woodhead, p. 126.
38 GL, MS 5563/1, pp. 355-56; GL, MS 5570/5, pp. 225, 241; GL, MS 6925; Brian Hobley and John Schofield, 'Excavations in the City of London: first interim report, 1974-1975', *Antiquaries Journal*, Vol. 57 (1977), p. 39.

39 Medway Archives, DRc/ESp1/4; Medway Archives, DRc/Ac/2, part 4b, ff. 3v, part 5, f. 13v, part 6, ff. 9r, 14v, 17v; Medway Archives, DRc/Ac/4, part 11, ff. 9r, 38v-40r, 48r; LMA, COL/SP/05/074, 26 April 1774.
40 TNA, C 7/258/75.
41 Schofield, Plate 6 and pp. 74-78.
42 CC, minute book 1683-1712, pp. 186, 192, 197, 201, 229, 233-34. The same plan is attached to all five leases: CC, Estate/8/1C/1; Estate/8/1C/2; Estate/35/1C/11; Estate/35/1C/12; Estate/35/2C/1. Leybourn was working for the Clothworkers in 1690 and the plan could have been his, but the lettering differs from that of plans known to have been by him.
43 CC, Estate/8/1C/1.
44 CC, minute book 1683-1712, p. 422; LMA, COL/SJ/27/470, No. 86; Strype, book 2, p. 82; William Maitland, *The History of London* (1775), vol. 2, book 2, p. 778.
45 Strype, book 2, p. 82.
46 LMA, catalogue entries for insurance records relating to Billiter Square.
47 CC, Estate/29/1A/24.
48 CC, catalogue entries for Estate/35; Alfred Povah, *The Annals of the Parishes of St. Olave Hart Street and Allhallows Staining in the City of London* (1894), p. 314.
49 GL, MS 184/4, ff. 47-48.
50 CCLD, 48.14.
51 Stow, vol. 1, p. 301; *City of London Livery Companies' Commission* (C.4073 I, 1884), vol. 2, pp. 349-52.
52 GC, Court minute book 1682-88, ff. 120v, 127r; TNA, C 7/143/31.
53 For garden houses, see Roger H. Leech, *The Town House in Medieval and Early Modern Bristol* (2014), pp. 229-80.
54 GC, Court minute book 1639-42, f. 139r-v; GC, 1731, B393; GC, Court minute book 1654-57, f. 66v; TNA, PROB 11/248/81.
55 Walter S. Prideaux, *Memorials of the Goldsmiths' Company* [1896], vol. 2, pp. 3-4, 9, 13, 94-95; GC, 1725, B393, entries for Ward's plan 17, No. 116; GC, Court minute book 1654-57, f. 154r.
56 Prideaux, *Memorials*, vol. 2, pp. 79-80; GC, Court minute book 1654-57, ff. 91r, 99r, 111v; GC, 1725, B393, entries for Ward's plan 17, Nos. 24, 65, 70, 80.
57 Strype, book 3, p. 94; Henry A. Harben, *A Dictionary of London* (1918), p. 321.
58 GC, 1731, B393, ff. 12v-13r.
59 *Oxford Dictionary of National Biography* (2004), Thomas Andrews; GC, B IV 165 (ii), 1699 deed; GC, 1731, B393; GC, 2839, B393; LMA, COL/CHD/LA/03/025/009/029, p. 38.
60 GC, 1725, B393, entries for Ward's plan 14; GC, 2839, B393.
61 GC, 1731, B393; GC, 2839, B393. Values are not recorded for Nos. 13-19 and 21-26.
62 Strype, book 2, pp. 108, 109.
63 TNA, C 24/1253, No. 40.
64 GC, 1731, B393, ff. 16v-17r; Hearth tax, p. 860; Woodhead, p. 33.
65 TNA, E 179/252/23; GC, 1725, B393, entries for Ward's plan 7.
66 Strype, book 3, p. 121; TNA, C 11/1396/18.
67 Leases of Nos. 2-6, 10 and 12-13 summarised in GC, 1725, B393, entries for Ward's plan 7.
68 Philip E. Jones, 'The estates of the Corporation of London', *Guildhall Miscellany*, No. 7 (1956), pp. 6-10; LMA, COL/AC/13/005/23, note by Joan Hardinge.
69 CCLD, COL/CCS/RM11/06757 and 06753. The Bridge House property included tenements in Bishopsgate to the north, but the leases of 1649 and 1698 were confined to the inn. A lease of 1656 to Hardmett of a tenement in Bishopsgate (not expiring until 1717) has 'Angell Inn' written on it in pencil, but this is clearly an error (CCLD, COL/CCS/RM11/06760).
70 LMA, COL/CC/BHC/01/004, pp. 36-37.
71 LMA, COL/AC/13/005/23, note by Joan Hardinge.
72 Entry based mainly on Centre for Metropolitan History, Life in the Suburbs Project, Houndsditch notes.
73 LMA, CLRO card index to property references in Repertories, Houndsditch.
74 Strype, book 2, p. 109.
75 CLJ, 001, ff. 178v-179r.
76 CLJ, 004, ff. 227v-229v.
77 CLJ, 004, ff. 210v, 217r-v, 224v, 225r.
78 CLJ, 004, f. 268v.
79 CLJ, 006, ff. 251r-252v; CCLD, 77.4.
80 e.g. Goldsmith Street (Prideaux, *Memorials*, vol. 2, p. 165); Cullum Street (Strype, book 2, p. 89).
81 See Marjorie B. Honeybourne, 'The precinct of the Greyfriars', *LTR*, vol. 16 (1932), pp. 18-22, 39-45; Holder, pp. 108, 384.
82 LMA, CLC/B/169/MS39190, e.g. 1700 lease. The point was noted by Honeybourne, 'Precinct', pp. 20-22.
83 Ibid.; C.L. Kingsford, 'Historical notes on mediaeval London houses', *LTR*, vol. 11 (1917), pp. 56-58; Graham Rees and Maria Wakely, *Publishing, Politics and Culture: The King's Printers in the Reign of James I and VI* (2009), pp. 61-62, 188; Philip E. Jones (ed.), *The Fire Court*, vol. 1 (1966), p. 142; TNA, PROB 11/234/646.
84 Honeybourne, 'Precinct', p. 20n; LMA, CLC/B/169/MS39190, 1688 lease.
85 George W. Edwards, 'The Bull and Mouth Meeting house, its site and environs', *Friends Quarterly* (April 1955), p. 78.
86 LMA, CLC/B/169/MS39192; LMA, CLC/B/169/MS39190, 1671 lease.
87 Jones, *Fire Court*, vol. 1, p. 142; LMA, CLC/B/169/MS39192.
88 LMA, CLC/B/169/MS39190, 1683 mortgage.
89 LMA, CLC/B/169/MS39190, passim; Nomura International, lease of 1668.
90 The figure is given in TNA, C 7/204/67.
91 LMA, MS 12819/13, 1717-18, p. 31.
92 Thomas Delaune, *Angliae metropolis* (1690).
93 J. A. Chartres, 'The capital's provincial eyes: London's inns in the early eighteenth century', *London Journal*, vol. 3 (1977), p. 32; Strype, book 3, p. 121.
94 Harben, *Dictionary of London*, p. 115; Edwards, 'Bull and Mouth Meeting house', pp. 78-82; Ben Weinreb and Christopher Hibbert (eds), *The London Encyclopaedia* (1983 edn), p. 634.
95 http://www.rbt.org.uk/estate/index.htm.
96 RBT, E21/1/2.
97 TNA, catalogue entries for Thomas Badeslade; Bendall, vol. 2, p. 19.
98 RBT, catalogue entry for E21/4/1.
99 TNA, E 179/143/370; RBT, catalogue entry for E 21/4/24; LMA, CLA/002/02/01/1723. The upper floors apparently extended over part of the yard at the back, and therefore part of the yard probably belonged to this house (hence the cistern in the yard in 1681). The 1673 inventory of Edward Hilton, citizen and haberdasher, who is recorded two doors

eastwards from Davis in 1666, cannot be securely related to a house in the elevation (Hearth tax, p. 924; TNA, PROB 4/4679).
100 RBT, E 21/1/3; Hearth tax, p. 924; TNA, E 179/143/370; RBT, catalogue entry for E 21/12/7; LMA, CLA/002/02/01/1150.
101 RBT, E1/1/2, f. 208; LMA, CLA/002/02/01/3014.
102 RBT, catalogue entry for E21/5/10; RBT, E1/1/2, f. 202; RBT, E21/5/13.
103 Stow, vol. 1, pp. 99, 143-44; Hearth tax, p. 924.
104 See http://www.rbt.org.uk/estate/London/images.htm.
105 http://pubshistory.com/LondonPubs/StAndrew Undershaft/ShipTurtleTavern.shtml.
106 *SOL*, vol. 36, *The Parish of St. Paul Covent Garden* (1970), pp. 1, 6, 20, 268, 296-97, 300-03, 306-09; TNA, C 8/84/53. Jones claimed four houses were to be built in the north-south alley (making a total of seventeen), but the plan shows three.
107 TNA, SP 16/400, No. 100; *Calendar of State Papers Domestic*, 1638-39, p. 395; TNA, C 8/84/53; TNA, PC 2/49, f. 244.
108 TNA, C 8/84/53; *SOL*, vol. 36, pp. 199, 268, Fig. 3; TNA, C 6/5/171.
109 *SOL*, vol. 36, pp. 182-83.
110 LMA, CLC/275/MS33392/001; LMA, CLC/275/MS33183, ff. 234v-38r.
111 TNA, C 5/580/72; TNA, C 5/580/95; LMA, CLC/275/MS33183, ff. 220v, 234v-38r; LMA, CLC/275/MS33360/003, No. 135. The cellar under Wilson's kitchen was excluded from the lease in both 1672 and 1676.
112 TNA, C 5/580/95.
113 i.e. Widow Miller 1678-80 (next to Daniel Stephens, innholder at the Unicorn), John Wymer 1675-84 (Widow Wymer from 1685), Mr Causern (assumed to be Costin) 1673-85, and Thomas Parr 1673-85 (SLHL, St Mary Newington poor rates 1673-95). Both observations on the ending of leases could be additions, though in the same hand as each other and the rest of the text on leases.
114 The Attorney-General and deponents referred to the Unicorn in Blackman Street, occupied by Charles Bowles and Daniel Stephens (TNA, E 112/606, No. 29, schedule; TNA, E 134/3&4Jas2/Hil22), but the Crown's Unicorn Inn was in St Saviour's parish, existed long before 1607, had a different set of owners and occupants, and was close to the Queen's Pike Garden, which was near Bankside (TNA, C 66/1426, No. 1; TNA, E 367/1541; *SOL*, vol. 22, *Bankside* (1950), p. 57).
115 TNA, E134/3&4Jas2/Hil22; TNA, PROB 11/365/332.
116 Three gabled buildings in Blackman Street apparently of the seventeenth century seem to be on the northernmost part of the site; see *John Tallis's London Street Views 1838-40* (LTS No. 160, 2002), part 31, Nos. 44-46. On the back of the plan is a sketch of tenements in Blackman Street, with another row of tenements and a large orchard behind, which seems to be the property north of the Boar's Head.
117 Lambeth Palace Library, VH 96/1775.
118 Strype, book 4, p. 31.
119 TNA, catalogue entry for PROB 11/450/131.
120 Lambeth Palace Library, VH96/656.
121 Lambeth Palace Library, VH96/1962.
122 Woodhead, pp. 97-98.
123 Westminster City Archives, St Margaret's rate list, E 203.
124 These plans are also at HH, CPM Supp 54 and 55, and there is a later version of the larger one at BL, Add MS 74221.
125 SLHL, catalogue of West estate papers; TNA, C 11/1413/4. Age at death from monument in St Mary Bermondsey.
126 Bendall, vol. 2, p. 189; SLHL, St Mary Magdalen, Bermondsey, poor rate 1712; TNA, C 24/1349, Nos. 52 and 91.
127 HH, Deeds 90A, Jones to Mountague 1654, Salisbury to Miller 1678; HH, Legal 157/4; HH, Deeds 100, Nos. 18, 22, 25, 37, 40. Only some of Miller's land passed to Steavens; see BL, Add Ch 76643.
128 SLSL, West Box 40; SLSL, St Mary Magdalen, Bermondsey, poor rate 1712.
129 It is catalogued as 88 East St, but corresponds on the 1915 OS 25-inch map to No. 89 rather than No. 88.
130 TNA, PROB 11/532/103; SLSL, St Mary Magdalen, Bermondsey, poor rate 1712.
131 HH, Deeds 90B, Salisbury to Denton 1693; SLHL, West Box D, No. 411; SLSL, West Box 40.
132 SLSL, West Box 37.
133 HH, Deeds 90A, Salisbury to Myers 1636; Plan 75; TNA, catalogue entry for Richard Doble 1678.
134 TNA, C 11/2234/47; TNA, PROB 11/532/103; TNA, C 11/497/25; Joseph Bullman, Neil Hegarty and Brian Hill, *The Secret History of our Streets: London* (2012), pp. 28, 67-68.

Notes to 'Plans of Building Types', pages 135-212

1 Peter Jackson, *London Bridge* (1971), p. 40; LMA, COL/CC/BHC/05/001, pp. 106, 115.
2 LMA, COL/CC/BHC/05/001, pp. 106, 115, 131; LMA, CLA/007/FN/03/016, 23 March 1632/33, 25 May 1633. For Darvoll, LMA, CLA/007/FN/03/015, April 1627, and 019/A, March 1666. There are similar plans possibly derived from Plan 62 at LMA, COL/SVD/PL/03/001 (by J. Russell) and Wren Society, *Miscellaneous Designs and Drawings by Sir Chr. Wren and Others*, vol. 12 (1935), plate XXVI.
3 Bruce Watson, Trevor Brigham and Tony Dyson, *London Bridge – 2000 Years of a River Crossing* (MOLAS monograph 8, 2001), pp. 83, 85; LMA, COL/CC/BHC/05/001, p. 115.
4 Jackson, *London Bridge*, p. 31; SMLH, p. 117.
5 The only other plan found of a house on the Bridge in the period covered is of one on the south-west part in 1695 and is to similar effect, showing a square room 20 feet by 12 feet 9 inches with a staircase in one corner (CCLD, COL/CCS/RM11/02490). For slightly later plans (to similar effect, but sometimes with a back room), see LMA, COL/CCS/PL/01/128.
6 Watson, Brigham and Dyson, *London Bridge*, pp. 110-12.
7 Strype, book 1, p. 57; Watson, Brigham and Dyson, *London Bridge*, p. 85. See also Plan 7.
8 LMA, COL/CC/BHC/05/001, pp. 131-32. See also Michael J. Chandler, 'London Bridge before the Great Fire', *Guildhall Miscellany*, No. 1 (1952), pp. 19-21; James Robertson, 'Persuading the citizens? Charles I and London Bridge', *Historical Research*, vol. 79 (2006), pp. 512-33.
9 LMA, COL/CC/BHC/05/001, p. 112.
10 SMLH, pp. 9, 11; Stow, vol. 1, pp. 19, 20, 126-27, 129; LMA, COL/PL/02/G/006.
11 LMA, COL/CC/CLC/03/006, p. 190.

12 Entry based mainly on LMA, COL/CC/CLC/03/003, ff. 21, 33; Walter Bell, F. Cottrill and Charles Spon, *London Wall through Eighteen Centuries* (1937).
13 Stow, vol. 1, p. 32; Strype, book 1, p. 17; LMA, COL/CHD/CT/01/30, f. 122r.
14 SMLH, p. 11; Henry A. Harben, *A Dictionary of London* (1918), p. 373.
15 William Maitland and others, *The History of London from its Foundation to the Present Time* (1756), vol. 1, p. 31. I owe this reference to John Schofield.
16 LMA, COL/PL/02/G/006, f. 4; LMA, COL/CC/CLC/03/007, p. 198, and 008, p. 31.
17 For the location, see LMA, COL/SVD/PL/05/0037.
18 CCLD, 33.11; LMA, COL/SJ/27/467, No. 184.
19 Maitland, *History of London*, vol. 1, p. 31.
20 CLJ, 004, ff. 115v, 124r; CCLD, 48.13.
21 CCLD, 163.34.
22 CLJ, 005, ff. 258-60; CCLD, 60.25; Maitland, *History of London*, vol. 1, p. 31.
23 CLJ, 007, ff. 217r, 228r-229v, 238r-239v, 022, ff. 71v-72r. Leybourn's plan of 1676 shows an earlier watchhouse almost opposite Coleman Street but in the roadway (LMA, COL/PL/02/G/006, f. 13).
24 Gustav Milne, *The Port of Medieval London* (2003), pp. 178-79; Henry G. Roseveare, '"The damned combination": the Port of London and the wharfingers' cartel of 1695', *London Journal*, vol. 21 (1996), pp. 97-111; LMA, CLA/008/EM/02/01/002, ff. 27v, 77v, 99r; BL, Add MS 5100, No. 56; *Oxford Dictionary of National Biography* (2004), Josiah Child.
25 BL, Add MS 5100, No. 56; Roseveare, '"Damned combination"', p. 100.
26 CCLD, 52.5. The north-west part of Botolph Wharf was excavated in 1982 (Museum of London sitecode BIG82), and the post-Fire plans will be compared with the excavated walls in due course (information from John Schofield).
27 GL, MS 5570/2, pp. 776-77, 824-25, 917.
28 BL, Add MS 5085, No. 19; *The Survey of Building Sites in the City of London after the Great Fire*, vol. 2 (LTS No. 101, 1964), f. 164, vol. 4 (LTS No. 98, 1962), f. 119.
29 GL, MS 5570/5, pp. 132, 143, 161, 173, 188, 197.
30 Bodleian Library, MS North c32 (1) and c33 (12); GL, MS 5570/6, pp. 258, 262, 274, 279; TNA, CUST 143/123, p. 150a.
31 John Norman Daynes, *A Short History of the Ancient Mistery of the Dyers of the City of London* (1965), pp. 16, 34; GL, MS 32588/5, Nos. 78 and 79.
32 This and the next paragraph are based mainly on Dyers' Company, 'Green Book'; GL, MS 32588/4, No. 57 (plan); GL, MS 32588/5, Nos. 98 (plan), 102 (plan), 103 (plan).
33 GL, MS 8164/2, p. 453.
34 BL, Add MS 5099, ff. 339-47.
35 Daynes, *Short History*, pp. 29, 36-37.
36 Dyers' Company, 'Green Book'; Daynes, *Short History*, p. 40.
37 Entry based mainly on TNA, RAIL 635/102; Philip Norman, 'Notes on the later history of the Steelyard in London', *Archaeologia*, vol. 61 (1909), pp. 389-426; LMA, A/LSC/79 (the extracts on which Norman's article was based); J.M. Lappenberg, *Urkundliche geschichte des Hansischen Stahlhofes zu London* (1851), pp. 199-202. For patching up, TNA, C 118/412, Almaine merchants v. Jacobsen, No. 40.
38 TNA, C 11/471/35; TNA, C 118/412, Almaine merchants v. Jacobsen, No. 37. Theodore Jacobsen seems to have rebuilt part of the Allhallows Lane frontage.

39 Ibid., Nos. 23, 30.
40 For George Seagood, City Carpenter in 1679-81, catalogue entry for LMA, COL/SJ/09/021. For the viewers (1675 and 1679 respectively to at least 1691), LMA, COL/SJ/27/467 and 468. John Bridges was citizen and tyler and bricklayer in 1672 (TNA, catalogue entry for Centre for Buckinghamshire Studies, D-LE/4/18).
41 On the back of one of the vellum copies of the plan (TNA, RAIL 635/102, No. 25) is written 'Prod d.10 Febr. 1714'.
42 The drawing of the Thames Street facade in T.M.M. Baker, *London: Rebuilding the City after the Great Fire* (2000), p. 33, shows the warehouse built in 1754.
43 TNA, C 118/412, Almaine merchants v. Jacobsen, No. 24.
44 Widow Lynes was not yet a widow in 1658 (HH, Legal 187, Salisbury to Worrall 1692); Dober's will was proved in 1678 (TNA, catalogue entry for PROB 11/356/128).
45 HH, Legal 94/8; HH, Legal 61/17; HH deeds cited below.
46 HH, Deeds 100, No. 35; TNA, catalogue entries for PROB 11/431/171, PROB 11/356/128.
47 HH, Legal 94/8; TNA, PROB 11/376/289.
48 HH, Deed 237/7; HH, General 62/11.
49 HH, Deeds 90A, Salisbury to Swett 1636; HH, Legal 187, Salisbury to Worrall.
50 Ibid.; HH, Deeds 100, No. 26.
51 HH, Deeds 90A, Salisbury to Case 1636; TNA, catalogue entry for PROB 11/185/40.
52 Peter Earle, *The Making of the English Middle Class* (1989), pp. 17, 19.
53 There are also many plans showing tenters, e.g. CLPB, A117.
54 Martha Carlin, *Medieval Southwark* (1996), pp. 55-57; LMA, CLA/007/EM/04/12, pp. 115-16; Simon Blatherwick and Richard Bluer, *Great Houses, Moats and Mills on the South Bank of the Thames: Medieval and Tudor Southwark and Rotherhithe* (MOLAS monograph 47, 2009), pp. 59, 104, 127.
55 LMA, COL/CCS/PL/01/049B; LMA, CLA/007/FN/03/020, 16 October 1680, 8 January, 21 May, 30 July 1681.
56 TNA, C 6/218/7.
57 Ibid.; TNA, C 6/216/12; LMA, CLA/007/FN/02/028, 1682-83.
58 LMA, CLA/007/FN/02/040, 1730-31 and 1731-32; LMA, CLA/007/FN/02/045, 1767-68; TNA, PROB 11/937/137; LMA, COL/CC/BHC/01/012, p. 366.
59 Blatherwick and Bluer, *Great Houses, Moats and Mills*, pp. 59, 76-77, 82, 98; MCO, Lease book M, 1631-41, f. 256; MCO, Lease book P, 1657-67, f. 673.
60 TNA, C 10/172/58; MCO, 128/44.
61 MCO, 129/27; MCO, Lease book P, 1657-67, f. 673; TNA, C 10/172/58.
62 MCO, 129/44; MCO, 128/53.
63 MCO, lease book R, 1673-83, p. 457; MCO, 129/24.
64 LMA, CLA/007/EM/05/02/009, p. 26.
65 LMA, CLA/007/EM/02/H/104; LMA, CLA/007/EM/02/K/049; LMA, CLA/007/FN/02/107, 1633-34; TNA, PROB 11/240/39.
66 LMA, COL/CCS/PL/01/205/37, 38 and 44.
67 GL, MS 5570/4, pp. 379, 396, 416, 425, 459, 517, 602, 642; TNA, C 6/237/15; TNA, C 6/203/14; GL, MS 5570/5, pp. 517, 520, 594; TNA, C 6/320/12.
68 GL, MS 5570/6, pp. 255, 264; GL, MS 5860/2, p. 13; Peter Mathias, *The Brewing Industry in England 1700-1830* (1959), p. 313; Richard Byrne, *Prisons and Punishments of London* (1989), p. 51.
69 LMA, CLC/B/169/MS39259.
70 LMA, CLC/B/169/MS39246, lease of 1680.

71 S. H. Higgins, *A History of Bleaching* (1924), pp. 9-10; G. Turnbull, *A History of the Calico Printing Industry of Great Britain* (1951), p. 3.
72 HH, Deeds 90B, Salisbury to Langstraffe 1677.
73 Partly based on another plan of the same area at the same date: HH, CPM Supp 52.
74 Ibid.; HH, Legal 157/4.
75 Ibid.; R. Campbell, *The London Tradesman* (1747), pp. 299-300.
76 L. A. Clarkson, 'The organization of the English leather industry in the late sixteenth and seventeenth centuries', *Economic History Review*, 2nd ser., vol. 13 (1960), pp. 245-46; Kevin Reilly, 'The leather production industry in Bermondsey – the archaeological evidence', in Roy Thomson and Quita Mould (eds), *Leather Tanneries – The Archaeological Evidence* (2011), p. 157.
77 R.S. Thomson, 'Tanning – man's first manufacturing process?', *Transactions of the Newcomen Society*, vol. 53 (1981-82), pp. 139-56; Roy Thomson, 'Skin, leather and tanning – some definitions', in Thomson and Mould, *Leather Tanneries*, pp. 3-7; John Cherry, 'Leather', in John Blair and Nigel Ramsay (eds), *English Medieval Industries* (1991), pp. 296-97, 300; Clarkson, 'Organization', pp. 246-47; William Jones, *Dictionary of Industrial Archaeology* (2006), pp. 380-81.
78 The verb 'kill' indicated the use of alkali to remove fatty materials, but contact with alkalis would damage the bark, so it would be surprising to find killhouse and millhouse adjoining (indeed they had moved together). A 'kill' could be a small stream, which could have been used for preparing tan bark extracts or oozes. A kiln (the lease refers to a 'kilnhouse') is unlikely as use of warm water leads to inferior leather and was forbidden by law. The killhouse is too small to be a slaughterhouse. I am grateful to Roy Thomson for advice on these matters.
79 TNA, PROB 31/142, No. 461; TNA, C 11/2056/8.
80 CLJ, 005, ff. 2r, 27r, 29v.
81 Campbell, *London Tradesman*, pp. 147-49; Elizabeth Glover, *The Gold and Silver Wyre-Drawers* (1979), pp. 1-6; Horace Stewart, *History of the Worshipful Company of Gold and Silver Wyre-Drawers* (1891), p. 1.
82 Campbell, *London Tradesman*, pp. 147, 149-50.
83 Craig Spence, *London in the 1690s: A Social Atlas* (2000), pp. 134, 136.
84 It abutted north on land leased to John Hunt, which was Cross Dagger Court (CLPB, B12).
85 CLJ, 005, f. 214r.
86 Cliff Webb, *London Apprentices*, vol. 21, *Founders' Company 1643-1800* (1998), pp. 1, 46.
87 Centre for Metropolitan History, Life in the Suburbs project, notes on Houndsditch, site M; CLJ, 004, ff. 202r, 207r, 219v, 244r.
88 TNA, C 11/710/26.
89 Betty R. Masters, *The Public Markets of the City of London surveyed by William Leybourn in 1677* (LTS No. 117, 1974), pp. 13-14.
90 Entry based mainly on Masters, *Public markets*; Mark Samuel, 'The fifteenth-century garner at Leadenhall, London', *Antiquaries Journal*, vol. 69 (1989), pp. 119-53; Ian Archer, Caroline Barron and Vanessa Harding (eds), *Hugh Alley's Caveat: The Markets of London in 1598* (LTS No. 137, 1988), pp. 4-5, 7-8, 87-88.
91 Strype, book 2, p. 89.
92 Probably a maker or seller of horse collars.
93 CLJ, 001, ff. 47v-48r; Ogilby and Morgan's map; CCLD,

35.32. Sir Robert Jeffery, or Geffery, also held the next plot to the south, which was probably the one for which a new lease was granted in 1673 (ibid; Masters, *Public Markets*, p. 29).
94 LMA, CLA/008/EM/02/01/001, f. 53r, and 002, f. 2r.
95 Howes, quoted in W.J. Passingham, *London's Markets: Their Origin and History* [1935], p. 5; LMA, CLRO card index of property references in Repertories, Smithfield.
96 LMA, P69/SEP/B/019/MS03146/001 and 002.
97 LMA, COL/CC/CLC/03/005, p. 175; CLJ, 007, f. 145v.
98 LMA, CLJ, 004, f. 171v; LMA, P69/SEP/D/045/MS03170/001A, f. 7.
99 Archer *et al*, *Hugh Alley's Caveat*, p. 94.
100 LMA, P69/SEP/D/045/MS03170/001, 1 September 1719.
101 LMA, P69/SEP/B/001/MS03149/002, p. 339; LMA, P69/SEP/D/045/MS03170/001A and 001 (especially 001A, f. 13; 001, 24 May 1711, 8 July 1712, 5 August 1718, 1 September 1719); LMA, P69/SEP/D/046/MS03167/001.
102 CCLD, 56.12; CCLD, 74.28; Rocque's map; CLJ, 020, f. 7r; CCLD, 4.12; LMA, P69/SEP/D/045/MS03170/001, 7 January 1755.
103 Ben Weinreb and Christopher Hibbert, *The London Encyclopaedia* (1993 edn), p. 813.
104 Entry based mainly on CLJ, 001, ff. 17v-18v, 36v-37v, 41r-v, 60v, 64r-66r, 92v; CLJ, 003, ff. 4v, 71r-v, 185r-v, 203r-v, 208r, 214v-215r, 236v; LMA, COL/CC/CLC/03/005, p. 50.
105 CLPB, A34.
106 LMA, COL/WD/03/022; *John Tallis's London Street Views 1838-1840* (LTS No. 160, 2002), p. 76 (22-23 Farringdon Street).
107 See Robert Latham and William Matthews, *The Diary of Samuel Pepys*, vol. 10 (*Companion*) (1983), pp. 416-18; Earle, *Making of the English Middle Class*, pp. 51-55.
108 GL, MS 5570/2, p. 338; GL, MS 6945/1, Nos. 532, 533.
109 GL, MS 5570/3, pp. 379, 382-83, 401, 410, 415-16, 817, 821, 830-31, 837, 872, 876-77, 887-88, 902; GL, 6945/1, No. 532; Hearth tax, vol. 2, p. 703. When some rooms said to belong to the inn were to be investigated in 1641, the viewers were to take with them 'a plott of the Starre Inne', indicating that one already existed (GL, MS 5570/3, p. 547).
110 GL, MS 6945/1, No. 535; GL, MS 5570/5, pp. 142, 149, 158; Latham and Matthews, *Diary of Samuel Pepys*, vol. 10, p. 395.
111 TNA, PROB 5/3653.
112 GL, MS 6945/1, lease to Shipton 1657.
113 Thomas Delaune, *Angliae Metropolis* (1690); TNA, PROB 5/3653; *A Complete Guide to all Persons who have any Trade or Concern with the City of London* (1755, 1765); *Kentish Post*, 1 January, 11 June 1755; GL, MS 21536, p. 10.
114 Thomas Delaune, *The Present State of London* (1681). The inn is not mentioned in John Taylor, *The Carriers Cosmographie* (1637).
115 Bendall, vol. 2, p. 276.
116 Delaune, *Angliae Metropolis*; Strype, book 3, p. 93.
117 William Rendle and Philip Norman, *The Inns of old Southwark and their Associations* (1888), p. 279; Delaune, *Present State*.
118 TNA, E 44/494; *A List of the 400 Hackney-coaches licensed in July and August, 1662...* (1664), p. 12.
119 LMA, H01/ST/A/006/002, 24 October 1689.
120 Rendle and Norman, *Inns of old Southwark*, p. 282.
121 Carlin, *Medieval Southwark*, pp. 53, 54n.
122 MCO, Lease book R (1673-83), p. 132; MCO, Surrey leases, bundle 4; TNA, C 24/1211, No. 80; TNA, C 9/162/31; Rendle and Norman, *Inns of old Southwark*, p. 112.
123 Entry mainly based on GC, B IV, 135 (i), 1672 lease; GC,

1725, B393, pp. 237-43 (including lease of 1722); GC, 1731, B393, f. 3r.

124 Harben, *Dictionary of London*, p. 307; *City of London Livery Companies' Commission* (C.4073 I, 1884), vol. 2, p. 354.

125 GC, Court minute book 1651-54, f. 169r; GC, Court minute book 1669-73, f. 278r.

126 TNA, C 11/2611/29; Walter Sherburne Prideaux, *Memorials of the Goldsmiths' Company* [1896], vol. 2, p. 201; Ralph Rylance, *The Epicure's Almanack* (2013 edn., Janet Ing Freeman, ed.), p. 75n.

127 Entry based on John Schofield and Richard Lea, *Holy Trinity Priory, Aldgate, City of London* (MOLAS monograph 24, 2005), pp. 30-40; CLJ, 008, ff. 45r, 63r-v, 212v.

128 LMA, COL/CC/CLC/03/009, f. 23v.

129 CCLD, 52.42; Strype, book 2, p. 109.

130 e.g. CLPB, B2, 47, 48.

131 CCLD, 56.26.

132 LMA, CLA/009/01/031, No. 4.

133 Joseph P. Ward, *Metropolitan Communities: Trade Guilds, Identity, and Change in Early Modern London* (1997), pp. 2, 4, 8-9, 29-39; George Unwin, *The Gilds and Companies of London* (1908), pp. 342-44; Earle, *Making of the English Middle Class*, pp. 250-60.

134 SMLH, pp. 44, 47.

135 Entry based mainly on Randall Monier-Williams, *The Tallow Chandlers of London*, vol. 4 (1977), pp. 270, 280-82; Gordon Phillips, *Seven Centuries of Light: the Tallow Chandlers Company* (1999), pp. 19, 21.

136 GL, MS 6153/4, ff. 3v, 4r, 15v.

137 GL, MS 6153/4, ff. 38r, 71v, 80r.

138 Elizabeth Glover, *Men of Metal: History of the Armourers and Brasiers of the City of London* (2008), pp. 21-22, 49, 109, 148, 162-66; Strype, book 3, p. 64; British Museum, Crace Collection, XXXVII, 30.

139 GL, MS 12071/4, f. 32v.

140 Entry based on Priscilla Metcalf, *The Halls of the Fishmongers' Company* (1977), pp. 13-15, 62-91.

141 Entry based mainly on John Newman, 'Nicholas Stone's Goldsmiths' Hall: Design and practice in the 1630s', *Architectural History*, vol. 14 (1971), pp. 30-39, 138-41; Prideaux, *Memorials*, vol. 1, pp. 4, 160-66, vol. 2, pp. 158-66, 313, 319.

142 GC, 1725, B393, p. 15; GC, 2104, B395.

143 Anthony Homes-Walker, *Sixes & Sevens: A Short History of the Skinners' Company* (2005), pp. 21-22; SMLH, p. 179.

144 TNA, PROB 11/438/211; TNA, C 5/144/1; TNA, C 10/248/3; GL, MS 30708/6, pp. 176, 309, 344, 390, 412.

145 Entry based on Ian Grainger and Christopher Phillpotts, *The Royal Navy Victualling Yard, East Smithfield, London* (MOLA monograph 45, 2010).

146 TNA, SP16/279, No. 70.

147 Entry based mainly on T. F. Reddaway, 'Sir Christopher Wren's Navy Office', *Bulletin of the Institute of Historical Research*, vol. 30 (1957), pp. 175-88; Celina Fox, 'The ingenious Mr Dummer: rationalizing the Royal Navy in late seventeenth-century England', *eBLJ* (2007), article 10.

148 Giles Worsley, 'Taking Hooke seriously', *Georgian Group Journal*, vol. 14 (2004), p. 1.

149 Latham and Matthews, *Diary of Samuel Pepys*, vol. 10, p. 299.

150 Entry based mainly on *SOL*, vol. 25, *St George's Fields* (1955), pp. 5, 9-12.

151 *Calendar of State Papers Domestic*, Addenda 1625-49, p. 451; George W. Marshall (ed.), *Le Neve's Pedigrees of the Knights* (Harleian Society, vol. 8, 1873), p. 324.

152 Strype, book 4, p. 30.

153 Entry based mainly on *SOL*, vol. 22, *Bankside* (1950), pp. 10-11; David J. Johnson, *Southwark and the City* (1969), pp. 97, 130-31, 223, 285; Bendall, vol. 2, p. 89.

154 LMA, COL/CC/BHC/01/003, p. 77.

155 Entry based mainly on *SOL*, vol. 20, *Trafalgar Square and Neighbourhood* (1940), pp. 7-9; H.M. Colvin (ed.), *The History of the King's Works*, vol. 4, *1485-1660*, part 2 (1982), pp. 162-64; ibid., vol. 5, *1660-1782* (1976), pp. 207-09. The plan was drawn before any stables were allocated to the Prince of Wales (April 1716); before the first eight-horse stable in the long range in the Great Mews and the house at the back of the latter were converted for the Prince of Wales's dog-keeper and kennels (June 1716); before the ruinous stable next to the gateway to Hedge Lane was taken down (November 1716); before the two ruinous equerries' lodgings (Nos. 50-51) were repaired (December 1716); and before a stable was repaired for the young princesses (October 1719); it was later than 1713, when a list of equerries includes only two of those referred to on the plan, and when Hawley was granted No. 58 (July 1713) (*Calendar of Treasury Letter Books*, 1713, p. 765; ibid., 1716, 10 January, 8 June; TNA, WORK 6/6, pp. 138-41, 168, 201-02; TNA, WORK 4/1, pp. 46, 95, 109, 126, and 13 November 1716, 28 October 1719; TNA, MPE 1/560; CRES 2/619). The note on the plan, in a different hand, indicating the number of stables used by the royal family is evidently a later addition, as the plan does not allocate any stables to the Prince of Wales or the young princesses.

156 TNA, T1/337/99 and 100.

157 Paul Jeffery, *The City Churches of Sir Christopher Wren* (1996), pp. 327-28.

158 Basil F. Clarke, *Parish Churches of London* (1966), p. 36.

159 LMA, P69/ANN/B/021/MS01061/017, 30 May 1702.

160 The large house was not quite on the corner of Church Entry and Ireland Yard. See the plan at Kent Archives Office, U145/E25, with the four houses on the west side of Church Entry backing onto the Apothecaries' garden and another south of them facing Glasshouse Yard.

161 John Leake's post-Fire plan shows the church on the west side of Church Entry but the deed leaves little doubt that it was on the east side; see Irwin Smith, *Shakespeare's Blackfriars Playhouse* (1966), pp. 62-63.

162 Holder, pp. 49-50, 370, 373-75; Alfred W. Clapham and Walter H. Godfrey, *Some Famous Buildings and their Story* [1913], pp. 254, 258, 260.

163 TNA, C 24/1168, No. 32; TNA, C 24/1189, No. 5; TNA, C 24/1220, No. 107.

164 LMA, P69/BOT2/D/022/MS03606/002.

165 Centre for Metropolitan History, Life in the Suburbs project, notes on St Botolph Aldgate.

166 CLJ, 005, f. 223r.

167 Entry based mainly on E. H. Pearce, *Annals of Christ's Hospital* (1901), pp. 45-64, 71, 147, 211, 300-01.

168 Weinreb and Hibbert, *London Encyclopaedia*, pp. 162, 634.

169 Entry based on Richard O. Havery, *History of the Middle Temple* (2011), pp. 76, 79-80.

170 Kenneth Nicholls Palmer, *Ceremonial Barges of the River Thames* (1977), pp. 24, 33; GL, MS 5570/3, pp. 472, 553, 589, 714, 807, 811, 840, 898; CC, catalogue entry for Estate/29/1A/1 and 5; Kieron Tyler and Hugh Willmott, *John Baker's late 17th-century Glasshouse at Vauxhall* (MOLAS monograph 28, 2005), pp. 2, 6-7.

171 GL, MS 5570/4, pp. 159, 170, 188, 193, 312, 333; CC, Estate 29/1A/6 and 7.
172 Palmer, *Ceremonial Barges*, p. 5; CC, catalogue entry for Estate/29; CC, Estate/29/1A/26; Tyler and Willmott, *John Baker's late 17th-century Glasshouse*, pp. 26-27.
173 Entry based on Prideaux, *Memorials*, pp. 105, 111-12, 143, 312-13; GL, MS 30708/4, ff. 49, 61, 120; GC, 1926, B393; Palmer, *Ceremonial Barges*, pp. 38, 42; Lambeth Palace Library, catalogue of deeds in series TA; Lambeth Palace Library, TD 210. The latter (a map of Lambeth in 1812) shows the exact site; plot numbers are identifiable from the catalogue of deeds in series TA.
174 T. F. Reddaway, *The Rebuilding of London after the Great Fire* (1940), pp. 190, 192, 295; LMA, COL/SJ/09/017 (Misc.MSS.160.15). The plans of the waterside laystalls are now attached to a later lease. The Mile End plan is at LMA, COL/CCS/PL/02/106. GL, MS 184/4, f. 46 also refers to a laystall at Bunhill by the Artillery Ground.
175 GL, MS 184/4, ff. 46-48; LMA, COL/SJ/27/212 (Misc.MSS.108.3).
176 CCLD, 38.10; LMA, COL/SJ/27/212; TNA, C 6/262/26; TNA, C 7/161/26; TNA, C 7/594/57. For Humfrey's 'troubles', see Masters, *Public Markets*, pp. 18-19.
177 CCLD, 38.10; LMA, COL/SJ/27/212.
178 LMA, COL/WD/03/019; Peter Hounsell, *London's Rubbish* (2013), pp. 12, 50.
179 Carole Rawcliffe, *Urban Bodies: Communal Health in Late Medieval English Towns and Cities* (2013), p. 142; Ernest L. Sabine, 'Latrines and cesspools of mediaeval London', *Speculum*, vol. 9 (1934), pp. 307-08; P.E. Jones, 'Whittington's longhouse', *LTR*, vol. 23 (1972), pp. 27-34; LMA, COL/CC/CLC/07/001, f. 63v; LMA, COL/CC/CLC/07/003, pp. 14, 154, 157-58, 171-72.
180 Rawcliffe, *Urban Bodies*, p. 141; L. F. Salzman, *Building in England down to 1540* (1967), p. 282; Henry Thomas Riley (ed.), *Munimenta Guildhallae Londoniensis: Liber Albus, Liber Custumarum, et Liber Horn*, vol. 2 (1860), part 1, p. cxii, part 2, pp. 450-51; Helena M. Chew and William Kellaway (eds), *London Assize of Nuisance 1301-1431* (London Record Society, vol. 10, 1973), p. 45.
181 BL, Add MS 5101, f. 135r; Reginald R. Sharpe, *Calendar of Wills Proved and Enrolled in the Court of Husting, London, A.D. 1258-A.D. 1688*, part 2.1 (1890), pp. 275-77; LMA, COL/CHD/CT/01/011, f. 30. The latter identifies the land let to John and Elizabeth Place and sub-let to Bartholomew Fish as formerly Philpot's, including the rooms over the longhouse. Philpot was given land by Richard II, which may be relevant, as the original longhouse was a royal foundation (Stow, vol. 1, p. 220).
182 BL, Add MS 5101, ff. 134v-135r; BL, Add MS 5099, f. 146r-v; Ann Saunders and John Schofield (eds), *Tudor London: A Map and a View* (LTS No. 159, 2001), Plate II.
183 BL, Add MS 5101, ff. 133r-135v; LMA, COL/CC/CLC/07/002, f. 72v; LMA, COL/CC/CLC/07/003, p. 28; Jones, 'Whittington's longhouse', pp. 28-29; LMA, COL/CC/CLC/07/001, ff. 66r-v.
184 LMA, COL/PL/01/076/E/04.
185 One of the six-monthly contracts for street sweeping in the ward refers to cleaning 'the Longhouse' once a week, in January 1726, but none of the others do (LMA, CLC/W/MA/002/MS04829).
186 BL, Add MS 5099, ff. 145v-147v; BL, Add MS 5101, ff. 135v-136r; BL, Add MS 5095, ff. 301v, 307v, 313v.
187 CLJ, 034, f. 50v; Jones, 'Whittington's longhouse', p. 34.

Notes to 'Plans of Houses', pages 213-278

1 LMA, CLC/210/G/A/004A/MS35934.
2 It was not found in LMA, CLC/B/169, or at Nomura International. The earliest surviving lease seems to be from 1669 (CLC/B/169/MS39256/001).
3 LMA, MS 12819/9, 1663-64.
4 Ibid., 1666-67; LMA, MS 12819/10, 1667-68; LMA, CLC/210/G/BLC/002/MS13443/001; LMA, CLC/210/G/BBH/001/MS12918/003, 1667 lease; Nomura International, 1667 lease. The plan refers in the abuttals to Mr Ward, who occupied a tenement in Greyfriars belonging to Christ's Hospital in 1639 (LMA, MS 12806/4, f. 292v), but he was apparently not a tenant directly of the Hospital and is not further recorded. When the 31-year lease granted in 1619 was renewed it ran until 1669, suggesting a new 21-year lease in about 1648 (LMA, MS 12806/3, f. 213r; LMA, MS 12806/6, p. 143), but this has not been traced in the Hospital's minutes.
5 Holder, p. 98; LMA, MS 12806/3, f. 207r.
6 Hearth tax, p. 714.
7 See R. B. McKerrow (ed.), *A Dictionary of Printers and Booksellers in England, Scotland and Ireland, and of Foreign Printers of English Books 1557-1640* (1910); Henry R. Plomer, *A Dictionary of the Booksellers and Printers who were at Work in England, Scotland and Ireland from 1641 to 1667* (1907); *Calendar of State Papers Domestic, 1649-50*, pp. 522-24.
8 LMA, MS 12806/3, p. 441; Alfred B. Beaven, *The Aldermen of the City of London*, vol. 2 (1913), p. xxv; TNA, PROB 11/215/761; LMA, MS 12806/6, pp. 143, 309-10, 391, 421; Ogilby and Morgan's map 1676. By 1640 Acton was living in Wood Street (GC, Court minute book 1639-42, ff. 41r, 46r, 84v).
9 LMA, MS 12819/10, 1667-68 to 1671-72. For examples, see LMA, CLC/B/169/MS39256/001.
10 Schofield, pp. 106-07.
11 Woodward, p. 62; Edmund Frederick Du Cane, *Some Account of the Family of Du Quesne* (1876), pp. 7, 13, 16, 18; Derek Keene and Vanessa Harding, *Historical Gazetteer of London before the Great Fire: Cheapside* (1987), pp. 713-23.
12 TNA, PROB 11/338/334; TNA, PROB 11/542/162; *Victoria History of the Counties of England – Surrey*, vol. 4 (1912), p. 98.
13 LMA, CLC/210/G/A/061/MS22633/001, p. 33; LMA, CLC/210/G/A/061/MS22633/003, p. 58; LMA, SC/GL/MPC/313/q7712790.
14 Entry based on Wren Society, vol. 13 (1936), *Designs and Drawings by Sir Christopher Wren for St. Paul's Cathedral, the Residentiaries' Houses, and the Deanery*, pp. 52-54.
15 GL, MS 6956, No. 952; Hearth tax, p. 681.
16 GL, MS 5570/4, p. 331; GL, MS 5570/5, pp. 294-95, 297; Woodhead, p. 125; GL, MS 6956, No. 951.
17 GL, MS 6956, No. 953; GL, MS 5860/1, No. 19.
18 GL, MS 5570/6, pp. 124, 531; GL, MS 6956.
19 Entry based mainly on CCLD 39.1; CCLD, 50.19; M. Melville Balfour, '"Judge" Jeffreys' house in Aldermanbury:

an historic City mansion', *LAMAS*, ns vol. 6 (1929-32), pp. 177-98; LMA, COL/CCS/PL/02/110A. For the context, see David Bowsher, Tony Dyson, Nick Holder, and Isca Howell, *The London Guildhall: An Archaeological History of a Neighbourhood from Early Medieval to Modern Times* (MOLAS monograph 36, 2007), especially pp. 239-40, 252, 284-85.
20 GL, MS 184/4, f. 39v.
21 COL/WD/03/018; OS 1:1056 map of 1873, London sheet 7.65.
22 Entry based mainly on J. Armitage Robinson, *The Abbot's House at Westminster* (1911); John Goodall, 'Monastic splendour: Cheyneygates, Westminster Abbey, London', *Country Life*, 6 January 2010, pp. 38-44.
23 Hearth tax, p. 1686.
24 DC, minute book 1667-1705, ff. 1v, 29r, 31r; A.H. Johnson, *The History of the Worshipful Company of the Drapers of London*, vol. 4 (1922), p. 480.
25 Ibid.; DC, a.351.
26 Corpus Christi, Cambridge, 09L/H11, 09L/H15b; TNA, C 7/375/100 and 110.
27 Corpus Christi, Cambridge, 09L/H15b; LMA, COL/WD/03/011.
28 SBH, uncatalogued leases, box 1, assignment from Lewys to Nelmes and Allington 1666; SBH, rentals in HB1/6 to HB1/10; SBH, HA1/6, ff. 50r, 59r-v, 62v; SBH, HA1/7, ff. 10r, 16r, 41v, 92v, 93v; TNA, E 179/252/23.
29 Plan 16 above; Plomer, *Dictionary*, pp. 139-40; SBH, HB1/10.
30 CCLD, 56.2; LMA, COL/CC/CLC/03/009, ff. 23-24.
31 Entry based mainly on CCLD, 33.22; CCLD, 70.1; CCLD, 41.21; CCLD, 66.2; CLJ, 007, ff. 134v, 231v.
32 GL, MS 184/4, f. 38r.
33 TNA, E 179/252/23.
34 LMA, COL/CC/CLC/11/012, No. 345 (1693).
35 GL, MS 39821, 8/8; GL, MS 11653A/1, pp. 49-50; Charles Welch, *Modern History of the City of London* (1896), p. 17.
36 Craig Spence, *London in the 1690s: A Social Atlas* (2000), pp. 120-21.
37 LMA, X109/197 (Repertory 73), ff. 79, 159, 217; *The Survey of Building Sites in the City of London after the Great Fire*, vol. 2 (LTS No. 101, 1964), f. 145; T.F. Reddaway, *The Rebuilding of London after the Great Fire* (1940), pp. 145-50; GL, MS 184/4, f. 32r; LMA, COL/CHD/CT/01/016, f. 21r; LMA, COL/CHD/CT/01/30, f. 135r.
38 CLJ, 009, ff. 33-34; CCLD, 42.16. Both in 1701 and 1721-22, the description in the lease or schedule places the kitchen on an upper floor and the plan places it on the ground floor.
39 Cornmeters weighed and recorded wheat delivered out of vessels or warehouses.
40 CLJ, 003, ff. 35v, 38v; CCLD, 68.18; Strype, book 2, p. 53.
41 LMA, COL/CCS/SO/01/09/009.
42 Fig. 284; GL, MS 184/4, ff. 28v 29r.
43 CCLD, 66.15.
44 LMA, COL/CCS/SO/01/09/009.
45 Ben Weinreb and Christopher Hibbert (eds), *The London Encyclopaedia* (1995 edn), p. 996; CCLD 38.1; CCLD 48.10.
46 Weinreb and Hibbert, *London Encyclopaedia*, p. 996.
47 Centre for Metropolitan History, Life in the Suburbs project, Minories notes, sites 12 and 13; LMA, CLA/008/EM/02/01/002, f. 108v ; CCLD, 54.5; TNA, C 11/15/35.
48 CLJ, 004, f. 273v; LMA, CLA/008/EM/02/02/011, f. 26v; Basil Duke Henning, *The House of Commons, 1660-90* (History of Parliament Trust, 1983), vol. 1, p. 369; LMA, COL/CHD/CT/01/30, f. 131r.
49 Entry based mainly on Centre for Metropolitan History, Life in the Suburbs project, Houndsditch notes, site 13.
50 CLJ, 004, ff. 162v-163r, 166v-167v.
51 CLJ, 004, ff. 135r-136v, 138r, 158v; CCLD, 52.21. The north and east abuttal is Flying Horse Yard on the lease but Inn on Ogilby and Morgan's map; the southern abuttal is indicated by measurements on the leases and LMA, P69/BOT4/C/001/MS05419/002.
52 CC, Charity/Lese/G/C/38. CC, Charity/Lese/G/A/1/47 identifies the property as 70 Holborn Hill. Lese left the house he lived in called the Rainbow and a little house backwards to his servant for ten years, and after that to the Company together with the house next adjoining to the west occupied by William Cox, but on Plan 142 the property does not abut on any other land belonging to Lese, and no other property on Holborn Hill came to the Company (CL/G/7/6). Almost certainly the front and back houses were left to the servant and the middle house (between them rather than to the west) was the one occupied by Cox.
53 CC, minute book 1639-49, f. 25r.
54 CC, Charity/Lese/G/C/38; CC, Charity/Lese/G/C/7 to 9; CC, CL/G/7/6.
55 *SOL*, vol. 36, *The Parish of St. Paul Covent Garden* (1970), p. 29.
56 Entry based mainly on LMA, CLC/210/G/BLC/002/MS13443/001; sas-space.sas.ac.uk/4696 (accessed 19 July 2014).
57 Schofield, p. 89.
58 LMA, MS 12819/9, 1666-67; LMA, MS 12819/10, 1667-68; above, p. 16.
59 LMA, H01/ST/E/067/039/014; LMA, copy of National Register of Archives list of St Thomas's Hospital deeds, pp. 131-32. I am grateful to Stephen Humphrey for advice on the location.
60 LMA, H01/ST/D/07/003, 26 August 1681, 28 September 1682, 18 January 1684. On the back of the plan is written 'Nathaniel Hanwell & Richard [?] Finch', and another copy (LMA, H01/ST/E/114/017) has text in a different hand. Finch described himself in his will of 1716 as living in St Thomas's Hospital (TNA, PROB 11/553/36).
61 LMA, H01/ST/E/65/B/001/001; TNA, PROB 11/346/354.
62 LMA, H01/ST/E67/06/29.
63 TNA, PROB 31/142, No. 461.
64 LMA, HO1/ST/E/067/026/07a.
65 It was not the same Glasshouse Alley as on Rocque's and Horwood's maps.
66 Entry based mainly on LMA, CLC/210/G/A/008/MS12834/002, pp. 227, 238; Schofield, pp. 146-49; LMA, CLC/210/G/BCA/047/MS13018, 13021 and 13021A. The hearth tax for 1664 records Henry Gerrard 3, Robert Heard 14, Henry Weaver 3, William Furnace 4 (Hearth tax, p. 1673).
67 Furnis agreed to make his house half a storey higher in 1656 (LMA, MS 12806/5, p. 456), and in 1683 there was a single garret 24 by 18 feet, whereas in c.1607 there were two garrets 16½ by 11 and 17½ by 12 feet.
68 LMA, CLC/210/G/A/008/MS12834/002, p. 227; LMA, CLC/210/G/BCA/047/MS13018, 13021 and 13021A. Gerrard's lease of 1683 does not list the rooms.
69 Entry based mainly on LMA, CLC/210/G/BCA/097/MS13071; LMA, MS 12806/8, p. 659; LMA, MS 12806/9, ff. 9, 112v, 117r.
70 Order to begin at LMA, CLC/210/G/BCA/080/MS13053, 1 December 1699; payment at LMA, MS 12819/12, casual

payments, 4 December 1702.
71 Bendall, vol. 2, p. 501; LMA, MS 12819/11, 10 November 1686, 13 April 1695; LMA, MS 12819/12, casual payments, 26 October 1698, 17 June, 20 November 1699, 15 July 1700, 4 December 1702; GL, MS 13283. See also GL, MS 22714.
72 SOL, vol. 10, St. Margaret, Westminster (1926), pp. 78-81; McKellar, p. 173.
73 Their names and those of other tenants have been written on Treswell's plan of c.1585 (Schofield, Plate 2).
74 LMA, CLC/210/G/A/061/MS22633/002, p. 120.
75 Schofield, pp. 68-69 (where the house is shown as divided into two in 1612).
76 See CCLD, 42.3. In 1700 it abutted east on property in 'Angle Court', Crutched Friars, which was Crossley's Court on Ogilby and Morgan's map and Three Tun Court on Rocque's (CCLD, 75.38).
77 CLJ, 001, ff. 50v, 70r-71v, 005, f. 246r-v, 006, f. 103v; CCLD, 75.38.
78 McKellar, pp. 101-03; Plan 7; LMA, COL/CC/BHC/01/004, p. 4; LMA, COL/CA/01/01/110, p. 113; TNA, catalogue entry for LMA, COL/SJ/09/021
79 Entry based mainly on CCLD, 38.12; CCLD, 48.16. For the other half of the pair, see CLPB, A22.
80 Strype, book 3, p. 51.
81 LMA, COL/CC/CLC/04/01, No. 208. Bavins are bundles of brushwood.
82 See Dorian Gerhold, 'Where did the Great Fire begin?', LAMAS, forthcoming 2016.
83 LMA, COL/CC/CLC/04/01, No. 208.
84 Ibid.; LMA, COL/CC/CLC/03/005, pp. 12, 71, 90, 92.
85 CCLD, 48.1; [Edward Hatton], A New View of London (1708), vol. 1, p. 56; CLJ, 007, f. 155r.
86 For the stone see http://collections.museumoflondon.org.uk/online/object/119401.html.
87 CCLD, 40.9; LMA, CLA/008/EM/02/02/011, f. 49r; Walter Bell, F. Cottrill and Charles Spon, London Wall through Eighteen Centuries (1937), p. 101. The lease describes the location as the Postern near Moorgate.
88 LMA, CLRO card index of Comptroller's City Lands deeds, places, Basinghall Postern.
89 e.g. OS 1:2500, London Sheet 63, 1894 (Godfrey edition).
90 CCLD, 56.28; CLJ, 005, f. 105r; Henry A. Harben, A Dictionary of London (1918), p. 226.
91 CCLD, 39.3; CLJ, 002, ff. 132v, 140v.
92 LMA, CLA/008/EM/02/02/011, f. 60v; CLJ, 004, 51v; CCLD, 52.1.
93 CCLD, 48.19; CCLD, 51.1; Peter Newman, Company of Adventurers, vol. 1 (1985), p. 339; E. E. Rich, The History of the Hudson's Bay Company 1670-1870, vol. 1, 1670-1763 (1958), p. 335. CCLD, 48.19 shows that the passage was separate from and to the west of Culver Court. The passage is not shown on Rocque's map.
94 Centre for Metropolitan History, Life in the Suburbs project, Houndsditch notes, sites A and B; CLJ, 004, ff. 200v, 203v, 206v.
95 CCLD, 53.19. Shoemakers' Row is the location stated in the lease. The long garden shown could be fitted in on Ogilby and Morgan's map only north-east of St James Duke's Place.
96 CCLD, 66.10; CLJ, 006, f. 33v.
97 Bell, London Wall, p. 101; CLJ, 006, f. 160v; CCLD, 57.5.
98 CLJ, 007, ff. 50v, 53r-54r.
99 CCLD, 65.2.
100 CCLD, 51.30; CLJ, 005, ff. 90r, 102r; TNA, catalogue entry for PROB 11/564/157.
101 Harben, Dictionary of London, pp. 84-85; Marjorie B. Honeybourne, 'The reconstructed map of London under Richard II', LTR, vol. 22 (1965), p. 47; Mary D. Lobel (ed.), The British Atlas of Historic Towns, vol. 3, The City of London (1989), p. 66; TNA, DL/4/89/44; CLJ, 007, ff. 227v-228v.
102 CLPB, A17; CLJ, 002, ff. 10r, 18v, 26v.
103 CCLD, 60.18.
104 CCLD, 42.3.
105 GL, MS 6165/1; GL, MS 6153/4, f. 37r.
106 CCLD, 68.7.
107 Entry based mainly on GL, Haberdashers' deeds, 1996/14, Box 1/15, Nos. 2, 7; GL, MS 15842/3, pp. 336, 349, 377, 379.
108 GL, MS 15842/3, p. 347; TNA, catalogue entry for PROB 11/140/298.
109 The leases dated 10 April 1691 record the term as 61 years although the extension from 51 to 61 years was agreed only on 6 July 1692. Probably the leases were sealed only in 1692.
110 GL, Haberdashers' deeds, 1996/14, Box 1/15, No. 8; GL, MS 33602/1, p. 2.
111 Strype, book 3, p. 93; Henry Camphin, 'Grub Street', LAMAS, vol. 3 (1870), p. 228; City of London Livery Companies' Commission (C.4073 III, 1884), vol. 4, p. 459; Fig. 326.
112 LMA, MS 12806/9, pp. 551-52, 724. All four leases have the same reference.
113 LMA, CLC/210/G/BBH/003A/MS22643.
114 CLJ, 001, ff. 7v, 11v, 33v, 007, ff. 13r, 29r-v; CLPB, B33a; CCLD, 62.8.
115 Dolphin Court is misplaced to the City in Hearth Tax, p. 117.
116 Michael Power, 'Shadwell: the development of a London suburban community in the seventeenth century', London Journal, vol. 4 (1978), p. 30.
117 COL/CHD/CT/01/023, p. 76.
118 SBH, uncatalogued leases, box 6, 1636 lease to Zacharie. For a larger development by Zacharie in Stepney, see Introduction, note 170.
119 LMA, CLA/008/EM/02/01/002, ff. 87v, 97v; CLJ, 002, ff. 92v, 98v, 106v; CCLD, 42.23.
120 Peter Barber, London: A History in Maps (LTS No. 173, 2012), pp. 148-49.
121 CCLD, 58.9; LMA, CLA/008/EM/02/01/002, f. 88v; CLJ, 004, f. 258r, 006, ff. 240v-241r.
122 CCLD, 51.26.
123 CCLD, 61.18.
124 CCLD, 56.7 describes it as without Cripplegate and abutting west on Fore Street. In 1696 it was said to be near Cripplegate and was leased with two houses north of the White Horse Inn (CCLD, 67.4).
125 CCLD, 56.7.
126 CLJ, 005, ff. 140v, 141r.
127 CLJ, 007, ff. 90v-92r.
128 CCLD, 62.27. They must have been about half-way along the passage, as they were in St Dionis Backchurch parish and did not adjoin Lime Street.
129 CCLD, 19.22; CLJ, 007, f. 247r.
130 Other examples are the Merchant Taylors' Company's on Tower Hill, with two storeys (GL, MS 34216, f. 16; see Stephen Freeth, 'The Tower Hill almshouses of the Merchant Taylors' Company', LTR, vol. 30 (2010), pp. 17-28) and Edmondson's almshouses at Bow, two storeys around a courtyard (DC, Y327/1).
131 Entry based on GL, MS 30708/5, pp. 361, 362, 363, 365, 370, 385, 393, 398, 431, 434, 439, 461, 462, 491; GL, MS 30951, f. 158; GL, MS 30708/6, pp. 162, 167, 192; TNA, catalogue reference for Lambeth Palace Library, VH 99/3/3; James

Foster Wadmore, *Some Account of the Worshipful Company of Skinners of London* (1902), pp. 255-56.
132 Anthony Homes-Walker, *Sixes & Sevens: A Short History of the Skinners' Company* (2005), pp. 45-46.
133 LMA, CLA/023/DW/01/288, mm. 1-2; LMA, P69/ALH5/B/003/MS05090/003, p. 56.
134 LMA, P69/ALH5/A/002/MS05084, lists of almsfolk and pensions at end; LMA, P69/ALH5/B/001/MS05342/01, 18 May 1710.
135 LMA, P69/ALH5/B/003/MS05090/003, pp. 209-10; LMA, P69/ALH5/B/001/MS05342/01, 23 November 1736, 1 March 1736/37.
136 CLJ, 020, ff. 175r, 176r; *The Endowed Charities of the City of London* (1829), p. 49; LMA, COL/PL/02/G/006, pp. 9-10.
137 Entry based on LMA, X109/227, pp. 113-20, 613-14; Wilfrid Scott-Giles and Bernard Slater, *The History of Emanuel School 1594-1964* (1977).
138 Morgan's map of 1682.
139 Dan Cruickshank and Neil Burton, *Life in the Georgian City* (1990), pp. 54, 137.
140 An unrelated note on the back is dated January 1673, a few months before the first building lease.
141 Manolo Guerci, 'Salisbury House in London 1599-1694: the Strand palaces of Sir Robert Cecil', *Architectural History*, vol. 52 (2009), p. 36; HH, summary of documents on London properties, Salisbury House 1670-71; TNA, MPA 1/40.
142 HH, Legal 224/17.
143 HH, London plans No. 15 seems to show what was built; one of the Strand houses was described as the lodge of Great Salisbury House. TNA, C 5/266/4 confirms the 29 houses.
144 HH, Deeds 106/15, 174/13, 200/14, 211/32; HH, London plans No. 15.
145 HH, Legal 224/17.
146 Strype, book 4, p. 120, book 6, p. 75.
147 TNA, C 6/424/62.
148 McKellar, p. 48; LMA, E/PYM/002.
149 TNA, C 5/266/4, Sadler's answer.
150 TNA, C 6/424/62; TNA, C 7/164/69.
151 TNA, C 7/164/69.
152 TNA, C 6/424/62; TNA, C 7/164/69; TNA, C 5/266/4; Strype, book 4, p. 120.
153 Hugh Phillips, *The Thames about 1750* (1951), p. 108; SOL, vol. 18, *The Strand* (1937), p. 223.
154 LMA, E/PYM/001 to 003.
155 SOL, vol. 33, *The Parish of St Anne Soho* (1966), pp. 29-32; TNA, C 6/259/81.
156 LMA, E/PYM/017, 019.
157 LMA, E/PYM/023, 414, 579 to 582, 586, 587, 590 to 597.
158 TNA, C 6/257/61.
159 TNA, C 10/499/58 and 83; LMA, E/PYM/023.
160 Westminster City Archives, F418, microfilm 1560, St Martin's rate book 1691; Roger North, *The Lives of the Right. Hon. Frances North, Baron Guilford ...* (1826), vol. 3, p. 210.
161 Norman G. Brett-James, *The Growth of Stuart London* (1935), p. 377; Weinreb and Hibbert, *London Encyclopaedia*, p. 26.
162 Entry based on SOL, vol. 46, *South and East Clerkenwell* (2008), pp. 247-48, 263-65.
163 Entry based mainly on SOL, vols 33-34, *The Parish of St. Anne Soho* (1966), vol. 33, pp. 154-58, vol. 34, plates 118-19.
164 The nearest parallel is the Meal Market (Plan 93).
165 Northamptonshire RO, BH(K)1103, articles.

IMAGE ACKNOWLEDGEMENTS

Images are reproduced by kind permission of the following (see Appendix 1 for document references for plans):

The Worshipful Company of Fishmongers, dust jacket, frontispiece, 76, 101, 103, 106, 160, 176, 200-01, 218, 220, 262

The Worshipful Company of Tallow Chandlers, 1, 98, 215, 321

The Worshipful Company of Dyers, 2, 162

© Trustees of the British Museum, 3, 4, 7, 10-13, 26, 31, 64, 66, 84, 119, 128, 145, 148, 150, 194, 202, 204, 210, 216, 239, 284, 311, 346, 352, 359

Courtesy of the Goldsmiths' Company, 5, 112-15, 208, 221-23

© The British Library Board, 6 (Sloane MS 3254A, f. 5), 16 (Maps Crace II.58), 227-30, 235, 236

London Metropolitan Archives, City of London, 8, 9, 32, 90, 104, 118, 120-25, 129, 141, 143, 144, 147, 149, 153, 155-57, 173, 183, 186-88, 191, 192, 193, 198, 199, 207, 209, 212-14, 233, 234, 240, 245, 246, 251, 255, 257, 265, 279-82, 285-87, 299, 301-10, 312-19, 323, 326, 329-38, 340, 343-45, 348, 353-56, 358, 362, 363

The Worshipful Company of Joiners, 14

Courtesy of the Clothworkers' Company, 15, 56, 58, 88, 109, 249, 288, 291, 297

Grub Street Project (University of Saskatchewan), 17

The Governors of Sutton's Hospital in Charterhouse, 18, 20-22

MOLA (Museum of London Archaeology), 19

Guy's and St Thomas' Charity, 23, 24, 182, 205, 290

The National Archives, 25, 34-36, 39, 40, 52, 134, 165-71, 226, 231-32, 238 (MPB 1/1)

The Burghley House Collection, 28, 29

By courtesy of the Marquess of Salisbury, 30, 37, 46, 172, 181, 347, 349, 350

The Society of Antiquaries of London, 33, 85, 117, 138, 146, 161, 219

Richard Lea, 38

© Crown Copyright 2015, OS GV-197584, 41, 44, 78, 102, 195

© Museum of London, 42

The Worshipful Company of Drapers, 43, 77, 81, 82, 273, 274

The Bodleian Libraries, the University of Oxford, 45, 55 (LP 73), 89, 203

Manolo Guerci, 47

RIBA Library Drawings Collection, 48

Courtesy of the Mercers' Company/photograph by Louis Sinclair, 49

By permission of the Pepys Library, Magdalene College, Cambridge, 50

Collection of the Duke of Northumberland, Alnwick Castle, 51

Courtesy of St Bartholomew's Hospital Archives, 53, 54, 61, 63, 65, 92, 276, 298

Look and Learn/Peter Jackson Collection, 59, 60

Reproduced by permission of the Provost and Fellows of Eton College, 67-72

Middlesex Guildhall Art Collection Trust, 73

© National Portrait Gallery, London, 75, 159, 263, 266

Nick Holder, 79, 80

The Warden and Fellows of All Souls College, Oxford, 83

By kind permission of Christ's Hospital Foundation, 86, 87, 126, 247, 289, 292-96, 327, 328

Reproduced by permission of Historic England, 91

Reproduced with the permission of the Worshipful Company of Stationers and Newspaper Makers, 94-97

The Worshipful Company of Armourers, 99, 100, 217

Medway Archives and Local Studies Centre, 107, 108

By permission of the Comptroller and City Solicitor, City of London, 111, 151, 152, 158, 175, 185, 190, 196, 211, 252, 254, 277, 278, 300, 320, 322, 341

Nomura International plc, 127, 178, 179, 256 (photo Nick Holder)

Reproduced by permission of the Rochester Bridge Trust, 130-33

Bridewell Royal Hospital, 136, 137

Copyright: Dean and Chapter of Westminster, 139, 268-70

Southwark Local History Library & Archive/West Estate collection, 140, 142

The President and Fellows of Magdalen College Oxford, 174, 206

The Worshipful Company of Skinners, 224, 250, 339

By kind permission of the PCC of St Peter-upon-Cornhill, 241

The Priest-in-Charge, St Andrew by the Wardrobe, 243

Parish of St Botolph without Aldgate, 244

By kind permission of the Masters of the Bench of the Honourable Society of the Middle Temple, 248

Dean and Chapter of St Paul's Cathedral, 259, 261

John Crook, 271

With the permission of the Master and Fellows of Corpus Christi College, Cambridge, 275

The Worshipful Company of Haberdashers, 324

Mr Jonathan Pym, 353-56

Original documents held at Northamptonshire Record Office, 360, 361

AUTHOR'S ACKNOWLEDGEMENTS

My first debt is to the Council and officers of the London Topographical Society for having had faith in this project from an early stage. I have been greatly helped by Sheila O'Connell as LTS editor and Graham Maney as designer and printer. John Schofield and Vanessa Harding read an earlier version of the whole text and Peter Barber the introduction, and all made many valuable observations. The Comptroller and City Solicitor's Department, especially Tina Armstrong, made it possible for me to see many of the plans among the Comptroller's City Lands deeds. More archivists, librarians and others have helped me than it is possible to list, but it would be unjust not to mention Jessica Collins (Clothworkers' Company); Penny Fussell (Drapers' Company); Ian Mackintosh (Dyers' Company); Raya McGeorge and Peter Capon (Fishmongers' Company); David Beasley and Sophia Tobin (Goldsmiths' Company); Robin Harcourt-Williams and Sarah Whale (Hatfield House); Jeremy Smith and Wendy Hawke (London Metropolitan Archives); Robin Darwall-Smith (Magdalen College, Oxford); Kate Jarman (St Bartholomew's Hospital); and Stephen Porter and Emma Morris (Sutton's Hospital in Charterhouse). Livery companies have been extremely generous as regards photographs and permissions, and so have many others. Vanessa Harding introduced me to the records of the Centre for Metropolitan History's Life in the Suburbs project. John Crook, Helen Esmonde, Manolo Guerci, Paula Henderson, Nick Holder, Stephen Humphrey, Richard Lea, Roger Leech, Allison Muri (Grub Street Project), Robin Myers, Mike Shaw, John Schofield and Roy Thomson provided information, advice, reconstruction drawings or photographs. My wife Lis provided much appreciated support and encouragement throughout.

INDEX

All references are to pages; *italics* denote pages on which illustrations occur.
Alphabetisation uses the word-by-word system.
With very few exceptions the appendices are unindexed.
Designations in parentheses after personal names should in most cases be preceded by 'citizen and ...'
and denote liveries rather than actual occupations (see p. 36).

Abchurch Lane, house 225-26, *225*
Acorn Alley 110-13, *110-11*
Act for Rebuilding the City of London (1667) 4, 19, 20, 22
Acton, William 214
Addle Hill, Chandlers' Rents 94-95, *94*
Albone, Francis (chemist) 245
Aldermanbury, Jeffreys' house 219-21
Aldermanbury Postern 254
   house 250, *250*
Aldgate 137
   pre-Fire houses 21
Aldgate High Street 206
   house 249, *249*
alehouses (*see also* inns and taverns) 181-82
   Blue Anchor 181, *181*
   Boar's Head 130
   Fore Street 181, *181*
   Horseshoe 250
   Ship 130
   Thames Street 261
Alexander, Daniel, Shafts Alley 124
Allhallows London Wall 265
Allington, William 226-27
almshouses 264-68
   Dyers' 144, 145-46
   Lawrence Camp's 265, *265*
   Old Jewry 98
   Skinners' 264, *264*, *265*
   Whitefriars 86, 88
Ambrose, William (brewer) 157
Anderton's Coffee House 181
Andrews, Thomas 110
Andrews, William (founder) 164
Angel Court 113-15, *114*, *115*
Angel Inn 113-15
Archer, John Wykeham
   view of Cecil Street 273
   view of Sherborne Lane house 22
architects, as surveyors 16-17
Arlington Street 273-75, *274*, *275*
Armitage, The (Hermitage) 60

Armourers' Company, land
   Bishopsgate Street 95
   Old Jewry 97
   plan book 15
Armourers' Hall 185-87, *186*
Arnald, Thomas 16
Ashton, Stephen 231
Athew, Thomas (joiner) 203
Audley, Sir Thomas 50
Austin Friars 78-82, *78-79*, *81*, 225
   houses 82, 224-25, *224*
Ave Maria Lane 92-93
Avis, Joseph 270

back-to-back houses 36, 95, 211, 256
Bacon, Sir Nicholas 48, 88
Badeslade, Thomas 14-15, 122-23
bakeries
   Houndsditch 164
   Perpoole Lane 164-65, *165*
   Tothill Street 240
Ball, John, houses in Thames Street 150
Banks, Richard (freemason) 232
Barbican (site) 107, 157
Barbon, Nicholas 270
bargehouses 208-09, *208*, *209*
Barker, John 164
Barnett, John (draper) 247
Barnham Street 8, 256-57, *257*
Baron, Charles (clothworker) 241
Bartholomew Fair 170
Basil, Simon, Great Salisbury House 57-58
Basinghall Postern, houses 244-45, *244*, *245*
Bassishaw Alley 219
Bateman, Sir James 277
Battle Bridge 152
Battle Mills (Southwark) 152-53, *153*
Bear Alley 172
Beard, Robert (coachman) 177
Becket, Thomas, chapel of 136
Bedford, Earl of 124

Beech, Francis 139
Beef Market (Leadenhall) 165, 167, *168*, 169
Belitha, Edward (haberdasher) 100
Bennet, Charles, Earl of Arlington 273
Bennet Street 273
Bermondsey
   Cherry Garden 152
   Coopers Yard 133, *133*
   East Lane 132-34, *133*, *134*, 160
   Grange Road, houses 236
   Salisbury Lane 132-34, *133*
   tannery 160, *160*
   West Lane (site) 152
   wharves 151-52, *151*
   whiting ground and rope walk 159-60, *159*
Bermondsey Street (formerly Barnesby Street) 155
Bermondsey Wall 132-34, *134*, 152, 160
Beveridge, Dr William 204
Bevington Street (site) 152, 160
Biggs, ?William 17, 191, 209, 264
Billiter Lane 98-100, *99*, *100*, 106
Billiter Square 106
Billiter Street 246
Bird, Sir William 214
Bishopsgate 137-38, *137*, *138*
   demolished 138
   house outside 233, *233*
   rebuilt 137
Bishopsgate Street 95-96, *96*, 110-15
   house 250, *250*
Black Raven Alley 102-03, *103*
Blackfriars, Church Entry 204-05, *204*
Blackman Street 128-30, *128-29*
blacksmiths 130
Blanch Appleton (courtyard), houses 252, *252*
bleaching (whiting) ground (Bermondsey) 159-60, *159*

312

Bludder, Henry (Deputy Surveyor of the Victuals) 194
Bludworth, Sir Thomas 57
   mansion 112-13, *112, 113*
Blue Anchor (Duke's Place) 181, *181*
Boar's Head (Southwark) 130, 178, *178*
Boazio, Baptista 9
Bodley, Sir Thomas 63
   house 62-63, 67, 226
Boggest, Damaris 152
Bond, Henry 15
Boover, John (poulterer) 181
Borough High Street
   Boar's Head Inn 130, 178, *178*
   Catherine Wheel Inn 177-78
   King's Bench Prison 198-99
   Southwark Counter and Sessions House 199-200
Botolph Wharf 142, *142*
Bottle Alley 95-96, *96*
Bouverie Street (site) 86, 237
Bowen, Adam 9
Bower, Anne 243
Bowles, Thomas, print of Fenchurch Street 247
bowling alleys
   Cecil House 43
   Greyfriars precinct 71
   Jewin Street 107, 108
Bradshaw, John 221
Bradshaw, Lawrence (Surveyor of the King's Works) 43
Braidwood Street 155
Bread Street, house plans 72-77, *73, 74, 75*
breweries
   Bridge House 155-56, *155*
   Cousin Lane 107
   Morgan's Lane 154
   Peacock Brewhouse 8, 156-57, *156*
   Pye Corner 157-59, *158*
   Rose 104
brick
   for houses 20, 29
   how depicted on plans 19
Bridewell Hospital, Wapping estate 126
Bridge House Brewhouse 155-56, *155*
Britannia Place (Bottle Alley) 95
Broad Court, houses 262, *262*
Bromfield, Sir Edward 57
Brookes, Thomas (carpenter) 163
Buck, Nathaniel and Samuel, panorama (1749)(details) *146, 211*
Buckingham Gate *see* Emanuel Hospital
Buckley's Court (Houndsditch) 116, *117*
builders, as surveyors 15-16
building materials 20
   how depicted on plans 19
building plans (i.e. for intended buildings) 8-9
Bull and Mouth Inn 120, *121*

Bull and Mouth Street 118-21, *118-19, 120*
bastion 141, *141*
Burghley House (formerly Cecil House) 43-45, *44*
Burnt Yard (Blanch Appleton), houses 252, *252*
Burrows, Peter 88
   house *90*
Burt, Robert (carpenter) 256
Butcher Row (site) 260
Butchers' Hall Lane 85-86
Butler, Charles (feltmaker) 250

Cable Street (site) 260
Caesar's Buildings (Middle Temple) 207, *208*
Caine, Captain John 185
Calthorp, Sir Martin 80
Calvert, Felix 157
Calvert, Thomas 157
Camomile Street, houses 263, *263*
Camp, Lawrence, almshouses 265-66, *265, 266*
Cannon Street Station (site) 41, 56, 211, 253
Canterbury, Dean and Chapter 209
Carp and King (house) 233
Carpenter, John (vintner) 180
carrier services 121, 176, 177
Carter Lane 2
Carteret, Sir Edward 240
Carteret Street, houses 239-40, *239*
Carthusian monks 38
Cartwright, Thomas (mason) 225
Cary, Daniel (brewer) 157-59
Catherine Street 126
Catherine Wheel Inn (Southwark) 177-78, *177*
Cavell, William, Southwark Counter and Sessions House 199-200
Cecil, Robert, 1st Earl of Salisbury 57, *58*
Cecil, Sir William 3, 8, 43, *45*
Cecil House (Strand) 43-45, *44*
first scale plan 3
Cecil Street, proposed houses 268-72, *271, 272, 273*
Chambers, Richard 57
Chandlers' Rents 94-95, *94*
chapel, London Bridge 136
Charles I, King, wishes respecting London Bridge 136
Charterhouse 37-39
   Pardon Chapel 38
   serving hatch 38
   water supply 37, *38*
Charterhouse Yard, houses 276-77, *276, 277*
Cheapside
   house plans 3, 72-77, *73, 74, 75*
      Humphrey Coke 39-41, *40*
   post-Fire house 21
   shops 25

   view 21
Cherry Garden (Bermondsey) 152
Chick Lane 171
Child, Sir Josiah 142, *142*
china shop 124
Chiswell Street 182
Chiverton, Sir Richard 56
Christ Church 86
Christ's Hospital 69, *71*, 206-07, *207*
   Bull and Mouth property 121
   cost of survey 19, 20
   Greyfriars Court 214
   Houndsditch 235
   Newgate Street property 85-86, *85*
   Pye Corner property 157
   Round Woolstaple 237
   Southwark property 256
   surveys by Treswell 4, 10
   Tothill Street land 240
Church Alley (later King Edward Street) 86
Church Entry (Blackfriars) 204-05, *204*
churches 203-06
Cibber, (Caius) Gabriel 151
Cinnamon Street 126
City Artificers 12
City Lands Committee 7, 8
   requirements on lease plans 5, 6, 12-13
Claret, William W. (attrib.), portrait of Jeffreys 221
Clark, Job (joiner) 145, *146*
Clarke, Giles 240
Clarke, Rupert 240
Clerk of the Works (City) 12
Clothworkers' Company
   bargehouse 208-09
   Fenchurch Street property 65
   Holborn Hill property 234
   properties affected by Fire 29
   residence for beadle 8
   Smithfield property 63
   survey by Ward 14
   surveys by Treswell 4, 5, 10
   Whitefriars property 86-88, *87*
Clothworkers' Court 105-07, *105*
coaching inns *see* inns
coffee houses
   Anderton's 181
   Hudson's 140
Coffyn, John 4, 88-90
Coke, Humphrey 9, 39-41
Colchester Bay Hall (Leadenhall Market) 167
Coleman Alley (Finsbury) 161, *162, 163*
Coleman Street (*see also* Armourers' Hall) 141
College of Physicians 137
Collins, William (innholder) 251
Conyers, William (bricklayer) 16, 214, 235
Coopers Yard (Bermondsey) 133, *133*

Copperplate Map (*c*.1555) 3, 115, 212
Cordwainers' Company 4
Cornhill
  houses 24
  Weighhouse Yard 227-28, *228*
Counter Court (Southwark) 200
Counter prison (Southwark) 199-200
Courthope, Edward (goldsmith) 233
Cousin Lane 107, *107*
Covent Garden, Rose Street 124-26, *125*
Cow Lane 63-64, *64*, *65*, 171
Cox, Samuel (distiller) 262
Cox, William (haberdasher) 234-35
Craig's Court 60
Crash Mills (Wapping) 50-53, *53*
Creechurch Lane, house 251, *251*
Creechurch Place (site) 50
Crippes, Sarah 251
Cripplegate 138
Critz, John de (the elder), painting of Robert Cecil 58
Cromwell, Thomas
  house 79, *79*, *80*
  property 2
Cross Dagger Court 163
Cross Keys Inn (Whitecross Street) 176-77, *176*
Crosse, Johnshall 8, 273
Crown and Greenbury Quays 144
Crowther, John
  view of Haberdashers' Square 256
  view of Skinners' Almshouses 265
Crucifix Lane 256
Crutched Friars (*see also* Navy Office) house 240, *240*
Culver Court 247
curriery 164
Cursitors' Hall 3, 47-48, *47*, *48*
Custom House 144
customers, for plans 5-9

Dacre, Anne, Lady 266
Darcy, Sir Edward, mansion 106
Darell, Sir Sampson (Surveyor of the Victuals) 192
Darvoll, Joseph 9, 135, 155
Darvoll, William (plaisterer) 103
Daynes, John 16
  Peter Du Cane's house 214-16
Daynes, Richard 16
deaneries
  St Paul's 216-17, *216*, *217*
  Westminster Abbey 221-23
Devonshire, William (turner) 252
Devonshire Row (site) 110
Dickenson, William (girdler) 261
Dickinson, William 16
  Westminster Abbey Deanery 221-23
Dirty Lane 131
Dober, Richard (shipwright) 133
docks
  Dowgate 107, 210
  London 51

dog kennel, Horn Tavern 180
Dolle, Anthony (saddler) 157
Dolphin, The (Billiter Lane) 98-100
Dolphin Court, houses 259-60, *259*
Dowgate Dock 107, 210
Dowgate Hill (*see also* Erber, The; Skinners' Hall; Tallow Chandlers' Hall)
  houses 253, *253*
Dowgate Laystall 210, *210*, *211*
Drake, Sir Francis 56
Drapers' Company
  The Erber 54-57
  Throgmorton Street 79, *79*, *80*
Drapers' Hall 224, *225*
Drinkwater, Francis 247
Du Cane, Peter, house, Pancras Lane 214-16, *215*, *216*
Duke's Place (*see also* Shoemakers' Row) 50, 139
  Blue Anchor 181, *181*
  Broad Court 262
  house 246, *246*
  Mitre Court 227, *227*
  Mitre Tavern 180-81, *180*
Dummer, Edmund 194-95
dyeing and dyehouses *103*, 144, 145, 160
Dyers' Company 144-45
  plan book 7
Dyers' Hall 145, *146*
Dyers' Hall Wharf 144-46, *145*

East Lane (Bermondsey) 132-34, *133*, *134*, 160
East Smithfield, Navy Victualling Yard 192-94
Edwards, William & Co (ironmongers) 146
Elizabeth I, Queen
  acquires St Mary Graces site 192
  coach-house 200
  statue 138
Emanuel Hospital 266-68, *266*, *267*
Erber, The (mansion, Dowgate Hill) 3, 54-57, *54-55*, *56*
estate plans 2-5
Eton College, Bread Street/Cheapside property 72
Evans, Jonathan (tailor) 246
Exeter House *see* Cecil House

Farriner, Thomas 243
Farringdon Road 172
feltmakers 155
Fenchurch Avenue 107
Fenchurch Buildings 246
Fenchurch Street 65-66, *66*, 247
  houses 246-47, *246*, *247*
  Papillon's house 217-19, *218*
Fetter Lane 88-90, *89*
Finch, John (grocer) 247
fines 36, 286-90

Finsbury (*see also* Great Swordbearers Alley)
  silver-spinning 161-63
Finsbury Yard, stables 182-83, *183*
Fire Court 88, 142, 144
Fire of London *see* Great Fire (1666)
Fish, Bartholomew (fletcher) 212
Fish Market (Leadenhall) 167
Fisher, George 131-32
Fishmongers' Company 144
  bargehouse 208-09
  Billiter Lane 98
  Papillon's house 217
  Peacock Brewhouse 157
  plan book *ii*
  Star Inn 173
  Thames Street land 102, *103*
Fishmongers' Hall 187-88, *187*, *188*
Fitch, John (bricklayer) 219, 227, 229
Fitch, Thomas (carpenter) 219
Fleet Ditch or Channel 13, 103-05, *104*
Fleet Lane 3, 40, *41*
Fleet Street, Horn Tavern 179-80, *179*
Flemming, Christopher, Throgmorton Street and Austin Friars 78-82
Flockton Street (formerly Salisbury Lane) 132
Floral Street 124, 126
Flying Horse Yard (Houndsditch) 182, *182*
Foltrop, John (City Carpenter) 243
Fore Street 245, 250
  alehouse 181, *181*
  houses 242, *242*, 254, *254*, 262
fortifications, plans 3
foundries, Old Bethlehem 163-64, *163*
Friend, John (hydrographer) 16, 132
Frith, Matthew (bricklayer) 274
Frith Street, houses 277-78, *277*, *278*
Furnis, William (grocer) 237-38

Gamon, Thomas (carpenter) 95
gardens
  of bargehouses 208
  Billiter Lane 99
  Cecil House 43, 45
  Cursitors' Hall 45
  Du Cane's house 216
  earliest plan 43
  The Erber 56
  Fenchurch Street 66
  Great Swordbearers Alley 260
  Greyfriars Court 214
  Greyfriars precinct 70-71
  Holy Trinity Aldgate 50
  of houses 27
  Jeffreys' house 221
  Jewin Street 107
  St Bartholomew's precinct 68
  Stationers' Hall 92
Gardyner, Richard 60-61
Garrick Street 126
Garway, William 80, 82
Gascoyne, Joel 9

gates, City, rebuilt after Great Fire 137-38
Gauden, Sir Denis 237
General Post Office 207
Gerrard, Henry (salter) 237-38
Glasshouse Alley 237
Glaziers' Hall 77-78, *77*
Goat Alley (Finsbury) 161, *162*, 263
gold and silver wire drawing 161-63
Goldsmiths' Alley 107-09, *108*, *109*
Goldsmiths' Company
   acquires Horn Tavern site 180
   acquires Jews' Garden 107
   bargehouse 209
   Bishopsgate Street alleys 110-12
   Bludworth's house 113
Goldsmiths' Hall 189-90, *189*, *190*
Gouge, Thomas 204
Gould, James 16, 144
   Dyers' Company plan book 7
Grange Road (Bermondsey)
   houses 236, *236*
   tannery 160
Gravel Lane 126-28, *127*, *128*
Great College Street (site) 131
Great Fire (1666) (*see also* Act for Rebuilding)
   origin 243
   and increased use of plans 4, 28-29
   papists blamed 244
   rebuilding after 22, 28-29
   unusual survivals 29
Great Peter Street (site) 131
Great Salisbury House (Strand) 57-58, *57*, *58*
Great Swordbearers Alley (Finsbury), houses 260-61, *260*
Greatorex, Ralph 15
Green, Peter, lease from Savoy Hospital 41
Green Market (Leadenhall) 168
Greenyard (Leadenhall) 135, 165, 167, *169*
Gregory, Arthur 9
Gresham Street (site) 113
Greyfriars Court 213-14, *213-14*
Greyfriars precinct (former) 69-71, *70-71*, 120
Grocers' Alley, house 243, *243*
ground plans 3-4
Grub Street, silver-spinner's shed 163, *163*
Gucht, Michael van der, portrait of John Ward *14*
Guerci, Manolo, reconstruction of Great Salisbury House 58
gunsmith's house 130
Guy's Hospital (site) 152

Haberdashers' Square, houses 255-56, *255*, *256*
Haiward, William 9
Handy, Hugh 15

Hanseatic League 41
   cartouche and arms *151*
   rebuilds Bishopsgate 138
Hanwell, Nathaniel 161
   life and work 15-16
   payment for surveys 19
   Grange Road (Bermondsey) 236
   houses etc. in Southwark 8
Hardy, John (pewterer) 262
Harp Lane 90-91, *91*
Harris, Daniel (cooper) 244
Harris, Richard 125-26
Hart Street (London Wall), houses 249, *249*
Hatton, George 149
Hawthorne, Henry (surveyor) 43
Hay's Wharf 152, 156
Hayward, William (merchant taylor) 123
hearth tax 31
heating, houses 26
Hendrick, Joseph 248
Henley, Thomas (?carpenter) 164-65
Henshaw, Walter, St Botolph Aldgate 15, 205-06
Herb Market (Leadenhall) 165
Hermitage (Armitage, Whitehall) 60
Hermitage (Wapping) 3, 50-53, *51*, *52*, *53*
Herne, Nathaniel (merchant) 187
Hicks, Sir Baptist 73-75, *76*
High Holborn, houses 241
Hilditch, Ralph 153
Hobbs, John 16
   Barnham Street 256
   Tothill and Carteret Streets 239-40
Hodge, John 270-72
Holborn Conduit 171
Holborn Hill, houses 234-35, *234*
Holder, Nick, reconstructions 79, 80
Holgill, Christopher, lease from Savoy Hospital 39-40
Hollar, Wenceslaus
   Cornhill (detail) *24*
   Exeter House (detail) *45*
   London Bridge (detail) *137*
   Nonsuch House (detail) *46*
   Northumberland House 60
   St Paul's 83
Holy Trinity Aldgate 3, *180*, *181*, 258
   former precinct 48-50, *49*, *50*
Hooke, Robert 137, 149, 165, 194
Horn Tavern (Fleet Street) 179-80, *179*
Horsemonger Lane 130
Horsepond (Smithfield) 170
Horseshoe Alehouse 250
Horsley Down 155
Horwood, Richard, map (1814) 155, 260, 275
Houndsditch 115-17, *116-17*
   Flying Horse Yard 182, *182*
   houses 232, 233, 235, *235*, 248, *248*
   workshops 164, *164*

house plans 213-78
   Abchurch Lane 225
   Aldermanbury Postern 250, *250*
   Aldgate High Street 249, *249*
   Arlington Sreet 274, *275*
   Austin Friars 224
   Ave Maria Lane 93
   Barnham Street 256-57, *257*
   Basinghall Postern 244-45, *244*, *245*
   Bishopsgate Street 233, 250, *250*
   Bread Street 72-77
   Broad Court 262, *262*
   Camomile Street 263, *263*
   Carteret Street 239-40, *239*
   Cecil Street 271, *272*
   Charterhouse Yard 276-77, *276*
   Cheapside 39-41, 72-77
   Creechurch Lane 251, *251*
   Crutched Friars 240, *240*
   Dolphin Court 259-60, *259*
   Dowgate Hill 253, *253*
   Du Cane's house *215*
   Duke's Place 246, *246*
   Fenchurch Street 246, *246*
   Fleet Lane 40, *41*
   Fore Street 242, *242*, 254, *254*, 262, *262*
   Frith Street 277-78, *277*
   Grange Road (Bermondsey) 236, *236*
   Great Swordbearers Alley 260-61, *261*
   Grocers' Alley 243, *243*
   Hart Street 249, *249*
   High Holborn 241, *241*
   Holborn Hill 234-35, *234*
   Houndsditch 116-17, 164, 233, 235, 248
   Jeffreys' house 220
   Leadenhall Street *101*, 122
   Lime Street 263, *263*
   Little Britain 226
   Mark Lane 242-43, *242*
   Mincing Lane 229
   Minories 232
   Mitre Court 227
   Newgate Street 241, *241*
   Old Bethlehem 163
   Papillon's house 218
   Pudding Lane 243-44, *244*
   Rose Alley 258-59, *258*
   Round Woolstaple (Westminster) 237-38, *238*
   Salisbury Street 269
   Shoemakers' Row 248, *261*
   Thames Street 261, *261*
   Throgmorton Street 79
   Tothill Street 239-40, *239*
   Tower Hill 245, *245*
   Tower Street *91*
   Weighhouse Yard 228
   Whitefriars 237, *237*
   Wormwood Street 251, *251*

houses
  back-to-back 36, 95, 211, 256
  gardens 27
  heating 26
  privies 27
  rooms 23-26
  stables 27
  subdivision 20, 22
  types 22-23
  water supply 26-27
houses (views, elevations etc.)
  Angel Court 115
  Fetter Lane 89
  Leadenhall Street 102, 122, 123, 124
  London Bridge 136
  Shafts Alley 124
  Sherborne Lane 22
  Thames Street 150
  Throgmorton Street 80
  Whitehall 61
houses of easement
  domestic 27
  Queenhithe 211-12, 211, 212
Howard, Henry, Earl of
    Northampton 58, 59
Howard, John (mariner) 232
Hudson's Bay Company 247
Hudson's Coffee House 140
Humfrey, Toby 210
Hunt, William Henry, view of Great
    Mews 203
Hutchinson, Joseph (carpenter) 16, 235

industries 152-64
inns and taverns (see also alehouses;
    Star Inn) 172-80
  Angel 113-15
  Boar's Head 178, 178
  Bull and Mouth 121
  Catherine Wheel 177-78
  Cross Keys 176-77, 176
  Horn 179-80, 179
  King's Arms 200
  Leadenhall Street 102
  Mitre 180-81, 180
  Ship and Turtle 123, 124
  Unicorn 129, 130
  used as lace market 121
  used as meal markets 171
ironmongers 146
Ironmongers' Company 5, 18
Isle of Ducks 155

Jackson, Peter, reconstruction of
    Fenchurch Street houses 66, 67
Jackson, Thomas (draper) 249, 254
Jacob's Island 132
Jacobsen, Jacob 146
Jacobsen, Theodore 149-51
James, John (armourer) 164
Jeffreys, George (later Lord Chief
    Justice), house 219-21, 220
Jeffreys, Jeffrey (merchant) 131
Jennings, John 176-77

Jerman, Edward (carpenter) 187, 209
Jerusalem Chamber (Westminster
    Abbey) 221, 223
Jeston, Roger (haberdasher) 255
Jewin Street 107-09, 108, 108, 109
Jewry Street (Poor Jewry Lane) 139
Jews' Garden 107
Joiners' Company, Master and
    Court 28
Jones, Inigo 125, 189
justices of the peace, Surrey 200

Kerwin, William (City Mason) 50
killhouse (tanning) 161, 305n78
King, Gregory, sketch for St
    Katherine's map 17, 18
King Edward Street (site) 86
King's Bench Prison 198-99, 198
King's Printing House 120
Kneller, Sir Godfrey, portrait of
    Papillon 219
Knowles, Israel (carpenter) 216
Knowles, John 163

lace, sold at Bull and Mouth 121
Lady, The (Thames Street) 102-03
Lamb's Passage 261
landowners, London 1-2
Lands, Heber (surveyor) 14, 20, 118,
    157
Langstraffe, Robert (whitster) 160
Lawrence, Sir John 212
Lawrence, Roger 16
Lawrence, William (joiner) 263
laystalls 210
Lea, Richard, reconstruction of Holy
    Trinity precinct 50
Leaden Porch 217
Leadenhall, Greenyard 135, 165
Leadenhall Building (site) 124
Leadenhall Market 165-69, 166-67,
    168, 169
Leadenhall Street 100-02, 101, 102
  houses 122-24, 122, 123, 124
Leake, John 16
lease plans 5-7
leases 27-28
Legal Quays 142, 229
Leigh, Samuel, panorama
    (1829)(detail) 209
Lem, Joseph 16
Lens, Bernard, Fishmongers' Hall 187
Lenthall, Sir John 198
Lewin, Edmund 137-38, 155-56
Lewing, Gamaliel (carpenter) 262
Leybourn, William 11
  life and works 11-12
  error corrected by Olley 18, 139
  payment for surveys 19
  Battle Mills 152-53
  Billiter Lane 98-100
  Bishopsgate 137-38, 137
  Boar's Head Inn 178
  Botolph Wharf 142

Catherine Wheel Inn 177-78
Chandlers' Rents 94-95
Clothworkers' property 29
Cousin Lane 107
Dowgate Hill 253
Dowgate Laystall 210
Fishmongers' Company plan
    book ii
Fishmongers' Hall 187-88
Fore Street 254
Leadenhall Market 165-69
Leadenhall Street 100-02
London Wall 137-38, 137
Ludgate 138
Morgan's Lane 154
Peacock Brewhouse 156-57
Porter's Key 143-44
Queenhithe house of easement
    211-12
St Paul's Deanery 216-17
Smithfield sheep pens 170
Star Inn 172-76
Stationers' Hall 92
survey for Tallow Chandlers 6
Tallow Chandlers' Hall 184-85
Thames Street 102-03
Thomas Papillon's house 217-19
Whitefriars houses 237
Lime Street, houses 263, 263
Litlyngton, Abbot 221
Little Britain 62-63
  Bodley's house 62-63, 67, 226,
    226-27, 226
Little Dorrit Court (site) 177
Little St Bartholomew's see St
    Bartholomew the Less
Liverpool Street (site) 164
Liverpool Street Station (site) 95
livery companies, plan books 5, 7
livery halls 183-92
Llewellyn, Martin
  life 10-11
  Greyfriars precinct 69-71
  St Bartholomew the Less 71-72
  St Bartholomew's precinct 4, 67-69
Lock, Thomas (carpenter) 187
Locke Yard 130
Lodge, William, picture of Star Inn
    175
London Bridge 135-37, 135, 136
  chapel 136
  lost plan (1587) 9
  Nonsuch House 3, 45-47, 46
  road widening 46, 137
  waterworks 135, 136
London Docks 51
London Wall 67, 137-41, 245, 249
  bastions
    Houndsditch 232
    Poor Jewry Lane 139, 139
    Shoemakers' Row 139, 139
    Windsor Court 140, 140
Long Acre 124, 125

longhouse, Queenhithe 211-12, *211, 212*
Love Alley (Love Lane) 97
Loveday, Thomas (turner) 230
Ludgate 138, *138*
Ludgate Hill 103-05, *104*

Magdalen College (Oxford) 154, 178
Maiden Lane 112-13
Malling Abbey 154
Mansell, Edward 9, 11
  Greyfriars precinct 69-71
mansions 213-23
Mark Lane, houses 242, *242*
markets 165-72
  Queenhithe 212
Marshalsea Court 200
mathematicians, as surveyors 13-15
Mayes, William (cordwainer) 88
Mazahod, Jacob (merchant) 251
Maze Ponds 152
Meal Market 171-72, *171, 172*
meat, Leadenhall Market 167
Mercers' Company, bargehouse 208-09
Merchant Taylors' Company 4, 228
mews, meaning 200
Micklethwait, Thomas (merchant taylor) 258-59
Middle Exchange 268
Middle Temple, Caesar's Buildings 207, *208*
Middleton, Richard (freemason) 242
Mile End *see* Skinners' Almshouses
military plans 3
Mill Bank Square 132
Millbank 131-32, *131*
Miller, Thomas (bricklayer) 132
Miller, Thomas (leatherseller) 236
mills
  Battle Mills 152-53, *153*
  Crash Mills (Wapping) 50-53, *53*
  tidal 152-53
Milton, John 76, *76*
Milton Street (formerly Grub Street) 163, 255
Mincing Lane, houses 229-30, *229*
Minories, houses 232, *232*
Mitre Court (Duke's Place) 227
Mitre Square (site) 50
Mitre Street 259
Mitre Tavern (Duke's Place) 180-81, *180*
models, by Llewellyn 10-11
Molins, William 173-75
Monger, Peter (brewer) 232
monks, Carthusian 38
Monkwell Street 140
Monmouth House 277
Monument, The 243
Morgan, Edmund 154
Morgan, William
  map (1682) 32-33, 132
    Salisbury Street 270

Southwark 155
panorama (1682), Porter's Key *144*
Morgan's Lane (Southwark) 154-55, *154, 155,* 178
Morris, Peter 135

Nail Gallery (Leadenhall) 167
Nash, Frederick, view of Bull and Mouth Inn *121*
Navy Office 194-97, *195, 196-97*
Navy Victualling Yard 192-94
Neckinger Wall Ditch 160
Nelmes, Richard 226-27
Nevill's Alley 4, 88-90, *89, 90*
New Fetter Lane (site) 90
New Fish Street Hill *see* Star Inn
New Street (site) 110
Newberry, Lewis (skinner) 264
Newbold, Augustine 98
Newgate 71, 138
Newgate Street 69
  house 241, *241*
Nicholls, John 172
Nicholls, Sutton
  views of Bishopsgate and Ludgate *138*
  view of Charterhouse Yard *277*
  view of Royal Mews *202*
Noble Street 113
Noke, James (merchant) 229
Nomura House (site) 121
Nonsuch House 3, 45-47, *46*
Norden, John, view of St Thomas's chapel *136*
Northampton House (Strand) 58-59, *59, 60,* 202
Northumberland, Earls of 120
Northumberland Avenue (site) 59
Northumberland House *see* Northampton House
Northumberland Place (house) 120
Norton, Roger (stationer) 227

official buildings 192-206
Ogilby, John and Morgan, William, map
  non-pictorial nature 3
  Bludworth's mansion *113*
  Burnt Yard 252
  Cousin Lane 107
  Du Cane's house *216*
  Dyers' Hall Wharf *145*
  Finsbury Stables 182
  Great Swordbearers Alley 261
  Haberdashers' Square 256
  Jeffreys' house garden *221*
  Leather Lane 164
  Nevill's Alley 88
  Old Bethlehem 164
  Papillon's house *217*
  Peacock Brewhouse *157*
  Pudding Lane 244
  Pye Corner *159*

St Bartholomew's precinct 69
Steelyard 146
Old Bethlehem, foundries 163-64, *163*
Old Fish Street Hill *see* Glaziers' Hall
Old Fleet Lane 172
Old Jewry 97-98
Oliver, John
  corrections to Leybourn's plans 18, 165
  London Wall 137
  and Merchant Taylors 4
  Skinners' Hall 191
  Steelyard 149
  Wood Street Compter 231
Olley, Isaac
  life and works 13
  Aldermanbury Postern 250, *250*
  Aldgate High Street 249
  alehouse in Fore Street 181
  Basinghall Postern 245
  bastions of London Wall 140-41, *140, 141*
  Bishopsgate Street 250
  Broad Court 262
  Camomile Street 263
  Creechurch Lane 251
  Fenchurch Street 246-47
  Flying Horse Yard 182
  Fore Street 254, 262
  foundries 163-64
  Hart Street 249, *249*
  Houndsditch 115-17, (?)248
  house outside Bishopsgate 233
  Lime Street 263
  Mincing Lane 229-30
  Minories, houses 232
  Mitre Tavern 180-81
  Pudding Lane 243-44
  St Botolph Aldgate 205-06
  Shoemakers' Row 261
  silver-spinners' sheds 161-63
  stables in Finsbury Yard 182-83
  Thames Street 261
  Wormwood Street 251
Olley, John
  life and works 12-13
  corrects Leybourn's plans 18, 139
  Angel Court and Bishopsgate Street 113-15
  Basinghall Postern 244-45
  Blue Anchor 181
  Dolphin Court 259-60
  Emanuel Hospital 266-68
  Flying Horse Yard 182
  Fore Street 242
  Grocers' Alley 243, *243*
  Houndsditch 115-17, 164, (?)248
  (?)Houndsditch houses 232
  house outside Bishopsgate 233
  Jeffreys' house 219-21
  Lawrence Camp's almshouses 265-66
  Leadenhall Market 165-69

London Wall
  bastions 139, *139*
  partial demolition 137
  Mark Lane 242-43
  Meal Market 171-72
  Mincing Lane 229-30
  Minories, houses 232
  Mitre Court 227
  property values 113
  Rose Alley 258-59
  Tower Hill 245
  Weighhouse Yard 227-28
  Wood Street Compter 230-31
Owfeild, Roger 98-100

Page, Gilbert (barber surgeon) 228
Palace of Westminster (site) 131
Palace Yard Square 132
Pancras Lane, Peter Du Cane's house 214-16, *215, 216*
'paper buildings' 88
Papillon, Thomas, house 217-19, *218*
papists, blamed for Great Fire 244
Parker, Sir John 60
Parliament Street (site) 237
Parratt, Edward (saddler) 182
Parrett, John (fishmonger) 103
Parsons, Samuel 9, 15
Paul's Cross 84, *84*
Paybody, Edmund 255-56
Peacock Brewhouse 8, 156-57, *156*
pedlars, Leadenhall Market 168
Penson, Thomas, Fishmongers' Company plan book *ii*
Pepys, Samuel 194
Percy, Algernon, 10th Earl of Northumberland 59
Perpoole Lane, bakery 164-65, *165*
Petty France 62-63, *62, 63*
Phillips, Luke 182
Philpot, Sir John 212
Pickleherring Mill 152, 154, *154*
pictorial features 3
Pincock Lane 86
Pindar Street (site) 110
Pipeborers Wharf 156
pissing cistern, Jeffreys' house 219
plan books, livery companies 5, 7
plans
  costs and payments 19-20, 284-86
  defined 1
  features 19
plots (= plans) 1
Pluckenett, Thomas 16
Poor Jewry Lane 139
population, London 1, 29
Porter, John 144
Porter's Key 143-44, *143*
Portpool Lane (formerly Perpoole Lane) 164-65
Portsmouth, first scale map 3
Post Office 207
Poston, Roger (merchant taylor) 242
Poultney, Thomas (joiner) 203

Powell, Philemon 180
Prestwood, George (carpenter) 107
Primrose Alley 110-13, *110-11*
Primrose Street (site) 110
printing houses
  Christ's Hospital 86
  Greyfriars Court 214
  King's 120
  Little Britain 227
prisons
  King's Bench 198-99
  Ludgate 138
  Peacock Brewhouse site 157
  Southwark Counter 199-200
  Wood Street Compter 230-31
privies, houses 27
Provost, John (merchant) 229
public lavatories *see* houses of easement
Pudding Lane 174, *175*
  house 243-44, *244*
Pullison, Sir Thomas 56
Pye Corner brewhouse 157-59, *158*
Pym, William 8, 273

Quakers 121
Queen Anne's Gate (site) 240
Queen Victoria Street (site) 78, 95, 216
Queenhithe, house of easement 211-12, *211, 212*

Ratcliff *see* Dolphin Court
Rawle, S., Mitre Tavern *180*
Rebuilding Act (1667) 4, 19, 20, 22
Red Cross Alley 130
rents 286-90
Rochester, Dean and Chapter, land on Ludgate Hill 103-05
Rochester Bridge Trust 123
Rocque, John, map 155
  Coleman and Goat Alleys 163
  Cross Keys Inn 177
  Dolphin Court 260
  Edlins Wharf 132
  Meal Yard 172
  Unicorn Yard 130
  Union Brewhouse 241
Rogers, John 3
Rookes, Richard 260
rooms, houses 23-26
rope walk (Bermondsey) 159-60, *159*
Rose Alley, houses 258-59, *258*
Rose brewhouse 104
Rose Street (Covent Garden) 8, 124-26, *125*
Rossington, Richard (builder) 270
Round Woolstaple (Westminster), houses 237-38, *238*
Rowe, Isaac 16
  Round Woolstaple 237-38
Rowley, John 15
Rowton, John (cordwainer) 248

Royal Mews (Westminster) 200-02, *201, 202*
Royal Mint 194
Russell, Margaret 242-43
Russell, Robert (skinner) 90
Ryder, Richard, houses on Holborn Hill 234-35

St Andrew by the Wardrobe 95, 205
St Andrew Undershaft 124
St Ann Blackfriars 204-05
St Bartholomew the Less 71-72, *72*
  churchyard 62, 67
  view from south *72*
St Bartholomew's Hospital
  former Greyfriars land 69
  land in Harp Lane 90
  Little Britain 226
  Newgate Street 241
St Bartholomew's precinct 3, 62
  Martin Llewellyn 67-69, *68*
St Botolph Aldgate 205-06, *205*
St George's Court (Fleet Street) 41
St Gregory's church 84
St James Duke's Place 246
St James's Park 273
St John Zachary 113
St Katherine Coleman, parish 246
St Katherine's precinct, sketch 17, *18*
St Margaret Fish Street Hill 135
St Margaret's church (Southwark) 199
St Martin in the Fields, land 202
St Martin's le Grand 120
St Mary Abchurch 226
St Mary Graces 50, 192
St Mary Somerset 78
St Michael le Querne, parish 39
St Michael Queenhithe 212
St Nicholas Cole Abbey 78
St Paul's Cathedral 83-84, *83*
St Paul's Deanery 216-17, *216, 217*
St Peter upon Cornhill 203-04, *203, 204*
St Sepulchre 170-01, 182
St Thomas's Chapel (London Bridge) 136
St Thomas's Hospital, property 41, 161, 177, 209, 237
Saintloe, John (fishmonger) and Mary 144
Salisbury, Earls of
  property in Bermondsey 132, 152, 160
  property in Strand 57-58, 268-72
Salisbury Lane (Bermondsey) 132-34, *133*
Salisbury Street, proposed houses 268-72, *269*
Sancroft, William 216
Saunders, Thomas 178
Savoy Hospital 3, 39-41
Saxton, John (carpenter) 16
scale, plans 3

Scarborow, Mr, house in Abchurch Lane 225-26
schools, Christ's Hospital 206-07
'Scotland' (off Whitehall) 60-61
Scott's Yard (Bush Lane) 57
Seagood, George (City Carpenter) 149
Seagood, Thomas 149
Selby, Anthony (draper) 229
Shafts Alley (Sharps Alley) 124, *124*
Shaler, Edward (gentleman) 243
Sharps Alley (Shafts Alley) 124, *124*
Shaw, Henry, print of Christ's Hospital *71*
Shaw, Sir John 175
sheep pens, Smithfield 170-71, *170, 171*
Shelton, John (saddler) 227
Shepherd, T. H.
  Catherine Wheel Inn *177*
  Emanuel Hospital *267*
  Leadenhall Street houses *102*
  Tallow Chandlers' Hall *185*
Sherborne Lane 225
  house *22*
Shewin, William (pinmaker) 236
Ship (alehouse) 130
Ship and Turtle (inn) 123, *124*
shipwrights 133, 152
Shoe Lane 234
Shoemakers' Row 139, 140, 246
  houses 248, *248*, 261, *261*
shops 19, 24-25
  china 124
  St Botolph Aldgate 206, *206*
Siderfin, Thomas 130
silver-spinners' sheds 161-63, *162*
Skinners' Almshouses 264, *264, 265*
Skinners' Company, bargehouse 209, *209*
Skinners' Hall 191-92, *191, 192*
slaughterhouse, Cross Keys Inn 176
Smith, Elizabeth (tanner) 161, 236
Smith, Henry (merchant taylor) 123
Smith, J. T., print of Wood Street Compter *231*
Smith, John 14, 240
Smith, John (scrivener) 106
Smith, Nathaniel (tanner) 161
Smith, Robert (cordwainer) 139
Smithfield (*see also* West Smithfield)
  new market buildings 171
  sheep pens 170-71, *170, 171*
Smythson, John, Northampton House 58-59
Soane, Thomas (grocer) 142
Society of Friends 121
Somerset House 195
Southwark Counter and Sessions House 199-200, *199, 200*
Southwark fire (1676) 177-78
Spade Alley 132
sponging houses 243
stables 121, 130

Finsbury Yard 182-83, *183*
Fishmongers' Hall 187
Flying Horse Yard 182, *182*
houses 27
Navy Office 197
Stanton, William (dyer) 254
Staples, Leonard (dyer) 210
Star Inn (New Fish Street Hill) 8, 29, 172-76, *173, 174, 175*
Stationers' Hall 92-93, *92*
Steavens, Sir William 132-34
Steelyard 41-43, *42*, 146-51, *147, 148-49*
  Master's dwelling *150*
  view from river *150*
Stephens, Daniel 230
Stepping, Daniel 161
Sterne, Thomas 135
Stewkley, Sir Thomas 121
Stoakes, Richard (mariner) 232
stocks
  Coleman Street 141
  Smithfield 170, 171
Stocks Market, shops 25
Stone, Nicholas (King's Master Mason) 124, 126, 189
Stony Lane (Southwark) 155
Stow, John
  on Bishopsgate 95
  on the Erber 56
  on Glaziers' Hall 78
  on Jews' Garden 107
  on Leadenhall Street 100
Strand *see* Cecil House; Great Salisbury House; Northampton House
Strand Palace Hotel (site) 45
street widening 28, 128
  Clothworker's property 29
  London Bridge 46, 137
Strype, John
map (1720) 34-35
  on Armourers' Hall 185
  on Bottle Alley 95
  on Bull and Mouth 121
  on Cross Keys Inn 177
  on Haberdashers' Square 256
  on Houndsditch 115
  on Leadenhall 165
  on London Bridge 136
  on Mincing Lane 230
  on 'Stationers' Rents' 93
  on Unicorn Inn 130
Stuart, Robert (barber surgeon) 140
Sufferance Quays 142
Suffolk House *see* Northampton House
Sun Court (formerly Weighhouse Yard) 228
surveying 17-20
  costs and payments 19-20, 284-86
  methods 17-18
  styles 19
surveyors 9-17

Symonds, John 9
  Cursitors' Hall 47-48
  Holy Trinity Aldgate 48-50

Tallow Chandlers' Company 95, 253
  plan book 6, 8, 18
Tallow Chandlers' Hall 184-85, *184, 185*
tanning and tanneries, Grange Road 160-61, *160*
Tasker, John 103-05
taverns *see* alehouses; inns and taverns
Temple *see* Middle Temple
tennis court, Cecil House 43
Terrell, William (ropemaker) 160
Thames Street (*see also* Fishmongers' Hall) 102-03, *103*, 142, 144, 145
  houses *150*, 261, *261*
Thomas, William 277
Thomas More Street (site) 50
Thompson, William 241
Throgmorton Street 78-82, *78-79, 80, 81*, 225
Titcombe, Joseph
  life and work 15
  plan book 18
  payment for surveys 19
  Armourers' Hall 185-87
  Bottle Alley and Bishopsgate Street 95-96
  Old Jewry 97-98
toilets *see* houses of easement; privies
Toms, William Henry
  view of Bishopsgate Street *115*
  view of St Bartholomew the Less *72*
Tooley Street 153, 155
Tothill Street, houses 8, 239-40, *239*
Tower Bridge Road (site) 161, 236
Tower Hill, house 245, *245*
Tower Street 90-91, *91*
Trafalgar Square (site) 200-01
Treswell, Ralph
  life 10
  Clothworkers' Court 106
  Fenchurch Street 65-66
  Houndsditch 235
  Mews 202
  Round Woolstaple 237
  West Smithfield and Cow Lane 63-64
Treswell, Robert 10
  Whitehall 60-61
Trinity Square (site) 245
Tudor Street (site) 86, 237

Unicorn Inn (Southwark) *129*, 130
upper storeys 7, 19, 22
Urwin, Gilbert 241

Vaughan Way (site) 51
Vauxhall Bridge (site) 209
Vincent, John (combmaker) 250

Visscher, Claes Janz., detail of
    Steelyard 42

Walker, James (brewer) 157
Walnut Tree Yard 110-13, *110-11*
Walpole, Sir Robert 275
Wapping *see* Crash Mills; Hermitage
    (Wapping)
Wapping Street 126-28, *127*
Ward, John (girdler) 124-25
    Rose Street *124*
Ward, John (surveyor)
    life and works 14, 17, *14*
    cartouche from plan *15*
    payment for surveys 19-20
    Bludworth's mansion 112-13
    Goldsmiths' Hall 189-90
    Horn Tavern 179-80
    Jewin Street 107
    Navy Office 194
    Primrose and Acorn Alleys etc.
        110-13
Wardrobe Terrace 95
warehouses 229-30
warfare, plans used for 2-3
Warren, Thomas (bricklayer) 216
Warren, William (draper) 248
water supply
    Charterhouse 2, 37-38
    houses 26-27
    Papillon's house 219
waterworks, London Bridge 135, *136*
Watkins, W., print of Bull and Mouth
    Inn *121*
weaving workshops 108, *109*, 112

Webb, Francis 157
Weighhouse Yard, Cornhill 227-28,
    228
West Lane (Bermondsey)(site) 152
West Smithfield 63-64, *64*
Westminster *see* Round Woolstaple
Westminster Abbey
    Deanery 221-23
    Jerusalem Chamber 221, 223
Westminster School 221
wharves 142-52
Wheatsheaf Yard 172
Whincop, Samuel 231
Whistler, Henry (gentleman) 226
White, Daniel 178
White, Robert, print of Leybourn *11*
White Bear (Cheapside property)
    72-73, 75-77
White Market (Leadenhall) 167
Whitecock Alley 145
Whitecross Street (*see also* Cross Keys
    Inn; Peacock Brewhouse) 161
Whitefriars 86-88, *87*
    houses 237, *237*
Whitehall 60-61
    houses at north end *61*
White's Court 217
whiting ground (Bermondsey) 159-60,
    159
Whitmore, Sir Thomas 214
Whittington, Richard 211
Whitwang, Sarah 250
Wildgoose Alley 149
Willey, John (baker) 164
Williams, 'Ma:' 204-05

Williams, Richard (clothworker) 228
Williamson, Daniel 178
Wilson, John 126, 128
Wilson, Joseph (wine cooper) 244
Wilson, Lewis (vintner) 228
Wilson, Samuel (merchant) 244
Wilson Grove (formerly Salisbury
    Street) 133
Windmill Alley 97
Windsor Court (Monkwell Street)
    140
Winn, Sir Rowland 276
Withers, Nathaniel 161
Wood, Robert (farrier) 240
Wood Street Compter, Keeper's house
    230-31, *230*, *231*
Woodward, Matthew (cornchandler)
    263
Wool Hall (Leadenhall Market) 167
workshops, Houndsditch 164, *164*
Wormwood Street
    house 251, *251*
    Lawrence Camp's almshouses
        265-66, *265*, *266*
Worster, Henry (draper) 253
Wren, Sir Christopher 194, 204
Wright, John (merchant taylor) 236,
    261

Yeats, Nicholas and Collins, J., print
    of Cheapside *25*
Yevele, Henry (mason) 154

Zacharie, Francis (brewer) 260